The Lord Protector

The Lord Protector
Religion and Politics in the Life of Oliver Cromwell

Robert S. Paul

The Lutterworth Press

The Lutterworth Press

P.O. Box 60
Cambridge
CB1 2NT
United Kingdom

www.lutterworth.com.
publishing@lutterworth.com

Paperback ISBN: 978 0 7188 9679 9
PDF ISBN: 978 0 7188 9680 5
ePub ISBN: 978 0 7188 9681 2

British Library Cataloguing in Publication Data
A record is available from the British Library

First published by The Lutterworth Press, 1955
This edition published 2023

Copyright © Robert S. Paul, 1955

All rights reserved. No part of this edition may be reproduced, stored electronically or in any retrieval system, or transmitted in any form or by any means, electronic, mechanical, photocopying, recording, or otherwise, without prior written permission from the Publisher (permissions@lutterworth.com).

To Eunice

Contents

Preface   9
Introduction   11

1. Formative Influences   17
2. Early Political Experience   43
3. From the Beginning of the Civil War to the Spring of 1644   56
4. The Civil War: Spring 1644 to the Self-Denying Ordinance   71
5. The Civil War: Spring 1645 to the End of the First Civil War   94
6. From the Fall of Oxford to the Army Debates, July 1647   106
7. The Army Debates of 1647   127
8. Carisbrooke to the Outbreak of the Second Civil War   151
9. The Second Civil War   164
10. The Execution of the King   181
11. The Beginnings of the Commonwealth Military and Political Problems   196
12. The Irish Campaign and Its Moral Issues   207
13. The Scottish Campaign: Dunbar   219
14. The Scottish Campaign: Worcester   234
15. From Worcester to the Expulsion of the Rump   249
16. Experiments at Home and Abroad   275

17.	Princeps: The Constitution and the Major-Generals	296
18.	Princeps: Home and Foreign Policy	322
19.	The Kingship and the End	350
20.	Judgement	381

Appendices

1.	Letter to Mr. Storie, January II, 1635/6	397
2.	Biblical Analysis of Cromwell's Letter to Mrs. St. John, October 23, 1638	399
3.	Extract from "Vindiciae Veritatis"	401
4.	Letter to Robert Hammond, November 6, 1648	403
5.	Letter to Robert Hammond, November 25, 1648	406
6.	The "Saddle Letter" Account	411
7.	Selected Letters	413
8.	Professor W.C. Abbott and Oliver Cromwell	415

Select Bibliography   419

Index   425

Preface

Ralph Waldo Emerson's observation that "there is properly no history; only biography" would be a commonplace by now, were it not for a moderate reaction which declares that there is properly no biography; only history. Perhaps the protest is a necessary corrective to the enthusiastic Carlyles and Macaulays who expounded history as an epic of the world's great ones, and who regarded the facts of history as little more than the homage paid to the eternal Hero by his generation. Whatever needs to be said in qualification of the reaction, it is a healthy reminder that a man cannot be separated from his environment – that there is for us, heroes included, a time to be born, and that we are bound to it, and conditioned by it.

Nevertheless, when we have said that, there still remains something within human character which is unique, timeless and which eludes definition. Oliver Cromwell is an illustration of this. Biographies of the Lord Protector have appeared regularly since the time of his death, and will probably continue to appear at regular intervals, because beyond the factors of time and place one recognizes within his personality an irreducible element which remains an enigma. So to Dr. S.R. Gardiner Cromwell was "the most typical Englishman of all time", to Sir Ernest Barker he was "the incarnation ... of the genius of English Nonconformity", to Wilbur Cortez Abbott he was the prototype, if not the archetype, of modern dictatorship.

The place of Oliver Cromwell in English history, however, has an importance beyond the riddle of his own personality, for the seventeenth century may well be described as the meeting ground of the ages of Faith and the Age of Reason, and within such a setting Cromwell is in any case a figure worthy of careful study. His significance is made more pointed by the fact that his Independent or Congregational churchmanship, with roots in Separatism and spiritual "democracy", appears to run counter to so much within his life, and we submit that the issues raised by his life and thought must therefore be of interest not only to historians and students of political institutions, but also to any who are concerned about the relationship between personal religion and the call to public action.

At this point I must give grateful acknowledgment to those who have played more than a modest part in the appearance of this book. I am well aware that my own interest in that borderland which separates the pastoral meadows of theology from the urban rush of politics was first stimulated by the former Principal of Mansfield College, Oxford, Dr. Nathaniel Micklem. To him and to Canon Claud Jenkins, the Regius Professor of Church History at Oxford, I can only pay a respectful tribute for all the help and encouragement they gave me in the earlier stages of my researches. Sir Ernest Barker and Dr. Geoffrey Nuttall both read through the script in its original form, and gave me valuable advice, although I am sure that none of these gentlemen would necessarily wish to accept all my conclusions. I must also acknowledge a debt to Dr. Norman Sykes, the Dixie Professor of Church History at Cambridge, for so readily giving me the opportunity of perusing certain unpublished MSS. of the late Sir Charles Firth, and to the Harvard University Press for permission to quote extensively from the works of the late Professor W.C. Abbott. I also wish to thank Mr. C.E. Wells of the Morgan-Wells Studio Service for the photograph of the Cromwell statue used as frontispiece.

I wish to thank Miss L. Schofield, Mrs. J. Dowling, and Miss G. Maddy for helping to type the MS. A special word of gratitude is due to Miss Edna Wakeley and Mrs. Joyce Youngman for their work upon the original typescript, to the Rev. E.T.D. James for preparing the index and Miss S.M. Burrough for proof corrections, and finally to my wife, who in addition to invaluable and painstaking work upon the MS. was reluctantly obliged, from the first day of our honeymoon, to take the Lord Protector into our family as a more or less permanent and nonpaying guest.

To her this book is dedicated in grateful and penitent homage.

Introduction

The late W.C. Abbott of Harvard listed nearly 3,700 works dealing with Cromwell,[1] and any addition to that list demands a very formidable excuse on the part of the author. The only justification that can be offered is the enigma of Cromwell's character itself.

It fascinates because it is full of paradox, and yet the paradox within his life was not merely political: it was not simply that of a man who began by fighting for individual liberties and ended by becoming an absolute dictator. The issue is complicated by religion, and at its deepest level the contradiction is between the Independent[2] who held "democratic" ideas in ecclesiastical matters, and the man who tried to remedy England's political impasse by becoming Lord Protector. To solve the dilemma historians have resorted to a wide variety of theories, the most simple being that of the royalists, who by denying the genuineness of Cromwell's religion are able to present the picture of a black-hearted tyrant who schemed for power from the beginning, while at the other end of the political rainbow there is the answer of nineteenth-century Liberalism – Cromwell the Great Democrat, who was forced by circumstance into absolutism. It would seem that between Clarendon's royalist convention of the "brave bad man" and Carlyle's noble "hero" there is a great gulf fixed, and if this is so, there can be no answer to the dilemma, and one's estimate of Cromwell must be consigned to the arbitration of prejudice.

Although there have been modern attempts to cut the Gordian knot and present a "realistic" view of Cromwell,[3] most of the

---

1. *A Bibliography of Oliver Cromwell* (Harvard University Press, 1929). Also Addenda to the Bibliography in *The Writings and Speeches of Oliver Cromwell* (Harvard University Press, 4 vols., 1937–47), IV.
2. Where capitalized, the word is intended in its ecclesiastical sense.
3. Cf. G. R. Stirling Taylor, *Oliver Cromwell* (1928); W.C. Abbott, *Writings and Speeches of Oliver Cromwell* (hereafter abbreviated to *W.S.* in references). The place of publication is mentioned in first references to books, and where it is not specified it must be presumed to be London.

theories fail because they reflect not so much the background of Cromwell's England as ideas current at the time of writing. No aspect of the seventeenth century has suffered so much in this respect as that of religion. G.M. Trevelyan has observed that in pre-Restoration England "it would have been difficult to find more than a handful of men who openly avowed a disbelief in the miraculous sanctions of the Christian faith, in one or other of its forms".[4] By the great majority of people in the seventeenth century the reality of God and the Devil, Heaven and Hell, was never doubted, and yet historians have more often than not ignored the fact that such beliefs were bound not only to colour the thought of that time, but also to condition the life and conduct of the people who held them. Hence if we are to attempt to understand Cromwell's career it is of the utmost importance that we should discover to what extent he shared the theological beliefs common to his time.

A similar facet of the same problem is to be seen in the usual treatment given to Cromwell's association with Independency. To treat the possibility of Cromwell's acceptance of these ecclesiastical views as a matter of incidental importance is entirely to misunderstand the Independent's emphasis upon membership in the Church. It is therefore of some importance to discover whether Cromwell regarded his Christian responsibility seriously enough to have joined an Independent Church. If he did, the relationship between religion and politics in his life may shed light not only upon his character but also upon the later development of political consciousness in English Nonconformity.

If this book then starts from Thomas Carlyle's premise that "a man's religion is the chief fact with regard to him", it does so not with any hope of weaning any from their cherished prejudices about the great Oliver, but upon the ground that religion was an indispensable part of the seventeenth-century environment, and that without giving it its due place we cannot hope to understand either the man or his age. At the same time, if religion and life were so closely related within seventeenth-century Puritanism we should also expect to discover that the mundane situations of political experience were not without significance in our understanding of Cromwell's religion.

To attempt an extended discourse on Cromwellian biography

---

4. *English Social History* (1944), 232.

Introduction

would be to invite comparison with W.C. Abbott's exhaustive survey,[5] and yet we cannot ignore the subject entirely, if only because Abbott's own great work needs to be given the place it deserves.

Throughout this book the original authorities have been regarded as primary, but it is clear that in travelling such a well-trodden historical path any writer must owe an immense debt to historians like S.R. Gardiner, C.H. Firth, and W.C. Abbott whose researches made the way plain. The debt to Abbott's *Writings and Speeches of Oliver Cromwell* is evident, and its text of Cromwell's written and spoken word is accepted as authoritative. My previous debt to Mrs. S.C. Lomas's edition of Carlyle's *Letters and Speeches of Oliver Cromwell* is almost equally great.[6]

Of the early biographies James Heath's *Flagellum* was perhaps the most important,[7] more for the extent of its influence than for its value as history. Carlyle regarded it as "the chief fountain indeed of all the foolish lies that have been circulated about Oliver since",[8] and W.C. Abbott's restrained irony is perhaps even more damning.[9] There is a passage in Galsworthy's *Loyalties* where it is remarked of one of the characters who was facing libel, "If he's as innocent as Christ, mud will stick to him", and that seems to have been the avowed principle of James Heath: he discovers a murderer in the Cromwell ancestry, he passes on with evident relish gossip of Cromwell's crude manners, and he is at pains to hint at an immoral relationship between Cromwell and Mrs. Lambert.[10] At the same time it is for his collection of anecdotes that Heath's book has more value than many more reputable volumes, for its author has provided us with some

---

5. Cf. Introduction, *A Bibliography of Oliver Cromwell*.
6. New York and London, 1904, 3 vols. References to this edition appear as *L-C*.
7. *Flagellum: Or the Life and Death, Birth and Burial of Oliver Cromwell The late Usurper* (1663). All references are to the second enlarged edition of the same year.
8. *L-C*, I, 12.
9. "Thus what the newspapers of his day omitted, Heath supplied, following, or founding, that great journalistic principle of giving the people what they want – abuse and personal gossip; and, based on these unfailing recipes for popularity, it is small wonder that his book was a success." *Bibliography of O.C.*, p. xviii.
10. *Op. cit.*, 128. There was no basis for the rumour in fact, but it was a favourite subject in Restoration "comedy"; cf. *Cromwell's Conspiracy. A Tragy-comedy Relating to our latter Times*, by "A Person of Quality" (1660). The importance of Heath is that his gossip was retailed by men like Dr. Bates and Sir W. Dugdale.

material – albeit of a doubtful kind – for a period of the Lord Protector's life which is otherwise more or less a blank.

In contrast, Samuel Carrington, whose favourable biography had appeared four years earlier, in a book of over two hundred pages,[11] devotes only two pages to his hero's early life, and only nine pages to the whole period of the Civil War up to the invasion of Ireland! The same criticism to a lesser degree must be levelled against the anonymous author of *The Perfect Politician*, although it is undoubtedly the best of the early lives.[12] The rest of the earlier biographies range from the almost useless panegyrics of Henry D'Awbeney and Richard Fleckno[e][13] to more sanely-balanced works published anonymously by Isaac Kimber[14] and John Banks[15] at the beginning of the eighteenth century, but our interest in them is limited, since their material is largely secondhand. The Rev. Mark Noble's *Memoirs of the Protectoral House of Cromwell*, published in 1784,[16] falls, however, within an entirely different category. As Mrs. S.C. Lomas has shown,[17] for all Carlyle's gibes at "poor Noble", the work was one of painstaking and often invaluable research, and really introduces the period of modern scholarship in Cromwellian studies.

Of Carlyle's own contribution it is sufficient to say that style, temperament, and literary prestige united in him to make him the ideal prophet, and the *Letters and Speeches of Oliver Cromwell*[18] presented for the first time material which stimulated the great reassessment of the seventeenth century associated with the names of Dr. S.R. Gardiner and Sir Charles Firth. All later biographies of Cromwell are dependent upon the literary

---

11. *The H story of the Life and Death of His most Serene Highness, Oliver, Late Lord Protector*, etc. (1659), dedicated to the Lord Protector Richard.
12. *The Perfect Politician: Or, A Full View of the Life and Actions (Military and Civil) of O. Cromwel.* (1660), attributed to Henry Fletcher and William Raybould; (cf. Abbot, *Bibliography of O.C.*, 135, item 1066.) Quotations from 3rd edition (1681).
13. *Historie and policie re-viewed, in the heroick transactions of his most serene highness, Oliver, Late Lord Protector, from his cradle to his tomb* (1659), by H.D.; and *The Idea of His Highness Oliver, late Lord Protector*, &c. (1659) by Richard Fleckno. The latter can be compared with *Panegyrici Cromwello* (1654) by the Roman Catholic chaplain of the Portuguese Ambassador.
14. *The Life of Oliver Cromwell, Lord Protector of the Commonwealth of England, impartially collected* (1724).
15. *A short critical review of the political life of Oliver Cromwell* (1739) "by a Gentleman of the Middle Temple".
16. Two vols. References are to the 3rd edition of 1787.
17. *L-C*, I, p. liv *seq*. Cf. *Ibid.*, 13 f, for Carlyle's remarks on Noble.
18. First published 1845.

evidence amassed by Carlyle and the detailed research of Gardiner and Firth, from the "popular" books of John Morley and Frederic Harrison at the beginning of this century, to the recent biographies by John Buchan, Hilaire Belloc, Maurice Ashley and G.R. Stirling Taylor. All these books, however, were written prior to the monumental work of the late Wilbur Cortez Abbott. His debt to previous scholars like Gardiner, Firth, and Mrs. Lomas is recognizable and, as we shall discover, his interpretation is often open to serious criticism, but this in no way detracts from a piece of scholarship which perhaps marks the greatest advance in Cromwellian studies since the publication of S.R. Gardiner's histories.[19]

---

19. *History of the Great Civil War 1642-43* (1886-91, 3 vols.); *History of the Commonwealth and Protectorate 1643-60* (1894-1901, 3 vols.). References are to the 4 vol. editions of 1893 and 1903.

Chapter One

Formative Influences

I

The family into which Oliver Cromwell was born owed its fortunes directly to the break-up of the monastic orders and to the Protestant Establishment. Its wealth can be traced to Richard Williams, nephew to Henry VIII's chief adviser and agent in the dissolution of the monasteries, Thomas Cromwell, Earl of Essex.[1] This Richard Williams adopted his uncle's surname, "Cromwell" or "Crumwell", in return for his patronage; he was knighted while his uncle was still in power and managed to retain the King's favour after Thomas Cromwell's fall, and he passed on a considerable fortune to his son, Sir Henry "Cromwell", who was knighted by Elizabeth, and whose liberality earned him the title "the golden knight".

Sir Henry was a vigorous local organizer against the threat of the Armada – an activity in keeping with one whose wealth was bound up with the Protestant succession – and of his daughters, one became the mother of Major-General Whalley, and another became the mother of John Hampden. His heir was knighted "Sir Oliver Cromwell" at the accession of James I, and one of his younger sons was Robert Cromwell, the father of the future Lord Protector. Sir Oliver Cromwell was a man "who from love of ostentation pushed his father's liberality to extravagance",[2] and eventually had to sell Hinchinbrook House to the Montagus, who thus became the leading family within the shire; which seems to have led to some rivalry between them and the Cromwells. Sir Henry's second son, Robert, inherited an estate at Huntingdon,

---

1. Thomas Cromwell's sister married Morgan Williams, a man from Glamorganshire who had settled in London. Her son, Richard, followed his uncle to Court, and for his help in the dissolution of the monasteries he was granted the Benedictine Priory at Hinchinbrook, Neath Abbey in Glamorganshire, together with many rich properties in the eastern counties and much that was formerly held by the rich abbey of Ramsey. Cf. Noble, *Protectoral-House* I, 14–17, and J.L. Sanford, *Studies and Illustrations of the Great Rebellion* (1858), 178 note; also *W.S.* I, 5.
2. C.H. Firth, *Oliver Cromwell* (1903), 3.

worth about £300 in the money of that time,[3] and he married Elizabeth, the young widowed daughter of William Steward of Ely, who brought with her a jointure of £60 a year. Her great-uncle, Robert Steward, had been the last Catholic Prior of Ely, and with the change in national religion, the first Protestant Dean of Ely Cathedral. In view of Oliver's later influence in the fen country, it is interesting to note Dr. Trevelyan's judgment that Ely Cathedral had for centuries maintained a dominant position over the "County Palatine" of Ely, and indeed, over the whole of Fenland.[4]

From this it will be seen that the fortunes of the family into which Oliver Cromwell was born were strongly linked to the Protestant succession, and primarily to the Anglican settlement of Elizabeth as offering the best hopes of stable government, and hence the continued enjoyment of their wealth.

Oliver's father did the things appropriate to a country gentleman of standing in those days. He was a bailiff of Huntingdon, a Justice of the Peace, a Commissioner of Sewers,[5] and, besides other offices of local importance, he sat at Westminster for the borough in 1593. Dr. George Bates, who hated the Protector cordially, admits that he was "born of honest parents",[6] and even James Heath was not able to discover anything to the disparagement of Robert Cromwell, apart from the fact that Oliver's mother kept a brew-house, "and thought it no disparagement to sustain the Estate and Port of a younger brother, as Mr. Robert Cromwell was, by those lawful means; however, not so reputable as other gains and Trades are accounted".[7]

Oliver was baptized on April 29, 1599, in the church of St. John, Huntingdon, the second son of his parents. A comparison of the portraits of Robert Cromwell and his wife Elizabeth suggests

---

3. Three or four times as much in pre-1939 money. Mr. Hilaire Belloc's estimate of Robert Cromwell's estate as "perhaps four or five thousand all told" seems to be far too high. Cf. Belloc, *Cromwell* (1934), 29. Cf. the article by Mr. Isaac Foot, in *The Contemporary Review,* Vol. CXLVI, July–December 1934, 556–63.
4. *English Social History,* 149.
5. i.e. fen drainage.
6. *Elenchus Motuum Nuperorum in Anglia: Or, a short Historical Account of the Rise and Progress of the Late Troubles in England* (English translation, 1683), 237. First part of the Latin edition was published 1649/50, second part 1661–63, third part (by Thomas Skinner) 1676.
7. *Flagellum,* 8. Walter Cromwell, maternal grandfather of Richard Williams, had been a brewer among other things. These facts probably account for royalist gibes at Oliver as a brewer.

Formative Influences   19

that she had the stronger character.[8] She came from a family with strong Puritan leanings,[9] and in this way she may have influenced her husband, for while there is no reason to doubt that Robert Cromwell was a loyal member of the established Church, his choice of school and college for Oliver suggests that he had Puritan sympathies.[10]

There were good reasons for Puritanism to flourish in the Cromwell family. The family fortunes were entirely dependent upon the Protestant succession, and at the time Oliver was born, less than fifty years had elapsed since the Catholic reversion under Mary. The threat of the Armada was still too recent for Englishmen to forget the Catholic menace from abroad, while the tendencies at court gave cause for disquiet; the truculence of James I at the Hampton Court Conference in 1603, the discovery of the Gunpowder Plot in 1605, and the weak Stuart foreign policy towards Spain all tended to encourage Puritan reaction among those families which had most to lose in the event of a Catholic triumph.

East Anglia was certainly infected with Puritan ideas earlier than most of the country, to some extent because of its geographical relationship with Holland.[11] Also, the religious persecutions in Europe were bringing Protestant refugees to this country, many of them weavers who settled near the cloth manufacturing town of Norwich. The city was becoming something of a Puritan centre, and it is not surprising to find here some of the first experiments in religious Separatism which eventually spread throughout the eastern counties.[12]

These counties, too, contained the seats and estates of great Puritan landowning families like those of Cecil, Montagu,

---

8. Cf. *W.S.*, I, 13, and the portraits in John Morley's *Oliver Cromwell* (1900 edn.).
9. Oliver's uncle, Sir Robert Steward, was a Puritan. Cf. *Flagellum*, 13; *Elenchus*, 238.
10. Cf. *infra*, p. 29 ff. Sidney Sussex College was noted for an unconsecrated chapel and lack of sympathy with Laud's reforms; G.M. Edwards, *Sidney Sussex College* (1899), 42 f., 100; J.B. Mullinger, *History of Cambridge University* (Cambridge, 3 vols., 1873, 1884, 1911), III, 130 and n.
11. The ports and mercantile centres tended to be Puritan; *English Social History*, 241.
12. Robert Browne's views spread through the surrounding counties at least as far as Bury St. Edmunds; R.W. Dale, *History of English Congregationalism* (1907), 120–5; H. M. Dexter, *The Congregationalism of the last three hundred years* (U.S.A., 1879), 70; Williston Walker, *The Creeds and Platforms of Congregationalism* (New York, 1893), 10 n. 4.

Devereux, and Rich, together with many lesser names, like the Barringtons of Essex, the Hampdens of Buckinghamshire, and the Cromwells of Huntingdonshire, all of which had built fortunes on the ruins of the old Church. The Puritan nobility extended its protection to persecuted members of the party,[13] and as family alliances grew, the influence of the new ideas became ever wider and stronger. To this we must add the influence of Puritan teaching in the University of Cambridge,[14] and the fact that the standard of preaching and ministration held by the Puritans contrasted very favourably with the general slackness and ignorance of the older clergy.[15]

In a sense these influences are all too abstract to be assessed accurately or to be over-stressed, but they indicate that the young Cromwell was born and bred in a part of the country which was alive to the new religious temper. Such influences must be seen in relationship to the ideas of prelacy remembered by an impressionable youth from the episcopal visitation of Huntingdon by the Bishop of Lincoln when Cromwell was five years old, or the impression of monarchy gained from the lavish entertainment of James I at Hinchinbrook in 1603.

II

Oliver was born the second of three sons in a family which contained seven daughters, but since his brothers, Henry and Robert, died in childhood, he was left his father's heir in a family circle which was predominantly feminine. At the end of his year at Cambridge, when he was barely eighteen years of age, his father died[16] and left him at the head of the family. There is not much material to estimate the effect on Oliver of this feminine

---

13. For the protection afforded Robert Browne by his kinsman William Cecil, Lord Burleigh, see *Dale, Hist, of English Cong'ism*, 124 f., 132 f. Lord Warwick gave protection to Jeremiah Burroughes, after the latter had been deprived by Bishop Wren; *A Vindication of Mr. Burroughes Against Mr. Edwards his foule Aspersions in his spreading Gangraena, and his angry Antiapologia*, etc. (1644), 19.
14. Martin Bucer's influence at Cambridge had been in marked contrast to Peter Martyr's failure to impress Oxford, J.B. Mullinger, *Hist, of Cam. Univ.*, II, 109–25. The Marian exiles returned in full force to Cambridge, *ibid.*, 171–4, and the University had recently witnessed the brief but influential tenure of office of Thomas Cartwright.
15. For Richard Baxter's description of the low state of the clergy intellectually and morally during his boyhood, see *Reliquiae Baxterianae* (1696), ed. Matthew Sylvester, Pt. I, 1.
16. He was buried at All Saints, Huntingdon, on June 24, 1617.

family circle, but there may have been a tendency for a few years to revolt from maternal control.

Of his boyhood and youth we know very little that is reliable. Heath informs us that he received his earliest education under "the slighted Governance of a Mistris", until "his Father removed him to the Tuition of Dr. Beard Schoolmaster of the Free-School of that Town, where his Book began to persecute him, and Learning to Commence his great and irreconcileable Enemy".[17] Of Dr. Thomas Beard's influence we shall have more to say, but speaking of Cromwell's character at this early stage, Heath speaks of the "Vices which were so predominant and visible in him" that Dr. Beard was unable to make any impression on "his obstinate and perverse inclination";[18] then, as if warming to the subject, the author of the *Flagellum* says that "Among the rest of those ill qualities which fructuated in him at this age, He was very notorious for robbing of Orchards", which crime was continued to such excess by "this Apple-Dragon" that the offence "ripened in him afterwards to the throwing down of all Law or Conscience, and the stealing and tasting of the forbidden fruit of Sovereignty".[19]

A modern reader will discover less significance in these youthful escapades than did James Heath, writing just after the Restoration, but the local gossip probably had a residuum of truth in it, and there is no reason to think that young Oliver Cromwell was any more pious than the average lad of his age. There is, however, a persistent rumour, duly recorded by Heath, that as a youth Cromwell had curious dreams and presages of future greatness,[20] and a similar story is told by Dr. Bates, who says that as a child Cromwell reported that "one appeared to him in the likeness of a Man, who told him that he should be a King",[21] and that Dr. Beard whipped him for it.

There is also the account of Oliver's part in a play, *The Five Senses* (placed by Heath at Huntingdon, and by Carrington during Cromwell's year at Cambridge)[22] in which the youthful

---

17. *Flagellum*, 4.
18. *Ibid.*, 5.
19. *Ibid.*
20. *Ibid.*, 6.
21. *Elenchus*, 337. Probably it was copied from Heath.
22. Carrington, *Hist, of the Life and Death of Oliver*, 3. However, in the 1657 edition of Anthony Brewer's *Lingua, or the Combat of the Tongue and the Five Senses*, it says, "First acted at Trinity College, Cambridge, after at the Free School at Huntingdon", and this may explain the confusion; cf. Abbott, *W.S.*, I, 24 n. 13.

Cromwell is reported to have set a crown upon his head and added "beyond his Cue some Majestical mighty words".[23] It sounds, as Professor Abbott has remarked, "too apt to be true", and yet we must admit it is the kind of incident which, in the light of future events, would have remained in people's memories.

There is considerable divergence of opinion as to the extent Oliver benefited by his education at Cambridge. Carrington says that while there he perfectly acquired the Latin tongue, "which Language as all men know he made use of to treat with Strangers".[24] A more fulsome account of his university career, and even more vague, comes from the sycophantic pen of Richard Fleckno, who observed that "He was bred a scholar in the University where, during his youth, he gave the first Essay of that Admirable vivacity of spirit, profoundnesse of judgement, and indefatigable industry, which afterwards inform'd all the Actions of his life".[25]

The royalist writers were rather less vague concerning Cromwell's scholastic accomplishments, and purport to give us some, idea how that "vivacity of spirit, profoundness of judgement, and indefatigable industry" were employed.[26] Sir William Dugdale says that in Cambridge Oliver "made no great proficiency in any kind of Learning; but then and afterwards sorting himself with Drinking Companions, and the ruder sort of people (being of a rough and blustering disposition) he had the name of a Royster amongst those that knew him".[27] Heath says that Cromwell was placed in Sidney Sussex College "more to satisfie his Fathers curiosity and desire, than out of any hopes of Completing him in his Studies", and adds that while he was there "he was more Famous for his Exercises in the Feilds than in the Schools, (in which he never had the honour of, because no worth and merit to a degree)[28] being one of the chief Matchmakers and Players at Foot-ball, Cudgels, or any other boysterous sport or game".[29]

That an undergraduate, not yet seventeen years of age, preferred

---

23. *Flagellum*, 6 f.
24. *Hist. of the Life and Death of Oliver*, 4; cf. *infra*, p. 33 n. 3.
25. *The Idea of His Highness*, 4. Fleckno was apparently a Catholic priest (cf. Leslie Stephen's article in the *Dictionary of National Biography*, VII, 260).
26. Although all their accounts may have been based upon the *Flagellum*.
27. *A Short View of the Late Troubles in England* (Oxford, 1681), 459.
28. Heath's bias excels itself here. Cromwell left Cambridge on the death of his father; even had that not been the case, it was common practice for gentry to spend a short time at the university without proceeding to a degree.
29. *Flagellum*, 7 f.

sport to books would hardly be cause for remark in modern times, but in the seventeenth century university "organized games and athletics did not exist, and sports were either discouraged or forbidden".[30] Games which in these days would be regarded as healthy amusements were regarded at this time as evidence of youthful dissipation, and the author of the *Elenchus* cursorily dismisses Cromwell's year as an undergraduate by saying, "he laid an unsolid Foundation of learning at Cambridge; but he was soon cloy'd with Studies, delighting more in Horses, and in Pastimes abroad in the Fields".[31]

Since all our information regarding Cromwell's boyhood and youth comes through his most violent detractors, it is almost impossible to form a just estimate of his character, although the very silence of Carrington may indicate that according to the judgment of the day there was little to single out for praise. But allowing for the use which the Restoration writers make of the available data, there is not much in these "uncontrolled debaucheries" which would to-day be regarded as evidence of an uncommonly vicious spirit. Boys of all ages seem to run to type, and we cannot err far in judgment if we represent him as a fairly boisterous youth, with not much time for books, but with a keen interest in active outdoor life and considerable prowess in the arts of personal combat.

At the same time we should not ignore the dreams of future greatness, in which both Heath and Carrington saw the evidence that they each wanted to see. Such grandiose imaginings are not uncommon, especially in lads brought up in the shadow of other people's wealth, and it would appear that Oliver, like many other highly-strung boys, indulged in his day-dreams without evincing much of the application necessary for achievement. The dreams did not prove, however, what James Heath tries to prove, that Cromwell schemed for personal power from his earliest days, and the words of Mr. Hilaire Belloc – by no means the least critical of his biographers – are a useful corrective to Heath's bias:

> If there is one thing certain about the moral character of Cromwell, to the man who reads him and remembers his reading impartially, it is that he was not ambitious.
>
> He lived to be over forty-five without making any effort at fame

---

30. Trevelyan, *English Social History*, 184.
31. *Op. cit.*, 237.

or power; and no man ever develops the desire for them long after youth has passed.[32]

III

We must return to discuss the influence of one whom most of Cromwell's biographers dismiss with little more than the note that Oliver was placed under "Thomas Beard – a Puritan schoolmaster, who wrote pedantic Latin plays, proved that the Pope was Antichrist, and showed in his *Theatre of God's Judgements* that human crimes never go unpunished by God even in this world".[33] It is to be doubted whether Dr. Beard's influence can be dismissed as briefly as that.

Dr. Beard seems to have maintained close connections with the Cromwell family, and Oliver appears to have held him in respect throughout life. As a friend of Robert Cromwell, Thomas Beard had attested his will,[34] and subsequently he acted with Oliver in several offices of local importance; they were signatories together of the Parliamentary indenture for the election of the Huntingdon burgesses in 1620,[35] they were Justices of the Peace for the borough in 1630,[36] while Beard was prominent among those who signed the indenture which saw the election of Oliver as a burgess for Huntingdon in 1627/8.[37] It was largely to uphold Dr. Beard's views against the Bishop of Winchester's nominee, Dr. Alablaster, that Oliver Cromwell make his maiden speech at Westminster on February 11, 1629. From this it would appear that he never lost his respect, or perhaps his affection, for Thomas Beard.

Although Dr. Beard remained within the Church of England, he was a rigid Calvinist and an uncompromising Puritan. He was a graduate of Cambridge,[38] and had been appointed Master of the Hospital and Grammar School of St. John the Baptist,

---

32. Belloc, *Cromwell*, 64.
33. Firth, *Oliver Cromwell*, 5. Notable exceptions, however, are W.C. Abbott and Hilaire Belloc; cf. *W.S.*, I, 22–6, Belloc, *Cromwell*, 59.
34. Copy of the will, *W.S.*, I, 29 f.
35. *Ibid.*, 46.
36. Noble, *Protectoral-House*, I, 102.
37. *W.S.*, I, 52.
38. Matriculated at Jesus College, 1584; A. B. 1587/8; A. M. 1591; S. T. B. 1602; S. T. P. ("Bird") 1614. *The Book of Matriculations and Degrees ... in the University of Cambridge from 1544 to 1659* (Cambridge, 1913), compiled by John Venn and J. A. Venn, *in loco*.

Huntingdon, in 1604, but his Puritan zeal was such that he added to this the office of "lecturer" in the town. An indenture dated March 23 1625/6 indicates not only the respect in which he was held by the people of Huntingdon, but also his own enthusiasm for the new thought in undertaking this additional labour.[39]

It is, however, in his writings that the significance of Dr. Beard in our study of Cromwell really appears, and of these his earliest and most popular work is the most important. *The Theatre of God's Judgements*,[40] according to its title-page, is a collection of histories from secular and sacred authors "concerning the admirable judgements of God upon the transgressors of his commandments". In other words, it developed the thesis of God's immediate concern in the events of history, and His active participation by granting rewards and punishments to His servants and His enemies. Dr. Beard's book was entirely concerned with pointing out the punishments visited upon the latter, and his purpose was to induce such people by the fear of God's wrath to turn from the error of their ways.

Eternal punishment for the wicked and reward for the good, was taken for granted in the doctrine of Providence accepted in the seventeenth century, but the important thing to notice is the extension of the doctrine to a belief that divine rewards and punishments Were operative "euen in this life", and particularly the way in which Beard applied his thesis, for it illustrates the attitude taken by Puritans towards their sovereigns, which so infuriated James I. In Beard's view the justice of God manifests itself "chiefly towardes them which are in the highest places of account, who being more hardned and bold to sinne, doe as boldly exempt themselues from all corrections and punishments due vnto them, being altogether vnwilling to be subiect to anie law of iustice whatsoever".[41]

He went on to emphasize that princes are subject both to the Law of God and of Nature, and we should remember that the same thing had been said twenty years earlier in the House of

---

39. An extract from the indenture is quoted in the article on Thomas Beard in the *D.N.B.* A Puritan "lecturer" was a minister appointed by zealous Puritans to supplement local preaching.
40. First published 1597. It was partly translated from the French, to which Beard added over three hundred additional historical examples.
41. *Op. cit.*, 7.

Commons, with unpleasant results for the one who said it.⁴² Since then, the issue which Peter Wentworth had raised – the limits to the royal prerogative, and the rights of Parliament to discuss national religion – had become increasingly prominent, and the political tension had been heightened by the House of Commons' challenge to the Crown in the granting of monopolies and the levying of subsidies. Thomas Beard's comments upon the limitations of absolute power among the Kings of Persia and Pharaohs of Egypt must have been received with a good deal of interest "for", he said, "they had not so much authoritie as to iudge betwixt man and man or to levy subsidies and such like by their owne powers; neither to punish any man through choler, or any ouerweening conceit, but were alwaies tied to obserue iustice and equitie in all causes".⁴³

It is obvious that these comments pointed towards the struggle between the Stuarts and their Parliaments, and the *Theatre of God's Judgements* maintained a steady popularity, running into four editions within the first fifty years of the seventeenth century.⁴⁴ As W.C. Abbott has said, "it is scarcely conceivable that Oliver Cromwell did not read Beard's book",⁴⁵ and that alone would make it of interest, but the fact that it advocated a doctrine that was at the centre of Cromwell's thought and conduct promotes the *Theatre* to considerable historical importance.⁴⁶

The relevance of the book to contemporary events in the early

---

42. Peter Wentworth, in the debate on Freedom of Speech, February 8, 1576. He was committed to the Tower, where he remained until March 12; cf. G.W. Prothero, *Select Statutes and other Constitutional Documents illustrative of the reigns of Elizabeth and James I* (Oxford, 1913, 4th edn.). Wentworth said, "For the Queen's Majesty is the head of the law, and must of necessity maintain the law: for by the law her Majesty is made justly our Queen, and by it she is most chiefly maintained … The King ought not to be tinder man, but under God and under the law, because the law doth make him a King …" (*Ibid.*, 120-22). The speaker was quoting Bracton, "Ipse autem rex non debet esse sub homine sed sub deo et sub lege, quia lex facit regem …". Henry de Bracton, *De Legibus et Consuetudinibus Angliae* (6 vols., 1878-83), I, 38; cf. 1, 268, edited by Sir Travers Twiss.
43. *Theatre*, 10.
44. 1597, 1612, 1631, 1648.
45. *W.S.*, I, 25.
46. "Though Oliver afterwards learned to modify the crudeness of this teaching, the doctrine that success or failure was an indication of Divine Favour or disfavour never left him, and he was able, in the days of his greatness, to point unhesitatingly to the results of Naseby and Worcester as evidence that God Himself approved of the victorious cause." S.R. Gardiner, *Oliver Cromwell* (New Impression, 1925), 3.

seventeenth century was enhanced by the interpretation of eschatology accepted by the majority of Puritans – an interpretation which identified the "latter days" of the Bible with the time in which they were living. Thomas Beard shared this view,[47] and the *Theatre* served as an introduction to his later publication, *Antichrist the Pope of Rome*,[48] which as its title indicates, set out to prove that the Pope was Antichrist. Both the interpretation of Providence held by Beard and the apocalyptic view of contemporary history were common enough in Puritanism, but in view of the fact that Cromwell came to hold these views very strongly,[49] we feel it is not extravagant to trace here the powerful influence of his Calvinist schoolmaster.

The appearance of the Authorized Version of the Bible in 1611 was the one tangible success from the otherwise miserable débâcle of Puritanism at Hampton Court in 1603, and the Bible was perhaps the greatest single influence on the life and thought of Cromwell. It has been said that "for him a single volume comprehended all literature, and that volume was the Bible",[50] and while the statement needs modification, it is true that his amazing knowledge of the Bible made up for any deficiencies in literature. But great and continuous as the influence of the Authorized Version undoubtedly was, it must have been a later influence, for it did not appear until Cromwell was twelve years old. The Bible of Cromwell's schooldays was the Genevan Bible, with its blackletter type and its remarkable annotations.

It would be from this Bible that Dr. Beard would teach the Scriptures, and it should be noted that the commentary provided in the Genevan Version was based on the same theology that appears in Dr. Beard's books. This commentary must have been of very great importance in helping to produce the hatred of Roman Catholicism which was characteristic of Englishmen – and particularly Puritans – during the first half of the seventeenth century, for it must be remembered that at the end of Elizabeth's reign there was a general desire for more religious

---

47. *Theatre*, 3.
48. Published 1625.
49. Writing to the Governor of Edinburgh Castle, Cromwell mentioned our Lord's care not to meddle with secular power, and added, "This was not practised by the Church since our Saviour's time, till Anti-christ, assuming the infallible chair ... practised this authoritatively over civil governors." September 12, 1650, *W.S.*, II, 338; *L-C*, II, 127–8 (CXLVIII).
50. John Morley, *Oliver Cromwell*, II; cf. *ibid.*, 50–2.

teaching, which the Queen was reluctant to permit[51] and the clergy unable to supply; hence, to a very large degree the Genevan Bible and its commentary had to meet that need.

Although practically all Cromwell's words indicate a knowledge of the Authorized Version rather than the Genevan, there are definite traces of the latter in one of his earliest letters, October 13, 1638,[52] but by 1638 the new version had been in existence nearly thirty years and had rapidly supplanted the older book, and therefore it is possible that these traces of the Genevan Version were drawn from Scripture memorized almost thirty years before under the vigilant eye of Dr. Beard;[53] no small testimony to the learned schoolmaster's faculty for implanting seeds of knowledge in the young.

The influence of the Authorized Version was something which extended throughout Cromwell's life; but it is not quite true to say that the Bible "comprehended all literature". In his letter to Richard Mayor, written just before Cromwell sailed for Ireland, he sets down his wishes regarding Richard Cromwell's education:

> I would have him mind and understand business, read a little history, study the mathematics and cosmography: – these are good with subordination to the things of God. Better than idleness, or mere outward worldly contents. These fit for public services, for which a man is born.[54]

Similarly in a letter to Richard himself he advises him, "Recreate yourself with Sir Walter Raughleye's History: it's a body of history, and will add much more to your understanding than fragments of story".[55]

This does not sound like one who despised human learning, but it shows the emphasis which Cromwell placed upon history as a study that would give a man "understanding"; and if history can be described as the secular study of Providence, we are again reminded of the *Theatre of God's Judgements* and the theology behind it.

---

51. Cf. Elizabeth's letter against "prophesyings". Prothero, *Statutes and Const. Docs.*, 205 f.
52. Cf. Analysis, *infra*, p. 399. Letter reproduced in full, *infra*, p. 36 f., W.S., I, 96 f.; L-C, 1, 89 f. (II).
53. This seems the most likely explanation for the Genevan references, although there may have been other, or contributory reasons, such as the continued use of the G. V. in Robert Cromwell's home.
54. August 13, 1649, W.S., II, 102 f.; L-C, I, 451.
55. April 2, 1650, W.S., II, 236 f.; L-C, II, 53 f.

IV

The influence of Thomas Beard on Cromwell was at least the influence of one with whom we know him to have been in fairly close contact for thirty years or more. In trying to estimate the influence of Cromwell's stay in Cambridge, on the other hand, we know very little, except that he was there for only one year. We have already noted a general consensus of opinion that as an undergraduate he was fonder of field sports than of his books, although there is no need to accept the royalist suggestion that he therefore kept bad company.[56] Notices of his time in Cambridge, however, are very fragmentary, and Sidney Sussex College has little more than the bare statement of his admission.[57]

The Cambridge to which Cromwell went in 1616 was undergoing change. It has been seen that the university had been under strong Puritan influence,[58] culminating in Thomas Cartwright's Lady Margaret professorship, an appointment which J.B. Mullinger regarded as significant evidence of the strength of the party.[59] Cartwright's acceptance of the chair appears to have been inconsistent with his antagonism to episcopacy,[60] but although he held the position for only a year, his influence upon the university can hardly be denied. Although the Puritans within Cambridge were probably a minority, they were men of authority and ability, and exerted an influence out of all proportion to their numbers,[61] but by the end of the century it was a declining influence, for Cartwright retired to Warwick and died just before the ill-fated Hampton Court Conference of 1603.[62] In their Millenary Petition to James,[63] the Puritans had attacked among other

---

56. *Supra*, p. 22 f. On March 23, 1646, Cromwell wrote to Lord Howard on behalf of Thomas Edwards (a contemporary at Sidney Sussex College), and whom he described as "a most religious man" for as long as he had known him. Not much can be inferred from this, but it does not suggest Oliver kept bad company while at Cambridge; *W.S.*, I, 431; *L-C*, III, 328 (Supplement 18).
57. Edwards, *Sidney Sussex College,* 1899, 73.
58. *Supra*, p. 20 n. 2.
59. Mullinger, *Hist. of Cambridge University,* II, 207–9.
60. It is important to notice the tenacity with which many Puritans held their appointments within the Establishment. This was received with scorn by the Separatists; cf. the extract from the examination of Henry Barrow and John Greenwood. Prothero, *Statutes and Const. Docs.,* 223.
61. Mullinger, *Hist. of Cambridge University,* II, 194 f., 299 f.
62. Died December 1603, Conference January 1603/4.
63. April 1603.

things the sources of college revenues, and they met with a sharp rebuff from the university in a grace which passed the Senate on June 9, 1603, to the effect that "Whosoever by word, writing or other way, should in the university openly oppose the doctrine or discipline of the Church of England, or any part thereof, should *ipso facto* be suspended from any degree taken or to be taken".[64] This was followed in 1604 by the enactment in Convocation of canons which sought *inter alia* to enforce uniformity of dress in ecclesiastical ministrations, and especially the wearing of the surplice. Hitherto this had been successfully evaded in the chapels of the two recent Puritan foundations, Emmanuel College and Sidney Sussex College.[65] It is of some interest to see that Sidney Sussex College should be associated with Emmanuel, which from its foundation had been regarded as a centre of extreme Puritanism.[66] It is evident, however, that by the beginning of the seventeenth century the university had moved towards compliance, and it is of importance to notice that within a university swinging towards conformity, Cromwell entered a college which had a brief but decidedly Puritan tradition.

Of Richard Howlet, Cromwell's tutor, we can say little. He went subsequently to Ireland and became Dean of Cashel.[67] A former pupil of his, Dr. Bramhall, Bishop of Derry, said that he had never known him to quarrel with anyone, and described him as "A moderate man in his tenets, far from Dr. Ward's rigidity and his way".[68] He was recommended to William Laud by Archbishop Ussher as "an able man and very fit for government",[69] and these testimonials suggest an efficient if somewhat compliant and colourless personality, which may be the main reason why we know so little of him. Writing of Cromwell's undergraduate days, however, the author of *The Perfect Politician* says that Oliver's tutor observed that he was not "so much addicted to Speculation, as to Action".[70] As far as we know, that is the only comment made by Richard Howlet about his celebrated pupil.

64. *Ibid.*, II, 448.
65. Founded 1596.
66. Founded by Sir Walter Mildmay, 1584, *ibid.*, 310 ff. Two Blundell scholarships were transferred from Emmanuel to Sidney Sussex. Cf. *ibid.*, 198.
67. Cf. note by Mrs. Lomas, *L-C,* I, 36. He was installed as Dean, March 9, 1638/9.
68. Quoted *ibid.*, from *State Papers Dom. Ireland,* Car. I, cclvi, 107, 108; cf. *Cal. S. P. Ireland* (1633–47), 196 (July 12, 1638).
69. *L-C,* I, 36 n.
70. *Op. cit.*, 2.

On the other hand, the material available for Dr. Ward, Master of Sidney Sussex during Cromwell's stay in Cambridge, is almost too profuse, since it is difficult to tell what is relevant. Samuel Ward came from an impecunious family, and had been admitted to Christ's College in 1589 while it was still Puritan in temper.[71] He was subsequently elected a Fellow of Emmanuel, and later became the third Master of Sidney Sussex, and Lady Margaret Professor of Divinity.[72]

His Puritan views and personal piety have been recorded for us in his *Diary*, and in other MSS. in the possession of Sidney Sussex College, some of which have been edited for us in *Two Elizabethan Puritan Diaries*, by Dr. M.M. Knappen.[73] Dr. Ward's character would not be of much interest to us, however, were it not for the fact that in a small college like Sidney Sussex the Master must have had a good deal to do with the undergraduates. As Lady Margaret Professor he eventually had considerable prestige throughout the university, but his influence upon a small college with practically no established traditions must have been felt at every point through college life, especially at a time when attendance at college chapel was compulsory.[74]

The first thing we notice about Samuel Ward is the introspective piety of his Calvinism. His *Diary* is often little more than a daily catalogue of faults and failings, usually morbid and often ludicrous: "Sept. 15, 1595. My 'crapula' in eating peares in a morning and other things which might have diminished my health. As also my to much gluttony at dinner tyme. My unfitness to do anything after dinner"[75] [*sic*.]

A good deal of Ward's self-examination sounds less like confession of sin than sensible advice to himself for the avoidance of future illness through over-eating, although he would have

---

71. Edmund Barwell's appointment as Head had been secured with the support of Sir Walter Mildmay (an old student of Christ's), and had been regarded as a victory for the reforming party, although Barwell proved to be singularly ineffective. William Perkins, the most competent tutor in Christ's at that time, fell under suspicion for his Puritan views, and was called before the Vice-Chancellor in 1587. Mullinger, *Hist. of Cambridge University*, II, 472 f.
72. J.B. Mullinger confuses him with a contemporary, Samuel Ward of Ipswich, one of the foundation fellows of Sidney Sussex College; cf. *ibid.*, II, 359; Edwards, *S.S.C.*, 45, 67 ff. The Samuel Ward with whom we are concerned was a student of Christ's, Fellow of Emmanuel, 1595, master of Sidney Sussex, 1610, and Lady Margaret Professor, 1623.
73. Chicago, 1933.
74. Trevelyan, *English Social History*, 184.
75. *Two Elizabethan Puritan Diaries*, III.

regarded the resultant distemper as a "judgment" of God. Samuel Ward's morbidity did not decrease with the years.[76] He accepted implicitly the same interpretation of Providence that we have noted in Dr. Beard, but whereas the latter emphasized the background of God's transcendent purpose within history, Dr. Ward stressed the imminence of God's intervention in the history of the individual. As J.P. Mullinger has written of him, "as he summed up each day's experience nothing appeared too trivial to form an indictment against himself, nothing in the course of events so ordinary as not to furnish a theme for wonder or to constitute a mystery".[77] Yet we must appreciate Ward's background if we are to understand his theology. He alone of his family had managed to win his way to a university and against the constant threat of poverty he had managed to maintain himself through the generous gifts and influence of his patrons. An impediment in his speech almost prevented his intention of taking holy orders, but against all disabilities he succeeded and achieved very considerable academic eminence. Such a career in a life governed by the ideas of "Election" and "Grace" could only mean to Samuel Ward God's personal care and intervention on his behalf.

The movement away from Puritanism during the last years of Elizabeth's reign was observed by Samuel Ward with extreme disfavour. This is quite clear from many extracts in his *Diary* – as, for example, when at Emmanuel College in 1604 he observed "two plots laid to bring our College to the wearing of the surplice".[78] Ward managed to quieten his conscience enough to conform – the wearing of the surplice was to him "an indifferent ceremony" – – but only because he could discern "no way of escape"; the future colour of national churchmanship had been decided by the Hampton Court Conference, and he saw no reason to suffer for being "singular".

His tendency towards compliance apparently grew with the years,[79] for later Dr. Ward embarked upon the most unpuritanical course of accepting plural livings,[80] and before the death of James

---

76. In his *Considerations* (1621) we have his detailed account of his reasons for and against asking a certain lady to be his wife! *Ibid*, 121–3.
77. *Hist. of Cambridge University*, II, 491.
78. Extract from the *Diary* (Edwards, S.S.C., 68 f.). This is not *Two Elizabethan Puritan Diaries*.
79. For Ward's early Puritanism, cf. Knappen's Introduction, *ibid.*, 37–41.
80. *Ibid.*, 41.

Formative Influences 33

he had become a royal chaplain,[81] but if we examine Ward's theology as distinct from his conformity in Church Order, we find that so far from giving up his original views he remained a rigid Calvinist throughout.[82] He took a strong Calvinist stand at the Synod of Dort in 1619, and was one of the signatories of the *Joynt Attestation*, the Calvinist reply to the Arminianism of Dr. Richard Montagu's *Appello*. Later on he was invited, together with the Master of St. Catherine's, to represent the university at the Westminster Assembly – an indication that he was regarded by the Presbyterians then in power as sufficiently sound in doctrine; Dr. Ward retained the temper of Calvin and the same doctrine of Providence that Cromwell had learned from Thomas Beard. For this reason, we suggest that as a formative influence upon the future Lord Protector he is not to be disregarded.

It is difficult to place Cromwell's year at Cambridge in its proper perspective; it was a comparatively short period and he left without a degree, although there is no reason to suggest that he left devoid of learning,[83] but perhaps the period can best be considered as a continuation of his early life and schooldays, and it is for Samuel Ward's re-emphasis of Dr. Beard's theology that we feel the year cannot be lightly dismissed: while at the university Oliver did not escape the atmosphere of the *Theatre of God's Judgements* and the august theology that inspired it.

---

81. *Ibid.*, 42.
82. Sir Simonds D'Ewes described a visit he made to Cambridge in 1635, when he heard a candidate for the B.D. degree assert both the doctrine of Justification by works and that the outward act of baptism expiated sin. He commented that the "brasen-faced asserting of these Popish points, especially the denying of Justification by faith, was abhorred by myself and all the orthodox hearers in the Commencement House; and Dr. Ward, the Lady Margaret Professor, and Master of Sidney College, sitting moderator the same day, openly rebuked the same Nevel for broaching those gross heresies, contrary not only to canonical Scripture, to the articles and homilies of our Church, but to the tenets and writings of all our Protestant divines, as well Lutheran as Calvinistic. I supped the same night in Sidney College, with the same Dr. Ward, where we both lamented the times that this wicked Nevel durst so impudently and openly maintain the vilest and most feculent points of all Popery." *The Autobiography and Correspondence of Sir Simonds D'Ewes, Bart., during the reigns of James I and Charles I* (1845, 2 vols.). Edited by J. P. Halliwell, II, 124.
83. *Supra*, p. 22–3. "Mr. Waller assures us, that he had a good knowledge of the Greek and Latin histories; nor must it be forgot that he ever patronized men of learning and science; and Dr. Manton says he had a very valuable and well-chosen library; all which does not seem to lead us to suppose him averse to learning, or that he was without a competent share of it himself, making allowance for the short time he was at college." Noble, *Protectoral-House*, 1, 96.

V

Cromwell's biographer, Carrington, says that he was intended for civil law, but that he "dived not over deep into this Study".[84] There is a persistent tradition that after leaving Cambridge Cromwell studied at Lincoln's Inn, probably because his father, grandfather, and two of his uncles had been there.[85] Professor Abbott thinks that he may possibly have been at Gray's Inn,[86] but in any case there is no direct evidence of any kind that he joined any of the Inns of Court.[87] James Heath says that, having left the University, Cromwell's "uncontrolled debaucheries did publiquely declare, for Drinking, Wenching, and the like outrages of licentious youth, none so infam'd as this young Tarquin",[88] and suggests that he was sent to London to study Law in the hope that his vices "might passe in the throng".[89] Needless to say, there is no evidence to support this slander – indeed, there is such a complete lack of data regarding Cromwell's time in London that even Heath cannot find crumbs with which to feed his malice; the only thing he can suggest is that the very nature of the place so affected Cromwell that he "spent his time in an inward spight".[90]

Heath's dilemma of having, for once, no fact or fiction which might be used for further blackening Cromwell's character, is not without its historical importance, for if such a persistent traducer could find no clear record of Cromwell's stay at Lincoln's Inn, it indicates the doubt which exists about the years between Cambridge and his coming of age. His marriage on August 22, 1620,[91] however, to Elizabeth, the daughter of Sir James Bourchier,[92] suggests that he must have been in or near

---

84. *The History of the Life and Death, etc.,* 4.
85. *W.S.,* I, 13, 33.
86. *Ibid.,* 33 ff.
87. Except the engraving of his lying in state, which says that he was "educated at Cambridge afterward of Lincons Inn". Cf. Abbott, *Bibliography of O. C.,* p. xv.
88. *Flagellum,* 8.
89. *Ibid.,* 9.
90. *Ibid.*
91. At St. Giles, Cripplegate; cf. *W.S.,* I, 35.
92. Cf. *Flagellum,* 14, J. Allanson Picton, *Oliver Cromwell: the man and his mission* (and edn., 1883), 33. John Buchan calls him Sir "John" Bourchier, and there was a Sir John Bourchier listed among the regicides (cf. Hansard, *Parliamentary History of England from the earliest times, etc.* (1807, etc.), IV, 48), who descended from John Bourchier, natural son of Lord Berners. This

London for some part of the time. Sir James was a city merchant owning an estate at Felstead in Essex and a house at Tower Hill, and he was related to the Hampdens.

There was always a bond of very deep affection between Cromwell and his wife: "there was never a vibrant man of eminent public activity so simply devoted to his home and so certainly satisfied with his marriage. He gave example of what is meant, in any sane and just definition, by the word chastity."[93] Yet although his wife must have been one of the greatest influences of his life, there is no material on which to base an estimate of that influence. Whether or not the increased responsibilities of marriage were responsible for bringing about his religious conversion we cannot say, but all the biographers are agreed that Cromwell was converted some time during his early married life.

Noble suggests that this conversion took place some time before Oliver was returned to Westminster for the borough of Huntingdon in 1628.[94] Heath, who is usually vague on matters of chronology, seems to place it earlier than that, although he is more interested in explaining the change of manners as a ruse by Oliver to augment a dwindling patrimony, than in historical accuracy.[95] Bearing in mind the fact that all the stories of Cromwell's dissipated youth are derived from royalists like Heath, and remembering the sober protestantism of his home and education, it is at least arguable that his religious experience may have been by way of gradual development rather than by sudden change. The story of the conversion may be no more than the attempt of writers like Heath to explain the transition between the early debauchee they depict, and the religious enthusiast Cromwell is known to have become, and the rhapsodical religion of Cromwell's letters might have been no more than his reaction to an attack of melancholia in the forms of expression popular among Puritans at that time.

Upon examination, however, it will be found that the reasons

---

man is described by Noble as "a rigid independent and republican, he was very dissatisfied with Cromwell's usurpation". Noble, *The lives of the Regicides, etc.* (1798), I, 102–4. This was clearly not the father of Cromwell's wife, of whom Noble commented, "Sir James was of so new a family, that he had his coat of arms granted him in Oct. 1610." *Protectoral-House,* I, 123 f.

93. Belloc, *Cromwell,* 55.
94. Cf. *Protectoral-House,* I, 100 f.
95. *Flagellum,* 12–14.

for believing that there was a comparatively sudden conversion are too weighty to be ignored. James Heath was obviously puzzled by the change, and his attempts to explain it as a subtle piece of financial duplicity are not very convincing. On October 13, 1638, the year of the Scottish National Covenant, Oliver Cromwell wrote the following letter to the wife of his cousin, Oliver St. John:

> Dear Cousin,
>
> I thankfully acknowledge your love in your kind remembrance of me upon this opportunity. Alas, you do too highly prize my lines, and my company. I may be ashamed to own your expressions, considering how unprofitable I am, and the mean improvement of my talent.
>
> Yet to honour my God by declaring what He hath done for my soul, in this I am confident, and I will be so. Truly, then, this I find: That He giveth springs in a dry and barren wilderness where no water is. I live (you know where) in Mesheck, which they say signifies *Prolonging*; in Kedar, which signifieth *Blackness*: yet the Lord forsaketh me not. Though He do prolong, yet He will (I trust) bring me to His tabernacle, to His resting-place. My soul is with the congregation of the firstborn, my body rests in hope, and if here I may honour my God either by doing or by suffering, I shall be most glad.
>
> Truly no poor creature hath more cause to put forth himself in the cause of his God than I. I have had plentiful wages beforehand, and I am sure I shall never earn the least mite. The Lord accept me in His Son, and give me to walk in the light, as He is the light. He it is that enlighteneth our blackness, our darkness. I dare not say, He hideth His face from me. He giveth me to see light in His light. One beam in a dark place hath exceeding much refreshment in it. Blessed be His Name for shining upon so dark a heart as mine! You know what my manner of life hath been. Oh, I lived in and loved darkness, and hated the light. I was a chief, the chief of sinners. This is true; I hated godliness, yet God had mercy on me. O the riches of His mercy! Praise Him for me, pray for me, that who hath begun a good work would perfect it to the day of He Christ.
>
> Salute all my good friends in that family whereof you are yet a member. I am much bound unto them for their love. I bless the Lord for them; and that my son, by their procurement, is so well. Let him have your prayers, your counsel; let me have them.
>
> Salute your husband and sister for me. He is not a man of his word! He promised to write about Mr. Wrath of Epping; but as yet

Formative Influences

I received no letters. Put him in mind to do what with conveniency may be done for the poor cousin I did solicit him about. Once more farewell. The Lord be with you; so prayeth

Your truly loving Cousin
Oliver Cromwell.[96]

The Scriptural phrases of this letter may be a style affected by Puritans, but the letter as a whole is certainly that of one who has been through an unforgettable religious experience: "You know what my manner of life hath been. Oh, I lived in and loved darkness, and hated the light. I was a chief, the chief of sinners." These confessions ought not perhaps to be taken too literally, since the apostle Paul spoke in terms no less extravagant of his own life before being converted to Christ,[97] but they do indicate the fact of an evangelical experience in Cromwell's life. Mr. Hilaire Belloc saw the importance of this when he wrote, "No Calvin, no Cromwell. You shall not understand the mind of Cromwell, nor any of the innumerable minds who have known themselves, from that day till yesterday, to be Elect of God, until you have felt the fierce blast from the furnace which Jean Cauvin of Noyon in Picardy kindled."[98]

Some form of religious conversion is implicit in the religion of Calvin's *Institutes,* for it emphasizes that in the face of Man's sin, we are saved by the Grace of God alone.[99] The selection of one man for salvation and another man for damnation was predetermined within the fore-knowledge of God, and the "Elect" were chosen not because of their natural merits, but because God in His grace had awakened in their hearts the faith which alone could merit salvation. Once a man grasped the full assurance of God's promise to him, he would pour out his heart in praise and thanksgiving for this unmerited gift: the certainty of his own salvation gave to the Puritan a tremendous sense of his unrepayable debt to Almighty God. "The Puritans", wrote Lord Macaulay, "were men whose minds had derived a peculiar

---

96. *W.S.,* I, 96 f.; *L-C,* I, 89 f. (II). Cf. *infra,* p. 339 for analysis of the Biblical phrases.
97. I Timothy 1:15. "Seriously to argue from such language as this that Cromwell's early life was vicious, is as monstrous as it would be to argue that Bunyan was a reprobate from the remorseful charges of *Grace Abounding.*" John Morley, *Oliver Cromwell,* 14 f.
98. *Cromwell,* 35 f.
99. John Calvin, *The Institutes of Religion* (translation by Henry Beveridge, Edinburgh, 1863), 2 volume edn. (I, 254–5), Bk. II, iii, 5–6.

character from the daily contemplation of superior beings and eternal interests. Not content with acknowledging, in general terms, an overruling Providence, they habitually ascribed every event to the will of the Great Being, for whose power nothing was too vast, for whose inspection nothing was too minute. To know Him, to serve Him, to enjoy Him, was with them the great end of existence."[100] Cromwell's humility before God in the letter to Mrs. St. John reminds us with what overwhelming gratitude Samuel Ward rehearsed God's goodness to him: it is Christianity lived in the spirit of St. Paul, and it had been called into being by an experience similar to that of the Damascus road. Henceforth all events in life were related to the certainty of eternal salvation, and we may apply to Cromwell the words with which Lord Macaulay described the typical Puritan of the seventeenth century, for he came to share a faith which believed that "it was for him that the sun had been darkened, that the rocks had been rent, that the dead had risen, that all nature had shuddered at the sufferings of her expiring God".[101] This Paulinism with its idea of special choice – or "election" – by "grace", is for our purpose the most important feature of Cromwell's conversion, since it leads on directly to the question of his vocation: God had chosen him, Oliver Cromwell, for salvation, and henceforth he was, however unworthily, the "chosen vessel" of the Lord.[102] But the very nature of such religion suggests a conception of Providence which held God to be responsible for every detail of the individual's life, no less than for every circumstance of history, and once the evangelical experience was his, Cromwell could not help breathing the same air as Samuel Ward and Thomas Beard; for good or ill he would enter into the legacy of his earlier training.

Is it possible to arrive at a date for this religious change? Cromwell was undoubtedly subject to periodic attacks of melancholia which seem to have borne some relationship to his religious experience, and we know that he had an attack in 1628, and that the London physician, Sir Theodore Mayerne, diagnosed his condition as *valde melancholicus*.[103] Dr. Simcott, Cromwell's family doctor at this time, assured Sir Philip Warwick "that for many years his Patient was a most splenetick man, and had phansyes

---

100. *Essay on Milton* (Oxford Plain Texts, 1909), 49.
101. *Ibid.,* 50.
102. Cf. Acts 9:15.
103. Sir Henry Ellis, *Original Letters illustrative of English History* (and series, 4 vols., 1827), III, 248.

about the cross in that town". The physician said that he had often been called to Oliver's at night in the belief that he was dying.[104] These fancies may have been the outcome of a deep religious struggle in a highly strung nature, or they may have been pathological; in either case we can imagine that they would deepen the sense of self-condemnation and intensify the desire for the assurance of divine forgiveness.

Bishop Burnet said that Cromwell had "led a very strict life for about eight years before the wars", and from this it would appear that Cromwell was converted just before 1629–30,[105] but it is easier to hazard guesses than to speak with any certainty.[106] Perhaps the first piece of positive evidence is from Cromwell's own correspondence. His earliest extant letter was written from Huntingdon on October 14, 1626, to ask Mr. Henry Downhall of St. John's College, Cambridge, to stand godfather for his son, Richard, who had been born on the fourth of the month.[107] While courteous, the style is straightforward and businesslike, and utterly devoid of Biblical quotations – a complete contrast to the letter to Mrs. St. John, quoted previously.[108] We must agree with one of Cromwell's former biographers when he observes that "it is impossible to believe that the man who on such an occasion could write to a valued friend without one word of gratitude for divine favours, or any reference to his growing responsibilities in life, could have been already so full of religious fervour as his later letters show that he became".[109]

It is reasonable, therefore, to assume that his conversion occurred between the dates of these letters, October 1626 and

---

104. *Memoires*, 1681, 249. Hypochondria was common in the seventeenth century; cf. Ward's *Diary*, and the concern of Richard Baxter and Sir Simonds D'Ewes for their health.
105. *History of My Own Time* (2 vols., 1897–1900), edited by O. Airey, I, 121. As a Scot, Burnet would date the beginning of the wars from either the outbreak of the first Bishops' War in 1638 or from the riots of the previous year.
106. Dr. S.R. Gardiner coupled the fact that Cromwell was ill in 1628 with the occurrence of his name in the register of St. John's Church, Huntingdon, as undergoing ecclesiastical censure. Dr. Gardiner admits the entries appear to be forged, but suggests that they were inserted later with Oliver's knowledge as a sign of penitence, and he infers from this that Cromwell was converted in 1628. The date is a good one, but the argument is weak, since Oliver was hardly likely to be elected to Parliament for the borough (1628), and be appointed a J.P. (1630) if he had recently been publicly censured. Cf. Gardiner, *Oliver Cromwell*, 5; *W.S.*, I, 51 f.
107. *W.S.*, I, 50 f.; *L-C*, III, 221 (Appendix 1), *infra*, p. 413 (Appendix VII).
108. *Supra*, p. 36 f.
109. J. Allanson Picton, *Oliver Cromwell*, 47.

October 1638. Two other letters fall within this period, and of these, the first does not help us very much, being purely a business letter to a complete stranger about some hawks which had strayed;[110] but the second, to Mr. Storie, appealing in restrained but unmistakable Biblical language for the continued financial support of a "lecture" not only identifies Cromwell with the Puritanism of his time, but shows him to be actively interested in its promotion.[111] This narrows the time for his conversion to between October 1626 and January 1635/6.

Unfortunately we have no more literary evidence to help us define the date more positively, but there are several facts about Cromwell's life at this time which may assist us. A tradition has persisted that about the time he removed from Huntingdon to St. Ives in 1631, he had seriously considered emigrating to New England, and this would suggest that by this time he had sympathies with the Separatist settlers of America.[112] Heath says that he was dissuaded from going by the death of his uncle, Sir Thomas Steward, and the inheritance left to him.[113] In 1628 Oliver was elected to Parliament as a member for Huntingdon borough, and in the following year he made his first recorded speech on an issue which showed him to be strongly against the "flat popery" preached by a certain Dr. Alablaster.[114] Dr. Beard had signed the indenture which returned Cromwell to Westminster, and it was in defertce of his old schoolmaster that Oliver had attacked Dr. Alablaster's preaching in the Commons; in 1630 we find that both Oliver and Dr. Beard are appointed justices for the borough.

These events indicate a close relationship between Oliver and

---

110. To John Newdigate, April 1, 1631, W.S., I, 70; L-C, III,. 313 f. (Supplement 1).
111. Appendix I.
112. Cf. Sir William Dugdale, *A Short View*, 459. By this time Cromwell had begun to support "popular" (i.e. puritan) movements: in 1630 he strongly opposed the change in the local government of Huntingdon, he was fined for refusal to take knighthood, and in 1633-4 he continued the work begun by his uncle, Sir Thomas Steward, by championing the fen-dwellers against the Crown and the "Adventurers" in the Fen-Drainage scheme. For further light on these incidents, see W.S., I, 66 ff.; Noble, *Protectoral-House*, I, 108 f.; J.L. Sanford, *Studies and Illustrations of the Great Rebellion* (1858), 232-7; Cal. S.P. Dom. (1619-23), 96; ibid. (1631-33), 23, 501; ibid. (1637), 447, 503; ibid. (1638-39), 301; Lord Clarendon, *The Life of Edward, Earl of Clarendon* (Oxford, 1857 edn.), I, 88 (reference to book and section).
113. *Flagellum*, 16.
114. W.S., I, 61 f., February 11, 1628/9; cf. Bulstrode Whitelocke, *Memorials of English Affairs*, etc. (1732 edn. corrected and enlarged), 12.

Formative Influences 41

his old schoolmaster since 1628, and we are forced to ask ourselves whether that relationship would have been likely if Beard's former pupil were still persisting in the course of folly attributed to him by his early biographers. We must therefore either regard the accounts of Cromwell's earliest wildness entirely as royalist fabrications, or else date his conversion between the years 1626 and 1628. Further, perhaps the date should allow for a period before his election to Westminster when the new convert would be very much "on trial", and this indicates a date just before 1628, as Mark Noble suggested.[115]

The royalist accounts of Cromwell's early life, while they may be modified, cannot be entirely disregarded, since the temperate Sir Philip Warwick says that

> The first years of his manhood were spent in a dissolute course of life, in good fellowship and gaming, which afterwards he seemed very sensible of and sorrowful for; and as if it had bin a good spirit, that had guided him therein, he used a good method upon his conversion; for he declared, he was ready to make restitution unto any man, who would accuse him, or whom he could accuse himselfe to have wronged: (to his honour I speak this. ...)[116]

Sir Philip's mention of "good fellowship, and gaming", however, is very different from the complete depravity attributed to Cromwell by the Restoration writers like Heath and Dugdale, and it seems a more credible picture of his young manhood, although to Cromwell himself, this way of life would appear as having been spent in "darkness" and hating the "light". It is difficult to see how he would ever have persuaded Elizabeth Bourchier to marry him, or her father to accept him into the family, if the character given him by Heath and Dugdale had been authentic.

In summary, therefore, it is suggested that Cromwell was converted after an emotional struggle which may have culminated or had its sequel in the illness of 1628, but by the time Charles I acceded to the throne Oliver must have been sufficiently "sound" in his religious views for the Puritan Dr. Beard to be one of his foremost supporters in his nomination for Parliament, and from this time onwards he gives every evidence of being decidedly Puritan in his views.

---

115. *Protectoral-House*, I, 100 f.
116. *Memoires*, 249 f. Cromwell acted up to this principle, and it is reported that he paid back a certain Mr. Calton £30 that he had won unfairly. *Flagellum*, 15 f.; *The Perfect Politician*, 2 f.

We must, however, see the implications of his conversion in relation to the formative influences of family, environment and education, for it made him not only a "good" man, but also a partisan and an advocate: "Election" implied personal choice, and once Cromwell accepted this salvation he accepted also a vocation from God. Our interest is to see how this was interpreted.

Chapter Two

Early Political Experience

John Morley once wrote that "the English have never been less insular in thought and interest than they were in the seventeenth century",[1] and the reason is to be found in the continental roots of Puritanism and their own recent history. Englishmen remembered the threat of the Spanish Armada and the persecutions of Queen Mary's reign, they did not forget the recent Gunpowder Plot, and they were alarmed at the reported increase in the number of Popish recusants and the spread of Jesuit influence throughout their country; but all these facts were given added point when the Englishman looked across the Channel and saw the religious struggle being waged throughout the continent. In the struggle against Spain and the Empire, in the stubborn opposition of the Rochellais to Richelieu and in the victories of Gustavus Adolphus, the English Puritan felt that his own battles were being fought, and when Frederick, the Elector Palatine, was forced into exile, when La Rochelle was forced to capitulate, and when Wallenstein swept through central Europe, the Puritan felt that it was time for all true Englishmen to take a hand. "Puritans felt", wrote Sir Charles Firth, "that these German drums were a call to England to be up and doing. With anxious or exultant eyes, they followed each turn of fate in the death-struggle of Catholicism and Protestantism. ... When Tilly fled before Gustavus at the Breitenfeld, Eliot cried that now 'Fortune and Hope were met'. When Gustavus fell at Lützen, every Puritan's heart sank within him."[2] It was a cosmic struggle in which all the Powers of Light and Darkness were engaged, and this being so James I's vacillating foreign policy seemed to be criminal folly, Charles I's home policy appeared to be betrayal and the ecclesiastical measures sponsored by William Laud were seen not as a reasoned attempt to put the Anglican Church on a

---

1. Morley, *Oliver Cromwell*, 1899, 42.
2. Firth, *Oliver Cromwell*, 24 f.

surer ecclesiastical foundation, but as an attempt to reintroduce Romanism: the constitutional struggle between the Stuarts and their Parliaments must be seen against the background of this fear and hatred of Catholicism. To a certain extent the fact that religious and constitutional issues arose at the same time may be regarded as an accident resulting from the peculiar inheritance which Charles received from his father both in policy and in temperament, but although we can see them as separate issues, there was no such clear dividing line to the people taking part.

I

Like hundreds of his fellow-Englishmen, Cromwell was educated and trained in constitutional issues through the petty affairs of local politics.

In 1630 he vigorously opposed the change in the local government of Huntingdon. He seems to have expressed himself somewhat bluntly, and he was committed to custody for his plain speech.[3] Henry Montagu, Earl of Manchester, was appointed to arbitrate, and although the earl condemned Cromwell's bluntness he ordered the charter to be amended to meet his objections, and the matter seems to have ended there.[4] By this time Cromwell was siding with the "popular" interests of the town, which were also identified with Puritanism, and he was fined for his refusal to take knighthood.[5] Whether or not these clashes with authority influenced him in his decision to leave Huntingdon, he joined with his mother on May 7, 1631, in selling most of their property there. A tradition persisted for some years that about this time Oliver seriously thought of emigrating. It may be that the acceptance of a lease for a stock-farm in St. Ives was rather in the nature of an experiment, the success or failure of which might well determine whether or not he would remain in England. He failed in a legal action undertaken to gain control of his uncle Sir Thomas Steward's estate; the old man Was apparently not competent to administer it himself.[6] The rights and wrongs of the

---

3. Oliver was supported by a certain William Kilborne, *W.S.*, I, 66–8.
4. Report transcribed in *W.S.*, I, 68 f. Cf. Noble, *Protectoral-House*, I, 108 f.; J.L. Sanford, *Studies and Illustrations*, 232–7.
5. *W.S.*, I, 71. List of those who paid the fine from *Cal. S. P. Dom.* (1631–33), 23.
6. The royalist writers naturally put the worst possible construction on this incident. Cf. Sir William Dugdale, *A Short View*, 459.

dispute are not very clear but Oliver continued to be Sir Thomas's heir.

In St. Ives he spent his time as a typical country farmer, and his responsibilities never rose very high.[7] Apart from a remarkable long-lived local rumour that he often attended church with his neck swathed in red flannel to protect his throat from the damp,[8] the most we know of his religion is from his letter to Mr. Storie.[9] There is no reason to suppose that at this time he considered himself anything but a loyal member of the Church of England, but his kinsman, John Williams, Bishop of Lincoln, who was living at Buckden, near Huntingdon, at this time, testified that he was "a common spokesman for sectaries, and maintained their part with great stubbornness".[10] We have already mentioned Cromwell's interest in the Puritan lecture at Huntingdon, and Mark Noble gives us some indication of how the letter to Mr. Storie came to be written.[11] He says that:

> It is somewhat to be wondered at, that we should not find complaints from archbishop Laud, in his visitation of the puritanism of the county of Huntingdon, but not a word drops from the primate respecting it, except a lectureship in the town of Huntingdon, which he desires the king may be disallowed, because the lecturer was removable by lay persons, to which his majesty assents; this was in 1633.[12]

Noble suggests that this lecture was the one about which Oliver wrote to Mr. Storie, and if that is so it is not without considerable significance, for although it would be straining the evidence to suggest that since the lecture was "removable by lay persons" Cromwell had accepted Independency, it does at any rate argue that the lecture at Huntingdon had a bias that way. The letter is couched sufficiently in the language and expression of the Bible to show that Oliver Cromwell was taking his religion seriously; and at this time, on the top of his failures, the news came in

---

7. Parish returns, *W.S.*, I, 78.
8. Noble, *Protectoral-House*, I, 105 n.
9. Appendix I.
10. The bishop's full description of his kinsman is given in *Old Parliamentary Hist.*, II, 463 f., n.
11. January 11, 1635, *W.S.*, I, 80 f.; *L-C*, I, 79 f. (I); *infra*, p. 397.
12. *Protectoral-House*, I, 258 f. For the reasons which lead us substantially to accept Noble's belief that the letter to Mr. Storie and the Huntingdon lecture suppressed by Laud bear some connection, the reader should refer to the note in Appendix I.

January 1636 that his fortunes were once more re-established by reason of his uncle's death.[13]

Oliver removed to the house of his uncle in Ely, where he soon began to take a hand in the affairs of the neighbourhood. As Sir Thomas's heir he became lessee to a number of properties from the Cathedral Chapter,[14] and he seems to have shown an active interest in the administration of one of the ecclesiastical charities,[15] which brought him into close contact with the cathedral authorities. Whether or not these associations with the dignitaries of the Establishment lessened his respect for them, his interest in Separatism increased rather than decreased, "Nor did he omit any other duty or civility, or Office of love to any, especially to those of the Household, as they termed the people of the Separation".[16] The letter to Mrs. St. John, which belongs to this period, gives us a clear picture of his religious enthusiasm,[17] and it is evident that Cromwell was ripe for a break with the Established Church.

Charles I was by this time set upon his ill-fated attempt to impose episcopacy on the Scots,[18] and in the light of future events it is surely not without significance that Oliver declared, "My soul is with the congregation of the firstborn, my body rests in hope,[19] and if here I may honour my God either by doing or by suffering, I shall be most glad." He was destined both to do and to suffer before very long, for in the same year the dispute about the fens came to a head, and in May 1639 there died, at the age of eighteen, "a most promising young man, who feared God more than most", Robert Cromwell, his eldest son.[20]

One of the minor failures of Stuart administration had been its management of the Fen Drainage scheme. The enterprise had

---

13. Cf. *Flagellum*, 16.
14. Leases, *W.S.*, I, 85–8, 89 f., 97–101.
15. *W.S.*, I, 89, 95, "Parsons' Charity".
16. *Flagellum*, 17.
17. *Supra*, p. 36 f., October 13, 1638.
18. The year of the National Covenant. Charles was trying to raise funds for his war.
19. This may be an oblique reference to his ecclesiastical position, i.e. another way of saying, "My *soul* is with those who have separated from the Church, although I still remain with the Establishment in hope of its reformation, but whatever happens I shall be prepared to do whatever is required."
20. See the notice of burial in Felstead parish register; Mrs. Lomas's note, *L-C*, I, 42.

been well-conceived and it had been started in 1604, but in 1634 the Crown contracted out of the project by putting the drainage into the hands of a private company of "Adventurers", with the Earl of Bedford at its head. The shareholders of this company were to be rewarded with 95,000 acres of the reclaimed land when the work was complete, 12,000 were to be handed over to the Crown, and another 40,000 were to be held by the company towards the upkeep of the embankments and works.

There had been a certain amount of opposition from fendwellers and others who imagined that their livelihood or their property was endangered; and in this Sir Thomas Steward appears to have played a leading part.[21] But when after three years the Adventurers adjudged the work complete and began to parcel out the land the opposition developed into serious rioting,[22] and it fell to Oliver to continue the work of his uncle, for it was reported that upon payment of a groat by the commoners for each cow they had upon the land he would hold the Adventurers in suit for five years. Meanwhile the inhabitants would continue to enjoy their traditional rights.[23] The trouble was not restricted to the local people for dissension broke out among the shareholders themselves and eventually the Crown intervened and reinstated the Dutch engineer Cornelius Yermuyden who had been responsible for the first failure: the shareholders protested that they were not getting their due, the local people protested at the loss of their commonage, and the fen-dwellers protested at the loss of their occupations. It was for the poorer people that Cromwell began to raise his voice "in which adventure, his boldness and Eloquence gained him so much credit".[24] As a result of the agitation the inhabitants of the district were confirmed in their rights until such time as the drainage was complete; but part of the royal share had been sold to the Earl of Manchester's son, Edward Montagu, Lord Mandeville, who had proceeded with enclosures which the local people in their turn started to pull down. The Lords at once rose in support of their colleague, and in the House of Commons Cromwell rose to the support of the commoners.[25] In the hearing which followed, under the chairmanship

---

21. *Cal. S. P. Dom.* (1619–23), 96.
22. *Ibid.* (1637), 447, 503; (1638–39), 301.
23. *Ibid.* (1631–33), 501.
24. Dugdale, *A Short View,* 460.
25. D'Ewes *Diary,* quoted in Sanford, *Studies,* 368 f.

of Edward Hyde, Cromwell appears to have spoken with more vehemence than grace.[26] He made no attempt to hide his warts; but although royalist writers suggest he was courting popularity, there is consistent evidence that he never lost the opportunity of helping those who stirred his pity: it is seen in his sympathy for the Separatists, his interest in public charities, and in his persistent championship of poor people threatened with dispossession and ruin. John Maidstone, one of his servants during the Protectorate, gives the following description of Oliver which we may regard as reasonably authentic:

> His body was wel compact and strong, his stature under 6 foot (I believe about two inches); his head so shaped, as you might see it a storehouse and a shop both of a vast treasury of natural parts. His temper exceedingly fyery, as I have known, but the flame of it kept downe, for the most part, or soon allayed with thos moral endowments he had. He was naturally compassionate towards objects in distresse, even to an effeminate measure; though God had made him a heart, wherein was left very little roume for any fear, but what was due to himselfe, of which there was a large proportion; yet did he exceed in tendernesse toward sufferers. A larger soul, I thinke, hath seldome dwelt in a house of clay, than his was.[27]

That was one side of Cromwell's nature, but we must look to John Hampden for insight into other qualities within him that were soon to be drawn out, for after the fen dispute Hampden remarked to a contemporary in the House of Commons that Cromwell was "an active person, and one that would sit well at the mark".[28]

II

Cromwell's sympathies, like those of many of his countrymen, were wholly with the Scots in the Bishops' War of 1638-39.[29] The

---

26. Cf. Lord Clarendon, *The Life of Edward Earl of Clarendon*, I, 88.
27. Maidstone to John Winthrop, Governor of Connecticut, March 24, 1659, *Thurloe State Papers* (7 vols., edited by T. Birch, 1742), I, 766. Also quoted in *Old Parliamentary History*, II, 466 n.
28. Sir Philip Warwick, *Memoires*, 251.
29. *Flagellum*, 17. Oliver's indiscreet speeches about the Bishops' War may possibly link up with the strange case of Captain Napier, who called at the lodgings of a Mrs. Cromwell in Drury Lane at this time, and hinted at an English plot to bring in the Scots. *Cal. S. P. Dom* (1637-38), 591 f.

fiasco of the First Bishops' War led directly to the Short Parliament of 1640,[30] and when Charles suffered a further discomfiture that year at the hands of the Scots,[31] he had to turn to Parliament. The Long Parliament began its course in November 1640, and in both these calls to Westminster Cromwell was elected for the borough of Cambridge.

He took no part in the impeachment and attainder of Thomas Wentworth, Earl of Strafford, but he was increasingly involved in religious and moral issues. One of the earliest impressions we have of him in Parliament is that of Sir Philip Warwick, who says:

> The first time that I ever took notice of him, was in the very beginning of the Parliament held in November 1640, when I vainly thought my selfe a courtly young gentleman: (for we courtiers valued ourselves much upon our good cloaths.) I came one morning into the House well clad, and perceived a Gentleman speaking (whom I knew not) very ordinarily apparelled: for it was a plain cloth-sute, which seemed to have bin made by an ill country-taylor; his linen was plain, and not very clean; and I remember a speck or two of blood upon his little band, which was not much larger than his collar; his hatt was without a hatt-band; his stature was of a good size, his sword stuck close to his side, his countenance swoln and reddish, his voice sharp and untunable, and his eloquence full of fervour.

The occasion of Oliver's speech was in defence of "a servant of Mr. Prynn's" – John Lilburne – who had been imprisoned for circulating a protest against the worldliness of the court. Sir Philip was not very impressed with the matter of the speech Oliver made on this occasion, and commented that it lessened his respect for Parliament to discover that the speaker "was very much hearkened unto".[32]

It was on some such occasion as this that Lord Digby, following Cromwell out of the debate, enquired of John Hampden who the man was; Hampden replied, "That slovenly fellow which you see before us, who hath no ornament in his speech; I say that sloven, if we should come to a breach with the King (which

---

30. April 13–May 5, 1640. The Short Parliament was dissolved by Charles when the members demanded that the king should give up his claim to Ship Money in return for subsidies.
31. The Second Bishops' War.
32. *Memoires*, 247 f.

God forbid) in such case will be one of the greatest men of England."[33]

By this time he had become a radical in the matter of ecclesiastical organization, and he supported the "Root and Branch Petition" which sought to abolish episcopacy.[34] In the debate of February 9, 1640/1, the House of Commons discussed whether the petition of 15,000 signatories against episcopacy should be heard, and Sir John Strangways, who moved its rejection, argued that "if we make a parity in the church we must come to a parity in the Commonwealth". This was hotly denied by Cromwell, who went on to say that "he did not understand why that gentleman that last spake should make an inference of parity from the Church to the Commonwealth". He went on to question Church revenues, and asserted that he "was more convinced touching the irregularity of bishops than ever before, because like the Roman Hierarchy they would not endure to have their condition come to trial".[35] We may think that Sir John Strangways had seen more deeply into the issues between Church and State than had Oliver at this point. King James had laid down the principle when he had declared at the Hampton Court conference, "No bishop, no king!", and that logic was soon to be accepted, so that the supporter of episcopacy became almost automatically the supporter of divine-right monarchy – a fact that is well illustrated by the secession from the Parliamentary cause of very many members of both Houses who had previously opposed the royal claims, but who could not accept the radical ecclesiastical measures introduced in 1640 and 1641. Oliver's reaction suggests that, although he had come to certain conclusions about the organization of the Church, he had not yet thought out the implications of those views, and this is borne out by Sir Philip Warwick who said that in a conversation with himself and Sir Thomas Chichely, Cromwell declared, "I can tell you, Sirs,

---

33. Sir Richard Bulstrode, *Memoirs and reflections upon the reign and government of King Charles I and Charles II* (1721), 192 f. Cromwell was becoming increasingly active in ecclesiastical causes. He was placed on committees to consider the petition of William Prynne and Henry Burton for their release, and to reconsider the case of Dr. John Bastwick. He served on a sub-committee of the Grand Committee on Religion, and on committees for considering claims arising out of the fen dispute, and to examine complaints against Bishop Wren of Ely.
34. Presented in December 1640.
35. *The Journal of Sir Simonds D'Ewes*, edited by Wallace Notestein (New Haven, U.S.A., 1923), 340.

what I would not have; tho' I cannot, what I would." In the same month we find him writing:[36]

> Sir,
> I desire you to send me the reasons of the Scots to enforce their desire of Uniformity in Religion, expressed in their 8th Article; I mean that which I had before of you. I would peruse it against we fall upon that debate, which will be speedily. Yours,
>
> Oliver Cromwell.[37]

This was a reference to proposals for peace advanced by the Scottish Commissioners. He, together with many like him, had looked to the Scots' army as a close ally in the struggle against Charles, and there was much to be said in favour of a Presbyterian system of Church government; but what were the implications of this Scottish demand for uniformity? How would it affect the status and the freedom of the Separatist groups which he had learned to respect? He was not at all sure that uniformity, as the Scots seemed to interpret it, would be the best for the country; but on this he was certain – he did not want Anglican episcopacy.

He therefore threw his whole weight into the abolition of the episcopate, joining with Sir Henry Vane the younger in drafting the famous "Root and Branch" Bill,[38] which was presented to the House of Commons by Sir Edward Dering on May 22, 1641, and after the discovery of a royalist plot to rescue Strafford he proposed that the bishops should be excluded from the House of Lords "before we proceed in this".[39] Later on (September 8) he moved that afternoon sermons should be held in all parishes of England "at the charge of the inhabitants of those parishes wheere ther are no sermons in the afternoone"[40] – which seems a rather petulant way of asserting the right to hear religious lectures.

From the King's point of view things were going from bad to worse. Strafford and Laud were left to their fate, and within a

---

36. *Memoires,* 176 f. "Oliver had not come to any settled principles in religion, at least in church government." Noble, *Protectoral-House,* I, 114 n.
37. To Mr. Willingham, February 1640/1, *W.S.,* I, 125; *L-C,* I, 96 (III).
38. The fact that Cromwell was working on this may account in some measure for his obscurity at Strafford's trial a fortnight previously.
39. *Harleian MSS.* 5047, f. 63a, cited by Abbott, *W.S.,* I, 134 n. Cromwell also spoke against the appointment of five new bishops in October. D'Ewes, *Diary, Harl. MSS.* 162, f. 53b, 54b; *Commons Journals,* II, 298 (1742).
40. D'Ewes, *Diary, Harl. MSS.* 164, f. 101a.

year the centralization within Church and State for which Elizabeth and the Stuarts had striven had been utterly destroyed. The Scots became even more distrustful of royal intentions when a plot was discovered to seize their leaders, and it was at this point that the news came of the outrages in Ireland. While Charles was in the north, the Irish attempted to seize Dublin, but being prevented they attacked and massacred many English and Scots families in Ulster. It is difficult to appreciate the fear and horror with which the news of this massacre was received in England: Richard Baxter, writing later of the Civil War, said that it was hastened "above all by the terrible massacre in Ireland and the Threatenings of the Rebels to invade England".[41] There is no doubt that accounts of the massacre were wildly exaggerated, for even after the Restoration Lucy Hutchinson still believed that over 200,000 Protestants had been killed![42] The King's tardiness in declaring the Irish insurgents to be rebels roused deep suspicions "that the rebellion in Ireland received countenance from the king and queen of England",[43] and upon Cromwell the effect of hearing the news was that he immediately subscribed £500 from his modest estate for use against the Irish. The effect of the massacre of October 1641 did not diminish with the course of years, and it became hardened into the one great religious prejudice of Cromwell's life – a hatred of things Catholic, and, in particular, an overwhelming detestation of the Catholic Irish.[44]

The suspicion which fell upon Charles enabled the Parliamentary opposition to exert still more pressure upon him, and the rising temper culminated in the stormy passage of the Grand

---

41. *Reliquiae Baxterianae*, I, 26.
42. "While the king was in Scotland, that cursed rebellion in Ireland broke out wherein above 200,000 were massacred in two months' space, being surprised, and many of them most inhumanly butchered and tormented; and besides the slain, abundance of poor families stripped and sent naked away out of all their possessions; and, had not the providence of God miraculously prevented the surprise of Dublin Castle the night it should have been seized, there had not been any remnant of the protestant name left in that country." *Memoirs of the Life of Colonel Hutchinson* by Lucy Hutchinson (Everyman edition), 75. For other exaggerations by responsible authorities, see *Rel. Baxt.*, I, 28 f., and Clarendon, *History of the Rebellion and Civil Wars in England* (Oxford, 1849 edn.), IV, 26. (N.B. – references to this work are to book and section. Clarendon estimates that 40,000-50,000 English lost their lives.)
43. *Memoirs of Col. Hutchinson*, 75.
44. Cf. Belloc, *Cromwell*, 129. Cf. his letter attempting to justify his action at Drogheda, *W.S.*, II, 127; *L-C*, I, 469 (CV), also his Declaration to the Irish Catholic clergy, January 1649/50, *W.S.*, II, 198; *L-C*, II, 8.

Early Political Experience 53

Remonstrance.[45] Its supporters introduced it to the House of Commons at rather a late hour, but there was some opposition and the debate was postponed until the following day. Eventually after a bitterly contested debate which lasted throughout the day and into the small hours of the next morning, the Remonstrance was passed by nine votes, and Cromwell assured Lord Falkland that had the remonstrance been rejected, "he would have sold all he had the next morning, and never seen England more; and he knew there were many other honest men of the same resolution".[46] The Remonstrance divided Parliament even more sharply into Puritan Parliamentarians and Anglican Royalists. In the petition which accompanied it, the King's concurrence was asked "for depriving the Bishops of their votes in Parliament, and abridging their immoderate power usurped over the Clergy", and for uniting all who were opposed to the Papists "by removing some oppressive and unnecessary ceremonies by which divers weak consciences have been scrupled, and seem to be divided from the rest". The rest of the Remonstrance collected into one amorphous document "all the grievances which the combined ingenuity of Pym and his followers could collect to discredit Charles's administration".[47] The Grand Remonstrance led directly to the impeachment of the five members,[48] and this in turn to Charles's clumsy attempt to arrest them in person;[49] and that ill-advised action made civil war almost inevitable.

III

In this chapter we have seen the beginnings of Cromwell's public life. It was with ecclesiastical issues that he was most concerned, as might be expected; but there were other ways in which he had to trace out the implications of his new-found religion, for he had yet to work out positive views on the nature of the Church. "He was more convinced touching the irregularity of Bishops than ever before", and he opposed them, not by separating from the Established Church, but by using every opportunity which presented itself to bring the Church of England

---

45. Gardiner, *Constitutional Documents*, 202–36. Presented to Charles, December 1, 1641.
46. Clarendon, *History of the Rebellion*, IV, 51, 52.
47. *W.S.*, I, 143. Not even the fen dispute was overlooked. Cf. Item 32.
48. Lord Kimbolton, Pym, Stroud, Hampden, Holies.
49. Whitelocke, *Memorials*, 52.

into conformity with his own views.[50] He tried to get the bishops excluded from the House of Lords he was instrumental in getting afternoon lectures established, he attacked the Book of Common Prayer, and in all these things he was trying to remove the "oppressive and unnecessary ceremonies by which divers weak consciences have been scrupled". He was obviously not opposed to the idea of a national Church, but he would like to see a national Church in which the Separatists were included and the bishops were excluded. As yet, however, he is undecided about what form of ecclesiastical organization he would like to see within the Church; the political power to which Parliament, and in particular the House of Commons, aspired, implied Presbyterianism, but[51] Cromwell wanted further information on that.

At the same time he would have to consider his religion in relationship to the nation and the time in which he was living. The Separatists regarded themselves as citizens of heaven, and held themselves apart from the affairs of this life; but the call of the hour was for men who would engage wholeheartedly in the struggle on the level of politics and perhaps warfare. This meant that the Separatists would have to re-think their position in relationship to civil society. While they were in exile, or meeting together in the obscurity of some country manor-house, they could ignore such questions, but when they found themselves forced to shape the pattern of a new commonwealth in America, or in England as they became involved in the struggle against Charles I, these questions could not be ignored. It is therefore

---

50. The Independents of the Westminster Assembly admitted that at first they had looked no further "then the dark part, the evil of those superstitions adjoyned to the worship of God, which have been the common stumbling block and offence of many a thousand tender consciences", before they tried to formulate positive ideas of what the true Church should be like. *Apologeticall Narration humbly submitted to the Honourable Houses of Parliament* (1646), 2.

51. It has not been sufficiently realized that to some extent the ecclesiastical settlement of Elizabeth implied a form of Presbyterianism. By the Act of Uniformity (I Eliz., Cap. II) every Englishman was to be *(ipso facto)* a member of the Church of England. It meant that, as far as the State was concerned, England was a country consisting only of Christians, and the House of Commons was therefore an elected body representing not only the civil interests of the English people, but also the laity of the *Church* in England. This was an accidental result of uniformity, but when the House of Commons claimed the right to discuss religion it became a kind of national General Assembly. To *control* national religion, however, the Commons would have first to abolish the bishops, and secondly, to maintain uniformity (since only by so doing could they claim to represent the Church). Hence Presbyterianism and parliamentary supremacy were allied causes.

a period of experiment in the realm of Moral Theology, and as Cromwell accepted responsibility for leadership and government, his life, to a large degree, personifies both the problems and the answers given.

Chapter Three

From the Beginning of the Civil War to the Spring of 1644

I

Although before the break of war Cromwell's ecclesiastical views could not be clearly defined, he was one of the first to sign the Protestation of the Commons which promised "To maintain and defend as far as Lawfully I may, with my life, power and estate, the True Reformed Protestant Religion, expressed in the Doctrine of the Church of England, against all Popery and Popish Innovations."[1] The question of religious toleration did not arise, and those who signed the Protestation did so as members of the national Church, reserving to themselves their own interpretation of the "True Reformed Protestant Religion".

Oliver took a far more active part in the preliminary moves leading up to war than has been generally supposed,[2] and when hostilities broke out he was one of the first to support the parliamentary cause.[3] On July 15, 1642, he moved that an order be made to allow the townsmen of Cambridge to raise two companies of volunteers and to appoint captains for them, and he was re-imbursed for the £100 he had spent on helping to arm the county.[4] In August of the same year he seized the castle and

---

1. May 3, 1641, *W.S.*, I, 127; *L-C*, III, 225 (Appendix 3), John Vicars, *Jehovah-jireh. God in the Mount of Englands Parliamentary Chronicle* (1644), 34. As a burgess of Cambridge Cromwell commended the Protestation to the Mayor and Aldermen of that town, and Carlyle has pointed out that although his fellow burgess, John Lowry, signed the letter, Oliver appears to have written it; *W.S.*, I, 127 f.; *L-C*, III, 226 f.
2. *W.S.*, I, 127, 149-97 *passim.*
3. February 7, 1642/3: "Mr Cromwell offers to lend Three hundred Pounds for the service of the Commonwealth." *Commons Journals*, II, 408; cf. John Rushworth, *Historical Collecitons* (7 vols., 1659, 1680, 1692, 1701), V, 564 (erroneously given in *L-C*, I, 111 n. as "Rushworth, IV, 564").
4. *Cal. State Papers Domestic, Charles I*, Vol. 491, No. 71, July 15, 1642, and see Nos. 71(i) and (ii) for related papers. Cf. *C.K.*, II, 674.

magazine of Cambridge,[5] crushed an attempt by the Bishop of Ely to put the King's Commission of Array into effect, and set three of the college heads as prisoners to London. He then returned to London to join the army of Robert Devereux, Earl of Essex, in time to be present at the battle of Edgehill on October 23,[6] and it was probably just after this unsatisfactory battle that he addressed some pungent remarks to John Hampden on the state of the parliamentary cavalry:

> Your troopers, said I, are most of them old decayed serving men and tapsters, and such kind of fellows, and, said I, their troopers are gentlemen's sons, younger sons, persons of quality: do you think that the spirits of such base and mean fellows will ever be able to encounter gentlemen that have honour, courage and resolution in them? Truly I pressed him in this manner conscientiously, and truly I did tell him, You must get men of a spirit, - and take it not ill what I saay, I know you will not, - of a spirit that is like to go as far as a gentlemen will go, or else I am sure you will be beaten still.[7]

By the end of the year 1643 the whole of the north, with the exception of Lancashire and Hull, and the whole of the west, with the exception of Gloucester, Plymouth and a few ports on the Dorset coast, were secure in the hands of the King, and it was only from the eastern counties – the Eastern Associaation – that Parliament received the least glimmer of hope. Early in January Oliver had suppressed the proclamation of the King's Commission of Array for Hertfordshire at St. Albans,[8] and his correspondence gives us some idea of his activity.[9] It is not surprising that by January 26 we find that he was become raised to the rank

---

5. Sir Philip Stapleton reported "That Mr. Cromwell, in Cambridgeshire, has seixed the Magazine in the Castle of Cambridge; and hath hindered the Carrying of the Plate from that University; which, as some report, was to the Value of Twenty thousand Pounds, or thereabouts". *C.J.,* II, 724, August 15, 1642. Cf. F. J. Varley, *Cambridge during the Civil War* (Cambridge, 1935).
6. Royalists have thrown doubt on whether Cromwell was ever at Edgehill (Holles, *Memoirs,* 17; Dugdale, *Short View,* 110), but a comparison should be made with the contemporary record in Vicars, *Jehovah-jireh,* 198. The question is investigated fully by Sir Charles Firth in his article "The Raising of the Ironsides", *Transactions of the Royal Historical Society,* XIII, 19n., and W. .C. Abbott, *W.S.,* I, 204.
7. The incident was recalled by Cromwell in his speech to the Second Protectorate Parliament, April 13, 1657, *W.S.,* IV, 471; *L-C,* III, 65.
8. Vicars, *Jehovah-jireh,* 246; *C. J.,* II, 100.
9. *W.S.,* I, 208, *L-C,* III, 314 (Supp. 2, December 17, 1642), and to Robert Barnard, January 23, 1642/3, *W.S,* I, 210, *L-C,* I, 115 f. (IV).

of colonel[10] and directed the defence of the eastern counties from Cambridge against the threat of attack by Lord Capel.[11] The number of his troops increased rapidly, and by September 1643 the single troop of October 1642 had grown to be a double regiment of fourteen full troops.[12]

During the early months of 1643 he was appealing for money;[13] he crushed the royalists at Lowestoft[14] and Lynn[15], and by the end of April he had captured Crowland. Laudatory epithets were fashionable but we cannot begrudge John Vicars's description as "the valiant and active Collonel Cromwell".

II

The threat with which Cromwell was most concerned at the end of the first few months of 1643 was that which developed from the Marquis of Newcastle's army in the north. In May Essex had ordered the forces of the eastern and east-midland counties to combine for the relief of Lincolnshire, and, if possible, to effect a junction with the Fairfaxes, who were more or less isolated in Yorkshire. The local commanders, however, showed little inclination to leave their own areas.[16] Cromwell proceeded to Grantham, the agreed rendezvous, where he met and defeated a far superior royalist force from Newark,[17] thereby tasting the fruits of personal victory in the field for the first time.[18] As Dr.

---

10. *Ibid.*, I, 117 n. (by Mrs. Lomas) for the date; also C.H. Firth, "The Raising of the Ironsides", article in the *Transactions of the Royal Historical Society*, XIII, 22 and notes.
11. To the Deputy-Lieutenants of Norfolk, and to Sir John Hobert, Sir Thomas Richardson and other knights and baronets of Norfolk, dated January 26 and 27, 1642/3 respectively, *W.S.*, I, 211–12; *L-C*, III, 228-30 (App. 4). Of. *Jehovah-jireh* 273.
12. *Rel. Baxt.*, I, 94.
13. *W.S.*, I, 218; *L-C*, I, 120 f. (V), and see also the appeal sent out to the "Inhabitants of Fen Drayton in the Hundred of Papworth" to help with funds for the fortification of Cambridge against Capel, *W.S.*, I, 217; *L-C*, I, 118 f., March 8, 1642/3. Cf. *W.S.*, I, 220 f.; *L-C*, I, 127 (VI).
14. *Jehovah-jireh*, 285. See letter from John Cory to Sir John Potts, quoted *L-C*, I, 122–4 (March 17).
15. *Ibid.*, 124, note by Mrs. Lomas, *W.S.*, I, 219.
16. Letter May 2, 1643, *W.S.*, I, 228 f.; *L-C*, I, 132 f. (IX).
17. *Jehovah-jireh*, 332. In view of the treachery of the Hotham family the presence of this superior Cavalier force may not have been entirely an accident. *Ibid.*, 366.
18. Cf. his letter to Sir Miles Hobart, May 13, 1643, *W.S.*, I, 230; *L-C*, 134, f. (X).

S.R. Gardiner has said, "The whole fortune of the Civil War was in that nameless skirmish."[19] In his account of the victory Cromwell exaggerated his own weakness and emphasized the greatness of God's intervention on their behalf[20] – "with this handful it pleased God to cast the scale", and "by God's providence they were immediately routed". The connection between God's intervening Providence and this particular body of men has begun to take shape in Cromwell's mind, and was soon to be shared also by his troops.

Despite the victory of the Fairfaxes at Wakefield,[21] the secret treachery of the Hothams and the mutual distrust of the commanders sent to relieve York led to a break-up of the coalition and left Fairfax to be defeated at Adwalton Moor,[22] and Sir John Meldrum, who had been sent north to command this group of forces and root out the treachery,[23] succeeded in apprehending Captain John Hotham, but failed in his main task of preventing the Queen from reaching Oxford. Oliver captured Stamford, beat off a raid from Newark on Peterborough, stormed Burleigh House, and hurried to effect a junction with Meldrum for the relief of Lord Willoughby's force in Gainsborough. At Edgehill Rupert's cavalry had been irresistible but uncontrolled, but at Gainsborough, Cromwell, after the initial success of his first charge, quickly drew up his disciplined troops and was able to take Cavendish's cavalry reserve in the rear. As a result the royalist force was completely destroyed and Cavendish was himself killed. After the battle, however, Cromwell found himself in the presence of Newcastle's main army, and retreat was inevitable; but it was conducted with consummate skill.[24]

---

19. *Great Civil War*, I, 143 (1893, 4 volume edition).
20. Joshua Sprigge, writing of Cromwell just before the battle of Naseby, said that he expected that "God would do great things by small means". *Anglia Rediviva; Englands Recovery* (1647), 43.
21. See the *Short Memorials of Thomas Lord Fairfax* (1699), edited by Brian Fairfax, 28–35; *Jehovah-jireh*, 337-f.
22. Fairfax, *Short Memorials*, 36–44. Cf. letter signed by the commanders June 2, *W.S.*, I, 234 f., also Cromwell's letter to the Commissioners of the Association at Cambridge, June 13, 1643, *W.S.* I, 235 f.
23. For the story of Hotham's treachery see *Jehovah-jireh*, 665–7; *L-C*, I, 133 f. n., 138 f., 150, 255. Meldrum's success was short-lived, for Hotham escaped from Nottingham Castle to Hull.
24. Cf. letter to William Lenthall, July 29, *W.S.*, I, 240–2; *L-C*, III, 230-2 (App. 5), to Sir John Wraye, July 30, *W.S.*, I, 243 f.; *L-C*, III, 233–5 (App. 5); and to some Suffolk gentlemen July 31, *W.S.*, I, 244–6; *L-C*, I, 140-3 (XII); *Jehovah-jireh*, 278 f.

Oliver was fully conscious of his victory: in the letter to some gentlemen of Suffolk he said, "Truly God follows you with encouragements, who is the God of blessings:[25] and I beseech you let Him not lose His blessings upon us. They come in season, and with all the advantages of heartening: as if God should say, Up and be doing, and I will help you and stand by you. There is nothing to be feared but our own sin and sloth."[26] John Buchan observed that at Gainsborough Oliver "achieved two of the most difficult feats of a cavalry commander, to attack an enemy in formation with troops disordered by difficult ground, and to withdraw weary men in the face of a fresh foe in overwhelming numbers. Gainsborough had clinched the lesson of Grantham."[27] One of Oliver's contemporaries commented later with some insight that this "was the beginning of his great Fortunes".[28] He had behind him a fine body of troops drawn from counties where he was known and respected – yeomen and their sons who had enlisted under his personal leadership "upon matter of conscience", and "thus being well armed within, by the satisfaction of their own Consciences, and without, by good Iron Arms, they would as one man, stand firmly, and charge desperately".[29]

An interesting event occurred about this time which stands apart from the military situation, but which is not unconnected with it. On August 3, 1643, *The Souldiers Pocket Bible* was published. It was a short book of Scriptural texts from the Genevan Version, taken chiefly from the Old Testament,[30] and provided a

---

25. "God of blessings" – reminiscent of Ezekiel 34:26 or Ephesians 1:3.
26. Carlyle noted that this paragraph was omitted in Rushworth and the newspapers (*L-C*, I, 140 n. 2). Cf. Rushworth, VI, 278 f.
27. *Oliver Cromwell*, 174 f.
28. Whitelocke, *Memorials* (1732), 72.
29. *Ibid.*
30. *The Souldiers Pocket Bible: Containing the most (if not all) those places contained in holy Scripture, which doe shew the qualifications of his inner man, that is a fit souldier to fight the Lords Battels, both before he fight, in the fight, and after the fight: Which Scriptures are reduced to several heads, and fitly applied to the Souldiers severall occasions, and so may supply the want of the whole Bible: which a Souldier cannot conveniently carry about him: And may see also useful for any Christian to meditate upon, now in this miserable time of Warre.* Imprimatur, Edm. Calamy (1643). Cf. the reprint in facsimile under the title *Cromwell's Soldier's Bible*, 1895. The anonymous author of the Introduction to the 1895 facsimile edition says that the extracts "with two exceptions only, are taken out of the Old Testament". This is incorrect as there are several references to the New Testament: Luke 3:14 (p. 2); Eph. 4:10 (p. 3); James 1:5 (p. 4); Matt. 10:28; 5:44 (p. 6); 2 Cor. 12:14 in error for 2 Cor. 12:9 (p. 14); 2 Cor. 1:10; 1 Cor. 29:15 in error for 1 Chron. 39:13 (p. 15).

From the Beginning of the Civil War to the Spring of 1644 61

guide for the devout soldier in all the vicissitudes of warfare. There is no reason to suppose that Cromwell had any hand in the compilation of this little book, or even that it was in any general circulation among the Parliamentary soldiers,[31] but it provides an important clue to our understanding of the relationship between religion and life in Cromwell's career.

There was bound to be moral tension as soon as the Separatist left the exclusiveness of exile and proscription and accepted social and civic duties. The same problem had faced the early Church when it ceased to be a persecuted sect, and with centuries of political activity behind it, the Roman Catholic Church tacitly had come to accept the fact that the Christian "ethic"[32] could not be enforced upon all men. It therefore recognized a double standard of Christian morality: the ethic of Christian perfection, which was attempted by comparatively few – priests and monastics – and a lower standard of morality, to which "Christian" laymen were required to conform.[33] Upon the basis of this recognition Rome had built up the science of Moral Theology. On the other hand, to Reformed theologians, and particularly to Separatists, the Church was by definition a company of people "called to be saints",[34] i.e. bent on attaining the perfection of the Christian ethic, and this expressly denies a double standard. Their ideal

---

31. C.H. Firth, *Cromwell's Army* (1902), 331–3.
32. The terms "ethics" and "morals" are used here in the specialized sense in which they are defined by Dr. Kirk in his chapter on "Moral Theology" in *The Study Of Theology* (ed. by K.E. Kirk, 1939), 363 f.; i.e. the "ethic" is the highest possible standard of conduct.
33. "Status religiosus seu stabilis in communi vivendi modus, quo fideles, praeter communia praecepta, evangelica quoque consilia servanda, per vota obedientiae, castitatis et paupertatis suscipiunt, ab omnibus in honore habendus est." *Codex juris canonici* (1933), 487. The phrase "praeter communia praecepta" implies a double standard. Perhaps the finest recent study of the tension between the secular and the spiritual is Mr. Aldous Huxley's study of the life of Père Joseph (François de Tremblay), the Franciscan monk who became Richelieu's lieutenant. *Grey Eminence* (1941).
34. Dr. John Owen wrote, "The Scripture doth in general represent the kingdom or church of Christ to consist of persons called *saints,* separated from the world. ... Those who know aught of these things will not profess that persons openly profane, vicious, sensual, wicked, and ignorant, are approved and owned of Christ as the subjects of his kingdom, or that it is his will that we should receive them into the communion of the church, 2 Tim. 3:1–5." *True Nature of a Gospel Church* (*Works,* 1853, XVI, 11 f.). Cf. also Thomas Goodwin, *The Government of the Churches of Christ,* Bk. I, Chapter I (*Works,* 1865, vol. XI, s)- However, John Calvin, with the conception of a State Church in mind, understood the problem, and hinted at the need of a formulated Moral Theology to meet it. *Institutes,* IV, 1, 9.

was possible as long as they were exiles enjoying seclusion from the responsibilities of citizenship,[35] but it required modification as soon as they returned to take up normal civic obligations, and to an even greater extent when they undertook the responsibilities of civil government. They discovered that the care of civil government was something that they could not entrust to others, and that they had to negotiate with, and accept responsibility for those to whom saintliness had little attraction.

The *Souldiers Pocket Bible,* with its predominant appeal to the Old Testament, indicates the unconscious answer which the seventeenth-century Puritans gave to the problem, and which in their view would be at once "Christian" and practicable within the secular community. They met the problem not by denying the duty of Christians to strive after the Christian Ethic, but on the basis of the Reformation's appeal to the Bible, and in particular by the division of Scripture into two "ethical" standards: the Old Testament defined a Christian's standards of conduct as he was a citizen of an earthly kingdom, and the New Testament defined his conduct as a citizen of Heaven. Both these standards were regarded as equally authoritative within their respective spheres, but to the Puritan it was a "dual ethic" rather than a double standard of morality. This position was not adopted consciously, and it was subject to considerable modification, but, on the basis of the Puritan's Biblical faith, it was the obvious way to meet the problem, and it suggests why historians have always found a cleavage or "dualism" between the conduct of the Puritan in politics or business and his devotional life.[36]

III

The urgency of the military position after the retreat from Gainsborough is emphasized by the general brevity of Cromwell's

---

35. "We had no new Common-wealths to rear, to frame Church-government unto, whereof any one piece might stand in the others light, to cause the least variation by us from the Primitive Pattern; we had no State-ends or Political interests to comply with; No Kingdoms in our eye to subdue unto our mould. ... We had nothing else to doe but simply and singly to consider how to worship God acceptably, and so most according to his word. ..." *Apologeticall Narration,* 3 f.
36. See Ernst Troeltsch, *The Social Teaching of the Christian Churches* (translation by Olive Wyon, 1931), 158 ff., A. S. P. Woodhouse, *Puritanism and Liberty* (1938), Introduction.

letters.[37] Fortunately for the Associated Counties Newcastle turned aside to besiege the Fairfaxes in Hull, and the threat to the eastern counties[38] did not materialize, although in his letter to the Deputy Lieutenants of Suffolk, August 29, 1643, Cromwell did not regard the danger as completely passed.[39] The primary importance of this letter, however, is in its description of the type of man which Oliver selected for his troops. He reminded the gentlemen of Suffolk that "a few honest men are better than numbers", adding the comment that "if you choose godly honest men to be captains of horse, honest men will follow them". He went on to advise his supporters:

> The King is exceedingly strong in the West. If you be able to foil a force at the first coming of it, you will have reputation; and that is of great advantage in our affairs. God hath given it to our handful; let us endeavour to keep it. I had rather have a plain russet-coated captain that knows what he fights for, and loves what he knows, than that which you call a gentleman and is nothing else. I honour a gentleman that is so indeed.[40]

The "russet-coated captain that knows what he fights for, and loves what he knows" could well have been a self-portrait. Cromwell was completely single-minded in the cause, and to him the issues were simplified to the clear-cut distinction of black and white. In that he differed from the Lord General of the Parliamentary army and a good many more officers within those ranks, and "over them", says Professor Abbott, "as over his enemies, he had the enormous advantage of absolute conviction of the utter righteousness of that cause and of himself, the utter wrongness of those on the other side".[41] Such enthusiasm in an officer can be infectious. Moreover, his letters show not only pride at seeing his troops grow into a formidable fighting force, but also concern for their material well-being: he was completely at one with his-

---

37. See Willoughby's letter (*W.S.*, I, 251; *L-C*, I, 146 f.). Cromwell himself wrote to the eastern counties of the probability of Newcastle advancing "into your bowels"; see the letters to the Committee of Suffolk (July 31, *W.S.*, I, 244 f. *L-C*, I, 140–3, XII) and to the Deputy Lieutenants of Essex, August 1, 4, 6 (*W.S.*, I, 247 f., 250, 251; *L-C*, III, 315 f., Supp. 4) and two letters to the Commissioners at Cambridge, August 6 and 8 (*W.S.*, I, 251, 252 f.; *L-C*, I, 147–50, XIV and XV).
38. See the notes to the Deputy Lieutenants of Essex, August 29, *W.S.*, I, 255.
39. *W.S.*, I, 256; *L-C*, I, 154 (XVI).
40. Cf. also his letter to Oliver St. John, September 11, 1643. *W.S.*, I, 258; *L-C* I, 155 f. (XVII).
41. *W.S.*, I, 190.

men. When the troops of a certain Captain Margery were accused of confiscating horses from the Suffolk gentry, Oliver rose at once to their defence and continued in a vein which showed that the real criticism went a good deal deeper:[42]

> Gentlemen, it may be it provokes some spirits to see such plain men made Captains of Horse. It had been well that men of honour and birth had entered into these employments, but why do they not appear? Who would have hindered them? But seeing it was necessary the work must go on, better plain men than none, but best to have men patient of wants, faithful and conscientious in the employment, and such, I hope, these will approve themselves to be.

It appears that there was considerable feeling against the inferior social standing of some of Cromwell's officers, but he maintained that integrity alone should govern a man's appointment.[43] Important as this principle undoubtedly is, however, Oliver viewed it and judged it as primarily a religious question: he was concerned with the selection of "godly honest men" in the sure belief that these men, irrespective of social class, would prove the most valiant in the Civil War, and events proved him right. The social criticism was the outcome of a religious criticism which struck deeply at the first principle on which his Troop had been formed, for it was of the essence of Independency and its kindred sects that the old privileges attaching to birth and aristocracy were superseded by the new responsibilities of being a child of Grace.[44] At first Oliver denied that his men were Anabaptists, but he soon shifted his ground to defend his employment of all Christians:[45] from religious principles, therefore, he established a principle which has become an axiom of Democracy, that neither class nor sect should debar a man from public service.[46] The

---

42. To the Deputy Lieutenants of Suffolk, September 28, 1643. *W.S.*, I, 261 f.; *L-C*, I, 159 ff. (XVIII).
43. The Royalists gibed at the humble origins of Cromwell's officers. Major-General Berry (at this time one of Cromwell's captains) was reported to have been a collier, and one of Clarendon's later correspondents described Vice-Admiral Lawson as "originally a kind of fisherman at Scarborough", who gained "preferment to a Newcastle collier". *Clarendon State Papers* (1786), III, 640 (Sambourne to Hyde, January 7, 1659/60).
44. John 3:1–7.
45. Letters to Crawford (quoted *infra*) and to Oliver St. John, September II, 1643. It should be noted that Anabaptists were identified with all the excesses of their continental co-religionists at Munster in 1533.
46. Cf. letter to Sir Thomas Barrington, October 6, 1643. *W.S.*, I, 264 f.; *L-C*, III, 317 (Supp. 5).

From the Beginning of the Civil War to the Spring of 1644   65

traitors, Sir John Hotham and his son Captain Hotham, had described the forces of their accusers as "a company of Brownists, Anabaptists, Factious, inferiour persons, &c."[47] and this appears to have been directed against Oliver's troops. It is not unlikely that the connection of this kind of snobbery with Hotham's treachery was one reason why Oliver reacted so vigorously to criticism of his soldiers' social status and orthodoxy. Such detractors were in the main those who were most attracted to Scottish presbyterianism, and they received their most crushing retort in Cromwell's protest to the Scots Major-General Crawford for his treatment of a subordinate officer:

> Surely you are not well advised thus to turn off one so faithful to the Cause, and so able to serve you as this man is. Give me leave to tell you, I cannot be of your judgment; that if a man notorious for wickedness, for oaths, for drinking, hath as great a share in your affection as one that fears an oath, that fears to sin, that this doth commend your election of men to serve as fit instruments in this work.
>
> Ay, but the man is an Anabaptist. Are you sure of that? Admit he be, shall that render him incapable to serve the public? He is indiscreet. It may be so, in some things, we have all human infirmities. I tell you, if you had none but such indiscreet men about you, and would be pleased to use them kindly, you would find as good a fence to you as any you have yet chosen.
>
> Sir, the State, in choosing men to serve them, takes no notice of their opinions, if they be willing faithfully to serve them, that satisfies. I advised you formerly to bear with men of different minds from yourself; if you had done it when I advised you to it, I think you would not have had so many stumblingblocks in your way. ... Take heed of being sharp, or too easily sharpened by others, against those to whom you can object little but that they square not with you in every opinion concerning matters of religion.[48]

This defence did not spring simply from the impatience of one good soldier at the harsh treatment meted out on irrelevant grounds to fellow-officers; the unity of Cromwell and his troops went deeper, and can be shown to have been curiously related to his ecclesiastical position. Had his views become settled? Can we accept the evidence of others that at a comparatively early date

---

47. *Jehovah-jireh,* 367.
48. March 10, 1643/4, *W.S.,* I, 277 f.; *L-C,* I, 170 f. (XX). See note, *Ibid.,* 170 for the identity of the man in question (Lt.-Col. Warner).

in the Civil War Cromwell was regarded as an Independent?[49] Up to the outbreak of the Civil War he does not seem to have severed his connection with the Church of England, nor are there any records of his membership of any Independent Church, and anyone conversant with the forms of Independency during the seventeenth century will see in this a serious argument against the "sincerity" of Cromwell's churchmanship, for almost above all things else, to be an "Independent"[50] meant to accept the obligations of covenanted membership within a "gathered church".[51] There is a considerable difference between a patronage of Independency and membership of an Independent Church, and we should expect to find some indications of membership if Cromwell had become as well known a practising Independent as the contemporary authorities suggest.

It is here that we must mention Richard Baxter's description of a strange incident which probably happened at the beginning of 1643. Writing of the events which led up to the Self-Denying Ordinance of 1644, Baxter said that Cromwell "had gathered together as many of the Religious Party, especially of the Sectaries as he could get",[52] and going on to comment on the attendant evils, he said,

> I reprehended my self also, who had before rejected an Invitation from Cromwell: When he lay at Cambridge long before with that famous Troop which he began his Army with, his Officers purposed to make their Troop a gathered Church, and they all subscribed an Invitation to me to be their Pastor, and sent it to me to Coventry: I sent them a Denial, reproving their Attempt, and told them wherein my Judgment was against the Lawfulness and Convenience of their

---

49. Robert Baillie always identified Cromwell with Independency. *The Letters and Journals of Robert Baillie, A.M.* (edited by David Laing, Edinburgh, 1841, 3 vols.), II, 153, 203, 209, 229, 230.
50. The term "Independent" covers a very wide variety of church practice in the seventeenth century. The Independents "occupy ... the whole interval between the Right, where the Puritan church-type is dominant, and the Left where the Puritan sect-type is not less supreme. No fact is more prominent than the existence of the two types side by side, or than their mutual influence particularly in the Centre Party, where indeed they merge." A. S. P. Woodhouse, *Puritanism and Liberty*, Introduction, p. 36. Professor Woodhouse uses the terms "church-type" and "sect-type" in the sense defined by Troeltsch (cf. *Social Teaching*, 593-8, 622 f.).
51. i.e. a congregation gathered from the world which had covenanted together to obey the Word of God, and gospel ordinances.
52. *Rel. Bax.*, I, 47.

way, and so I heard no more from them: And afterward meeting Cromwell at Leicester he expostulated with me for denying them.[53]

This is clearly a very important passage. It indicates not only where the roots of Cromwell's unity with his troops really lay, but also it resolves the mystery of his churchmanship. It is reliable evidence that he not only embraced the Independents' ecclesiastical position early in the Civil War, but also set about the curious task of forming his troop of horse into an Independent Church – a kind of militant congregation. In fact this is explicitly stated in the index of *Reliquiae Baxterianae*, where in reference to this incident under Cromwell's name, it says, "he invites Mr. Baxter to be Chaplain and Pastour to his Regiment when he was forming it into a Church".[54] In other words, the formation of the Ironsides had a religious significance, and it appears to have been Oliver's aim to bind them together not only as an efficient fighting machine, but also spiritually: they were united *as a Church* by the one type of churchmanship which could embrace in equality all shades of Puritan opinion. If this be so, then it throws new light on certain parts of Cromwell's career, for it not only explains the nature of the unity between him and his men, but also why he became known as "the great Independent" without his name ever having been connected with any particular local Church.[55]

This unity between Cromwell and his troops was, however, to have a theological significance beyond its importance in defining his churchmanship. He came to think of himself and his troops as welded together into a single instrument in the hand of the Almighty,[56] and he seems almost to have regarded the very unworthiness with which others charged them as the special reason for God's choice of them as His "instrument". He does

---

53. *Rel. Bax.*, I, 51. It appears that Captain Berry was instrumental in the invitation being sent to Baxter. Cf. Firth's article "The later history of the Ironsides" in the *TranS.R. Hist. Soc.* (New Series, 1901), XV, 3, also Sir James Berry and S.G. Lee, *A Cromwellian Major General* (Oxford, 1938), 14. Regarding the date of this call, it should be noted that by March 1643 Cromwell's original troop had become five troops. It seems therefore that the invitation was sent to Baxter soon after Cromwell became a colonel. Baxter was in Coventry for two years after the Battle of Edgehill.
54. *Rel. Bax., in loc.*
55. The importance of Baxter's testimony in solving the question of Cromwell's churchmanship was pointed out by the author in an article previously published in the Congregational Historical Society *Transactions*, Vol. XVI, No. 3 (September 1950), 118–31.
56. *Supra*, p. 63 f.

not provide arguments for this choice, but he accepts it as a fact manifestly demonstrated by the success granted to his troops. The Puritan did not attempt to explain why or how God predestined him to salvation and others to damnation, but once he had become convinced that he was "elect of God", he was bound to God's will by ties of gratitude and complete humility to his Redeemer, which nevertheless became unconquerable pride before his fellow-men; before God he had nothing to commend him, but before men he was a "chosen vessel", ready to shoulder impossible tasks in the certain knowledge that while he could achieve nothing by himself, in the strength of the One to whom all things were possible no task was too great. "The Puritan", wrote Macaulay, "was made up of two different men, the one all self-abasement, penitence, gratitude, passion; the other proud, calm, inflexible, sagacious. He prostrated himself in the dust before his Maker: but he set his foot on the neck of his king."[57] When Oliver wrote to Sir Thomas Barrington, "truly I count not myself worthy to be employed by God", we are reminded of the similar protestations voiced by the Old Testament prophets,[58] who, for all their protests, knew they had been set aside for special tasks by the Lord God. Oliver and his troops had begun to share a corporate sense of vocation under God,[59] and it remains for us to see how he interpreted his own task as their successes became more and more identified with his leadership.

IV

The addition of cavalry from Hull to Oliver's strength gave him a considerable cavalry force with which to join the Earl of Manchester.[60] This army engaged an equal number of cavaliers at Winceby on October II, 1643, where Oliver had a remarkable escape from death, having been knocked down and crushed by the horse which had been shot from under him.[61] The Earl of Manchester had succeeded Lord Grey of Wark as Major-General

---

57. *Essay on Milton.*
58. Cf. Exodus 3: II – 4:10; Isaiah 6:5; Jeremiah 1:6.
59. Cf. *Rel. Bax.*, I, 51.
60. Rushworth, *Historical Collections,* VI, 280; Fairfax, *Short Memorials,* 65.
61. Vicars, *God's Ark overtopping the World's wave, or the 3rd part of the Parliamentary Chronicle* (1644), 46. Rushworth, despite different details, has obviously based his account on Vicars. Rushworth notes that although Manchester had not so many Colours as the Royalists he had as many men. Rushworth, VI, 281 f.

of the Eastern Association on August 9, 1643, and he very soon re-occupied Lincoln and Gainsborough, so that Lord Fairfax was able to sally forth from Hull and force the Marquis of Newcastle to raise the siege.

Sixteen hundred and forty-three was "a year of significant deaths".[62] The Royalists had suffered, but Parliament lost the more heavily, for John Hampden had been mortally wounded in a skirmish at Chalgrove Field on June 18, and Pym died on December 8 after an illness. John Pym, more than any other man, had been the architect of the Rebellion, and at the time these losses seemed irreparable. Parliament was thrown back upon Scottish aid, but the Scots were intent on introducing the Presbyterian Church government into England. It was, however, this very prospect that brought to the fore Independents like young Sir Henry Vane and Oliver Cromwell.[63] Oliver acted for all practical purposes as Manchester's second in command ever since the latter had assumed command of the Eastern Association, and his ability was granted official recognition by his appointment as Lieutenant-General to Manchester on January 21, 1644, and to membership of the Committee of Both Kingdoms at its inception in February, 1644.[64]

Judged by the course of the Civil War as a whole the military activity of Cromwell at this stage was of local importance, but, with the passing of Pym and the appointment of Oliver as Lieutenant-General to the Earl of Manchester, the stage was reset and a new leading actor made his appearance. All the factors which might produce the Protectorate were already present, including those intangible factors which belonged to Cromwell's beliefs and character. But perhaps the most significant fact of these early months of the war was the complete success of Cromwell and his troops in all that they undertook, and this conjunction of military success with the contemporary ideas of Providence could not but strengthen Oliver's convictions about the righteousness

---

62. Buchan, *Oliver Cromwell,* 171.
63. For the opposition of the Independents in the Westminster Assembly at this time, see *W.S.,* I, 269.
64. Correspondence of this period is the note to the Committees of Ely, January 10, 1643/4, *L-C,* III, 318 (Supp. 6); *W.S.,* I, 268 f., also a note to Mr. Edwards, treasurer for Wisbech, January 19, *W.S.,* I, 271; the letter to Sir Samuel Luke, March 8, *W.S.,* I, 276 f.; *L-C,* III, 236 (App. 6); and an interesting letter to the Rev. Mr. Hitch, choirmaster of Ely Cathedral demanding that in the interests of public order he should desist from his "unedifying and offensive" choral service, January 10, *W.S.,* I, 270; *L-C,* I, 167 (XIX).

of his Cause, and hence his own vocation under God. For this reason we must give due weight to his military career as a most important influence in the development of his thought.

Chapter Four

The Civil War: Spring 1644 to the Self-Denying Ordinance

I

By the spring of 1644 serious political differences were beginning to appear between the Presbyterians and Independents. Many Presbyterians hoped for a negotiated peace, which would not leave the King humiliated by total defeat, and they imagined this could best be achieved by a policy of continuous defence. They feared the radical and religious elements which were appearing within the parliamentary party as much as they feared the royal prerogative,[1] and peers like Essex, Willoughby and Manchester had a strong landed interest which often allowed territorial considerations to outweigh military strategy. There was a tendency on the part of county forces to avoid action outside their own boundaries, and thus Parliament could never produce an effective field army strong enough to bring the King's army to a decisive battle: localized armies produced static warfare and military stalemate.

On the other hand the Independents argued that lasting peace would not be attained by a precarious balance of power: they sought a complete parliamentary victory which would leave the King powerless to make war.

This difference appears to be entirely secular, but, as Mr. Bruce points out, the division became more and more identified with the ecclesiastical distinction between Presbyterians and Independents.[2] The Presbyterians looked for the reformation of the Church of England from the "popish" elements remaining in its organization and liturgy, but they did not desire to abolish the Establishment; indeed, the ordinance of February 5, 1644, requiring all Englishmen over the age of eighteen to sign the Covenant, implied uniformity as comprehensive as that of Elizabeth's

---

1. *The Quarrel between the Earl of Manchester and Oliver Cromwell*, edited by John Bruce and David Mason (Camden Society), 1875, p. xxxii.
2. *Ibid.*, pp. xxxi–xxxviii.

Settlement. They hoped that the conclusions of the Westminster Assembly of Divines would be ratified by Parliament, and that the establishment of Presbyterianism would provide the basis of any peace terms offered to Charles, whereas the Independents could never expect their system to be accepted by Charles even if the autonomy of local congregations did not preclude the idea of an established Church altogether.[3] Their plea was for religious toleration, and Independency therefore gathered to itself all the sects whose hope of survival depended upon this principle, or which advanced the even wider claim of Liberty of Conscience.[4] Since Charles would never accept such limitations to religious uniformity while he had power to resist, their only hope was in the complete defeat of the King and a dictated peace. They sought peace not by vain endeavours "to come to terms with an opponent who refused to admit the constitutional *status* of those with whom he treated, but by directing all the national energies to obtain a victorious close of the war".[5]

But the proceedings of the Westminster Assembly showed that they had as little to hope from their Presbyterian "brethren" as from the King, and in the event of a negotiated peace the Independents stood to find themselves in a worse position than at the beginning of the war. The only chance they had of achieving their end was by gaining control themselves and establishing an ecclesiastical system based on religious toleration.

There could be no doubt to which of these parties the Earl of Manchester would belong. As a known Presbyterian[6] he had

---

3. This had certainly been true of the followers of Robert Browne, but the principle of local autonomy had been severely modified by the "Congregationalist" Independents of the Westminster Assembly. These men were responsible for the Establishment of the Protectorate and were influenced by John Cotton's State Churches in America. Cf. *infra*, p. 75, n. 3.
4. The sects tended to favour Liberty of Conscience in inverse proportion to their numbers. For the relationship between Toleration and Liberty of Conscience, see the first few chapters in *The Contest for Liberty of Conscience in England* by Wallace St. John (Chicago, U.S.A., 1900).
5. Bruce, *op. cit.*, p. xxxiii.
6. "His Lordship hath often, in the hearing of many witnesses, thus expressed himselfe solemnly. I could contentedly part with halfe my estate, upon condition the discipline of Christ was established, and a good Ministry settled in every Congregation of the Kingdome, yea with those conditions, how gladly could I betake my selfe unto a Country life, and leave all other contentments in the World. ... I know no man, who attends the Campe, lesse self-seeking, and more desirous to issue the Warres, in a comfortable Peace, than my Lord Manchester." (Ashe, *A true Relation of the most Chiefe Occurrences at, and since the late Battell at Newbery*, 1644).

been appointed one of ten peers to sit in the Westminster Assembly, his territorial interests kept his mind centred upon the local defence of the eastern counties, and as a peer he had a natural aversion from radical elements which threatened the ancient constitution of England. On the other hand Cromwell had become an Independent,[7] and it is against the background of differences which were religious, political and personal that we must view the events which led up to the Self-Denying Ordinance.

II

Before Major-General Crawford entered the Army of the Eastern Association Cromwell and Manchester had worked well together, and the Rev. Robert Baillie, one of the Scottish Commissioners, said that Manchester, "a sweet meek man", allowed Cromwell to control the Army "at his pleasure". Of Cromwell himself he said that he was "a very wise and active head, universallie well beloved, as religious and stoutt; being a known Independent, the most of the sojours who loved new wayes putt themselves under his command".[8] In February 1644, however, following the entry of Scotland into the English war, Laurence Crawford, a Scotsman of rigid Presbyterian views, became Major-General to the Earl of Manchester's army.

There were undoubtedly personal reasons why Crawford and Cromwell would find it difficult to agree, for Crawford was as strong a personality as Oliver himself, and as a professional soldier with continental experience he would expect his views to be accepted in preference to those of a gentleman-farmer turned officer. Furthermore, Oliver was an Englishman with very little love for the Scots. But when due allowance is made for all the personal factors, the real reason for the breach was ecclesiastical and theological. Parliament, as the price of Scotland's entry into the English war, had signed the Solemn League and Covenant, and it appeared logical to Crawford that Presbyterian uniformity should be enforced in honour of the treaty obligations. He could not be expected to understand the variety of sects he found in

---

7. This alone can account for Cromwell's attitude during the next few months. If ambition had been his motive he would surely have stood to gain more by giving his support to the influential Presbyterian party. The only reasonable explanation for his position is that he had become a convinced Independent.
8. *Letters and Journals*, II, 229.

the army of the Association, and he soon began to take strong measures against some of his less orthodox officers.[9] The relationship between the two men rapidly deteriorated; but Crawford's animosity against Oliver would not have been of any great consequence had there not been a corresponding readiness in the Earl of Manchester to listen to it, and it is clear that something occurred to harden this easy-going nature.

Manchester was a sincere Presbyterian; as one of the King's commissioners at Ripon in 1640 he had been assiduously courted by the Scots.[10] From January 22 to April 16, 1644, the King had held a royalist "Parliament" at Oxford, and there had been rumours that peace overtures might be made. Because of this there was a military lull and Manchester took the opportunity to devote his energies to some of his ecclesiastical duties.[11] He attended the meetings of the Westminster Assembly and conducted an official visitation of the University of Cambridge, in company with his two Presbyterian chaplains Ash[e][12] and Goode," ejecting men of the wrong sort from their masterships or fellowships, and putting into their places Puritan ministers and scholars recommended by the Westminster Assembly".[13] Oliver on the other hand was spending most of his labours in military organization, or minor skirmishes. Therefore Manchester was no longer under his immediate influence, but both in the Assembly and with his chaplains he was under strong Presbyterian pressure, and at a time when Presbyterians were very bitter against the Independents for their opposition in the Assembly. Oliver was the acknowledged friend of the dissenters of the Assembly, who by reason of their minority had been forced to adopt a policy of obstruction in order to gain time,[14] but this policy was not likely to impress a lay peer who in face of the majority's strength might easily be convinced that the minority opinion was irrelevant and factious: Robert Baillie wrote of the Independents in the Assembly:

---

9. See Crawford's MS., *Narrative of the Earl of Manchester's Campaign* in Bruce and Masson's *Manchester's Quarrel, etc.*, 59–70, and see Cromwell's letter regarding Lt. Warner, *supra*, p. 65.
10. Clarendon, *History of the Rebellion*, II, 108.
11. Cf. *Manchester's Quarrel*, p. xxi.
12. Simeon Ashe had been educated at Emmanuel College, Cambridge. He was a strict Presbyterian.
13. Masson, *Manchester's Quarrel*, p. xxi.
14. September 16, 1644; Baillie, *Letters and Journals*, II, 230.

beside all the errour and great evill which is their way, they have been the only men who hes keeped this poor church in an anarchie so long a time, who have preferred the advancement of their private new fancies to the kingdom of Christ, who hes lossed many a thousand souls through the long confusion occasioned by their willfulness only.[15]

Manchester would have agreed, and was the more ready to listen to Crawford.

The differences between Manchester and Cromwell arose ultimately out of different interpretations of the doctrine of the Church.[16] The Presbyterian desire for religious uniformity was founded upon the conception of a single unified Church and ecclesiastical discipline, which had been taken over from Calvin. The claim of the Independent rested upon the authority of the Holy Spirit within the local congregation as a microcosm of the Universal Church, and this meant that they could not logically deny a similar claim by other Christians equally sincere: it implied Liberty of Conscience, although not all Independents would go as far as that.[17]

Then again, the respective attitudes of Presbyterians and Independents to the war turned on the extent to which they were prepared to trust the civil magistrate with power in ecclesiastical matters. A strict reading of Calvin would suggest that, granted the establishment of "true religion", any further resistance to the King would become sin against "God's anointed",[18] and this is substantially the attitude taken by Essex, Manchester and their colleagues in 1644. The Independents of the Asssembly considered themselves followers of Geneva no less than their Presbyterian colleagues, but reformation of religion "according to the Word of God" for which the Solemn League and Covenant

---

15. Public Letter, April 2, *Letters and Journals*, II, 147.
16. Cf. *supra*, p. 71–2.
17. The Independents of the Westminster Assembly had been chosen for their closeness to the Presbyterian views. Jeremiah Burroughes in his *Irenicum* defined the limits to which he and his friends would carry toleration; "the Devil must not be left alone, though he be got into mens consciences. God hath appointed no City of Refuge for him; if he flies to mens consciences, as Ioab did to the homes of the Altar, he must be fetched from thence. ..." (*Irenicum, to the Lovers of Truth and Peace, Heart-Divisions opened In the Causes and Evils of them* (1646), 29 ff.) Later in the same book he denied that Independents would tolerate Roman Catholics, Arians, or Moslems, but he summarized the Independent attitude in the following words – "we come as farre as we have light to guide us, we dare not step one step in the dark; if we doe we shall certainly sinne". (*Ibid.*, 47.)
18. *Institutes*, IV, xx, 23, 29; cf. 32.

provided, meant something very different for them; nor would "true religion", in the view of Independents, ever find its place within the nation while religious uniformity was exercised to the oppression of the People of God. Therefore, according to their engagement in the Solemn League and Covenant, and according to Calvin's own principles, they held they were entitled to resist for as long as it was necessary.

The conflict was felt throughout the parliamentary party: it had assumed national importance. The typical Presbyterian attitude to the conduct of the war had been personified in the Earl of Essex and his heavy defensive strategy, and it was becoming increasingly clear that, if the war was to be won decisively, its management must be taken out of the hands of the present Commander-in-Chief and his associates, and placed in the hands of one who would pursue the task with vigour. We know from Robert Baillie that the Independents came to regard Cromwell as the man for this task.[19]

It appears that there was in London a small but very influential group of politicians which had attached itself to the Independent party. These men had supported the Solemn League and Covenant in order to gain the support of the Scots, but had obstructed the Scots when they sought to impose religious uniformity upon England.[20] Robert Baillie complained bitterly about this apparent change of front. In some of Baillie's earlier letters Sir Henry Vane is seen working very closely with the Scots,[21] and Baillie as late as April 2, 1644, commenting upon the Independents' influence upon Members of Parliament, confidently said "Sir Harie Vane, whatever be his judgement, yet less nor more, does not owne them, and gives them no encouragement",[22] but by September the same year a Toleration measure had been introduced to the House of Commons, and Baillie complained that "Our greatest friends, Sir Henry Vane and the Solicitor [St. John], are the main procurers of all this; and that without any regard to us, who have saved their nation, and brought these two persons to the height of the power now they enjoy, and use to our prejudice".[23] Sir Henry Vane and St. John had become the political

---

19. *Letters and Journals*, II, 229 f.
20. Cf. Holles, *Memoirs* (1699), 15–17.
21. *Letters and Journals*, II, 89, 117, 133 f., 141, 145 f., 230.
22. *Ibid.*, 146.
23. *Ibid.*, 230, to Dickson, September 16, 1644. Cf. *Ibid.*, 235. Similarly *Ibid.*, 231, Public Letter, October 1644. Cf. *Ibid.*, 179, 235–7.

The Civil War: Spring 1644 to the Self-Denying Ordinance 77

leaders of Independency and through the newly created Committee of Both Kingdoms they were exerting considerable power in the affairs of the nation.

The appearance of these leaders transformed the position of the Independents: it gave the Party real influence at Westminster, and above all it gave to Independency a centre of political direction which had little to learn from the Scots in the methods of political management. Undoubtedly some of those who joined the Independent party did so because they were so deeply implicated in the rebellion as to make any thought of compromise with Charles unthinkable, and they were drawn to Independency for motives of self-preservation. The leaders, however, realized that in warfare the most effective argument is an army, and they began to look about for a general who could be relied upon. It appears that Sir William Waller was the first soldier to be approached, for after his defeat at Roundaway Down[24] he found himself surrounded with numerous friends from the Independent party when he returned to London:

> In that heat (as the sun is ever hottest after a cloud) I had an offer from them of a very considerable army to be raised, and putt under my command, with a constant maintenance for it, if I would engage myself to entertein none but godly officers, such as should be recommended to me. Unto which I replied, that I desired nothing more than to have such officers about me, as might be remarkable for that spott, as Moses calleth it; but I wished them to consider that there went more to the making of an officer than single honesty. ...
>
> I then found they had it in their designe to modell and form an army, that should be all of their owne party, and devoted to their owne ends. Upon this we differed. I trusted not them, nor they me, and so we agreed. From that time forward I may date the expiration of their friendship.[25]

It is clear from this where the idea of an Independent army had originated, and it is equally clear that in 1643 Cromwell was not considered as its commander, but by the middle of 1644 the position was very different, for the Independent leaders discovered that they had among their own number one who had not only assiduously been building up an army of "godly officers",

---

24. July 13, 1643.
25. *Vindication of the Character and Conduct of Sir William Waller*, written by himself and edited anonymously (1793), 13–15.

but who had won for himself a reputation as a brilliantly successful cavalry leader. Moreover, he needed no persuasion as to either the righteousness of "their designe" or its ultimate success.

III

It was under the shadow of this political struggle that the operations were undertaken jointly against the Marquis of Newcastle in the city of York at the end of April 1644, by the armies of Fairfax and Manchester, and the Scots under the Earl of Leven and David Lesley. The Marquis of Newcastle was about to give up the city when Rupert marched to his relief, and on July 2 the battle of Marston Moor was fought.[26] The Parliamentary army attacked early in the summer evening, gaining the tactical advantage of surprise, and Oliver's troopers on the left wing swept through Byron's cavalry only to be halted by the charge of Rupert and Molineux's regiment. At this critical juncture Oliver himself was grazed in the neck by a pistol shot fired so close that the flash momentarily blinded him. It was probably the most critical moment of his career and of the Puritan cause, but at that moment the royalist pressure slackened to meet an attack on its flank delivered by David Lesley with the reserve of "800 ill-mounted Scots".[27] It does no discredit to Cromwell to suggest that this temporary relief gave him just the chance he needed to gather himself, to rally his men and send them forward to drive the royalists before them through Wilstrop Wood.

Oliver's next move was a stroke of genius, for on almost the whole of the remaining front the forces of Parliament had been routed, and both the Earl of Leven and Lord Fairfax fled from the field. The left wing, and Major-General Crawford's men in the left-centre had been successful, but apart from Baillie's isolated band of Scots on the right nothing else remained of the Parliamentary army. Cromwell paused in the pursuit, reformed his troops, and, wheeling right to the extreme opposite wing to his own, he attacked and defeated the cavalry under Sir Charles Lucas that was slowly annihilating Baillie's Scots. The rest of Goring's cavalry returned from plundering the Parliamentary

---

26. For detailed discussion of the battle, see Sir C.H. Firth's article "Marston Moor" in the *Trans. R.H.S.* (New Series, 1898), Vol. XII.
27. Buchan, *Oliver Cromwell*, 188.

baggage too late to be of any assistance to their cause, for with the remaining Scots and the infantry under Crawford, Oliver attacked Newcastle's Whitecoats in the royalist centre, who, lacking cavalry support, died fighting.

The latent suspicion between Independents and Presbyterians immediately showed itself when the reports of the battle reached London, both sides claiming the victory, and neither side daring to concede any credit to the other. The Scots were particularly at pains to discredit Cromwell, ascribing the victory to David Lesley. Robert Baillie's correspondence reflects the intense anxiety of the Scottish commissioners in London to secure the settlement of Presbyterianism before the Independents could use their reports of the battle to gain the concession of religious toleration.[28] The Scots' embarrassment was the greater because the Earl of Manchester's chaplain, Simeon Ashe, had written an authoritative account of the battle that gave more credit to Cromwell "than we are informed is his due", and which was likely to weigh a good deal with the more moderate Presbyterians of the English Parliament.[29] The account mentions the good service which was done by many of the Scots in the fighting, and adds that they "therefore very well deserve to be sharers in the honour of the day", but that hardly made up for the increase in Cromwell's prestige.

Baillie had received his account of the battle from two compatriots, Sir Adam Hepburne of Humby, and Lieutenant-Colonel William Crawford of Skeldon,[30] and from the latter he received the intelligence "that at the beginning of the fight, Cromwell got a little wound on the craige, which made him retire, so that he was not so much as present at the service; bot his troupers were led on by David Lesley".[31] This rumour that Cromwell was not even present – strangely reminiscent of a rumour

---

28. To Spang, July 12, 1644, *Letters and Journals*, II, 203. To Blair, July 16, *ibid.*, 209.
29. Vicars inserted Ashe's account verbatim in *God's Arke*, 273–8. Baillie suggested that Simeon Ashe's writings "which for the man's known integrity, are every word believed … should be first seen and pondered by some of yow there". *Letters and Journals*, II, 209.
30. *Letters and Journals*, II, 218. David Laing, the editor, confuses Lt.-Col. William Crawford of Nether Skeldon (or Skeddon) with the Major-General of Manchester's army (cf. *ibid.*, n. 3), but it is clear from Baillie's letter and from *Rushworth*, VI, 605, that "Skeldon Crawford" was a Lieutenant-Colonel of dragoons in the army of the Scots.
31. *Letters and Journals*, II, 218.

about Edgehill[32] – was spread assiduously by the Scots, and particularly by Cromwell's antagonist, Major-General Laurence Crawford.[33] With Scottish assistance this rumour persisted for some time, but it does not bear examination.[34] It is evident that Cromwell was wounded, but we must agree with Firth when he comments that "the supposition that Cromwell, so long as he remained in the field at all, would content himself with being the nominal commander, and allow Leslie, or Crawford, or any other man to assume his authority and take his responsibility, is utterly incompatible with Cromwell's character.[35] The Independents were undoubtedly using Oliver as a figure-head, but there is no evidence to show that he took any active part in this political campaign: the most that can be said about him is that he did "Herod like, suffer others to magnifie him".

It cannot be assumed, however, that Oliver was completely unaffected by all that others were saying about him. The Independent Party hailed him as a national hero for the victory at Marston Moor, and the tone of Simeon Ashe's account indicates that there were also some English Presbyterians who took a similar view. The pamphlet *Vindiciae Veritatis: the Scots designe discovered*,[36] gives a very clear idea of Cromwell's tremendous prestige within the Independent Party and the idea of Cromwell as the divinely chosen "Instrument" was already in the minds of some of his Independent admirers whether or not it had as yet occurred to Oliver himself. Indeed, Cromwell's letter to Walton, although admittedly a letter of condolence,[37] gloried in the great victory which he and his troops had, under God, achieved at Marston Moor, and we notice a significant recurrence of the first person plural: "We never charged but we routed the

---

32. *Supra*, p. 57 n. 2.
33. He is the authority behind Holles's account, *Memoirs*, 15–17.
34. Cf. Sir Charles Firth, *Trans. R.H.S.* (New Series), XII, 52 n., 53 n.
35. *Ibid.*, 61. Cf. the extract from *Vindiciae Veritatis* in Appendix III.
36. See Appendix III. Written by "N.F.", who is thought to be Nathaniel Fiennes, Lord Saye and Sele, the only member of the House of Lords who could be regarded as an Independent in religion. The pamphlet was for the most part written in 1647. The relevant parts of the tract are reprinted in the *English Historical Review*, No. 18, Vol. V, 351 f., April 1890.
37. July 5, 1644. See Appendix VII. Cromwell has been criticized because he made no mention of David Lesley's part in the battle in this letter (Gardiner, *Hist. of the Great Civil War*, II, 1 f.; Belloc, *Cromwell*, 77 f.). As Sir Charles Firth has shown, such details would have been entirely out of place in a private letter of condolence as this was. Firth, *Trans. R.H.S.*, XII, 61 f., *W.S.*, I, 287 n.

enemy.... God made them as stubble to our swords, we charged their regiments of foot with our horse, routed all we charged."[38] It is not difficult to detect in this a new note of assertion and confidence, which might mean that Marston Moor was as decisive for Cromwell personally as it was for the war generally.

IV

The feverish pamphleteering after Marston Moor was merely a premature eruption of forces which had been working beneath the surface for some time. The Presbyterians had been temporarily worsted, for not only had the Independents managed to get their reports of the victory to London before their rivals, but also it had to be admitted that a number of the Presbyterian commanders had left the field in undignified haste. Furthermore, popular national feeling was a good deal more ready to accept the accounts of Cromwell as the real victor than those ascribing the salvation of England to the Scots. Thus far the Independents had scored an important political success over the Presbyterians, but no one imagined that either party would be content to leave the matter there.

After the battle the three parliamentary armies divided and Manchester moved towards the Midlands. He was extremely unwilling to engage in another major battle that summer, and he had no intention of attacking Prince Rupert in Chester. On July 27 John Lilburne captured Tickhill Castle, and Manchester threatened to hang him for acting in defiance of his orders.[39] On August 1 the Earl informed the Committee of Both Kingdoms that, after a conference with Leven and Fairfax, the three commanders had decided to disregard the intelligence sent them by the Committee regarding Rupert's troops in Lancashire on the ground that it "was not such as we could rely upon". He went on to announce his intention "to be my selfe at Lincolne by Satterday

---

38. A similar sense of divine choice seems to have been shared by the troops themselves: "I found this generally among the Souldiers (especially in my noble Lord of Manchesters Regiments) to my hearts great content, that they all gave the Lord of Hosts all the glory of this victory, wherein they were onely instruments." Vicars, *God's Arke*, 274.
39. W.S., I, 289. It is of interest to note that soon after the battle of Marston Moor the three commanders addressed a request to the Committee of Both Kingdoms for the Settlement of the Church.

night, and shall attend the recruiting and refreshing of my forces with what speed I can".[40]

On August 10 he informed the Committee from Lincoln that since their instructions to proceed against Rupert appeared to him "so large a commission, and a worke so difficult, considering the weake condicion of the forces that are here with mee",[41] he had summoned his officers and together they had set out in some detail the reasons why the campaign ought not to be undertaken.[42] In the face of these excuses the Committee withdrew its order and asked Manchester to send a force to join with the local troops from the Midland counties to hinder Rupert's recruitment in those parts; but they did not get much response.

If local Parliamentary commanders were unwilling to move beyond their own boundaries, and regarded the conclusion of one successful engagement as an excuse for retiring at ease in their own counties, Parliament would never be able to fight anything but a local war. In view of the Earl of Essex's dire peril in the west Manchester was ordered west to take Waller's place, and to block the passage of Charles. He received his orders on September I, and by the time he had received notice[43] of the disaster to Essex's foot at Lostwithiel,[44] he had reached Huntingdon. Even then he did not march without a final grumble about his lack of recruits; but disagreement between the officers of the Eastern Association had reached such proportions that news of it had come to the ears of the Committee at Derby House. Similar quarrels had broken out in almost every army under Parliament about this time,[45] and so serious was the position that a letter was circulated to the principal Parliamentary commanders, calling upon them to "lay aside all Particulars, and unanimously and heartily joyn in all Counsels and Endeavours for the Public Service".[46]

There seems no doubt that some Independents had seen

---

40. *Manchester's Quarrel*, 5. See also the rest of his correspondence with Derby House, *ibid.*, 1–26.
41. *Ibid.*, 8 f.
42. *Ibid.*, 9.
43. September 8.
44. September 2.
45. Baillie alludes to this in his letter to William Spang, September 13, 1644. *Letters and Journals*, II, 226.
46. *Rushworth*, VI, 719 f.

The Civil War: Spring 1644 to the Self-Denying Ordinance

Essex's failure in the west as a new political opportunity and had not troubled to veil their joy at the Presbyterians' discomfiture,[47] but Cromwell's letter to Valentine Walton on September 5 reflects no such pleasure. He said:

> We do with grief of heart resent the sad condition of our Army in the West, and of affairs there. That business hath our hearts with it, and truly had we wings, we would fly thither. So soon as ever my Lord and the foot set me loose, there shall be no want in me to hasten what I can to that service, for indeed all other considerations are to be laid aside, and to give place to it, as being of far more importance. I hope the Kingdom shall see that, in the midst of our necessities, we shall serve them without disputes. We hope to forget our wants, which are exceeding great, and ill-cared for; and desire to refer the many slanders heaped upon us by false tongues to God, who will, in due time, make it appear to the world that we study the glory of God, the honour and liberty of the Parliament, for which we unanimously fight, without seeking our own interests. ...[48]
>
> We have some amongst us much slow in action: if we could all intend our own ends less, and our ease too, our business in this Army would go on wheels for expedition. Because some of us are enemies to rapine, and other wickednesses, we are said to be factious, to seek to maintain our opinions in religion by force, which we detest and abhor. I profess I could never satisfy myself of the justness of this War, but from the authority of the Parliament to maintain itself in its rights; and in this Cause I hope to approve myself an honest man and single-hearted. ...

Cromwell gives us a clue to where responsibility for delay really lay, and reading between the lines we can gather some idea of the dissensions and disputes within the command of Manchester's army. Just how deep those disputes were Cromwell had good cause to know: he still had to meet prejudice against his

---

47. "When we ware last at Huntington, ther was the first report that the Earle of Essex was routed, and that he had totally lost his artillery and fought [foot?] wherupon the Independents many of them ther did as it ware to show themselves soe joyfull as though it had been a victory new gained to themselves. Ther is many a gentleman I believe had as sad a hart as my selfe that day will beare me wittness of there rejoycing, the yett I doe believe that if the state should protest against that sect, and they should have noe command, the best part of them would be noe Independents, for ther is many of them of their opinion of their preferment. ..." From the Statement of the anonymous "Opponent of Cromwell", *Manchester's Quarrel*, 76 f.
48. *W.S.*, I, 292; *L-C*, I, 181 f. (XXIII).

"plain russet-coated captain",[49] but he had also to counter Crawford's increasing influence with Manchester, and the latter's short-sighted policy of deliberate inaction. On top of these irritations came the news of Essex's defeat and Skippon's surrender, which had been largely the result of ineffective strategy, divided command and unwillingness on the part of the Parliamentary generals to co-operate. It was obvious that something must be done to prevent similar calamities in the future, and it was at this time that the quarrel between Cromwell and Major-General Crawford came to a head. It is of interest to notice that Cromwell attacked the Scot first, and not Manchester, possibly in the hope that by removing Crawford he would be removing the main cause of the dissensions in the army of the Association at least.

The gap between September 11–22 in the correspondence between Manchester and the Committee at Derby House is due to the fact that the three chief officers of the Eastern Association's army were in London to have their differences thrashed out. Crawford was accused by Cromwell in general terms of religious intolerance; but Vane and St. John seem to have taken the opportunity of Cromwell's presence to get a general order for religious toleration through the House of Commons. Baillie furiously declared in one of his letters that while Cromwell was in town "the House of Commons without the least advertisement to any of us, or of the Assemblie, passes an order, that the grand committee of both Houses, Assemblie, and us shall consider of the means to unite us and the Independents; or if that be found impossible, to see how they may be tollerate".[50] As Robert Baillie saw only too clearly this was almost equivalent to an Act of Parliament for religious toleration. He went on to suggest that the quarrel had been hatched up by Cromwell and his Independent officers

---

49. The "Opponent of Cromwell" in his statement complained: "I shall declare Coll. Cromwell raysing of his regiment makes choyce of his officers, not such as weare souldiers or men of estate, but such as were common men, pore and of meane parentage, onely he would give them the title of godly pretious men. ...

"Looke what a company of troopers are thrust into other regiments by the head and shoulders, most of them Independents, whome they call Godly pretieouse men; nay, indeed to say the truth, allmost all our horse be mayd of that faction.

"If you looke on Coll. Russell's regiment, Coll. Mountegue's, Coll. Pickerin's, Coll. Rainsborough, all of them professed Independents intire, andbesides in most of our regiments they have crammed in one company or other that they or ther offecers must be Independents." *Manchester's Quarrel*, 72 ff.

50. *Letters and Journals*, II, 229 f. To D. [D]ickson, September 16, 1644

because they knew that the military situation made them indispensable.

But if this was the case, why did they allow the opportunity to impose their will to slip, for the charges against Crawford Were not pressed? Baillie himself was forced to admit that the plan of the Scottish Chancellor (John Campbell, Earl of Loudoun) to unite a new army under Essex stood a good chance of composing "the irreconcileable differences betwixt Cromwell and Crawford",[51] and it therefore seems more likely that in view of the military situation Cromwell and Crawford agreed to bury their differences. Furthermore, if Cromwell went to London to get a specific guarantee against interference with the opinions of his troops, he achieved his object by the order of the House of Commons without pressing for Crawford's removal.[52]

The general military plan was to arrange a conjunction of armies that would cut off and crush the King, but if Loudoun's plan appeared to solve the differences between various commanders, there is no evidence that the Earl of Manchester acted with any more enthusiasm. The Committee at Derby House found it necessary constantly to remind Manchester of its previous orders, and even to supplement its authority with special votes passed by the House of Commons. Manchester was at first blandly content to make excuses, but as the Committee became more insistent he showed a certain amount of peevish annoyance.[53]

His annoyance was not entirely ill-placed, for it must be admitted that Parliamentary commanders might well question to whom they owed ultimate allegiance. There were no less than four claimants to authority over Manchester's army – the Commander-in-Chief, Essex; the county committees, which had equipped the army for their own defence; the Committee of Both Kingdoms at Derby House; and lastly, the House of Commons, which constantly saw fit to augment all other orders with instructions of its own. Manchester's resentment, as a general officer and a peer, at this intrusion is understandable,[54] and although

---

51. *Ibid.*, 232.
52. Baillie thought the charges against Crawford were dropped through the astute management of the Scottish Commissioners – "we did so manage that businesse, that all their assayes so were in vaine". *Ibid.*, 235. On the other hand, if it was a guarantee of religious toleration that Cromwell desired, the Independents had brilliantly out-manoeuvred the Scots.
53. The full correspondence appears in *Manchester's Quarrel, passim.*
54. Cf. *Manchester's Quarrel,* lxiv n.

it by no means condones his slackness, the fact which emerges from this correspondence was that Parliament must have an army unfettered by local responsibilities, and responsible to the government through a centralized command. It was a solution which had occurred to Waller in July of that same year,[55] and which was becoming increasingly obvious; but Cromwell saw that the immediate problem was to ensure that half-hearted and incompetent leadership should be excluded.

V

It was in this mood of unwilling compliance that Manchester "co-operated" with Waller in the second battle of Newbury, October 27, 1644. He had, in the words of Dr. Gardiner, "fallen into the temper which sees a mountain in every molehill, and which prefers to do nothing rather than risk defeat".[56] The King was in a good defensive position at Newbury. A wide flanking movement was to be led by Cromwell and Balfour and stood good chance of success, but Manchester delayed his supporting attack until it was too late, and this enabled the royalist army to retire under cover of darkness towards Oxford.[57] Cromwell pursued, but his cavalry was tired, and the King escaped. Manchester then undertook a desultory investment of Donnington, which was entirely at his mercy, but the Parliamentary command was so completely disorganized that the King was able to return on November 9 and relieve the castle without any attempt being made to stop him. The Parliamentary generals seemed to lose all initiative. The general disappointment of Parliament's supporters was expressed in the letter sent to Manchester and the generals by the Committee at Derby House. The Committee stiffly expressed its regret that the enemy "met not with that opposition that was expected from an army that God had blessed lately with soe happy a victorie against them", and added that "soe long as the enemie continues in the field, wee cannot

---

55. Gardiner, quoting from Waller's correspondence with Derby House on the desertion of local levies to their own parts, gives the following extract: "My Lords, I write these particulars to let you know that an army compounded of these men will never go through with your service, and till you have an army merely your own, that you may command, it is in a manner impossible to do anything of importance." *Great Civil War,* II, 5.
56. *Ibid.,* 21.
57. Whitelocke, 109.

advise that you should goe to your winter quarters", but that some attempt should be made "to recover the advantage the enemie hath lately gained in releiving Dennington".[58]

Professor Masson has rightly observed that these words were really the prologue to the great impeachment of the Earl of Manchester, but the letter had a deeper significance. Propositions for peace were in the air, and the Committee warned Manchester that what had happened could be "very prejudicall to the publique affaires". The Committee suggested that the affairs of the army should be "managed with greater unanimitie and executed with more chee[r]fulness". It concluded with the explicit instructions that future operations should be "resolved upon by common advise of a councel of warre", and that Manchester should give them "frequent advertisements" of his plans.[59] He had earned the rebuke.

Similarly the *Commons Journals* reflect the displeasure of the House at the relief of Donnington Castle and Basing House;[60] on November 14 Sir Arthur Hazelrigge, who had been deputed by Manchester, Waller and Balfour to report to Parliament, gave his account, but the Commons called upon the Committee of Both Kingdoms to give a report,[61] and on the following day, having heard a report by those members of the Commons who were also members of that Committee, they ordered that Sir William Waller and Cromwell should make a full report on the military operations on the following Monday (November 25).

It was in these circumstances that the charge was presented against the Earl of Manchester. Cromwell declared:

> That the said Earl hath always been indisposed and backward to Engagements, and against the ending of the War by Sword; and for such a peace to which a Victory would be a disadvantage, and hath declared this by Principles express to that purpose, and a continued Series of Carriage and Actions answerable. And since the taking of York (as if Parliament had now advantage full enough) he hath declined whatever tended to further Advantage upon the Enemy, neglected and studiously shifted off opportunities to that purpose, (as if he thought the King too low, and Parliament too high) especially at Dennington-Castle. That he hath drawn the Army into, and detained them in such a Posture, as to give the

---

58. *Manchester's Quarrel*, 57 f.
59. *Ibid.*, 58.
60. Cf. *Ibid.*, lxvi–lxvii.
61. November 22, 1644.

Enemy fresh Advantages, and this before his Conjunctions with other Armies, by his own Absolute Will, against or without his Council of War, against many Commands from the Committee of Both Kingdoms, and with Contempt and vilifying those Commands. And since the Conjunction, sometimes against the Councils of War and sometimes perswading and deluding the Council to neglect one Opportunity with pretence of another, and that again of a third, and at last by perswading that it was not fit to fight at all.[62]

The grounds for these accusations were what we should have expected, and they are set out fully in the account known as *Cromwell's Narrative*,[63] which, even if not Cromwell's own work apparently gives us the substance of his speech in the House of Commons, and may have been notes rewritten for use as evidence in the following dispute.[64] The *Narrative* accuses the Earl of having "playnely declared himself against fighting", and of having summoned a Council of War in order to waste time. It was asserted that Manchester had advanced the argument against fighting "that if we beate the King 99 times he would be King still, and his posterity, and we subjects still; but if he beate us but once we should be hang'd, and our posterity be undonne".

After this it was not to be expected that Oliver would escape without a violent counter-attack from Manchester and his friends. Nor was the opposition to be disregarded, for practically all the peers would rally to the support of their colleague, the Scots would welcome the opportunity of attacking the acknowledged

---

62. *Rushworth*, VI, 732. Cf. Whitelocke, 116. Robert Baillie reported the news of the accusation in a Public Letter sent on December 1:
   "Lieutenant Generali Cromwell has publicklie, in the House of Commons, accused my Lord of Manchester of the neglect of fighting at Newbury. The neglect indeed was great; for, as we now are made sure, the King's armie was in that posture, that they took themselves for lost utterlie. Yet the fault is most unjustly charged on Manchester: It was common to all the Generali Officers then present, and to Cromwell himselfe as much as to any other. ..." *Letters and Journals*, II, 244 f.
63. Reprinted in *Manchester's Quarrel*, 78–95; W.S., I, 301–11.
64. Opinions on the authenticity of the *Narrative* differ. Masson held that the terseness and perspicuity were essentially Oliverian, and says "substantially and throughout, this Narrative appears to me to be Cromwell's own, with suggestions from Haselrig, and perhaps Waller". *Manchester's Quarrel*, lxviii n. Mr. Bruce, on the other hand, thought the style unlike that of Cromwell, and suggested it was the work of several hands. Dr. Gardiner seems to have accepted it (*Great Civil War*, II, 22 n.), but Mrs. Lomas refers to it as "the so-called Narrative of Oliver Cromwell". R.H. Abbott questions the authorship, but accepts it as substantially the charge brought by Cromwell against ManchesteR.W.S., I, 311 n.

hero of the sects, and there was a good proportion of influential Presbyterians in the House of Commons who detested Cromwell for the same reason. The counter-accusation rallied all these elements in a determined attempt to eliminate Cromwell. On November 28 Manchester made a long statement in his own defence in the House of Lords and on Monday, December 2, his narrative, committed to writing, was read to the Lords and approved. The Lords requested that a joint committee be set up with the Commons to discuss the accusations from both sides, and eventually the Commons received from the Earl of Manchester his reply to Cromwell's charge and a counter-accusation.[65] He accused Cromwell of being responsible for the King's escape after the relief of Donnington Castle,[66] and of having said "that he hoped to live to see never a nobleman in England"; he had expressed contempt for the Assembly of Divines and had called them persecutors, and he had declared that he could as soon draw his sword against the Scots as against any in the King's army. Furthermore, Manchester accused him of the fixed resolve to have none but Independents in the Army of the Association, so that "in case there should be propositions of peace or any conclusion of peace as might not stand with those ends that honest men should aim at, this army might prevent such a mischiefe".[67] There is nothing in this that we cannot believe of Oliver – indeed much of it seems to bear special point with regard to Cromwell's relationship with Major-General Crawford, but it is easy to see how these sentiments would shock the Earl of Manchester and his noble Presbyterian colleagues,[68] and it was to be expected that the Scots would exert all their power to get Cromwell removed.

Meanwhile a committee of both Houses, which had been suggested by the Lords, was set up and presided over by Zouch Tate, a Presbyterian "of the narrowest type",[69] but the Commons

---

65. The first narrative is in Rushworth, VI, 733–6; and the second (from the Tanner MSS.) is in *Camden Miscellany*, VIII (1852), edited by S.R. Gardiner.
66. Cf. Crawford's *Narrative. Manchester's Quarrel*, 66-7. Allowance must be made for Crawford's exaggerations, but it is interesting to notice that Crawford and Manchester agree in attributing to Sir Arthur Hazelrigge all that Cromwell accused Manchester of saying at the Council of War. Cf. *Ibid.*, 69, and Manchester's letter to the House of Lords, *Camden Miscellany*, VIII, and *Narrative, op. cit.*, 92 f.
67. *Camden Miscellany*, VIII; *L-C*, I, 184 n.
68. Cf. Holies, *Memoirs*, 18 f., and Baillie, Public Letter, December 1, 1644, *Letters and Journals*, II, 245.
69. *Great Civil War*, II, 91.

had set up a subsidiary committee of their own to discuss how far the Peers' attack on Cromwell constituted a breach of privilege,[70] and it can be seen that the quarrel was rapidly developing into a dispute between the two Houses of Parliament. There was the question of privilege and the dignity of the Lower House, and there was the fact that someone had to bear the responsibility for the fiasco at Donnington Castle. The correspondence between the Earl and Derby House could be quoted to show that the Committee of Both Kingdoms had been most seriously dissatisfied with Manchester's conduct from the time he left York, and this made many people realize that if the dispute came to a head the Earl would have to. give place.

It was perhaps because the Scots appreciated this that they tried other means to achieve their object – a "difficill exercise" hinted at by Baillie. The two lawyers, Bulstrode Whitelocke and John Maynard, were summoned privately to the house of the Earl of Essex, "no Excuse to be admitted", to advise on the best legal means to proceed against Cromwell. The meeting was held very late one night, early in December, and there were present besides the Earl of Essex himself, the Scottish Commissioners, headed by their Chancellor, Loudoun, and three of Cromwell's opponents in the Commons, Denzil Holies, Sir Philip Stapleton and Sir John Meyrick. The conference was under the chairmanship of Essex, but the Scots Chancellor took charge. He told the lawyers that they had been called there to advise on a legal point, and after mentioning that Cromwell was the friend neither of Essex nor of the Scots he observed that "It is thought requisite for us, and for the carrying on of the cause of the tway kingdoms, that this obstacle or remora may be removed out of the way".[71] Could Cromwell be proceeded against as an "Incendiary"? Both lawyers assured him that English law had machinery which could be used against such persons but doubted whether Cromwell could be brought into this category, and Whitelocke added that Cromwell was a person of great influence "and therefore there must be proofs, and the most clear and evident against him, to prevail with the Parliament to adjudge him to be an incendiary".[72] The Scots knew that if they were to get the Presbyterian Settlement accepted by the English Parliament they must not be involved in an unsuccessful impeachment; therefore nothing further came of the conference.

---

70. Cf. Whitelocke, 116.
71. Whitelocke, 116.
72. *Ibid.*

On Monday, December 9, Zouch Tate reported for his committee, but instead of giving a detailed account of the evidence, confined himself to stating in general terms that the chief causes of the division were pride and covetousness. Cromwell rose immediately and said that it was time to save the nation by a more speedy prosecution of war to a successful conclusion. He said:

> I do conceive if the Army be not put into another method, and the War more vigorously prosecuted, the People can bear the War no longer, and will enforce you to a dishonourable Peace.
>
> But this I would recommend to your prudence, Not to insist upon any complaint or oversight of any Commander-in-chief upon any occasion. ... Therefore waving a strict inquiry into the cause of these things, let us apply ourselves to the remedy; which is most necessary. And I hope we have such true English hearts, and zealous affections towards the general weal of our Mother Country, as no Members of either House will scruple to deny themselves, and their own private interests, for the public good; nor account it to be a dishonour done to them, whatever the Parliament shall resolve upon in this weighty matter.[73]

When Oliver returned to his seat Tate moved "That during the Time of this War, no Member of either House shall have or execute any Office or Command, Military or Civil, granted or conferred by both or either of the Houses of Parliament, or any Authority derived from both or either of the Houses".[74] The motion was seconded by Vane, and it was voted for by both parties, and in one vote the House of Commons had disposed of half her general officers including Essex, Manchester, Waller and Cromwell. This remarkable solution to the quarrel was received with a good deal of hesitancy by the Lords, and it was not until February 15, 1645, that it became law as the *New Model Ordinance*. The Scots were completely bewildered by the whole procedure.[75]

---

73. *W.S.*, I, 314 f.; *L-C,* I, 186–7. In the debate which followed Cromwell spoke for the loyalty of his troops (*W.S.*, I, 316; *L-C,* I 187 f.), and a summary of what may be another part of his contribution to the debate appears in Clarendon, *History,* VIII, 195; *W.S.*, I, 315 f.
74. *C.J.*, III, 718; *God's Arke* 74 f.; Whitelocke, 118.
75. Baillie, *Letters and Journals*, II, 247, December 26, 1644.

With the introduction of the Self-Denying Ordinance and the formation of the New Model Army we pass to a further stage of Cromwell's career, but the significant facts of 1644 were these – he and his troops had withstood all attempts to divide them, and that in battle they had been the match of Rupert's best cavalry. Cromwell had seen the weakness of those who opposed him revealed, not only in the defeat of royalist armies, but also in the failure of Essex and the futility of Manchester, and these facts could only reaffirm what some of the Independent party were proclaiming openly, that he and his men were God's chosen Instruments: "It must not be souldiers nor the Scots that must doe this worke, but it must be the godly to this purpose."[76]

If Cromwell was implicated in the manœuvres of the Independent politicians he remained essentially apart from them, and if he took part in a plot to get rid of Manchester's half-heartedness and incompetence, it was to combat what he conceived to be a greater evil. The Self-Denying Ordinance at once excluded the doubters and the waverers from their army commands. We cannot altogether agree with S.R. Gardiner's suggestion that it was proposed by Oliver in "a happy inspiration",[77] since Zouch Tate was "hardly the man to play into Cromwell's hands", but even if the measure were the result of hard bargaining behind the scenes at Westminster,[78] there can be no doubt that Cromwell fully expected to lay down his command.[79] On the other hand, if

---

76. Alleged statement by Cromwell quoted in the statement of the "Opponent of Oliver Cromwell", *Manchester's Quarrel*, 72.
77. *Great Civil War*, II, 91.
78. Clarendon's account of a plot by Vane to secure the Ordinance is confused but suggestive. *History*, VIII, 90–7.
79. "He had against him the Scots, the House of Lords, and a considerable minority of the House of Commons. If he wished personally to retain his command while expelling Manchester, he would surely have continued the prosecution of his adversary in the face of all obstacles, sooner than have sought to force his way back into military office in the teeth of the opposition he would have to encounter.... It is hard to avoid the conclusion that he was prepared to sacrifice not only his attack upon the commander whom he despised, but even his own unique position in the army." *Great Civil War*, II, 91 f. Four letters written during January support this view. They are notes on behalf of men who had served him, which suggests that he wanted to see these men suitably rewarded before he relinquished his command. The tone is that of an officer bidding farewell to his colleagues: to William Staines, January 6, 1644/5 (*W.S.*, I, 324; *L-C*, III, 319, Supp. 6); to the Sequestrators of the Isle of Ely, January 17 (*W.S.*, I, 325; *L-C*, III, 322, Supp. 9); to the Committee of Cambridge (?), January 21 (*W.S.*, I, 325; *L-C*, III, 320, Supp. 6); to the Committee of the Isle of Ely, January 30 (*W.S.*, I, 326).

he was raised to command again despite the Self-Denying Ordinance, then it could only be God's call. Meanwhile, like Gideon, he was prepared to wait, and watch for His sign.[80]

---

80. Judges 6:36–40.

Chapter Five

The Civil War: Spring 1645 to the End of the First Civil War

I

In view of the dramatic measure introduced at the end of 1644 it is remarkable enough that we should be concerned any further with the history of Oliver Cromwell. The Self-Denying Ordinance finally passed the House of Lords on April 3 with the amendment that officers were not compelled to relinquish their commands for a period of forty days. On February 27, 1645, news came that Melcombe Regis was surrounded by Royalists, and Cromwell was ordered temporarily to join Sir William Waller.[1] After this he proceeded to Windsor to deliver up his commission to Fairfax who was fitting out the New Model Army, for which the cavaliers as yet had little but contempt.[2] Instead of his discharge Oliver received from Derby House an urgent order to prevent the King from breaking out of Oxford. Sprigge's remark that Cromwell thought "of nothing lesse in all the World" than such an appointment[3] is perhaps a little too ingenuous, but although the politicians may have adroitly seized the opportunity for extending Cromwell's command, they could hardly have engineered the circumstances which made it necessary.

Cromwell's Oxford raid has been called "a brilliant little episode".[4] He prevented the junction of the King with Rupert, bluffed the surrender of Bletchingdon House,[5] and then turned

---

1. At first his regiment rebelled against the order until it became known that he was to accompany it. See *infra*, p. 96, for Waller's opinion of Oliver while the latter was under his command.
2. Whitelocke says "the New Model was by them in scorn called the New Noddle". *Memorials*, 140; cf. Joshua Sprigge, *Anglia Rediviva*, 12.
3. *Ibid.*, 10.
4. Buchan, *Oliver Cromwell*, 212.
5. Cromwell's account of these operations is given in two letters: April 25, *W.S.*, I, 339 f.; *L-C*, I, 192–4 (XXV); April 26 (dated by Carlyle 24), *W.S.*, I, 341 f.; *L-C*, III, 237 f. (App. 7).

his attention to the south-western approaches of Oxford.⁶ In a report to the Committee of Both Kingdoms of a minor victory at Bampton Bush, he said:⁷

> God does terrify them. It's good to take the season; and surely Goddelights that you have endeavoured to reform your armies; and I beg it may be done more and more. Bad men and discontented say it's faction. I wish to be of the faction that desires to avoid the oppression of the poor people of this miserable nation, upon whom [no] one can look without a bleeding heart.

He implicitly believed that God's hand was immediately guiding him: "I profess his very hand has led me. I preconsulted none of these things." To defeat the King and prevent further unnecessary bloodshed was the cause to which he was committed because, to him, it was clearly God's cause.

He met a repulse at Farringdon House⁸ but minor losses could in no way obscure the fact that the raids round about Oxford, in which he had co-operated with Major-General Brown's forces from Abingdon, had been exceptionally successful. The two commanders eventually sent word that Charles was moving out of Oxford to the north,⁹ and on hearing this, Parliament ordered that Cromwell "should be dispensed with for his personal attendance in the House and continue his Service and Command in the Army for 40 days longer, notwithstanding the Self-denying Ordinance".¹⁰ Sprigge says that "This was much spoken against by Essex his party, as a breach of that Ordinance", but while no doubt the Independents at Westminster were mainly responsible for prolonging Oliver's service, it is clear that they were supported by a good many moderates throughout the country. His own behaviour during this period was in every way "correct" and, as Vicars pointed out, the harmony between commanders

---

6. He defeated Sir "Richard" Vaughan at Bampton Bush, Sprigge, 12. There is some doubt about Vaughan's name. Sprigge gives the name as Sir William Vaughan; Cromwell, in the letter cited below, calls him Sir "Richard" Vaughan, and Whitelocke calls him "Sir H. Vaughan" (*op. cit.*, 144). Cf. also Vicars, *Burning-Bush*, 141 f.
7. April 28, W.S., I, 342 f.; *L-C*, III, 238 f. (App. 7).
8. Cf. three letters dated April 29 and 30, W.S., I, 344–5; *L-C*, I, 195 (XXVI and XXVII), and *ibid.*, III, 324 (Supp. 12); cf. also Sprigge, 12.
9. Whitelocke, 145.
10. *Ibid.* Cf. Sprigge, 16.

was in distinct contrast to the history of 1644.[11] He had obeyed without question the commands of Waller and Fairfax, he had co-operated with Brown, and promptly obeyed the Committee at Derby House. In Waller's view he had not up to this time shown "extraordinary parts", nor did Waller think that Cromwell professed to have them, "for, although he was blunt, he did not bear himself with pride or disdain. As an officer he was obedient, and did never dispute my orders, nor argue upon them".[12] Certainly Oliver could not afford to balance his reputation against a public scandal like that of the previous year, but having effected the desired reformation of the army there was no reason why he should. He must, however, watch his step, for there were many intent upon his downfall: Whitelocke reported the murmurs of Essex's friends,[13] and when a cavalry detachment was despatched under Colonel Vermuyden to serve with the Scots, Sprigge remarked naively that Cromwell was "for I know not what reason, not so acceptable to their Army".[14]

It was as well that he did not go north, for the King suddenly advanced against the eastern counties, and it was imperative that someone be appointed promptly to secure the defences. No one was better fitted than the one who had been from the start the soul of the Association, and on May 29 Cromwell set out for Aylesbury under the orders of the Committee of Both Kingdoms to defend the Isle of Ely and the eastern counties.[15]

---

11. "And heer I cannot omit to make mention of another singular mercy of God unto us in our Armies, Viz. The most excellent love and good agreement of Major Generali [*sic.*] Cromwell, and of Major Generali Brown (though both of brave and high Spirits) all the time of their being together at and about Oxford, and elsewhere ... as if David and Jonathan 2 soules were transmigrated, and mutally united in one body. O, if such sweetness and oneness of hearts and affections had been found among our Commanders formerly, wee had, certainly, now been in a farre better condition, than as yet wee are like to be in." *Burning- Bush,* 151. Vicars was a Presbyterian (cf. *ibid.,* 436, 457 f.).
12. *Recollections,* 124; cf. *W.S.,* I, 334; Sanford, *Studies,* 617.
13. Whitelocke, 145.
14. Sprigge, 20.
15. Cromwell's activity can be judged from his correspondence: May 31 (*W.S.,* I, 352); June 4, *ibid., L-C,* I, 197 f. (XXVIII); cf. also *W.S.* I, 353 f.; *L-C,* I, 199; III, 244 (App. 8).

II

The King's threat increased, and with the sack of Leicester[16] early in June the Common Council of London petitioned the Commons that the Commander-in-Chief be granted "power and encouragements to improve all present advantages without attending Commands and Directions from remote Counsels".[17] Fairfax was given a free hand, and was able to move off from Oxford and seek out the King, but he still lacked a competent cavalry commander, and on June 8 his council of war supported the petition of the City and urged the immediate appointment of Cromwell.[18]

To the modern reader this would seem to be but the outcome of Oliver's previous record, but to his contemporaries it must have been little short of a miracle that he remained in the army at all, and still more so that he should now be appointed Fairfax's second-in-command. He had seen the displacement of Essex, Manchester, Denbigh and Waller, together with a number of lesser commanders, and yet he was retained, at first, as concession to immediate military needs, but now by popular demand. He had kept his command in spite of the opposition of the House of Lords, the suspicion of the Scots and the legalism of the House of Commons, and one of the reasons was not unconnected with theology. The astuteness of the Independents at Westminster, the loyalty of his troops, and his own ability, could not of themselves have triumphed over the Self-Denying Ordinance had not the majority of Parliament's supporters regarded Cromwell as indispensable,[19] and they did so because they accepted a relationship between God's Providence and material success: "it was observed God was with him".

---

16. "... the conquerors pursued their advantage with the usual license of rapine and plunder, and miserably sacked the whole town, without any distinction of persons or places; churches and hospitals were made a prey to the enraged and greedy soldier, to the exceeding regret of the King." Clarendon, *History*, IX, 33.
17. *Burning-Bush*, 155. Cf. Baillie, *Letters and Journals*, II, 275, 286.
18. "Letters from the chief Officers of Horse under Sir T. F. to the Parliament, desiring that Colonel Cromwel might be Lieutenant General of the Horse under Sir Tho. Fairfax; and after some debate, the House ordered, that Sir T. F. should appoint Cromwel to command the Horse under him, as Lieutenant General if he thought fit." Whitelocke, *Memorials*, 149. Cf. *Cromwelliana* (1810) ed. James Caulfield, 18; cf. Sprigge, 10–11.
19. "Cromwell began to increase in the favour of the people, and of the Army and to grow great even to the envy of many." Whitelocke, 150.

Although the House of Lords demurred, the Commons assented to Cromwell's appointment to the New Model on June 10, 1645, and Sir Thomas Fairfax sent for him immediately. Oliver rode into Fairfax's camp on June 13, and the battle of Naseby took place on the following day. His troops on the right wing, occupying high but somewhat broken ground, halted and routed the charge of the royalist left wing under Sir Marmaduke Langdale, and, together with the dragoons (on the extreme left), crushed the royalist foot regiments in the centre. The King's horse guards, in reserve, were deflected from their charge at the last moment and galloped from the field.[20] Rupert, following his usual blind tactics, had cut through the Parliamentary left wing under Ireton and went on to attack the baggage train. He returned to find that the field was lost.[21]

Both sides had known that the battle could well decide the issue of the war, for if Charles had won he could have marched into the heart of the eastern counties, and, as Morley suggests, ultimately joined with Goring to attack London.[22] However, the King lost more than the lives of the superb Bluecoats at Naseby, for the capture of his private cabinet and correspondence proved beyond all doubt his duplicity during the previous negotiations for a compromise peace, and this vindicated the very policy which the Independents had advocated.[23]

In contrast, Cromwell's position was immeasurably enhanced. For the second time Cromwell's leadership had turned what had

---

20. Clarendon, H story, IX, 40.
21. The ferocity of the battle can be judged from the fact that, of the Parliamentary commanders, the Commander-in-Chief lost his helmet, while Major- General Skippon and Ireton were both grievously wounded. Cromwell himself had another narrow escape from death during the battle. *The Perfect Politician* (3rd edition), 12 f. The authoritative account for Naseby, as for the history of the New Model Army generally, is Sprigge's *Anglia Rediviva* (35–41). Other accounts are in Vicars's *Burning-Bush*, 158–62; Whitelocke, 150 f.; Clarendon, *H story*, IX, 37-42; and a brief account in Baillie's *Letters and Journals*, II, 286 f. See also W.S., I, 354–9; *L-C*, III, 241–3.
22. Morley, *Cromwell*, 184. Sprigge was very pessimistic, and Baillie showed no faith in the New Model Army. *Anglia Rediviva*, 42; *Letters and Journals*, II, 164 f., 287.
23. The papers were published by order of Parliament under the title *The Kings cabinet opened; or certain packets of secret letters and papers, written with the Kings own hand and taken in his Cabinet at Naseby Field*, (1645). A summary of the contents of the cabinet appears in Vicars, *Burning-Bush*, 176. The discovery of the King's intention to bring in the Irish together with proof of his duplicity and of the Queen's attempts to engineer the invasion of England from France, Spain, or Holland, meant that Charles lost credit with moderate elements within the nation at large.

appeared to be inevitable defeat into resounding victory, and this time no Scots were present to belittle what he had done.[24] His prestige can be seen in the immediate order in the House of Commons that he should remain Lieutenant-General under Fairfax during the good pleasure of Parliament, notwithstanding the Self-Denying Ordinance,[25] an order which the distrust of the Lords limited to three months.[26] The silence of the Scots was significant: Robert Baillie enquired of a certain Mr. Cranford about the intentions of the Scots army should Fairfax be beaten, or "if Cromwell be victor", and hinted at a plan to raise an army under Essex to act in conjunction with the Scots.[27] In a letter to Lauderdale of the same date he protested that Fairfax had sent his report through "ane horrible Antitriastrian", against whom the whole Assembly of Divines had marched in a body to protest to Parliament, and that in Cromwell's report of Naseby he had desired the House of Commons "not to discourage those who had ventured their life for them and to come out expressly with their much-desyred libertie of conscience".[28] The displeasure of the Presbyterians influenced the House of Commons to omit printing the closing paragraphs of the letter,[29] but these paragraphs show that "whatever else may have been the result of the victory at Naseby, it loosed Cromwell's tongue":[30]

> Honest men served you faithfully in this action. Sir, they are trusty; I beseech you in the name of God not to discourage them. I wish this action may beget thankfulness and humility in all that are concerned in it. He that ventures his life for the liberty of his country, I wish he trust God for the liberty of his conscience, and you for the liberty he fights for.[31]

Robert Baillie had some reason for suspicion. We know that for some time Cromwell had been gathering religious dissenters into his ranks as a matter of deliberate policy,[32] and he was

---

24. Sprigge, 43 f. Cf. Oliver's letter after the battle of Langport, July 1645, the relevant passages of which are quoted *infra*, p. 100 f.
25. Whitelocke, 151.
26. *Ibid.*, 152.
27. June 17, 1645, *Letters und Journals*, II, 278.
28. *Ibid.*, 280.
29. Gardiner, *Great Civil War*, II, 252 f. Cf. Mrs. S.C. Lomas in *L-C*, I, 205, n. 1.
30. Gardiner, *op, cit.*, II, 252.
31. To William Lenthall, June 14, *W.S.*, I, 360; *L-C*, 1, 204 f. (XXIX). Cf. also the note to Sir Samuel Luke, June 15, *W.S.*, I, 360 f.; *L-C*, III, 325 (Supp. 14).
32. *Reliquiae Baxterianae*, I, 30 f.

probably fully prepared to create an army which, in the last resort, would fight for liberty of conscience.[33] If the attempt to impose Presbyterian uniformity made Oliver as ready to draw sword against the Scots as against the King, Baillie's correspondence gives ample proof that the Scots regarded Cromwell as a far greater menace than Charles Stuart. After Naseby Baillie expressed the hope that Parliament and the King might come to terms quickly, otherwise, he said, "I am feared of the sequell", for although it appeared as if the power of royalism was now broken, he observed that "some feares the insolence of others, to whom alone the Lord has given the victory of that day". He added the comment that "it wes never more necessare to haste up all possible recruits to our army".[34]

The ways of Providence must have been a great problem to the Rev. Mr. Baillie, for the uncanny success of the man who triumphed in every military operation and over every political trap presented an undoubted threat to his most cherished beliefs; but Baillie's observations were sinister, for they meant that even at this stage the campaign of Dunbar and Worcester was likely to be a sad necessity.

After the defeat of Goring at Langport, in a letter to a member at Westminster,[35] Cromwell wrote:

> You have heard of Naseby; it was a happy victory ... God was pleased to use His servants; and if men will be malicious and swell with envy, we know Who hath said, If they will not see, yet they shall see, and be ashamed for their envy at His people.[36] I can say this of Naseby, that when I saw the enemy draw up and march in gallant order towards us, and we a company of poor ignorant men, to seek how to order our battle – the General having commanded me to order all the horse – I could not (riding alone about my business) but smile out to God in praises, in assurance of victory, because God would, by things that are not, bring to naught things that are.[37] Of which I had great assurance; and God did it. O that men would therefore praise the Lord, and declare the wonders that He doth for the children of men![38]

---

33. *Ibid.*, I, 57.
34. Public Letter, June 17, *Letters and Journals*, II, 287.
35. July 10, *W.S.*, I, 364–6; *L-C*, III, 245–7 (App. 9).
36. Isaiah 26: II (A.V.).
37. 1 Corinthians 1:28.
38. Psalm 107:8, 15, 21, 31.

The Civil War: Spring 1645 to the End of the First Civil War 101

There can be no doubt of the religious enthusiasm which these victories awakened in the writer:[39] military success was the final vindication of the Independents' policy which he believed to be the Will of God.

III

From the battle of Langport, July 10, 1645, to the fall of Oxford, June 24, 1646, the Civil War became a series of sieges in which the few minor field actions were hardly more than brief skirmishes. Bridgewater was captured on July 23, 1645, Bath was taken without bloodshed (July 29) and Sherborne Castle was stormed after a fortnight's siege (August 2–15), and in the meantime Cromwell dealt with the local clubmen.[40] On August 12 his commission was renewed for a further four months, and if it seems to us that Parliament could have dispensed with his military services at this stage, it should be remembered that in London the war appeared by no means over with Charles hovering on the Welsh border and with the sudden onset of Montrose's amazing victories in Scotland.[41]

With the fall of Sherborne the New Model was free to proceed against Prince Rupert in Bristol, where the defenders were hampered by the ravages of the plague. Charles made a desperate attempt at recovery by striking from Doncaster into the heart of the Eastern Association, and he reached Huntingdon and Bedford. Meanwhile in the operations against Bristol Fairfax and

---

39. Hilaire Belloc says that Cromwell's account of Naseby "is a falsehood the quality of which would be spoilt if one were to pile up adjectives upon it". *Cromwell*, 79. He points out that the nucleus of Cromwell's men, far from being "poor and ignorant men", were tried veterans. But Belloc himself explains the extravagance of this language when he shows that Cromwell's desire was simply to magnify the God whom he worshipped: "Cromwell was not a vain man; he was a devoted, enthusiastic man. He was as he believed the instrument of his implacable God, and if he continually exalted that instrument and held his tongue about other inferior instruments who appear to have been pretty useful, it was probably more because he was ... singing the praises not of Oliver but of Jehovah whom Oliver served." *Ibid.*, 80 f.
40. Cf. Sprigge, 77–9. The clubmen were bands of local volunteers which had united to expel all soldiers from their borders.
41. Even while Fairfax and Cromwell were engaged against Sherborne, Montrose was marching against Glasgow, and August 15 saw the fall both of Sherborne to the English Parliament and of Glasgow to Montrose. The officers of the New Model sent a letter of condolence to the Earl of Leven, and promised, perhaps not without some relish, to march to Scotland's assistance once England had been cleared. September 3, 1645, Sprigge, 96 f.; *W.S.*, I, 371 f.

Cromwell had a narrow escape from death when a cannon-ball "grazed upon the Fort within two hands breadth of them".[42] Joshua Sprigge also noted that whereas the plague had been taking a weekly toll of about 100 lives within the city, only one soldier from the New Model was heard to die of it; and to Sprigge these were clear evidences of God's favour.[43]

The assault commenced on September 10, 1645, but when the royalists fired the town Fairfax agreed to give terms,[44] and in his report to the Speaker of the House of Commons[45] Oliver again made his plea for religious toleration:

> Presbyterians, Independents, all had here the same spirit of faith and prayer; the same pretence and answer; they agree here, know no names of difference: pity it is it should be otherwise anywhere All that believe, have the real unity, which is most glorious, because inward and spiritual, in the Body, and to the Head.[46] As for being united in forms, commonly called Uniformity, every Christian will for peace-sake study and do, as far as conscience will permit; and from brethren, in things of the mind we look for no compulsion, but that of light and reason.

After the surrender of Bristol the army divided, and Cromwell was sent to Devizes,[47] which capitulated upon terms on September 21, 1645[48] Fairfax had elected to go further west, leaving Cromwell to attack Winchester and the formidable Basing House. Winchester Castle eventually capitulated on the night of October 5–6,[49] and then, joining Colonel Dalbier,[50] Cromwell prepared to assault Basing House which, defended by its Catholic owner, John Paulet, Marquis of Winchester, had ruined the reputation

---

42. Sprigge, 109.
43. *Ibid.*, 112. See also Cromwell's letter to Lenthall cited below. The presence of the plague in Bristol had been the most important argument advanced against investing the city when the matter had been discussed by the Council of War.
44. Sprigge, 105–9.
45. September 14, *W.S.*, I, 374–8; *L-C*, I, 212–8 (XXXI).
46. Cf. Ephesians 4:3–8.
47. Note to the governor and terms. *W.S.*, I, 379 f.
48. At the same time Col. Pickering, acting under Cromwell's orders took Laycock House on September 24, and Col. Rainsborough captured Berkeley on the 26th. Sprigge, 122–4.
49. Letter to William Lenthall, October 6, *W.S.*, I, 381 f.; *L-C*, I, 220 f. (XXXII). The terms are given in *W.S.*, I, 382–3. See Sprigge, 128 f., who supposes the letter to have been addressed to Fairfax, and was followed by Carlyle, but on this point see *W.S.*, I, 382 n.
50. It appears from Holles's *Memoirs*, 17, that Dalbier was jealous of the praise accorded to Oliver.

of so many parliamentary commanders. It was stormed and sacked on October 14, 1645,[51] and since Montrose was now a fugitive after his defeat at Philiphaugh,[52] the writing was clearly on the wall.

The rest of the military activities up to the fall of Oxford on June 24, 1646, followed the now familiar pattern of siege and capitulation. Indeed, the obvious perplexity which sincere royalists had in reconciling the evil fortunes of their cause with the claims of the one for whom they were fighting, may partly explain the rapid collapse of their strongest garrisons after the battle of Langport. Some might interpret their ill successes as a judgment of God on the immorality of the royal armies, but there must have been many who had begun to reflect deeply on the wisdom of continuing the struggle, "lest haply they be found even to fight against God".[53] There was no Puritan monopoly on the doctrine of Providence, as the correspondence between Sir Thomas Fairfax and Sir Ralph Hopton in Cornwall shows very clearly.[54] Hopton surrendered on March 14, 1646, Exeter accepted terms on April 9, and "every day brought the news of the loss of some garrison".[55]

Charles was determined at all costs to avoid being surrounded in Oxford and having to surrender to Fairfax's army, "which he was advertised from all hands would treat him very barbarously".[56] Therefore, on April 27 he made his way in disguise out of Oxford, and arrived at the Scots' camp at Newark on May 5, leaving the "Home of Lost Causes" to surrender on June 24. The first Civil War flickered to an end.

---

51. Hugh Peters later reported that Oliver had "spent much time in prayer the night before the storm; and seldom fighting without some Text of Scripture before him. This time he rested upon that blessed word of God, written in the *hundred-and-fifteenth* Psalm, eighth verse, They that make them are like unto them [i.e. idols], so is every one that trusteth in them, which, with some verses going before, was now accomplished". L-C, I, 227; Sprigge, 139–42. Cf. Cromwell's letter to Lenthall, October 14, W.S., I, 386 f.; L-C, I, 223–5 (XXXIII); Sprigge, 137–9. An account of the action at Basing House is also in Vicars, *Burning-Bush*, 289 f.
52. September 23, 1645.
53. Acts 5:39.
54. Sprigge, *Anglia Rediviva*, 206–12
55. Clarendon, *History*, X, 31.
56. *Ibid.*, X, 32.

IV

Looking at the period from the distance of three hundred years, the ultimate Parliamentary victory after Naseby never seems to have been seriously in doubt, but it must have appeared very differently at the time. Whenever the question of Cromwell's commission came under review some new danger appeared – royalist activity in the west during the early months of 1645, the sack of Leicester in June, and the success of Montrose in the autumn of that year. Added to which there was the coincidence that Fairfax needed a cavalry commander, whereas he might just as well have needed a Major-General of Infantry or a Lieutenant-General of the Ordnance to complete his army. In the face of these needs and Cromwell's record Parliament was practically forced to keep him in the army: events seemed to concur in demanding his retention.

In view of the contemporary ideas on Providence it became possible virtually to hold only one of two contradictory theories about Cromwell – either he was a Heaven-sent deliverer, or he was a Satanic tyrant. The theory of the Satanic tyrant, which came into popularity at the Restoration, can be seen growing in the writings of such men as Robert Baillie, Clement Walker[57] and Denzil Holies,[58] while the Independents regarded him as a man sent "to the kingdom for such a time as this":[59] his continued service with the army, his escapes from death, and above all his military success, all pointed that way. In his letters Cromwell himself speaks with a new confidence, and we notice his growing concern about the devastation caused by the war.[60] The King had been defeated, but there was still the problem of settling the nation in peace. If Oliver retained any influence now that the

---

57. *The Compleat History of Independency* (1648).
58. Holies regarded all the peculiar circumstances which demanded Cromwell's presence in the army after the Self-Denying Ordinance as hatched up by the Independents. *Memoirs*, 35 f.
59. Esther 4:14.
60. Cf. the Self-Denying speech, and also his letter of April 28, 1645, *supra*, p. 91 and p. 95. Cromwell always found time to intercede on behalf of others. Cf. his letters, July 27, 1646, to Thomas Knyvett, on behalf of the parishioners of the Rev. Robert Browne, *W.S.*, I, 408; *L-C*, I, 237 (XXXVI); July 31, to Fairfax, on behalf of Adjutant Fleming, *W.S.*, 1, 408 f.; *L-C*, 1, 238 f. (XXXVII); certificate on behalf of the royalist John Heron, August 18, *W.S.*, I, 411 f.; and his letter to Rushworth, August 26, on behalf of Henry Lilburne, *ibid.*, 412; *L-C*, 243 (XXXIX).

fighting had ceased we should expect him to turn all his energies towards the permanent settlement of the country; but that settlement would have to be one which would guarantee beyond all doubt those religious liberties for which he and his men had fought.

Chapter Six

From the Fall of Oxford to the Army Debates, July 1647

I

"It is in the involved and complicated events of these months", I writes R.H. Abbott, "that there rests in large part the various charges of hypocrisy, double-dealing or treachery levelled against Cromwell."[1] Yet Cromwell appears to have had very little to do with the Parliamentary activity in the summer of 1646, or in the negotiations leading up to the Propositions of Newcastle in the July and August of that year.

The situation should have been entirely in the hands of the members at Westminster, but the end of the fighting had found them politically unprepared. The fact that the King was in the custody of the Scots had aroused English national feeling, and although Charles had very few material assets, he was still, in his Person, the most important factor in the problem of settlement. Moreover, the King himself did not underestimate the fact that he was indispensable to the constitution of the country. In a etter to Lord Digby in March he had said that he expected to be able "to draw either the Presbyterians or the Independents to side with me for extirpating one the other, that I shall be really king again".[2] This explains much that happened, in the twelve months that followed the fall of Oxford. It was not easy to conclude lasting peace while Charles pursued this policy, but he showed clearly his intention to put it into effect. A flood of correspondence from his pen attempted to set at loggerheads England and Scotland, Parliament and the Army, and the ground in which he sowed his seed had been prepared by national and religious antipathies which had developed during the war.

The Presbyterians were prepared to bring back Charles on

---

1. *W.S.*, I, 435.
2. March 26, 1646, Thomas Carte, *An History of the life of James, duke of Ormonde* (1735–86, 3 vols.), III, 452; cf. *L-C*, I, 235.

almost any terms if they could assure the abolition of episcopacy and the establishment of Presbyterianism in England, but the Independents and the Army feared this quite as much as any resettlement of the Anglican Church. For a time they had the support of a number of moderate politicians who distrusted Scottish interference in English affairs, but this support would disappear as soon as Charles came into English hands.

Cromwell's sympathies both as an Independent and as a soldier were mainly with the Army, but not entirely so. From the very early days of the war he had looked to the House of Commons for authority and support – it had been the means of his advancement, it had supported him against Manchester, and it had been responsible for his continued commission. He still looked to Parliament as the legal authority by which arms had first been taken against the King, and any undermining of its authority could only weaken its position and thus prolong the country's uncertainty.[3]

Parliament was occupied with a threefold problem. First, Charles must be transferred to English hands and the Scottish army induced to return to Scotland; secondly, the English army must be substantially reduced; thirdly, plans must be laid for the reconquest of Ireland. It was obvious that if the New Model Army could be relieved of its present officers and used in Ireland, the second and third of these problems would have been solved, but before this could be attempted Parliament would have to do something about the soldiers' arrears of pay.

On September 14 the death of the Earl of Essex removed the obvious rival to Fairfax, and the one man whose prestige might have done much to allay criticism of a Presbyterian settlement. He was certainly the Independents' most formidable opponent, and Clarendon reports that they "were wonderfully exalted with his death".[4] His death appeared so opportune that "it was loudly said by many of his friends that he was poisoned".[5] He died from a chill contracted while hunting.[6]

---

3. Earlier in the year, just before Henry Ireton's marriage to his daughter Bridget, Cromwell had criticized Ireton in the Commons for forwarding to him a proposal by Charles to surrender, instead of sending it directly to Parliament. It was a point of etiquette, but it reaffirmed the principle that the Army was the servant of Parliament. Cf. *W.S.*, I, 401; *G.C.W.*, III, 95 f. See also Cromwell's letter to Walton, September 5, 1644, *supra*, p. 83.
4. *History*, X, 81. Cf. Clement Walker, *History of Independency*, Pt. I, 43.
5. Clarendon, *History*, X, 80.
6. Ludlow, *Memoirs* (1894, 2 vols.), ed. C.H. Firth, I, 144.

Cromwell transferred his activities from the Army to the political sphere during the autumn of 1646. By virtue of his reputation and his ability he was assuming a new importance among those who were responsible for the day to day administration of the country.[7] The routine business of government had to be carried on, and until the regular form of the constitution could be resumed the machinery of war had to be adapted. It was government by Parliamentary committees. In December, while negotiations with Charles and with the Scots were being conducted by Parliament, Cromwell was placed on no less than five special committees, and the experience he had of this piecemeal administration – open as it was to corruption and private interest – seems to have left an indelible mark on his memory.[8] Yet immersed as he was in the details of executive government his personal piety was never far from the surface.[9]

II

Two days before the articles with the Scots were signed[10] Cromwell wrote to Sir Thomas Fairfax to report on the course of the negotiations, and he added some news of a move directed

---

7. Summary of his activities. *W.S.*, I, 414 f. Three documents signed by him during October illustrate the administration of the country; to Fairfax, October 6, *W.S.*, 1, 414; *L-C,* I, 245 (XL); to Jenner, October 29, *W.S.*, 1, 417; *L-C* III, 327 (Supp. 17); resolution regarding the security of the Channel Isles, *W.S.*, I, 418, October 30.
8. See his speech, April 21, 1657. *W.S.*, IV, 486 f.; *L-C*, III, 94 f.
9. Cf. his letter to Bridget Ireton, October 25, *W.S.*, 1, 416; *L-C*, I, 246 (XLI): "Your Sister Claypole is (I trust in mercy) exercised with some perplexed thoughts. She sees her own vanity and carnal mind, bewailing it; she seeks after (as I hope also) that which will satisfy. And thus to be a seeker is to be of the best sect next to a finder; and such an one shall every faithful humble seeker be at the end. Happy seeker, happy finder! Who ever tasted that the Lord is gracious, without some sense of self, vanity, and badness? Who ever tasted that graciousness of His, and could go less in desire, and less in pressing after full enjoyment? Dear Heart, press on; let not husband, let not anything cool thy affections after Christ." Cf. Isaiah 55:6; Jeremiah 29:13. There was a sect called the "Seekers" which held itself very loosely to recognized religious forms, and Sir Charles Firth has suggested that Cromwell may have had leanings towards this (Firth, *Oliver Cromwell,* 149 f.). This surely strains the sense of Cromwell's words, for here a "seeker" is simply contrasted with a "finder" (i.e. one of the elect).
10. The articles were signed on December 23, 1646. The amount of the indemnity to be handed to the Scots had been fixed by September 1 at £400,000. Half of this sum was to be paid before the Scots left England, and the rest by instalments. Cf. *W.S.*, I, 421–4, 425.

against the Army by the Common Council of the City.[11] This forecast the trend of events during the next few months, for with the departure of the Scots in February the influence of the Presbyterians in London and Parliament increased.[12] Charles reached Holmby House with the Parliamentary commissioners on February 16 convinced by the enthusiastic crowds, which had lined his route, of his people's loyalty.[13] The Presbyterians in Parliament seemed to be in complete control and with the person of the King in their hands they now turned their attention to the reduction of the Army.[14] They sought to solve the Army problem and to deal with the situation in Ireland in one comprehensive measure[15] by planning to enlist the demobilized soldiers under new officers for the reconquest of Ireland. At the same time they tried to curb the power and authority of the senior officers by voting that apart from Sir Thomas Fairfax no officer should hold rank above that of colonel and that no member of the Commons should hold command in England,[16] a measure obviously directed against officers like Cromwell and Ireton.

Cromwell himself was taken seriously ill just before this, and the move might have succeeded had not the continued neglect of the soldiers' pay aroused the hostility of the rank and file, and caused them to rally to the support of their officers. Charles had recently appeared favourable to the proposal of establishing Presbyterianism for three years,[17] and the Independents in the Army were faced with the return of constitutional government at the expense of the religious freedom for which they had fought and suffered. However, the discovery of more royal correspondence revealed that the King had no intention of keeping his

---
11. December 21, *W.S.*, I, 420 f.; *L-C*, I, 248 f. (XLII).
12. While the Scots army remained on English soil many of the moderates in Parliament had tended to support the Independents as a counterbalance to Scottish influence.
13. Cf. Whitelocke, 238.
14. February 18, 1646/7. A reduction of 400 cavalry and dragoons was passed without a division. Cf. *G.C.W.*, III, 217.
15. Whitelocke, 240.
16. March 8, *C.J.*, V, 107–8; Whitelocke, 239; *W.S.*, I, 427 f. Cf. *G.C.W.*, III, 219 f.
17. See the suggested answer to the Propositions drawn up for the King by certain Members of Parliament, and forwarded by M. de Bellifèvre to Mazarin to be laid before Queen Henrietta Maria. Gardiner, *Const. Docs.*, 309–11 (January 29/February 8, 1646/7). Charles later agreed to the proposal to retain the Presbyterian establishment for three years, and control of the militia for ten in his third answer to the Newcastle Propositions. Cf. *infra*, p. 115 n. 15.

bargain with Parliament longer than it suited his purpose to do so. The French agent Bellièvre reported to Cardinal Mazarin that it was the King's boast "Qu'il est certain qu'ayant patience six mois toutes choses se brouilleront, en sorte que ses affaires se feront sans qu'il s'en mesle",[18] and in an intercepted letter to an old cavalier Charles told the latter to hold himself in readiness.[19] This intelligence did not impress Parliament with any conviction of the King's good faith, and the negotiations came to an abrupt end.

By March 7 Cromwell had recovered from his illness, and was writing about it to Fairfax:[20]

> Sir,
> It hath pleased God to raise me out of a dangerous sickness; and I do most willingly acknowledge that the Lord hath (in this visitation) exercised the bowels of a Father toward me.[21] I received in myself the sentence of death, that I might learn to trust in him that raiseth from the dead, and have no confidence in the flesh.[22] It's a blessed thing to die daily,[23] for what is there in this world to be accounted of. The best men according to the flesh, and things, are lighter than vanity. I find this only good, to love the Lord and his poor despised people, to do for them, and be ready to suffer with them;[24] and he that is found worthy of this hath obtained great favour from the Lord; and he that is established in this shall (being conformed to Christ and the rest of the Body) participate in the glory of a Resurrection which will answer all.

There was to him in his recovery something of a miracle. He had not so far taken any part in the quarrel which was developing, but the resolution of March 8 obviously affected him most, and by it he was inevitably drawn into the dispute. On March 11 he remarked to Fairfax in a letter[25] that "there want not in all places men who have so much malice against the army as besots them".

---

18. *Record Office Transcripts*, quoted G.C.W., III, 215.
19. *Ibid.* Gardiner unfortunately gives us no clue where this letter can be traced, although Whitelocke has the following note regarding a letter in cypher intercepted from Charles: "The King's letter in Characters referred to Mr. Wakerly to open the meaning of it." Whitelocke, 237. For notes of other intercepted correspondence, cf. *ibid.*, 243, 248.
20. *W.S.*, I, 428 f.; *L-C*, I, 295 f. (LIV). Abbott points out that it was dated wrongly by Carlyle. Cf. *W.S.*, I, 429 n.
21. A typical Biblical expression. Cf. Jeremiah 31:20; Philemon 12.
22. Philippians 3:3 f.
23. 1 Corinthians 15:31.
24. Cf. Acts 5:41; Romans 8:17; 2 Timothy 2:12.
25. *W.S.*, I, 430; *L-C*, I, 252 (XLIII).

In the postscript to this letter he reveals that some Londoners were raising men against the Army "to prevent [the sectaries?[26]] from cutting the Presbyterians' throats!" He added the comment, "These are fine tricks to mock God with."

Under the influence of the wealthy merchants of the City and the Presbyterians of the surrounding counties,[27] Parliament ordered Fairfax not to quarter within twenty-five miles of London, which Cromwell seems to have regarded as reasonable,[28] since it was necessary not to give any grounds for charges of intimidation against the Army.[29] He was trying to keep Army and Parliament from an open breach, and he protested in Parliament, "In the presence of Almighty God, before whom he stood, that he knew the Army would disband and lay down their Arms at their dore, whensoever they should command them".[30] At the same time he had good cause for bitterness against the members at Westminster, and when walking one day with Edmund Ludlow in Sir Robert Cotton's garden, he declared bitterly "that it was a miserable thing to serve a Parliament, to whom let a man be never so faithful, if one pragmatical fellow amongst them rise up and asperse him, he shall never wipe it off".[31] He even considered leaving England to enlist under the Elector Palatine.[32]

On March 21 a Parliamentary deputation met Fairfax and forty-three of his officers in Saffron Walden Church to discuss the terms of disbandment, but the officers wanted to have fuller details. The troopers themselves drew up a somewhat violent petition,[33] which was modified by the officers, and eventually addressed to the General. Freedom from impressment, pensions for widows and orphans, arrears and indemnity were not in themselves unreasonable demands, but they aroused a storm at Westminster, and Cromwell himself "inveighed bitterly against the

---

26. Carlyle inserts "us soldiers". The text is doubtful.
27. It is interesting to note that several of the petitions which came into Parliament expressing distrust of the Army came from the Associated Counties. Petitions from Suffolk and Essex, Whitelocke, 238, 239. Cf. G.C.W., III, 216, 220 f.
28. To Fairfax, March 19, 1646/7. W.S., I, 430 f.; L~C, I, 254 (XLIV).
29. Steps were taken against officers who disobeyed the limit. Cf. ibid.
30. Walker, History of Independency, Pt. I, 31.
31. Memoirs, I, 144 f. Gardiner dates this conversation about this time, and he is followed by Firth and Abbott. Cf. G.C.W., III, 221; Ludlow, Memoirs, I, 145 (note by Firth); W.S., I, 433. See also Whitelocke's remarks about Parliament's ingratitude to the soldiers. Whitelocke, 236 f.
32. Cf. G.C.W., III, 222 n.
33. Whitelocke, 240.

presumption"[34] – not because he was unsympathetic but because the soldiers' procedure appeared to be dictatorial. The Levellers[35] within the Army immediately charged him with lack of good faith and Cromwell received the first of a remarkable series of letters from John Lilburne.[36] It was addressed "To the Man whom God hath honoured, and will further honour, if he continue honouring him, Lieu. Generali Cromwell", and having mentioned his previous obligations to Cromwell[37] Lilburne went on to plead:

> O deere Cromwell the Lord open thine eyes and make thy heart sensible of those snares that are laid for thee in that vote of the House of Commons of two thousand five hundred pounds per annum ... as poor Mordecai in the bitterness of his spirit sayd unto Queen Esther, so say I to thee ... thou great man, Cromwell, Think not with thyself, that thou shalt escape in the Parliament House, more than all the rest of the Lambs poor despised redeemed ones, and therefore, O Cromwell, if thou altogether holdest thy peace, (or stoppest or underminest, as thou dost, our and the Armies petitions) at this time, then shall enlargement and deliverance arise to us poor afilicted ones, (that have hitherto doted too much on thee, O Cromwell) from another place then from you silken Independents (the broken reeds of Egypt in the House and Army) but both thou and thy Fathers House shall be destroyed: but who knoweth whether thou art come out of thy sicknesse, and to such a height in the kingdome, for such a time as this? And therefore if thou wilt pluck up thy resolutions like a man that will persevere to be a man for God, and goe on bravely in the feare and name of God, and say with Esther, If I perish I perish; but if thou would not, know that heare before God, I arraigne thee at his dreadful Barre, and there accuse thee of delusions and faire words, deceitfully, for betraying us, our wives and children into Haman-like tyranicall clutches of Holies and Stapleton ... and the rest of that bloody and devouring faction, that hath designed us to utter ruine and destruction, and this land and Kingdome to vassalage and slavery, against whom we are sufficiently able to preserve our selves if it were not for thee,

---

34. Clarendon, *History*, X, 88. Cf. Wildman, *Putney Projects* (1647), a. R.H. Abbott says that Cromwell was supported by Ireton, but the point seems doubtful. *W.S.*, I, 434. Cf. *G.C.W.*, III, 224.
35. An influential republican movement among the rank and file of the Army, which sought to reduce social distinctions.
36. March 25, 1646/7. Printed later in Lilbume's pamphlet, *Jonah's Cry out of the Whales belley: Or, Certain Epistles writ by Lieu. Coll. John Lilburne unto Lieu. Generali Cromwell, and Mr. John Goodwin*, etc. (July 16, 1647).
37. *Supra*, p. 49.

O Cromwell, that are led by the nose by two unworthy covetous earth-wormes, Vaine and St. John. ... Sir I am jealous over you with the hight of Godly jealousie. ...

The letter deserves to be quoted at length because of its importance. It gives clear proof that there were radical elements in the Army which were prepared to take independent political action, but it is equally significant as an indication of Cromwell's prestige, and for the style in which it was written. Cromwell was not being charged with double dealing, as Abbott suggests,[38] but with being "led by the nose" by the Independent politicians; the charge of duplicity was not to come until later. But Lilburne urges Cromwell to take the lead in championing the soldiers' demands, and he brings to bear the full force of a Biblical exposition upon the words of Mordecai the Jew to Queen Esther:[39] "Who knoweth", he writes, drawing the parallel, "whether thou art come out of thy sicknesse, and to such a height in the kingdome, for such a time as this?" The tone of his writing is not that of a critical letter, but that of a passionately delivered sermon: Lilburne was, in fact, "prophesying" to Cromwell on behalf of the "poor afflicted ones" of the Army, and their dependents. This makes the letter important. Cromwell would always listen to forthright language, but here Lilburne was claiming to expound not Expediency but God's Will, and his words assumed an authority which, according to the principles of his own churchmanship, Cromwell dared not ignore.

III

Intelligence having been received[40] that the petition, which Fairfax had been ordered to suppress, was still in circulation, certain officers were called to the bar of the House to answer charges relating to it,[41] and the climax came on March 30 with a hasty resolution rushed through the House by Holies condemning the Army petition, and declaring that those who continued to promote it "shall be looked upon, and proceeded against, as Enemies to the State, and Disturbers of the Public

---

38. *W.S.*, I, 434.
39. Esther 4:13 f.
40. March 27 and 29.
41. Robert and Thomas Hammond, Pride and Ireton. Whitelocke, 241 Ireton was already at Westminster.

Peace".[42] It was a foolish and precipitate measure of immature statesmanship, for it contributed neither to the security of Parliament nor to the solution of the problem.

The accused officers successfully defended themselves in the House, and there was nothing to do but to let them return to their regiments with the request that they should use their influence to counteract the petition.[43] An attempt at compromise was made with the appointment of Skippon as future commander of the army in Ireland with the rank of Field-Marshal, and Massey as Lieutenant-General,[44] but on April 15 at Saffron Walden, about two hundred officers asked that their old generals might continue with them in Ireland,[45] and when some of the commissioners present suggested that the spokesmen were speaking only for themselves, "the Officers cryed out, All, All, – Declareing thereby their unanimity in those desires".[46]

During the month of April Cromwell seems to have held aloof from both Parliament and the Army, and S.R. Gardiner has suggested "that Cromwell was now passing through one of those long periods of hesitation which with him always preceded important action".[47] It is probable that he hoped to avoid being implicated any further, but it is characteristic of him that, before making a big decision, there should be a period of inactivity which is very difficult to explain. He did not resign his responsibility, nor did he definitely assume it, but he seems to have stood apart from the situation until it became clearer, and until events gave him the lead for intervention: he was waiting for a "providence". It is perhaps not without significance that on April 10 Lilburne sent another letter, reproving him for his silence;[48] but the lead for which Cromwell had been waiting was not long in coming. On April 27 the House of Commons decided to pay the army six weeks of its arrears but on April 30 three troopers,

---

42. Accepted by the Lords, *Declaration*, March 30, *Journals of the House of Lords* [*L.J:*], IX, 115. Whitelocke, 242.
43. April 1. Cf. Whitelocke, 242.
44. *Ibid.*
45. *Clarke Papers*, I, 7.
46. *Ibid.* The following day most of the cavalry officers and a hundred of the infantry officers signed an appeal to Parliament to give them back their old generals. *Moderate Intelligencer*, April 15–22.
47. S.R. Gardiner, *G.C.W.*, III, 241. Holies suggested that Oliver held aloof so that the disorders might increase! *Memoirs*, 239.
48. *Jonah's Cry*, 6.

Allen, Sexby and Shepperd,[49] representing eight troops of Horse, arrived with letters which voiced grievances similar to those of a month earlier.[50] Parliament became alarmed and ordered Cromwell, Skippon, Ireton and Fleetwood to report at once on the situation, authorizing them to promise that an ordinance of Indemnity would be prepared and that a considerable amount of the arrears would be paid before disbandment.[51] This was a considerable concession and it promised a reasonable expectation of composing the differences, but Parliament had become conciliatory too late, and the presence of Regimental Agitators indicated within the ranks of the Army the existence of a well-organized system for the soldiers' mutual defence. On May 2, Cromwell, Skippon and Ireton arrived at Saffron Walden, but the situation became very delicate when it was learned that overt moves were being made to muster forces against the Army.[52]

The publication of the King's third answer to the Newcastle Propositions[53] put the soldiers in a serious position, and it is not surprising that in these circumstances the soldiers themselves should think of bargaining with Charles for better conditions. It was reported that "some of the Foote about Cambridgeshire give out that they will goe for Holdenby and fetch the king".[54] It is possible that if such overtures were made they originated with Ireton.[55] He had not the same scruples about withstanding Parliamentary authority as had Cromwell, and it was in his regiment at Ipswich that the idea of using the King to oppose Parliament had first been suggested.[56] This was the position when the military commissioners from Parliament entered upon their negotiations at Saffron Walden – a situation of precarious balance

---

49. Whitelocke, 245. This is the first official appearance of regimental "agitators". Cf. *G.C.W.*, III, 236 f., 243 f.
50. Copies were also given to Cromwell and Skippon, who both handed the letters in to Parliament; see the *Examination of the 3 troopers on April 30th, Clarke Papers*, I, 430–3 (App. B).
51. *W.S.*, I, 439 f.
52. Newsletter from an officer, May 3. *Clarke Papers,* I, 21 f.
53. Gardiner, *Const. Docs.,* 311–6; Charles to the House of Lords, May 12, 1647, *L.J.,* IX, 193; Charles to Bampfield, May 16, Colonel Joseph Bampfield's *Apologie* (1684), 24; Whitelocke, 247 (May 18). Charles conceded Presbyterian establishment for three years, and control of the militia for ten.
54. Relation from Walden, May 5, *Clarke Papers,* I, 25. The rumour was repudiated at the conference at Saffron Walden. Whitelocke, 246.
55. Suggested by Gardiner. *G.C.W.,* III, 239–41.
56. Letter from Suffolk, April 20 from *Portland MSS,* quoted by Gardiner, *G.C.W.,* III, 236 f. Gardiner commented that "when such a man as Ireton shifts his ground, he shifts it without much warning". *Ibid.,* 240.

where an ill-timed expression of intolerance on the part of Parliament, or the least show of violence on the part of the soldiers, might bring renewed strife.

On May 7 Skippon explained that his command in Ireland was "altogether unthought of, unsought for",[57] to which Colonel Robert Hammond replied bluntly that they appreciated Skippon's good qualities and "should as freely goe with him as any, except the Generali and Lieutenant Generall".[58] On May 15 about two hundred officers assembled, and the whole day was devoted to discussing their grievances;[59] on the following day[60] the debate showed some heat,[61] but towards the end Cromwell was able to announce that the vote of six weeks' arrears had been raised by Parliament to eight weeks, and that an Act of Indemnity had "already passed the House of Commons".[62] He went on to remind the men that if the authority of Parliament fell, "nothing can follow but confusion", and he called upon them now, as they had fought hitherto to establish that authority, to pledge themselves to preserve it. After the conference the Commissioners sent a brief account to Lenthall,[63] and admitted that they "found the army under a deep sense of some sufferings, and the common soldiers much unsettled"; but it now looked as if the concessions would be honoured and the negotiations crowned with success.[64]

The situation, however, was obscured by mutual suspicion.[65]

---

57. *C.P.,* I, 29.
58. The Commissioners sent a full report to Lenthall- - May 8. *W.S.,* I, 443; *L-C,* III, 249 f. (App. 10).
59. *C.P.,* I, 33–45.
60. Whalley presented a declaration signed by 223 officers: *Declaration of the Armie under Sir Thomas Fairfax, as it was lately presented at Saffron Walden in Essex unto Major Generali Skippon, Lieutenant Generali Cromwell, etc.* (1646) [*sic*.]. Gardiner has pointed out that the strongest evidence of Cromwell's loyalty to Parliament at this time is the silence of Major Huntington, who later turned against him. Huntington blamed Ireton for the Declaration presented by Whalley on May 16. Ireton had told the Agitators "that it was lawfull and fit for us to deny disbanding till we had received equall and full satisfaction for our past Services". *Sundry reasons inducing Major Huntington to lay down his Commission* (1648), 2. Cf. *G.C.W.,* III, 246 f., n.
61. *C.P.,* I, 45–78.
62. *Ibid.,* 72-3; *W.S.,* I, 445 f.; *L-C,* III, 330 f. (Supp. 21). Cf. Whitelocke 247.
63. *W.S.,* I, 446 f., May 17. A fuller report, with a covering note by Cromwell and Fleetwood, was sent later. May 20, *W.S.,* I, 447–50; *C.P.,* I, 94-9; *L-C,* III, 331 (Supp. 22).
64. *C.J.,* V, 181 See Whitelocke's remarks about the two parties. Whitelocke, 248.; Whitelocke, 248.
65. See Whitelocke's remarks about the two parties. Whitelocke, 248.

The House of Lords, on May 20, invited Charles to come to Oatlands. Parliament did not believe Cromwell's assurance that the Army would disband,[66] and the concessions were given less out of any change of heart than from the expedient of gaining time.[67] The Presbyterians expected renewed warfare and they had been preparing to that end.[68] Two days after Cromwell and his colleagues had presented their report, the Presbyterians opened secret negotiations with the Scots through Lauderdale, and with the French through the agent Bellièvre, for the removal of the King's person from England to Scotland,[69] and on May 25 measures were forced through Parliament for the immediate disbandment of the New Model Army, with the precaution that each regiment should be disbanded at a different place. No mention was made of implementing any further the promises already made, and the soldiers were peremptorily given the choice between dismissal or enlistment for Ireland.[70] Everything achieved at Saffron Walden was lost. A letter, which was probably written by Ireton to Cromwell,[71] expresses the bitterness of the soldiers at some length:

> Truly Sir, I am loath to express what their sense is of this. Tis in vaine to say anything on their behalfe; I only dread the consequences, and desire that on all sides there may be more moderation and temper. I doubt the disobleiging of soe faithfull an Army will be repented of; provocation and exasperation makes men thinke of that they never intended. They are posses't, as farr as I can discerne with this opinion, That if they be thus scornfully dealt withall for their faithfull services whilst the Sword is in their hands, what shall their usage be when they are dissolved?

---

66. Letter of Intelligence, May 24, *Clarendon MSS.* 2520. Cf. *G.C.W.*, III, 258; *W.S.*, I, 451.
67. *G.C.W.*, III, 259. Cf. Whitelocke, 248.
68. On April 16 an Ordinance had been passed giving the Common Council of London power to appoint a new committee for the control of its militia, and Presbyterian officers had immediately been nominated. Parliament approved the nominations on May 4. Whitelocke, 245.
69. Joachimi to the States General, May 26/June 7, *Additional MSS.* 17,677, S. 456 f. (Misprinted 17,667 in *G.C.W.*, III, 259 n.) The rapidity with which the Presbyterians moved may have been due to Bellièvre. Cf. his despatch to Mazarin, June 3/13, deploring their procrastination, quoted in *C.P.*, I, p. xxiv.
70. It passed the Commons on May 25, and the Lords on the 27th. *C.J.*, V, 183; *L.J.*, IX, 207; Whitelocke, 248.
71. *C.P.*, I, 101; cf. *ibid*, 102 n., where Sir Charles Firth shows that although the letter was dated May 25 it was almost certainly not written until the 27th. He also discusses the authorship. Cf. also *G.C.W.*, III, 261 and n.

That was the question which was as much in the minds of the officers as of the men.[72]

On May 29 a meeting of officers at Bury St. Edmunds recommended a general rendezvous,[73] and when the Parliamentary committee appointed to supervise the disbanding of Fairfax's regiment at Chelmsford[74] arrived they found that the soldiers had gone.[75] The Army had to act quickly, for already it had defied the explicit order of the constitutional authority for which it had been fighting, and it must by all means prevent the premature agreement between Parliament and the King. On the other hand, if the action of the Army was illegal and treasonable, the intrigues of the Presbyterians in Parliament with foreign powers were no less open to question: legally Parliament may have been right, but morally and politically its attitude to the Army was wholly indefensible.

Up to this time Cromwell had supported Parliament even to the extent of arousing the criticism and distrust of many who had previously followed him into battle. Skippon's reputation had suffered, for it was reported that "Major Generali Skippon is quite lost in the Army by endeavouring to please both sides".[76] Fairfax had already joined the troops, but Cromwell and Fleetwood were still in London, and there was some speculation as to whether they would be arrested.[77] But Cromwell had decided to throw in his lot with the Army, and one of the considerations which led him to this decision must have been the need to hold the men together, for already Rainsborough's regiment had mutinied and had been pacified only with great difficulty.[78] A Leveller, John Harris(?), writing against Oliver later, reported a meeting in his house at Drury Lane on May 31, 1647, when in order to anticipate a move by the Presbyterians to remove the

---

72. Cf. a letter by an army agent forwarded post-haste to the AgitatorS.C.P., I, 100. The last part of the letter shows that the Agitators had their own system of intelligence; the rest of the despatch was in a numerical cypher.
73. C.P., I, III. Letter of Intelligence; Whitelocke, 249.
74. Letter from Fairfax to Skippon, May 28. C.P., I, 106 f. Letter from Derby House to Fairfax, May 31. Ibid., 113 f.
75. It is clear that the situation was almost out of hand. Ireton, Okey (Robert?), Lilbume and Rich were asked to draw up "Heads of Advice", and "They show the necessity of the Officers complying with the Soldiers, who would have a general Rendezvous, without their Officers, if not by their consent". Whitelocke, 249.
76. Letter of Intelligence, C.P., I, 113.
77. Cf. Masson, The Life of Milton (7 vols., 1859–80), III, 537 f.; Clarendon, History, X, 88.
78. G.C.W., III, 264. Cf. Whitelocke, 249.

King, it was agreed that Cornet Joyce should proceed at once to Oxford, win the support of the garrison, and either prevent the removal of the King from Holmby, or conduct him to a place of greater security.[79]

IV

It is clear that Cromwell knew something about Cornet Joyce's exploit before it was undertaken, but the extent of his knowledge and the extent to which Joyce accurately understood and obeyed his instructions is not so clear. Joyce, having secured the support of the Oxford garrison on June 1, arrived at Holmby [Holdenby] the following day, and it seems that most of the guards, apart from the Presbyterian, Colonel Graves, who commanded them, had already been won over by agents from the Army.[80] Graves escaped, and after the place had been secured Joyce sent a letter back to London[81] with instructions (according to Holies) that it should be delivered to Cromwell, or failing him, Sir Arthur Hazelrigge or Fleetwood.[82]

Immediately the news reached London Cromwell and Fleetwood left the city before any action could be taken against them. Leveller writers, such as Harris and John Lilburne, asserted later that Cromwell, anticipating a similar move by the Presbyterians, authorized the whole design, but it should be remembered that the source behind their reports was Joyce at a time when he had good reason to lay the blame elsewhere.[83] Sir Philip Warwick says that a number of officers, among whom were Cromwell and Ireton, made a point of informing Charles that he had been removed from Holmby "without their privity, knowledge, or consent",[84] and this is strongly supported by other authorities.[85] John

---

79. W.S., I, 452, quoted from *The Grande Design*; also in G.C.W., III, 266 f. n.
80. "Pye's Regiment and Graves' are all engaged with the army. ... All the Dragoones at Holdenby are come in upon Engagement to the Army; soe now they are all of a piece. ..." Letter of Intelligence, *C.P.*, I, 113.
81. *C.P.*, I, 118 f.; W.S., I, 453. The letter was misdated June 4 for June 3 – possibly an indication of overwrought nerves on the part of the writer; cf. Firth's note, *C.P.*, I, 118.
82. Holies, *Memoirs*, 97.
83. Cf. Major Huntington, *Sundry Reasons*, 3 f.; *A Narrative of the late Lord General Cromwell's Anger against Lieut.-Col. Joyce* (1659). Cf. *Harleian Miscellany*, V (1810), 558; *C.P.*, I, p. xxvii.
84. *Memoires*, 229.
85. See a letter to Lenthall, June 7, quoted in *Old Parliamentary History*, XV, 410, and a Newsletter of the same date, *C.P.*, I, 125.

Rushworth printed a "True and Impartial Narration" of the incident (which can be shown on very good internal evidence to have been very largely the work of Joyce himself)[86] which says that after the disappearance of Colonel Graves, some of his "damning Blades" swore that they would fetch a relief force, "and therefore", the writer continues, "to prevent Disturbance and Blood, and for the Peace-sake of the Kingdom, all declared unanimously, that they thought it most convenient to secure the King in another place". This suggests that the decision to remove the King from Holmby was taken on the spot by Joyce with the unanimous consent of the soldiers he took with him.

Cromwell and Ireton insisted that they knew nothing of the proposal to escort the King away from Holmby,[87] but it is obvious that they knew a good deal about Joyce's expedition.[88] Fairfax, when he heard the news, told Ireton that he did not like it, and demanded who had given the order. Ireton admitted that he had given the order for Joyce to go, but "onely for securing the King there, and not for taking him away from thence".[89] Meanwhile Cromwell came in on this interview and defended what had been done on the grounds that it had merely prevented Graves from removing Charles by the direct order of Parliament.[90] Joyce may have acted on his own initiative, or he may have followed a policy agreed by the Agitators and others who wanted to force the hands of the General Officers, but what was done could not be undone, and the material facts were that Charles was now firmly in the hands of the soldiers and that Cromwell had irrevocably sided with the Army against Parliament.

---

86. See Prof. Masson's reasons given in *Milton,* III, 542 n. The full text of the "*True and Impartial Narration*" is given, Rushworth, VII, 513–17.
87. Cromwell's integrity in this matter is accepted by Gardiner (*G.C.W.,* III, 250–74, 282-4 n.); Firth (*C.P.,* I, p. xxiv–xxxi); Mrs. S.C. Lomas (*L-C,* I, 262 n.); R.H. Abbott (*W.S.,* I, 452–6, 461–5).
88. When Fairfax proposed disciplinary action against Joyce, "the Officers, whether for fear of the distemper'd Soldiers, or rather (as I suspected) a secret allowance of what was done, made all my endeavours ineffectual". Fairfax, *Short Memorials,* 116 f.
89. *Sundry Reasons,* 3.
90. There was a comprehensive plot to get the King to Scotland, and to put him at the head of an army to subjugate the Independent Army under Fairfax. Letter from Dr. Denton to Ralph Verney, June 4, 1647, *Verney MSS.,* quoted *G.C.W.,* III, 259 n.; *C.P.,* I, p. xxv.

V

The King chose to proceed to Newmarket, but meanwhile the news of Cornet Joyce's exploit so alarmed Parliament that on June 3 the House of Commons voted in favour of considering the payment of arrears in full, and expunged from its records Holies's resolution.[91] The Presbyterian leaders appealed secretly to the Scots for aid, ordered Major-General Massey to call out the city militia,[92] and promised, in a message to the Queen and the Prince of Wales, that they would support another Scottish invasion of England, if the Prince would lead it.[93] On the other hand, the Army held a second rendezvous at Kentford Heath near Newmarket on June 5, and issued a *Humble Representation*,[94] in which the soldiers demanded the names of the members responsible for the resolution of March 30.[95] At this rendezvous the troops entered into a *Solemn Engagement*,[96] and specifically charged the Presbyterian leaders with fomenting warfare.[97]

Immediately on learning of Joyce's arrival at Holmby, Fairfax had despatched Colonel Whalley's regiment to protect the King, and two further regiments were sent when it became known that Charles had been removed. Cromwell himself gave Whalley instructions "to use anything but force to cause His Majesty to return",[98] but Charles firmly refused to go back,[99] and made his way steadily to Newmarket, being visited on the way by Fairfax, Cromwell and other officers, at Childerley.

Meanwhile the Houses of Parliament were drawn further away

---

91. Whitelocke, 250. Cf. *supra*, p. 113 f.
92. *Ibid*, 252.
93. *G.C.W.*, III, 278.
94. Rushworth, VII, 505–10.
95. Unknown to the soldiers it had been erased from the records on June 4.
96. Rushworth, VII, 510–12.
97. Gardiner has shown that the main part of this paper was drawn up by the Agitators, but there are two interesting clauses at the end which appear to have been inserted at the instigation of Cromwell. The first of these established a Council of the General Officers together with two commissioned officers and two other representatives from each regiment. The other clause denied that the Army intended the overthrow of Presbyterianism for the establishment of Independency, but that it would "study to promote such an Establishment of common and equal Right and Freedom to the whole, as all might equally partake of", i.e. the Army would support the establishment of Presbyterianism on condition that freedom of conscience was allowed. *G.C.W.*, III, 281 f.
98. Memoirs of *Sir John Berkeley* (1699), 13.
99. Whitelocke, 251.

from the Army by influence exerted from two new quarters. Large numbers of "Reformadoes" – men who had changed sides in the war and ended by serving under Essex, Waller or Massey – had been pouring into London, and were rioting.[100] Members of the Houses were threatened on their way to Westminster, but realizing that it might be able to use these men against Fairfax's army, Parliament voted £10,000 to their use.[101] At the same time the city demanded that a force of cavalry should be raised for the capital's defence. On the day that Parliament was voting money to the use of Reformadoes Fairfax wrote to the House giving details of what had happened.[102] By June 10 the Army had reached Triploe Heath near Cambridge, and was drawn up to receive the Parliamentary Commissioners, but before the Commissioners arrived the soldiers had been instructed "to be very silent and civill towards the said Commissioners". The soldiers had also been promised that if necessary the Army would seize the Cinque Ports to prevent the loss of treasure abroad, and that plans would be formulated to meet the possible invasion by the Scots.[103] The Commissioners could make little impression on the Army in this mood.[104]

The appeal by the Lord Mayor and City Fathers to Parliament for adequate defence gave the Army officers cause to address themselves directly to the Common Council of the city. Accordingly a letter was sent from the officers' quarters at Royston,0[105] which bears all the marks of Cromwellian inspiration and, possibly, authorship. The letter stated that all the Army wanted was "satisfaction to our demands as soldiers; and reparation upon those who have, to the uttermost, improved all opportunities and advantages, by false suggestions, misrepresentations and otherwise, for the destruction of this army with a perpetual blot of ignominy upon it".[106] To some extent, as Gardiner points out, this

---

100. *Ibid.*
101. *Ibid.*, 252.
102. There was another letter from Fairfax on the 8th. Rushworth, VII, 550 f.
103. Letter to Skippon, June 10. *C.P.,* I, 127 f.
104. Whitelocke, 252.
105. *W.S.,* I, 459–61; *L-C,* I, 266–9 (Army Manifesto); Rushworth, VII, 554 f.
106. *W.S.,* I, 459 f.; *L-C,* I, 267 f. "We have said before, and profess it now, We desire no alteration of the Civil Government. We desire not to intermeddle with, or in the least to interrupt, the settling of the Presbyterian. Government. Nor do we seek to open a way to licentious liberty, under pretence of obtaining ease for tender consciences." This is exactly the same attitude to the ecclesiastical settlement as we found in the last clause of the *Solemn Engagement.* Cf. Rushworth, VII, 510–12.

letter "displays Cromwell as concealing from himself that he was really executing a change of front",[107] but if it had been a complete change of front John Lilburne would not have had cause to protest to him as he did later on July 1. It would perhaps be truer to say that Cromwell was not so much executing a change of front, as advancing to a new position, from which he saw the Army as truer representatives of the people than the members at Westminster: if Parliament was unable or unwilling to assume its prime responsibility of establishing a just peace, then other instruments, under God, would have to take a hand.

VI

The Army marched on London and quartered at St. Albans.[108] The London-trained bands were called out but refused to move. Petitions in support of the Army's demands began to flow in to Fairfax from those very counties that a few months previously had been petitioning Parliament against his army.[109] A declaration drafted by Ireton and signed on June 14, defined more exactly the Army's attitude to those who had opposed it[110] and specifically accused the eleven Members of Parliament to whom the Army took exception. They were entering the sphere of politics in no uncertain manner – "Here", as Denzil Holies wrote later, "they first take upon them openly to intermeddle with the business of the kingdom",[111] and there is no doubt that, having now sided with the Army, Cromwell's hand, and that of his nearest associate Ireton, can be seen guiding the policy of the Army. Lilburne sent Cromwell an enthusiastic letter[112] congratulating him for his "active paines" in the common cause, and giving him a good deal

---

107. *G.C.W.*, III, 287 f.
108. Ignoring the feverish command of the Lords to keep outside a thirty mile limit. *L.J.*, IX, 256–8. The Commons immediately extended the limit to forty mileS.C.J., V, 209.
109. Essex, Norfolk and Suffolk, Whitelocke, 252. A reply was drafted by the officers to the petitioners, in which it was again expressly stated, "We meddle not with matters of Religion or Church Government, leaving those to Parliament". *W.S.*, I, 466 f.; *C.P.*, I, 130–2.
110. Rushworth, VII, 564–70; Whitelocke, 253 f. The Declaration suggested placing authority of government into the hands of men "approved at least for moral righteousness". Gardiner pointed out that this was an interesting forecast of the Little Parliament. *G.C.W.*, III, 294 n.
111. *Memoirs*.
112. June 22, *Jonah's Cry*, 7 f.

of sound counsel.[113] He suggested that the Army leaders should "with all candor ... endevour to understand the King and let him understand you, and seale with him as becomes honest men that play above boord, and doe their actions in the sight of God, for the good of all". This policy the Army leaders took immediate steps to pursue.

On June 24, 1647, the Army sent the *Humble Remonstrance*[114] to London, and on the same day Charles left Newmarket with the Parliamentary Commissioners, arriving at Royston on the 25th.[115] Cromwell wrote to Whalley,[116] informing him that Dr. Hammond and some other chaplains to the King were making their way towards him, and pointing out that, although the Parliamentary Commissioners might try to obstruct, "now you can be as civil as some others that pretend to be more". Accordingly on Sunday, June 27, Charles attended divine service according to the Anglican rite, and as Cromwell had foreseen, the Commissioners were immediately instructed to remove the chaplains.

Sir Allen Apsley, who had defended Barnstaple for the King, and was then on his way to France, delivered a letter to Sir John Berkeley from Cromwell.[117] Oliver reminded Berkeley of a conversation he had had fourteen months earlier with Lambert at the rendition of Exeter, when the Royalist had suggested that if the Independent officers intervened "to restore the King and People" to their ancient rights this "would so ingratiate them with both, that they would voluntarily invest them with as much trust and power as subjects are capable of". In his account of the new approach from Cromwell Berkeley goes on to say:

> To this discourse of mind, they now informed me, at that time, they had only given a hearing, but no consent, as proceeding from an interest much divided from theirs: but that they had since found,

---

113. He advised him "immediately to march with a Declaration of peace and love to the body of the Citie", which would enable the Army's friends in London to take action against the eleven members, but he was emphatic in advising the Army leaders not to attempt to condemn the eleven members to death by Ordinance. He was at pains to prove the illegality of such a course. *Ibid.*
114. Rushworth, VII, 585–91; Whitelocke, 255.
115. With the approach of the Army the eleven members requested permission to withdraw from the House. On June 28 the Army had reached Uxbridge, and on July 1 ten of the higher officers were appointed by Fairfax to meet representatives from Parliament. Whitelocke, 256.
116. *W.S.*, I, 468 f.; *L-C*, III, 332 (Supp. 23); *C.P.*, I, 140.
117. Berkeley, *Memoirs*, 6–10.

by experience, all, or the most part, of it so reasonable, that they were resolved to put it in practice, as I might perceive by what had already passed. They desired for the present nothing of me, but that I would present them humbly to the Queen and Prince, and be suitor to them in their names, not to condemn them absolutely, but to suspend their opinion of them, and their pretensions towards his Majesty, and judge them rather by their future behaviour; of the innocence whereof they had already given some testimonies to the world, and would do more and more, daily. When I should have done this office, they desired I would come over into England, and become an eye-witness of their proceedings.[118]

The Army leaders must have intended what they said, otherwise it is unlikely that they would have been content for Berkeley to hold a watching brief; but such negotiations were almost bound to fail, not only because it was "an interest much divided from theirs", but also because of the different standards of thought and conduct accepted by the two parties: Charles frankly distrusted Cromwell and the other officers because they never mentioned anything about their personal aggrandizement. Some years later Cardinal de Retz had a conversation about Cromwell with Bellièvre:

Je vous entends, répondit le Président de Bellièvre, & je vous arrête en même tems, pour vous dire ce que j'ai appris de Cromwel, (M. de Bellièvre l'avoit vu & connu en Angleterre.) Il me disoit un jour, que l'on ne montait jamais si haut, que quand on ne sait où l'on va.[119]

The French cardinal did not understand the saying, and dismissed the author of it as a madman. Others have found in it a cryptic expression of Cromwell's ambition. It would be simpler and more true to Cromwell's thought to interpret the words by the doctrine of Providence – for Providence was leading him to a position within the State of which the obscure farmer of St. Ives had never dreamed. French cardinals and English royalists found such an essentially simple faith unbelievable – they were the words of a fool, or of a hypocrite. Cromwell had said to Sir John Berkeley on June 12, "that whatever the world might judge of them, they would be found no seekers of themselves farther

---

118. Berkeley, *Memoirs*, 10.
119. *Mémoiresédu Cardinal de Retz* (Amsterdam, 1719), II, 384 f. See also Gardiner's reasons for dating this incident between Cromwell and Bellièvre about this time. *G.C.W.*, III, 316 n.

than to have leave to live as subjects ought to do, and to preserve their consciences".[120] The King and his advisers could not accept this as ingenuous, and Sir Allen Apsley warned Sir John Berkeley that he would have to deal with "subtil men, that govern'd themselves by other Maxims than the rest of the World".[121] In a world of diplomacy it is often difficult for "honest men that play above boord, and doe their actions in the sight of God", to convince others of their good faith.

---

120. Berkeley, *Memoirs*, 16.
121. *Ibid.*, 10.

Chapter Seven

The Army Debates of 1647

I

The officers and Agitators met in a General Council of War at Reading on the morning of July 16, 1647.[1] The temper of the Army had not been improved by a widespread rumour that Colonel Poyntz intended to betray the Northern Army into the hands of the Scots,[2] and therefore the Council met in the knowledge that it must resolve its differences without delay.

The meetings of this Council set the stage for all future army debates during the interregnum. They are important for many reasons – they show us how the Army regarded itself as representative of the whole nation, and they illustrate the Urgency behind the desire for a just peace;[3] but for our better understanding of Cromwell their importance can hardly be over-emphasized, not only because we trace through them the growth of his political ideas, but also because they demonstrate in a most striking way the "church" relationship between him and his troops, and present us with a clear picture of ecclesiastical discipline existing side by side with military discipline in Fairfax's incredible army.

The occasion on July 16[4] was to discuss a *Representation*[5] by the Agitators, urging the immediate march of the Army upon London. At the opening of the afternoon session Cromwell introduced the debate by emphasizing that their task was to prepare something which would present a reasonable chance of peaceful

---

1. The Agitators were admitted to this Council in order to maintain unity. Cf. Newsletter [by John Rushworth?], *C.P.I.*, 214 f. The *Clarke Papers* give a full account of the Army Debates of 1647. A. S. P. Woodhouse in *Puritanism and Liberty* gives full accounts of the later debates at Putney and Whitehall, and gives a summary of the Reading debates in an appendix. R.H. Abbott and Mrs. Lomas report Cromwell's speeches in full, linked by the argument of the rest of the debate. For the sake of consistency, we have used Abbott's text for Cromwell's own words.
2. Poyntz was arrested by his own men, but released by order of Fairfax.
3. Cf. the utterances of officers such as Capt. Clarke and Lt.-Col. Jubbes, who cannot be placed in any group with precision. *Ibid.*, 180; Woodhouse, 99.
4. *C.P.*, I, 176–82; *W.S.*, I, 475–7; *L-C*, III, 333 f. (Supp. 24).
5. *C.P.*, I, 170–5.

settlement for the nation,⁶ and he argued strongly for a treaty with Parliament to secure their rights, rather than any display of force.⁷ One of the Agitators, Allen, assured the General that he and the men he represented did not question the integrity of the officers, but because they were suspicious of the men with whom they had to treat, they thought immediate action was less dangerous than delay.⁸ In reply Cromwell suggested that the most hasty method was not always the most effective: their enemies in Parliament were not "upon the gaining hand" but the exercise of force would tend "to make them gain more". To this Allen replied that they had long hoped for a Parliament of the kind he had described, "a Parliament soe reformed as might back this present power",⁹ but their friends at Westminster constantly appeared to be losing ground, and they would continue so unless the Army marched to London.

What was to be regarded as the ultimate authority within the State? Allen, quite clearly, regarded the "power" of the Army as independent of, and even superior to, the authority of Parliament. Cromwell on the other hand still respected Parliament as the authority which they had fought to uphold, and was seeking a way to reconcile the Army's power with the Parliament's authority, before the rash use of the former not only destroyed the last constitutional link with the past, but also denied the principles of their first resistance. His plea for a treaty, however confused in its expression, maintained the honour of both sides: he wanted reform, whereas the Agitators intended revolution.

Henry Ireton appears to stand with Cromwell at this point, but there is a subtle difference between the two men. Ireton was far less distressed at the possible use of force against Parliament – indeed, he was of the opinion that the use of force would be inevitable-r-but he was concerned that the Army should have a constitutional excuse for its actions. He had no such ideals about Parliamentary unanimity as Cromwell had, for he frankly admitted, "what reason have I to expect that other men should trust mee more than I should trust to them?"¹⁰ but he insisted that the Army should have a "legal" excuse for its actions.

---

6. *W.S.*, I, 478; *L-C*, III, 335; *C.P.*, I, 184; Woodhouse, 412.
7. *W.S.*, I, 478 f.; *L-C*, III, 336; *C.P.*, I, 185 f., Woodhouse, 413.
8. *C.P.*, I, 189–93. Similar arguments had been expressed previously by Captain Clarke.
9. *C.P.*, I, 193; Woodhouse, 415.
10. *C.P.*, I, 194 f.; Woodhouse, 415.

The Army Debates of 1647

The Agitators believed – and it is clear that Ireton shared their belief – that whatever concessions the soldiers had gained from Parliament had, in Edward Sexby's phrase, been wrung from it "rather out of feare then love",[11] and that since the power had been put by Providence unto the hands of the soldiery it was their duty to use it.[12] Ultimately Cromwell would have agreed but he still hoped Parliament would become purged, not by external threats, but by its own action.[13] On the following day, July 17, Ireton presented his *Heads of Proposals*,[14] and on the 18th Fairfax appointed a committee of twelve officers to perfect the proposals.[15] With this action the Army made its first attempt at legislating for the country.

II

Meanwhile the King had been provided with a preview of these proposals before they were officially presented to him.[16] Sir John Berkeley seems to have regarded them as very moderate, and told the King that he would have suspected them more than he did if they had demanded less. He further advised Charles that "never was crown so near lost, so cheaply recover'd, as his Majesty's would be, if they agreed upon such terms".[17] The King, however, was obsessed with the idea that his consent was indispensable to the constitutional settlement of the country.[18] Reports from London indicated that the Army was unpopular in

---

11. *C.P.*, I, 207 f.
12. Although some of the Agitators were more secular in their approach to political theory than Cromwell, they all accepted the view of Providence that associated military success with the signs of God's favour. Cf. Woodhouse's introduction to *Puritanism and Liberty*, 54 ff.
13. *W.S.*, I, 481 f.; *L-C*, III, 339 f.; *C.P.*, I, 192 f.; Woodhouse, 414 f.
14. Text of the *Heads of Proposals*, Rushworth, VII, 731; Gardiner, *Const. Docs.*, 316–26; Woodhouse, 422–6 (Extracts). Ireton was aided in drafting the proposals by Cromwell and Lambert. Cf. Whitelocke, 254. See also the report of the proceedings in the Army Council on July 17, *C.P.*, I, 211–14, in which Ireton explains how he had been deputed to draw up the propositions. His defensive statement and the rather ambiguous comments by William Allen show how Ireton was regarded with suspicion by the Agitators.
15. Fairfax's order appointing the council. *C.P.*, I, 216 f. Cf. Woodhouse, 421 f.
16. Berkeley, *Memoirs*, 30 ff.
17. *Ibid.*
18. After receiving Berkeley's advice "his Majesty broke from me with the expression, Well! I shall see them glad 'ere long to accept more equal terms". *Ibid.*, 32.

the City, and Charles thought that the Army leaders would be forced to accept his terms. It is true that earlier accounts of the preparations being made against the Army had been grave, but after July 16 the Presbyterian majority in the House of Commons had dropped, and Fairfax was confirmed in his command of all the land forces in the country.[19] The following day, in view of the Army's approach, the Commons gave the eleven members permission to withdraw.[20] Cromwell, Waller, Hammond and Rich assured the Parliamentary Commissioners in the name of the General and the Army that they were satisfied with the action and would be prepared to consider a settlement. The situation at that point promised well, and is reminiscent of the position immediately after the Saffron Walden Conference – Parliament apparently doing its best to conciliate the soldiers, and Cromwell using his influence to prevent violence. But just as the May crisis had been turned by a reaction in Parliament itself, so now the situation was altered by a reaction within the City. On July 21 an engagement was signed at Skinners' Hall by apprentices, watermen and "reformadoes" to maintain the Covenant, and to bring the King back to Westminster on his terms of May 12,[21] and on the 26th a petition demanding the repeal of Parliamentary control of the city militia was presented to the Houses by a turbulent crowd. Both Houses were intimidated into a hasty assent, and a mob of rioters entered the Commons and held the Speaker in his chair while a resolution was passed recalling the King to London.[22]

None of the constitutional forms of public authority could effect its will, and it was no longer a question whether or not force would be used to bring Parliament to a decision, but which form of power would become dominant, the New Model Army or the London mob. On July 30 when the House reassembled fifty-seven members had fled to the Army for protection,[23] and neither House had a Speaker. The members left at Westminster were quite unabashed. They proceeded to hurry Presbyterian

---

19. *L.J.*, IX, 338; Whitelocke, 259.
20. *C.J.*, V, 251 f. This occurred exactly two months after Cromwell had read the report from Saffron Walden in the Commons.
21. This occurred exactly two months after Cromwell had read the report from Saffron Walden in the Commons.
22. For an account of the riots, cf. *C.P.*, I, 217 f.
23. Cf. Walker, *Hist. of Independency*, Pt. I, 40 f.; Ludlow, *Memoirs*, I, 161 f.; and Sir Charles Firth's note, *C.P.*, I, 218–19. The fact that the Earl of Manchester sought refuge with the Army suggests that the threat was real enough.

legislation through the Houses, and they forbade Fairfax to come within thirty miles of the city, in spite of the fact that the Army was already at Colnbrook, between Windsor and Twickenham. It was probably just before the news of the London riots reached Charles that Major Huntington delivered a message to Ireton from the King[24] to say that he had decided to put his entire dependence upon them, and that if they "proved honest men" they would prevent further bloodshed. Ireton received this assurance with very great jubilation, and vowed that they would be "the veriest knaves that ever lived" if they failed to keep their promises "because the King by not declaring against us had given us great advantage against our Adversaries".

However, when the news came to Charles of the city riots and the votes of Parliament calling for his return, it put an entirely different complexion on matters. He not only went back on his word, but he was guilty of a gross error of political judgment, for instead of seeing that these events were likely to bring the Army to London, he imagined that the officers would be thrown back on him. The Earl of Lauderdale had assured him of the support of the Scots and English Presbyterians, and he now felt he could raise his terms. Hence when the *Proposals* were presented to him officially he rejected them with scorn which was the amazement of even his own supporters. He even went out of his way to inform the officers that he regretted nothing so much as his action in the Bill against Strafford, and that he intended to have the Church "establish'd according to Law". He hoped God had forgiven him the sin of allowing episcopacy to be given up in Scotland, and he reiterated several times, "You cannot be without me; You will fall to ruin if I do not sustain you." Sir John Berkeley and John Ashburnham, the King's agents, were just as much at a loss to understand this conduct as were the officers, and although Charles eventually moderated his tone, it was too late, for Rainsborough had already slipped out of the conference and sent off a report to the regiments.[25]

After this exhibition of royal intransigence Cromwell grew somewhat cooler in his attitude towards the King,[26] and he expostulated to Ashburnham that he could not be trusted. He charged the King with having intrigued "to raise new troubles",

---

24. *Sundry Reasons*, 7 f.
25. Berkeley, *Memoirs*, 34 f.
26. Clarendon, *History*, X, 125.

and he [Cromwell] "would not be answerable if any thing fell out amiss and contrary to expectation".[27] The fears were not ungrounded. The Army had approached Charles because, in view of their own experience of Parliament, the soldiers felt that failure to reach a settlement may not have been entirely due to the King, but they would not have to suffer many indignities from Charles before returning to the attitude Baxter had noticed after Naseby.[28] However, even after the conference reported above, the Army officers still tried to reconcile the King to their proposals and when Berkeley asked them how they proposed to obtain the concurrence of Parliament, it was Rainsborough who bluntly intimated that Parliament would not be given much choice in the matter.[29] But while Charles felt he had the power to raise his terms he would continue to prevaricate. He could not see that although he was undoubtedly indispensable to the legal settlement of the country, the Army had already shown that it was ready to dispense with legality. The stubbornness which resulted from his failure to recognize his position *de facto* as distinct from his position *de jure* was the one real hindrance at this time to final settlement.[30]

From Colnbrook the Army advanced to Hounslow Heath[31] where, on August 4, 1647, it received an anxious plea from the Common Council of London that there should be no further bloodshed: official London, at any rate, was beginning to feel some remorse at its share in recent events. In reply, the Army denounced as illegal the choice of new Speakers "by some gentlemen of Westminster", and the votes passed in the absence of the Speakers.[32] On the following day the nine peers and fifty-seven Members of Parliament who had taken refuge with Fairfax subscribed to an engagement to live and die with him and the Army,[33] and on August 6 the Army marched into the city.[34] There

---

27. *Ibid.*
28. *Reliquiae Baxterianae*, I, 57.
29. Berkeley, *Memoirs*, 36 f.
30. Cromwell and Ireton had been able to control the rank and file so far because the first suggestion of negotiating with Charles had come from them. As the rank and file lost confidence in Charles it became suspicious of Cromwell and Ireton for persisting in negotiations. Cf. Berkeley's *Memoirs*, 24–6, 39–46, *passim*; Clarendon, *History*, X, 126.
31. August 3, 1647.
32. *L.J.*, IX, 375–8.
33. *Ibid.*, 385; Rushworth, VII, 755.
34. Whitelocke, 264.

was nothing for the remaining members at Westminster to do but to submit with as good a grace as possible.[35] Fairfax was made Governor of the Tower, and Colonel Tichborne was installed as Lieutenant; a day of public Thanksgiving was ordered, and a gratuity of a month's pay was ordered for the rank and file of the Army, while the city hastened to make its separate peace by inviting Fairfax and his officers to a banquet, which the General declined.[36]

The Members of Parliament, however, realized no more than did the King the real danger that confronted them in the radical movement within the Army.[37] They saw the Levellers chiefly as an embarrassment to Cromwell and Ireton, and not as a well-organized body of responsible opinion with a political theory of its own based upon the common rights of man. Cromwell, however much he might dislike the use of force against Parliament, had as his first aim the maintenance of Army unity and discipline, and he would not hold out indefinitely against the Levellers' pressure. His remarks at Reading did not deny the principle of purging Parliament, but had urged that Parliament should be given time to purge itself. There was a limit to his patience, and on one occasion, exasperated by some piece of Presbyterian truculence, he remarked to Ludlow in the House, "These men will never leave till the army pull them out by the ears."[38] On August 18, at Kingston, the Army Council drew up a declaration in support of the demand for a parliamentary purge, and on August 20 a new attempt was to be made to outlaw the proceedings conducted in the Speakers' absence. The officers who were

---

35. The Commons resolved that, "This House doth approve the Coming up of the General and the Army, for the secure and safe Sitting of the Parliament: And that Thanks be given to the General and Army for the same." *C.J.*, V, 268. The Lords went even further, and resolved that "This House doth approve the Declaration of Sir Thomas Fairfax, and his Proceedings in bringing up the Army". *L.J.*, IX, 379.
36. Whitelocke, 264.
37. The Lords desired the concurrence of the lower House in an Ordinance declaring null and void all those acts performed by the Houses during the period July 26-August 6. This motion was lost by two votes. The resolutions of the House during that period were repealed, but the implication of a vote declaring them null and void, as Abbott has pointed out, would have been to render those members responsible for these measures liable to censure or punishment for unconstitutional proceedings. The extreme Presbyterians by this vote virtually secured confirmation of the legality of their sitting without the Speakers. Whitelocke, 264; *C.J.*, V, 270; *W.S.*, I, 495.
38. *Memoirs*, I, 148. For the date of this incident cf. *ibid*, note; *G.C.W.*, III, 350 n.; *W.S.*, I, 496 n.; Huntington, *Sundry Reasons*, 8.

Members of Parliament, having left a party of soldiers at the door and stationed a regiment in Hyde Park, succeeded in getting the measure passed. It was Ireton's method.

III

The fact that Henry Ireton seems to have had a growing influence upon his father-in-law helps to explain some of the charges of inconsistency against the latter. The influence was real enough to be noticed by some of their near associates among the General Officers, and Clarendon tells us that Sir John Berkeley was the more ready to believe his informants in the Army Council – Watson and Staines[39] – "because they seemed very much to blame Ireton's stubbornness towards the king, and to fear that he often prevailed upon Cromwell against his own inclinations".

Charles's agents were quick to work upon any suspicion which existed between the Agitators and their higher officers. Berkeley himself had a very extensive correspondence with Levellers in the Army, and other royalist sympathizers were active in spreading rumours of a personal engagement between Cromwell and the King, which increased the suspicions of the rank and file. A good deal of this suspicion rested on the very flimsy circumstantial evidence that "Cromwel's and Ireton's door was open to us [the royalists] when it was shut to them".[40]

The position of Cromwell and Ireton was not enviable. The fleet was infected with royalism,[41] and the influence of the Leveller movement was growing in the Army. They were distrusted by the King,[42] Parliament and Levellers, and although they maintained

---

39. Dr. William Staines [or Stane], Quarter-Master General, and Leonard Watson, Scoutmaster-General. *History,* X, 135.
40. Berkeley, *Memoirs,* 41. Cf. *Ibid.,* 39–40. While John Lilburne was in prison, Sir Lewis Dives, a royalist fellow-prisoner, steadily fed him with rumours that Cromwell and Ireton had a secret accommodation with Charles, since "he judged it for the King's service to divide Cromwel and the Army". Berkeley also records that Lady Carlisle assiduously spread a rumour that Cromwell had a personal agreement with the King and was to be created Earl of Essex.
41. Vice-Admiral Batten resigned his commission, and Rainsborough was appointed in his place. Whitelocke, 271. The sailors, however, refused to serve under the latter, and in the following spring Batten sailed with eleven ships to join Rupert in Holland.
42. On August 26, 1647, they had voted for a modified form of the Newcastle Propositions being sent to Charles, and he could not understand how they could do this when their own proposals were before him. (Bates, *Elenchus* (1685 edn.), Pt. I, 88; Dugdale, *Short View,* 264 f.) It was, however, one way

their control over the Army Council, it was extremely tenuous.[43] When Major Francis White bluntly declared in the Army Council that there was "no superintendent Authority in this kingdom but what is exercised by the power and force of the sword", he was stating no more than many would take to be a sober estimate of the truth.[44] Everything depended on the speed with which a settlement could be concluded, and Cromwell and Ireton sought desperately to find a way out of the impasse. They showed themselves ready to negotiate with all elements in the situation. Cromwell visited Lilburne in prison, to secure from him the promise that he would not stir up the Army to mutiny if he were released,[45] and he even went so far to conciliate the Presbyterians as to announce openly his disinclination "to cast down the foundation of Presbytery and set up Independency".[46] He was in the midst of men who feared and distrusted him, and he knew it. On September 14, writing to Michael Jones in Ireland to congratulate him on his victory at Dungan Hill he said that,[47] "though it may be for the present a cloud may lie over our actions, to them who are not acquainted with the grounds of our t[ransactions?]; yet we doubt not but God will clear our integrity and innocency from any other ends we aim at but his glory and the public good".

It rings true: the evidence is that Cromwell was honestly striving to reach the basis for a settlement, but within the Council he had to face the bitter antagonism of Rainsborough who led a group which was opposed to any further negotiation with Charles,[48] and it is clear that Henry Marten headed a similar group in the Commons. On September 17, 1647, Marten

---

of showing Charles what he could expect from Parliament. When he saw the new parliamentary terms he promptly showed his preference for the Army's proposals, and commended them as the basis for all future discussion. Whitelocke, 269.

43. It is possible that the waning prestige of the Army leaders may have had something to do with the refusal of the city to raise a loan of £50,000 for the Army's support. Whitelocke, 268, 269.
44. *A Copy of a Letter ... by Francis White* (1647). White was expelled from the Council for uttering these words.
45. But on September 14 Cromwell supported a motion to search for precedents regarding the jurisdiction of the Lords in Lilburne's case. Lilburne, *An Additional Plea* (1647); *C.J.*, V, 301.
46. *Two Declarations from Sir Thomas Fairfax and the Generali Councill* (September 7, 1647).
47. *W.S.*, I, 505 f.; *L-C*, I, 277 f. (XLVI).
48. Ford to Hopton, September 20, *Clarendon MSS.* 2597. A quarrel was occasioned by Cromwell's insistence that negotiations with Charles should continue.

proposed that no further addresses be made to the King,[49] and the temper of the House can be judged from the fact that on the 23rd it voted that certain of the Newcastle Propositions, including the parts abolishing episcopacy, should be submitted once more to the King, and that only one more application should be made. During these debates Cromwell, Ireton, Vane, St. John and Fiennes had urged the method of a personal treaty between Parliament and the King, and a royalist newsletter of the period commented that their "Civilities are visible".[50]

The same could not be said of Charles. The royal obstinacy increased with the arrival of the Scottish Earls of Lanark and Loudoun to join their colleague Lauderdale,[51] and this renewed Scottish diplomacy reopened the possibility of invasion from the north.[52] There was a rumour that Cromwell believed that further negotiation with Charles was useless, and that Ireton had disagreed and offered to relinquish his commission;[53] but although their negotiations with the King had broken down by October 20, Cromwell made a speech three hours long on that day and "spoke very favourably of the King, concluding that it was necessary to re-establish him as soon as possible".[54] The evidence therefore shows that, although in their negotiations with the King Cromwell and Ireton had failed, they still hoped for a settlement with him, if not through the Army, then through Parliament. The hardening of Parliament's attitude towards Charles seemed to provide the Army officers with a new opportunity to press their terms, and it would have seemed to be wiser from their point of view not to urge too far the idea of a personal treaty between Charles and the Houses. Why then did Cromwell speak in the King's favour on October 20? Was it to impress Charles by his sincerity, or was it because he sincerely feared the result of a complete break with the King?

---

49. Ford to Hopton, September 28, *Clarendon MSS.* 2604. Cf. Whitelocke, 271.
50. *Clarendon MSS.* 2602. Cf. *C.P.,* I, 230 n.
51. October II, Letter of Intelligence, *Clarendon MS.* 2622. For Cromwell's very full activities during these days see his letter to Fairfax, October 13. *W.S.,* I, 510; *L-C,* I, 278 f. (XLVII); and *W.S.,* I, 508 f.
52. Cf. Cromwell's letter to Fairfax recommending the appointment of Col. Robert Overton to command at Hull, October 22. *W.S.,* I, 513 f.; *L-C,* I, 280 f. (XLVIII).
53. Letter of Intelligence, *Clarendon MSS.* 2622.
54. Newsletter, *Record Office (Roman) Transcripts,* October 22/November 1, quoted Gardiner, *G.C.W.,* III, 381; *W.S.* I, 512 (translation).

IV

The importance of the Army debates at Putney and Whitehall in 1647 makes a further examination of them unavoidable. The first of the meetings opened on October 28 under the chairmanship of Cromwell, in the absence of Fairfax through sickness, and at this meeting the Agitators presented the first draft of the *Agreement of the People*,[55] which they and their Leveller friends had prepared as a counterblast to both the *Newcastle Propositions* and Ireton's *Heads of Proposals*. Yet for all their radical constitutional ideas these men were theologically men of their own time. "We have been by Providence put upon strange things," Edward Sexby said, "such as the ancientest here doth scarce remember. The Army acting to these ends, Providence hath been with us, and yet we have found little fruit of our endeavours." Their efforts to settle the country had not been blessed because they had "gone to Egypt for help":[56] they had tried to please a King who would never be pleased unless they all cut their throats, and they had tried to please a Parliament whose members were rotten. Then turning to Cromwell and Ireton, the Agitator expressed what was in the minds of a good number of his associates. "Your credits and reputation", he said, "have been much blasted, upon these two considerations. The one is for seeking to settle this kingdom in such a way wherein we thought to have satisfied all men, and we have dissatisfied them – I mean in relation to the King. The other is in reference to a Parliamentary authority." Sexby's words were specially important because they challenged the very theological basis on which Cromwell claimed to act. "You are convinced God will have you to act on," Sexby said to Cromwell and Ireton, but if they were to be justified in that belief they must either reconcile their doctrine of Providence with their very evident failure in diplomacy, or make way for other "instruments" of the Divine Purpose.

Cromwell and Ireton did not immediately answer this objection – indeed, they could not, but they were able to defend the action they had taken hitherto. Cromwell said that he had acted on the authority of the General Council of the Army, and when

---

55. Text in Woodhouse, 443 ff.; Gardiner, *Const. Docs.*, 333 ff.
56. See Isaiah 30, 31. Lilburne in his letter to Cromwell, March 25, 1646/47, had called the Independents of Westminster "the broken reeds of Egypt". Cf. *supra*, p. 112.

he had expressed any contrary opinion in Parliament he had merely exercised his right as a private member of the House,[57] while Henry Ireton added that although he had no wish to set up either King or Parliament in any sense that would imperil the best interests of the kingdom, he "would not seek, nor will join with them that do seek, the destruction either of Parliament or King".[58]

When the Agitators' detailed proposals were read it was obvious, as Cromwell observed, that they were introducing a form of government radically different from that which the country had traditionally held "since it hath been a nation",[59] and Cromwell was afraid the change would bring about the disintegration of the country into mutually hostile counties or districts. Cromwell pleaded that they should look at the proposals with "reason and judgment", but this at once presented him with a theological difficulty, for how could he allow "reason" to have precedence over "faith"? "I know a man may answer all difficulties with faith", he said, "and faith will answer all difficulties really where it is, but", he added, "we are very apt all of us to call that faith that perhaps may be but carnal imagination and carnal reasonings." Faith might be used as an excuse for any rashness – "we ought to consider the consequences, and God hath given us our reason that we may do this". It was a brief digression which had little to do directly with the point at issue, but it shows us the way his mind worked.

Oliver returned, however, to a faith which was based upon Providence – the conviction that as God had revealed His will in the success of this Army, so now He would reveal it again by granting them united counsels, and he promised the Agitators, "I shall offer nothing to you but that I think in my heart and conscience tends to the uniting of us and to the begetting a right understanding among us." Anyone could formulate a system of government better than the existing unhappy state of the country, but they must examine how far they could go in such proposals. The Army must honour the terms of its previous contracts – "he that departs from that that is a real engagement and a real tie upon him, I think he transgresses without faith, for … God does expect from men the performance of every honest obligation".

---

57. Colonel Rainsborough defended Cromwell on this point. Woodhouse, 4; *C.P.,* I, 232.
58. Woodhouse, 4 f.; *C.P.,* I, 233.
59. *W.S.,* I, 518 ff.; *L-C,* III, 350 ff.; Woodhouse, 7–10; *C.P.,* I, 236–40.

The stand which Cromwell was making on this point has a deeper significance. Some historians have suggested that there was a complete separation in Puritan thought between the Kingdom of Grace and the world of affairs. A.S.P. Woodhouse has called it the "principle of segregation", which he suggests "completely secularizes one division of existence".[60] We must question that. We suggest that – whatever the ultimate results of Reformation teaching[61] – that tendency which has often been taken for secularization in Puritanism began as an Old Testament ethic based upon justice and interpreted by Law. The conception of "the dual ethic" provides us with an explanation of Puritan conduct very different from that of "the principle of segregation", and on the basis of Reformation biblicism it does more justice to the essentially theological attitude of the Puritan towards the whole of life.[62] It is supported by these speeches. The King – and indeed, Parliament – had no special claim to be treated by the Army officers with Christian charity, but as Cromwell urged throughout the debates, "he that departs from that that is a real engagement and a real tie upon him, I think he transgresses without faith". It meant the recognition of certain standards and responsibilities even towards erstwhile enemies which were just as much a part of the Law of God as those which were binding upon Christian friends; and the basis of these rules of behaviour was to be found in the Old Testament and the Mosaic Covenant.

The debate continued. Ireton admitted that there was much in the Agitators' proposals that he would "rejoice to see obtained", but they were not free to enforce a constitution of their own choosing,[63] and Cromwell declared his willingness even to resign from the Army rather than be an obstacle to its unity or a hindrance to national settlement. With all this emphasis on the Army's "engagements" some of those present began to wonder somewhat anxiously the extent to which they had been committed by their officers, and at least one of the Levellers present seemed willing for Cromwell to resign.[64]

One of the most remarkable speeches, however, came from

---

60. Woodhouse, *op. cit.*. Introduction, 57–60.
61. Cf. Professor R.H. Tawney, *Religion and the Rise of Capitalism* (1926), especially chapter IV.
62. *Supra*, p. 54 f., 60–2.
63. Woodhouse, 12; *C.P.*, I, 243.
64. The "Bedfordshire Man". Woodhouse, 18; *C.P.*, I, 251 f.

Lieutenant-Colonel Goffe.[65] He regretted that God seemed to have withdrawn Himself from their counsels, but he pointed out that in the events of their time "God does seem evidently to be throwing down the glory of all flesh", and there was the clear warning that if they were not prepared to humble themselves before Him they would come under His judgment. With Cromwell's proffered resignation in mind, he went on:

> It is not enough for us to say, "If we have offended we will leave the world, we will go and confess to the Lord what we have done amiss, but we will do no more so." Aaron went up to Hor and died; and Moses was favoured to see the land of Canaan – he did not voluntarily lay himself aside. I hope our strayings from God are not so great but that a conversion and true humiliation may recover us again; and I desire that we may be serious in this, and not despise any other instruments that God will use.

Within its context Goffe's speech was of some importance, for he was here "prophesying" to Cromwell just as Lilburne had done. As one of the Lieutenant-General's old officers he knew the sense of vocation with which those troops had been first imbued, and he was clearly unwilling lightly to dispense with Oliver's leadership. But he was speaking in terms not of persuasion but of conversion, his censures were not military or political but ecclesiastical, and he used the same theology and sense of vocation that was central in Cromwell's thought to press home his arguments. Cromwell made no comment, except to agree to Goffe's suggestion that they should meet for prayer, and to suggest that they ought to do it as speedily as possible, but Ireton professed himself to have been profoundly moved and warmly welcomed the idea of a prayer meeting on the next day.[66]

On this conciliatory note the debate might have adjourned, but it did not, for, however much some might welcome the turn taken by the discussion, there were signs of impatience from the political wing, and this led Cromwell to assure the Levellers that although some might think that he and Ireton were "wedded and glued to forms of government", they were far from being

---

65. Woodhouse, 19–31; *C.P.*, I, 353–5.
66. The fact that these officers so readily accepted the suggestion is regarded by Woodhouse as evidence of their facility in "the lower tactics of debate"; but Cromwell's suggestion was to hold the prayer meeting on the following morning and the Council did not usually take place until the afternoon, so it can hardly be represented as an astute move to gain time.

committed to that extent. "I say no more but this," he said, "I pray God judge between you and us when we do meet, whether we come with engaged spirits to uphold our own resolutions and opinions, or whether we shall lay down ourselves to be ruled by that which he[67] shall communicate."[68] And for all practical purposes the debate on October 28, 1647, closed at that point.

V

The debate on the following day[69] opened with speeches of an exhortatory character and Goffe addressed the company at some length, describing how the previous night he had been kept awake pondering "the conjunction that is between Antichrist, or that mystery of iniquity in the world carried on by men that call themselves the church … with kings and great men".[70] According to the Apocalypse, the work of Christ and His "saints" during the last days was to destroy this "mystery of iniquity", and although "it is a scruple among the Saints, how far they should use the sword; yet God hath made use of them in that work". He wanted them to enquire whether some of their recent actions – "I mean in our compliance with that party which God hath engaged us to destroy" – had not obstructed God's work. On the other hand, he addressed himself also to those who were too ready to throw over the work of Cromwell and Ireton, and warned them to "take heed of rejecting any of the Saints of God before God rejects them", especially "if God be pleased to show any of his servants that he hath made use of [them] as great instruments in his hand". He reminded them of the recent march on London, for God had provided them with a far better opportunity for effecting their desires than when the proposal had been first mooted. He concluded with the hope that they might discover unity in their counsels.

This speech was couched in the extravagant phraseology of the fervent Fifth Monarchist, but it should not be dismissed too lightly as a religious harangue, for the speaker was not so much debating in an Army Council as exercising his gift of prophecy

---

67. i.e. God.
68. *W.S.*, I, 528; *L-C*, III, 363; Woodhouse, 37; *C.P.*, I, 279.
69. October 29, 1647, Woodhouse, 38–95; *C.P.*, I, 280–363; *W.S.*, I, 529–36 *L-C*, III, 363–72 (Supp. 25).
70. i.e. the relationship between popery and monarchism.

to the "church".[71] He felt that he had a special commission to communicate to the Council a message which would heal their divisions, and he addressed that message authoritatively to both groups. But his speech, however well intentioned, does not seem to have evoked much enthusiasm. The next speaker did not refer to it,[72] and Cromwell suggested that there should be an adjournment, so that they might pursue private discussions – to which Colonel Rainsborough said bluntly that in his view the more public the discussions were the better.

The debate became rather confused and some heat was generated. Ireton denied that he was committed in any way to a personal engagement with the King,[73] and vowed that even if God saw fit to destroy the whole social and civil constitution of the Country he hoped he would be ready to accept it, but he added, "I hope too he will so lead this Army, that they may not incur sin, or bring scandal upon the name of God, and the name of the people of God, that are both so nearly concerned in what this Army does." For this reason he wanted them first of all to examine how far the Army itself was already committed by its public pronouncements, and furthermore "I would have us consider of this", he declared, "that our ways and workings and actings, and the actings of the Army, so far as the counsels of those prevail in it who have anything of the spirit of Jesus Christ, may appear suitable to that spirit."

In this we approach again the problem of moral theology with which these men were wrestling:[74] it was not sufficient that the Army should regard itself as the instrument of God's purpose, or that events should seem to confirm this sense of vocation, for another factor entered into its public actions, namely, whether or not those actions were intrinsically moral. The subjective sense of vocation and the equally subjective interpretation of Providence must be judged by the Spirit of Jesus Christ. This does not mean that Ireton thought that the whole New Testament ethic was applicable in secular affairs – in dealing with enemies he would not have gone beyond the equity of the Mosaic Law – but it does mean that he conceived this standard to be established within the Christian Gospel and interpreted by the Christian conscience.

---

71. See the account of the Rev. John Saltmarsh's "prophetic" mission to Fairfax's headquarters in 1647. Whitelocke, 285.
72. Robert Everard, Woodhouse, 42; C.P, I, 285 f.
73. Woodhouse, 48–52; C.P., I, 294–8.
74. *Supra* p. 138–9.

On the question of practical procedure, Ireton agreed that the *Agreement* should be read first, and the various engagements of the Army discussed in so far as they were affected by its provisions.[75] A heated argument developed upon the first article, manhood suffrage, with Ireton trying to retain the old basis of a property qualification, and Rainsborough just as stubbornly opposing him,[76] until Edward Sexby entered the debate and gave vent to all the pent-up bitterness which he and his fellow-Levellers felt:[77]

> We have engaged in this kingdom and ventured our lives, and it was all for this: to recover our birthrights and privileges as Englishmen; and by the arguments urged there is none. There are many thousands of us soldiers that have ventured our lives; we have had little propriety in the kingdom as to our estates, yet we have had a birthright. But it seems now, except a man hath a fixed estate in this kingdom, he hath no right in this kingdom. I wonder we were so much deceived. If we had not a right to the kingdom, we were mercenary soldiers. ... I shall tell you in a word my resolution. I am resolved to give my birthright to none. Whatsoever may come in the way, and [whatsoever may] be thought, I will give it to none.

He bluntly accused those who were opposing the *Agreement* of "a distrust of Providence". This could be expected to draw forth the strongest reaction from Cromwell, who said that he was more dissatisfied with what Sexby had said than with anything he had heard hitherto, "because it did savour so much of will", and he went on to propose that they wasted no more time but decided on what they were agreed. They were agreed that the existing form of representation ought to be revised, and to this end he proposed the appointment of a committee to discuss how it best could be accomplished.

This was by no means the end of the debate, but Cromwell's

---

75. Suggested by Rainsborough and supported by Maximilian Petty. Wood-house, 48.
76. Colonel Rainsborough protested, "I am a poor man, therefore I must be [op] pressed: if I have no interest in the kingdom, I must suffer by all their laws be they right or wrong. Nay thus: a gentleman lives in a country and hath three or four lordships, as some men have (God knows how they got them); and when a Parliament is called he must be a Parliament-man; and it may be he sees some poor men, they live near this man, he can crush them – I have known an invasion to make sure he hath turned the poor men out of doors." *Ibid.*, 59.
77. *Ibid.*, 69 f.; *C.P.*, I, 322 f. The radical party advanced the view, widely believed in Stuart times, that manhood suffrage had been every Englishman's right before the Norman Conquest.

show of spirit was not without its effect, and the rest of the speeches were in a more subdued tone.[78] However, although the impression left at the end of this debate is that of complete disunity, there is also the feeling that the last word had yet to be spoken. Cromwell himself, although he utterly disagreed with the propositions advanced by the Levellers, seems to have left the direction of his case to his son-in-law. Yet Ireton's lengthy speeches seem to have been made primarily to prevent a premature decision rather than to present anything constructive. One can discern a subtle lull underlying the situation, as if Cromwell and Ireton were waiting for something to happen. On the practical side it was agreed that the committee should meet on the following day, October 30, at the Quartermaster-General's quarters.[79]

Meanwhile, Charles was pursuing his own policy of intrigue with the Scottish Commissioners; there was a good deal to give Cromwell reason to hesitate.

VI

The debate on October 29 had opened on a high religious level, but had degenerated as tempers became more frayed. On Monday, November 1, Cromwell asked them to present their experiences of God's answer to their prayer for guidance.[80] Captain Allen said that his experience, and that of other godly people, was that the negative voice of the King and the House of Lords should be abolished;[81] Captain John Carter remarked that he no longer found the inclination in his heart to pray for the King that he had had formerly,[82] and Commissary-General Cowling observed that the sword was the only thing that had recovered their rights, and was the only thing "which he ever read in the word of God had recovered the rights of the people".[83] So far it would seem that religion provided but a very thin covering for ideas which had a strong anti-monarchical bias.

---

78. Even Rainsborough apologized "for some passion and some reflections".
79. The main provisions agreed were the dissolution of Parliament by September 1, 1648, biennial Parliaments, the election of a Council of State by Parliament, equal electoral districts, and the suffrage to include all free-born Englishmen who had helped in the war. Cf. *C.P.*, I, 363–7.
80. Woodhouse, 95–124; *C.P.*, I, 367–406; summaries in *W.S.*, I, 539–46; *L-C*, III, 372–82.
81. Woodhouse, 95 f.; *C.P.*, I, 367 f.
82. Woodhouse, 96; *C.P.*, I, 368.
83. *Ibid.*

When eventually Oliver gave his own views he commended some of the things that had been said about the abolition of the royal veto, but he reminded them that the King was king by contract,[84] and that their own position was bound up with that of Parliament: they could not deny the validity of the existing Parliament without at the same time destroying their own justification for existence. In his view, however, forms of government were not of supreme importance, and he instanced the Jews who had been governed successively by Patriarchs, Judges, and both elective and hereditary Kings: "If you should change the government to the best of it," he said, "it is but a moral thing. It is but, as Paul says, 'dross and dung in comparison of Christ.'"[85] As an expression of Cromwell's political convictions that explains a good deal of his later experiments in constitutional matters.

Several of those present expressed their views, but it was quite evident that within the Army Council there was an increasingly clear division of thought, not only in constitutional matters between Cromwell and Ireton on the one hand and the Levellers on the other, but also regarding the very purpose of the debate between what we might call the political and ecclesiastical wings of the Council. Lieutenant-Colonel John Jubbes might rehearse the fruits of the Holy Spirit in the soul with considerable eloquence and unction and Goffe might call upon them to "wait upon God", but Colonel Rainsborough refused to be impressed and the Agitator, William Allen, wanted things brought to an issue.

Edward Sexby again brought an edge into the debate which it had not had hitherto. In a hint which was none too well covered he said that all the Army's difficulties were due to the fact that some of their number had acted on their own. "I think", he commented, "that we have gone about to heal Babylon when she would not. We have gone about to wash a blackamoor, to wash him white which he will not. We are going about to set up that power which God will destroy."

In reply Oliver made what was perhaps his most important speech of the debates. He thought there was need for caution in what some speakers forecast so readily in God's name, and he pointed out that Sexby's exegesis was dubious: the point was only valid if indeed one could be sure that it was "Babylon" which they had set out to heal. He went on to review their situation:

---

84. *W.S.*, I, 539; Woodhouse, 96, In this passage Abbott's text is to be preferred.
85. Philippians 3:8.

Truly we have heard many speaking to us; and I cannot but think that in many of those things, God hath spoke to us. I cannot but think that in most that have spoke there have been some things of God made forth to us; and yet there hath been several contradictions in what hath been spoken. But certainly God is not the author of contradictions. The contradictions are not so much in the end as in the way. I cannot see but that we all speak to the same end, and the mistakes are only in the way. The end is to deliver this nation from oppression and slavery, to accomplish that work that God hath carried us on in, to establish our hopes of an end of justice and righteousness in it. We agree thus far. I think we may go thus far further, that we all apprehend danger from the power of the King and from the Lords. ... I do to my best observation find an unanimity amongst us all that we would set up neither. Thus far I find us to be agreed, and thus far as we are agreed, I think it is of God. But there are circumstances in which we differ as in relation to this.[86]

As in a Quaker meeting, or in the Church Meeting of a gathered Church, Oliver was trying to state "the sense of the meeting",[87] and having outlined the ground of their unity, he proceeded to state the cause of their differences. He divined, probably correctly, that these differences were due fundamentally to fear – fear primarily for their own safety,[88] but fear also, on the part of Ireton, of the anarchy which might result from a complete breakdown of the traditional constitution, and he commented, "Truly I think it hath pleased God to lead me to a true and clear stating our agreement and our difference; and if this be so we are the better prepared to go [on]."

In his closing paragraphs he warned those present not to be carried away with "apprehensions that God will destroy these persons or that power", for it was always possible to be mistaken, and even if God had the intention to destroy particular people or forms of authority He could do so without necessitating them "to do a thing which is scandalous, or sin, or which would bring dishonour to His name". Oliver was referring to the immediate debating-point of the Army's commitments through its published statements, but we cannot help looking past this issue to the figure of Charles himself. Did Oliver, even at this stage, consider the King's fall to be inevitable? There is a grim detachment about these words: it was God's business, not his,

---

86. *W.S.*, I, 543 f.; *L-C*, III, 377 f.
87. As he had at the end of the debate on October 29.
88. Cf. Abbott, *W.S.*, I, 526 f.

for "what God would have us do, He does not desire we should step out of the way for it".[89] He was stating not what he meant to effect, but what he believed had already been decreed by Providence, and therefore quite out of his power either to promote or retard except as led by God.

This was by no means the end of the debate,[90] but there was no speech more sombrely prophetic of the future than this. Despite Oliver's attempt to state the sense of the meeting the occasion ended on the note of complete disagreement between the higher officers and the Agitators. The discussion ended with the protest of the Leveller Major John Wildman to the former, "If God will open your hearts to provide so that the king will not do me injury, I shall be glad of it. If not, I am but a single man, I shall venture myself and share in the common bottom."

The rest of the debates at Putney in November 1647 are not reported as fully as we could wish,[91] but the pattern had been laid down. The Agitators' increasing hostility to Charles was demonstrated in the face of the General officers' suspected sympathy with the royal cause, and even the growth of some sympathy with Charles in the ranks.[92] On November 5 Fairfax resumed his chairmanship of the Council, and with Cromwell probably at Westminster, Ireton was left to carry the burden of debate. Rainsborough succeeded in getting the Council to pass a vote of "No addresses", and Ireton left as a sign of his dissent.[93] Matters had reached a deadlock, and on November 8, after a very critical speech from a certain Captain Bray, Cromwell succeeded in getting the officers and Agitators returned to their regiments. He and Ireton had negotiated with all in their efforts to reach a

---

89. Cf. Ireton's speech, *supra*, p. 142. The theory that Cromwell engineered Charles's escape from Hampton Court so that he might more easily accuse him, revived in recent years by the late Hilaire Belloc, has been answered by Isaac Foot in the *Contemporary Review* (Vol. CXLVI, July–December, 1934), 556–63. Cf. Belloc, *Cromwell*, 243–5.
90. Cf. Woodhouse, 107–24; *C.P.*, 383–406.
91. *C.P.*, I, 407–18, 440–2 (App. E).
92. A meeting of the committee of officers opened on November 3 with a story of the General wearing the King's colours, and a report that the soldiers were saying, "Let my Colonel be for the Devil and he will, I will be for the King," *Ibid.*, 410.
93. Newsletter from Putney, November 8/18, *ibid.*, 441. On the following day (November 6) Parliament voted that Charles should henceforth assent to all Ordinances presented to him, which indicates that the members at Westminster were moving in the same direction.

settlement, and had found themselves, having achieved nothing, distrusted by all. He could do no more but wait upon Providence.

VII

It is possible at this point to trace out the development of ideas which were presented during the course of the debates of 1647, and to see how they affected Cromwell's sense of vocation. The first thing which appears remarkable to the modern reader is that constitutional issues, which have become political commonplaces, were all fought out on the theological level: "the Puritan turned to the theological aspects of a question as naturally as the modern man turns to the economic; and his first instinct was to seek guidance within the covers of his Bible."[94] A.S.P. Woodhouse argues that in this Puritanism was merely using the idiom of its day, and suggests that theology and Scripture were employed in these debates simply to justify a policy which had been predetermined on political grounds. Undoubtedly this was sometimes true, especially in the speeches of politically-minded and theologically-equipped Levellers like Edward Sexby. But if it were entirely true of the debates it would do scant justice to what Woodhouse himself has said about the Puritan conception of underlying unity between the twofold scheme of Nature and Grace:[95] God's will was supreme in Heaven and on Earth, within Church and State. An extensive knowledge of Scripture and a sound grasp of Christian doctrine were inevitably the weapons which the Puritan used in political debate, and they were necessary because his political ideas arose primarily from his understanding of Providence and the Christian doctrine of Man. Edward Sexby's most damaging criticisms of Cromwell and Ireton were made on the basis of their accepted theology,[96] but he could make them only because that theological basis mattered.

The debates underline Cromwell's uncertainty in trying to interpret God's Will for the nation, and in particular the difficulty of understanding the Army's immediate task. But although the next move was obscure, the general principle was clear, "the end is to deliver this nation from oppression and slavery, to accomplish that work which God hath carried us on in, to establish

---

94. Woodhouse, Introduction, 39.
95. *Ibid.*
96. *Supra*, p. 137 f.

our hopes of an end of justice and righteousness in it".[97] Meanwhile it was reasonable to wait. The prominence given by some of the speakers to the march on London in July[98] suggests that Cromwell's prestige among the rank and file of the Army probably stood higher than one might expect from the tone of some of the speeches for the stand he had taken then. The riots of July 21–30 and the flight of some of the members had provided a "providential" opportunity for the Army to march, and he had been more responsible than any other for preventing hasty action which would have blackened the Army's reputation in the eyes of the nation.

However, in our understanding of Cromwell perhaps the great significance of the Army Councils was less in what they said or did, than in what they were. What are we to say of constitutional debates that begin with a prayer and testimony meeting, and throughout which the argument is conducted by means of Biblical exposition, where exegesis is more important than political definitions and theology than the theory of government? How are we to interpret the discussions of a military council where the General will listen patiently to the advice and open criticism of representatives from the ranks, and in which it is regarded as reasonable that he should offer to resign rather than break the unity of the meeting? If it is regarded simply as a military council it is, of course, fantastic; but it is not fantastic if it is regarded as the "Church Meeting" of a congregation in arms. Because of this, and because they were possessed of "the Spirit", the utterances of men like Goffe and Jubbes were received by Cromwell and Ireton with respect, and this may in large measure explain their noticeable movement away from the King. But we must not forget that more practical reasons were leading them in the same direction: there was the paramount necessity of maintaining armed unity, there was their own experience of the King's intractability, and there was his complicity in the Scots' designs for his escape.[99] The "prophesyings" must be seen within the context of these practical factors.

Cromwell's character is too complex to be explained by a simple motive: despite high resolve, motives of expediency and

---

97. *Supra*, p. 146.
98. Cf. Woodhouse, 41, 98; *C.P.*, I, 285, 371.
99. Cf. Clarendon, *History*, X, 125.

self-preservation must also have been operative. His sensitiveness to the charge of having a personal agreement with Charles does not prove that such an agreement existed, but it may have been mooted by the royalists, and even discussed with him, and the offer to relinquish his command may have been made with the idea of gaining a free hand.[100] But when this is said, the principle that had governed his actions hitherto had been to wait for a clear "providence" that he could accept as God's leading, for it was in historical events that Cromwell saw the hand of God, and it was in historical situations that he sought His answer. Such a period of waiting may be seen through the course of these debates, and we should interpret the protracted discussions in this light: Cromwell and Ireton were waiting for a further "extraordinary dispensation" of God's Will.

---

100. It was reported that members of his family had been received at Charles's court. *Clarendon S.P.*, II, Appendix xl (November 1, 1647).

Chapter Eight

Carisbrooke to the Outbreak of the Second Civil War

I

On October 22, 1647, the Scottish Commissioners, Loudoun, Lauderdale and Lanark had delivered a written covenant to Charles that if he escaped the Scots would give him every aid in the recovery of his throne.¹ Charles, however, had given his word not to attempt to escape, and until he had freed himself from that obligation he would do nothing. He evaded the difficulty by a characteristic manœuvre, which left his enemies, if anything, more convinced of his faithlessness than if he had simply broken parole.² It is a curious commentary on Charles that had he been either more honest or less honest he would have probably escaped with both his life and his throne. On October 31 Whalley increased the guard over the King and on November 1 Berkeley, Ashburnham and most of the royalist courtiers were ordered away from Hampton Court.

The King can hardly be blamed for wishing to escape, and plans were hurriedly pushed forward during the first few days of November. Ashburnham counselled Charles to throw himself boldly on the goodwill of the Presbyterians within the city, for in the event of a popular royalist rising there, the Scottish army would march south in its support. The King, however, refused either to go to London or to escape to France and it was finally decided that the probable destination should be the Isle of Wight, where Colonel Robert Hammond – who was known to have royalist sympathies – was the newly appointed Parliamentary

---

1. *G.C.W.*, IV, 1.
2. Ashburnham had given his parole that the King would not attempt to escape, and had indicated to Whalley that Charles's word was pledged with his. On the King's orders Ashburnham now withdrew his parole on the grounds that the increasing Scottish influence at Court made him unable to guarantee the King's actions. Charles interpreted this as freeing himself from all obligations, and when asked to renew parole refused to do so.

governor.³ Preparations for the escape were complete by November 10.

On the following day Colonel Harrison, the fifth monarchy visionary, denounced Charles in the Council of Officers at Putney as "a man of Bloud" who ought to be set on trial,⁴ and although Oliver urged prudence the arguments he presented were a virtual acceptance of the King's guilt.⁵ He realized, however, that if the extremists had their way they would unite against the Army every other force, military and civil, in England and Scotland, and he was determined at all costs to prevent any attempt at summary justice. He immediately warned Colonel Whalley,⁶ and Whalley showed this letter to Charles to convince him of the officers' concern for his safety. On the other hand, nothing could have suited the King's plan better,⁷ since he was able to represent the letter as an attempt to make him "a close prisoner" under the pretence of saving his life.⁸ He escaped from Hampton Court at 9 p.m. on November 11, escorted by Sir John Berkeley and John Ashburnham, but the royal party had no clear-cut plan,⁹ and they eventually arrived at Carisbrooke.¹⁰

The view that Cromwell inveigled Charles to Carisbrooke, in order to further his own schemes, seems to be based on the following lines of Andrew Marvell:

"Twining subtle fears with hope
He wove a net of such a scope
That Charles himself might chase

---

3. Robert Hammond was a kinsman of Cromwell by his marriage with Hampden's daughter, but he was also nephew to Dr. Henry Hammond, chaplain to the King. The Isle of Wight was within reach of France, and Robert Hammond was known to be somewhat sympathetic with the royal cause. At the same time his connections with Cromwell would enable Charles to keep in touch with the Army leaders.
4. *C.P.,* IV, 417–18; abbreviated account, *W.S.,* I, 551; *L-C,* III, 382 (Supp. 25 (4)).
5. He cited the arguments put forward for sparing the life of Joab – Abner's assassin. 2 Samuel, 3:27–39.
6. Letter to Whalley, *W.S.,* I, 551 f.; *L-C,* I, 285 (Letter L).
7. This point is made by Abbott *(op. cit.,* I, 552). Cf. Berkeley, *Memoirs,* 54.
8. King to Whalley, *L.J.,* IX, 520; quoted *W.S.* I, 552.
9. Berkeley, *Memoirs,* 54–7. Cf. Clarendon, *History,* X, 136.
10. The King was very angry when Ashburnham and Berkeley foolishly disclosed his whereabouts to Hammond, since he was probably hoping to use the safety of his person as a means of bargaining with Hammond for his freedom of action. Cf. Berkeley, *Memoirs,* 57–66.

To Carisbrooke's narrow case,
And thence the royal actor borne
The tragic scaffold might adorn."[11]

However, Marvell was not the only one of Cromwell's later admirers who praised him for what they assumed to be examples of his consummate skill in statecraft,[12] and the theory of the "Carisbrooke trap", which was promulgated by Dr. Bates,[13] and which has been revived by Hilaire Belloc, is not tenable, since it is clear that the plan originated in the counsels of Ashburnham and Berkeley.[14]

Charles had escaped from the power of the extremists and was now in the custody of one of Cromwell's relatives. This roused the Leveller party to a new pitch of abuse against Cromwell:[15] Colonel Rainsborough and Henry Marten talked of impeaching him, and others apparently contemplated a less formal kind of assassination.[16] A rendezvous of the Army had been called for November 15 at Corkbush Field near Ware, and anticipating trouble the officers drew up the *Remonstrance from his Excellency Sir Thomas Fairfax and his Council of War* which although published in Fairfax's name showed clear signs of Cromwell's inspiration. It accepted some of the Agitators' proposals, but condemned them for obstruction and sedition. Fairfax threatened to lay down his commission if military discipline was not immediately restored, and a declaration of approval was appended for the signatures of officers and men.[17]

On arrival at the rendezvous the officers found not only the regiments which had been ordered to meet the General, but also

---

11. Quoted *W.S.*, I, 554.
12. Cf. *The Perfect Politician*, the title-page of which bore the motto "Qui nescit Dissimulare, nescit Regnare"; also Flecknoe's *The Idea of His Highness Oliver* (1659) and Carrington's *The History of the Life and Death of ... Oliver* (1659).
13. *Elenchus*, Pt. I, 88–90.
14. Cf. *supra*, p. 151–2. The theory of the "Carisbrooke trap" is rejected by most scholars. Cf. Abbott, *W.S.*, I, 553–5; Gardiner, *G.C.W.*, IV, 16 n.; Buchan, *Oliver Cromwell*, 259. Clarendon did not blame Cromwell for Charles's flight to Carisbrooke, although he did draw attention to Cromwell's pleasure at learning of Charles's safe arrival there. *History*, X, 138. There were good reasons for Cromwell to be satisfied, for the King had not gone directly either to London or to the Scots. Furthermore, the King's flight made the Parliament realize how dependent it was upon the Army against a new rising. *Ibid.*, X, 139. Cf. *supra*, p. 147 n. 1.
15. Clarendon, *History*, X, 140.
16. Cf. William Kiffin, *Walwyn's Wiles* (1649), 18 f.
17. *W.S.*, I, 560.

those of Robert Lilburne and Fleetwood, which had been ordered elsewhere.[18] This was a flagrant act of mutiny. The men appeared with copies of the *Agreement* in their hats inscribed "England's freedom! Soldiers' rights!" It was a critical situation which would have had incalculable results if it had not been tackled promptly. Waving aside some officers who approached him with copies of the *Agreement*, Cromwell went to the mutinous troops with drawn sword, and upon their refusal to take down the papers, he commenced to do so himself, arresting three of the ringleaders. This unnerved the troopers and they tore the papers from their hats. The three men arrested were condemned to death by summary court-martial, and army discipline was completely restored.[19]

Cromwell's action at Corkbush Field should not be underestimated, for practically single-handed he had defied the mutineers. If he had ever intended to break with Charles simply for the sake of his own security or ambition, that moment on November 15 would have been the time to have done so. The significance of his action against the Levellers for the peace of the kingdom at large is reflected in the grudging admiration of Clarendon, who said that if the Levellers' meeting "had not been encountered at that time with that rough and brisk temper of Cromwell, it would presently have produced all imaginable confusion in the parliament, army, and kingdom".[20]

II

Although the headquarters of the Army was moved from Putney to Windsor, the Army showed that it could still maintain its influence over the city, by inducing the latter to make good its arrears of pay;[21] but again the Army leaders found themselves forced to change their political position. On November 16 Charles forwarded proposals to Westminster which went a long

---

18. Four horse and three foot regiments had been ordered to the rendezvous. Lilburne's regiment had been ordered north to watch the possible approach of the Scots' army, but it had driven off most of its officers and marched to the rendezvous. *G.C.W.*, IV, 23.
19. They threw dice for their lives and only one, a trooper named Arnold, was shot. At other rendezvous there was apparently no unrest.
20. *History*, X, 140. Cromwell was thanked by the House for his action, November 19. Whitelocke, 279.
21. Colonel Hewson was ordered to march to London to collect the money, and the Commons, alarmed at the prospect of another military occupation, prevailed upon the authorities in the city to provide the necessary means. Cromwell was asked to write to secure Hewson's withdrawal. Whitelocke, 280.

way to meet the differences between him and Parliament – the best opportunity of settlement[22] that had occurred since the failure of the Army *Proposals*. By this time, however, the Army officers could not look upon the prospect of agreement between King and Parliament with anything other than concern, for no group could allow success to its rival without fearing for its own safety. It would be unreasonable to place too much emphasis on the motive of personal security with men who, over a period of years, had constantly risked their lives in war, but R.H. Abbott is right to show that at this stage of the struggle it must have had its place.[23] On the evening of November 18 or 19[24] Ireton remarked "with a discontented countenance" at the Kingston headquarters that he hoped the proposed settlement between the King and Parliament "would be such a peace as we might with a safe conscience fight against them both".[25] He perhaps had more reason than any to know that despite the King's very specious proposal of liberty for those who could not "in conscience submit" to the established Church, if they relinquished power such a settlement would not prevent the suppression of Independency and their own deaths or exile. He was suspicious that the King and the Presbyterians were intriguing to out-manœuvre the Army politically, and an indication that this suspicion was not without foundation came in the Scottish Commissioners' protest to Parliament against the treatment given to the King since his removal to Holmby House:[26] a planned diplomatic offensive was being launched, which aimed at leaving the Independents without allies and, as the only obstacles to settlement, detested by the public. They had therefore either to lead or perish.

---

22. Charles still upheld episcopacy but he conceded the establishment of Presbyterianism for three years, and that presbyters might help bishops in ordination. He proposed freedom of conscience for all except atheists and Roman Catholics. He agreed to relinquish control of the militia for his own lifetime, if it might revert to his heirs, and he recommended that Parliament should consider the Army proposals concerning parliamentary elections. He again requested that the settlement should be by means of a "personal treaty" in London. Cf. Charles's letter to the House of Lords; Gardiner, *Const. Docs.,* 328–32; Whitelocke, 279 f.
23. *W.S.*, I, 562 f.
24. Probably the 19th, since the King's letter appears under that date in Whitelocke, 279 f.
25. Major Huntington, *Sundry Reasons*. Ireton's curious phrase "with a safe conscience" indicates his search for moral grounds on which he might base his position.
26. February 16, 1647.

Independent influence in the Houses of Parliament was, however, able to delay an immediate reply to the King, and when the answer was formulated it was drafted on a rather different basis,[27] but from the point of view of national settlement the Independents were on unstable ground: they were a small minority, and the Army, which presented them with what power they had, had no constitutional authority. Their plea for toleration may justify them in the eyes of modern historians, but the majority of their countrymen regarded it as an unnecessary and dangerous innovation, and if in order to achieve settlement they became the scapegoats, their contemporaries would have delivered them to their fate without a qualm.

Yet in their determination to gain liberty of conscience, the Independents were defending a principle of far more value than their individual safety. If they could have trusted Charles to honour his word in granting this liberty as a permanent right, his terms might well have been accepted, but it is clear that by the time the Four Bills had passed the House of Lords on December 14, 1647, something had happened which had confirmed the officers' distrust, and which radically altered their attitude to the King. Gardiner believed that the most likely explanation for this was in the "Saddle Letter" story, which appears in Thomas Morrice's *Life of the Earl of Orrery*. On being asked by Lord Broghill why the Army did not come to terms with Charles in 1647, Cromwell is reported to have told the story of the intercepted "saddle letter", which revealed to him and Ireton the King's intention to unite with the Scots against them.[28]

Some such incident must have taken place. Dugdale said that

---

27. After receiving the letter from the King, the House of Lords shelved it for nine days, and then on November 25 they appointed a committee to select from the Newcastle and Hampton Court propositions certain articles as a basis for counter-proposals. They proposed to keep the militia directly under the control of Parliament for twenty years, and thereafter indirectly, by requiring the sanction of Parliament for its use. They also demanded that the King's declarations against the Houses should be revoked, that royal honours granted since the flight of Secretary Windebank should be annulled, and that Parliament should have the right of adjourning to any place it thought fit. On November 24 these recommendations were sent to the Commons to be drafted into Bills, and they passed the Lords as Bills on December 14. Gardiner, *Const. Docs.*, 335–47.
28. The "Saddle Letter" account is given in Appendix VI. Cf. *A Collection of State Letters of ... Roger Boyle ... first Earl of Orrery*, by Rev. Thomas Morrice (1743), I, 15. Cf. *G.C.W.*, IV, 27–31; *W.S.*, I, 564. The story is accepted as substantially authentic by Gardiner (see above), Firth (cited by Gardiner, *G.C W.*, IV, 27 n.), Buchan, *Oliver Cromwell*, 261; and to some extent by Abbott, *W.S.*, I, 563–7.

Carisbrooke to the Outbreak of the Second Civil War

Cromwell was reputed to favour the King's restoration, but that some time after Charles had been brought to Hampton Court[29] a letter was intercepted from the Queen which revealed that the Scots were raising a new army to put the King back on the throne. When he was interrogated about this Charles denied any knowledge of it, and his reaction convinced Cromwell and Ireton that "his Majesty was not to be further trusted".[30] Another account connects this letter from the Queen with the "saddle letter", and suggests that in reply to the Queen's plea that he should not "yield too much to the traitors", Charles had assured her that he would not regard any promises as binding as soon as he had the power to break them.[31]

R.H. Abbott has suggested that while there is truth in these accounts, the change of attitude towards the King was sufficiently accounted for by the situation itself, for Cromwell and Ireton "were confronted by a world of enemies, which, save for the Levellers, centered in the King",[32] but whatever may be said of Ireton, Cromwell's complete *volte-face* needs more explanation than is provided by the general situation, and it seems evident that this is to be found in revelations of the King's postbag.[33]

III

The new proposals[34] submitted to Charles included an ecclesiastical settlement based upon a modified form of Presbyterianism, with toleration for all except Roman Catholics and those who worshipped by the Book of Common Prayer.[35] The provision of toleration was included for the Independents, but they were well aware that it was a precarious concession.

On November 25 there was a meeting of the General Council

---

29. Charles was held at Hampton Court from August 24, 1647, until he went to Carisbrooke, November 11, 1647.
30. Dugdale, *Short View*, 378.
31. Joseph Spence, *Anecdotes* (ed. 1820), 271 f. The evidence regarding this is discussed fully in *G.C.W.*, IV, 27-32, and *W.S.*, I, 563-7.
32. *W.S.*, I, 567.
33. If a letter from the Queen arrived while Charles was at Hampton Court, Cromwell would be expecting him to attempt an immediate escape to the Scots. This may explain the tension in the Army Debate of November 1, and Cromwell's relief on reading Hammond's letter. The discovery of the "Saddle Letter", or some similar correspondence, would confirm the previous fears.
34. Four Bills, to which were added 23 qualifications and 12 propositions.
35. Gardiner, *Const. Docs.*, 345 f.

of the Army, and on the following day Sir John Berkeley arrived with letters from the King and from Robert Hammond asking for the officers' support in re-establishing Charles on the throne.[36] Berkeley described how he was overtaken near Windsor by Cornet Joyce, who informed him that the Agitators had been discussing whether or not the King ought to be brought to a trial, and that it was his, Joyce's, opinion that he should. Berkeley did not receive a very warm welcome when he reached Fairfax's headquarters.[37] He managed to get into contact with one of the General Officers with whom he had had dealings previously,[38] who informed him that Cromwell and Ireton had spoken against the King in the Army Council, and that Cromwell had observed (with regard to the Levellers) that "if we cannot bring the Army to our sense, we must go to theirs, a Schism being evidently destructive".[39] The following day, Berkeley, having sent Captain Cook to Cromwell, received the reply "that he durst not see me, it being dangerous to us both, and bid me be assured, that he would serve his Majesty as long as he could without his own ruin; but desired that I should not expect he should perish for his sake".[40]

It cannot be wondered that Berkeley's informant, and a good many more, had come to regard Cromwell and Ireton's changes of front as examples of extreme perfidy. Throughout the period that followed the fall of Oxford these officers had seemed to veer as their interest dictated, sometimes appearing to support the King, sometimes acting against him; and yet the reasons for their changes in policy were to be found less in any caprice or ambition than in the actions of their enemies. Just as England during the eighteenth century altered her alliances to conform to a policy based on the Balance of Power, and gained an unenviable reputation in the process, so Cromwell and Ireton can be shown to have followed certain fundamental principles – the well-being of the people – which they equated with the well-being of the "people of God" – and the maintenance of Army unity. Their changing attitude to the King must be seen in the light of these basic factors. They now incurred considerable risk in attempting a *rapprochement* with the Levellers, since they had no guarantee

---

36. *Memoirs*, 68–76.
37. *Ibid.*, 70.
38. Clarendon, *History*, X, 148. Cf. *ibid*., X, 135.
39. Berkeley, *Memoirs*, 74.
40. *Ibid.*, 76.

that their overtures would be accepted, and there can be no explanation for the move, unless they had become convinced that Charles was committed to their destruction, and that the Levellers had been right where they had been wrong: it is significant that the change of front was, to some extent, reflected by Fairfax himself.[41]

Cromwell made a public confession of his "conversion", for Berkeley's informant went on to say:

> Cromwel bent all his Thoughts to make his peace with the Party that was most opposite to the King, in which Peters was instrumental. He acknowledg'd (as he had formerly done upon the like occasion) that the Glories of the World had so dazzled his eyes, that he could not discern clearly the great Works the Lord was doing; that he was resolved to humble himself, and desire the Prayers of the Saints, that God would be pleased to forgive him his Self-seeking. These Arts ... perfected his Reconciliation, and he was reinstated in the Fellowship of the Faithful.[42]

It is all too easy to dismiss such an expression of penitence as pious humbug, but it was not necessarily insincere. If it can be accepted as approximating to what actually happened it is a remarkable illustration of ecclesiastical discipline in the seventeenth century, and further evidence of the "church" relationship between Cromwell and his troops.

IV

Whatever confirmation was needed of the King's intentions was provided when Charles's *Engagement*[43] with the Scots became known, for in the event of the English army's refusal to disband, it provided that to secure their common aims,[44] "an army should be sent from Scotland into England", while on the religious level it went on to say,

> that an effectual course shall be taken by Act of Parliament, and all other ways needful or expedient for suppressing the opinions and

---
41. Berkeley, *Memoirs*, 70.
42. *Ibid.*, 74 f.
43. First submitted to the Scots on December 15, 1647, and agreed to on the 26th. *Clarendon MSS.*, 2685, 2686; Gardiner, *Const. Docs.*, 347–52; *G.C.W.*, IV, 39–41.
44. *Const. Docs.*, 349–50.

practices of Anti-Trinitarians, Anabaptists, Anti-nomians, Arminians, Familists, Brownists, Separatists, Independents, Libertines, and Seekers, and generally for suppressing all blasphemy, heresy, schism.

Thus the Independent officers were forced more and more to come to terms with the Levellers. On Tuesday, December 21, at a Council held at Windsor the mutineers were forgiven, and on the following day a great prayer meeting was held in which the officers, including Ireton, made "such sweet musick as the heavens never before knew".[45] The meetings continued for some days, and Clarendon writes "at this conference, the preliminaries whereof were always fastings and prayers made at the very council by Cromwell or Ireton, or some other inspired person, as most of the officers were, it was resolved, that the king should be prosecuted for his life as a criminal person".[46] On December 26 the Scots secured additional articles from the King, and two days later the King replied to the Four Bills and propositions submitted by Parliament. On the same day Hammond dismissed Berkeley, Ashburnham and Legge, probably on receiving instructions from Cromwell.[47]

Having made up his mind, Cromwell did not take long to make his views known at Westminster, and in the debate on the King's reply to the Four Bills in the Commons he declared that the King was a man of great ability, "but that he was so great a dissembler, and so false a man, that he was not to be trusted". He instanced the King's simultaneous dealings with the Army and the Scots with the inevitable threat of further war, and he concluded "that they might no farther trouble themselves with sending messages to him".[48] When the House decided by 141 votes to 92 not to approach the King again, many of the Presbyterians remaining at Westminster left, and the Independents seized the initiative: the Committee of Safety was revived, for the security of the State, and to conduct diplomatic relations with other countries,[49] and this was probably the first step in the establishment of the Commonwealth. Cromwell sent a full report of

---

45. *Clarendon S.P.,* II, App. xlv; *Perfect Diurnall,* December 31 (p. 1864).
46. Clarendon, *History,* X, 147. Cf. Whitelocke, 284–5, who says that the meeting was devoted to expressions of penitence from officers who desired to be readmitted to the favour of the General.
47. ? December 1647, *W.S.,* I, 574 f.; *L-C,* III, 383 (Supp. 26).
48. January 3, 1647/8. Clarendon, *History,* X, 146.
49. *C.J.,* V, 416; Whitelocke, 286; Walker, *Hist. of Independency,* 71 f.

what had happened to Hammond, and his relief at the course of events is obvious. He added that, "this business hath been (I trust) a mighty providence to this poor Kingdom and to us all. The House of Commons is very sensible of the King's dealings, and of our brethren's, in this late transaction". He asked Hammond to inform him if he should discover "juggling", for it could be of "admirable use at this time".[50]

But the problem of national settlement was no nearer solution. Therefore Oliver seems to have branched out into a series of social activities, aimed at uniting the various parties,[51] and the period is important because it marks the point at which Cromwell began to exercise the strategy of a national statesman. He expressed himself persuaded of the desirability of a Common-wealth, "but not of the feasibleness of it",[52] and he made unsuccessful attempts to bring together Presbyterians and Independents in a common ecclesiastical policy.[53] It could not be expected, however, that these activities would pass without comment: the scurrilous ballad *O Brave Oliver,* which became popular, is an expression of the suppressed hatred, and perhaps even more of the suppressed fear, with which Cromwell's career was being watched.[54]

A personal attack on Charles's character was developed by the revival of the old charge that he, together with the Duke of Buckingham, had been responsible for James I's death. There was no truth in this rumour, but a resolution supporting the charge passed the Commons,[55] Cromwell going so far as to move the expulsion of Selden, who had dared question the motion.[56] It

---

50. January 3, 1647/8, *W.S.,* I, 577–8; *L-C,* I, 289–91.
51. An example of this activity is seen in the party given at his house in King Street, attended by the Independent officers and Republicans to seek a solution of their differences. Ludlow, *Memoirs,* I, 184–6.
52. *Ibid.*
53. Ludlow made the acute observation that the inability of these two groups to agree was the fact that "one ... would endure no superior, the other no equal". *Memoirs,* I, 184. For Cromwell's attempts to win over Henry Marten and Sir Henry Vane, see *ibid.,* 186 f.; *W.S.,* I, 580.
54. Perhaps reference should be made to the possible influence of the Elizabethan tragedies on the public mind (e.g. Dr. Faustus, Tamberlaine, Macbeth). Pride and success led directly to the downfall of the "hero" through the agency of demonic powers, and current theology emphasized the same things – character must be either black or white, consigned irrevocably to hell or heaven. Cf. *W.S.,* I, 582–3.
55. Clarendon, *History,* X, 148–51.
56. Letter of Intelligence, February 17, *Clarendon MSS.* 2724, 2725; *Clarendon S.P.,* II, App. xlv.

is possible that Cromwell himself, now convinced to his own satisfaction of Charles's utter worthlessness, believed the libel, but it had an unfortunate effect on public opinion, for it tended to reduce the issues to a struggle between two opposed personalities, and it was bound to recoil on to the heads of its sponsors: if Cromwell was on his way to becoming the nation's ruler, it meant also that Charles was "about to become a martyr, then a saint".[57]

On the other hand, whatever the appearances to the contrary, Cromwell's personal ambitions were still very modest. One of the curious things which the study of his life brings to light is the way in which insignificant personal matters obtrude themselves into the main stream of national events, and take upon themselves an importance out of all proportion to their comparative irrelevance at the time. Cromwell's eldest son, Richard, was courting the daughter of Richard Mayor, an obscure country squire, and nothing is less like the action of an ambitious man than to give his blessing to such a match.[58]

But although these private affairs were due to have a happy issue, national matters did not proceed so smoothly: there was a strong royalist reaction throughout the country during the months of April and May in 1648, and on April 6 we find Cromwell informing the governor of Carisbrooke of a new attempt to rescue the King on March 20.[59] The state of affairs in Ireland gave grave cause for concern,[60] London was hostile,[61] the Scots were awaiting the opportunity to invade, and Wales was on the brink of open rebellion. The Army leaders were hated by everybody, and in their search for allies they seem, for a very short time, even to have approached the King again.[62] On April 28, as an attempt to pacify the city, Parliament voted not to alter "the fundamental government by King, Lords and Commons",[63] and

---

57. Abbott, W.S., I, 584.
58. The correspondence about this matter shows that the personal piety of the young lady's family weighed more heavily in Cromwell's estimation than the question of a suitable dowry. Cf. the letter to Colonel Richard Norton, February 25, 1647/8, W.S., I, 585; *L-C,* I, 292 f. (LIII). See also later letters to Norton, March 28, April 3, 1648; W.S., 1, 590 f.; *L-C,* I, 298, 300–2 (LV, LVI). See W.S., I, 587–9 for Cromwell's fortune in relation to other fortunes made in the war.
59. To Hammond, April 6, 1648. W.S., I, 594; *L-C,* I, 302 f. (LVII).
60. See letter to Sir Adam Loftus, April 3, 1648. W.S., I, 593.
61. Walker, *Hist. Independency,* Pt. I, 83; Whitelocke, 299.
62. Cf. *Tricks of the State,* quoted in *G.C.W.,* IV, 99 n.
63. Carried by 165 votes to 99, *C.J.,* V, 547.

hence, when the Council of War met on the following day at Windsor, Cromwell and his colleagues found themselves in an almost impossible position. Cromwell asked that they should examine what they had done hitherto, "as well as our ways particularly as private Christians, to see if any iniquity could be found in them, and what it was, that if possible we might find it out, and so remove the cause of such sad rebukes which were upon us by reason of our iniquities".[64] The piety is not accidental, but a note of desperation runs through it. They had tried everything to reach a settlement without success, and their best efforts had gained them only distrust and hatred. In view of their belief in Providence the failure could be explained only by their own personal sin. But in what had they been at fault? For two days they sought God's answer in prayer, and then on the third day came the news that Adjutant-General Fleming had been killed in a general royalist uprising in the south of Wales. This was the answer to their prayers: they had trusted one who had proved that he would always be the cause of bloodshed. They vowed grimly to reduce the nation again to obedience, but this time there was added the significant rider that Charles Stuart would be brought to justice for the blood which had been shed in his name.[65]

---

64. *W.S.*, I, 598 f. Abbott does not accept the royalist accounts of Cromwell's speeches at this conference.
65. Allen's *Narrative*, cited in *W.S.*, I, 599.

Chapter Nine

The Second Civil War
(May 1648–December 1648)

I

The royalists had timed the new war well. The Scots were ready to invade, and England itself was seething with resentment against the government and its army. The Army appeared to be divided: many of those who were about to be disbanded were royalist in sympathy, and the Leveller elements were undermining the authority of the higher officers. The rising was centred in three main areas. In the far north, Sir Marmaduke Langdale brought out troops to clear the way for a Scottish invasion. Secondly, there was a general uprising in Wales, led by two disaffected officers of the Parliamentary army, Colonel Poyer and Colonel Laugharne. Thirdly, a revolt broke out in the south-eastern counties – previously regarded as a Parliamentary stronghold. Fairfax decided to deal with this immediate threat to the capital himself, but Cromwell, with the main force, was detailed to tackle the danger in Wales.[1] He was preceded by Colonel Horton, who met the mutineers on May 8 at St. Fagan's and defeated them.

This was heartening to the government, but it by no means crushed the rebellion even in the Principality, and the seizure of Berwick and Carlisle by Langdale and Sir Philip Musgrave opened the way to the Scots. On May 3 a letter was delivered from the Scots to Parliament demanding the reimposition of the Covenant and the Presbyterian discipline, together with the disbandment of Fairfax's army and the readmittance of the excluded Presbyterian members. On May 4, two thousand petitioners from the county of Essex agitated that the King be restored and that the Army be disbanded,[2] and this was followed by a petition from "divers hundreds" from the county of Surrey, which developed

---

1. Lambert, himself a Yorkshireman, was sent to the north, and Sir Hardress Waller was sent to keep the south-western counties from rising.
2. Whitelocke, 304.

into a riot.³ In the face of this pressure Parliament passed a strict law against blasphemy,⁴ and allowed the city authorities to control the London Militia. The support of the Presbyterians showed that the royalist threat was formidable, and with rebellion continuing in Kent the possibility of an invasion from the Continent could not be overlooked.⁵

Meanwhile, in a speech to his troops at Gloucester on May 8, Cromwell called upon them "to arm themselves with the same resolution as formerly".⁶ The news of Colonel Horton's success at St. Fagan's was not without its effect in London.⁷ As the pattern of the insurrection became clearer Charles's Presbyterian sympathizers in the city and in Parliament became more and more uneasy: Poyer had declared for the King and Prayer Book, and none of the petitions from the counties mentioned anything about the Covenant.⁸ Horton's victory had prevented the immediate organization of a royalist field force in Wales, and although there was still plenty of hard fighting to be done there, it was limited to the reduction of those towns which had been captured during the period of initial surprise. The general situation was grave,⁹ and

---

3. *Ibid.*, 306.
4. i.e. against the sects. *Ibid.*, 303.
5. *Ibid.*, 304.
6. John Hancock to – ?, May 8, in *The Declaration of Lieutenant-Generall Cromwell concerning his present design and engagement against Col. PoyeR.W.S.*, I, 606. Two of Cromwell's letters belong to this period, both of them brief: to Fairfax, regarding the garrisoning of Bristol, May 9, and on the same date to Captain Roberts to put the Gloucester militia on their guard. *W.S.*, I, 606 f.; *L-C*, III, 384 f. (Supp. 27 and 28).
7. The news reached London on May 11. Whitelocke, 305.
8. *Ibid.*, 304. Cf. *G.C.W.*, IV, 126. See also a newsletter from London, May 12 (*C.P.*, II, 6 f.) – "To observe the strange alteration the defeating of the Welsh hath made in all sorts is admirable. The disaffected to the army of the religious Presbyterians now fawne upon them, partly for feare of you, and partly in that they thinke you will keepe downe the Royall partie, which threatened them att their doores in the streetes to their faces with destruction, and putt noe difference beetweene Presbyter and Independant. ... When letters were read in the House of the defeate, how many Royalists hunge downe their heads, and went out, nott staying the conclusion; from all which you may see clearly how necessary itt is to bee alway in action with your army, and iff nott heere, yett elsewhere ... the Citty talke as if they would alsoe joyne with you against the Royall partie, butt trust them nott; for all that are nott fooles, unlesse your frends, are for Kinge and Byshopps."
9. Fairfax and Ireton were engaged in reducing Kent, and London was directly threatened by the Earl of Norwich (George Goring) and later by Capel. Lambert was maintaining himself only with difficulty in the north owing to the betrayal of Pontefract and the loss of Scarborough. The south-west was fairly quiet, but North Wales was still in revolt. Cf. *G.C.W.*, IV, 127–62.

Cromwell pursued the total reduction of South Wales with vigour, for his immediate task was clear. He was out to destroy those who had not scrupled to renew the bloodshed in the face of God's Providence, and against such Oliver was implacable. In his report after the fall of Pembroke[10] he made special point of requesting that Colonel Poyer and those officers who had formerly served Parliament should be excepted from pardon, "because they have sinned against so much light, and against so many evidences of Divine Presence going along with and prospering a righteous cause, in the management of which they themselves had a share".[11]

II

Although the fall of Pembroke meant the virtual end of resistance in southern Wales, the position was still critical, with Lambert falling back in the path of Hamilton's invading Scots. The Parliamentary commander in the north could only limit his activities to harassing cavalry action until further support could be sent, and Cromwell lost no time in obeying the summons to join Lambert.[12] He proceeded to Leicester, where he picked up much needed supplies on August 18, and received letters appointing him Commander-in-Chief of the army in the north.[13] He then ordered Lambert to avoid any general action until the rest of the available forces were able to join him.

There was a considerable agitation against Cromwell in London at this time, but if the release of John Lilburne was calculated to embarrass the Lieutenant-General the manœuvre entirely misfired,[14] for his enemies ignored the fact that, despite real

---

10. Summons to Poyer, July 10, and terms. *W.S.*, I, 620 f., *L-C*, III, 386 (Supp. 30).
11. July 11, *W.S.*, I, 621; *L-C*, I, 324 (LXII). For the centrality of religious freedom within Cromwell's mind see his letter congratulating Fairfax on the success at Maidstone and in the south. June 28, *W.S.*, I, 618 f.; *L-C*, I, 319-22 (LXI).
12. For his precautions before leaving Wales see letters to the Mayor of Haverfordwest, July 12 and 14. *W.S.*, I, 622 f.; *L-C*, III, 254 f. (App. 11).
13. Cf. note from Derby House in *W.S.*, I, 626 from *Cal. S.P. Dom.* (1648-49), 227.
14. Abbott has pointed out that apart from the general sympathy for the King in the country, there was a noticeable movement towards the King at West-minster. The Lords (August 1) rejected a resolution declaring that "those who invited the Scots are traitors". *W.S.*, I, 626 f. Cromwell was being personally attacked in the narrative given by Major Robert Huntington which was inserted in the *Lords Journals.*

The Second Civil War 167

differences, the two main groups in the Army were entirely united in their opposition to the cavaliers and the Scots.[15] A similar united aim might have bound together the very diverse elements of the royalist insurrection in opposition to Independency, but their mutual distrust was stronger than their common purpose: the suspicions and hesitation of the Presbyterians in London probably decided the issue of the second civil war.

Cromwell pushed on to Pontefract and while he was here a *Declaration* was addressed to the City of Bristol in his name. Ostensibly it was a public declaration of thanks for the city's help during the siege of Pembroke, but it was in fact a personal apologia against the calumnies published in London,[16] and in it he declared that he and his troops were ready to resign their power as soon as they might live "free from tyranny and persecution". But from what party could they gain this assurance? Certainly not from the King, and equally certainly not from the Presbyterians, whether English or Scots; and unless they were prepared to consign the country to anarchy this left nothing but their own personal rule.

On learning that Hamilton had chosen the Lancashire route, Cromwell quickly crossed to the west by the valley of the river Ribble, and moved towards Preston with the intention of cutting the Scots' line of retreat. The royalist army was foolishly strung out in a long line with apparently very little liaison between the commanders. Monro's Anglo-Irish army was far to the north, Langdale's forces were just north of Preston, with Hamilton himself in the town, while Middleton and Callander with the cavalry were sixteen miles to the south on the road to Wigan. Cromwell

---

15. "... although Oliver had his hands full with Poyer, Goring, Holland, and Hamilton and Langdale the last year; but especially with the general odium that was then in both Houses against him, upon the notable Impeachment of his Major Huntingdon [August 2, 1648], and I then by my absolute freedom was a little up, and could have at my pleasure been revenged of him, if I had so pleased either by divisions in his Army, which was easily then in my power; or by joyning in impeaching him with Major Huntingdon; which I had matter enough to do, and was earnestly solicited to do it again and agaun, and might have had money enough to boot in my then low and exhausted condition to have done it, yet I scorned it, and rather applied my hand to help him up againe, as not loving a Scotch interest." *The legal Fundamental Liberties of the People of England* (1649), 28, by John Lilburne; reprinted in *C.P.*, II, 254. Cf. Ludlow, *Memoirs*, I, 200 f., note by C.H. Firth.
16. *The Declaration of Lieutenant-General Cromwell concerning the citizens of London*, August 14, 1648. *W.S.*, I, 629 f.

attacked in the centre on August 17, 1648, and drove Langdale's broken forces into Preston town,[17] thus splitting Hamilton's army and blocking the escape route of their main force. Hamilton made a stand on August 20 at Winwick, but the royalists were beaten back with the loss of about three thousand men, and when Cromwell reached them at Warrington, Lieutenant-General William Baillie surrendered with the remainder of the infantry. On the 25th the cavalry capitulated to Lambert at Uttoxeter, and since Fairfax had almost crushed opposition in the southern counties,[18] this meant that the second civil war was coming to an end,[19] although isolated garrisons like Pontefract had to be reduced with some difficulty.

Cromwell, of course, regarded this victory as an added vindication of the "godly", and declared it was "nothing but the hand of God".[20] He added:

> Wherever anything in this world is exalted, or exalts itself, God will put it down, for this is the day wherein He alone will be exalted. It is not fit for me to give advice, nor to say a word what use should be made of this, more than to pray you, and all that acknowledge God, that they would exalt Him, and not hate His people, who are as the apple of His eye,[21] and for whom even Kings shall be reproved;[22] and that you would take courage to do the work of the Lord, in fulfilling the end of your magistracy, in seeking the peace and welfare of the people of this Land, that all that will live quietly and peaceably may have countenance from you, and they that are implacable and will not leave troubling the Land may speedily be destroyed out of the land.

The issue of religious freedom was implicit, but so also were the future dealings with Charles, and the implications of the letter were certainly not lost on the King's supporters.[23]

Orders had to be sent to continue the pursuit of Hamilton's

---

17. Letter to Committee of Lancashire, August 17. *W.S.*, I, 632 f.; *L-C*, I, 329 f. (LXIII).
18. Fall of Maidstone, June 1, 1648; capitulation of Colchester, August 28, 1648.
19. Authorities for the battle of Preston are fully listed in *W.S.*, I, 633 n., to which might be added the account of Ludlow's *Memoirs,* I, 200–2.
20. To Lenthall, *W.S.*, I, 634–8; *L-C,* I, 336–44 (LXIV).
21. Deuteronomy 32:10, Psalm 17:8, Lamentations 2:18, Zechariah 2:8. In all these places it refers to Israel, the people of God.
22. 1 Chronicles 16:21.
23. Clement Walker, *History of Independency,* Pt. 1, 136.

army,[24] but from Oliver's private correspondence we see that he continued in a state of godly rapture for some time. Writing to the Independent peer, Lord Wharton, on September 2, on a private matter, he again opened his heart:[25]

> When we think of our God, what are we.[26] Oh, His mercy to the whole society of saints, despised, jeered saints! Let them mock on. Would we were all saints. The best of us are (God knows) poor weak saints, yet saints; if not sheep, yet lambs, and must be fed.[27] We have daily bread and shall have it, in despite of all enemies. There's enough in our Father's house.[28] ... I think, through these outward mercies (as we call them), faith, patience, love, hope, all are exercised and perfected, yea, Christ formed, and grows to a perfect man within us.[29]

Such private letters are important because they illustrate how "these outward mercies" produced an almost mystical state of religious fervour in Cromwell after his great victories; but some of his colleagues at Westminster – notably Sir Henry Vane – were rather less sure about the connection between divine providence and Oliver's "outward mercies".[30] The politicians had to some extent deliberately fostered the idea of a divinely inspired commander,[31] and the design had succeeded beyond all expectations.

---

24. See Cromwell's letters to Sir Henry Cholmley and Sir Ed. Rodes, August 20, 1648. *W.S.*, I, 639; *L-C*, I, 345 f. (LXV); Lord Grey of Groby, of the same date. *W.S.*, I, 640; to the Committee at York, August 23. *W.S.*, I, 640; *L-C*, I, 346 (LXVI); and to Derby House, same date. *W.S.*, I, 641 f.; *L-C*, III, 256 f. (App. 12).
25. *W.S.*, I, 646; *L-C*, I, 353 f. (LXVIII). Abbott's text is to be preferred.
26. Psalm 8:3–4.
27. John 21:15.
28. Cromwell seems to get rather involved between the "daily bread" petition of the Lord's Prayer (Matthew 6:11, Luke 11:3), the Bread of Life discourse in John 6:31–5, and our Lord's words in Matthew 7:9–11 (Luke 11:11–13).
29. A paraphrase of Ephesians 4:13, with a trace of Galatians 4:19.
30. "Remember my love to my dear brother H. V[ane]. I pray he may make not too little, nor I too much, of outward dispensations. God preserve us all, that we, in simplicity of our spirits, may patiently attend upon them. Let us all not be careful what use men will make of these actings. They shall, will they, nill they, fulfil the good pleasure of God, and so shall serve our generations." To Oliver St. John, *W.S.*, I, 644 f., *L-C*, I, 350 f. *LXVIII*. In this letter Cromwell goes on to quote Isaiah 8, which foretells the destruction of the alliance against Judah. It is however, important to notice that the notes of the Genevan Version margin – which still had to supply the lack of comment in the A.V. – applied the chapter from verse 9 onwards to the Church. Its comment on verse 12, for example, was, "Consent not ye that are godly, to the league and friendship that this people seeke with strangers and idolators", and its comments upon verses 13 and 14 were also to the point.
31. *Supra*, pp. 77–8, 80 f.

They might now begin to wonder at the effect the fiction was having upon Cromwell himself, for his letters indicate that in simple faith Oliver was really coming to believe the myth about himself. After the fighting was over this would lead to complications.

III

Cromwell was now free to settle outstanding issues with Scotland, and he accordingly moved towards the border. The Scots began to have some misgivings whether he would content himself simply with recapturing the English towns of Berwick and Carlisle,[32] and in view of the disunited state of that embarrassed country they were in no condition to meet an invasion. Political developments took place rapidly. It was clear that Scotland had connived at Hamilton's invasion, and had broken her treaty obligations, for none could pretend that the occupation of English towns was necessary at that time for her defence.[33] Therefore the Marquis of Argyle, and those ministers who had originally opposed the Hamilton project, left the Scottish estates with the intention of treating Cromwell's army as an ally. Argyle was soon joined by the Chancellor, Loudoun, and by the Earl of Leven.

Cromwell advanced to Berwick and demanded its surrender in terms which suggested a request in the name of the Almighty.[34] On September 16, 1648, having been enlightened by a letter from Loudoun as to the recent developments within Scottish affairs, Cromwell wrote a cordial letter of amity to Argyle and his

---

32. These towns by an agreement of 1646-47 were not to be garrisoned without the consent of both kingdoms (cf. *W.S.*, I, 653 n.).
33. Robert Baillie wrote to Spang on June 26, 1648: "The world knew there was no danger to us from them, [i.e. the Malignants who had taken Berwick and Carlisle,] for they had been with us in Edinburgh, and their enterprize upon Berwick and Carlisle was generally beleaved not to have been undertaken without some of our privities." *Letters and Journals*, III, 44.
34. From Alnwick, September 15, "I need not use any arguments to convince you of the justice hereof. The witness that God hath borne against your army in their invasion of this kingdom which desired to sit in peace by you, doth at once manifest His dislike of the injury done to a nation that meant you no harm, but hath been all along desirous to keep amity and brotherly affection and agreement with you.

"If you deny me in this, we must make a second appeal to God, putting ourselves upon Him, in endeavouring to obtain our rights, and let Him be judge between us." *W.S.*, I, 650 f.; *L-C*, I, 357 f. (LXX). Lodovic Lesley, the Governor, replied that he held the town in trust for the Committee of Estates and must await their orders.

friends,³⁵ but in a letter to Loudoun two days later he took good care to drive home the lesson of Preston, suggesting that God's reason for allowing the royalist rising was in order to make His people in both Scotland and England realize their need for unity.³⁶

Meanwhile the English Parliament was pursuing a policy which would hardly have met with his approval. On September 2, the Houses, reinforced by the excluded Presbyterians, repealed the Vote of No Addresses, and, despite the bitter opposition of the Republicans like Ludlow, reopened negotiations with Charles at Newport.³⁷ Cromwell's attitude was probably reflected in the protest of the regiments at Newcastle and Berwick against renewed negotiations with Charles and a strong protest was also voiced by Henry Ireton. When Ludlow went to Colchester to urge Fairfax to march on London, Ireton advised caution,³⁸ but the officers were not impressed by Charles's opinion that Hamilton's defeat was "the worst news that ever came to England".³⁹ Impatient of the King's attitude at Newport, Ireton then came out strongly on the side of the Republicans, and urged Fairfax to purge the House.

With the approval of Argyle and his supporters, Cromwell crossed the Tweed on September 19.⁴⁰ On the 22nd he met Argyle and other representative Scots, who agreed to the occupation of Berwick and Carlisle by the English,⁴¹ and on October 4 he accepted the invitation to enter Edinburgh, "where he was received with all solemnity, and the respect due to the deliverer of

---

35. *W.S.*, I, 652 f.; *L-C*, I, 358 f. (LXXI).
36. September 18. *W.S.*, I, 653 f.; *L-C*, I, 362–5 (LXXIII).
37. A time limit of forty days had been set for the discussions, starting on September 18. Charles eventually agreed to withdraw his declarations against Parliament, but nullified the concession by stipulating that nothing was to be valid unless agreement was reached on all points.
38. Ludlow, *Memoirs*, I, 204. Ludlow's journey was made about September 6. Cf. *G.C.W.*, IV, 212 f.
39. Ludlow, *Memoirs*, I, 203.
40. Letter to Derby House, September 20. *W.S.*, I, 656 f.; *L-C*, III, 258–60 (App. 13). He immediately took strict measures to ensure the good behaviour of his troops in Scotland. Proclamation, September 20, *W.S.*, I, 656; *L-C*, I, 366 f. Cf. Clarendon, *History*, XI, 99, also cf. September 21, *W.S.*, I, 659; *L-C*, I, 367 f. (LXXIV).
41. Lodovic Lesley, the Governor of Berwick, insisted on referring the question to his superior, the Earl of Lanark, who had joined Monro. Lanark, however, had no choice but to agree, and the necessary orders came through on September 29. Cromwell recommended to Fairfax that the care of Berwick be placed in the hands of Sir Arthur Hazelrigge, Governor of Newcastle.

their country".⁴² The following day he took the opportunity to address a vigorous appeal to the Scottish Committee of Estates, and in forthright terms blamed Scotland's failure to control her royalists for the suffering caused in England by Hamilton's Scottish army.⁴³

In the meetings that took place in Edinburgh an interesting point emerges regarding Cromwell's political principles. One of the Scottish ministers, the Reverend Robert Blair, asked the English General for his views on monarchy and religious toleration, to which Cromwell is reputed to have said that he favoured monarchical government, but that he did not favour toleration. But when Blair questioned him about his attitude to the Presbyterian church-government Cromwell refused to be drawn, protesting, "O now, Mr. Blair, you article me too severely, you must pardon me that I give you not a present answer to this; I must have some time to deliberate."⁴⁴ Before one is tempted to dismiss Cromwell in Robert Blair's terms as "an egregious dissembler and a great liar", it must be remembered that "toleration" had become a political term with unpleasant connections, and was generally represented to mean the free exercise of all heterodox sects without control, and this was far from the position of the group of Independents to which Cromwell belonged, as later history illustrates.⁴⁵ Similarly, while Cromwell shared the Army's disillusion about the King, there is evidence to show that he had not as yet any alternative to offer to the Stuart monarchy.⁴⁶ In point of fact, the agreement concluded

---

42. Clarendon, *History,* XI, 99. Cf. Ludlow, *Memoirs,* I, 203; Whitelocke, 343.
43. October s, *W.S.,* I, 663 f.; *L-C,* I, 375–7 (LXXVII).
44. William Row, *Life of Robert Blair* (edited by Thomas M'Crie, 1848), 210. Cf. *W.S.,* I, 666.
45. i.e. the ecclesiastical policy of the Protectorate. Jeremiah Burroughes, one of the dissenting Independents in the Westminster Assembly, had written, "They who are for a Congregationall way, doe not hold absolute liberty for all religions." *Irenicum: to the lovers of Truth and Peace* (1646), 41. He went on to point out, however, that persuasion and example were the only ways to combat error, and force was not to be used. Lilburne reported that in November 1658 he and his friends had a sharp discourse with Ireton, "our principall difference lying at his desire in the too strict restraining Liberty of Conscience and in keeping a power in the Parliament to punish where no visible Law is transgressed". Later on at the meetings in Windsor Lilburne reported, "a long and tedious tug we had with Commissary Generell Ireton only, yea sometimes whole nights together, Principally about Liberty of Conscience, and the Parliaments punishing where no Law provides, and very angry and Lordly in his debates many times he was". *Fundamental Liberties,* 31, 34 f. Cf. *C.P.,* II, 259, 264.
46. Cf. Ludlow's *Memoirs,* I, 184–6.

The Second Civil War   173

between Cromwell and the Scots suggests the expedient by which they sought to compromise between adherance to monarchy and distrust of the King.[47]

IV

Meanwhile Colonel Rainsborough, who had been sent by Fairfax to reduce the castle of Pontefract, was captured in a sally by the garrison, and killed while trying to escape.[48] His death was interpreted by the Army as the deliberate assassination of the one who had first proposed that the King should be brought to trial.[49] Cromwell came up to take charge of the siege, and to exact vengeance from those responsible for the "murder".

Charles, who in order to facilitate negotiations had been allowed to stay in Newport on parole, had again been planning to escape with the help of his host, William Hopkins.[50] The conclusion of the Thirty Years' War on the Continent opened the possibility of foreign intervention in English affairs, and the Queen had been very busy trying to build an alliance to come to her husband's aid.[51] On October 27 Charles had been asked to disavow the Duke of Ormonde who had landed the previous day in Ireland, but his evasive answer left no doubt that Ormonde's plan had his blessing. The idea of ending the farce by bringing the King to trial had definitely taken root in the Army, and was fostered by the Levellers throughout the country,[52] but it is difficult to say how far Cromwell and Ireton shared these sentiments completely, although it is probable that Ireton was more radical in this than his father-in-law. There is, however, one piece of

---

47. "Whoever considers the wariness in the wording and timing this protestation, the best end whereof could be no other than the keeping the king always in prison, and so governing without him in both kingdoms, (which was thought to have been the purpose and agreement of Cromwell and Argyle when they parted) must conclude, that both the commissioners, and they who sent them, laboured and considered more what they were to say in the future, than what they were to do to prevent the present mischief they seemed to apprehend." Clarendon, *History,* XII, 10.
48. Clarendon, *History,* XI, 123.
49. *W.S.,* I, 673.
50. Cf. *G.C.W.,* IV, 220 f., and also the King's letter to the Prince of Wales. Clarendon, *History,* XI, 191 (November 25, 1648).
51. Peace of Westphalia signed October 14 /24, 1648.
52. Petitions from Oxfordshire and Leicestershire brought to the House of Commons on September 30, and petitions from Sir W. Constable's regiment on October 10. Cf. *G.C.W.,* IV, 227.

important evidence which helps us to see the trend of Cromwell's thought, and this is the pseudonymous letter which he wrote to Robert Hammond on November 6, 1648.[53]

In this letter three things stand out clearly: first, Cromwell defends the radical movement within the Army by reminding Hammond, with his crypto-royalist sympathies, that it was easy "to take offence at things called Levellers, and run into an extremity on the other hand, meddling with an accursed thing". Secondly, in his view, the choice between Presbyterianism and moderate episcopacy was "a hard choice", and there was no necessity for either, although he felt that Charles would find it easier to tyrannize with the system "that he likes and serves his turn", than with the other which he heartily detested. Thirdly, he implied that in their readiness to establish moderate episcopacy, the Independent politicians had gone too far to meet the King, but he defended himself against those who thought he had gone too far in conciliating the Scots. It was fitting that they should discuss their differences with Scotland peaceably, and in answer to the opinion that he should have defeated the Scots rather than come to terms with them, he observed that it would not have been too difficult, "but I think not Christian". As for the suggestion that it would have been better to leave the Argyle and Hamilton parties in a state of balance Cromwell commented that "by the providence of God it is perfectly come to pass", although he added that it was "not by our wisdom".

From this letter we get an impression which is rather different from the "greeting devil" of Robert Blair's judgment. Which of the two is correct? Perhaps both are to some extent true. The fundamental principles of Cromwell's action are rather to be found in a letter to a personal friend than in the impressions of one who was admittedly hostile to him. On the other hand we cannot entirely discount Blair, however much he may have misinterpreted Cromwell's motives. Cromwell did dissemble, whether he was conscious of doing so or not, by making out the points of difference between himself and the Scots to be less important than in fact they were.

A further point arises of some importance to the future of the

---

53. Because of its importance we reproduce in full in Appendix IV. *W. S.,* I, 676-8; *L-C,* III, 389-92 (Supp. 35); *C.P.,* II, 49-53. C.H. Firth and S.R. Gardiner were the first to identify this letter as written by Cromwell. For their reasons and the identification of the pseudonymous names, see *C.P.,* II, *loc. cit.*; *G.C.W.,* IV, 248 and notes; *L-C,* III, 388 f.; *W.S.,* I, 676.

country, for if Cromwell regarded neither Presbyterianism nor Episcopacy as necessary for settlement, we can only assume that he desired the establishment of an ecclesiastical policy which would enable all "the godly people" to unite, and of all the systems of church government which had been advanced the Congregational theory[54] was the only one which made this possible; but this could only be achieved after the subjugation of the Presbyterians in the English Parliament, and the virtual elimination of Charles from English politics.

This does not mean that at this point Cromwell intended to effect a thoroughgoing purge of Parliament, or to enforce the King's death – Parliament might "purge" itself, and Charles might be either deprived of his regal power, or deposed in favour of one of his sons – but it does indicate how Cromwell's ecclesiastical views were likely to influence his political action. Furthermore, these tendencies should be seen in relationship to two significant facts which were noticed by John Lilburne, for after leaving prison Lilburne went north to make "diligent scrutinies" into rumours about Cromwell, which in his view "savoured more of intended self-exalting, than ... the through-advancement of ... the Liberties and Freedoms of the Nation".[55] At the same time, Lilburne affirms that it was generally agreed among the officers "first to cut off the King's Head", and then to "thoroughly purge, if not dissolve, the Parliament".[56]

On November 20 a Remonstrance was handed in to the House of Commons from certain officers in the Army, the first article of which was "That the King should be brought to Justice, as the Capital Cause of all".[57] Negotiations between the King and Parliament had broken down on November 24 with Charles's refusal

---

54. The word "Congregational" seems to have been sometimes used to distinguish those whose Independent polity was modified to "a middle way betwixt that which is falsely charged upon us, Brownism, and that which is the contention of these times, the authoritative Presbyteriall Government". *The Apologeticall Narration* (1646). Cf. the quotation from Burroughes, *supra*, p. 172, n. 4. These "Congregationalists" were to be Cromwell's chief advisers in ecclesiastical matters.
55. *Fundamental Liberties*, 29; C.P., II, 255.
56. Ibid., 256. Cf. 259.
57. Whitelocke, 355. The full title of the Remonstrance was, *A Remonstrance of his Excellency, Thomas Lord Fairfax, General of the Parliament's Forces, and of the General Council of Officers held at St. Albans, the 16th of November*. It was adopted on the 18th, and reached Westminster on the 20th. See C.P., II, 54 f.; G.C.W., IV, 233 n., and also the letter from Ireton to Hammond quoted in W.S. 685.

to give up episcopacy, and on the 29th a full Council of the Army expressed their apprehension of any treaty with the King, and of any Accommodation with him, or Restitution of him there-upon".[58] Lilburne noticed that Henry Ireton had become the moving spirit in the Army councils at this point.

On November 25 the General Council of Officers at Windsor resolved that an order be sent "requiringe that the person of the Kinge be secured as formerly in Carisbrooke Castle untill some resolution to our Remonstrance or otherwise further order shall be given from his Excellency".[59]

V

Meanwhile Cromwell was at Pontefract, and on November 20 he wrote a letter to Fairfax from his leaguer which was not without its ominous note. "I find", he said, "a very great sense in the officers of the regiments of the sufferings and the ruin of this poor kingdom, and in them all a very great zeal to have impartial justice done upon Offenders; and I must confess, I do in all, from my heart, concur with them; and I verily think and am persuaded they are the things which God puts into our hearts."[60]

Abbott has raised the question why Cromwell was content to remain at Pontefract when he might have been more profitably employed in the discussions at army headquarters and suggests that Oliver purposely avoided action because it was good policy not to be involved.[61] This does not really answer the question. Presumably, as an officer he was still under orders, but apart from that, one of the most striking things about his career as we

---

58. Whitelocke, 359.
59. *C.P.*, II, 55. A Prayer Meeting was held on November 26 in which those present sought God "to direct them in the great businesse now in hand, that they may bee instruments that justice may be done upon those who have caused so much bloud to be shed, and that righteousnesse and iudgment may flowe in the land". Newsletter from Windsor, *ibid.*, 58. News had been received on the evening of November 25 that Colonel Ewers had secured the person of the King, and on the 27th instructions were sent to Ewers that if necessary he was to convey Charles to Hurst Castle for safety, *ibid.*, 59. On the 26th (the same day as the Prayer Meeting) Fairfax received petitions from the forces in South Wales that "the Kinge might be speedily brought to justice". *Ibid.*
60. *W.S.*, I, 690 f.; *L-C*, I, 390 f. (LXXXIII). Cromwell was very bitter against all who had rebelled in the second civil war; this is reflected in a letter to Jenner and Ashe, November 20. *W.S.*, I, 691 f.; *L-C*, I, 386–8 (LXXXII). Abbott contrasts this with his courtesy to Sir John Digby who had held Newark during the first civil war for the King, November 22. *W.S.*, I, 693. Cf. *supra*, p. 166.
61. *W.S.*, I, 695 f.

have traced it, is that in times of tension and crisis there were curious periods of inactivity preceding every big decision he made. There is no apparent explanation for such lacunae in his affairs except the one which he gave himself, that he was waiting upon God, i.e. waiting for God's hand to show itself in events, to guide him into the next step. More often than not the occasion for his action superficially gives him the appearance of being an opportunist, but to Cromwell himself there was nothing fortuitous in such a sign.

The correspondence which passed between him and Ireton at this time might have been invaluable, but it has not survived,[62] probably because it was too dangerous to be kept – a negative indication both of the subject dealt with and perhaps of the way in which it was approached. On the other hand there is another invaluable letter to Colonel Robert Hammond, written at a time when the course of events made the latter contemplate resigning his post. It would be hard to overemphasize the importance of this letter[63] in any attempt to trace Cromwell's thought at this time. We can discern Cromwell's exalted faith in the lessons of "outward providences", which he proceeded to apply to Hammond's particular case. Hammond was reminded that God had searched him out and forced him to take responsibility when he had thought of escaping by retiring to the governorship of the Isle of Wight, and in a remarkable passage Cromwell has summed up his own interpretation of the doctrine of Providence as it affected individuals:

> Dear Robin, thou and I were never worthy to be door-keepers in this service. If thou wilt seek, seek to know the mind of God in all that chain of Providence, whereby God brought thee thither, and that person to thee; how, before and since, God has ordered him, and affairs concerning him: and then tell me, whether there be not some glorious and high meaning in all this, above what thou hast yet attained? And, laying aside thy fleshly reason, seek of the Lord to teach thee what that is; and He will do it.

On the question of Civil Authority, Cromwell reached the conclusion that where the security of the State was at issue, the Army was a lawful power ordained by God to "oppose one name of authority, for those ends, as well as another". However, these

---

62. *W.S.*, I, 695.
63. November 25, 1648. *W.S.*, I, 696–9; *L-C*, I, 393–400 (LXXXV); Appendix V.

were but "fleshly reasonings", and he reverted to his favourite argument: "My dear friend, let us look into providences; surely they mean somewhat. They hang so together; have been so constant, so clear and unclouded." In the face of his serious qualms, Hammond was reminded that it was this same Providence which now was moving the hearts of the great majority of the "Saints" towards unanimity within the Army. "And to conclude," the writer added, "we in this Northern Army were in a waiting posture, desiring to see what the Lord would lead us to."

Judge this letter simply on political grounds, and it may be interpreted as you will,[64] but that would be to risk misreading the main point about Cromwell's rise to power which the letter illustrates – namely, that the constant element in his career was not his politics but his theological approach to politics. Major Huntington had recognized that despite conservative preferences, Cromwell did not regard any particular form as sacrosanct,[65] and the passage on civil government emphasizes this. He was moving to new political grounds, but the theological principles underlying the change were those that we have met hitherto: the Army had been "called of God to fight against the King", and had a divine vocation to oppose any authority – King or Parliament – should the safety of the State be endangered.

R.H. Abbott has complained that the letter gives no clue either to the reason of Cromwell's continued stay at Knottingley,

---

64. Historians differ. Gardiner sees the letter as a change of front: "Cromwell strove to justify his change of ground in the spirit of one who argues because he has made up his mind, not in that of one who has resolved to follow the argument whithersoever it may lead him." *G.C.W.*, IV, 252. But compare Buchan, *Cromwell*, 292; Morley, *Cromwell*, 257 f.; Abbott, *W.S.*, I, 699–701; Firth, *Oliver Cromwell*, 212–14.

65. In presenting his charges against Cromwell before Parliament on August 1, 1648, Major Robert Huntington summarized what he believed to be Cromwell's canons of political conduct:

"1. That every single man is Judge of just and right, as to the good and ill of a Kingdome.

"2. That the interest of honest men is the interest of the Kingdome, and that onely those are deemed honest by him that are comfortable to his Judgement and practice, may appear in many particulars. ...

"3. That it is lawfull to passe through any formes of Government for the accomplishing his ends, and therefore either to purge the houses, and support the remaining Party by force everlastingly, or put a period to them by force, is lawfull and suitable to the interest of honest men.

"4. That it is lawfull to play the knave with a knave." *Sundry Reasons* (August 2, 1648), 13 f. The charge was inscribed also in the *Lords' Journals*; *L.J.*, X, 411.

or to his views about the future,⁶⁶ but the latter point is surely answered in what Oliver said about the Army's sense of unity, while as to the reason for his continuance at Knottingley, he states quite clearly that the northern army was in "a waiting posture ... desiring to see what the Lord would lead us to". It may be difficult for a modern to understand the attitude of a man of action who was quite prepared to wait for an apparently fortuitous event and call it "providence", yet it is the only way in which Cromwell's periods of silence can be understood, and to disregard this fact is to risk misunderstanding completely the importance and reality of Providence in his life and thought. It is clear that the publication of the Army *Declaration* had caused him and the northern army to throw in their lot with their colleagues, and to this extent he was committed to the policy which aimed at bringing Charles to trial, and the possible purging of the Houses of Parliament; but the signal for action – the providential moment – had not yet come, and until it did come, Cromwell would be prepared to wait.

Abbott has reminded us that although it is not necessary to assume with the royalists that Cromwell plotted the King's death and his own ascendancy from the beginning, "yet somewhere along the way the idea that he might be called to the highest post must have occurred to him".⁶⁷ The idea of him as the divinely inspired hero appears even as early as Marston Moor, and the opinion of other people must have had some effect on the formation of Cromwell's views of his own vocation, but by itself it would have had little effect; the basis of his sense of divine calling – when at last he could be certain of it – could only rest in the relationship between his providential success on the one hand, and on the other the need for one who was strong enough to settle the nation permanently.

Oliver and Charles stand in tragic contrast. Colonel Ewer had already replaced Hammond with orders to convey the King to Hurst Castle, and the significance of this was not lost upon the royal prisoner. In the letter written on November 25 to the Prince of Wales, Charles wrote:⁶⁸

> We know not but this may be the last time we may speak to you or the world publicly: we are sensible into what hands we are fallen;

---

66. *W.S.,* I, 701.
67. *W.S.,* I, 701 f.
68. From Clarendon, *History*, XI, 191.

and yet, we bless God, we have those inward refreshments the malice of our enemies cannot perturb. We have learned to busy ourself in retiring into ourself and therefore can the better digest what befalls us; not doubting but God's providence will restrain our enemies' power, and turn their fierceness to his praise.

There is not much of this passage with which Cromwell would not have grimly agreed: he, too, was resigned to the Divine Will, but it was with the consciousness that he had yet to accomplish even greater tasks than he had performed hitherto in the name of his God.

Chapter Ten

The Execution of the King (December 1648–January 1649)

I

We now enter upon a chapter of English history which has probably been covered more thoroughly than any other, and we shall deliberately direct our attention away from the tragic figure of the King in order that we may better be able to understand the part played by Cromwell.

Robert Hammond was suspect, and on November 28 he was arrested at Farnham. Ireton and the Levellers agreed at Windsor that a conference on future policy should be called between the chief parties within Parliament and the Army, and Cromwell was summoned from the north.[1] The Army entered London on December 1. Three days later the news arrived that the King had been transferred to Hurst Castle, and in the meantime a committee of Levellers and Independents drafted a revised *Agreement of the People*. Parliament was impotent but unco-operative, and accordingly the officers carried out the "purge" which had been threatened so often previously. Colonel Pride, with the help of Lord Grey of Groby, ejected about forty Presbyterian Members of Parliament, leaving the immediate political horizon clear for the Army's friends at Westminster.[2] Cromwell probably arrived in London on the evening of Pride's purge.[3]

The truncated Parliament promptly obeyed most of the Army's demands. It expelled the eleven members,[4] it cancelled

---

1. Fairfax to Cromwell, November 28. *C.P.*, II, 62 f.
2. Whitelocke, 359 f.
3. December 6, 1648. "Lieutenant-General Cromwell the night after the interruption of the House arrived from Scotland [*sic.*], and lay at Whitehall, where, and at other places, he declared that he had not been acquainted with this design; yet since it was done, he was glad of it, and would endeavour to maintain it." Ludlow, *Memoirs*, I, 211 f. For the Army's Declaration to the Commons, November 30, cf. Whitelocke, 358.
4. Sir John Clot[s]worthy, John Glyn, Col. Edward Harley, Denzil Holies, Sir William Lewis, Col. Walter Long, Major-General Edward Massey, Sir John Maynard, Major-General Poyntz, Sir Philip Stapleton, Sir William Waller.

the votes authorizing the treaty of Newport, it revoked the repeal of the Vote of No Addresses; but it wished to dismiss the military leaders of the Second Civil War with fines and banishment, and this lenient treatment met with Cromwell's strong disapproval.[5] On December 14 certain former Army officers of known Presbyterian leanings were arrested on the charge of calling in the Scots.[6] Cromwell visited the Duke of Hamilton several times in prison, possibly expecting to get evidence not only of the complicity of the Presbyterians but also of the King,[7] but despite rumours to the contrary,[8] Hamilton protested his sole responsibility for the invasion.[9] On one of the two occasions when Cromwell attended the Army debates on the new *Agreement of the People* it was resolved that the King should be transferred to Windsor Castle "in order to the bringing of him speedily to justice",[10] and a committee was appointed to put this into effect.[11] Charles arrived at Windsor on December 23.[12]

Cromwell's activities show that he was more and more involved in the direction of affairs.[13] On December 18 Cromwell, Whitelocke, Sir Thomas Widdrington, Colonel Dean and the Speaker, "had a long Discourse together about the present Affairs",[14] and there was a similar conference on December 21.[15] Although we have no information of what passed at these

---

5. Abbott has drawn attention to a brief Certificate signed by Cromwell on December 8, 1648, on behalf of a former royalist, John Kellond, and has made the important point that such favours were in sharp contrast to Cromwell's attitude to those who had taken part in Hamilton's invasion. *W.S.*, I, 709. Cf. *supra*, p. 176, n. 3.
6. Major-General Browne, Sir John Clotworthy, Sir William Waller and others. Whitelocke, 361. Cf. Pride's demands to the House of Commons, *ibid.*, 360.
7. *Mercurius Pragmaticus*, December 14 and 18.
8. *Mercurius Elenticus*, December 12–19; *Perfect Diurnall*, December 14. and *William, dukes of Hamilton* (1677), 379.
9. *Mercurius Pragmaticus*, December 18; Gilbert Burnet, *Memoires of*...
10. December 15, at Whitehall. His other appearance was December 29. *C.P.*, II, 272 f. (Table of Attendance).
11. It was further resolved that the Earl of Holland, Sir Lewis Dives, Sir John Owen and Sir Henry Lingen should be brought to trial, together with others accused of espionage. *C.P.*, II, 132.
12. Cf. letter from the Council of Officers to Lieutenant-Colonel Cobbett for the custody of Charles from Hurst Castle to Windsor. *C.P.*, II, 132.
13. Whitelocke seems to have observed the signs of Cromwell's new authority. Under December 19 he writes, "A Visit to Lieutenant-General Cromwell, who lay in one of the King's rich beds in Whitehall." This was written many years later, but the fact that it was noticed is significant. Whitelocke, 362.
14. *Ibid.*
15. *Ibid.*, 363.

conferences, Whitelocke and Widdrington met on the 22nd to draw up proposals for healing the breach between Army and Parliament and restoring the excluded Members, and it is possible that Cromwell was trying to obtain a compromise settlement which would stop short of bringing Charles to the block, for Whitelocke appears to have been genuinely shocked when the proposal to bring the King to trial was mooted in the Commons on the 23rd. On the other hand, Cromwell's recommendation of Dr. Dorislaus – soon to be the King's chief prosecutor – to Doctor's Commons in Trinity Hall, on December 18,[16] may be no less significant.

The other evidence points in this direction. On December 22 Cromwell and Ireton wrote to Harrison, and to Colonel Whitchcott the governor of Windsor Castle, and the letters emphasize the care with which the King's movements were being controlled.[17] On the following day the Council of Officers drew up a series of eight articles of instruction for Colonel Tomlinson, "for the immediate securing of the King's person from escape",[18] and the only article which failed to be passed unanimously was the fifth, forbidding Tomlinson to allow anyone to speak to Charles except in the presence of a guard, and this was opposed by Cromwell alone.[19] On the same day the remaining Members of the House of Commons established a committee to consider "how to proceed in a way of Justice against the King, and other capital Offenders".[20] The wording leaves no doubt that the verdict would be a foregone conclusion.

Cromwell was in a leading position, but by no means a dominating position. S.R. Gardiner has amassed considerable evidence which suggests that even at this point he was trying to save Charles's life.[21] There were rumours that Ireton wished to keep the King imprisoned until he had given up the right of veto, the claim on Church lands, and his support for the Scots, and that in Cromwell's view the King's trial ought to be deferred until those who had instigated the last war had been brought to trial. Clement Walker suggests that the Council of War intended to keep Charles a close prisoner, and so "to mortifie him by degrees,

---

16. *W.S.*, I, 712; *L-C*, I, 403 f. (LXXXVI).
17. *W.S.*, I, 713–15; *L-C*, III, 395–8 (Supp. 38 and 39).
18. *C.P.*, II, 144–6.
19. Sir Charles Firth's note. *Ibid.*, 146 n.
20. *C.J.*, VI, 102.
21. *G.C.W.*, IV, 281–7.

and worke him to their desires". He adds the important comment:

> When it was first moved in the House of Commons to proceed capitally against the King; Cromwell stood up and told them, That if any man moved this upon designe, he should thinke him the greatest Traytour in the World; but since providence and necessity had cast them upon it, he should pray God blesse their Councels, though he were not provided on the sodaine to give them counsel.[22]

Neither Ireton nor Cromwell would hesitate to push forward the trial because they had any doubts of the King's guilt, or because they regarded his person as sacrosanct; but there were grave reasons for hesitation, and certain facts stand out which enable us to get a general impression of Cromwell's position. First, the evidence listed by Gardiner indicates that Cromwell was trying up to this point to postpone or prevent the actual trial; secondly, in his willingness to assume more authority we see Cromwell trying to control the course of national events; thirdly, the scrupulous care with which the King was guarded suggests that the officers wanted to keep the disposal of his person in their own hands. In summary, we have the picture of Cromwell trying to rise to the top in order to ride the coming storm, anxious to prevent the execution of the King so far as he could without compromising his own position, but ready, if the situation could be resolved in no other way, to bring the King to trial and exact without further scruple the penalty which he believed Charles so justly deserved.

On Christmas Day a committee met to consider the method of proceeding against Charles.[23] Cromwell urged the Council of Officers to spare Charles's life upon the condition that he accepted provisions entrusted to the Earl of Denbigh to present to the King on that day. By the 28th it had become known that Charles had refused to give audience to Denbigh,[24] and the procedure for bringing the King to trial was hurried forward.[25] Now that the decision had been taken both the verdict and the penalty were

---

22. *History of Independency*, Pt. II (*Anarchia Angltcana*), 54. The order of the Council of War is clearly that of December 23, but Walker and Whitelocke, probably following the newspapers, both date it December 37 (Whitelocke, 365).
23. Whitelocke, 364.
24. *G.C.W.*, IV, 285 f.
25. Whitelocke, 365.

The Execution of the King

foregone conclusions. It is hardly necessary to point out that to attaint by means of Ordinance, and to charge the King with High Treason (or any other crime), was quite outside the bounds of the Law, since English law is founded upon the sovereignty of the King. But new forms of sovereignty were being advanced for which the Common Law made no provision, and until these new ideas had been defined there was no law but that of force, qualified to some extent by ill-defined beliefs in a Natural Law.[26] Charles had shown by his refusal to come to terms that it was to be war to the death, and we cannot altogether blame his opponents if they decided – the laws of England notwithstanding – that it would be no more than justice if the first to die should be Charles Stuart.

II

Having decided, whoever else drew back, it would not be Cromwell. On January 1, 1648/9 the House of Commons declared that it was High Treason for the King of England to levy war against the Parliament and Kingdom of England, and when the Lords refused to pass the Ordinance for the King's trial,[27] this gave the Commons the excuse to assume the dignity of "Supreme Authority" within the nation.[28] On January 2, 1649, an Ordinance to try Charles by court-martial was introduced, and although the approval of the Upper House and the Scots was still wanting,[29] the Commons proceeded to pass an "Act of the Commons in England assembled in Parliament for the erecting of a High Court of Justice, for trying Charles Stuart, King of England".[30] One hundred and thirty-five judges were nominated, and the second name to appear, after that of Fairfax, was that of Oliver Cromwell. The High Court met on the 8th to settle the preliminaries of the trial, and on the following day a public proclamation invited witnesses to appear against the King;[31] but no witnesses were invited to appear in the defence, nor was the

---

26. Some indication of this appeal to Natural Law is perhaps to be traced in the charge that the King had offended against the "Liberties of the Subject" and broken "the fundamental Laws and Liberties" of the kingdom.
27. Whitelocke, 366 f.; *L.J.*, X, 641. Cf. *W.S.*, I, 723.
28. Whitelocke, 366 f.
29. *Ibid.*, 367.
30. January 6, 1649. C.H. Firth and R.S. Rait (editors), *Acts and Ordinances of the Interregnum* (3 vols., 1911), I, 1, 253.
31. Walker, *History of Independency*, Pt. II, 68.

proclamation published much beyond the capital. The officers were perfectly well aware of the extreme unpopularity of the King's trial within the nation at large, and speed was essential.[32] Even so, there was dangerous opposition from some Presbyterian ministers in the City. Cromwell evidently wanted to put the whole procedure on a more popular basis: he disapproved of the attitude of the Commons to the Peers, on the grounds that the two Houses ought to stand together,[33] and he opposed the suggestion that the public should be excluded from the trial, but was overruled.[34] This suggests that in the events which followed he did not have complete control. At the same time no one man held more responsibility than he did – he was appointed to every important committee, and if his was not the sole deciding voice in the nation's affairs, it was certainly the single voice that carried most weight.[35]

The preliminaries having been settled, and the officers of the court selected with some difficulty, the order of the hearing was determined. On January 18 the High Court began to examine the evidence submitted by the prosecution.[36] The King was brought from Windsor to St. James's Palace, and in anticipation of the result asked that he might be attended by one of his own chaplains. With the appointment of Dr. Juxon, the Bishop of London, the stage was set for the climax of the tragedy.[37] It was reported at the trial of Henry Marten in 1660 that on January 19, 1649, when news came of the King's arrival –

> Cromwell run to the window, looking on the King as he came up the Garden, he turned white as the wall, returning to the board he speaks to Bradshaw and Sir Henry Mildmay, how they and Sir William Brereton had concluded on such a businesse, then turning to the board, said thus. My Masters, he is come, he is come, and now we are doing that great work that the whole nation will be full of: Therefore I desire you to let us resolve what answere we shall

---

32. Cf. the debate on the *Agreement of the People* in the Army Council on January 6, in which both Cromwell and Ireton show that they knew the general unpopularity of what was happening. *C.P.*, II, 170 f.
33. Cf. the letter January 12. *Clarendon S.P.*, II, 1–li.
34. Thomas Walkeley at the trial of Hugh Peters in 1660. *The Exact and Impartial Account of the Arraignment, Trial and Judgment of the nine and twenty regicides* (1660), 160 f.; *State Trials*, V, 1124.
35. This is perhaps corroborated by the rumour that his kinsman Colonel John Cromwell came as an envoy from the Prince of Wales with a blank paper signed by the Prince, and embossed with his signet, for Cromwell to fill in his own terms in return for the King's life. *Flagellum* (2nd edn.), 67–9.
36. Whitelocke, 369.
37. *Ibid.*, 370.

The Execution of the King

give the King when he comes before us, for the first Question that he will ask us will be: by what authority and Commission we do try him? to which none answered presently. Then after a little space Henry Marten ... said, In the name of the Commons and Parliament assembled, and all the good people of England.[38]

On the following day the High Court – with the significant absence of Fairfax – sat in Westminster Hall, and the trial had begun.[39]

The wording of the charge itself is of interest, since it developed at some length the accusation that Charles had been responsible not only for the first Civil War, but that he

> hath renewed, or caused to be renewed, the said Warre against the Parliament, and good people of this Nation, in this present yeare, one thousand six hundred forty and eight, in the Counties of Kent, Essex, Surrey, Sussex, Middlesex, and many other Counties and places in England and Wales, and also by Sea. ... By which cruell and unnaturall Warres by Him, the said Charles Stuart, levied, continued, and renewed, as aforesaid, much Innocent bloud of the Free-people of this Nation hath been spilt.[40]

Algernon Sydney came up to town about this time, and heard that he had been nominated as one of the King's judges. He arrived in the Painted Chamber during the preliminary discussions regarding the procedure of the trial, and he said that having listened to the debate for a time,

> I did positively oppose Cromwell, Bradshaw, and others, whoe would have the triall to goe on, and drewe my reasons from theis tow points: First, the King could be tried by noe court; secondly, that noe man could be tried by that court. This being alleged in vaine, and Cromwell using these formal words, (I tell you we will cut off his head, with the crowne upon it,) I ... went out of the roome and never returned.[41]

Cromwell's attitude was fixed, but so was that of Charles. All testimonies agree as to the dignity with which he carried himself throughout the proceedings of the next few days: the high doctrine of the Divine Right of Kings appears at its best in the way he refused to acknowledge the jurisdiction of the judges, and asserted

---

38. Sir Purbeck Temple in *The Exact and Impartial Account*, 248. Cf. *State Trials*, V, 1201.
39. Walker, *History of Independency*, Pt. II, 87 ff.; Whitelocke, 370.
40. *History of Independency*, Pt. II, 89 f.
41. *Sydney Papers*, edited by R.W. Blencowe (1825), 237.

"their duty was due to him, and his superiority over them".[42] Nor was the King's nobility of carriage without its effect upon those who witnessed the scene. On the very first day there had been a protest from the gallery by no less a person than Lady Fairfax,[43] and during the course of the proceedings later there were those among the judges who were made uneasy by the King's perfect self-possession and control. At his trial in 1660 Colonel John Downes said that he protested during the trial, and managed to get a temporary adjournment. He was soundly rated by Cromwell who declared that they were dealing with "the hardest-hearted man that lives upon the earth", and "desired the Court, without any more ado, would go and do their duty".[44] This incident apparently took place on Saturday, January 27, after Charles had asked to be heard by the Lords and Commons in the Painted Chamber, but the request was refused, largely upon the opposition offered by Cromwell. When the Court reassembled Bradshaw announced its decision, and after a lengthy speech "much aggravating the Kings offences, and mis-applying both Law and History to his present purpose",[45] the clerk read the sentence.

It was, however, one thing to condemn the King to death but quite another matter to provide authority enough to carry out the sentence, and the King's judges had to implement the verdict without delay.[46] There was considerable reluctance among some of those who had taken full part in events up to this point to set their signatures to the warrant of execution, and if the evidence of the regicides at the Restoration can be trusted, something more than persuasion was needed to keep these men to their previous decision.[47] The same difficulty was experienced in getting officers

---

42. Clarendon, *History,* XI, 233.
43. *Ibid.,* 235.
44. *State Trials,* V, 1212 f. The testimony was corroborated by another of the regicides, Thomas Waite. *Ibid.,* 1215 f.
45. Walker, *History of Independency,* Pt. II, 102.
46. There had been a good deal of diplomatic activity to get the sentence postponed or reversed. The States General of Holland sent ambassadors, Louis XIV of France approached both Fairfax and Cromwell, the Scots tried to intervene, and the Prince of Wales negotiated with Fairfax and Cromwell privately. Cf. Whitelocke, 369, 374, 376; MS. de Brienne in F. Guizot, *The History of Oliver Cromwell and the English Commonwealth* (translated by A. Scoble, 2nd edn., 2 vols., 1854), I, 327 f.; Clarendon, *History,* XI, 229. Cf. *supra,* p. 186, n. 4.
47. Cf. Thomas Waite's evidence at his own trial. *State Trials,* V, 1219. See also Richard Ingoldsby's story, Clarendon, *History,* XVI, 225.

The Execution of the King

to take part in the execution, and from the later testimony of Colonel Hunks who was first approached to draw up the warrant for the executioner, we learn that, "Cromwell would have no delay".

There is a rumour, recounted by James Heath, that on the day of the execution Cromwell called a meeting of some of the officers to discuss whether the death of Charles could be avoided, "for he was not ignorant, he said, what calumny that Action would draw upon the Army and themselves in particular"; but Heath says that it was suggested that they should "seek God to know his mind in it", and Cromwell delivered himself of such a lengry prayer that a messenger arrived in the middle of it to announce that the King was dead; whereupon Cromwell "declared unto them, that it was not the pleasure of God he should live, and therefore he feared they had done ill to tempt him against his will; or words to that effect".[48]

III

Charles I was beheaded on January 30, 1649. The dignity and heroism with which he had conducted himself throughout the trial did not desert him on that day, and it erased completely the memory of his previous arrogance and misgovernment. As Edward Hyde wrote later, Charles at the time of his death "had as great a share in the hearts and affections of his subjects in general, was as much beloved, esteemed, and longed for by the people in general of the three nations, as any of his predecessors had ever been".[49] The lines of the Puritan poet, Andrew Marvell, are the picture that the King impressed upon the nation at his execution:

---

48. *Flagellum,* 69 f. Although this story is obviously suspect, it may be supported by the account given by Sir Thomas Herbert, who with Juxon after the execution, happened to meet Fairfax. The General was apparently returning from a discourse or prayer meeting in Harrison's rooms, and he appeared not to know that the execution had taken place, but shortly after "they were met by another great commander, Cromwell, who knew what had so lately passed; for he told them, They should have Orders for the King's burial speedily". Thomas Herbert, *Threnodia Carolina* (included in *Memoirs of the two last years of the Reign of Charles I,* 1711).
49. Clarendon, *History,* XI, 243. For accounts of the execution cf. Whitelocke, 374 f.; Clarendon, *History,* XI, 244; Walker, *History of Independency,* Pt. II, 110–13.

> "He nothing common did or mean
> Upon that memorable Scene;
> But with his keener Eye
> The Axes edge did try:
> Nor call'd the Gods with vulgar spite
> To vindicate his helpless Right,
> But bow'd his comely Head,
> Down as upon a Bed."

But the poet added lines which were far more significant to the future of the country when he addressed the lines to Cromwell:

> "But thou the Wars and Fortunes Son
> March indefatigably on."[50]

Beneath all the events which led up to the King's death, and beneath the series of successes that was bringing Cromwell to the fore, there was the half-formed feeling that Fate was somehow taking a hand. Of Charles's downfall even Clarendon admitted that "there were so many miraculous circumstances contributed to his ruin, that men might well think that heaven and earth conspired it, and that the stars designed it".[51] Charles's words in Westminster Hall and from the scaffold left no doubt about the depth and sincerity of his personal piety, but there was considerable heart-searching as to how the King's personal religion was to be reconciled with his cruel fate. An example of this is to be seen in Sir Philip Warwick, who frankly confessed the uneasy questionings which the King's death brought to his mind:

> And now we are come unto the last stage of this good Prince's life; and this leads us, tho' not to fathom the depth, yet to discern the course of divine Providence, which hitherto had led him through such a labyrinth of various fortunes, that knowing his goodness and Christian patience, I ever expected (and there were often rational hopes to feed that desire) such a deliverance from God on his behalfe, as he had other times afforded unto David, by teaching his

---

50. *Horatian Ode on Cromwell's return from Ireland.* Cf. the lines of the poet Dryden about Cromwell:
    "His grandeur he derived from heaven alone;
    For he was great ere fortune made him so;
    And wars, like mists that rise against the sun,
    Made him the greater seem, not greater grow."
    Heroic stanzas on the late protector Oliver Cromwell, printed in Banks's *A Short Critical Review,* 322–6.
51. Clarendon, *History,* XI, 243.

hands to fight, and giving victory unto his Anointed. But his end (I speak it to my shame) as it flung me into great melancholy, so it did into some dissidence.[52]

The tension could be resolved in only one of two ways, for either – in spite of his piety – the King deserved his fate, or else he was a saint, a royal martyr, in whose sufferings royalists did not hesitate to find a parallel in the sufferings of Christ. "Thus he died greater than he had lived."[53]

What then of Cromwell, and those who were associated with him? Bishop Burnet, a shrewd judge of men and events, thought that "Ireton was the person that drove it on; for Cromwell was all the time in some suspense about it".[54] A good deal of the evidence we have is open to question, being the work either of avowed royalists, or of men who were fighting for their lives at the Restoration and who were ready to lay blame elsewhere as a means of saving themselves. The words of Mrs. Hutchinson about the attitude of her own husband show that not all the regicides were coerced by Cromwell:

> The gentlemen that were appointed his [the King's] judges, and divers others, saw in him a disposition so bent on the ruin of all that opposed him, and of all the righteous and just things they had contended for, that it was upon the consciences of many of them, that if they did not execute justice upon him, God would require at their hands all the blood and desolation which should ensue by their suffering him to escape, when God had brought him into their hands. Although the malice of the malignant party and their apostate brethren seemed to threaten them, yet they thought they ought to cast themselves upon God, while they acted with a good conscience for him and for their country. Some of them afterwards, for excuse, belied themselves, and said they were under the awe of the army, and overpersuaded by Cromwell, and the like; but it is certain that all men herein were left to their free liberty of acting, neither persuaded nor compelled.[55]

It is hardly reasonable to suppose that any great number of those taking part could have been coerced by any single person to propagate an act which they sincerely believed to be judicial

---

52. Warwick, *Memoires*, 206 f.
53. Burnet, *History of My Own Time*, I, 80.
54. *Ibid.*, I, 79.
55. Lucy Hutchinson, *Memoirs of Colonel Hutchinson* (Everyman edn.), 266 f. It should be remembered, however, that Colonel Hutchinson's republican views were well known; he was in any case a near relative of Ireton. Cf. *ibid.*, 285.

murder. Mrs. Hutchinson says that they tried to hold back, not out of respect for Charles or the monarchy, but because they feared the possible reprisals, and that strikes the truer note, for it helps to explain Cromwell's brusqueness with them: he would not have much patience with men who were afraid to stand by the logic of their own principles.

Yet when due allowance is made for the weakness of the testimonies, everything points to the fact that Cromwell dominated the scene of Charles's trial. At its blackest we have the picture of undue haste in the preparation of the case, of an illegal trial, of the suppression of all opposition and of pressure used to secure accomplices, and however the evidence is sifted the shadow of some or all of these charges remains. Yet the criticism of Cromwell in these proceedings is for the means adopted, and not for the end pursued, for on the wider question of how far the death of Charles was inevitable more needs to be said.

There is little one can say about the legality of the High Court of Justice. It had been set up by a narrow majority vote of a truncated House of Commons,[56] and without any recognition by the Upper House, but even if it had been set up by the unanimous votes of both Houses it would still have been outside the bounds of English law. Legally Cromwell and his associates had no grounds on which to instigate proceedings against the King, and Gardiner is undoubtedly right when he says that "those who promoted this charge threw their case away by forsaking the political ground on which they were strong for the legal ground on which they were weak".[57] They made the fundamental mistake of trying to judge the King as if he were a subject under the Common Law of the land, whereas the moral ground on which the struggle against Charles had been undertaken was at a level beyond that of the Common Law.

Charles may have realized this when he proceeded from his purely legal ground of questioning the Court's jurisdiction to point the consequences of this arbitrary procedure for the nation as a whole.[58] On the other hand, it is fatally easy to see the King's

---

56. Twenty-six to twenty votes.
57. *G.C.W.*, IV, 300.
58. "... truly, if it were onely my own particular case, I would have satisfied My Selfe with the Protestation I made here the last time, against the Legality of this Court, and that a King cannot be Tryed by any Superiour Jurisdiction upon Earth: but it is not My case alone, it is the Freedome, and the Liberties of the People of England, and (doe you pretend what you will) I stand more for their

championship of common rights on this occasion, and to forget the previous history of his reign, his own arbitrary demands, his duplicity, and his willingness to hold the country to ransom by refusing to negotiate honestly. Cromwell's curt dismissal of Downes' protest was uttered in the conviction that they were dealing with "the hardest-hearted man that lives upon the earth", and although it is to be regretted that in his trial Charles was not allowed rights granted to every free-born Englishman by the constitution, yet we can also see justice in the claim that there should be no sentimentality in dealing with a man simply because he was King. Cromwell held the view that there was nothing sacrosanct about monarchy, except in so far as it carried with it responsibilities which ought to be kept the more scrupulously in that they were divinely given. If Charles were guilty then he ought to be punished despite legal precedent and public sentiment: Colonel Hutchinson's opinion would be his – he saw in the King "a disposition so bent on the ruin of all that opposed him, and of all the righteous and just things they had contended for, that ... if they did not execute justice upon him, God would require at their hands all the blood which would ensue". This much is clear from Cromwell's arguments presented to the Scots' Commissioners during the trial:

> he thought a breach of trust in a king ought to be punished more than any crime whatsoever. He said, as to their covenant, they swore to the preservation of the king's person in defence of the true religion: if then it appeared that the settlement of the true religion was obstructed only by the king, so that they could not come at it but by putting him out of the way, then their oath could not bind them to the preserving him any longer. He said also, their covenant did bind them to bring all malignants, incendiaries, and enemies to the cause, to condign punishment: and was not this to be exercised impartially? What were all those on whom public justice had been done, especially those who suffered for joining with Montrose, but small offenders acting by commission from the king, who was therefore the principal, and so the most guilty.[59]

Compare this with the legal arguments put forward at the trial and we can see that here is the heart of the charge against the

---

Liberties; for if Power without Law may make Lawes, nay, alter Fundamentall Lawes of the Kingdome, I doe not know what Subject he is in England that can be sure of his Life, or any thing that he calls his owne." Walker, *H story of Independency*, Pt. II, 93 f.

59. Burnet, *History of My Owm Time*, I, Burnet heard the story from Lieutenant-General Drummond.

King. The indictment was unique and of a higher nature even than High Treason, and since there was no regular machinery by which such a case might be tried, Cromwell and his colleagues set up clumsy machinery of their own. It was illegal machinery because the charges were in fact higher than those of which the Law took cognizance, and it broke down because they tried to translate into terms of English Common Law crimes which called into question the very foundation of the Law itself. No serious historian could condone the methods used, but, granted their premises and their convictions, the justice of their claim must be admitted: arbitrary power was being used to destroy arbitrary power.

In the public's view, however, this struggle was being reduced more and more to the issue between two personalities; but there is no reason to suppose that Cromwell at this time had thought of it in this form. He saw the issue as between Charles's will on the one hand, and the principles of the Rebellion on the other. That was an over-simplification, but it was his position. The impasse had resulted because the King had been defeated by commoners and he was unwilling to resume his executive position on their terms. A recent biographer of Cromwell has suggested that an "experienced solicitor could have drawn up a reasonable settlement between Charles and his people – even although the King was so much of a fool and so great a deceiver";[60] but as long as the King remained "so much of a fool and so great a deceiver" that is to be doubted, and the plight of the country was too pitiful to warrant longer expenditure of time on solutions calling for mutual trust and co-operation where there was no possibility of anything but distrust and obstinacy. Charles's death threw open the possibility of stable government on a new foundation, in a way which was quite impossible while he was alive.

It must be clear that the religious issue, as it was the heart of the opposition to Charles during the war, had a good deal to do with his death. Bishop Burnet noted that at the time of the trial and execution there were not more than about 8,000 soldiers stationed around London, "but these were selected out of the whole army, as the most engaged in enthusiasm; and they were kept at prayer in their way almost day and night, except when they were upon duty".[61] Even among the most "enthusiastic" of

---

60. G. R. Stirling-Taylor, *Oliver Cromwell*, 240.
61. *History of My Own Time*, I, 79. On January 5 a certain Elizabeth Poole of Abingdon appeared before the Army Council at Whitehall – not to submit

the Army's supporters, however, there were some who looked upon the execution of the King with misgiving, but never once did Cromwell indicate by word or sign any remorse or penitence at the part he played in the King's death.

Whether or not the legend which gathered round the memories of Lord Southampton is fact or fiction, the solemn judgment of the nocturnal visitant in the story may well have been Cromwell's own judgment on the execution of Charles I:

> The night after King Charles was beheaded my Lord Southampton and a friend of his got leave to sit up by the body in the Banqueting House at Whitehall. As they were sitting very melancholy there, about two o'clock in the morning they heard the tread of somebody coming very slowly up stairs. By-and-by the door opened and a man entered very much muffled up in his cloak, and his face quite hid in it. He approached the body, considered it very attentively for some time, and then shook his head, sighed out the words, "Cruel necessity!" He then departed in the same slow and concealed manner as he had come. Lord Southampton used to say that he could not distinguish anything of his face; but that by his voice and gait he took him to be Oliver Cromwell.[62]

"Cruel necessity!" That carries the authentic note of Cromwell's verdict.

---

factual evidence, but to deliver a revelation she had had from God, to the effect that Charles should not be executed, but "that you may binde his hands and hold him fast under". The most remarkable thing about Mrs. Poole's vision was that it should have been so seriously considered by the Army Council. *C.P.*, II, 163–9.

62. Spence, *Anecdotes*, 273-5. Cf. *Flagellum*, 70.

Chapter Eleven

The Beginnings of the Commonwealth Military and Political Problems (February-August 1649)

I

General Considerations

In the execution of Charles, what Cromwell deemed to be morally right very conveniently coincided with what he regarded as politically expedient; but with the death of the King, the leaders of the rebellion knew that they had closed the door to compromise, and that they would be forced to provide alternative government: they dared not allow the new State to fail. This fact really dominates the rest of Cromwell's life.

There were three practical problems with which those who were now left at the head of affairs had to deal immediately: first they had to establish stable administration in the midst of the chaos left by the civil wars; secondly, they had to defend the new State against almost universal hatred at home and abroad, and thirdly, related to these previous factors, they must take steps to make their government more representative. In this situation the governing remnant in the House of Commons soon found itself in a dilemma, for the Levellers were blindly pressing for a new election when the country was decidedly royalist in sympathy.

However, an interim government could hardly be regarded as definitive. On January 29, 1649 an "act" was passed which exchanged the authority of "the King in Parliament" for that of "Custodes Libertatis Angliae, Auctoritate Parliamenti"[1] – a conveniently vague title to describe conveniently unspecified persons, Those who had voted on December 5 in favour of further negotiation on the basis of the King's reply to the Commons were excluded from their seats;[2] a committee was set up to

---
 1. Whitelocke, 374.
 2. Those who had been absent from the division were not allowed to resume their seats until they had expressed their disapproval of the previous resolution.

The Beginnings of the Commonwealth Military

exclude from office those who had in any way supported Charles in the wars, and on February 6, 1649, having refused to discuss the future constitution with the remaining peers, the House of Commons proceeded to abolish the House of Lords.[3] A thorough-going policy of repression against former royalists was fore-shadowed in the establishment of a new High Court of Justice, with Bradshaw as its President, and it is significant that while Bradshaw was preoccupied with these legal matters, Cromwell was chosen as first chairman of the new Council of State, in which had been vested the executive power of the Commonwealth.[4]

II

Suppression of the Leveller Mutinies

An Independent group firmly held the reins of government. England was governed by a closed oligarchy, and although the House of Commons had declared that the people of England were, under God, "the original of all just power",[5] it is clear there was to be no hasty appeal to this Authority: the political temper of the people was such that the leaders of the Commonwealth could not afford to take the risk.[6]

On the other hand this could not but raise the anger of the Levellers, who had presented their doctrinaire opinions to the Commons in the *Agreement of the People* on January 20, only to find them shelved. While John Milton was declaring on behalf of the government that "all men naturally were born free, being the image and resemblance of God himself",[7] the setting

---

3. *C.J.*, VI, 132. March 19, 1649. Monarchy abolished March 17.
4. Abbott notes that Cromwell was the only member of the government who was a General officer of the Army, a member of the Commons, an ex-member both of the Committee of Both Kingdoms and of the High Court of Justice, and a signer of the King's Death Warrant: "if he was not officially the head of the new government, the current opinion expressed in news and satires was correct – he was indisputably *primus inter pares,* the head and front of the revolutionary party and movement, its chief support as well as its directing force." *W.S.*, II, 15.
5. Whitelocke, 336, January 4, 1648/9. England was not formally a republic until May 19, 1649 when an "act" was passed making it a republic or Free state.
6. The extreme popularity of the *Eikon Basilike,* which appeared soon after the execution was an indication of the latent royalism within the nation. Milton was commissioned to reply and produced *The Tenure of Kings and Magistrates,* and *Eikonoklastes.*
7. *Tenure of Kings and Magistrates (Milton's Prose* (World Classics, 1925), edited by Malcolm W. Wallace, 331).

up of the Council of State and the refusal of the old House of Commons to give place to a more representative body, seemed to be but the forging of new bands for old. The Levellers felt they had been cheated. They had united with the Independents over the trial of the King, and now they wanted to see the beginnings of a true democracy – complete religious freedom, freedom for the press, universal manhood suffrage, annual parliaments. Theoretically their position was unanswerable, but they lacked the political realism to see that at that time their policy would have been the shortest method of bringing back the Stuarts.

Leveller pamphlets were now added to Presbyterian libels and royalist lampoons[8] in criticism of the government: Lilburne with *England's New Chaines Discovered*,[9] and a second pamphlet from his pen soon joined the first.[10] Cromwell and the Independents were accused of being ruled not by "principles of honesty or Conscience, but (as meer Politicians) are governed altogether by occasion as they see a possibility of making progress to their Designes; which course of theirs, they ever termed, a waiting upon Providence, that under the colour of Religion they might deceive the more securely".[11] This attack is perhaps of more than ordinary interest, because in the opposite attitudes of Cromwell and Lilburne we see the tension presented to the Puritan when he was forced to act politically. Cromwell was finding the need of a formulated moral theology and was trying to meet the need on the basis of his professed beliefs; Lilburne on the other hand held the Separatist position of an undivided Christian ethic, and refused to admit any such problem.

Cromwell was quick to appreciate the danger which threatened the new State from the Leveller agitation. On February 22 the Army Council recommended that legislation be passed to punish any civilians involved in disaffecting the troops,[12] and when Lilburne's petition was followed by a Remonstrance, presented on March 1 by eight troopers who brazenly admitted their complicity in the production of *England's New Chaines*, the

---

8. For royalist pamphlets, cf. *W.S.*, II, 1–3.
9. The pamphlet was appended to a petition which Lilburne presented to the Commons, a summary of which appears in Walker, *History of Independency*, Pt. II, 133–5.
10. *A second Part of England's New Chains*, with Overton, Prince, and Walwyn. Summary in Walker, *History*, Pt. II, 135 f.
11. *Ibid.*, 135.
12. *C.P.*, II, 190–2. Passed February 26.

petitioners were promptly court-martialled[13] and cashiered.[14] On March 27 Lilburne's book was pronounced seditious by the House, and on the following day he and the others implicated[15] were arraigned before the Council of State.[16] The security of the infant State was quite clearly the first consideration in the mind of Cromwell, and the vehement chaffings of Lilburne and his friends would hardly have called forth such violent reaction had they not occurred at a time when a host of dissident factions was appearing from turbulent Fifth Monarchists to the pacifist "True Levellers" or Diggers.[17] The Leveller agitation must be seen against this background, and until unity was re-established the position was extremely critical.

In Ireland Michael Jones, the governor of Dublin, was more or less enclosed in the city and his troops were disaffected. If the Marquis of Ormonde could resolve the suspicions existing between the Presbyterians, native Catholics, and English Cavaliers he would have at his disposal a formidable force with which to invade England, covered by Prince Rupert's naval squadron. Ireland was a dangerous thorn in England's side, but on April 17, 1649, when the troops to go to Ireland were chosen, some refused to go abroad until the Leveller demands had been met, and threw down their arms.[18] On April 24 a mutiny broke out in Whalley's regiment, and all attempts to calm the men by persuasion failed

---

13. March 3.
14. March 6. They subsequently published *The Hunting of the Foxes from Newmarket and Triploe Heath to Whitehall, by 5 small Beagles.*
15. Overton, Prince, Walwyn.
16. Lilburne heard Cromwell in the Council urging that the strictest measures should be employed in crushing the Levellers: "I tel you Sir, you have no other way to deale with these men, but to break them in pieces; and thumping upon the Councel Table againe, he said Sir, let me tel you that which is true, if you do not breake them, they will break you; yea, and bring all the guilt of the blood and treasure shed and spent in this Kingdom upon your heads and shoulders..." John Lilburne, *The Picture of the Council of State* (1649), 15.
17. The principles of equality which Lilburne would apply to political representation Winstanley and the Diggers applied also to the sphere of economics and they introduced the idea of common ownership. The appearance of this "left wing" was an embarrassment to the Levellers. The Diggers were harmless enough, but the government was startled into ordering Fairfax to suppress their communal experiment at St. George's Hill, Weybridge. For Digger writings see Woodhouse, *Puritanism and Liberty,* 379-86; and Gardiner, *Commonwealth and Protectorate,* I, 43 f. n.
18. Three hundred in Hewson's regiment alone. Gardiner, *Commonwealth and Protectorate,* I, 44-5. The soldiers had been told that if they did not wish to proceed to Ireland they could stay in England, but would have to retire from the army.

until Cromwell and Fairfax arrived. Fifteen of the recalcitrants were court-martialled, and six were condemned to death, but Cromwell interceded and only one, Robert Lockyer, was shot.[19] Colonel Scrope's regiment, supported by Ireton's, most of Reynolds', and both Skippon's and Harrison's regiments refused to go to Ireland until their demands had been met, and on May 6 some of the troops, having issued a manifesto of their case,[20] held an irregular rendezvous at Banbury. This was crushed by Colonel Reynolds, but the leader, a cashiered corporal, William Thompson, managed to escape to Scrope's mutinous regiment at Salisbury.

The mutiny might now reach serious proportions, and the Generals acted promptly. Cromwell and Fairfax first reviewed their own regiments in Hyde Park, and Cromwell promised that those who thought martial law was a burden could take their pay and leave the army.[21] As a result the Generals were able to set out for Salisbury on May II with a force of two regiments of horse and three of foot on which they could rely.[22] Eventually the mutineers were overtaken by Cromwell's cavalry at Burford Bridge, where one man was killed, four hundred captured,[23] and the rest dispersed throughout the locality. On May 17 William Thompson, the original leader of the mutiny, was overtaken with his last few supporters by Colonel Reynolds, and was killed refusing quarter. With his death the Leveller mutinies flickered to an end.

---

19. The court martial was on April 26. In petitioning against Lockyer's sentence his friends unfortunately suggested that all sentences promulgated by courts martial were illegal by the Petition of Right and Common Law. As Gardiner has pointed out, if this theory were allowed to stand it would have brought military chaos. Cf. *Commonwealth and Protectorate*, I, 46. At Lockyer's funeral on April 29 crowds of Londoners wore the sea-green favour of the Levellers – an indication perhaps more of dissatisfaction with the government than of general Leveller sympathies. Cf. Whitelocke, 399.
20. *England's Standard Advanced*. On May 1 a new "Agreement of the People" had been issued.
21. *W.S.*, II, 67, from *Perfect Occurrences* (May 5, p. 509). The reference to martial law was obviously directed at the protest regarding Robert Lockyer's sentence.
22. On reaching Andover Cromwell appealed to each regiment for loyalty against the Leveller mutineers, and although some of the soldiers objected to action against their former comrades, his appeal was successful.
23. Walker gives the number of captured as 180. *History*, Pt. II, 178, but cf. Gardiner, *Commonwealth and Protectorate*, I, 53, n., and *W.S.*, II, 70. Four were condemned to death, although one was spared. The men shot were Comet Thompson, brother of the leader of the mutineers, and two corporals, Church and Perkins. Comet Denne pleaded for his life and was spared.

These disturbances were important not because they reached any great proportions but because of the promptitude with which Cromwell acted. The unity of the Army was an absolute priority for the security of the new State, and those who threatened to disrupt it must be crushed; but the comparative leniency with which the rank and file were treated was perhaps a no less important factor in re-establishing this unity than the military operations undertaken against them.

III

The Choice of the Commander for Ireland

Although the Leveller mutinies retarded the immediate military programme with regard to Ireland, preparations had been started.[24] The government was extremely sensitive to anything affecting the Irish situation, and when at the end of January it was reported that a small squadron under Rupert had arrived off Kinsale, the Commons immediately voted the increase of thirty ships to the Commonwealth's naval strength! The control of the navy was now in the hands of a small and efficient committee headed by Vane, and a squadron was immediately despatched to serve off the Irish coast under Ayscough. When on February 26 Michael Jones reported on the Irish military situation it was clear that help could not be any longer delayed,[25] and on March 9 the Council of State was instructed by the House to confer with the Committee of the Army about preparations for an expeditionary force.[26] It estimated that a force of twelve thousand should be sent to Ireland.[27]

---

24. The reduction of Ireland had been expressly stated as one of the matters with which the Council of State was to concern itself, under the directions given to it at its inception.
25. Cf. the brief account of the Irish position in *W.S.*, II, 13. On February 26 Cromwell was instructed to arrange for posts between Chester and Holyhead to facilitate communications with Jones. *Cal. S.P. Dom.* (1649–50), 19. The following day was spent discussing how Jones could be helped, and on the steps to be taken to free the Channel Isles.
26. *Cal. S.P. Dom.* (1649–50), 31–2. Two days later Colonel Audley Mervin – one-time commander under Ormonde, but at that time a prisoner in the Tower – was ordered to surrender all his Irish documents. *Ibid.*, 33.
27. A small committee (Cromwell with eight others) had been appointed on March 2 to investigate the raising and financing of an Irish expedition. It covered ground far wider than its commission, and reviewed the whole question of army strength. It proposed a standing force of 44,373 at a monthly cost of £120,000. *Ibid.*, 28. Cf. Walker's figure of £160,000 per month, *History*, Pt. II, 139 f.

Bradshaw was now free to take up his position as President of the Council of State, and Cromwell could devote himself exclusively to military problems.[28] The question of the command of the forces in Ireland was raised almost immediately. It would seem logical that since the possibility of a direct invasion of England from the European mainland could not be entirely discounted, Fairfax's position as Commander-in-Chief would keep him in England with the home army. This meant that another officer would have to be appointed to the command in Ireland, and Cromwell was the obvious choice, both by reason of his record, and as Fairfax's second-in-command. He was offered the post and considered the matter for about a week. During a speech to the Army Council on March 23, he observed, "I had rather be overrun with a Cavalierish interest than a Scotch interest; I had rather be overrun with a Scotch interest, than an Irish interest; and I think of all this is most dangerous ... for all the world knows their barbarism."[29] Religious prejudice, national prejudice and personal antipathy were here combined with a native foresight in military matters to reinforce these predilections, and furthermore, in offsetting the general unpopularity of the new government in England against his countrymen's hatred of foreign domination, he shewed himself to be a very shrewd judge of the Englishman's temper.[30]

Cromwell accepted the command,[31] but, although the choice seems to have been almost inevitable when the political position at home is considered, it seems strange that he was invited to take the command, and perhaps even stranger that he accepted it. It would have seemed more expedient to remain in England, where he could keep his hold upon the political situation. None of those who were suspicious of his personal ambitions expected him to be rash enough to assume the active command in Ireland. The

---

28. Hamilton, Holland, and Capel were executed on March 9. On the day Bradshaw was invested with his new office, Cromwell was appointed, together with Cornelius Holland, Sir Henry Mildmay, and Valentine Walton to confer with the navy commissioners with regard to the ships to be used in the expedition. *Cal. S.P. Dom.* (1649–50), 33.
29. *W.S.*, II, 36–9; *L-C*, III, 400–5 (Supp. 42); *C.P.*, II, 200 ff.
30. "Truly it is [come] thus far, that the quarrel is brought to this state, that we can hardly return unto that tyranny that formerly we were under the yoke of ... but we must at the same time be subject to the kingdom of Scotland or the kingdom of Ireland, for the bringing in of the King. Now that should awaken all Englishmen, who perhaps are willing enough he should have come in upon an accommodation, but not [that] he must come from Ireland or Scotland."
31. Reported to the Council of State, March 29.

Presbyterians thought that "he never did intend to go thither in person; or that if he did, his absence from England would give them all the advantages they could wish",[32] and the Cavaliers expected him first to establish his personal ascendancy both in the Army and in the State before he would take the risk of leaving England.[33] This might have been the policy of a man bent solely on personal power, but the subjugation of Ireland was clearly the first step to be taken in the defence of the Commonwealth of England, and that was the primary consideration at this time in the mind of Oliver Cromwell. He accepted the command to safeguard the results of the Rebellion, and the time might come when the same motive would force him to personal supremacy within the State. Towards this the sense of his own vocation and England's increasing difficulties were leading him, but the modest settlement of his heir in marriage to Dorothy Mayor of Hursley is a small, but significant, indication that in Cromwell's mind these two factors had not yet fully become one.[34]

IV

Preparations for Ireland

On April 1 Cromwell took part in a meeting for prayer and exhortation of a kind which was common in the councils of the Army, and according to Clement Walker, he "spent an hower in prayer, and an hower and an halfe in a Sermon. In his prayer he desired God to take off from him the Government of this mighty People of England", which Walker regarded as "an audatious, ambitious, and hypocriticall imitation of Moses".[35] Walker went on to say, "It is now reported of him, that he pretendeth to Inspirations; and that when any great or weighty matter is propounded, he usually retireth for a quarter or halfe an hower, and then returneth and delivereth out the Oracles of

---

32. Clarendon, *History*, XII, 71.
33. Carte, *Original Letters*, I, 265.
34. A great deal of his correspondence during these months relates to the projected marriage. To the Rev. Robinson, February 1, 1648/9, *W.S.*, II, 8; *L-C*, 411–12 (LXXXVII); to Mayor, February 12, 26, March 8, 14, 25, 30, *W.S.*, 12 f., 21, 27 f. 29 f., 40 f., 46 f.; *L-C*, I, 414 f., 418 f., 420, 424–7, 428 f., 430 f. (LXXXVIII, LXXXIX, XC, XCII, XCIII, XCIV). See also *supra*, p. 162. The marriage took place at Hursley on April 30. For Cromwell's letters to Mayor during April – 6, 15, 28, cf. *W.S.*, II, 52, 56, 61 f.; *L-C*, I, 431 f., 432–4, III, 406 f. (XCV, XCVI, Supp. 43).
35. Cf. Numbers 11:10–15.

the Spirit."[36] Allowing for the author's antipathy, the passage suggests that Cromwell had a definite sense of mission; but the occasion was important for another reason, for here he invited to be his chaplain in Ireland[37] the minister of Coggeshall, John Owen, who was to become the Melanchthon of "orthodox" Independency and Cromwell's chief adviser in ecclesiastical affairs. The choice of Owen to be his spiritual adviser and Oliver's attempt to settle church government in England[38] were a significant foreshadowing of his future ecclesiastical policy.

In Ireland the position had worsened. Ormonde had succeeded temporarily in uniting English Royalists and Irish Catholics, and during May both Michael Jones and George Monk had been hard pressed. Ormonde had captured Drogheda and was preparing to attack Jones, while Monk, deserted by the Ulster Scots, was left isolated at Dundalk. His immediate opponent was Owen Roe O'Neill with six thousand Irish Catholics, but fortunately for the Parliamentary commander O'Neill lacked supplies and was willing to do business with both sides. As a result he concluded a treaty with O'Neill on May 8, by which the latter promised not to make terms with any enemies of the English Commonwealth for a period of three months.[39]

---

36. *Hist. of Independency,* Pt. II, 153 f.
37. For Cromwell's meeting with Owen in the house of Fairfax, cf. Andrew Thompson's *Life of Owen* in Goold's edition of Owen's *Works* (24 vols., Edinburgh, 1850–55), I, p. xlii; Masson, *Life of Milton,* V, 76.
38. On or about April 12, "Cromwell moved in the House of Commons, That the Presbyterian Government might be settled, promising his endevours thereto; but whether he meant a Classicall or Congregationall Presbytery (which differs little or nothing from Independency) he did not declare; and here lyeth the fallacy, he likewise moved, that the secured and secluded Members might againe be invited into the House: they sent their Agents both Laymen and Ministers (amongst whom Mr. Marshall, Nye, Carrell, Goodwin and Hugh Peters were chief) to cajole and decoy the Ministers, Citizens, and expulsed Members, with discourses and propositions." Walker, *Hist. of Independency,* Pt. II, 157. The distinction which Clement Walker draws between Presbyterian church government and the type of church government advocated by Philip Nye, Joseph Caryl, Thomas Goodwin, and Hugh Peters, was a real one. Stephen Marshall was counted to be a moderate Presbyterian, but the other divines mentioned were all members of that group of "Congregationalists" who in the Westminster Assembly had represented their own views as a *via media* between Presbytery and Brownism. Cf. *supra,* p. 175, n. 1. John Owen and Thomas Goodwin preached before the House on June 7, and the following day the House recommended that they should be preferred to the headships of two Oxford colleges. Whitelocke, 406.
39. It is clear from Monk's letter to Cromwell on May 25 that the latter knew of the agreement, and Walker asserts that it was concluded directly upon Cromwell's authority. [Cf. *Hist. of Independency,* Pt. II, 233-46, and *The True State of*

On May 19, 1649, the "Act" was passed which constituted the people of England a "Commonwealth and Free State",[40] but the attempts against Cromwell's life,[41] and the assassination of the Commonwealth's ambassador, Dr. Dorislaus, at The Hague earlier in May were indications of the hatred and uncertainty which faced the new State. Rupert's successful relief of the Scilly Isles added a new incentive to press forward the preparations for Ireland. On June 15 Ireton was appointed Cromwell's second-in-command and on the 22nd Cromwell's commission was read before the House,[42] but on that day Ormonde began the siege of Dublin, and the time factor had become urgent.[43] The difficulty of finding money for the expedition led many to question whether it would ever set sail.[44]

At length, after a prayer meeting at Whitehall on July 11,[45] Cromwell set out, reaching Bristol on the 14th.[46] It was at this juncture that two items of news arrived from Ireland which radically affected the situation. First Monk arrived with the news of how he had been forced to capitulate upon terms to Inchiquin,[47] and this put the English government in a difficulty, for it meant that the treaty with the Catholic O'Neill was likely to be revealed, and the Irish expedition would hardly appear to be the holy Protestant crusade that it had been represented to be to the nation at large. Fortunately for those at the head of affairs, Monk

---

the Transactions of Col. George Monk with Owen-Roe-Mac- O'Neill (1649), reprinted in Gilbert, *Contemporary History of Ireland* (1879–80), II, 221.] Although Cromwell's part in the matter cannot be proved, it should be noted that Jones was trying to foment differences between O'Neill and Ormonde with Cromwell's full knowledge. Cf. *W.S.*, II, 83.

40. Cf. Whitelocke, 403.
41. On June 7 a public dinner was delayed by the discovery that the linch-pin had been removed from Cromwell's coach. From this time we find the extremer Levellers intriguing with the Royalists, and it was from this desperate alliance that the attempts on Cromwell's life were generated. Cf. letter to Cromwell from the Council of State, May 16. *Cal. S.P. Dom.* (1649–50), 143.
42. Whitelocke, 410; *C.J.*, VI, 239 f.
43. Cf. Cromwell's speech accepting the appointment in Clarendon, *History*, XII, 72.
44. *W.S.*, II, 84.
45. Whitelocke, 413.
46. Cf. his letter to Mayor from Bristol, July 19. *W.S.*, II, 95; *L-C*, I, 448 f. (XCIX).
47. With the capture of Drogheda by Inchiquin, Sir George Munro and Lord Montgomery had declared for the King, and O'Neill, largely through the incompetence of his troops, had been forced to retreat to Londonderry. Without hope of relief, Monk had surrendered but most of his garrison had re-enlisted under the Royalist commander.

could be persuaded to accept full responsibility, and he was officially reprimanded.[48]

But while the government was busy trying to save its face over Monk, there came the heartening news of Michael Jones's victory over Ormonde at Rathmines. Cromwell's account of it shows us the effect this news had upon him personally just before he set sail for Ireland:[49] "These things seem to strengthen our faith and love, against more difficult times." A sign of ultimate victory in Ireland had been given by Michael Jones's timely success, just as some months earlier victory in the second Civil War had been heralded by Colonel Horton's success at St. Fagan's. Cromwell therefore departed for Ireland in one of his exalted moods: all things were for the time forgotten in his enthusiasm for "this astonishing mercy; so great and seasonable",[50] which was to him the augury of success, and set the seal to the holy crusade.

R.H. Abbott, commenting upon the Leveller mutinies, wrote that unless the Commonwealth leaders found "a man of sufficiently strong, even ruthless determination, ability and political astuteness, they were doomed to fail".[51] The same might be said with regard to the situation in all its complexity which faced the infant republic, and there can be no doubt that Cromwell was coming to regard himself as the man destined to save the Great Rebellion from failure and his country from chaos – a vocation which must be fulfilled in those public services "for which a man is born".[52]

---

48. Walker, *History,* Pt. II, 230 f.; Whitelocke, 419.
49. To Richard Mayor, August 13, 1649. *W.S.,* II, 102 f.; *L-* C, I, 450 f. (C).
50. *Ibid.*
51. *W.S.,* II, 63.
52. Letter to Mayor; cf. note 2 above.

Chapter Twelve

The Irish Campaign and Its Moral Issues (August 1649 – May 1650)

I

The battles of Cromwell's earlier career were important because they helped to build up in him the all-important conception of a divinely-appointed vocation. Doubtless the successes in Ireland added further to the strength of his conviction, but the attitude with which he accepted the Irish command suggests that a sense of mission had already taken shape in his mind, and if this was the case then it is likely that he would see in the sequence of future events only those things which would support the theory.

The Irish expedition is important for another reason, namely, the moral issues raised by Cromwell's treatment of the Irish, particularly at Drogheda and Wexford. Certainly these massacres appear as the blackest deeds of his career.[1] The incidents of the Irish campaign, however, cannot be considered apart from the rest of Cromwell's career. A man does not suddenly become barbarous, except through madness, or because circumstances unexpectedly bring to life dormant passions; and there are certain factors which had become part of Cromwell's character and which became roused while he was in Ireland – distorted history, religious and national prejudices, and antagonisms created or accentuated by the civil wars. Undoubtedly first among these factors was the horror which had been engendered in England by the exaggerated accounts of the Irish massacre of English Protestant settlers in 1641. The evidence of Richard Baxter, Lucy Hutchinson and Edmund Ludlow shows how the massacre

---

1. S.R. Gardiner, one of Cromwell's staunchest champions, has pointed out that in England, except at Basing House, Cromwell had been uniformly merciful, but "he now treated Irishmen worse than he treated Englishmen". *Comm. & Prot.*, I, 125, n. 2.

gripped the imagination of normally sober-minded Englishmen.[2] In 1645 a preacher before the House of Commons had declaimed, "Behold Scotland comes with her thousands of slain men; England with her ten thousands; Ireland with her millions."[3] Cromwell did no more than share this distorted thinking about Ireland, but it coloured all his relationships with that country,[4] and to this hatred of Ireland for one specific deed, there was added the Puritan hatred of Roman Catholicism as the system of Antichrist. We must also take account of the English contempt for the Irish nation as a race: Lord Clarendon described Ulster as "the seat of the old Irish, who retained the rites, customs, manners, and ignorance of their ancestors, without any kind of reformation in either".[5] Then we must add to the foregoing the sense of mission with which Cromwell entered the Irish campaign.

There remains one final consideration which was entirely practical. Of the Irish campaign the Lord Lieutenant might well take to himself the words of Macbeth:

> "If it were done, when 'tis done, then 'twere well
> It were done quickly. ..."

Whether one looks at the situation from the point of view of bringing the ruinous bloodshed to a speedy end, from the point of view of the stability of the Commonwealth, or from the point of view of Cromwell's personal career, it was essential that the war in Ireland should be won decisively at the earliest possible moment. As we have seen, in Cromwell's mind the good of the people and the stability of the Commonwealth were one and the same thing, and this was in process of becoming identified completely with his own career.[6] Speed was therefore essential.

---

2. Cf. *supra*, p. 52 f., and Ludlow, *Memoirs,* I, 20 f.
3. Peter Sterry, on November 25, 1645; published as *The Spirits Conviction of Sinne* (1645), 15.
4. For Cromwell's preoccupation with Irish affairs up to this point cf. *W.S.*, I, 162, 164–5, 180, 185, 215, 258–9, 411, 438, 571, 573. For a comparison between the atrocities committed by the Irish and those committed by English and Scots in Ireland cf. the Appendix to Warburton's edition of Clarendon's *History* (Vol. VII, p. 209–45).
5. *History,* XI, 146.
6. In his *Impeachment of High Treason against Oliver Cromwell and Henry Ireton,* published about this time, John Lilburne accused Cromwell of aspiring to the chief position in the State. Lilburne often showed keen insight into Cromwell's intentions, although he never correctly divined his motives. As a result of this publication the House of Commons on August 20 issued a warrant for Lilburne's arrest. *Cal. S.P. Dom.* (1649–50), 544.

II

Drogheda and Wexford

After landing in Ireland on August 15, Cromwell's speech to the people of Dublin gave the keynote to his campaign,[7] and he moved almost immediately upon Drogheda, about thirty miles to the north of Dublin, and on the mouth of the Boyne. It was governed by Sir Arthur Aston, who had lost a leg previously in an accident as governor of Oxford for Charles I. He was a Roman Catholic, and, apart from one regiment, most of the men under him were Irish Catholics. Ludlow says that Cromwell well knew the importance of this action and therefore "resolved to put all upon it".[8] On September 3 he was before Drogheda with his army, and on the 10th he summoned Aston to surrender; on the following day he attacked the town. The fighting must have been particularly fierce and bloody, for the English were thrown back from the walls twice, and Colonel Castle was killed at the head of his men. Writing of the next assault Dr. Bates says:

> But this having been twice unsuccessfully attempted, he himself [i.e. Cromwell], with Ireton, commanding the Attack, with Indignation and Courage, redoubled by the former repulses, they make the way which they found not, into the Town, and put to the Sword all they meet, without favour or compassion.[9]

In his letter to Bradshaw Cromwell described the first repulses they suffered, and then added that "being thus entered, we refused them quarter", and he gave it as his considered opinion that not thirty of the whole garrison escaped. He informed the President of the Council that since this action the enemy had evacuated Trim and Dundalk,[10] commenting, "truly I believe this bitterness will save much effusion of blood",[11] and in a fuller account to Lenthall he accepted full responsibility for the order

---

7. *W.S.*, II, 107. On the 23rd Cromwell issued a declaration to defend the inhabitants of Dublin from being plundered (*ibid.*, 110; *L-C*, III, 410 f., Supp. 48), and on the following day a similar declaration to cover the whole country, *W.S.*, II, III.
8. Ludlow, *Memoirs*, I, 233.
9. *Elenchus Motuum*, Pt. 2, 27.
10. Summons to Dundalk. *W.S.*, II, 122; *L-C*, I, 463 f. (CIII).
11. September 16. *W.S.*, II, 124 f.; *L-C*, I, 464 f. (CIV).

which led to the massacre.[12] His own justification for the action is to be found in the comment,

> I am persuaded that this is a righteous judgment of God upon these barbarous wretches, who have imbrued their hands in so much innocent blood;[13] and that it will tend to prevent the effusion of blood for the future, which are the satisfactory grounds to such actions, which otherwise cannot but work remorse and regret.

Such was Cromwell's massacre of Drogheda, where, in contrast to the iron discipline with which he had held his troops throughout the civil wars in England, he not only relaxed his control, but sanctioned a holocaust, thereby blackening the name for justice tempered with mercy which up to that point had been deservedly his.

Cromwell's army immediately made its way south to the port of Wexford, which, standing in a deeply sheltered harbour at the south-eastern corner of Ireland, was in a position to cover the Bristol and English Channels, and the citizens of Wexford had made good use of this geographical position to send their privateers to prey upon the merchantmen of England in the Narrow Seas.

On October 3 Cromwell sent his formal summons to the governor, Colonel David Synnott, but the latter tried to gain time until relief had arrived.[14] Ormonde himself visited Wexford to confer with the governor, and on the day following Sir Edmund Butler arrived with further reinforcements and to take command of the defence.[15] Cromwell's artillery made two large breaches in the defences, and the governor suggested terms far higher than he could hope to get from Cromwell at any time,[16] let alone in the latter's present mood. The final article of the suggested terms indicated that the people of Wexford were perhaps beginning to

---

12. September 17th. *W.S.*, II, 125–8; *L-C*, I, 466–72 (CV).
13. Mrs. S.C. Lomas has the following note at this point: "Cromwell seems to have held all Ireland responsible for the massacres of eight years before. There can have been few – if any – at Drogheda who had taken part in them; certainly not the officers, certainly not the English soldiers, and almost certainly not Ormond's own regiment, raised in his ancestral domains round Kilkenny." *L-C*, I, 469 n., cf. Gardiner, *Comm. & Prot.*, I, 125.
14. Lord Iveagh with 1,500 Ulstermen. For a full account of Cromwell's dealings with Synnott, cf. *W.S.*, II, 135–9; *L-C*, I, 476–88.
15. October 11. He arrived with 500 foot and 500 horse.
16. For the full terms suggested, cf. *L-C*, I, 483–5.

suffer some qualms of conscience about the private activities of their frigates in recent years.[17] In reply Cromwell offered reasonable conditions,[18] but the negotiations were suddenly cut short when the commander of the castle, Captain Stafford, surrendered to Cromwell and thus enabled him to turn the castle guns on the town. When the English appeared on the ramparts of the castle, the enemy quitted the town walls, and the English, seeing their advantage, immediately stormed the town and killed all who came in their way. About three hundred defenders were drowned while trying to escape in two overcrowded boats, and in his account to Lenthall, Oliver added the comment that

> indeed it hath not without cause been deeply set upon our hearts, that, we intending better to this place than so great a ruin, hoping the town might be of more use to you and your army, yet God would not have it so; but, by an unexpected providence, in His righteous justice, brought a just judgment upon them, causing them to become a prey to the soldier, who in their piracies had made preys of so many families, and made with their bloods to answer the cruelties which they had exercised upon the lives of divers poor Protestants.[19]

III

From October 1649 to May 1650

Such then were the two massacres with which Cromwell began operations in Ireland, and the rest of the campaign in Ireland can be covered comparatively briefly.

Cromwell proceeded to Ross, where after some negotiations[20] the governor, Sir Lucas Taafe, eventually capitulated on terms. There was no recurrence of the fierce spirit shown at Drogheda, although it was not because Cromwell's love for Catholics had

---

17. "That no memory remain of any hostility or distance which was hitherto between the said Town and Castle on the one part, and the Parliament or State of England on the other part; but that all act and acts, transgressions, offences, depredations and other crimes, of what nature or quality soever, be they ever so transcendent, attempted or done, or supposed to be attempted or done, by the Inhabitants of the said Town or any other, heretofore or at present adhering to the said Town, either native or stranger, and every of them, – shall pass in oblivion; without chastisement, challenge, recompense, demand or questioning for them, or any of them, now or at any time hereafter."
18. *W.S.*, II, 139; *L-C*, I, 485 f.
19. October 14. *W.S.*, II, 140–3; *L-C*, I, 476–88. Cf. also his letter to Fairfax, October 15. *W.S.*, II, 144; *L-C*, III, 411 (Supp. 49).
20. Cf. the correspondence. *W.S.*, II, 144–8.

increased, as the blunt reply to the governor of Ross shows well enough.[21]

By this time sickness was beginning to spread through the invading army. Colonel Horton died in October,[22] Michael Jones in December,[23] and Cromwell himself became very ill as the weather deteriorated. He wrote, "I have been crazy in my health",[24] and admitted, "I scarce know an officer of forty amongst us that hath not been sick".[25] Owing to these privations the invaders failed to take Duncannon fort; but divisions were beginning to appear among their enemies. The declaration by the Irish Catholic bishops at Clonmacnoise of a "holy war" against the invaders only served to antagonize the English Protestant royalists, who now found themselves between Cromwell and the Pope, and as a result many from the enemies' garrisons in Munster came over to Cromwell's army; in this way Cork came into his hands. The coalition which faced him was beginning to break up,[26] but he was forced by the weather and illness among his troops to raise his siege at Waterford in November and go into winter quarters.

Nothing, however, occurred to shake Cromwell's faith in the absolute justice of the cause for which he was fighting. At the end of November he said in a letter to William Lenthall:[27]

> Sir, what can be said to these things? Is it an arm of flesh that doth these things? Is it the wisdom, and counsel, or strength of men? It is the Lord only. God will curse that man and his house that dares to think otherwise. Sir, you see the work is done by divine leading. ... And if it will not yet be received that these are seals of God's approbation of your great change of Government, which indeed was no more yours than these victories and successes are ours; yet let them with us say, even the most unsatisfied heart

---

21. "For that which you mention concerning liberty of conscience, I meddle not with any man's conscience. But if by liberty of conscience you mean a liberty to exercise the mass, I judge it best to use plain dealing, and to let you know, where the Parliament of England have power, that will not be allowed of." October 19, W. S., II, 146; *L-C,* I, 492 f. (CX).
22. Cf. Cromwell's letter to Lenthall, October 25. *W.S.,* II, 153; *L-C,* I, 495 f., postscript.
23. Cf. Cromwell's letter to Lenthall, December 19. *W. S.,* II, 177; *L-C,* I, 515 (CXVII).
24. To Mayor, November 19. *W.S.,* II, 159 f.; *L-C,* I, 498 (CXIII).
25. To the Speaker, November 20. *W.S.,* II, 162–5; *L-C,* I, 501–7 (CXV).
26. Owen O'Neill had died, and there was now no effective command over his troops.
27. November [25]. *W.S.,* II, 171–4; *L-C,* I, 507–12 (CXVI).

amongst them, that both are the righteous judgments and mighty works of God; that He hath pulled down the mighty from his seat,[28] that calls to an account innocent blood, that He thus breaks the enemies of His Church in pieces. And let them not be sullen, but praise the Lord, and think of us as they please.

Before Cromwell left Ireland he was to receive some reverses,[29] but when he departed on May 26 he left Ireton to finish the conquest in the knowledge that Irish opposition was virtually crushed. As he received daily evidence of the break-up of the enemy garrisons, he regarded the successes of the campaign as "the seals of God's approbation" and as "the righteous judgments and mighty works of God". A letter to his wavering friend, Lord Wharton,[30] shows that he completely identified his cause with the Will of God:

> It were a vain thing, by letter, to dispute over your doubts, or to undertake answer to your objections. I have heard them all; and I have rest from the trouble of them, and what has risen in my own heart; for which I desire to be humbly thankful. I do not condemn your reasonings; I doubt them. It's easy to object to the glorious actings of God, if we look too much upon instruments. I have heard computations made of the members in Parliament: Good kept out, most bad remaining; it has been so this nine years, yet what has God wrought. The greatest works last; and still is at work. Therefore take heed of this scandal.
>
> Be not offended at the manner; perhaps no other way was left. What if God accepted the zeal, as He did that of Phineas[31] whose reason might have called for a jury? What if the Lord have witnessed his approbation and acceptance to this also, not only by signal outward acts, but to the heart also? What if I fear my friend should withdraw his shoulder from the Lord's work (Oh, it's grievous to do so) through scandals, through false mistaken reasonings. ... You was desired to go along with us: I wish it still. Yet we are not triumphing; we may (for aught flesh knows) suffer after all this.

---

28. Luke 1:52.
29. At Kilkenny, on March 27, Sir Walter Butler capitulated, but with all the honours of war, and at Clonmel Cromwell received the biggest repulse of his career with the loss of 2,000 men, at the hands of Hugh O'Neill, Owen O'Neill's nephew. The Irish garrison succeeded in escaping under cover of darkness on May 10, leaving Cromwell to enter the town and to keep the articles of its surrender. However, when he eventually left Ireland on May 26 he had captured all the ports with the exception of Waterford, and had cleared the southern river valleys.
30. January 1, 1649/50. *W.S.*, II, 189 f.; *L-C*, I, 521–3 (CXVIII).
31. Numbers 25:6–8.

The Lord prepare us for His good pleasure! You were with us in the Form of things; why not in the Power?

Against the background of Drogheda and Wexford such letters appear to be the height of hypocrisy, but to dismiss them as such would be but a superficial reading both of the facts and of the man.

IV

Moral Considerations

This leads inevitably to a discussion of the moral issues raised by Cromwell's Irish campaign. Despite the fact that Abbott has spoken of an increasing sternness as shown at Drogheda and as "still more evident at Wexford",[32] Cromwell himself said of Wexford that he intended "better to this place",[33] and there is no reason to doubt his word. The massacre which took place at Wexford appears to have been a spontaneous act of those who were storming the town, and who still had the ugly precedent of Drogheda in their minds. This does not exonerate Cromwell, who had provided them with that precedent, and who did nothing to stop the butchery once it had started; but Drogheda raises the moral issues in their most acute form.

The question we must ask is not whether in the light of modern humanitarianism the massacres can be defended, but how far these actions were consistent with Cromwell's religious and moral conceptions as we have traced them hitherto; and to answer this question we need to look again at his religious and national prejudices, the standards of morality which he accepted, and the relationship between all these factors and that of military expediency.

With regard to Cromwell's prejudices against the Catholic Irish a good deal has been said already, but it is given point by the remarkable document which Cromwell compiled early in 1650, and addressed to the Irish Catholic prelates. On December 4, 1649, the Catholic prelates had met at Clonmacnoise and issued two manifestoes[34] calling upon all Catholics to unite against Cromwell. Cromwell's reply "combined statecraft, theology, religious

---

32. *W.S.*, II, 134.
33. Cf. Cromwell's letter to Lenthall quoted *supra*, p. an.
34. December 4 and 13.

The Irish Campaign and Its Moral Issues

emotion, arguments, persuasion and threats, in an amazing denunciation of the ecclesiastics who had ventured to speak for their people and their church". It was, as R.H. Abbott has said, "a declaration of war to the death on the Roman Catholic clergy and their adherents,"[35] but amid all the distortion, the ignorance of true facts, and the often faulty logic of this statement, the impression persists that the writer was utterly sincere.

Having upbraided the Catholic bishops for their "antichristian and dividing" conception of "clergy and laity", he went on to expostulate:

> By the grace of God, we fear not, we care not for your union. Your covenant is with death and hell; your union is like that of Simeon and Levi.[36] Associate yourselves, and you shall be broken in pieces; take counsel together, and it shall come to naught.[37] For though it becomes us to be humble in respect of ourselves, yet we can say to you, God is not with you. You say your union is against a common enemy. ...
>
> Who is it that created this common enemy? I suppose you mean Englishmen. The English! Remember, ye hypocrites, Ireland was once united to England. Englishmen had good inheritances which many of them purchased with their money; they or their ancestors, from many of you and your ancestors. They had good leases from Irishmen for long time to come; great stocks thereupon; houses and plantations erected at their cost and charge. They lived peaceably and honestly amongst you. You had generally equal benefit of the protection of England with them, and equal justice from the laws, saving what was necessary for the State (out of reasons of State) to put upon some few people apt to rebel upon the instigation of such as you. You broke this union! You, unprovoked, put the English to the most unheard-of and most barbarous massacre (without respect of sex or age) that ever the sun beheld. ... Is God, will God be, with you? I am confident He will not!

He denounced them as "a part of Antichrist, whose Kingdom the Scripture so expressly speaks should be laid in blood",[38] and went on to castigate the prelates soundly for keeping their people in ignorance, commenting that the only theological reason he had had from people for their opinions since he had come to Ireland

---

35. *W.S.*, II, 196. The text of the declaration is *ibid.*, 196–205; *L-C*, II, 5–23.
36. Genesis 34:25–31.
37. Isaiah 8:9 ff.
38. Revelation 6:9–11.

was that "indeed they did not trouble themselves about matters of religion but left that to the Church".

He left them in no doubt about his intention to extirpate the Roman Catholic religion, as far as it was practised openly, but he added,

> As for the people, what thoughts they have in matters of religion in their own breasts I cannot reach; but think it my duty, if they walk honestly and peaceably, not to cause them in the least to suffer for the same, but shall endeavour to walk patiently and in love towards them, to see if at any time it shall please God to give them another or a better mind. And all men under the power of England, within this dominion, are hereby required and enjoined strictly and religiously to do the same.

It has been observed that to claim that he did not meddle with any man's conscience and then to deny the Catholic liberty of worship "was as idle as if the Catholics had pretended that they did not meddle with conscience if they forbade the possession or use of the Bible, or hunted Puritan preachers out of all the pulpits".[39] They are not quite parallel cases. Cromwell lived at a time when the Inquisition was in operation, and he had been born when it was almost at the height of its power. Catholic Inquisitors like Torquemada[40] did not hesitate to coerce the very conscience that Cromwell here professes he cannot reach. Basically, his intolerance of the Roman Catholic faith was Catholicism's intolerance of all religion but its own: "you having chiefly made use of fire and sword, in all the changes in religion that you have made in the world".

Such was Cromwell's reply to the Irish bishops and it gave him the opportunity to state much that was positive in his own faith. The responsibility of the individual before God, the doctrine of the Priesthood of all Believers, the doctrine of Providence, freedom of conscience, are all mixed up here with a good deal of national prejudice and a hopelessly inadequate interpretation of Anglo-Irish history; but it is delivered with the passionate sincerity of a man who obviously believed every word he had written. However defective it is, "as an explanation of

---

39. Morley, *Cromwell,* 296.
40. Tomás de Torquemada (1420–98), Inquisitor-General of the Spanish Empire, 1481–98.

Cromwell's own conduct in Ireland, this Declaration is of supreme importance".[41] The author of it was perhaps no better nor any worse informed about Ireland than the rest of the nation that claimed sovereignty over that unhappy country, but the prejudices embodied in it have this significance that they belonged to a man who in a few years, and through a series of unparalleled military successes, had risen from civilian obscurity to be his country's most outstanding general, and who believed those successes – "falsely called the chance of war" – to be ordained by Providence. This Declaration must therefore be read by the side of the accounts of Drogheda and Wexford, for although it provides no excuse for Cromwell's actions there, it does much to explain why they happened.

Here we must remind ourselves of the way in which the Puritan turned to the Old Testament "ethics" for precedents in dealing with those who had no claim to his Christian charity – into which category Cromwell would certainly relegate all Irish Catholics. In answer to Lord Wharton's criticisms, it was to the grim morality of Phineas, who executed summary justice on his own initiative, that Cromwell appealed for justification.[42] Bishop Burnet reveals that this appeal to the Old Testament, which may have begun as an unconscious tendency, eventually became accepted practice, for he wrote:

> I had much discourse with one who knew Cromwell well, and all that set of men, on this head, and asked him how they could excuse all the prevarications, and other ill things, of which they were visibly guilty in the conduct of their affairs. He told me, they believed there were great occasions in which some men were called to great services, in the doing of which they were excused from the common rules of morality: such as were the practices of Ehud and Jael, Samson and David: and by this they fancied they had a privilege from observing the standing rules.[43]

When Cromwell entered Ireland he went in the spirit of

---

41. Gardiner, *Comm. & Prot.*, I, 148.
42. Cf. Numbers 25:6–8, and *supra*, p. 213.
43. *History of My Own Time*, I, 78. Cf. also this passage from a Puritan writer: "The laws indeed be few and brief, yet are they perfect and sufficient, and so large as the wisdom of God judged needful for regulating judgment in all ages and nations. For no action or case doth, or possibly can, fall out in this or other nations ... but the like did, or possibly might fall out in Israel." William Aspinwal, *Description of the Fifth Monarchy* (1653).

Samson towards the Philistines or of Samuel towards the Amalekites:[44] whatever his natural regret, he had no remorse.

The final consideration, however, was that of military expediency. We have already seen that Cromwell had sufficient reason for bringing the Irish campaign to a conclusion as soon as possible, and Ormonde would undoubtedly try to force the invaders into a series of protracted sieges, so that the Irish weather could accomplish by sickness what he could never hope to do by force of arms. The order given at Drogheda was given in the heat of the battle and may not have been premeditated, but having given the order Cromwell defended it on the military grounds that it would bring the war to a more speedy end.

Perhaps a modern example will help to give us a better understanding of Cromwell at this point.[45] On August 6, 1945, the first "atomic" bomb fell on the Japanese city of Hiroshima, and a few days later a similar bomb was dropped on Nagasaki; the two bombs, according to a conservative estimate, killed or maimed a total of one hundred thousand people, most of them civilians who died in circumstances of indescribable horror. Japan surrendered to the Allies on August 15, 1945, and, while it is outside the scope of our present study to discuss the rights and wrongs of this case, it should be noted that the reasons given by Cromwell for the massacre of the garrison of Drogheda were precisely the same as those advanced by the Allies to justify the use of the new bomb.[46] Although some civilians undoubtedly suffered at Drogheda, the order which Cromwell gave extended only to those in arms, and on any fair assessment it would appear that he could give points in humanity to an "enlightened" twentieth century. This is not offered in excuse for events which do blacken his name, but as an attempt to put the massacres at Drogheda and Wexford into proper perspective.

---

44. Cf. Judges 16:28–31; 1 Samuel 15.
45. The responsibility for the massacres has been bitterly argued, cf. the bibliography on the subject in W.S., II, 121, n. 45.
46. "A warning, clearly and solemnly explaining the powers of the new weapon, would possibly have ended the Japanese resistance. If it had not ended it, then the dropping of the bombs, as many still think, *would* have been justified, in the sense that it would have shortened the war (as it did) by many months, and saved infinitely more lives – including the lives of women and children – than were lost in the bombed areas." MR.E. H. Jeffs, in the editorial of *The Christian World,* October 24, 1946, p. 8.

Chapter Thirteen

The Scottish Campaign: Dunbar (May 1650 – January 1651)

I

The Supreme Command

The campaigns of Ireland and Scotland provide very different pictures of Cromwell, and yet together they form a single chapter in his rise to power, since the success of the former not only paved the way for the invasion of Scotland, but also led to his superseding Fairfax as Commander-in-Chief. When Cromwell resumed his seat in the Commons the Speaker, William Lenthall, expressed to him the hearty thanks of the House in an "eloquent Oration, setting forth the great Providence of God in those great and strange Works, which God had wrought by him, as the Instrument".[1] Every system of government has recourse to a theory by which it substantiates its own authority. Monarchy based itself on the "Divine Right of Kings", and although the Levellers had put forward as an alternative the divine rights of the People, this could not yet stir the popular imagination; but in the conception of a divinely-inspired and invincible leader – God's "Instrument" – there was already to hand a new theory of authority to take the place of the Divine Right of Kings. The need for leadership was making Cromwell's personal rule inevitable.[2]

Meanwhile the Commonwealth's practical difficulties remained. On February 5, 1649, in Edinburgh, the Prince of Wales had been proclaimed King of Great Britain, France and Ireland, on condition that he signed the Covenant, and he had not scrupled

---

1. *C.J.*, VI, 418.
2. "An ever-victorious commander with an aura of invincibility, compelling eloquence, profound conviction of the righteousness of his cause and the certainty of its success, and unconquerable resolution, was precisely what the Commonwealth most needed and what he now provided." R.H. Abbott, *W.S.*, II, 260.

to accept the condition. This made war between England and Scotland almost inevitable, and from England's point of view the great value of the rapid progress in Ireland had been to forestall a war on two fronts. Robert Baillie had commented gloomily on September 7, 1649, "it seems Ireland is lost; I think we shall be next tried".[3]

Fairfax was the one uncertain factor in the situation. His own ecclesiastical position veered between Presbyterianism and Independency,[4] and at first he seemed to approve the proposal to enter Scotland, but afterwards, "being hourly persuaded by the Presbyterian ministers and his own Lady, who was a great Patroness of them,[5] he declared himself unsatisfied that there was just ground for the Parliament of England to send their Army to invade Scotland".[6] The Council of State thereupon selected a committee to visit the Lord General[7] and it is evident that as leader of the deputation Cromwell used his best endeavours to persuade Fairfax to change his mind. In answer to Fairfax's objections he said that, despite the failure of the previous Scottish invasion, "they now intend a new Invasion upon us I do as really believe, and have as good Intelligence of it, as we can have of anything that is not yet acted". In his view, the English ought to strike first to prevent "the great Misery and Calamity of having an Army of Scots within our Country".[8] Fairfax however was adamant. Schemes had been hatched for the deposition of Fairfax, but Cromwell had firmly withstood any attempt to elevate himself at the expense of his former chief – even Ludlow had to admit he "really thought him in earnest".[9] Writing their memoirs in the light of later events, Ludlow and

---

3. Letter to Captain Titus. *Letters and Journals,* III, 102.
4. Cromwell had met John Owen for the first time in Fairfax's house. Cf. *supra,* 204 n. 2.
5. "During this time [i.e. about the time Charles I was conducted to Holmeby] Sir Thomas Fairfax himself lay at Nottingham, and the governor was sick in the castle. The general's lady was come along with him, having followed his camp to the siege of Oxford, and lain at his quarters all the while he abode there. She was exceeding kind to her husband's chaplains, independent ministers, till the army returned to be nearer London, and then the presbyterian ministers quite changed the lady into such a bitter aversion against them, that they could not endure to come into the general's presence while she was there; and the general had an unquiet, unpleasant life with her. ..." *Memoirs of the life of Col. Hutchinson* (Everyman edn.), 237.
6. Whitelocke, 460.
7. Cromwell, Lambert, Harrison, St. John and Whitelocke.
8. Whitelocke, 460 f.
9. By refusing to accept the supreme command. *Memoirs,* I, 243 f.

The Scottish Campaign: Dunbar

others interpreted his attitude as a further example of duplicity, but Lucy Hutchinson was more consistent.[10] Oliver had nothing to gain by trying to retain Fairfax as Commander-in-Chief. If he coveted the supreme command he had only to remain unobtrusively quiet to be appointed, but he "pressed that notwithstanding the unwillingness of the Lord Fairfax to command upon this occasion, they would yet continue him to be General of the army; professing for himself, that he would rather chuse to serve under him in his post, than to command the greatest army in Europe".[11]

Since the attempt to get Fairfax to change his decision was unsuccessful, an act was passed "for constituting and appointing Oliver Cromwell Esq; to be Captain General and Commander in Chief of all the Forces raised and to be raised by the Authority of Parliament within the Commonwealth of England."[12]

Just after this, in a private conversation, Edmund Ludlow frankly admitted to Cromwell that he had formerly entertained serious doubts about his motives, and in reply Cromwell assured the republican of his readiness to see the nation "settled in a free and equal Commonwealth" on the grounds that it was probably the best way to keep the Stuarts at bay. He confessed that he believed that they were passing through the events foretold in the 110th Psalm, and spent "at least an hour in the exposition of that Psalm".[13] In view of the Fifth Monarchist opinions which were held by men like Harrison, Overton and Goffe, and by such influential divines as John Goodwin,[14] it can hardly be supposed that Oliver would escape being affected by them, but it would be interesting to know how he applied this psalm to the events of his time.[15] To whom did he consider this psalm was addressed?

---

10. "To speak the truth of Cromwell, whereas many said he undermined Fairfax, it was false; for in Colonel Hutchinson's presence, he most effectually importuned him to keep his commission, lest it should discourage the army and the people at that juncture of time, but could by no means prevail, although he laboured for it almost all the night with most earnest endeavours. But this great man was then as immovable by his friends as pertinacious in obeying his wife." *Memoirs of Col. Hutchinson* (Everyman edn.), 274.
11. Ludlow, *Memoirs,* I, 243.
12. Whitelocke, 462.
13. Ludlow, Memoirs, I, 246.
14. Burnet, *History of My Own Time*, I, 120 f.
15. "The Lord said unto my Lord, Sit thou at my right hand, until I make thine enemies thy footstool.

What was to be his own part in the future theophany? According to a literal interpretation almost all these promises had been fulfilled to Cromwell himself: he had seen his enemies reduced to his feet, in the formation of the psalm-singing Ironsides "the rod of thy strength" had come out of Zion, and his own career was evidence that he had "the dew of his youth". Might not the rest of the psalm also be a promise to him? It is difficult to see how else he could have applied it.

If he interpreted Scripture in this way, then we have an important clue to resolving that tension between Cromwell's "democratic" Independency and his later autocratic government, for if he came to consider himself as a ruler in the Davidic sense, then he was bound to consider that the exercise of his magistracy would involve not only secular authority, but also the commission to speak with the prophetic imperative, "Thus saith the Lord". However much Congregational views might seem to foreshadow "a free and equal Commonwealth", they were counterbalanced by the high sense of personal vocation and prophetic authority held by those who were called into the ministry of Reformed churches.[16] If Cromwell came to regard himself *in loco pastoris* within the nation he would assume a "divine right" which would spring directly from his sense of vocation, in which the spiritual authority of the prophet would be joined to his exercise of secular power, and although this would be a dangerous theory, in the light of his theological beliefs and previous success it would be extremely plausible.

II

The Invasion of Scotland

The mood in which Cromwell marched into Scotland was

"The Lord shall send the rod of thy strength out of Zion: rule thou in the midst of thine enemies.

"Thy people shall be willing in the day of thy power, in the beauties of holiness from the womb of the morning: thou hast the dew of thy youth.

"The Lord hath sworn, and will not repent, Thou art a priest for ever after the order of Melchizedek.

"The Lord at thy right hand shall strike through kings in the day of his wrath.

"He shall judge among the heathen, he shall fill the places with the dead bodies; he shall wound the heads over many countries.

"He shall drink of the brook in the way: therefore shall he lift up the head."

16. See Owen's sermon on Jeremiah 3:15; *Works,* IX, 452–62; and Richard Baxter's *Reformed Pastor* (1655), especially the passages in Chapter II on discipline.

The Scottish Campaign: Dunbar

very different from that in which he had gone to Ireland, for although recent events had stirred up a good deal of enmity between the two countries, there was no cause for hatred like that of the Irish "massacre". The years of the Civil Wars had been spent on the whole in close alliance, and in all but Church polity the theology of the Scots was identical with that of Cromwell himself – a fact that he was more ready to admit than they were. Yet the national picture which confronted Cromwell in Scotland was not unlike that which faced him in Ireland. In both countries he was opposed by a national Church divided by factions, and by people whose only other point of unity was a King who was a foreigner and a "heretic". Hence, although Cromwell's temper was very different from what it had been in Ireland, his diplomatic policy was the same – to divide and rule.

The newly-created Lord General set out at the end of June with Fleetwood as his Lieutenant-General, Lambert as Major-General, and Whalley as Commissary. From Newcastle Cromwell and his officers issued a declaration to "all that are Saints, and Partakers of the Faith of God's Elect, in Scotland", in which they pointed out that the real issue at present was that of religious toleration:

> As for the Presbyterian, or any other form of church-government, they are not by the Covenant to be imposed by force; yet we do and are ready to embrace so much as doth, or shall be made appear to us to be according to the Word of God.[17] Are we to be dealt with as enemies, because we come not to your way? Is all religion wrapped up in that or any one form? Doth that name, or thing, give the difference between those that are the members of Christ and those that are not? We think not so. We say faith working by love is the true character of a Christian.[18]

The passage illustrates well both the proximity and the unbridgeable distance between Scottish Presbyterians and English Independents. The true strength of the Independent position was in its insistence that the individual conscience should be free to persuasion by the Holy Spirit. Although they went to Scotland with the sword, it was in defence of this principle, and

---

17. Sir Henry Vane had secured this proviso to the Solemn League and Covenant. The Independents felt they were on strong ground here, for the "dissenting brethren" had formulated their polity from Scripture while they were in exile, and while many of their Presbyterian colleagues remained in Anglican livings. Cf. *Apologeticall Narration*, 2.
18. *W.S.*, II, 283–8, signed by John Rushworth, secretary to the Army.

hence they persisted in greeting their opponents of the Kirk as Christian brethren. The Scots could not return the compliment, and their moral position was so much the weaker.

The English Army began to cross the Tweed on July 22, 1650, and reached Dunbar on the 25th, via Cockburnspath. David Lesley had denuded the country of men and provisions,[19] but at Dunbar supplies were unloaded from the fleet which was supporting the Army. Just about the same time Charles II was visiting Lesley's army and inspiring it with that "carnal courage at his presence" which Archibald Johnston of Wariston and his colleagues of the Kirk found so obnoxious.[20] From Dunbar the English Army moved up beyond Musselburgh to reconnoitre the Scottish lines and found that Lesley occupied an impregnable position, with fortifications extending to the sea at Leith, and manned by an army of thirty thousand. A frontal attack with an army but half that size was unthinkable, and the fortifications could not be outflanked. Therefore, after some preliminary skirmishing Cromwell retired to Musselburgh on July 30.[21]

While the two armies remained warily in their quarters, Cromwell again temporarily discarded the sword for the pen in a letter addressed to the General Assembly and Commissioners of the Scottish Kirk.[22] An interesting comparison could be made between this Declaration and that addressed to the Irish Prelates, for although he blamed the Scottish ministers for having "begotten prejudice", in the end he pleaded with them as a fellow Christian, "I beseech you, in the bowels of Christ, think it possible you may be mistaken".

In the meantime Lesley, who was for ever handicapped by the struggle for control in his army between the leaders of the Kirk

---

19. Lesley commanded under the nominal supreme command of his uncle, the Earl of Leven.
20. Bishop Burnet said that the King was allowed to visit the Scotch army only once, "but not to stay in it; for they were afraid he might gain too much upon the soldiers: so he was sent away". *History of My Own Time*, I, 94.
21. A hot action developed between the Scottish horse and the rearguard, in which Lambert was wounded and was for a time a prisoner. Cromwell arrived back at Musselburgh to find the place barricaded against him by some of the local people, and an attempt was made during the night by Major-General Montgomery and some cavaliers to break through to his headquarters. See letter to Bradshaw, July 30. *W.S.*, II, 299–301; *L-C*, II, 73–6 (CXXXV). Montgomery's failure enabled the Kirk to force Charles to exclude "Malignants" from the Scottish camp. *W.S.*, II, 301.
22. August 3, 1650. *W.S.*, II, 302 f.; *L-C*, II, 77–80 (CXXXVI).

The Scottish Campaign: Dunbar

and the King's cavaliers,[23] had moved to cover the road to Stirling to prevent the English outflanking him and cutting through to the sea.[24] As Cromwell moved north-west Lesley moved west to check him, and on August 27 the two armies met in the boggy ground near Gogar, but were unable to get to grips on such difficult terrain, and hence Cromwell ordered his army a second time to retire. The Scottish general saw the English move to the east, and fearing they would try to interpose between him and Edinburgh, he hastened to prevent this, but finding his fears groundless he blocked the English army's passage to Musselburgh. Cromwell avoided the threat only by making his tired troops do a rapid forced march along the coast road. Sickness was added to the difficulties of the invaders, as in Ireland, and so far neither by pen nor by sword had Cromwell been able to drive a wedge into the Scottish defence. Lesley had made no mistakes, and in his impregnable defensive position he had nothing to lose and everything to gain by being content to wait. There was nothing more for the English to do but return once more to Dunbar, and there await developments.[25]

III

Dunbar

The retreat began on August 31, and the Scottish Army followed so closely upon the invaders' heels that the English were never free from attacks until they entered Dunbar itself, and here Lesley turned off the road to occupy Doon Hill, which over-looked the town and commanded the road to Berwick and the south. This meant that the English could not escape from Dunbar except by sea, and from the hill Lesley commanded the situation: his strategy had been impeccable, and he had succeeded

---

23. The leaders of the Kirk were trying to force Charles to sign a declaration which would admit his father's guilt for the bloodshed of the Civil Wars, forswear Anglicans and Catholics, denounce his mother as an idolatress, and promise to impose Presbyterianism on England! The Kirk denied that it supported Charles until he signed this declaration, and Cromwell's letter to Lesley replied to this. The Scots used Cromwell as a lever to force Charles to sign; as a result, many most efficient royalist officers were expelled on theological grounds, and their place taken by staunch supporters of the Kirk.
24. Redhall, belonging to Sir James Hamilton, had been taken by Cromwell on August 24.
25. Before he left Musselburgh Cromwell wrote an account to the Council of State (?), August 30. W.S., II, 311 f.; *L-C*, II, 87 f. (CXXXVIII).

in out-generalling Cromwell. Dunbar itself could be easily fortified, and might be held indefinitely, for a stream running in a fairly steep ravine separated the two armies, and the town was out of range of Lesley's artillery. Moreover, the English had the advantage of warm, dry quarters within the town, whereas the Scots were forced to camp upon the exposed hillside; but when that is said, the initiative was now with the Scots, who outnumbered the English by about two to one.

When Cromwell learned on September 1 that Lesley had occupied Cockburnspath, he knew that he had been outmanoeuvred, and if he were defeated it would leave the Scots entirely free to stage a counter-invasion into England; in the existing state of unrest within that country, this might well have been fatal.[26] It is clear, however, that although Cromwell made dispositions to meet the possibility of Lesley's victory, and although his own position was desperate enough, he was confident of a successful outcome. When he looked back on his own feelings he was able to declare after the battle, "that because of their numbers, because of their advantages, because of their confidence, because of our weakness, because of our strait, we were in the Mount, and in the Mount the Lord would be seen; and ... He would find out a way of deliverance and salvation for us – and in deed we had our consolations and our hopes."[27] One eye-witness said that before the battle of Dunbar "Oliver was carried on with a divine impulse; he did laugh so excessively as if he had been drunk; his eyes sparkled with spirits."[28]

The armies were separated by the forty-foot ravine of the little Brock (or Spot) Burn, which was traversed by a cart track at a point where the glen was more shallow. An English outpost was stationed here in a keeper's cottage, and a preliminary skirmish took place over possession of this.[29] Cromwell called his officers to a day of prayer, and he liked to recall in later years that he felt

---

26. Cf. Burnet, *History of My Own Time*, I, 95. On September 2 Cromwell wrote post-haste to Sir Arthur Hazelrigge to warn him of the gravity of the situation, and to urge him to take all necessary precautions to counter the threat of invasion. *W.S.*, II, 314 f.; *L-C*, II, 92–3 (CXXXIX).
27. To Lenthall, September 4. *W.S.*, II, 321–5; *L-C*, II, 102–10 (CXL).
28. John Aubrey, quoting an eye-witness, *Miscellanies* (5th edn., Library of Old Authors, 1890), 113. Aubrey continued, "The same fit of laughter seized Oliver Cromwell, just before the battle of Naseby; as a kinsman of mine, and a great favourite of his, Colonel J. P. then present, testified." R.H. Abbott suggests that Aubrey's informant may have been John Pickering.*W.S.*, II, 319.
29. It was captured by the Scots and then recaptured in a counter-attack.

The Scottish Campaign: Dunbar

"such an enlargement of heart in prayer, and such quiet upon it, that he bade all about him take heart, for God had certainly heard them".[30] A short time after this, while walking with other officers in the Earl of Roxburgh's garden and viewing the Scottish Army stretched out over Doon Hill, Cromwell noticed a considerable movement in the enemy's camp. He at once declared, "God is delivering them into our hands, they are coming down to us." It appears that the leaders of the Kirk had urged an immediate attack upon "the sectaries", and that Lesley had counselled patience without much success. However, the Scots had moved down the hill towards the more level ground nearer the coast, and probably Lesley's plan was to swing his right wing round to block the Berwick road and thus entirely enclose the English Army in Dunbar before launching his attack,[31] but it meant that at the point where the ravine of the burn ran towards the steeper slopes of Doon Hill the left wing of the Scottish Army became enclosed in the narrow end of a natural funnel. At the same time, on the opposite wing near the coast there was room for cavalry to manoeuvre, and Cromwell saw that if the right wing of the Scottish cavalry could be broken and turned back into this funnel, between the ravine and the hill, Lesley's large numbers would become a hindrance, for in such a narrow space there would not be room for twenty-two thousand men to be effective.

His plan, however, depended entirely upon the success of the assault upon the Scottish right, and that in turn depended upon the discipline and precision of the initial manœuvre. The time chosen for the attack was daybreak September 3, and certain selected troops, under Lambert and the most experienced commanders,[32] crossed the burn during the night.

The Scottish troops spent an uncomfortable night in cold wind and rain among the stooks of corn, and many of their

---

30. Burnet, *History of My Own Time*, I, 95 f.
31. The English would then be able to escape only by the sea, or into hostile country, and be cut off from their ships. Sir Charles Firth shows that the Scots' movement to the right was considerable. *Oliver Cromwell*, 282.
32. One false move, and these picked troops would have been cut off. Lambert, who as Major-General would normally have commanded the foot in the centre, actually commanded the horse on the left wing, together with Harrison and Whalley. Colonel Monk was put in command of the centre, while Cromwell, with his own cavalry regiment and the veteran foot regiments of Pride and Overton, executed a wide enveloping movement to turn the Scottish right wing into the centre. It will be noticed, therefore, that all the weight and experience of Cromwell's army was concentrated in turning the Scots' right flank.

officers left their men in order to seek shelter for themselves in nearby villages.[33] On the other hand, the wintry conditions helped to cover the English moves, for just before dawn a strong body of troops crossed the ravine, and a feint attack was opened by a minor body of cavalry supported by the artillery on the Scottish left flank. Then the major attack on the right developed, and Monk, with the artillery in support, brought about a general engagement. The Scots rallied to meet Lambert's charge, while Monk could make little progress in the centre. Temporarily checked, Lambert charged again, a little more towards his left, while Cromwell – with Psalm sixty-eight upon his lips – struck on the extreme right flank of the Scottish army. Lambert's charge this time was completely successful, and the foot regiments Cromwell had with him broke through. Gradually, and then with increasing momentum, as Oliver had foreseen, the whole of the Scottish right wing began to turn into their own infantry, until very soon Lesley's army of twenty-two thousand men became a rabble stampeding into the bottleneck of escape.[34] As the rout developed into a pursuit, Cromwell halted his men to sing Psalm 117 in thanksgiving for victory – a spiritual exercise with certain practical advantages.[35] Of Lesley's great army three thousand were killed, and ten thousand were taken prisoner, while Cromwell's first estimate of his own losses was as low as twenty men.[36]

He was jubilant, as he had every reason to be, and we get a vivid picture of the strange frenzy which the success wrought upon him in the fact that immediately after the battle he wrote to everyone about it – to the Speaker,[37] Bradshaw,[38] Ireton,[39] Lord Wharton,[40] Hazelrigge,[41] Richard Mayor,[42] and to his own wife.[43]

---

33. Another unfortunate circumstance from the Scots' point of view was the fact that there was a general order to the infantry that none but the file leaders were to keep their match alight. Bates, *Elenchus Motuum*, II, 106.
34. John Hodgson, *Memoirs* (printed in *Original Memoirs written during the Great Civil War*, edited by Sir Walter Scott, 1806), 146–8. Hodgson gives credit for the plan to Lambert. *Ibid.*, 144–6.
35. It is the shortest psalm, having only two verses.
36. Cf. Cromwell's letter to Lenthall, September 4, 1650.
37. *W.S.*, II, 321–5; *L-C*, II, 102–10 (CXL).
38. September 4. *W.S.*, II, 326; *L-C*, II, 112–14 (CXLII).
39. September 4. *W.S.*, II, 327 f.; *L-C*, II, 116–18 (CXLV).
40. September 4. *W.S.*, II, 328 f.; *L-C*, II, 119 (CXLVI).
41. September 4. *W.S.*, II, 326 f.; *L-C*, II, 111–12 (CXLI).
42. September 4. *W.S.*, II, 329 f.; *L-C*, II, 115 f. (CXLIV).
43. September 4. *W.S.* II, 329; *L-C*, II, 114 f. (CXLIII).

The Scottish Campaign: Dunbar

Dunbar was to Cromwell nothing short of divine intervention on his behalf, the vindication of his faith and the principles for which he had fought, and in his letter to Lenthall he did not hesitate to press home the moral of the victory for the benefit of those who were at Westminster:

> We that serve you beg of you not to own us, but God alone; we pray you own His people more and more, for they are the chariots and horsemen of Israel.[44] Disown yourselves, but own your authority, and improve it to curb the proud and insolent, such as would disturb the tranquility of England, though under what specious pretences soever; relieve the oppressed, hear the groans of poor prisoners in England; be pleased to reform the abuses of all professions; and if there be any one that makes many poor to make a few rich, that suits not a Commonwealth. If He that strengthens your servants to fight, pleases to give you hearts to set upon these things, in order to His glory, and the glory of your Commonwealth, besides the benefit England shall feel thereby, you shall shine forth to other nations, who shall emulate the glory of such a pattern, and through the power of God turn into the like.

The letter reads less like a despatch from a successful general than the exhortation of a prophet, and perhaps the author intended it to be so. It summarized a political programme which Cromwell had already outlined to Edmund Ludlow as minimum requirements for the nation's health, and there was even a hint of future foreign policy, but the immediate significance of the letter was in the domestic affairs of England, for if the Lord General felt it incumbent upon him to speak thus in the name of his God to the present rulers at Westminster, what if they failed to pursue these ends?

If the letter to Lenthall drew the moral for the government, the letter he wrote to his wife pointed the lesson for himself:

> My Dearest,
>
> I have not leisure to write much, but I could chide thee that in many of thy letters thou writest to me, that I should not be unmindful of thee and thy little ones. Truly, if I love thee not too well, I think I err not on the other hand much. Thou art dearer to me than any creature; let that suffice.
>
> The Lord hath showed us an exceeding mercy: who can tell how great it is. My weak faith hath been upheld. I have been in my

---

44. 2 Kings 2:12. Cromwell's use of capitalization for the Divine pronouns should be noted. He tended to do this when profoundly moved to express his humility before God.

inward man marvellously supported; though I assure thee, I grow an old man, and feel infirmities of age marvellously stealing upon me. Would my corruptions did as fast decrease.

Primarily this is a love-letter, but it contained tremendous auguries for the future in the simple confession, "My weak faith hath been upheld."

IV

Edinburgh and the West

From a military point of view Dunbar was as decisive for Scottish hopes as Naseby had been for the hopes of Charles I. David Lesley's great army had been irretrievably crushed,[45] and the way was open for the English to attack Edinburgh and to win control of Scotland south of the Forth. The rest of the campaign indeed serves only to emphasize the completeness of the victory, which seems to have staggered even Cromwell's own friends, who hastened to counsel moderation, and to remind him that whereas those against whom he had fought previously "had the visible character of God's displeasure upon them", his present opponents were of the people "by and for whom these great deliverances are to be wrought".[46]

The Lord General himself, however, was far more interested in weaning the Scots from Charles Stuart than in pursuing them with any great severity.[47] David Lesley, with the remnants of his Dunbar army and a number of hastily gathered levies, took up a position at Stirling, and Charles was at Perth awaiting recruits from the royalist highlands. Rumour had it that the young King was not displeased with the Dunbar battle,[48] for, as Cromwell foresaw, Scottish affairs would now move away from the domination of the Kirk towards national royalism.[49] There were, however,

---

45. Lesley had been soundly criticized, but he was retained in his command. Baillie, *Letters and Journals*, III, 111, 132.
46. Letter from Oliver St. John. Cf. *L-C*, II, 117 n.
47. One of his first actions after the battle was to issue a Proclamation of clemency and aid for the wounded Scots left behind on the field of battle (*W.S.*, II, 320 f.), and in his letter to Hazelrigge, September 5, he shows himself to have been gravely concerned at the wretched plight of many of the Scots prisoners. *Ibid.*, 331 f.; *L-C*, III, 270 f. (App. 19).
48. Clarendon, *History*, XIII, 23.
49. "Surely it's probable the Kirk has done their do. I believe their King will set up upon his own score now, wherein he will find many friends, taking opportunity offered." To Hazelrigge, September 4. *W.S.*, II, 327; *L-C*, II, 112. Cf. Clarendon, *History*, XIII, 23.

still the extreme Covenanters of the West, like Strachan and Kerr, and Cromwell's immediate diplomatic aim was to drive a wedge between these men and the royal cause.[50] He first occupied the city of Edinburgh, from whence he conducted an offensive which was more theological than military against the governor of the castle. To the Presbyterian ministers who preferred to shelter there rather than accept his invitations to preach openly in the city Cromwell addressed some pertinent words on freedom of speech,[51] but he reserved his most withering scorn for their objection to the lay preaching within the ranks of the English Army.[52]

The Lord General was undecided what to do: the disunity of the forces opposed to him, the smallness of his own army numerically, and not least, the completeness of his victory, seem to have found him momentarily at a loss. He marched to Stirling and summoned the town, but returned to Edinburgh on September 20. An expedition to attack Charles in the county of

---

50. Strachan, Wariston, and others of the Covenanting party had held an abortive conference with Cromwell's officers in August. *W.S.*, II, 308 n.
51. The ministers of England are supported, and have liberty to preach the Gospel, though not to rail, nor, under pretence thereof to overtop the civil power, or debase it as they please. No man hath been troubled in England or Ireland for preaching the Gospel, nor has any minister been molested in Scotland since the coming of the army hither. The speaking truth becomes the ministers of Christ." September 9, 1650. *W.S.*, II, 335–6; *L-C*, II, 122 f. (CXLVII). For the ministers' reply to Cromwell through Dundas, cf. *L-C*, II, 124 f.
52. "Are you troubled that Christ is preached? Is preaching so inclusive in your function? Doth it scandalize the Reformed Kirks, and Scotland in particular? Is it against the Covenant? Away with the Covenant, if it be so! I thought the Covenant and these could have been willing that any should speak good of the name of Christ; if not, it is no Covenant of God's approving, nor the Kirks you mention in so much the Spouse of Christ. ... I hope He that ascended up on high [Ephesians 4:8 f.] may give His gifts to whom He please: and if those gifts be the seal of mission, be not envious though Eldad and Medad prophesy [Numbers 11:25–9]. You know who bids us covet earnestly the best gifts, but chiefly that we may prophesy [1 Corinthians 12:31 f.]; which the Apostle explains there to be a speaking to instruction and edification and comfort, which the instructed, edified and comforted, can best tell the energy and effect of. If such evidence be, I say again, take heed you envy not for your own sakes, lest you be guilty of a greater fault than Moses reproved in Joshua for envying for his sake [Numbers 11:25–9].

"Indeed you err through the mistake of the Scriptures. Approbation is an act of conveniency in respect of order; not of necessity to give faculty to preach the Gospel. Your pretended fear lest error should step in, is like the man that would keep all the wine out the country lest men should be drunk. It will be found an unjust and unwise jealousy, to deny a man the liberty he hath by nature upon a supposition he may abuse it. When he doth abuse it, judge." Sept. 12, W.S. II, 337–9, L.C, II. 125–31, (CXLVIII).

Fife was initiated, but almost immediately abandoned,[53] and an elaborate attempt to mine Edinburgh Castle was started, but the field of diplomacy seemed to offer most hope of success.[54]

Partly as a show of strength, and partly to conciliate the inhabitants, Cromwell made a brief visit to Glasgow,[55] but on his return he found that his attempts to draw the Western Covenanters away from Charles were not without their effect, for they had openly denounced the agreement with Charles and voiced doubts about his sincerity. Soon, as the result of a series of quarrels in Scottish affairs and of minor military action, the opposition in this quarter disappeared, and this simplified matters for the English,[56] for it left them with only the Army which Lesley commanded in the name of the King and the Estates to oppose them. Once Edinburgh Castle was reduced they would be free to march against Charles. Progress had been made in mining the castle, but eventually after protracted negotiations[57] and a desultory resistance, the governor, Sir Walter Dundas, capitulated to generous terms, and the garrison marched out on December 25.[58]

The fall of Edinburgh without anything more than a token resistance was received with fury at the court of the King,[59] and it was a sure sign that a wedge had been driven between the Estates and Charles on the one hand, and the more rigorous supporters of the Covenant on the other. This was sufficiently

---

53. The boats were ordered to Leith on September 27th, and men were actually embarked, but then recalled.
54. Cf. letter to Scottish Committee of Estates, October 9. *W.S.*, II, 349 f.; *L-C*, II, 140 f. (CL).
55. Perhaps it was to impress Glasgow with the orthodoxy of the English army that Captain Covell was court-martialled and cashiered there. Cf. Firth, *Cromwell's Army*, 347 f.; *W.S.*, II, 353 f. It is of interest to notice, too, that in addition to the chaplain, William Good, who accompanied the army, Cromwell had sent a request to Westminster that the Congregationalists, John Owen and Joseph Caryl, together with the popular Presbyterian preacher, Edward Bowles, should be sent to Scotland, September 17. Whitelocke, 471; cf. *W.S.*, II, 346.
56. Moss troopers were beginning to appear, similar to the English Clubmen. Many such groups were officered by cavaliers who had been purged from Lesley's army.
57. Negotiations with Dundas: December 12, 13, 14, 18. *W.S.*, II, 366-74; *L-C*, II, 153-63 (CLIV-CLX). Letter to Lenthall, December 24. *W.S.*, II, 376; *L-C*, II, 164 f. (CLXI).
58. It conveniently allowed the Independent army to keep Christmas as a day of Thanksgiving.
59. As members of the garrison arrived in Fife they were imprisoned. Dundas did not return to the King, but stayed to dine with Cromwell; both Strachan and Johnston of Wariston soon came behind the English lines.

signalized "with great solemnity and magnificence"[60] in the coronation of Charles at Scone on January 1, 1650/51, and from this time onward Cromwell could represent the war as a war against Scottish royalism.

---

60. Clarendon, *History,* XIII, 50.

Chapter Fourteen

The Scottish Campaign: Worcester (January – September 1651)

I

The Lord General's Illness

The English Commonwealth was now in a much stronger position than it had been a year before. Prince Rupert's squadron had been almost eliminated by Blake, and with the eclipse of the house of Orange in Holland,[1] and the outbreak of the Fronde in France, the two foreign powers most likely to take arms against the republic were temporarily silenced. Spain had taken the step of recognizing the Commonwealth in the hope of enlisting its services against France, Henry Ireton's clearing-up operations in Ireland, if not spectacular, were effective, and the Stuarts' only hope of recovery lay in Scotland; but with Cromwell in control of the south, Charles could not allow the situation there to remain static indefinitely.

For the first few months of 1651 the weather caused the suspension of military operations in Scotland, except for the clearance of the southern part of the country from moss troopers and the reduction of a few castles.[2] But Cromwell's responsibilities within the State were increasing, and he was now being kept fully informed by the Council of State of England's position both at home and abroad.[3] His personal prestige increased with his responsibilities. Parliament sent an engraver to prepare a cast of his features for a medal to celebrate Dunbar,[4] and he was elected

---

1. William II of Orange had died in November 1650, and De Witt had come to power.
2. Dumfries, Kirkcudbright, Kenmure Castle and Hume Castle taken. Monk took Tantallon Castle on February 23, and Fast Castle was taken a few days later.
3. *W.S.*, II, 386. The Council had voted that Cromwell should be kept fully informed of all important matters affecting the safety of the Commonwealth (January 24).
4. Not with Cromwell's consent. Cf. letter to the Committee of the Army, February 4, 1650/51. *W.S.*, II, 391; *L-C*, II, 175 f. (CLXV).

Chancellor of Oxford University.⁵ By these and similar means, "little by little, in his various capacities, he came more and more to be the center and directing force in the three kingdoms".⁶

On February 4, 1651, the Army set out in very rough weather for Linlithgow, but although the English reached Kilsyth on the 7th in an attempt to drive into Fife, the weather deteriorated so rapidly that they were forced back to Edinburgh. This excursion had serious results, for Cromwell was taken dangerously ill, and during the next three weeks suffered no less than three successive relapses.⁷ He seems to have recovered to some extent by March 4,⁸ but his illness gave rise to the gravest concern and it brought military operations almost to a standstill in Scotland. Meanwhile, rumours of his death sped all over the country, for Robert Baillie commented in his notes, "A word of Crumweel's death, Sabath, March 9, when I was within praying for the King, and against him", but on March 23 he added somewhat impatiently: "Rumours of Crumweel's miserabill dath continuing."⁹ Nothing illustrates better how the future of the Commonwealth seemed to centre in the person of Cromwell than the eagerness with which his enemies seized upon the possibility of his death.¹⁰ It was at this juncture that a serious royalist plot with ramifications throughout England was discovered. The government acted energetically – governors of garrisons were ordered back to their posts and the traitor Captain Browne Bushell¹¹ was executed as a warning to others of his kind; but the conjunction of the plot

---

5. To Dr. Greenwood, February 4. *W.S.*, II, 392; *L-C*, II, 180 f. (CLXVI). In this letter Cromwell regretted the fact that public duties prevented his active interest in the affairs of the university but promised "you shall not want my prayers that that seed and stock of piety and learning, so marvellously springing up amongst you, may be useful to that great and glorious Kingdom of our Lord Jesus Christ."
6. R.H. Abbott. *W.S.*, II, 386.
7. Apparently he was able to get through a certain amount of work in between the attacks; cf. letters to Dr. Greenwood, February 14, *W.S.*, II, 394; *L-C*, II, 182 f. (CLXVII); to the Justices of Wilts., February 23, *W.S.*, II, 395. He also signed a pass on February 25 and wrote to Westminster to raise Colonel Fenwick's regiment to a strength of 1,600. Cf. *ibid.*, 395.
8. i.e. sufficiently to write a note to Sir John Wollaston on that day (*W.S.*, II, 396); a letter on behalf of Colonel John Lilburne on March 8 (*ibid.*, 396 f.; *L-C*, II, 183 (CLXVIII)); to Lenthall, March 11, advocating the establishment of a university or university college at Durham from the endowment of the Dean and ChapteR.*W.S.*, II, 397 f.; *L-C*, II, 186 f. (CLXIX).
9. *Letters and Journals*, I, cix.
10. Cf. *infra*, p. 238 f.
11. Browne Bushell had voluntarily given up his ship to Rupert in 1640.

with Cromwell's sickness had given London cause for concern and the Council of State sent Mr. Jenkin Lloyd to Scotland to convey its condolences to the General, and doubtless also to discover what cause it might have for alarm. Meanwhile, the extent of the royalist plot only became known when Thomas Coke, One of those implicated, was captured in London.[12] Offered his life in exchange for information, Coke revealed that well-known people in practically every county were involved and he also accused certain popular Presbyterian ministers of London.[13] Of these, Christopher Love, Thomas Case and William Jenkins, together with five laymen, were arrested, and certain new dispositions were made in the Army to suppress any attempt at a general rising.

By the end of March Cromwell had recovered sufficiently to think again about taking the initiative against the Scots,[14] and by April 12 he wrote to his wife in deep thankfulness for his recovery.[15] Had he been in private life he would doubtless have regarded his recovery as a "providence", but coming as it did at this juncture in public affairs his illness could only have been to him a special providence which re-emphasized his complete dependence upon God. Indeed there are some grounds for thinking that the combination of his own sickness and the discovery of the royalist plot hardened Cromwell a good deal in his attitude towards the Scots,[16] for Colonel Kerr reported to Johnston of Wariston that he had been heard to utter some hard words about the Scottish ministry, and in the view of both Wariston and his friend this portended "the Lord's hardning him the mor by his seaknesse and preparing for a stroak".[17] Cromwell's coolness

---

12. Papers proving the complicity of Coke and others had been taken from Isaac Birkenhead.
13. Thomas Coke was the son of Charles I's Secretary of State. The ministers charged by him included Edmund Calamy, but the grandson of the latter makes no reference to this in his autobiography, although he says "he was very active in the Restoration of King Charles II, in 1660". *Historical account of my own Life*, I (1829), 55, by Edmund Calamy (2 vols.).
14. Blackness Castle blockaded and taken, and the relieving force cut off by Monk.
15. *W.S.*, II, 404 f.; *L-C*, II, 189 f. (CLXXI).
16. This change of attitude was noticed by Lady Wariston, Lady Ingliston, and by Wariston himself. *Diary of Sir Archibald Johnston of Wariston* (ed. Fleming, Edinburgh, 1919), 35–7.
17. *Ibid.*, 39. Cromwell joined the army at Hamilton on April 19. He went on to Glasgow and was sufficiently recovered to listen to three Scottish sermons the next day. Baillie, *Letters and Journals*, III 165.

towards Wariston may have been no more than his weariness at being repeatedly badgered about the Scottish registers, but when we remember his implacability towards the perpetrators of the Second Civil War, the revelation of England's danger brought to light by the recent plot and by his own illness might very well cause him to lose patience with Scottish waverers and their pretensions.

A brief excursion to Glasgow may have been an attempt to keep the city and university quiet by a show of strength,[18] but intelligence had been received of an attempt by Charles to pass the English Army and to invade England.[19] By the end of May the affairs of the Commonwealth were not progressing as favourably as its position in January seemed to forecast. Abroad its position had deteriorated,[20] in England the government had not yet recovered from the shock at discovering the strength of organized royalism throughout the country,[21] and in Scotland events had been held up by Cromwell's ill health. While he had been in Glasgow Cromwell had renewed his discussions with the Scottish theologians of the town and university, and R.H. Abbott suggested that what gold had accomplished in Ireland Oliver hoped "persuasion might achieve in Scotland, for his eloquence was as much a part of his equipment for the conquest of Scotland as his artillery, and scarcely less effective".[22] This is undoubtedly true, since he would not have employed theological argument if he had not thought it would prove effective, but we cannot simply dismiss it as a military expedient: the effectiveness of an argument is determined by its soundness, and Cromwell's readiness to enter theological controversy shows us how firmly his convictions were held.

---

18. As suggested by R.H. Abbott. *W.S.*, II, 409. Cromwell had returned to Edinburgh by May 2.
19. Letter to Harrison, May 3. *W.S.*, II, 411 f.; *L-C*, III, 276–7 (App. 20). Cf. Whitelocke. "It was conjectured that the Scots would decline any Engagement with the English, but weary them out and take the first Opportunity to get by them into England" (May 26). Whitelocke, 494.
20. Ascham, the newly appointed ambassador to Spain, had been murdered by English royalists almost as soon as he had arrived (May 27). Rupert had escaped from Blake and gone to Barbados, which had declared for Charles, and the warfare of privateers between English and French ships in the Channel was hindering commerce.
21. Perhaps this shock was the reason why waverers like Robert Hammond tried to re-enter the army. Hammond had retired on pension, but it is clear from Cromwell's reply to him on May 13 that Hammond had intimated a desire to return to the government's service. *W.S.*, II, 418; *L-C*, III, 431 (Supp. 65).
22. *W.S.*, II, 415.

Upon his return to Edinburgh the Lord General was perplexed about what next to do. Wariston says that Cromwell admitted he was never in more doubt what he should do, whether he should go into Fife, or back to the Borders, or to the West, and that his "perplexity maid him grow unweal".[23] With unconscious humour the Scot records that Cromwell became ill after he had received Wariston's last letter about the Scottish registers,[24] but whatever the reason – the weather, his own indecision, or as Wariston complacently asserts, his "unrighteous dealing" about the Scottish registers – Cromwell fell ill again and suffered several violent attacks in the space of a few days.

The news of this relapse again alarmed the members of the government in London and they immediately despatched Dr. Bates and Dr. Wright to join Cromwell's physician in Scotland. Whitelocke says that "there was some Damp upon the English Army by the Sickness of the General", and Parliament suggested that Oliver should retire to a healthier place in England and entrust the remainder of the Scottish campaign to anyone he thought fit.[25] It was observed, however, that the news of his illness did not so much depress the English "as it heightened the Scots, who were very much elevated with the fancy of his death; believing the slightest report of it to be the real truth, because it corresponded with their desires."[26]

The attack, although violent while it lasted, ended as suddenly as it had begun, and by the time Bates and Wright had reached Scotland Cromwell was well on the way to a good recovery. In the final paragraph of a letter to Bradshaw he commented upon a thought which must have passed through the minds of many at Westminster. "I wish", he said, "more steadiness in your affairs here than to depend, in the least, upon so frail a thing as I am. Indeed they do not, nor on any instrument."[27] Certain alterations in the command of the Army had already been made in Scotland, possibly as a precautionary measure,[28] but by June 9

---

23. *Diary*, 53.
24. *Ibid.*, 54 f.
25. Whitelocke, 494.
26. *The Perfect Politician: Or a Full View of the Life and Actions (Military and Civil) of O. Cromwel.* Probably written by Henry Fletcher, and first published in 1660. The quotation is from the 3rd edition of 1681, 130 f.
27. June 3. *W.S.*, II, 421; *L-C*, II, 201 f. (CLXXIV).
28. Lambert had been promoted Lieutenant-General in Fleetwood's place, Deane, although still commanding the fleet in the Firth of Forth, was made Major-General, and Monk became Lieutenant-General of the Ordnance.

Whitelocke records that Westminster had received "Letters of the General's good Recovery of Health again, and that the Doctors were returned from him".[29] That recovery had come none too soon, for the English had lost the initiative in Scotland and were hardly holding their own.[30]

Twice within a few months Cromwell had been laid low by illness, and twice he had been granted a miraculous recovery, and he was beginning to realize how much the stability of the Commonwealth was bound up in his own person. What, then, could be the meaning of his successive bouts of sickness, unless God was testing his faith?[31] What was he to learn from his recovery, unless it was God's sign that he had been raised up to finish the task he had begun? In a letter to Richard Mayor on June 28, which had some pertinent things to say about young Richard Cromwell's extravagances, he gives us some insight into the spiritual foundations of his own public career, for he commented that it was not fitting for his son to "make pleasures the business of his life, in a time when some precious Saints are bleeding, and breathing out their last, for the safety of the rest".[32] To do the will of God, and to work for these same "precious saints", this was the only business for a man worthy of the name: these were the reasons for undertaking the hazards of public services, "for which a man is born".[33]

II

The Expedition to Fife: Inverkeithing

Whatever theological inferences the Lord General drew from

---

29. Whitelocke, 494.
30. Colonel Alured had abandoned Dumfries, and Broghill Castle was eventually reoccupied by the Scots. The Clydesdale district had slipped from English control, and the same was beginning to happen throughout the whole of the western districts.
31. This conception of "special providences" can be seen in the diaries of Richard Rogers and Samuel Ward in *Two Elizabethan Puritan Diaries*. Compare, too, the following extract from the *Autobiography of Sir Simon D'Ewes, Bart.* (ed. J. O. Halliwell, 1845): "I suppose there scarce lives any man but hath escaped sickness and danger in his infancy; but that I should survive so many several hazards, is I believe altogether without parallel and almost past belief and therefore requireth the greater thankfulness from me: and did not evil times threaten a speedy ruin to truth and piety, I would hope to live to do good service both to Church and Commonwealth, and that it should appear that God had not delivered me out of so many perils but to some public end." I, 32.
32. *W.S.*, II, 425 f.; *L-C*, II, 209–11 (CLXXVIII).
33. Letter to Mayor, August 13, 1649.

his recovery, it was very soon evident that the period of military inactivity was at an end. Moving on June 30, 1651, the English forces advanced as far as Falkirk, and the Scots retreated, but Cromwell was quite unable to tempt Lesley from his position, nor was he able to engineer any means of outflanking the enemy. He was determined, however, to bring matters to an issue in Scotland, and since the Scots refused every offer of open battle Cromwell returned to a project which had been first mooted in the previous September:[34] "My Lord General having offered the Enemy Battle at Torwood, and finding it was their Intention to delay the War, took counsel to adventure the landing of some forces on the Fife side."[35] On July 17 Colonel Overton embarked from Leith with a comparatively small force to land at North Ferry, which was on a narrow peninsula of land on the Fife coast opposite Queensferry. Such a peninsula could be held against the whole Scottish Army if Overton could be given time to consolidate his position, but the English had to take the risk of Lesley quickly sending an overpowering force along the north bank of the estuary of the Forth and crushing the invaders as they landed. On the other hand, if the bridgehead could be maintained, Lesley's position at Stirling would become untenable and Cromwell would be in a position to drive into Fife, the centre of Scottish resistance. Lesley sent Major-General Sir John Browne with about four thousand men to deal with Overton,[36] but on the night of July 17 Lambert was sent over to take command, with two horse and two foot regiments. By Sunday, July 20, Lambert was on the peninsula in command of five thousand men. The two forces met at Inverkeithing at the neck of the peninsula, and for some time faced each other without moving, but Lambert, receiving news that Cromwell was retreating[37] and that Browne was receiving reinforcements, attacked immediately, and was completely successful.[38] The total number of troops engaged in the battle was less than half the Scottish army at Dunbar, and yet it has been

---

34. *Supra*, p. 231–2 and n.
35. From Lambert's letter. Whitelocke, 499.
36. Overton had about 1,400 men with him.
37. An erroneous report based on the movement of fresh dispositions in the English army.
38. Browne was fatally wounded; 2,000 Scots were killed, and there were 1,500–1,600 prisoners. Cf. letter cited in note 2 *infra* p. 241, also the letter to Lenthall, July 22. *W.S.*, II, 434; L-C, III, 433 (Supp. 67), and Lambert's account in Whitelocke, 499.

The Scottish Campaign: Worcester

pointed out that its results were hardly less important,[39] for with the way into Fife standing wide open, Lesley's impregnable position at Stirling had been turned, and the end of the war in Scotland was in sight.

To Cromwell himself it must have seemed like another miracle. At the end of June he had had very little idea how to bring matters to a head: the decision to land on the coast of Fife had been taken, "after waiting upon God, and not knowing what course to take", and later on in a letter he admitted that he and his officers were quite at a loss to know how they might get to grips with Lesley's army.[40] It seemed to be a repetition of the same Grace that had been with them at Dunbar: in both cases the English Army had faced an impasse, and in both cases a God-given inspiration had miraculously opened the way.

On hearing the news of Lambert's victory the first reaction of the Scots was to move with all their force and meet this threat to their rear, but having advanced a few miles it was clear that Cromwell would follow and they would then have the English on two sides of them. The Scottish army therefore returned to Stirling, leaving the initiative wholly in Cromwell's hands. He decided to exploit the situation in Fife to the full, and his troops began to embark on July 23. He reached Perth (St. Johnstons) on August 1, and having sent a summons to the governor,[41] he bombarded the town.

It was while he was before Perth that he received the not altogether unexpected news that the Scottish army was staging a counter-invasion. The move had been anticipated some time before, and with the breakdown of Lesley's Fabian defence it was to be expected that Charles would have his way and a more spectacular strategy would be employed. Indeed, Cromwell had not left the enemy generals very much choice of action. They were unwilling to meet his troops a second time in open battle, and short of being banished to the highlands or being completely surrounded, they had no choice but to march south and hope that they could gather enough strength from English royalists either to cut through the English militia, or to face Cromwell when he had caught up with them. Given the character of the

---

39. Abbott, *W.S.*, II, 431.
40. To William Lenthall, July 21. *W.S.*, II, 432 f.; *L-C*, II, 303-5 (CLXXV).
41. *W.S.*, II, 440; *L-C*, III, 434 (Supp. 68).

young Charles Stuart and his *émigré* courtiers, there could be no doubt that this flamboyant project would be most attractive to them.

Cromwell on the other hand had little to fear, since the country was still semi-mobilized as a result of the recent royalist plot, and an invasion by the Scots would unite Englishmen behind the government. His confidence is reflected in the fact that after hearing the news of the Scots' march south he continued his operations against Perth,[42] which surrendered on August 2.[43] From his letter to Lenthall announcing the surrender[44] it is clear that he had not only risked the Scottish invasion, but that to some extent he had engineered it, since only by transporting most of his army over the Forth could he shift Lesley from the position at Stirling. There was, so Cromwell believed, in every situation an inner "necessity" by which all things moved to their pre-destined end, and such a necessity was present in this desperate invasion of England. It would drive the Scottish Army to inevitable destruction, and bring a final settlement with the house of Stuart, which would end once and for all its power to disturb the peace of England.

III

Worcester

The Scots began to march for England on July 31, 1651, and by August 5 they were crossing the English borders. Charles was proclaimed King of England at Carlisle on the following day, and issued a general invitation to the English to join him, but the response was disappointing. The plain fact of the matter was that whatever the shortcomings of the Commonwealth government it had given England a certain measure of peace and security, and while the great majority of Englishmen was probably royalist at heart, they were not prepared to accept the depredations of another ruinous war in exchange for doubtful preferences in the matter of government. The attitude of those who did find themselves in Charles's army is described by the young Duke of Hamilton:

> We have quit Scotland, being scarcely able to maintain it; and

---

42. Harrison was despatched with a force of cavalry to harass the Scots' army.
43. The articles of surrendeR.W.S., II, 442.
44. August 4. *W.S.*, II, 443-5; *L-C*, II, 213-15 (CLXXX).

yet we grasp at all, and nothing but all will satisfy us, or to lose all. I confess I cannot tell you whether our hopes or fears are greatest: but we have one stout argument, despair; for we must now either stoutly fight it, or die.[45]

It was said that after Charles's proclamation to the country, some of the gentry joined him, but "only two thousand of the Common People"[46] and the efficiency with which the recent insurrection had been stamped out had a good deal to do with the general reluctance to join the royal cause. Contributory causes were the suddenness of the invasion, the efficiency of the Commonwealth in raising troops, and the memory of recent atrocities committed by the Scots in England.[47]

The Scots Army could survive only by a miracle of the kind granted to Cromwell at Dunbar, but miracles did not seem to be attracted to the Stuart cause. Harrison was in front of the invading army, and Lambert was in its rear; the Scots were marching into a hostile country where every county was mobilizing local forces to oppose them, and Cromwell, whose tactics had defeated their ablest general at Dunbar, whose strategy had outwitted him in Fife, and whose legendary invincibility had yet to be disproved, was marching inexorably towards them with the main body of the experienced English army. Cromwell set out for England on August 6, and took the easterly route, probably so that he could intervene more quickly in the event of the Scots striking for London. Lambert was at Penrith, about a day's journey behind Charles, and Harrison was at Ripon.

Meanwhile Fairfax was organizing the Yorkshire militia and Fleetwood was preparing the defence of the capital, while all over the country the county militia was put into readiness. Just as Lambert guided Hamilton to the west three years earlier, so now he and Harrison[48] shepherded Charles away from the capital and ushered him into the western cul-de-sac, although there were several reasons why Charles was not unwilling to keep to the western districts. His troops were badly in need of a rest and could be put in to garrison a fortified town, and he would be near three districts to which the Stuarts had never appealed in vain for recruits – Wales, Gloucester and Cornwall. On this

---

45. Hamilton to Crofts, August 8. Henry Cary, *Memorials of the great Civil War in England, 1646–52* (1842), II, 305 (2 vols.).
46. Bates, *Elenchus*, Pt. 2, 122 marginal note (1685 edn.).
47. *Ibid.*, 122–8.
48. Their forces had united on August 14th. *W.S.*, II, 448.

occasion, however, they failed to respond, but Charles succeeded in occupying Worcester on August 22.

The armies of the Commonwealth were beginning to converge. Fleetwood had advanced with his London troops as far as Banbury, and other formidable forces were stationed at Oxford, Reading and Bristol. Cromwell reached Leicester on the 23rd[49] and then turned west, and on the 24th a conference of General Officers was held at Warwick. On the 26th Robert Lilburne utterly defeated Lord Derby at Wigan, and on the following day Cromwell wrote a letter to Lord Wharton,[50] in which he pointed out that although Wharton and other waverers had "helped one another to stumble at the dispensations of God", now they had "an opportunity to associate with His people, in His work". He went on to observe that the task ahead did not need their help, "save as our Lord and Master needed the Beast,[51] to show His Humility, meekness and condescension: but you need it to declare your submission to, and owning yourself the Lord's and His people's."

The end of the civil war which had ravaged the country since 1642 was in sight. To Cromwell the issue had all the way through been a simple issue, and he protested to Wharton: "Do not say, you are now satisfied because it is the old quarrel; as if it had not been so, all this while"; whether the fighting had been against Anglican royalists, Irish Catholics, Scottish Presbyterians or republican Levellers it had been one and the same struggle for "the Lord against His and His people's enemies", and the proof was to be found in nine years of unbroken military success which God had granted to one who had single-mindedly undertaken the struggle in His name. Such an over-simplification, of course, was hardly possible to anyone but Cromwell himself, but we can no more expect him to understand why the issue appeared less simple than that to Wharton or Hammond, than we could expect him to understand the Roman Catholic prelates of Clonmacnoise. But although Cromwell did over-simplify the issues, that over-simplification was valid for him: one may doubt whether Cromwell was indeed "the instrument" of the Almighty's purpose in England, but one cannot doubt that Cromwell believed himself to be so.

---

49. At Ferrybridge he had met and conferred with Fairfax.
50. *W.S.*, II, 453; *L-C*, II, 219 (CLXXXI).
51. A reference to the as? on which Christ rode into Jerusalem on Palm Sunday.

The Scottish Campaign: Worcester

He now faced Charles in Worcester with a force of twenty-eight thousand men,[52] i.e. about double the strength of Charles's army, and Charles was caught in a strategic trap.[53] Cromwell obviously intended not only the defeat of Charles's army but also the complete destruction of royalism's power to wage war. For this reason, though there could hardly be any doubt about the ultimate result, he laid the plans with extreme care.[54] Boats were gathered to provide temporary bridges more or less at the confluence of the Severn and the Teme, and since the forces available were large enough, they were divided into two parts with the river between. Lambert and Harrison were stationed to the east on the hills to block any attempt by the defenders to break out towards London.

On September 3, exactly one year after the miraculous victory at Dunbar, "Cromwell himself in person (about 3. a Clock with his Life guard, and Collonel Hackers Regiment, and Collonel Ingoldsby's, and Fairfax's entire) passed over his Bridge of Boats upon the Severn",[55] and the attack had begun in earnest. At the same time, Fleetwood's men crossed the Teme by means of a bridge of boats and by fording the river lower down near the broken bridge at Powick. The battle cry was "The Lord of Hosts" as it had been at Dunbar.[56]

This battle on the western bank of the Severn was grimly contested, for the low scrub prevented the English cavalry from being very effective, but eventually weight of numbers pushed the defenders back to St. John's whence they were driven into the town and the west gate of Worcester was secured by the

---

52. Raised to 31,000 by the arrival of the Essex and Suffolk militia.
53. Hilaire Belloc thought that Cromwell was a bad strategist and that the moves leading to the Worcester battle were a major blunder. In view of the fact that Cromwell finished his operations before Perth before marching south, and in view of the care with which the Scottish army was shepherded away from London and every provision made for its total destruction, we feel more inclined to agree with John Buchan when he said that: "In the Worcester campaign ... he opened the door to the invader, and by a precise concentration at the right point made victory certain." Buchan, *Oliver Cromwell,* 401 f., cf. Belloc, *Cromwell,* 142.
54. He was probably ready to attack by September 2, but awaited his propitious day; cf. *W.S.,* II, 458. Clarendon wrote later that "Cromwell used none of the delay nor circumspection which was imagined, but directed the troops to fall on in all places at once". *H story,* XIII, 75. But Clarendon was not present.
55. *Flagellum,* 115(3rd edn.).
56. Robert Stapleton's letter to Westminster, September 3, 1651. Whitelocke, 507.

English Meanwhile, Charles decided on a daring move, which might well have retrieved the day. Putting himself at the head of his cavalry Charles rode out to the east and attacked Lambert and Harrison on the eastern slopes, and succeeded in pushing the Parliamentarians up Red Hill, but the resistance was just too stubborn for Charles to smash Lambert's force before Cromwell arrived from the western bank with the needed reinforcements. Even then it was only after three hours of stubborn fighting that Charles's Scottish army was beaten back into the city of Worcester. Fort Royal refused quarter and its garrison was slain by the Essex militia,[57] and then its guns were turned on the rest of the city holding out. About four thousand of the defenders escaped out of the north gate, but the great majority of these were taken during the next few weeks in the net which Cromwell had spread for them.

Hamilton's argument of despair had not been successful,[58] but it had proved itself a "stout argument", for Cromwell himself described the victory as "as stiff a contest, for four or five hours, as ever I have seen".[59] As at Drogheda, he had himself taken a full part in the actual fighting,[60] and at ten o'clock on the day of the battle, "being so weary, and scarce able to write", he dashed off a letter to Lenthall in his excitement to announce the victory. This was followed on the next day by a fuller account,[61] in which he declared, "The dimensions of this mercy are above my thoughts. It is, for aught I know, a crowning mercy. Surely if it be not, such a one we shall have."

Cromwell humbled himself before his Maker – it was his prayer that the fear of the Lord might keep all those who had been "so prospered, and blessed, and witnessed unto, humble and faithful", but he went on to urge Parliament in God's name to continue the good work.[62] It was his day. The victory had completely broken royalist hopes, and although Charles II managed to escape to France, most of those who had marched with him

---

57. In both of his letters to Lenthall on the 3rd and 4th, Cromwell emphasized the courage shown during the battle by the newly raised militia.
58. Cf. *supra*, p. 242 f.
59. September 3. *W.S.*, II, 461; *L-C*, II, 223 f. (CLXXXII).
60. *Merc. Pol.*, September 4; *Perf. Diurn.*, September 8.
61. *W.S.*, 11,462 f.; *L-C*, 11, 224–6 (CLXXXIII). Cf. Whitelocke, 507 f.
62. Cf. a letter written to Parliament on September 8 on behalf of the widow of a Worcester citizen who had been executed by Charles for his services to the Commonwealth. *W.S.*, 11,467; L-C, 111,278 f. (App. 22).

were captured.⁶³ Whitelocke, describing the reception which the Lord General received in London, says that "He carried himself with great Affability, and seeming Humility, and in all his Discourse about the Business of Worcester would seldom mention any thing of himself, but of the Gallantry of the Officers and Soldiers, and gave (as was due) all the Glory of the Action unto God".⁶⁴ But some who had come to know him best noticed that there was a significant change in his attitude. Although he had been long suspect by doctrinaire republicans like Ludlow and Hutchinson, it was apparently from the days which immediately followed Worcester that they began to discern signs of what they regarded as a fixed determination to seize the reins of government.⁶⁵ Later on Hugh Peters recalled that the alteration in Cromwell's demeanour after Worcester made such an impression upon him that on his own return to London at that time he confidently told a friend that the Lord General would make himself king.⁶⁶ This observation does not contradict what Whitelocke remarked about Oliver's "seeming humility", but rather does it illustrate the two sides of a single complex character – the one part all humility before God, and the other part, a divinely-inspired "instrument" speaking with prophetic authority.

Henceforth, Cromwell was to face battles of a different kind, but no subsequent failure could obliterate the fact that throughout nine years of almost continuous fighting, beginning as an inexperienced captain already in middle age, and emerging as the invincible Commander-in-Chief of the Commonwealth armies, "no single operation of war that he ever undertook had failed".⁶⁷ Worcester was the coping stone to a military career of unsurpassed fortune and brilliance. In a work on Cromwell's religion there would be no justification for dealing with his military successes if it were not for the fact that these victories had become an integral part of his religion: he held the simple conviction that they were due entirely to Almighty God. But he could not count it lightly that with all men to choose from, God had called *him*. Hence his "prophesying" to the men at Westminster and the authority with which he spoke and acted after Worcester. All his struggles, in politics and war, had been undertaken in the conviction

---

63. Clarendon, *History*, XIII, 78–82.
64. Whitelocke, 509.
65. Cf. Lucy Hutchinson's *Memoirs*, 284 (Everyman edn.).
66. Twice recorded in Ludlow's *Memoirs*, I, 344; II, 9.
67. Frederic Harrison, *Oliver Cromwell*, 167.

that they were necessary steps in the defeat of God's enemies and the settlement of the nation: the first object had now been gloriously achieved, could it be seriously thought that God intended to leave the second task incomplete?

Chapter Fifteen

From Worcester to the Expulsion of the Rump (September 1651 – April 1653)

I

To the majority of Cromwell's contemporaries the battle of Worcester meant far more than the climax of a brilliant military career, it foreshadowed an end to all the chaos and uncertainty of civil war; but the general relief needed a figurehead round which it could be expressed, and however much Oliver Cromwell might with due humility give thanks to God, the great mass of Englishmen found it easier to give thanks to Oliver.[1] "Cromwell came to London in great Solemnity and Triumph", wrote Whitelocke, "and he was entertained all the way as he passed to his House with Vollies of great and small Shot, and loud Acclamations and Shouts of the People."[2] In the first flush of its enthusiasm, and in reaction from the fear it had felt during the Scots' march south, Parliament showered honours on him: he was immediately voted estates worth £4,000 per annum, Hampton Court was prepared to be his official residence, and he was invited to select some suitable house near the capital, so that he could give Parliament the benefit of his advice regarding the future settlement of the country.[3]

This problem was exceedingly complex. Not only was there the task of imposing a new constitution upon a society which had its roots in monarchy, and the difficulty of providing a national "Representative" that would be sympathetic to the objects of the rebellion, but there was the further problem of the large

---

1. In this chapter we are concerned principally with the steps by which Cromwell expelled the Rump and assumed power in 1653, and the war with Holland and the financial situation of the Commonwealth – both matters of paramount importance to the course of English history at this time – are touched upon only in so far as they are likely to have affected our main subject.
2. Whitelocke, 509.
3. *C.J.*, VII, 13 f.

numbers of disenfranchised royalists, who must have a reasonable prospect of redeeming their citizenship if civil peace was to be established in anything more than name. In face of these formidable difficulties, the Parliament appears to have gone to work with a will: it ordered a fast day "to seek God for Counsel and Assistance"[4], it debated the vexed questions of its own dissolution and the election of a Representative to take its place,[5] and it discussed "an Act of Oblivion and General Pardon".[6]

Cromwell kept his finger firmly on the pulse of every department of the national government,[7] and the victory at Worcester had brought his name into the front rank of European figures: foreign states openly courted him or secretly manœuvred to win his favour,[8] and if he had exerted much pressure while the victory of Worcester was still green in the public memory, he might have been granted official recognition as temporary Head of the State. He made no such move.

Perhaps the reason for this was partly due to Henry Ireton's death in Ireland, a bare month after the fall of Limerick, the last large centre of Irish resistance.[9] Certainly the weeks which followed

---

4. Whitelocke, 510.
5. Wednesday, September 17. The debate on this was probably pushed on by Cromwell. He was deputed by the House to express thanks to the ministers who had preached to them on this occasion (Joseph Caryl and Nicholas Lockyer), and was teller in the division for dissolution, which was won by 33 votes to 26. Cf. Whitelocke, 510 (under September 27). See also the letter of Salvetti, the Tuscan agent, Gardiner, *Commonwealth and Protectorate*, II, 70 n.
6. Whitelocke, 510. Also an act for the maintenance of maimed soldiers and soldiers' widows.
7. Cf. *W.S.*, II, 469–98.
8. For a full account of the French, Spanish and other foreign attempts to win Cromwell's support, cf. *W.S.*, II, 489–92.
9. He died on November 26, 1651. Limerick fell on October 27. R.H. Abbott says, "Ireton's death was an important event in Cromwell's life. All the influence of that stem idealist had been in the direction of democratic, popular, almost communistic doctrines ... had he lived and retained his influence over his father-in-law, there is reason to believe that the ensuing events might have taken a somewhat different course. ..." (*W.S.*, II, 504). It must be agreed that Ireton's influence on Cromwell was very important, but there is every reason to believe it was just opposite to that which Abbott suggests. It is difficult to see how Abbott could suggest that Ireton was the democrat and that he "had stood at all times in opposition to the 'grandees' of the army", when it is obvious from the *Clarke Papers* that the Levellers considered Ireton to be the most inflexible "grandee" they had to face. The suggestion that Ireton held "almost communistic doctrines" is directly contrary to his stubborn defence of authority and private property, and to much material that Abbott has himself listed. Cf. *W.S.*, I, 516, 520, 524–5, 527 f., 532–8, 706, 711, 725; II, 24, 101; *Clarke Papers*, I, *passim*; Woodhouse, *Puritanism and Liberty*, 1–178 *passim*; *supra*, p. 137 f., 143. For Cromwell's sadness at Ireton's death, cf. Whitelocke, 516.

Worcester appear to have been a period of uncertainty. Of the ultimate end in view there cannot have been much doubt: the national settlement must be of a kind which would safeguard the results of the Rebellion, and there can have been little doubt in Oliver's mind that the Almighty intended to use him; but the way was narrow and often dark. In these circumstances he found it better to wait for God's clear leading, and he admitted as much in a letter written to his correspondent the Reverend John Cotton, of Boston, New England.[10] Cotton was a right-wing Independent of the same group as John Owen, Thomas Goodwin, Philip Nye and Hugh Peters. He was responsible for organizing the association of Independent churches which virtually became the State Church of Massachusetts, and his association with Cromwell is an additional proof of the latter's ecclesiastical position. Like Cotton, he sought to combine spiritual freedom with soundness of doctrine and due order in the Church – in neither civil nor ecclesiastical polity was Cromwell an anarchist – but the immediate importance for us of the letter to Cotton is the light it throws upon the Lord General's attitude to the situation of the moment. Beneath all the "seeming humility" we can discern a clear acceptance of his own vocation to govern, but he was undecided about the next step and was content to wait; and this probably explains his unwillingness to hasten the issue after Worcester – it was not lack of inner certainty about his own vocation, but an expectation that God would reveal His will more clearly. At the same time there was a growing popular belief that Cromwell was the man sent by God to match the hour. The Tuscan agent reported to his government that

> there cannot be discovered in him any ambition save for the public good, to which he brings all his spirit and power, which is so great and is used by his Excellency with such humility and respect toward

---

10. "Surely, Sir, the Lord is greatly to be feared, as to be praised! We need your prayers in this as much as ever. How shall we behave ourselves after such mercies? What is the Lord a-doing? What prophecies are now fulfilling? Who is a God like ours? To know His will, to do His will, are both of Him.

"I took this liberty from business, to salute you thus in a word. Truly I am ready to serve you and the rest of our brethren and the Churches with you. I am a poor weak creature, and not worthy the name of a worm; yet accepted to serve the Lord and His people. Indeed, my dear friend, between you and me, you know not me, my weaknesses, my inordinate passions, my unskilfulness and everyway unfitness to my work. Yet, yet the Lord, who will have mercy on whom He will, does as you see. Pray for me. Salute all Christian friends though unknown." October 2, 1651. *W.S.*, II, 482 f.; *L-C*, II, 240 f. (CLXXXIV).

every one, that he has come to be honoured and esteemed (besides for his great valour) as a man commanded by Heaven to establish this republic by divine service.[11]

Nevertheless, while Cromwell was waiting for the inspired moment, the rest of the country had a chance to recover its breath from the cheering. In particular the members of "the Rump"[12] began to see in the popular General a formidable threat to their own authority, and they sought to postpone their own dissolution. Their procrastination, together with the petty corruption of which some of the members were undoubtedly guilty, rapidly brought Parliament into disrepute with the Army officers. Major-General Harrison, a Fifth-Monarchist, wanted the Rump to make way for the Millennium. His views may have been extravagant, but he was soon to find an ally in the most popular of the officers, Major-General John Lambert, who was disgruntled by the abolition of the Deputyship of Ireland, to which he had recently been appointed after the death of Ireton.[13]

Cromwell now had to meet the opposition of former friends at Westminster. Sir Henry Vane and his colleagues, who had used Cromwell's prestige to forward the interests of their party, were beginning to think twice about the power which the general wielded, and to doubt their wisdom in creating the fiction of his divinely-inspired infallibility.[14] Their plan had been almost too

---

11. Amerigo Salvetti, October 3/13, 1651. Translation by Abbott (*W.S.*, II, 473) of letter quoted in Gardiner, *Commonwealth and Protectorate*, II, 59 n. (*Add. MSS.* 27,962, N. 252).
12. i.e. the truncated House of Commons.
13. Lambert was appointed in January 1651/2 (Whitelocke, 523), and by the end of that month he was in London making preparations. Lucy Hutchinson says that he treated the members of the Rump (to whom he owed his appointment) as "scarcely worth such a great man's nod" (*Memoirs*, Everyman edn., 286). Cromwell had previously given up his salary as Lord Lieutenant as redundant, and therefore the action of the House in abolishing the office on May 19 was quite logical, but it inevitably terminated Lambert's appointment (Whitelocke, 536). Although Mrs. Hutchinson blamed Cromwell for Lambert's displacement, from Ludlow it appears that Cromwell pressed for Lambert's retention as Deputy (*Memoirs*, I, 318 f.), and he certainly helped Lambert to meet the expenses of his equipage (Hutchinson, *Memoirs*, 287). When Lambert refused to take an inferior title Cromwell appointed Fleetwood, whose wife had recently died and who had made a match with the widowed Bridget Ireton.
14. "From the time of the defeat at Worcester, and the reduction of Scotland and Ireland to perfect obedience, Cromwell did not find the parliament so supple and so much to observe his orders as he expected they would have been. ... But that which troubled him most was the jealousy that his own party of independents had contracted against him; that party that had advanced him to the height he was at, and made him superior to all opposition, even his beloved

successful, and they had certainly not weighed the possibility that the general chosen would himself believe the fiction. To a large extent the men who had hitherto guided the political side of the Independent party's policy were politicians first and Independents incidentally – they were Independents in opposition to Presbyterian uniformity rather than because of any positive adherence to Independent churchmanship – which was very far from being Cromwell's position. On November 14, 1651, the Rump, by a majority of only two votes,[15] decided to dissolve, but not until November 3, 1654. This decision amounted almost to a personal defeat for Cromwell, and it shows that the glamour of Worcester's victory was beginning to fade. By 1654 he might have been displaced without arousing much outcry either from the public or from the rank and file of the Army, which by then would be considerably reduced.

The new political grouping arose out of the confusion through which England was seeking a solution to her constitutional problem, and the elections for the Council of State show that this centred in the attitude of the individual to Cromwell's position in the State.[16] By the end of November 1651, virtually nothing had been accomplished towards the settlement of the country on a peace-time basis, and this meant that the uncertainty would continue, for nothing lasting could be established until there was a government with a unified policy and effective power. The settlement of the nation must include an enlightened attitude towards the conquered party,[17] an ecclesiastical programme that could restore order in Church matters, a definite foreign policy, and the reduction of military strength to a size consonant not only with national security but also with national economy. On December 10 "Cromwell desired a Meeting with divers Members of Parliament and some of the chief Officers of the Army at the Speaker's House; and a great many being there, he proposed to

---

Vane, thought his power and authority to be too great for a commonwealth, and that he and his army had not dependence enough upon or submission to the parliament. ... He observed that those his old friends very frankly united themselves with his and their old enemies, the presbyterians, for the prosecution of the war with Holland, and obstructing all the overtures towards peace; which must in a short time exhaust the stock, and consequently disturb any settlement in the kingdom." Clarendon, *History*, XIV, 1 and 2.

15. 49–47.
16. November 19 and 20, 1651. *W.S.*, II, 501 f.
17. The problem at this time was probably not conceived quite in this way, but it is reflected in all the constitutional discussions of the interregnum.

them, That the old King being dead, and his son being defeated, he held it necessary to come to a Settlement of the Nation."[18] The lawyers present[19] were strongly in favour of a limited monarchy, while the soldiers were just as strongly in favour of a Republic. Cromwell's final comments were ambiguous, but their ambiguity makes them significant. He thought that Whitelocke's suggestion of a treaty with one of the older princes would be "a Business of more than ordinary Difficulty", but he thought that if it could be done with safety "a Settlement with somewhat of Monarchial Power in it, would be very effectual". What he had in mind was to be revealed to Whitelocke nearly a year later.[20]

Cromwell himself was becoming increasingly Head of the State in fact if not in name. Many of the problems which faced the country could not wait until the new constitution had been decided upon, drafted and accepted, and this meant that more and more he had to accept the responsibility for initiating interim proposals: foreign policy, national finance, and the ecclesiastical settlement could not be made to depend upon the good pleasure and agreement of the Rump. The immediate solution would be for the Rump to resign its authority into his hands, but this was not forthcoming: either out of innocence or out of wisdom his contemporaries were remaining perversely obtuse.

Meanwhile the ecclesiastical question came to the fore. The rapid growth of unorthodox sects meant that the Commonwealth government would have to formulate a clear ecclesiastical policy and stand firmly by it, for the cessation of hostilities had not brought any abatement of religious fanaticism.[21] The matter came to a head with the publication of a book of Socinian doctrine,[22]

---

18. Whitelocke, 516.
19. William Lenthall, Bulstrode Whitelocke and Sir Thomas Widdrington.
20. *Infra*, p. 259 f.
21. The Ranters held that sin was no longer sin to those who were "spiritual", and it can be seen that this might be held to justify any kind of vice. Nor was the average Englishman very much concerned with trying to distinguish between Ranters and the Quakers' doctrine of the inner light. George Fox himself, with his disrespect for the recognized forms of religion and authority, did much to get the Friends disliked (cf. *Commonwealth and Protectorate*, II, 90–5). In 1651-2 Ludovic Muggleton, and his cousin John Reeve, claimed to be "Two Heavenly Witnesses of the Apocalypse", and caused a public scandal, and in 1653, Vavasour Powell, a Welsh Fifth Monarchy revivalist, came to London and gathered immense crowds to hear his preaching. Amid the profusion of these enthusiasms the ordinary man was hardly equipped to discriminate.
22. February 1651/2. Socinius (1539–1603) was an Italian theologian Who had denied the divinity of Christ.

which offended the religious susceptibilities of all who held the doctrine of Christ's divinity – Presbyterians, Independents, Baptists and Quakers alike. Dr. John Owen headed a delegation of fifteen ministers which petitioned Parliament to suppress the book, and a committee of forty was appointed to consider it.[23] As a result of this protest a further committee was charged with formulating positive recommendations for religious settlement, and John Owen assumed a natural leadership in framing the proposals. He was a man admirably fitted for the task – an "orthodox" Independent, belonging to the group whose theories on church government were a "middle way" between Brownism and Presbyterianism, and a theologian of outstanding erudition and ability. Under Cromwell's patronage, Owen and his friends took the lead in the ecclesiastical affairs of the country,[24] and this again emphasizes Cromwell's own ecclesiastical position.[25] His own views on the religious settlement of the country were given in his speech at the dissolution of the first Protectorate Parliament on January 22, 1654/5, when he suggested that the Parliament could have made provisions for a "Godly Ministry", which "yet would have given a just liberty to Godly men of different judgements, men of the same faith with them that you call the Orthodox Ministry in England, as it is well known the Independents are, and many under the form of Baptism, who are sound in the

---

23. Deputation received on February 10, 1652. *The Racovian Catechism* was ordered to be burnt on April 2, 1652. It had been first published in Poland in 1642.
24. Independents were rapidly filling important posts in the universities. Thomas Goodwin had been appointed President of Magdalen College, Oxford. Samuel Winter was appointed Provost of Trinity College, Dublin, on June 3, 1652. Owen had been appointed Dean of Christ Church in 1651 and in 1652 Cromwell nominated him to be Vice-Chancellor (cf. Cromwell's letter to Convocation, September 9, 1652, W.S., II, 577 f.); less than a month later Cromwell delegated his powers as Chancellor of the University to a commission headed by the Vice-Chancellor (cf. October 16, W.S., II, 581 f; *L-C*, III, 284 f., (App. 25)) and this suggests that he had considerable confidence in Owen's ability.
25. A good deal of stress has been laid upon the mystical element in Cromwell's religion (Buchan, *Oliver Cromwell*, 67 f.; Dr. G.F. Nuttall, *The Holy Spirit in Puritan Faith and Experience* (Oxford 1946), 115 f.), which caused him to choose men like William Dell, John Saltmarsh and Peter Sterry as his chaplains. Yet Cromwell's mysticism was founded very squarely on Biblical doctrine: the Spirit of God "speaks without a written Word sometimes, yet according to it" (January 22, 1654/5, W.S., III, 592; *L-C*, II, 427). It seems, therefore, that while Cromwell's experimental religion drew him to men like Peter Sterry, his respect for order in ecclesiastical matters also drew to him men like Owen; although Sterry was a mystic religiously, ecclesiastically he belonged to John Owen's group. Cf. V. de Sola Pinto, *Peter Sterry* (Cambridge, 1934), 13 f., 19–24.

Faith". He looked for a union of all Christians who, while differing in lesser matters, were agreed upon the central Gospel truths, "looking at salvation only by faith in the blood of Christ".[26] This was virtually the position taken by Owen and his colleagues and embodied in their proposals and the "Fifteen fundamentals of Christianity" which the committee eventually presented to Parliament, and for which Owen took the major responsibility. In these propositions John Owen accepted the idea of an established State "Church" in which all "orthodox" Protestants could unite, and the administration of the system was put into the hands of two committees, part clerical and part lay – a central committee responsible for general oversight of the establishment and for the examination and ejection of unsuitable clergy and schoolmasters,[27] and local committees which were to be responsible for accepting ministers and schoolmasters into livings and appointments.[28] In addition, toleration was to be granted to all but those who denied the Christian religion.

The group of Independents to which Owen belonged had from the first insisted that while they did not hold "absolute liberty for all religions", the basis of evangelism must be persuasion and not coercion,[29] and the *Agreement of the People* had echoed the same breadth in its provision that none should be compelled to subscribe to the Establishment, "but only may be endeavoured to be won by sound doctrine, and the example of a good conversation".[30] The similarity between Owen's proposals and those set forward in the *Agreement of the People*[31] was not, one feels, the result of conscious imitation, but should be traced to a

---

26. W.S., III, 586; *L-C,* II, 416.
27. "Ejectors". They were to travel from one part of the country to another. *Commonwealth and Protectorate,* II, 99.
28. "Triers".
29. Cf. *supra,* p. 172, n. 4.
30. *Const. Docs.,* 370.
31. S.R. Gardiner has drawn attention to the similarity between Owen's proposals and the *Agreement of the People (Commonwealth and Protectorate,* II, 97. R.H. Abbott, apparently following Gardiner, notes the same thinG.W.S., II, 520). Both schemes allowed for an Established "Church" round which self-supporting nonconformist churches might be gathered in toleration, and both put definite limits to the extent of that toleration. *The Agreement of the People,* however, put the emphasis on public order, and even its threat of proscription against the Roman Catholics and Episcopalians seems to follow from its intention to withhold toleration only from those who threatened "the civil injury of others" *(Const. Docs.,* 370). Owen, on the other hand, as befitted a theologian, put the restriction on to a theological level by proscribing those who attacked the majesty or the honour of God.

common cause – the ecclesiastical views of Henry Ireton and the Army officers who had helped to formulate the *Agreement* were fundamentally the same as those held by John Owen and his colleagues: underlying both there was the same conception of catholicity within the Church. In this Owen had the full support of Oliver Cromwell.[32]

In foreign affairs there was also need for a unified policy, and it was obvious that until stable government had been established in England, the new Commonwealth could never play her full part in the affairs of Europe. The differences between Cromwell and the members of the Rump were a serious embarrassment in this respect, since other nations could only look askance at a country whose possible alliances might be changed at any moment. The embassy of Oliver St. John and Walter Strickland to the United Netherlands, which had proposed a Protestant Union, had been granted scant courtesy.[33] Privateering was going on between English and French ships in the Channel, and the recognition which Spain had granted to the Commonwealth was on a very precarious foundation. At the moment, however, England was able to hold the balance between the rival interests of France and Spain, and both these countries tried to gain the support of Cromwell.[34]

On the other hand, the relations with Protestant Holland deteriorated. It appears that Vane, and the Navy for which he was largely responsible – supported by important mercantile interests – pressed strongly for war, whereas Cromwell and the Army officers were, generally speaking, against it. War with Holland was bound to be a naval war, and the Army feared that its interests would be sacrificed to keep the Navy supplied, but in the main Cromwell's opposition was simply that of a good Protestant who thought England's power should be exerted against the enemies of the Faith rather than against her

---

32. In answer to someone who remarked that he would rather be a persecuting Saul than an indifferent Gallio, Cromwell declared, "I had rather that Mahometanism were permitted amongst us than that one of God's children should be persecuted." Preface to *The Fourth Paper by Major Butler*, signed by "R.W." [Roger Williams], quoted in Gardiner, *Commonwealth and Protectorate*, II, 100, cf. Gardiner's note, *ibid*.
33. St. John and Strickland asked for their recall at the end of May 1651. *W.S.*, II, 419 f.
34. Negotiations with Condé and de la Rivière. *W.S.*, II, 488–92. See also *ibid.;* 524–31.

coreligionists.³⁵ He did not, however, attempt to force his will against the popular current and the Dutch needed a lesson for the murder of Dr. Dorislaus, and their recent refusal to discuss closer union with the English Commonwealth. As the war continued,³⁶ however, Cromwell seems to have favoured it less and less. He could not, at will, bring the war to an end. He had the first and last words in all the necessary decisions of State, and yet he controlled the situation only in the same sense in which it may be said a good horseman controls a high-spirited horse: he "rode" the situation, but he never attempted to over-master it.

II

The first concern of England was the settlement at home; and in view of the Rump's reluctance to get rid of itself, the first step was to find a way in which a dissolution might be achieved. The Army officers began agitation against the Rump in the summer of 1652, in a way that could only be reminiscent of previous occasions.³⁷ On August 13, 1652, some Army officers presented a petition to Westminster, which, although it did not demand the immediate dissolution of Parliament, touched on all the major questions of settlement and reform,³⁸ and "reads like a Cromwellian programme".³⁹

---

35. Part of his distaste may have been due to the influence of Hugh Peters, who showed his dislike openly, and even took active steps to get the war stopped. (Cf. *Comm, and Prot.*, II, 187 f.). Peters went to the length of urging Ayscough to leave the service rather than fight. He was severely reprimanded, and as the result of popular indignation withdrew for a time from his post as preacher at Whitehall. *Ibid.*, 188. Cf. also *W.S.*, II, 567–9, 586.
36. The details are not of primary importance for our purpose. Gardiner gives a good account of the war. *Comm. and Prot.*, II, 149–52, 169–73, 176–220.
37. Clarendon alleged that Cromwell used the Council of Officers against the Members of Parliament. *History*, XIV, 3.
38. Whitelocke, 541. It had been published on August 10 in a slightly different form under the title, *A Declaration of the Armie to the Lord General Cromwel for the Dissolving this Present Parliament*.
39. *W.S.*, II, 572. It was presented by Whalley, Barkstead, Worsley, Goffe, Hacker, Okey. All but the last-named remained faithful to Cromwell to the end. Cf. *W.S.*, II, 571. Whitelocke commented, "Many were unsatisfied with this Petition, looking upon it as improper, if not arrogant for the Officers of the Army to dictate to the Parliament their Masters; and in Discourse of it with Cromwell, I advised him to stop this way of their petitioning, by the Officers of the Army with their Swords in their Hands, lest in time it might come too home to himself, but he seemed to slight or rather to have some Design by it in order to which he put them to prepare a way for him." Whitelocke, 541.

For nearly a year since the battle of Worcester the country had awaited positive signs of constitutional settlement, but without any encouragement. Financially, the Commonwealth was in sad straits: at the end of a ruinous civil war it had become involved in an expensive naval war, and its extraordinary means of revenue – the compositions of cavaliers, and the sale of delinquents' lands, church lands and royal property – were rapidly drying up. If the Commonwealth was to pay its way in the future it must find the means from regular taxation, but the maxim still held good, "no taxation without representation": if the old form of Parliament was no longer possible, the leaders of the Commonwealth must devise some new deliberate body where the chosen representatives of the nation – or at least the representatives of those who were to foot the bill – could voice their grievances. At the same time, it was imperative that there should be a stronger Executive, and the relationship between the executive and legislative branches of government must be defined. Cromwell's present relationship with Parliament was most unsatisfactory. He may have been for all practical purposes Head of the State, but he was still the paid servant of the Rump, and he lacked any form of constitutional recognition. Despite his real power and influence, he had been frustrated in home policy and foreign policy, and largely – so it appeared to him – by selfish and sectional interests. The dismissal of the Rump was the key to the whole position: it was the Rump which stood in the way of a new Representative, it was the Rump which was procrastinating over the country's settlement; it was the Rump which sought to curb Cromwell's power. Without this little handful of outdated and detested Parliamentarians he could hardly fail to become recognized as Head of the English Commonwealth.

It was about this time that Bulstrode Whitelocke was walking with Cromwell one evening in St. James's Park and discussing the affairs of the nation.[40] After the usual courtesies, Cromwell commented upon the dangerous situation of the Commonwealth, and Whitelocke agreed that their present danger was "greater than ever it was in the Field", and he gave some point to his remarks by instancing the "Factions and ambitious

---

40. About November 7, 1652. Whitelocke, 548–50; W.S., II, 587–92. Carlyle rejected the conversation as being too much "dimmed by just suspicion of dramaturgy" (L-C, II, 255), but it has been accepted as authentic by S. R, Gardiner and R.H. Abbott, *Comm. and Prot.*, II, 229–31, 231 n.; W.S., II, 587 and n.

Designs" of the Army as the greatest obstacle to peace, although he hastened to compliment the General on the admirable way in which he had kept discipline. Oliver said that the murmurings of the soldiers were due to the fact that "they are not rewarded according to their deserts, that others who have adventured least, have gained most", and he went on vigorously to criticize the Members of Parliament: "really their Pride, and Ambition, and Self-seeking, ingrossing all Places of Honour and Profit to themselves, and their Friends, and their daily breaking forth into new and violent Parties and Factions,[41] their delays of Business, and design to perpetuate themselves, and to continue the power in their own hands, ... and the scandalous Lives of some of the chief of them, these things (My Lord) do give too much ground for People to open their Mouths against them, and to dislike them". It was quite a comprehensive indictment, and he added that unless an authority could be created that could "keep things in better order", it would be impossible to prevent national ruin.

Whitelocke at once reminded Oliver that even the Lord General could not control the Members of Parliament, since his commission was from them. The lawyer was disposed to trust the good sense of his parliamentary colleagues when the time came to make a decision about the settlement, but Cromwell emphatically disagreed. Whereupon the following dialogue took place:

> **Whitelocke.** We our selves have acknowledged them the supreme Power, and taken our Commission and Authority in the highest concernments from them, and how to restrain and curb them after this, it will be hard to find out a way for it.
> **Cromwell.** What if a Man should take upon him to be King?
> **Whitelocke.** I think that remedy would be worse than the disease.

Questioned on this, Whitelocke pointed out that Cromwell already had control of the Militia, and although he had no veto, his wishes were not easily put aside, while foreign ambassadors all went directly to him. "So," he concluded, "I apprehend indeed less Envy and Danger and Pomp, but not less Power and real Opportunities of doing Good in your being General, than would be if you had assumed the Title of King." Oliver's real

---

41. Whitelocke has a full stop here, but the sense clearly demands a comma.

difficulty, however, was not that he lacked the power, but that he lacked the recognition and constitutional authority that the times demanded.[42]

Pressed to express his own views more clearly, Whitelocke suggested that the best solution for their present difficulties was for the Lord General to treat with Charles Stuart, for he would be able to make whatever terms he liked for the liberties of the nation, and to safeguard himself and his friends. But this was not the solution which Cromwell desired: the house of Stuart had been tried, and had been found wanting, and the defeats which they had suffered were sufficient testimony that God had witnessed against "that slighted cause":[43] the road back to the Stuarts was a closed road. Yet the country needed "a Settlement with somewhat of Monarchial power in it", and this could be achieved only by going forward to his own personal rule, not by returning by way of the Stuarts. The conception of his political mission under God had become crystallized: he might still be vague about the style and title, he might still not see his way clear to achieve it, and the Rump might still remain in the path, but of the reality and nature of that vocation he had no doubt.

From the point of view of Oliver's rise to power, November 1652 seems to be a decisive turning-point, for this was the month in which he opened his mind to Whitelocke, and the end of that month witnessed the defeat of Blake by Van Tromp in the Downs[44] – a "staggering blow" to the war party. England was desperately short of funds with which to continue the fight, and the Rump even suggested selling Hampton Court, which had been assigned to Cromwell after Worcester. The situation seemed to be working up to a trial of strength between Parliament and its Lord General. It is possible that even at the time of his conversation with Whitelocke Cromwell was contemplating

---

42. In his reply to Whitelocke's objections, he said he had heard "from some of your Profession" that, in the event of a return of the Stuarts, the servants of a *de facto* monarch would be legally exempt from reprisals; he also referred to the traditional reverence in which the conception of monarchy was held in England. Whitelocke on the other hand doubted – and perhaps with very good reason - - whether any law would defend them if Charles Stuart returned. Cromwell's arguments were used, in April 1657, by the lawyers to persuade him to accept the throne. Whitelocke was on that deputation, and the similarity between the arguments used suggests that he had remembered this conversation. Cf. *L-C*, III, 41–53, also *infra*, p. 362.
43. Speech January 22, 1654/5. W.S., III, 583; *L-C*, II, 411.
44. November 30, 1652.

putting an end to the war, but from this time onward the break with the Rump appears to have been inevitable.

III

In face of its fall in naval prestige the government was forced to raise the pay of the sailors by reducing the pay of the soldiers,[45] and by disbanding certain garrisons. This was unfortunate, for the Army officers were already disgusted at Parliament's lack of response in meeting their demands. There was an ominous echo of former days when a group of officers began to meet at Allhallows, in Thames Street, to pray for a new Representative, and in the first week of January 1653, the Council of Officers met at St. James's for prayer and preaching. Parliament was not slow to read the signs of the times and on January 6 it ordered that an Act for an equal Representative should be prepared immediately.[46] The situation was strangely parallel to that which had existed at Newmarket prior to the expulsion of the eleven members. The reputation and authority of Parliament was at the nadir: with the Army truculent and the City disaffected by the Dutch blockade, it had no power to implement its will and no popular support. It was a situation ripe for decisive action, and if the royalists had not been completely crushed there can be little doubt that they would have supplied it.

Early in January[47] the Council of Officers named a committee which later conferred with the Council of State,[48] and eventually this committee issued the Army's programme of successive parliaments, reform of the law, and limited liberty of conscience in religion. Cromwell would have no scruples about using the Council of Officers to offset the designs of the Rump, but he was not altogether a free agent, for among the officers themselves he was pushed on by two groups – one headed by Lambert, who out of revenge for the way he had been treated over Ireland was pressing for the Rump's immediate dismissal, and the other led by the Fifth-Monarchist, Harrison, "who", Cromwell remarked, "is an honest man, and aims at good things, yet from the impatience of his spirit will not wait the Lord's leisure, but hurries

---

45. Paulucci to Sagredo, January 7/17, 1653/3. *Cal. S.P. Ven.* (1653–54), 9.
46. *C.J.*, VII, 244.
47. January 8.
48. January 13.

me on to that which he and all honest men will have cause to repent".[49]

Some people, however, saw evidence that when the moment of "the Lord's leisure" arrived Oliver would not be unprepared. Royalist historians point out that in February the young Duke of Gloucester was sent to the Continent, which could be interpreted as the removal of a possible rival.[50] On the other hand, Parliament had taken the first step in the matter.[51] The conversation with Whitelocke should be remembered not only for Oliver's part in it, but also for the significant turn to the discussion introduced by the lawyer: there can be no doubt that had Cromwell been prepared to foreshadow the part of George Monk, he had the power and popularity to do it, and therefore the presence of the young prince was as much an embarrassment to the republicans at Westminster as it was to Oliver's own possible ambitions.

On February 19–20, 1652/53, Admiral Blake won a complete victory over Van Tromp, and this broke the hold the United Netherlands had kept on the English Channel and immeasurably strengthened the position of the war party. The Rump showed no signs of resigning; it was proposed to supplement the old Parliament by a series of by-elections instead of a "general" election, and Parliament began to look round for ways in which to clip the wings of its Commander-in-Chief. Cromwell himself was having to think his way through to new constitutional theories, for when the Council of Officers resolved to dismiss the Rump, he and Desborough had asked them what they would then call themselves, for "Parliament is not the supreme power, but that is the supreme power that calls it".[52] Oliver was still hesitant about destroying completely the one surviving link with the constitution of the past; yet in face of the general detestation of the Rump the time was rapidly approaching when whoever

---

49. Ludlow, *Memoirs*, Im 346. See also C.H. Firth's note, ibid. Ludlow himself was in Ireland at the time.
50. Clarendon, *History*, XIV. 87; Heath, *Chronicle of the Late Intestine War* (1663), 614 f.
51. On December 7, 1652, Parliament had ordered that the Duke of Gloucester should be sent to the mainland of Europe.
52. Newsletter, March 18, *Clarendon MSS.;* extract in *Engl. Hist. Rev.,* VIII (Firth, 1893), 528; W.S., II, 625. Cromwell went on to say that an additional reason for not ejecting the Parliament at that juncture was that it was occupied in negotiating a treaty with Holland. Another violent change in government would destroy the confidence of foreign states.

had the nerve to eject the members at Westminster would be more truly representative of the nation than were the members themselves.

IV

Meanwhile, the Bill of Elections continued to be discussed in all its aspects, and the Army grew more impatient of the delay.[53] Cromwell seems to have had considerable difficulty in restraining the officers from precipitate action, and his "sticking close to the House" caused him "to be daily railed upon by the preaching party, who say they must have both a new Parliament and General before the work be don".[54] The members of the Rump appear to have been saying much the same thing about Oliver, but for very different reasons. There were some heated exchanges which indicate that the tension was rapidly nearing breaking-point, and after one particularly violent altercation between Cromwell and Harrison, the former in exasperation threatened to resign his commission in favour of any officer that Parliament would approve. The Venetian envoy commented in a despatch to his government that since no one was ready to accept the responsibility "he may be considered more firmly established than ever, although much exasperated at bottom",[55] and this shows that although nothing could have been easier in theory than for the House to vote Cromwell out of his command, his authority within the Army was still indisputable and indispensable.

If the evidence of Cromwell's encounter with Edmund Calamy is to be trusted,[56] he had already made up his mind that the Rump

---

53. The main point at issue was whether the old Parliament was to resign and an entirely new Representative be elected, or whether the existing Parliament was to be augmented by a series of by-elections, as Vane and Marten proposed. Despite the obvious criticism of maintaining the unpopular members of the Rump in their seats (virtually for life), the plan had something to be said for it. As Henry Marten pointed out, the politicians who had brought the infant Commonwealth into being were best fitted to put it on its feet (Clarendon, *History*, XIV, 5), and the members of the Rump had become skilled in the business of government. Also, it would keep some continuity with the legally elected Parliament of 1642.
54. April 1. *Engl. Hist. Rev.*, VIII, 528 f., reprint from *Clarendon MSS.*; W.S. II, 626.
55. Paulucci to Sagredo, April 19/29. *Cal. S.P. Ven.* (1653–54), 60; W.S., II, 627.
56. The incident occurred about this time. At a meeting with the London clergy to ask them what they thought about the expulsion of the Rump, Edmund Calamy opposed it saying to Cromwell, "There will be nine in ten against you.

was to go, and Whitelocke says that "I still found him in distaste with the Parliament and hastening their dissolution".[57] In face of its rising unpopularity[58] the House hurried forward the Bill of Elections, until by the middle of April it wanted only its third reading to make it law; but still no solution had been reached on the point at issue. Both sides were afraid that their opponents would manipulate the membership of the new Representative: the Rump was afraid that if it resigned the Army would be able to overawe and influence the electors, and the Army officers knew that if the old Parliament became co-optative, the vacant seats would be filled with nominees of the existing members.[59] The two sides prepared for the crisis: republican soldiers like Major John Streater from Ireland,[60] and Sir Arthur Hazelrigge, the Governor of Newcastle, arrived in London to protest against the Army agitation, and the Council of State authorized Cromwell to grant a commission for Lambert to command in Scotland for six months.[61]

The opposing groups cut across all the accepted political divisions of the Civil War. Some on both sides were both officers in the Army and Members of Parliament; there were no clear-cut definitions. The best distinction, perhaps, is to be found in the terms "Cromwellian" and "anti-Cromwellian", for the underlying issue – despite the Fifth-Monarchy enthusiasms of Harrison – was Cromwell's position within the State. Gradually there had grown up, amid the chaos of those conflicting times, a strong party of men who saw in Cromwell the rock on which the new

---

    'Cromwell replied by asking, "But what if I should disarm the nine, and put the sword into the tenth man's hand; would not that do the business?'" (*W.S.*, II, 626, quoted from the *Life of Henry Neville*, 35; cf. Alex. Gordon's article on Calamy in *D.N.B.*) This has been interpreted as an example of Cromwell's political cynicism. (G. R. Stirling-Taylor, *Oliver Cromwell*, 298.) But perhaps he was merely facing Calamy with what Providence had already accomplished – God had disarmed the nine, and put the sword into the tenth man's hand. That interpretation would appear to be nearer the temper of Cromwell's thought.

57. Whitelocke, 553.
58. A further petition from the Army on April 7, Bordeaux to Brienne, April 21/May 1, 1653. *Archives des Affaires Etrangères*, lxii, fol. 117; quoted in *Comm. and Prot.*, II, 253 n.
59. Cf. Masson, *Life of Milton*, IV, 409 n.; *Comm. and Prot.*, II, 254 n.
60. Streater strongly opposed Cromwell in the Council of Officers: "Col. Streater persisted in his Resolution of giving reasons against it, and being slamm'd by Harrison with Christ's personal Raign, and that he was assured the Lord General sought not himself, but that King Jesus might take the Scepter; He presently replied; That Christ must come before Christmas, or else he would come too late." Heath, *Flagellum*, 129.
61. April 14, 1653. *Cal. S.P. Dom.* (1652–53), 260, 279. Cf. *Engl. Hist. Rev.*, VIII, 529 (April 8).

English society could be built, the one stable personality in the shifting sand of private interest and civil strife. It was not simply sentiment, although the nucleus of the party was the veteran officers who had followed him in battle, but among his supporters there were also politicians like Oliver St. John, divines like Owen, Caryl and Manton, and men of letters like Milton. More important still, Cromwell was supported by many ordinary people with no claim to eminence. Nothing is more remarkable in reading through his correspondence than to notice how, in the midst of the most urgent crises of state he always found time to write on behalf of those who requested his help.[62] If this was conscious policy, then Cromwell must have been a man of remarkable foresight and subtlety, but the letters appear to be the spontaneous reaction of one who, for a soldier, was unusually sensitive to the appeal of individual suffering. This concern for other people's welfare, however, was not without its practical effects, as R.H. Abbott noticed, for "he had probably come into contact with more persons than any man of his time, and he had improved his opportunities to attract and conciliate wherever possible".[63] His popularity has best been expressed in the verse of his most brilliant admirer, John Milton:

> "Cromwell, our cheif of men, who through a cloud
>   Not of warr onely, but detractions rude,
>   Guided by faith & matchless Fortitude
>   To peace & truth thy glorious Way hast plough'd,
> And on the neck of crowned Fortune proud
>   Hast reard Gods Trophies, & his work pursu'd,

---

62. The list of occasions of this kind during the months between Worcester and the fall of the Rump is formidable: letter on behalf of William Guise's widow, September 8, 1651, *W.S.*, II, 467; *L-C*, III, 278 f. (App. 22); on October 10(?) he interceded before Parliament on behalf of the children of the Earl of Kildare, *W.S.* II, 478; in October he favoured mercy for Lord Derby, *W.S.*, II, 487; November 24, 1651, letter on behalf of the widow of John Franklyn, M.P., *W.S.*, II, 500; *L-C*, III, 435 (Supp. 70); November 20, he supported a petition of more than 100 widows and children of Worcester victims, *W.S.*, II, 508; December 1651, letter on behalf of Mr. and Mrs. Fincham, *ibid.*, *L-C*, III, 281 f. (App. 24); February 24, 1651/2, he favoured leniency for Cavendish, *W.S.*, II, 515; February 24, letter to J.P's on behalf of wounded soldiery, *W.S.*, II, 521 f.; certificate on behalf of William Gutteridge, *ibid.*, 533; August 2, 1652, he tried to keep Lord Craven from forfeiture; August 27, letter on behalf of Daniel Searle's wife, *W.S.*, II, 575; *L-C*, III, 437 (Supp. 72); 24th, letter on behalf of widow Burden, *W.S.*, II, 574. Cf. earlier examples *supra*, p. 104 n., and notes on 182, 230.
63. *W.S.*, II, 509.

> While Darwen stream with blood of Scotts imbru'd,
> And Dunbarr feild resounds thy praises loud,
> And Worsters laureat wreath; yet much remaines
>   To conquer still; peace hath her victories
>   No less renowned then warr, new foes aries
> Threatning to bind our soules with secular chaines:
>   Helpe us to save our Conscience from the paw
> Of hireling wolves whose Gospell is their maw."[64]

V

Meanwhile, discussions were going on between the Army officers and members of the Rump. In a speech four years later Cromwell summarized his own objections to the Rump's proposals:

> there [was] a Bill framed, that Parliaments might always be sitting, [he said] and we did think, who are plain men, and I do think it still, that it had been, according to the foolish proverb, out of the frying-pan into the fire. For ... we should have had fine work then! We should have had a Council of State, and a Parliament of four-hundred men, executing arbitrary government without intermission, saving of one company; one Parliament leaping into the seat of another, while they left them warm. ... Why this design of theirs, it was no more but this, that Committees of Parliament should take upon them, and be instead of, the Courts of Westminster. ... and Committees erected to fetch men from the extremest parts of the nation to London, to attend Committees, to determine all things. ... And the Parliament assuming to itself the authority of the Three Estates that were before. ... and I thought, and we thought, and I think so still, that this was a pitiful remedy.[65]

Nevertheless, since the final debate on the Bill was due to take place on Wednesday, April 20, there appears to have been, on the previous day, an attempt at compromise.[66] The members of the Rump were afraid to leave the Army in control of the new elections, but the Army officers on the other hand suggested an interim government by a selected council of trusted men. The meeting adjourned and it was agreed to meet the next day. Early on the morning of April 20, however, the supporters of the

---

64. *To the Lord Generali Cromwell* (May 1652), "On the proposalls of certaine ministers at the Committee for the Propagation of the Gospell".
65. April 21, 1657. *W.S.*, IV, 484–97; *L-C*, III, 85–123.
66. Whitelocke, 554.

Rump's power arrived in the House in unusually large numbers and immediately called for a debate on the Bill of Elections. If the Bill had been passed forthwith Cromwell and the Army officers would have been in the very difficult position of opposing an "Act" of Parliament, and it would have been almost impossible to secure any appreciable modification to the idea of a co-optative Parliament. To Cromwell the procedure appeared to be a deliberate breach of faith.[67] Whitelocke reports that early on April 20 he went to Cromwell's lodgings, and the debate of the previous day was resumed. During this discussion word came that Parliament was sitting. Cromwell broke off the conference, and those who were members went to the House to discover that the Bill of Elections was being rushed through. Oliver was so enraged that he called out soldiers and stationed them at the doors.[68] He entered the House hurriedly, without even having dressed properly,[69] and listened with mounting anger to the course of the debate. Then he remarked to Harrison, who was sitting next to him, that "he judged the Parliament ripe for a dissolution and this to be the time of doing it",[70] and soon after this he rose from

---

67. "At the parting two or three of the chief ones, and very chiefest of them did tell us that they would endeavour to suspend farther proceedings about the bill for a new representative until they had a further conference. And upon this we had great satisfaction, and we did acquiesce, and had hope, if our expedient would receive a loving debate, that the next day we should have some such issue thereof as would have given satisfaction to all.

"They went away late at night; and the next morning, we considering how to order that which we had farther to offer to them in the evening, word was brought they were proceeding with a Representative, with all the eagerness they could. We did not believe persons of such quality could do it. A second and a third messenger told us they had almost finished it, and had brought it to that issue, with that haste as had never been known before; leaving out all things relating to the due exercise of the qualifications; and, as we have heard since, resolved to pass it only in paper, without engrossing it, for the quicker despatch of it. Thus, as we apprehended, would have been thrown away the liberties of the nation into the hands of those who had never fought for it. And upon this we thought it our duty not to suffer. And upon this the House was dissolved even when the Speaker was going to put the last question." Speech, July 4, 1653. *W.S.*, III, 59 f.; *L-C*, II, 287 f. (Speech I). Cf. *The Declaration of the Lord General and His Council of Officers*, April 22, 1653; *W.S.*, III, 5-8.
68. Whitelocke, 554.
69. See Algernon Sydney's account. R.W. Blencowe, *Sydney Papers* (1825), 139-41.
70. Ludlow, *Memoirs*, I, 351 f. Regarding the measure introduced to the House on the morning of April 20, Sir Charles Firth writes, "The objection of the army to it is plainly stated in their Declaration. The corrupt party in Parliament it affirms, 'long opposed and frequently declared themselves against having a new representative; and when they saw themselves necessitated to take the bill into consideration, they resolved to make use of it to recruit the House with persons

his place and began to speak. Algernon Sydney, who was present, says that Cromwell first spoke in commendation of the Parliament, and of the great changes it had brought about, "but afterwards he changed his style, told them of theyr ... faults; then he sayd, Perhaps you thinke this is not Parliamentary language, I confesse it is not, neither are you to expect any such from me."[71] He told the Members,

> that the Lord had done with them, and had chosen other instruments for the carrying on his work that were more worthy. This he spoke with so much passion and discomposure of mind, as if he had been distracted. Sir Peter Wentworth stood up to answer him, and said, that this was the first time that ever he had heard such unbecoming language given to the Parliament, and that it was the more horrid in that it came from their servant, and their servant whom they had so highly trusted and obliged: but as he was going on, the General stept into the midst of the House, where continuing his distracted language, he said, "Come, come, I will put an end to your prating"; then walking up and down the House like a mad-man, and kicking the ground with his feet, he cried out, "You are no Parliament, I say you are no Parliament; I will put an end to your sitting; call them in, call them in": whereupon the serjeant attending the Parliament opened the doors, and Lieutenant-Colonel Worsley with two files of musqueteers entred the House.

After the Lord General had accused various members with their sins both public and private, the mace was removed and Harrison helped the Speaker from his chair.

> Then Cromwel applied himself to the members of the House, who were in number between 80 and 100, and said to them, "It's you that have forced me to this, for I have sought the Lord night and day, that he would rather slay me than put me upon the doing of this work."[72]

At this point Alderman Allen, one of the Treasurers for the Army, begged Cromwell to allow affairs to resume their normal course, but the General immediately turned upon him, and

---

of the same spirit and temper, thereby to perpetuate their own sitting.' ... It was not the provision for the dissolution of the present Parliament Cromwell and the soldiers objected to, but the provisions relative to the constitution of the new Parliament." Firth, Ludlow's *Memoirs*, I, 351 n. The Army *Declaration* is given in *Flagellum*, 132–9. Cf. Masson, *Life of Milton*, IV, 405, and Cromwell's speech, July 4, quoted *supra*, p. 268 n 1.

71. Blencowe, *Sydney Papers,* 139.
72. Ludlow, *Memoirs,* I, 352–4.

accused him of misappropriating public funds. Then, as the members left, he told Sir Henry Vane that he might have prevented this but "he was a Juggler, and had not so much as common honesty".[73] Cromwell took the Act from the clerk, put it under his cloak, and locked the door behind him. The same day, in the afternoon, he visited the Council of State, accompanied by Major-General Lambert and Col. Harrison, and announced: "Gentlemen, if you are met here as private persons, you shall not be disturbed; but if as a Council of State, this is no place for you; and since you can't but know what was done at the House in the morning, so take notice, that the Parliament is dissolved."[74] Bradshaw protested that no power on earth could dissolve Parliament but itself, but, for all his protest, the Commonwealth was, for all practical purposes, at an end. The onus of government was now, for the rest of his life, wholly on the shoulders of the man who had taken the initiative.

VI

In writing of the relationship between religion and life in the career of any individual it is hard to avoid the use of the much-abused word "sincere". How far was Cromwell "sincere" in what he did on April 20, 1053? As Abbott has pointed out, "that he was 'sincere' at the moment of dissolution no one can doubt, for no one is ever more sincere than an angry man, and he was very angry at that moment".[75] Yet this does not answer the fundamental question. It may be that Cromwell was pushed on by forces beyond his control, that he had no intention of becoming England's ruler, and that his mistakes were due to sudden fits of justifiable anger:[76] it may well be that no theory completely explains the enigma of Cromwell, and that there were within him elements of Machiavelli's *Prince* as well as Bunyan's *Christian*.[77] There is no question of having to choose between two Cromwells – one black and the other white. Such an essentially simple choice may have been possible to Cromwell's contemporaries, but the historian finds a variety of motives operative, ranging from personal safety and self-interest to the most altruistic desire

---

73. *Sydney Papers*, 141.
74. Ludlow, *Memoirs*, I, 357.
75. *W.S.*, II, 650.
76. John Buchan, *Oliver Cromwell*, 423–5.
77. R.H. Abbott, *W.S.*, II, 655f.

to do God's Will, and the judgment in the end will depend very largely upon what the individual historian admits as evidence. However, even if one argues that he was self-deluded, no charge of fundamental hypocrisy will stand by the facts.

Hilaire Belloc cannot be accused of being over-sympathetic to the Lord Protector – according to the evidence he admitted, he found within Cromwell's actions "treasons, betrayals, falsehoods, acts of abominable cruelty, and false pretensions of motive", and yet he affirmed, "these do not make him black. They do not form one whole body of evil intention which would make us call him (as did Clarendon, who watched him closely) a bad man. ... The sin or turpitude is not part of a whole system of conduct springing from an evil root."[78] A part of the reason for this judgment is not hard to find, for whatever evidence is taken from secondary sources – the memoir writers, the historians, the political writers and pamphleteers – one cannot entirely discount the evidence of Cromwell's own written and spoken words; and in his correspondence both private and public, and in his public utterances, one must face the reality of his personal religion. He may have been on occasions untrue to "the heavenly vision", he may have misinterpreted it or been self-deluded, but the reality of that religion to him cannot be doubted: it had made him what he was.[79] We must seek to understand the Ejection of the Rump in the light of Cromwell's conversion, and all that this implied of being "elect" and "chosen"; it must be seen in the light of the theology which recognized the doctrine of Providence in the immediate concern of a personal Deity; and in the developing sense of corporate mission of the Commander and his troops from the formation of a fighting "Church" up to the fulfilment of their hopes at Worcester. Moreover, we must remember that the theology behind his personal religion had been burnt into Cromwell's character by the heat of his victories and the very success of his policy. Through all his experiences there was a

---

78. *Cromwell*, 63.
79. G. R. Stirling-Taylor in *Oliver Cromwell* submits that too many of Cromwell's biographers "have discussed him from the view-point of political and social and religious theories; and have paid more attention to the theories than the facts. There has been too great a readiness to listen respectfully to what Cromwell said he wished to do, and too little attention has been given to what, in fact, he did do." (*Op. cit*, 17.) The protest is justifiable, but the author has proceeded to disregard in the main all that Cromwell wrote or said, but accepted what others said about him. This makes Stirling-Taylor's book one more theory about Cromwell, and not a particularly convincing one.

certain inevitability about the rising crescendo of events. "Vocation" was by this time the word which summed up the central theme of Cromwell's life, and the saying attributed to him that "no one rises so high as he who does not know where he is going", is perhaps to be interpreted less as political opportunism than as the acceptance of divine leading – which perhaps explains why the French Cardinal de Retz found it so difficult to understand.[80]

There is little doubt that the ejection of the Rump brought Cromwell to a new high-level of personal popularity. In later years he boasted that not so much as a dog barked at the dismissal of the Members from Westminster,[81] and, with the exception of the comparatively small number of republicans, all sections of the population greeted the news with jubilation. Clarendon wrote later that "there needs not be any other description of the temper of the nation at that time, than the remembering that the dissolution of that body of men who had reigned so long over the three nations was generally very grateful and acceptable to the people", and he went on to say that the Army's published explanation "was looked upon as very reasonable".[82] The royalists were no less jubilant than were Cromwell's supporters themselves to see their old enemies at Westminster give place to Cromwell. Even in 1663 the memory of how the news was "received with all imaginable gladnesse" was fresh enough in the mind of James Heath to be recalled with the satirical comment that, "because there are so few good Acts in his [Cromwell's] Life, let the Reader score him One for the 23. [20] April 1653."[83] It is clear that the population united then to praise Cromwell's action as commendable and necessary, as his biographers now unite in condemning it as ill-advised. "By this so acceptable an Action", wrote the royalist physician, Dr. George Bates, "he so blotted out the Memory of his past Villanies, that for a time he was rather look'd upon as a Saviour; the Shouts and Bonfires that were made, sufficiently expressing the Joys of the People, for being delivered from so cruel a Yoke. They praise the Freedom the General took, in not fearing to charge his

---

80. *Mémoires du Cardinal de Retz*, II, 385; cf. *supra*, p. 125.
81. Speech to the first Protectorate Parliament, September 12, 1654. W.S., III, 453; L-C, II, 369.
82. *History*, XIV, 11.
83. *Flagellum*, 130, 131.

Impotent Masters to their Faces, with Vices that were publically talked of":[84] "now, as after Worcester," comments John Buchan, "he could have made himself king".[85]

Oliver had waited for the right moment. There had been that interval – so unsatisfactory for the biographer, so true to Cromwell's habit – spent quietly strengthening his position and authority, and awaiting the moment for decisive action.[86] When that moment came its choice was significant, for he chose an occasion when those who opposed him had apparently put themselves morally in the wrong: before God and Oliver the procedure of the Rump on April 20, 1653, appeared to be a definite breach of faith. Therefore the indignation of the Lord General was righteous indignation, and when he went to the House he went as a minister of God to execute wrath. His whole manner was that of the Old Testament prophet visiting the leaders of the nation and castigating them for their sins: his tempestuous bearing, "as if he had been distracted", and his specific charges against the corruption and bad faith of individual members, all bespoke his conscious assumption of prophetic authority. All this prophetic indignation and authority – his sense of personal commission by, and responsibility to, God alone – is epitomized in the classic imperative to the members as the soldiers began to file in, "In the name of God – Go!"

James Heath says that when Cromwell returned from the dissolution of the Rump he acquainted the officers with what had happened, and told them bluntly that he expected them to support him. He added that "when he went up into the House, he

---

84. *Elenchus*, II, 162. Cf. Dugdale, *Short View*, 405 f.
85. *Oliver Cromwell*, 425. Abbott has been unnecessarily sentimental about the Rump in his desire to uphold parliamentary authority, and this has led him into some contradiction. He has said that the dissolution "had been a great shock to public opinion", and that "the Nation was stunned by the suddenness of the stroke", although he has himself shown that the move had been generally expected. In the same way it is misleading to call the *Declaration* of the Council of Officers "a thoroughgoing denunciation of the late Parliament". On the contrary, by the contemporary standards it was a very moderate statement. Cf. *W.S.*, III, 1-15.
86. There is an interesting reference by Sir William Dugdale to Cromwell's practice of seeking guidance from God before any great decision: "And so much did he then pretend to Revelations; that when any weighty matter was propounded to him, he usually retired for a quarter of an hour, or more, and declared what was revealed to him." *Short View*, 391. Cf. Clement Walker's comment, *supra*, p. 203.

intended not to do it… and did not therefore consult with Flesh and Blood at all, nor did he premeditate the doing thereof, though he plainly saw the Parliament designed to spin an everlasting Thread."[87] The means by which Cromwell came to power meant that his future government was bound to be autocratic; but it was not an absolute dictatorship in the sense of being without limits. Cromwell could not disregard the Biblical conception of what was lawful and just, any more than he could disregard his Independent respect for liberty of conscience. Opposition to the fundamental programme of settlement would not be tolerated, because it was God's will rather than his own, and there was likely to be much heart-searching as to what might with justice be called "liberty of conscience" for such persons as Friends and Episcopalians, but in matters where the stability of the State was not involved his government was likely to be remarkable for its breadth and leniency.

In the introduction to this book mention was made of the paradox which exists between Cromwell the Independent and Cromwell the Lord Protector, and we are now able to see how the tension was resolved for Oliver himself: it was resolved in the "prophetic" function of Cromwell's political mission. On the fundamental questions of "healing and settling" he did not believe it was he himself who was speaking to the nation, but it was God speaking through him. His attitude to his parliaments and his public utterances breathe the spirit of the prophetic "Thus saith the Lord": it was not a denial of the Independents' principles of democracy, but a development of their contention that all government should be theocratic and therefore prophetic – it was to be a public ministry exercised on behalf of the whole nation.

---

87. *Flagellum*, 130. Cf. the appropriateness of Isaiah 61:1–4.

Chapter Sixteen
Experiments at Home and Abroad (1653)

I

Cromwell's task was no different from that which he had set before Parliament in 1644 – "to save a Nation out of a bleeding, nay almost dying condition, which the long continuance of this War hath already brought it into";[1] but if the task was in principle the same, in extent and complexity it was infinitely greater. The campaigns in Ireland and Scotland, the war with Holland, the growing apprehension abroad, and nine additional years of civil strife all made his task in 1653 the more difficult and urgent.

He had lost the advice of Henry Ireton, and if he had risen in personal prestige he had also alienated many of those who had been his loyal colleagues. He was very conscious that his present authority was based not upon his national popularity, but upon the supremacy of the Army, and even within the Army he was kept in check by the nice balance of Lambert's and Harrison's interests. Even the policy of his staunchest friends in pressing for his recognition as Head of the State could only result in fixing the responsibility of government more firmly upon him. He was very much alone, and in the welter of political confusion at home and of diplomatic uncertainties abroad he had only the clear call of events on which to base the certainty of his mission.

Government had to be undertaken both at home and abroad. If Europe could no longer ignore the new military power that had arisen at her north-western corner, neither could England afford to be indifferent to the continental powers. The Dutch war must be settled, regular diplomatic relations must be established and strong alliances contracted: a consistent foreign policy must be formulated and adhered to. At home, taxation must be put on a more equitable basis and the economy of the country

---
1. Speech, December 9, 1644. W.S., I, 314 f.; L-C, I, 186–7.

restored, the balance-sheet of delinquency must be finally struck, and a religious settlement must be introduced that would guarantee the maximum religious freedom consistent with public order and admit public responsibility for the cure of souls. All these matters were centred in the problem of the future national constitution, and in particular the problem of getting a representative body to take the place of the old Parliament: foreign states would hold aloof until there was a reasonably stable government with which they could negotiate, taxes could not be levied indefinitely without representation, an Act of Indemnity and Oblivion depended upon the good faith of a responsible government, and order could be brought into the chaotic state of the nation's religion only by an accepted national authority. The constitutional question was central.

II

For the immediate continuation of administration a decemvirate[2] was appointed, in which both Lambert and Harrison found places. It is clear that a struggle was going on behind the scenes between these two officers regarding the future form of government. Lambert favoured a close-knit oligarchy to which, perhaps, an "elected" parliament, carefully winnowed, might be added, whereas Harrison, under the influence of his apocalyptic Fifth-Monarchy visions, was pressing for a nominated council of seventy – the "Sanhedrim" of the New Israel;[3] but whatever struggles for power were going on at higher levels Cromwell was not seriously rivalled by anyone else: the responsibility for government was his, and he recognized it.[4]

It is comparatively easy to be wise after the event, but some such experiment as the Nominated Parliament was to be expected. A direct appeal to the whole electorate was obviously out

---

2. Seven officers and three civilians.
3. Ludlow, *Memoirs*, I, 358.
4. Cf. Cromwell's conversation with Major Salway and John Carew as reported by Ludlow, although it is apparent from the same conversation that he wanted to divest himself of his unlimited responsibility as soon as possible. (*Ibid*, 357 f.) After the defeat of the Dutch in May Cromwell invited the people to join in a day of Thanksgiving, and Whitelocke adds the comment, "This took the more with many People because it was not a Command and imposing Men, but only an Invitation of them to keep a Day of publick Thanksgiving." (Whitelocke, 558.) Whatever his power Cromwell knew that he still lacked recognition.

of the question, but money was needed, and an assembly with the appearance of being at least more representative than the Rump, and willing to vote taxes, was therefore to be preferred to a smaller council. On the other hand, the Army officers could hardly avoid proceeding by way of careful and selective nomination. The response to "the Declaration of the Lord General and his Council of Officers"[5] had been reassuring,[6] but it was to be expected that the main support for the new government would come from the gathered churches: Cromwell's victory was their victory, and they regarded his last coup as setting the seal to the day of their power. Although Harrison's dream of a "Sanhedrim" was impracticable, the Lord General had a good deal of sympathy, with those who believed that the time had come for the rule of "the saints". What then could better meet the situation than that out of every county men of this sort should be chosen from the godly congregations to represent the nation, and to share with him the responsibilities of government? The *Agreement of the People* had laid down the principle that for the first two national "Representatives"[7] that were to be elected after the wars none should be eligible "who have not voluntarily assisted Parliament against the King" either in person or in kind, and it was recommended "that, in all times, the persons to be chosen for this great trust may be men of courage, fearing God and hating covetousness".[8] The *Agreement* had been formulated by men who had been inspired by the religion of the gathered churches, and it was within these congregations that citizens of the type they had in mind were to be found: they were Puritan, they had loyally supported the Rebellion from the first, and an assembly of such men, Cromwell would argue, could be relied upon to maintain the revolutionary settlement and act in the country's interest.

Accordingly, nominations were invited and received from the congregations, and one hundred and fifty men were selected to constitute the new Representative. A significant pointer, however, to the subtle change in the way in which Cromwell now regarded his own status in the nation is the fact that he did not seek his own election to this body, and if the assembly was to be

---

5. April 22, 1653. *W.S.*, III, 5–8.
6. Cf. Whitelocke, 555–7; Clarendon, *History*, XIV, 11.
7. i.e. Parliaments.
8. Gardiner, *Constitutional Docs.*, 364.

regarded as in any sense the equivalent of a Parliament, this would be the first time since 1628 that Oliver Cromwell had not sat at Westminster as a member. The inference is clear – he now regarded himself as independent of, and even superior to the new Representative. On the basis of the selection made by the interim Council, writs were issued on June 6 to "divers persons fearing God, and of approved fidelity and honesty", who were informed under Oliver's signature that they were "by myself with the advice of my Council of Officers, nominated", and required "personally to be and appear at the Council Chamber in Whitehall, within the City of Westminster, upon the fourth day of July next". In such manner – avoiding the word "Parliament" – the Nominated Assembly of Puritan notables met on the day appointed to hear the Lord General deliver its commission.

III

Judged by any standard the occasion was remarkable, not to say unprecedented, and Oliver seems to have realized it. His speech[9] was lengthy, and it was delivered on a hot July day in an over-crowded room. He reviewed at great length the history of England since 1644, and asked his audience to weigh carefully the significance of that course of events which brought them to Westminster – whether there was not "a remarkable print of Providence set upon it, so that he who runs may read it".[10] Naturally he dwelt upon the dissolution of the Rump and defended the action taken. In the opinion of the officers, if the Rump had been successful the next Parliament would have consisted entirely of Presbyterians, and "though it be our desire to value and esteem persons of that judgment", he commented, "we had as good have delivered up our cause into the hands of any as into the hands of interested and biassed men; for it is one thing to live friendly and brotherly, to bear with a love a person of another judgment in religion; another thing to have any so far set into the saddle upon that account as that it should be in them to have all the rest of their brethren at mercy."[11]

When the Lord General began to consider the task which

---
  9. July 4, 1653. *W.S.*, III, 52–66; *L-C*, II, 272–303.
 10. Cf. Habakkuk 2:2.
 11. This was precisely the position of supremacy enjoyed by the Independents at that moment, and their claim to that position could only be justified by willingness to concede toleration to others.

faced the Assembly he said that it was the practice of those who gave up their authority into the hands of others "to lay a charge", but he added, although he seemed to speak of a charge, "it's a very humble one". Basing his words on Hosea 11:12 he told them that their commission was twofold – first, to rule the whole nation equitably, "to be as just towards an unbeliever as towards a believer"; and he confessed, "I have often said, foolishly, I had rather miscarry to a believer than to an unbeliever". Secondly, they had a duty to all Christians – "saints" – though of differing judgments, "and", he added, "if I did seem to speak anything that might seem to reflect upon those of the Presbyterian judgment, I think if you have not an interest of love for them you will hardly answer this of faithfulness to the Saints". Applying Isaiah 41:19 to their charge, he declared that "if the poorest Christian, the most mistaken Christian shall desire to live peaceably and quietly under you ... let him be protected".

The Lord General then let his vision fly over the great work which lay in prospect for this Assembly. Freely expounding further verses from Scripture,[12] he made a curious virtue of the necessity that had brought them to Westminster, and maintained that since none of them had sought nomination their call was obviously from God; "Therefore," he declared, "own your call!" He proceeded to a liberally adapted paraphrase of the sixty-eighth psalm, applying it as a prophecy to the existing condition of the Church, and he looked forward to the time when God would establish his Gospel Church and gather His people "out of the multitudes of the nations and people of this world". He asked their forgiveness for speaking for so long on such a hot day, and commending them to the grace of God and the guidance of His Spirit, he ended by affirming that he and his officers would be ready in the future, "as the Providence of God shall lead us, to be subservient to the work of God, and to that authority which we shall reckon God hath set over us".

A formal declaration was then read[13] in which the Lord General solemnly entrusted "the Supreme Authority and Government of this Commonwealth into the hands of the persons then met, who ... are to be held and acknowledged the Supreme Authority of the Nation".

Oliver's speech had been an oration to fit the occasion, but if

---

12. Psalm 110:3 and Isaiah 43:21.
13. *W.S.*, III, 67.

one judges it on the political level alone it is little more than a meaningless harangue. The clue to interpretation is in Oliver's own claim that it was a "Charge" – the kind of commissioning given to a Puritan minister at his Ordination or Induction to a pastorate.[14] It is the practice on such an occasion for the procedure to follow a clearly-defined pattern, in which a review of the steps leading to the ordinand's "call" and his acceptance, would proceed to the "Charge", or commissioning, delivered by a minister or member whose experience would enable him to speak with special authority. This was the pattern of Oliver's speech on July 4, 1653 – he was giving the Charges at the Ordination of the members of the Nominated Assembly, and their Induction into the pastorate of the Nation. Even in commending them to the guidance of the Holy Spirit he was using a phrase to which his churchmanship would give a significance beyond that of ordinary piety, for behind it would be the conception of the Congregational Church Meeting, or Synod, which professedly meets "under the guidance of the Holy Spirit" and seeks to discover "the mind of Christ". The whole form and spirit of Cromwell's speech suggest that he was thinking of the Nominated Assembly in these terms: England was to be governed by a "Church Meeting" set within the parish of the whole nation.[15]

At the same time, whatever the ecclesiastical significance of this occasion and of the speech which the Lord General delivered, the political undertones were present, and could not be disregarded. In home affairs a religious policy was envisaged which would make regular provision for a parish ministry but which would further be characterized by wide toleration, and although in respect of foreign policy Cromwell's remarks do not expressly foreshadow the Protestant League, they do give us some idea of the spirit in which it was conceived.

---

14. The term is still used to describe the address delivered at the Ordination and Induction of Congregational, Baptist and Presbyterian ministers.
15. In America the relationship between Church and State became so close that in New England the "Town Meeting" was simply the Congregational "Church Meeting" in its civic setting. Membership of the Congregational Church was (in Massachusetts and Connecticut) for many years a condition of full citizenship, and hence the Town Meetings of these States were assemblies very similar in conception to the Nominated Assembly. It appears that because of the identity between Church Meeting and Town Meeting the former fell into disuse in New England; among American Congregational Churches there is no regular Church Meeting of the kind known among their sister churches in England.

IV

For over ten years England had been preoccupied with her own affairs, and there had been no foreign policy in the generally accepted sense of that term. Since the death of Charles I – or, more accurately, since the arrival of Henrietta Maria on the Continent in 1644 – Parliament had had to keep one eye on continental affairs, but its interest was solely that of preventing foreign aid for the Pretender to the throne. The Dutch war signalized a departure, and indicated that mercantile interests were likely to play an important part in the future foreign policy of British governments; but that was in the future, and for the moment Cromwell controlled England's destiny. His views therefore become the most important factor in any discussion of English affairs, and because of this we shall expect to find religion continuing to play an important if not a dominant role in England's policy abroad.

Cromwell had inherited the war with the United Provinces and although he believed enough in the justice of England's cause not to favour an unconditional cessation of hostilities, a satisfactory peace with the Netherlands was his immediate aim in foreign affairs. The eclipse of the House of Orange, and the rise of the republicans of Holland with John de Witt as Grand Pensionary, meant that there was some hope of the pro-Stuart policy of the Dutch government being reversed, and a rapprochement with England being effected. There was a desire for peace on both sides, but not for peace at any price.

After the defeat of the Dutch fleet off the Gabbard Sands on June 2, 1653, de Witt cut through the unofficial diplomacy and sent four official envoys.[16] The Council of State did not wish to be too far committed,[17] and the Dutch found that before negotiations could begin properly they would have to concede that Van Tromp had been at fault in his attack off Folkestone – an admission of "war guilt".[18] Cromwell then brought forward a

---

16. Van Beverning and Nieupoort were from the province of Holland, van de Perre from Zealand, and Jongestaal from West Friesland. Negotiations were opened with the Council of State by the first arrival, van Beverning, on June 20.
17. Pending a clearer view of the foreign policy to be adopted by the new Legislature which had just been summoned.
18. On June 29 Cromwell seems to have suggested in a note to Nieupoort that the temporary dismissal of van Tromp might prepare the way for negotiations. In our discussion of the Anglo-Dutch negotiations we have relied to a large

revolutionary scheme which aimed to unite the British and Dutch republics, and suggested that for a start representatives of each nation might be immediately admitted to the governing body of the other. "You have appealed to the judgment of Heaven," he declared to the Dutch deputies. "The Lord has declared against you. After the defeats you have undergone, your only resource is to associate yourselves with your formidable neighbour to work together for the kingdom of Christ."[19]

This was a characteristic Oliverian approach to foreigners, and it would be equally typical of him that he should look from the triumph of Puritanism in the British Isles to the triumph of Protestantism throughout the world. To repair Britain's economy, to maintain the fruits of the Great Rebellion, to establish peace with the Netherlands and promote unity among Protestant peoples were all steps in the achievement of this dream. The Dutch, however, had had time to cool from the fervour of their crusade against Spain, and they neither shared nor understood Cromwell's vision. The negotiations therefore did not meet with much success.[20]

Possibly the deputies' attitude was influenced by the failure of the English fleet to maintain its blockade of the Dutch ports – a fact that received a good deal of popular criticism[21] – but in his speech to the Dutch envoys on July 13, 1653,[22] Cromwell soundly rated them for their reluctance to admit their country's guilt when God had so clearly witnessed against them. He urged them that their thoughts about the treaty "ought to go beyond mere consideration of profit", that "in England, God be thanked! the work was better understood than in the United Netherlands", and that the prime consideration must be "the preservation of freedom and the outspreading of the kingdom of Christ". In other words, he delivered to the Dutch a curtain-lecture of such a kind, that, despite its obvious sincerity to those familiar with

---

extent on the extracts from Beverning's diary and letters to the Council, quoted by R.H. Abbott from H. Scheurer's *Verbael Gehouden door de Heeren H. van Beverningk, W. Nieupoort, J. van de Perre, en A. P. Jongestaal* (1725, The Hague Archives).
19. From Beverning's diary, quoted in *W.S.*, III, 45.
20. The Dutch had suspicions that Cromwell had proposed hard terms in order to curry patriotic favour for his government, while the English thought de Witt had sent the deputies to win time for the Dutch fleet to refit.
21. See Cromwell's letter to Penn, July 9, 1653, *W.S.*, III, 69 f. The fleet probably returned to refit and to land Blake who was seriously ill.
22. *W.S.*, 111, 70–3, from *Verbael*.

his ways of thought, it could only be dismissed by the Dutch as a typical example of insular prejudice and insufferable English conceit.

When the English proposals were presented on July 21, it was discovered that they advanced a plan for an Anglo-Dutch Commonwealth so revolutionary that the Dutch feared it would mean the virtual absorption of the Netherlands into England. The example of Scotland was too recent,[23] and as further negotiations seemed useless, two of the envoys returned home,[24] although the position of the Dutch negotiators was made very much more difficult by the defeat administered by Monk to Van Tromp and de With[25] off Scheveningen on July 31, which resulted in Van Tromp's death.[26] The heavy losses on both sides in this engagement precluded any major naval action for some time, but de With's fleet was badly damaged by gales in October, and events again seemed to be shaping the victorious destiny of Cromwell and his country.

On August 6 Van Beverning managed to gain a long private conversation with the Lord General in St. James's Park.[27] The Dutchman pointed out that the English proposals took no cognizance of Holland's existing treaty obligations,[28] but Cromwell remarked that "the interests of the people remain always the supreme law".[29] Beverning was quick to reply that it would not augur well for the proposed treaty with England if the Netherlands held herself so loosely to her treaty obligations, and the Lord General "appeared to agree and let it pass". He stressed the commercial advantages of union and was extremely vague about the constitutional form of his proposed Anglo-Dutch State.

A formula for political union of the two sovereign republics was never found. Unofficial negotiations were carried on throughout

---

23. Nieupoort suggested that the proposals must have been taken straight from the settlement imposed upon Scotland the previous year! Jongestaal to Frederick William of Orange, July 19 /29, 1653. *Thurloe State Papers* (7 vols., 1742), I, 362.
24. Nieupoort and Jongestaal.
25. Witte Comeliszoon de With, Vice-Admiral: not to be confused with John de Witt, the Grand Pensionary.
26. Van Tromp was able to break the blockade and allow de With to escape from the Texel, but his fleet was defeated and he himself was killed.
27. *W.S.*, III, 84 f., from *Verbael*.
28. i.e. between the Netherlands and Denmark.
29. "Salus populi suprema lex esto." Cicero, *De Legibus*, III, iii, 8.

August and September, and on September 23 Sir Cornelius Vermuyden, as Cromwell's confidential envoy, approached Van de Perre with a new plan which stopped just short of political union.[30] The fact that political amalgamation was not pressed reflects upon Cromwell's constitutional difficulties at home, and his disillusionment with "government by the saints": until Britain had solved its own constitutional troubles it could hardly expect Holland or any other country to consider any wider union. Eventually even Oliver was convinced, and when open negotiations were resumed on November 17 and 18,[31] he said – with some regret – that suggestions for union would be put aside in view of Dutch objections. Yet it was clear in the ensuing discussion that although the English scheme had been officially discarded, Cromwell still hankered after it, and it is equally clear that the Dutch found the Lord General's preoccupation with the English proposals, and his tone of condescension, highly irritating. They had to remind him that "they clearly saw the mercy shown by God almighty to the English in their difficult situation and otherwise,[32] but thanks to God they enjoyed many commodities themselves!" If Cromwell understood the rebuke he showed no signs of having done so, and blandly advised them that since Britain offered so many advantages to the Dutch, they ought to rate closer relationships between the two countries more highly than anything else. "The English", he declared, "could say without boasting that God our Lord had brought their country in such a state that they could do without us ... but that we without their friendship could not continue our trade." It was in this spirit of virtuous superiority that on December 2 the Lord General presented the scheme of a treaty which the Dutch could not possibly accept, and hence they had no option but to break off negotiations, despite the news of further Dutch losses at sea.

Although the Lord General's attempt to bring about an Anglo-Dutch state or federation failed, his schemes indicate the general

---

30. It was proposed that the two governments should conclude an offensive and defensive alliance, that there should be mutual admission to commercial privileges and civil rights, and the plan implied a division of the world into British and Dutch "spheres of influence" for the double task of trade expansion and missionary enterprise! *Verbael,* 149–53, as cited in *W.S.,* III, 107.
31. *W.S.,* III, 122–5, from *Verbael,* 187–96.
32. A sharp reminder of the ineptitude of the Nominated Parliament and the turbulence of the Fifth Monarchists.

pattern that his foreign policy would follow. It has been justly remarked that the proposal for coupling together foreign trade and Protestant evangelism "was a conception only equalled, as it was perhaps suggested, by the success of its predecessor, commerce and Catholicism",[33] but it reminds us that a foreign policy does not consist of an alliance with one power. If the immediate problem was to reach a settlement with the Netherlands, friendship must also be sought with other states, and a policy must be defined towards the great Catholic powers. Most of these were likely to come into conflict with the new militant republic – France by reason of its proximity, and Spain and Portugal by reason of their trading interests; but there were good reasons why each wished to avoid an immediate open war with England, not least because of their mutual rivalries.

With an army waiting to be used and expecting to be paid, the Puritan republic was not likely to remain at peace for long,[34] and the relationship of the Catholic powers with England during these months reflects their anxiety. Spain, as an hereditary enemy of England since the death of Mary, was in the most obvious danger, but she had adroitly forestalled immediate war by promptly recognizing the republic as early as December 1650. Portugal did not seem to be in immediate danger. The Portuguese were traditionally accepted as England's oldest allies, and on the strength of this alliance John IV's ambassador tried to secure a new trade agreement, but found himself driven to such hard terms that his king refused to ratify the treaty. An unforeseen incident, however, suddenly strained relationships between England and Portugal near to breaking-point, and diplomatic circles were shocked into realizing that the new power could not be ignored.[35]

France, torn by the civil wars of the Fronde and more or less

---

33. R.H. Abbott, *W.S.*, III, 107.
34. Three possible lines of action were defined in the Council Meeting of April 20, 1654: war with France and alliance with Spain; war with Spain and alliance with France; "or to have had freindshipp with both, supposinge wee might have had good sums of money from both soe to doe". *C.P.*, III, 203.
35. Dom Panteleon Sa, the young brother of the Portuguese ambassador, expressed some disparaging comments about England in company with some companions one evening near the Exchange. A quarrel developed with Colonel Gerard, an English royalist, and the Portuguese escaped, but only to return with more colleagues and to pick a further quarrel in which two innocent men lost their lives. Dom Panteleon retreated to his brother's house, but diplomatic privilege was refused by Cromwell and he was executed for the murders. Clarendon, *History*, XIV, 38-40; Whitelocke, 569.

constantly at war with Spain, appeared to be the most open to attack, and her ships had engaged in unbroken privateering against English shipping in the Channel throughout the civil wars.[36] Furthermore, the Protestant citizens of Bordeaux were in revolt. Probably war with France would have been a certainty if intervention on behalf of the Bordellais could have had any possibility of success, but despite negotiations it was clear from the first that no foreign intervention could save them.[37] It was only the statesmanship of Cardinal Mazarin which kept his country treading carefully along the precarious path between war and peace with England, and it is difficult in retrospect to explain how he avoided open conflict during this critical period, for there were plenty of grounds for a declaration of war,[38] and there were inviting opportunities to be exploited. We are led to the conclusion that either Cromwell was not yet ready to embark upon foreign war, or else that he and Mazarin had reached a tacit understanding. Perhaps both suggestions contain elements of the truth. Clarendon, who as an exile in France was in a good position to judge the effects of Cromwell's foreign policy, said, "every day produced fresh evidence of the good intelligence between Cromwell and the cardinal".[39]

Meanwhile, if it was from the Catholic south that England was to pick its enemies, it was to the Protestant north that it would look for its friends. The fact that the Dutch had been granted preferential rates for the passage of their boats through the Sound had meant that the Baltic had become almost entirely closed to English trade, and an alliance with Sweden was desirable in order to counter-balance the existing alliance between Denmark and Holland. At the end of December, 1652, Lord Lisle had been accredited as ambassador to Sweden, but he had declined, and since then many had been approached without success. Recollection of the fate of Ascham in Madrid and of Dorislaus at

---

36. Not only was there a constant danger from French picaroons, but open engagements with the French Fleet were not unknown. In October Captain Hayton reported an engagement of this kind in which the French were worsted. Whitelocke, 566.
37. They surrendered on July 31, 1653.
38. See Cromwell's letter to Mazarin, July. *W.S.*, III, 74; *L-C*, III, 442 (Supp. 79a). There were also the actions of French privateers and French support for the royalist cause.
39. *History*, XIV, 34 and 53. Cf. the letter to Mazarin, June 9. *W.S.*, III, 35; *L-C*, III, 288 (App. 27), and the assurance that English ships would not be sent to the Garonne to aid the Spaniards. *W.S.*, III, 82 f.

The Hague would be a considerable deterrent. Eventually Bulstrode Whitelocke was persuaded, not without many misgivings, to accept the position.[40] This appointment, confirmed on October 29,[41] was the first time since the pacification of Britain that an envoy of the British Commonwealth had been commissioned with the specific task of concluding a foreign trade alliance,[42] and with the appointment of John Thurloe as head of the government's Intelligence in the preceding July, it marked the practical "arrival" of the Commonwealth in European affairs.

V

However spectacular the entry of the republic into European affairs might be, the real test of its permanence would be at home, and in summoning the assembly of Puritan representatives an attempt had been made to deal with the outstanding problem of constitutional settlement.

There were dependent problems, which if not equally far-reaching were certainly equally urgent, and there are indications that after the ejection of the Rump a determined attempt was made to cut through the Gordian knot of England's domestic difficulties, and to produce practical results quickly. The financial chaos was taken in hand. In April, 1653, the credits of the previous government were appropriated, the Commissioners for inspecting the Treasuries were required to report on the state of national finance,[43] a real attempt was made to get the soldiers' arrears settled and their regular pay guaranteed,[44] and an inquiry instigated into outstanding monies held by the officers for the men.[45] Cromwell's efforts met with the immediate approval of the soldiers, who declared "that in four hours so to speak he has

---

40. Cf. letter of invitation, September 2. *W.S.*, III, 97; *L-C*, III, 289 (App. 27).
41. Whitelocke, 567.
42. We may ignore Strickland and St. John's ill-fated embassy to the Netherlands in 1651.
43. *Cal. S.P. Dom.* (1652–53), 299. Also, despite the protests of the Spanish ambassador, a cargo of captured bullion and specie was "frozen" pending a decision on its ultimate fate.
44. See Cromwell's letter to the Commissioners for the monthly Assessment at Chester, June 10, *W.S.*, III, 37; and his similar letter to Gloucester, calendared in *L-C*, III, 441 (Supp. 79).
45. Letter to Lt -Col. Mitchell, May 18, 1653. *W.S.*, III, 28; *L-C*, III, 287 (App. 27).

effected what was denied them for whole years by the late parliament".[46]

His financial policy involved Ireland. By a boldly conceived stroke Cromwell and his colleagues sought at once to punish the Irish delinquents, settle the country with Protestants, and to repay the Commonwealth's debts. Roman Catholic priests and Irish soldiers were deported or allowed to emigrate,[47] and a High Court of Justice was set up to try the principal leaders of Irish resistance. As a result, the government had at its disposal a considerable amount of property; a proportion of this was to be divided among the "Adventurers",[48] the soldiers, and the nation's creditors. In addition, it was estimated that there would be enough land left to provide a useful annual income to the Treasury.

However the "settlement" of Ireland worked out in practice, it does not appear to have been vindictively conceived. It has been observed that the members of the High Court of Justice, "while vigorous, seemed to bear out the claims of their superiors that they were not 'men of blood',[49] and the plan for the redistribution and resettlement of Ireland aimed at leaving the peasantry unmolested. Granted the views about Ireland which Cromwell and his Council shared, it was a bold and imaginative way of meeting their immediate difficulties.[50]

In Scotland the work of pacification continued, but the officer in charge, Colonel Robert Lilburne, had all he could do to keep the Highlanders subdued[51] and the Kirk mollified. One significant fact in home affairs, however, which witnessed both to the completeness of English supremacy, and to the realism of the government, was the summons to representatives from Scotland and Ireland to sit at Westminster, and the creation of a single

---

46. Paulucci to Sagredo, June 15/25. *Cal. S.P. Ven.* (1653–54), 90.
47. Whitelocke, 553, 562.
48. i.e. those who had originally subscribed the funds for the reconquest of Ireland.
49. R.H. Abbott, *W.S.*, III, 43.
50. An act "touching the Adventurers for lands in Ireland" was mooted by the Council of State early in June (Whitelocke, 557), but it was left to the new Representative to take final action in the matter. On August 16, 1653, an order was made for an act "touching Publick Debts", and there were "Orders touching Arrears of Some Officers in Ireland; and for the sale of some Delinquents Lands to defray Publick Charges". *Ibid.* An act for the Irish Adventurers was passed on September 27, *Ibid.*, 565.
51. In September Whitelocke made special reference to the fact that "the highlanders were all quiet." *Ibid.*, 564.

executive and legislative authority of all three nations for the first time.

One of the first official actions of the Puritan nominees who came to Westminster was to vote themselves the dignity and title of a "Parliament",[52] but the trial of John Lilburne during these months showed that whatever grounds there were for the assumption of that title, it was certainly not founded upon popular consent.

Lilburne had been exiled after a dispute about a colliery in 1652 for his calumnies against Sir Arthur Hazelrigge. While abroad he had dealings with the Duke of Buckingham, but in defiance of the ban he returned to England in 1653, and was almost immediately arrested and committed to Newgate.[53] He had, however, become something of a national figure, and petitions immediately began to pour in to Parliament for his release.[54] On July 15 he was brought to trial, and he again defied the court in a way which captured the nation's imagination,[55] so that the jury brought in a verdict which was virtually one of acquittal.[56] Even the soldiers who lined the streets sounded their trumpets in his honour when the verdict became known.

The importance of Lilburne's trial was not in the fact that "Freeborn John" had once again escaped the gallows, but in the revelation of popular feeling which could not be misinterpreted by those responsible for government. Lilburne had a natural propensity for pretentious martyrdom – what Clarendon described as "a marvellous inclination and appetite to suffer in the defence or for the vindication of any oppressed truth"[57] – but the expression of jubilation at the verdict was due neither to his popularity nor to sympathy with his opinions – it simply reflected the general anxiety at the policy of the Nominated Parliament,

---

52. *Ibid.*, 564. *Diary of Thomas Burton* (ed. J.T. Rutt, 4 vols., 1828), I, i.
53. Whitelocke, 558. He published from prison several appeals to Cromwell and to the Council of State. For his petitions to Parliament, see *Burton's Diary*, I, ii, v.
54. Whitelocke, 558–61 *passim*.
55. In 1649, after one of his imprisonments he managed to appeal so successfully to popular sympathy that he was acquitted amid enthusiastic rejoicings.
56. August 20. The verdict was that Lilburne had done "nothing worthy of death". He was kept a close prisoner. See the chapter on Lilburne in *The Concern for Social Justice in the Puritan Revolution* (1948), 20–38, by Dr. W. Schenk; Whitelocke, 563; and *Burton's Diary*, I, viii–x.
57. *History*, XIV, 50. Clarendon misdates Lilburne's trial as 1655, instead of 1653.

which was demonstrating all the least reasonable features of Puritanism.

The Assembly contained a good number who were very far from the fanaticism attributed to this Parliament by its detractors.[58] Even Clarendon admitted that among its members there were "some few of the quality and degree of gentlemen, and who had estates, and such a proportion of credit and reputation as could consist with the guilt they had contracted", but he went on to say that the greater number were "inferior persons, of no quality or name, artificers of the meanest trades, known only by their gifts in praying and preaching".[59] S.R. Gardiner has estimated that there were eighty-four "moderates" and sixty Puritan radicals at Westminster,[60] and it was from the minority and its excesses that the Parliament gained its notoriety.

There were many reforms which this Parliament introduced that were truly enlightened. If the members' debates on national finance were stormy,[61] they showed a deep sense of responsibility,[62] even at the expense of the more powerful Army officers.[63] Bills were passed which, for the first time, legalized civil marriages, enforced the registration of births and deaths and the probate of wills. In its humanitarian legislation the Parliament was far in advance of its time, introducing acts for the care and maintenance of the mentally defective and lunatic, for the redress of prisoners' grievances, and for the relief of poor creditors and debtors.[64]

These reforms, however, were overshadowed by measures which went much further than the country was prepared to go, and threatened to disrupt the life of the nation completely. Religion had been the means by which the Nominated Parliament came into existence, and religion very soon appeared likely to be the reason for its eclipse. The clear division of interests between two parties within the House appeared when it was seriously proposed on July 15, 1653, to abolish tithes as the regular means

---

58. Cf. *W.S.*, III, so.
59. *History,* XIV, 15.
60. *Comm. and Prot.*, II, 308-10.
61. For Parliament's preoccupation with finance, cf. *Burton's Diary,* I, ii-iv, x.
62. Acts were considered regarding the arrears of Excise, the farming out of Excise, and for revising the inequalities in taxation. Whitelocke, 564, 566.
63. Cf. the reference to a debate on easing public charges by the multiplicity of officers. *Ibid,* 565.
64. *Ibid.,* 563, 564, 565. Cf. *Burton's Diary,* I, x, xi, xiv. A full list of the legislation is to be found in Firth and Rait, *Acts and Ordinances of the Interregnum,* II, 702-813.

of maintenance for the ministry. This drastic measure was lost by only twenty-five votes. This was hardly what Cromwell had meant when he had called upon the members to "encourage" the ministry, and such procedure did not inspire any confidence that a stable policy was to be expected from the new Supreme Authority.[65] A further example of the same kind is to be seen in the proposed reform of the legal system. Cromwell himself had expressed the wish that the costly and ambiguous processes of English Law might be clarified and simplified,[66] but he was not prepared for the summary abolition of the Court of Chancery as proposed by the Nominated Parliament in August, 1653, and his hesitation was certainly shared by the greater part of the nation.[67]

The more "advanced" Members of Parliament were stimulated to this and similar extreme measures by the irresponsible preaching of the Fifth Monarchist preachers, like the anabaptist, Christopher Feake, and the Welsh revivalist Vavasour Powel at Blackfriars, who called for the abolition of the Common Law and the substitution of the laws of Moses. The religious extravagance of such men, together with the multiplicity of heterodox sects, and the anti-clericalism of a large minority in Parliament, only served to aggravate a religious situation which Cromwell had been trying to settle and regularize.[68] The Lord Mayor's petition in September had been concerned that there should be some promise of stability in religious matters, but on October 6, when the Lord Mayor tried to prevent a soldier from preaching in St. Paul's churchyard, a riot developed. In the same month there

---

65. The concern of the average citizen was voiced in a petition of the Lord Mayor and Common Council of London to Parliament in September, "That the precious Truths of the Gospel may be preserved in Purity, and the Dispensers thereof, being approved, to be learned, Godly, and void of offence, may be sent forth to preach the Gospel.

"That their settled maintenance by Law, may be confirmed, and their just Properties preserved.

"That the Universities may be zealously countenanced and encouraged." Whitelocke, 564.

66. Ludlow, *Memoirs*, I, 246 f.

67. Under Friday, August 5, 1653, it is recorded: "The House, according to former order, took into consideration the business of the Court of Chancery.

Resolved, that the Court of Chancery of England shall be, forthwith, taken away." *Burton's Diary,* I, vi; cf. *Ibid.,* viii, xiii.

68. Abolition of tithes and reform of the law had long been main planks in the Levellers' platform, coupled with a pronounced anti-clericalism. Dr. W. Schenk stresses the connection between the Leveller movement and the more radical religious groups. *The Concern for Social Justice in the Puritan Revolution,* 68–79, 82 ff.

was an even more significant protest from "the Congregational Churches in the North", and the House itself voted, "That there shall be a Declaration giving fitting liberty to all that fear God, and for the preventing the Abuses against Magistrates, and for the Preservation of such that fear God among themselves without imposing one upon the other, and to discountenance all Blasphemies, damnable Heresies, and licentious Practices."[69]

Meanwhile, the Lord General called a conference which included the Independents, John Owen and Philip Nye, the Presbyterian, Stephen Marshall, and the Baptist, Henry Jessey, to discuss the religious situation in the country. His chaplain, Peter Sterry, was deputed to try and persuade Christopher Feake and his followers that their agitation was bringing the government into disrepute both at home and abroad.[70] The Fifth Monarchists refused either to be persuaded or subdued, and eventually Feake was committed to prison for his fulminations against Cromwell and the government.[71]

Cromwell was irritated and bewildered by the course events were taking. Because the Parliament was composed of "good" men he had looked for good government: he had expected reform of the legal system, and Parliament had threatened to abolish the Law altogether; he had desired a settlement in religion with reasonable liberty of conscience for all, but Parliament had attempted to deprive the ministry of its settled maintenance, and had encouraged the ravings of a new spiritual Babel; he had hoped for enlightened Christian legislation, but he was forced to realize that the course upon which the Parliament appeared to be set threatened to bring all government to the ground. In this spirit he wrote to Fleetwood in Ireland at the end of August:[72]

> Truly I never more needed all helps from my Christian friends than now! Fain would I have my service accepted of the saints (if the Lord will), but it is not so. Being of different judgments, and of each sort most seeking to propagate their own, that spirit of kindness that is to them all, is hardly accepted of any. I hope I can say it, my life has been a willing sacrifice, and I hope, – for them all. Yet it

---

69. Whitelocke, 566.
70. Van Beverning had attended some of the meetings at Blackfriars.
71. *Cal. S.P. Dom.* (1653–4), 308.
72. August 22. *W.S.*, III, 88 f.; *L-C*, II, 307 f. (CLXXXIX).

much falls out as when the two Hebrews were rebuked: you know upon whom they turned their displeasure.[73]

But the Lord is wise, and will, I trust, make manifest that I am no enemy. Oh, how easy is mercy to be abused: Persuade friends with you to be very sober. If the day of the Lord be so near (as some say), how should our moderation appear.[74] If every one (instead of contending) would justify his form "of judgment" by love and meekness, Wisdom would be justified of her children.[75]

There was very little in subsequent events to reassure Cromwell.[76] He was unanimously re-elected in the election for the new Council of State on November 1,[77] but there were dark rumours of designs to have him supplanted by Harrison. On the other hand, his supporters in Parliament used the pretext of a fresh royalist conspiracy to get a new High Court of Justice appointed: the fiasco of Lilburne's trial could not be allowed to recur.

Meanwhile, it seemed as if the radicals were proposing to abolish both the public ministry and the universities. A committee on tithes brought in proposals which were obviously framed by the more moderate party,[78] but these were decisively rejected by the House on December 10, and this left the way open for the opposition to launch a new attack on the public maintenance of the ministry generally. It was probably in apprehension of such a move that on December 12, 1653, Cromwell's supporters, taking a leaf from the Rump's book and arriving early at Westminster, proposed and carried the dissolution of the Parliament

---

73. Exodus 2:14. It was not the first time Cromwell had likened himself to Moses. Cf. *supra*, p. 203.
74. Philippians 4:5.
75. Matthew 11:19 (Luke 7:35). Cf. Wisdom 7:22-8.
76. The critical state of the country was reflected in a further outbreak of royalist plotting. Colonel Phillips and some colleagues were committed to the Tower for treason on August 13. They were joined on the 27th by Colonels Slingsby and Pinchbeake, and on the following day the wealthy Leveller, William Walwyn. This suggests that Cromwell feared a Royalist-Leveller attempt to overthrow him. In September bear-baiting was forbidden in Warwickshire to prevent royalists gathering under cover of the sport.
77. There were 113 voters present. Harrison was only thirteenth on the list of those elected.
78. They provided for the ejection of "all ministers who are not of good Behaviour and holy in Conversation, or not apt and able to teach, or hold forth the faithful Word, or be not diligent"; provision was also suggested for the union of small parishes within a three-mile radius of the place of public worship; it was suggested that where there were scruples against tithes, an assessment might be made by the local Justices of the Peace. Whitelocke, 570.

and delivered its authority back to the Lord General.[79] The Nominated Parliament was at an end.

VI

On September 12, 1654, reflecting on those months during which the Nominated Parliament sat, Cromwell commented ruefully, "what the event and issue of that meeting was, we may sadly remember: it hath much teaching in it, and I hope will make us all wiser for the future",[80] and even at the end of the Protectorate, he described this experiment as the story of his own "weakness and folly":[81] the shame and uncertainty of 1653 were never forgotten. Yet there is no obvious reason why the Nominated Parliament should have ended in failure. Other Parliaments had been no more representative and not nearly so conscientious, but had survived to enjoy a better reputation. What were the lessons which were to be learned from this attempt to govern the three nations by men chosen for their godliness?

First, it may be taken as an axiom of good government that the pace at which legislation is passed must approximate to the pace of public opinion. A conservative government may try to retard, and a radical government may try to accelerate reform, but as soon as any government begins to draw away from popular desire, it has ceased to be good government and may end by becoming a tyranny. This is what happened in 1653, for in the flush of Puritan idealism the members tried to give the nation not what the people wanted, but what they thought was good for them, and ordinary people resented it because they began to feel that the accepted pattern of English life was being threatened. Secondly, we are faced with the question how far the Christian ethic can be

---

79. "It was moved in the House, that the sitting of this Parliament any longer would not be for the good of the Commonwealth, and that it would be fit for them to resign up their Powers to the Lord General: This Motion was seconded by several other Members, and then the House rose.

"And the Speaker, with many Members of the House, with the Mace, went to Whitehall where they did, by a Writing under their Hands, resign to his Excellency the Powers; and Mr. Speaker attended with the Members, did present this Resignation of their Powers to his Excellency accordingly." Whitelocke, 570. Cf. *Burton's Diary*, I, xiv. The motion was proposed by Sir Charles Wolseley and seconded by Sir Anthony Ashley Cooper and Colonel Tichborne. *C.P.*, III, 9.

80. Speech to the first Protectorate Parliament. *W.S.*, III, 454; *L-C*, II, 37a (Speech III).
81. April 21, 1657. *W.S.*, IV, 489; *L-C*, III, 98 (Speech XIII).

or ought to be imposed upon a nation. Nations are predominantly secular, and the standard by which they are governed must be recognized by all as binding within the tacit contract of their common life: the basis is Justice rather than Love, for the former does not assume that men are better than they really are.[82]

We are back at the principle that we have called, for want of a better name, the "dual ethic". The course taken by the Nominated Parliament underlines the fact that to govern a nation on the basis of an ethic to which the majority of people cannot or will not aspire, is an imposition, and ultimately may be a breach of trust. In the realm of the secular the basis of political action will always be that of human justice rather than Christian love. This does not mean, however, that the categories with which the politician works are necessarily subchristian, for the Christian politician is called upon to apply the highest standard possible in relationship to the people he governs, and in this he is constantly inspired by the love or concern he bears for them as a Christian. The members of the Nominated Parliament did not understand these distinctions: the failure of the government by Puritan "saints" was their failure to distinguish clearly between or to reconcile adequately their vocational duty to God as individual Christians, and their vocational duty to God as civil representatives of their fellow men.

---

82. This is seen most pointedly in the policy of the Roman Catholic clerics who governed France throughout the first half of the seventeenth century, the Cardinals Richelieu and Mazarin, and the former's lieutenant, Père Joseph.

Chapter Seventeen

Princeps: The Constitution and the Major-Generals (1653 – 1656)

I

The Lord Protector

Lambert's written constitution, long prepared, was accepted, for there was no alternative, and this "Instrument of Government" was put into operation almost immediately. Hereby it was established "That the supreme legislative Authority of the Commonwealth of England, Scotland, and Ireland, and the Dominions thereunto belonging shall be and reside in one Person, and the people assembled in Parliament; the style of which person shall be, Lord Protector of the Commonwealth of England, Scotland, and Ireland."[1] Although this meant that the constitution was to return to the traditional form of a single person and Parliament, it also meant that this person was committed to accept any limitations which Parliament might impose. On the other hand, there were safeguards employed to prevent any hostile person from being elected to Parliament, or from sitting if they were elected,[2] and there was a definite provision that "the Persons elected shall not have the power to alter the Government as is hereby settled in a single Person and a Parliament".[3]

---

1. The text of the Instrument of Government is in Whitelocke, 571–7; Gardiner, *Const. Docs.*, 405–17. The Instrument nominated Cromwell "Lord Protector" for life; it provided that the Lord Protector was to control the militia and exercise his government with the consent of Parliament when it was sitting, or with the advice and consent of a council of twenty-one members; legislation was to be initiated by Parliament when in session, and the Lord Protector had no right of veto (if the Protector's consent was not given to a bill within twenty days, it still became law); provision was made for national religion, and there was to be religious freedom for all but Roman Catholics, Episcopalians, and such as "hold forth and practise licentiousness". The most significant articles, however, were those which ensured triennial Parliaments (which within the space of three months could not be dissolved without their own consent), and which ensured that Parliament should be summoned should the Lord Protector fail to summon it himself (Articles X–XII, XX).
2. Articles XIV–XVI.
3. Article XII.

Princeps: The Constitution and the Major-Generals

On December 12, 1653, Oliver Cromwell, His Excellency the Lord General (dressed as a civilian) took the oath administered to him by the Lord Commissioner Lisle, and became installed in the Court of Chancery as His Highness the Lord Protector, but the change in his habit could not conceal where his power resided. His oath of office declared that he had been "desired and advised, as well by several Persons of Interest and Fidelity in this Commonwealth, as the Officers of the Army", to take upon himself "the Protection of these Nations", and throughout the proceedings this emphasis on the military appeared and reappeared with an insistence which almost raised the Army to the status of a fourth estate of the realm.

For Cromwell himself the failure of the Nominated Parliament had meant far more than the breakdown of a constitutional experiment. It meant disillusionment. He was forced to realize that religious theories were not likely to meet political necessities. "The visionary and the practical man in him had been at strife, and the latter had triumphed, but the triumph left an uneasy conscience behind it."[4] The change of the temperature of the government was signalized by changes in the personnel of Cromwell's advisers. Thomas Harrison and the Fifth Monarchists went into eclipse as the republicans before them.[5] The new administration aimed at stability and rejected "enthusiasm", and from this time onward the Lord Protector relied on the advice and services of professional men. They were soldiers like Lambert, Monk, Desborough and Montagu; politiques like Sir Anthony Ashley Cooper, and Sir Charles Wolseley; clergymen like John Owen, Philip Nye and Thomas Goodwin; lawyers like Widdrington, Whitelocke and Lisle; merchants like Christopher Packe and Robert Tichborne; and behind all, the professional administrator, John Thurloe. Many of the Protector's court had been prominent in the affairs of the nation for some years, but with the exclusion of all other elements their influence now became predominant. They were bound to the Protectorate for a variety of reasons – some from personal loyalty, some from desire for settled government, and others for ambition – but whatever their motives in supporting the Protector, they were strictly

---

4. John Buchan, *Oliver Cromwell*, 439.
5. Harrison was deprived of his commission on December 21, and ordered to retire to his father's house in Staffordshire by February 13, 1654. He was kept under observation, arrested for a short period in September of that year, and relieved of his army command in December 1654.

realistic. Their position received its most dignified expression in the prose of Milton who pleading for equal rights and equal laws, added:[6]

> If there be any one who thinks that this is not liberty enough, he appears to me to be rather inflamed with the lust of ambition or of anarchy, than with the love of a genuine and well-regulated liberty; and particularly since the circumstances of the country, which has been so convulsed by the storms of faction, which are yet hardly still, do not permit us to adopt a more perfect or desirable form of government.
>
> For it is of no little consequence, O citizens, by what principles you are governed, either in acquiring liberty, or in retaining it when acquired. And unless that liberty which is of such a kind as arms can neither procure nor take away ... shall have taken deep root in your minds and hearts, there will not long be wanting one who will snatch from you by treachery what you have acquired by arms.

Cromwell's supporters saw the weaknesses of the situation and were ready to accept the Protectorate and all its implications for the maintenance of public order. The sincerity of many of them could not be doubted, but there were others who were simply time-servers to the rising star of Cromwell's fortune, and some who were not afraid to exploit the military power on which the Protectorate was based.[7] The influence of such men produced a gradual secularization, not so much in the policy as in the atmosphere of the Protectorate.

For the first eight months of the Protectorate Cromwell and his Council ruled by ordinance. Apart from the diatribes of the Fifth Monarchists and the sullen hostility of the republicans, it appears to have been a quiet period in the affairs of the nation: peace was concluded with the Dutch in April, 1654,[8] and there was at least the prospect of a parliament. Yet during these months the domestic and foreign policies of the Protectorate were initiated, and for some the signs must have appeared ominous. A

---

6. *Defensio Secunda pro populo Anglicano* (1654), *Milton's Prose* (World Classics), 403.
7. Cromwell protested to Colonel Hutchinson with regard to some of his arbitrary measures that "Lambert had put him upon all those violent actions". *Memoirs of Col. Hutchinson* (Everyman edn.), 298. The exchange of Ireton's influence for that of John Lambert may have been a much more significant factor in Cromwell's life than has been generally recognized.
8. Both Fifth Monarchists and Republicans wanted to continue the Dutch war and force the Dutch to a coalition. Cf. Ludlow, *Memoirs*, I, 378, note by C.H. Firth.

treason ordinance was passed to extend the penalties for treason to any who spoke or acted against the Instrument of Government. Fifth Monarchist preachers soon became liable to punishment under it, and since conviction would mean death, the Protector kept them imprisoned without trial.[9] It was a piece of humanitarianism which earned him no thanks, because the English hated arbitrary imprisonment more than the death sentence.[10] Edmund Ludlow in Ireland refused to sign the proclamation of the Protectorate, and hindered its publication for a fortnight.[11] The threat of future trouble is seen in the fact that although Ludlow resigned his position as one of the Commissioners for Ireland, he retained his commission as Lieutenant-General on the grounds "that as one had made use of the military sword to destroy the civil authority, so others might have an opportunity to restore it by the same means".[12] Cromwell could now count on the bitter enmity of many by whose help he had risen, and the tension which grew during the Protectorate can be sensed beneath the surface – the sullen opposition and fear of a government, not because it was harsh or vindictive, but because it appeared arbitrary in its actions and unlimited in its power.

Although Cromwell appeared to be absolute, his recognition as Lord Protector had in fact set bounds to the absolute power which he commanded as Captain General,[13] and while Parliament was not sitting, the powers of the Council, with Lambert at its head, were scarcely less extensive than those of the Protector. Although it was usual for the wishes of the Protector to be obeyed, it was not an invariable rule.[14] R.H. Abbott has suggested that the administration during these first eight months of the Protectorate was conducted in a way "not dissimilar from but with even more authority than that which had been exercised by

---

9. After a meeting on December 19, 1653, Feake and Powell were taken into temporary custody. They were released but rearrested in January 1654. Feake and another preacher, Simpson, were taken to Windsor Castle on January 28. *W.S.*, III, 147, 175 f.
10. Buchan, *Oliver Cromwell*, 445.
11. Ludlow, *Memoirs*, I, 374–6. Under February 16 Whitelocke notes that the Protector had been proclaimed in Dublin, "but not so soon nor so chearfully as he was in the North". Whitelocke, 581.
12. Ludlow, *Memoirs*, I, 377–8. Colonel Hutchinson was another republican who "would not act in any office under the protector's power". *Memoirs of Col. Hutchinson* (Everyman edn.), 293, 297–9.
13. Cf. *supra*, p. 296, n. 1.
14. He intervened in Irish affairs unsuccessfully on February 16 and March 20 1654. Cf. *W.S.*, 111, 198, 238.

Charles I and his Council in the period of 'personal government' against which they had risen in arms",[15] and he suggests that the root of Cromwell's difficulties was in the fact that although few doubted that within the circumstances "he was the man in all the British Isles best fitted for the headship of the state", even his eulogists "were unable to bridge the gap between the fact and the theory of his position in the state".[16]

The criticisms do not stand, and they would certainly not have been understood by Cromwell and his supporters.[17] Under the *Instrument* Cromwell had constitutional limits which Charles never had, and the position of the country in 1653–54 was radically different from what it had been in 1629–40, for Charles had imposed his personal rule on a country at peace, whereas Cromwell had to produce order out of the chaos caused by over ten years of civil war. Nor is it true to say that he and his supporters were unable to bridge the gap between the fact and theory of his position in the state. The answer which they presented was that of Cromwell's providential leading and vocation under God: in place of the Divine Right of Kingship, a new Divine Right of Vocation was asserted, founded squarely upon the doctrine of Providence, and although many may have been sceptical, the progress of Cromwell's career was too remarkable for this theory to be disregarded. For Cromwell himself the proofs had been too clear for him to doubt his high calling. Towards the end of his life

> He caused one of his Gentlemen often to read the tenth Chapter of Matthew's Gospel;[18] and twice a day himself rehearsed the 71 Psalm of David, which[19] hath so near a relation to his Fortune and

---

15. *Ibid.*, 157.
16. *Ibid.*, 180 f.
17. "A new parliament is summoned; and the right of election given to those to whom it was expedient. They meet; but do nothing; and, after having wearied themselves by their mutual dissensions, and fully exposed their incapacity to the observation of the country, they consent to a voluntary dissolution. In this state of desolation, to which we were reduced, you, O Cromwell! alone remained to conduct the government and to save the country. We all willingly yield the palm of sovereignty to your unrivalled ability and virtue. ..." Milton, *Defensio Secunda* (World Classics), 396. Even the royalist Dr. Bates admitted that the people were united under Cromwell from fear of the fanatics' excesses. *Elenchus Motuum*, Pt. II, 171.
18. This chapter begins with Christ's commission to the Twelve, and contains the promise of God's care for the disciple, together with Christ's warning of the opposition and difficulties that His followers would meet. Cf. vv, 22, 29–39.
19. See especially vv. 6–12.

to his Affairs, as that one would believe it had been a Prophesie purposely dictated by the holy Ghost for him; or else that this great Personage was the Mortal Figure of that great Favourite of God, who had done so many marvellous things with such slender beginnings, passing through so many obstacles, difficulties, and dangers.[20]

The parallel between his own career and that of the peasant lad who became King of Israel was extremely pointed, and the psalms assume an increasingly important place in his life.[21] The idea of David as the servant of the Lord[22] seems to be very near Cromwell's conception of himself: David was anointed as Israel's king not by any natural right, but by the direct choice of God, and he was called to govern Israel during the critical beginnings of her national history. Oliver Cromwell seems to have taken this as a pattern for himself, but since this conception of divine commission rested ultimately upon his own sense of vocation and his own interpretation of Providence, the bases of his call were too subjective to go unchallenged. Parliament was soon to challenge them.

II

Parliament and the "Single Person"

The first Protectorate Parliament was called to meet on September 3, 1654,[23] the auspicious anniversary of Dunbar and Worcester.[24] After addressing the members briefly in the Painted Chamber the Lord Protector dismissed them until the morrow. On the following day there was a procession of suitable solemnity[25] to hear a sermon preached by Dr. Thomas Goodwin in Westminster Abbey.[26] From the Abbey the members assembled

---

20. Carrington, *History of Oliver*, 230.
21. See R.E. Prothero, *The Psalms in Hunan Life* (1904), 229–36.
22. 2 Samuel 3:18; 4:5, 8; 1 Kings 3:6; 8:24–6, 66; Psalm 78:70; 89:3, etc.
23. Under the Instrument of Government there was a slight tendency to increase the representation of the counties at the expense of the smaller boroughs. Abbott says that, "taken all in all, in view of the peculiar circumstances, of the opposition to the Protectorate, and of the Council's veto power, the new Parliament was apparently a better and more representative body than might have been expected." W.S., III, 387. Cf. Gardiner, *Comm. and Prot.*, III, 167–78.
24. The day was a Sunday and offended the scruples of some of the members. See the *Diary* of Guibon Goddard, in the introduction to *Burton's Diary*, I, xviii.
25. Whitelocke, 599.
26. Goodwin's sermon has not survived, but from Cromwell's speech it appears to have been based upon the delivery of Israel from Egypt, and her entry into the Promised land by way of the desert. This simile was applied to the

once more in the Painted Chamber, where the Lord Protector greeted them "seated in a Chair of State set upon steps".[27]

There was an obvious contrast between this ceremony and the occasion fourteen months previously when Cromwell, as Captain General, had delivered the commission to the Nominated Parliament and "devolved" his trust upon them. There was no such attempt to resign his authority on the present occasion, and if the additional pomp and circumstance was indicative of Cromwell's altered status, it was no more significant than the altered style of his speech.[28] He could not refrain from some rehearsal of the providences of God, and his address did not lack its fair share of scriptural quotation, but the members were treated to a plain statement of their country's difficulties, from which the note of something even akin to despair was not entirely absent. "I must profess this to you", he said, "that if this day ... prove not healing, what shall we do?" He proceeded to describe the existing confused state of the country, where everyone claimed the right to advance his own arbitrary opinions; in particular he mentioned the Levellers[29] and those "many honest people, whose hearts are sincere" but who were under "the mistaken notion of the Fifth Monarchy".

While the nation was "rent and torn in spirit" Jesuits had entered the country, and the wealth of the nation had been wasted by naval war. The Protector went on to give an account of his stewardship – the reform of the legal system had been entrusted to lawyers of ability, steps had been taken for the regulation of the ministry, and a free Parliament had been called. Instead of facing the hostility of Europe they now had peace with the Dutch, treaties had been concluded with Sweden, Denmark, Portugal, and most of the Protestant states on the Continent, and there was a projected treaty with France. He explained the financial straits in which they were placed, and said it was "one of the great ends of calling this Parliament, that this ship of the Commonwealth may be brought into a safe harbour"; he concluded by assuring them that he spoke "as one that doth

---

circumstances in which England found herself at that time. The President of Magdalen College had had the degree of D.D. conferred upon him by Oxford University on December 23, 1653.
27. Whitelocke, 599.
28. W.S., III, 434–43; L-C, II, 339–59 (Speech II).
29. The Lord Protector confused the political demands of the Levellers with the social demands of the "True Levellers" (or Diggers).

resolve to be a fellow-servant with you". After the speech the members were dismissed to choose their Speaker,[30] so that they might lose no time in carrying on their work.[31]

We have already seen that the Instrument of Government forbade the members to alter the new constitution,[32] but there were ominous signs of future trouble. It was pointed out that the Treason Ordinance which had been published by the Lord Protector and the Council made it High Treason for anyone to speak against the present government, and it was claimed that this hindered Parliament's freedom of speech. It was moved that "notwithstanding that Ordinance, the House was free to debate the Government".[33]

It was clear from the first that Parliament intended to assert its supremacy over the Lord Protector, and it was proposed to alter the constitution so that it would read, "that the Government should be in the Parliament of England, &c; and a single person, qualified with such instructions as Parliament should think fit".[34] The members strongly asserted Parliament's exclusive right to the legislative function of government, and although the "Court Party" strenuously opposed the proposals, they appeared steadily to lose ground.[35] They urged that the supremacy of Parliament would give it the right to perpetuate itself, as the Long Parliament had done, and in so doing they advanced a theory of the Divine Right of the Protector as high as anything advanced by the Earl of Strafford: the co-ordinate power of Protector and Parliament was the foundation of the constitution, and "foundations were not to be altered or removed". They asserted that the sword and the present power were both "of God", and that, "the whole nation had concluded themselves and us from altering of it, by the sealing of the indenture of the

---

30. William Lenthall, the Speaker of the Long Parliament, was chosen. Goddard, *Burton's Diary*, I, xx.
31. The diary of Guibon Goddard (elected a burgess for Lynn in Norfolk), which is printed in the introduction to *Burton's Diary*, gives a detailed account of Cromwell's dealings with this Parliament. Goddard's reactions to the new government were typical of a good many of the elected members. He was critical of the Court Party – Cromwell's supporters – and suspicious of the Protector's powers, but he was not sufficiently opposed to relinquish his seat.
32. *Supra*, p. 296.
33. Goddard, *Burton's Diary*, I, xxiii (Cf. Whitelocke, 600). The proposal was turned down, but on the significant ground that it called in question something "which was never doubted".
34. Goddard, *Burton's Diary*, I, xxv.
35. *Ibid.*, xxvi.

return of the election".[36] Finally – and this was the fact which prevented all real compromise – Goddard says "they did not forbear to tell us plainly, that it must be so; that my Lord Protector must not be thought, that ever he would part with that power which he conceived was so fully in him".[37]

On the other hand, the opposing party, headed by the group of experienced republicans,[38] asserted the supremacy of Parliament in terms no less high, and they challenged not only the political ground of the Protectorate, but also its theological foundations: they pointed out, "That the providences of God are like a two-edged sword, which may be used both ways; and God in his providence, doth often permit of that which he doth not approve; and a thief may make as good a title to every purse which he takes by the highways".[39] This, of course, is the obvious flaw in an interpretation of Providence which identifies God's favour with success, but the republicans saw it only because the form of government they wanted had suffered eclipse; there had been no such denial of the popular view of Providence when the Long Parliament had been at its height.[40]

The Protector could not allow the House to assert its authority over his own, for that would mean not only that he could be put out of office and command, but also that there would be no check on Parliament in three matters where his experience had shown such a limitation to be necessary – prevention of perpetual parliaments, control of militia, and the settlement of religion. Therefore when it seemed that a proposal was about to be passed to which he could not possibly agree,[41] Cromwell summoned the members before him again in the Painted Chamber on September 12.[42] When they were assembled, the Protector told them roundly[43] that they were a free Parliament only so long as they owned the authority which called them there, and it appeared

---

36. Ibid., *xxix*.
37. Ibid.
38. Sir Arthur Hazelrigge, Thomas Scot, Lord President Bradshaw. Cf. Ludlow, *Memoirs*, I, 391.
39. Goddard, *Burton's Diary*, I, xxx. An argument repeated in later debates cf. *ibid.*, lxix.
40. Cf. *Memoirs of Col. Hutchinson* (Everyman edn.), 235, 269.
41. That the "Government should be in the Parliament and a single person, limited and restrained as the Parliament should think fit". September 11. Proposed by Matthew Hale, Goddard, *Burton's Diary*, I, xxxii.
42. Cf. *Ibid.*, xxxiii.
43. W.S., III, 451–62; *L-C*, II, 366–90 (Speech III). Summary in Whitelocke, 605.

Princeps: The Constitution and the Major-Generals

necessary for him to dilate somewhat on the nature of his office:

> I called not myself to this place, [he declared;] I say again, I called not myself to this place; of that, God is witness. And I have many witnesses who, I do believe, could readily lay down their lives to bear witness to the truth of that, that is to say, that I called not myself to this place. And being in it, I bear not witness to myself; but God and the people of these nations have borne testimony to it also.
>
> If my calling be from God, and my testimony from the people, God and the people shall take it from me, else I will not part with it. I should be false to the trust that God hath placed upon me, and to the interest of the people of these nations, if I should.

He traced his own history from the early days and through the civil wars, and he declared, "I begged to be dismissed of my charge; I begged it again and again. And God be judge between me and all men if I lie in this matter!" But despite his protest, and although he spoke of a "sinful" desire "to be quit of the power God had most providentially put into my hand", it was evident that he had no intention of being quit of it now, for he believed that he had been called to the task by God and the people. As proof of this he instanced his Installation, which, he said, "was not done in a corner"; he cited as further witnesses the judges and magistrates who acted under his commissions, the sherriffs who issued the writs for Parliament, and finally the members themselves and the whole electorate. "And thus," he added, "I have made good my second assertion, that I bear not witness to myself; but the good people of England, and you all, are my witnesses." From this he asserted his own Divine Right of Vocation, for "May not this character, this stamp, bear equal poise with any hereditary interest, which may have, and hath had, in the common law, matters of dispute and trial of learning? wherein many have exercised more wit, and spilt more blood, than I hope ever to live to see or hear of in this nation."

He defined three fundamentals of government: first, that the government should be by a single person and a Parliament; secondly, liberty of conscience;[44] thirdly, control of the Militia by

---

44. It is very interesting to notice that Cromwell used the *cuius regio, eius religio* principle (every monarch's defence for religious uniformity) to defend his own right to establish religious toleration. He said, "Every sect saith, Oh! Give me liberty. But give him it, and to his power he will not yield it to anybody else. Where is our ingenuity? Truly, that's a thing ought to be very reciprocal. The magistrate hath his supremacy, and he may settle religion according to his

the single person, since only by such power could the perpetuation of parliaments be prevented and the constitution defended. He pointed out that all the power of the Protector was to be shared, with Parliament or with the Council when Parliament was not sitting, and he declared that he would rather be rolled into his grave and buried with infamy than submit to the destruction of this government "so owned by God, so approved by men". The reasons for this – and they go to the heart of the difference between the arbitrariness of Charles I and the arbitrariness of Cromwell – were to be found in the situation in which the nation found itself, for he reminded the members that foreign states could look upon "a people that have been unhinged this twelve years' day, and unhinged still", and he added:

> if breaking should come upon us, and all because we would not settle when we might. ... Who can answer for these things to God, or to men; to the people that sent you hither, who looked for refreshment from you, who looked for nothing but peace, and quietness, and rest, and settlement? And when we shall come to give an account to them, we shall be able to say, Oh! we have quarrelled for, and we contested for the Liberty of England. Wherein forsooth? For the liberty of the people? I appeal to the Lord ... that the liberty of England, the liberty of the people, the avoiding of tyrannous impositions, either upon men as men, or Christians as Christians, is made so safe by this Act of Settlement, that it will speak sufficiently for itself.[45]

He brought his speech to an end by requiring each of the Members of Parliament to sign an engagement that they would be faithful to the Lord Protector, and not propose or give their

---

conscience. ... All the money of this nation would not have tempted men to fight upon such an account as they have engaged, if they had not had hopes of liberty, better than they had from Episcopacy, or than would have been afforded them from a Scottish Presbytery, or an English either, if it had made such steps or been as sharp and rigid as it threatened when it was first set up."

45. It can be suggested that Cromwell and his army had contributed substantially to the plight of the three nations, but it can also be argued that during the past few years they had stood between the nation and anarchy, and were in that position at this time. Cromwell saw his form of government as safeguarding the principles which had been won during the civil wars. Professor Abbott is near the truth when he writes that Cromwell's rule had one great advantage against which none could argue, and that "was its apparent inevitability. What was the alternative? To Republicans and Parliamentarians it was the supremacy of Parliament, but even they were bound to admit the necessity for an executive head. To Royalists it was obviously monarchy, but that was unthinkable to the men now in control, who had risked their lives to overthrow monarchy." W.S., III, 500.

consent to alter the Government "as it is settled in one single person, and a Parliament".[46] The speech was notable for its freedom from religious enthusiasm, but for all that it stated perhaps more clearly than any of his speeches the high doctrine of his vocation, and indicated without ambiguity the "providential" necessities on which that calling rested.

About one hundred and forty members signed the Recognition immediately, but the typical attitude of the remainder was illustrated in the action taken by the Norfolk members.[47] Obviously a good proportion of the remaining members intended to give way as little as possible to the Protector. On September 14, 1654, the House met and voted "that it was not intended by any thing in our former subscription, to preclude or restrain ourselves from the examining or altering of any of the articles in the Instrument of Government, saving only that of the first article of settling the government in a sole person and the Parliament".[48] Parliament was still truculent, and the Instrument of Government would not be accepted without substantial modification.

III

Parliament and Prerogative

The acceptance of the new constitution, even in a very much truncated form, would at least mean that the form of government was recognized and had been agreed by representatives of the people, but it was clear from the start that the Lord Protector

---

46. See the form of Recognition, W.S., III, 463; L-C, II, 391; Goddard, *Burton's Diary*, I, xxxv.
47. "Our Norfolk members did not presently (i.e. immediately) subscribe, saving only Mr. Frere (Freer, or Frere, had been a supporter of Cromwell in the Nominated Parliament. Cf. Gardiner, *Comm. and Prot.*, II, 310), who instantly subscribed it. The rest of our members did most of us dine together, purposely to consult what was fittest to be done in so great an exigent, in order to the discharge of our trust. And, truly, the subscription was, in effect, no more than we were restrained unto by our Indentures, and the thing would be done without us, and we had fairly contended for it: we had not given the question, but it was forced from us, and we were told that plainly it must be so. For these and several other considerations and reasons, which we thought ought to prevail with men preferring the peace of our countries and the safety of our people immediately concerned in this affair, before passions and humours, we thought fit rather to give way to present necessity, and to comply with it by submitting than refusing. Accordingly we did subscribe, all except Mr. Woodhouse, Mr. Hobart, and Mr. Church." Goddard, *Burton's Diary*, I, xxxv–vi.
48. *Ibid.*, I, xxxviii; Whitelocke, 605.

and the opposition regarded the Instrument of Government in quite different ways: Cromwell regarded it as the permanent guarantee of the Country's settlement, whereas the parliamentarians regarded it as a stepping-stone to full parliamentary sovereignty.[49]

Despite the fact that many of the more intractable members had been excluded, the Protector's powers were attacked wherever they could be attacked. His control of the militia, his powers of nominating to the Council, the estimates for taxation were all assaulted in turn. His office was declared to be elective and not hereditary,[50] the articles on religion were very hotly debated, without any practical result,[51] and the provisions for liberty of conscience were whittled down.[52] Against these bills the Lord Protector was to have no power of veto,[53] and it can hardly be wondered that the parliamentary committee which had attended him to discuss the articles on religion met with a decidedly cool reception.[54] It was eventually decided "that without the consent of the Lord Protector and Parliament, no Laws shall be made for the restraining of such tender consciences as shall differ in Doctrine, worship and Discipline from the publick Profession, and shall not abuse this Liberty, to the Civil Injury of others or the Disturbance of the publick Peace",[55] but Parliament showed its inclination in the matter by ordering two books by the Unitarian John Biddle to be burnt publicly, and their author to be committed to prison.[56]

---

49. This was illustrated in the debate on the Protector's veto. Both parties in the House agreed that the Protector should have the power of vetoing legislation which sought to perpetuate the sitting of parliaments, but a stormy debate raged on whether this right should be declared "to be" or "shall be" in the Protector. In insisting on the former the Court Party argued that the Protector possessed his power as Head of the State, while the Parliamentary Party maintained that he would have this right only by the authority of Parliament, and presumably at a future date the power might be removed. Goddard, *Burton's Diary*, I, lxxiv.
50. *Ibid.*, I, li.
51. *Ibid.*, lix-lx; Whitelocke, 609.
52. Although it was voted that no laws should be passed to force anyone to accept the form of religion recognized by the state, it was also voted that bills should be introduced "compelling people to come to church upon the sabbath- day", and for the suppression of certain "damnable heresies" which were to be enumerated by Parliament.
53. Goddard, *Burton's Diary*, I, cxiii.
54. *Ibid.*, I, lxxix.
55. Whitelocke. 609. The last clause was directed against the Fifth Monarchists and Quakers.
56. *Ibid.*, Goddard, *Burton's Diary*, I, cxxiii-cxxx.

Princeps: The Constitution and the Major-Generals

The attitude adopted by Parliament towards the Protector's known will in religion is typical of its attitude throughout the session. Whenever the Protector's ordinances were brought into the discussion there was always a strong body of the House which was unwilling to admit their validity;[57] the debate on December 5, 1654, on parliamentary representation and the appointment of Judges, was described by Goddard as "a day of the greatest dispute of business that I had known in the whole Parliament".[58] They also voted "That no Law should be altered or repealed, nor new Laws made, nor any Tax imposed, but by assent of Parliament",[59] and that the Protector should not have the right to pardon treason or murder.[60] The civil estimates were limited to £200,000 p.a.,[61] and the Chancery Ordinance was suspended.[62]

The break ultimately came over the question of the militia. On Wednesday, January 10, 1655, it had been proposed that before voting on the Bill which would settle the constitution, a conference should be sought to discuss outstanding issues with the Lord Protector, but that motion was lost.[63] The question of the militia was debated the following week without any agreement being reached, but on the last occasion it was declared that "the militia of this Commonwealth ought not to be raised, formed, or made use of, but by common consent of the people assembled in Parliament".[64]

On Monday, January 22, 1655, taking advantage of the fact that by lunar reckoning the five months allowed for the Parliament had elapsed, the Lord Protector dissolved Parliament, and in so doing denied himself the ratification of the constitution that he desired and looked for. In his speech[65] he reminded them that from the day they had signed the Recognition they had had no hindrance from him but during the whole of their sitting he had

---

57. Whitelocke, 607 f. Goddard comments, "It was moved, that the former Ordinance of the Lord Protector, to the same purpose, be suspended; but could not prevail." *Burton's Diary*, I, lxii, cf. *ibid.*, xc.
58. *Ibid.*, cxii.
59. Whitelocke, 608.
60. *Ibid.*, 609.
61. *Ibid.*; Goddard, *Burton's Diary*, I, cxxii.
62. Whitelocke, 608; Goddard, *Burton's Diary*, I, xcvi.
63. The voting was 95–107. *Ibid.*, cxxvii.
64. Voting 109–82. *Ibid.*, cxxxi–iii.
65. W.S., III, 579–93; *L-C*, II, 404–30 (Speech IV); Whitelocke, 610–18.

not heard from them,[66] and under their shadow subversive elements had sheltered. Nothing had been done to establish religion on a sound basis, or to give a just liberty to the conscience of others; on the contrary, he observed:

> Is there not yet upon the spirits of men a strange itch? Nothing will satisfy them, unless they can put their finger upon their brethren's consciences, to pinch them there. To do this was no part of the contest we had with the common adversary; for religion was not the thing at first contested for, but God brought it to that issue at last, and gave it unto us by way of redundancy, and at last it proved to be that which was most dear to us. ... Is it ingenuous to ask liberty, and not to give it? What greater hypocrisy than for those who were oppressed by the Bishops, to become the greatest oppressors themselves, so soon as their yoke was removed?[67]

He asked the members to judge whether they had made the best use of their time, and commented, "you have wholly elapsed your time, and done just nothing". He declared that even the Long Parliament would have acted differently, and "As for myself, I desire not to keep it [the form of government] an hour longer than I may preserve England in its just rights, and may protect the people of God in such a just liberty of their consciences". The country needed settlement, but it seemed fated not to have it: "I would be loath to call it fate, that were too paganish a word – but there is something in it, that we have not our expectations."

Then with an eye upon future criticism of his inevitable return to arbitrary government, he said that although some would think it was wrong to raise taxation without Parliament, he had another argument for the people – "whether they prefer the having of their will, though it be their destruction, rather than comply with things of necessity? That will excuse me." He was indignant that it had been suggested that these "necessities" were a creation of his own ambition, and he warned them that they were in danger of the unforgivable sin,[68] "therefore whatsoever you may judge men for, and say, this man is cunning, and politic, and subtle, take heed, again I say, how you judge of his [God's] revolutions, as the products of men's inventions." He upbraided the members

---

66. This was not strictly true, since committees had been sent to confer with him on religion, and regarding the dismantling of certain fortified towns. Cf. Goddard, *Burton's Diary*, I, lxxix, xci–xciii.
67. Cf. *supra*, p. 305, n. 1; *infra*, p. 324-33 *passim*.
68. Cf. Mark 3:28-30 (Matthew 12:31-2; Luke 12:10).

for their neglect of the Army, when it was thirty weeks in arrears in Scotland, and he concluded by saying, "I know not what the Cornish-men, or the Lincolnshire-men may think, or other counties, but I believe they will all think they are not safe. ... And if it be my liberty to walk abroad in the fields, or to take a journey, yet it is not my wisdom to do so when my house is on fire."

It was a rambling speech, but there were good grounds for Cromwell's insistence that the country was in danger; indeed, those whose business was the actual task of defence had no doubt about the matter.[69] The Levellers and royalists were plotting together, Fifth Monarchists were keeping up a constant stream of abuse, Scotland was still unpacified, Fleetwood was having trouble in Ireland, and the ill-fated West Indian expedition under Penn and Venables had just set sail.

Cromwell was exasperated because other people did not see the dangers nor accept them as sufficient justification for his actions. In a letter to a friend just before the dissolution of Parliament,[70] he declared that, "were it not that I know whom I have believed,[71] the comforts of all my friends would not support me, no not one day". During the session of his first Parliament he had carried the burden of government despite bad health and domestic troubles,[72] and he had sustained a serious accident.[73] The strain of government was beginning to tell upon him, and he was deeply conscious of people's criticisms.[74]

---

69. Cf. Blake's observations: "I cannot but exceedingly wonder, that there should yet remaine so strong a spiritt of prejudice and animosity in the minds of men, who profes themselves most affectionate patriots, as to postpone the necessary wayes and meanes for preservation of the commonwealth, especially in such a time of concurrence of the mischievous plots and desseins both of old and new enemies, tending all to the distinction of the same." Blake to Thurloe, March 14, 1654/5. *Thurloe S.P.,* III, 232.
70. To Lt.-Col. Wilkes, January 1654/5. *W.S.,* III, 572 f.; *L-C,* III, 459–61 (Supp. 98); *C.P.,* III, 239–42.
71. 2 Timothy 1:12.
72. His wife and daughter had been ill, and his mother had died.
73. His coach horses bolted and he was pitched from the coach and dragged some distance by his feet before the horses were stopped.
74. "Whosoever labours to walk with an even foot between the several interests of the people of God for healing and accommodating their differences is sure to have reproaches and anger from some of all sorts. And truly this is much of my portion at the present, so unwilling are men to be healed and atoned; and although it be thus with me, yet the Lord will not let it be always so. If I have innocency and integrity the Lord hath mercy and truth, and will own it. If in these things I have made myself my aim, and designed to bring affairs to this

It has been said that Cromwell failed to observe that the general criticism which he had to face was to be explained "not by the sinfulness of mankind but by a common detestation of a Government based on the power of the sword".[75] But would the troubles of the three nations have disappeared had Cromwell resigned? There is nothing to suggest that England's foreign enemies would suddenly have become friendly, that Scotland and Ireland would have become amenable, or that the Cavaliers, the Fifth Monarchists and the Republicans would have agreed about the constitutional settlement of the country. Anarchy would have resulted, and hence if there is justification for the opposition to the Protectorate, there is at least equal justification for Cromwell's claim that he and the Army prevented the nation from suffering a worse fate. The Lord Protector saw this very clearly, and perhaps that was the reason for his blindness to shortcomings nearer home.

IV

The Insurrection of 1655

The tension within the nation was due to the fact that "there was an irrepressible conflict between a Parliament which regarded itself as the representative of the nation and a Protector who regarded himself as appointed by God to save that nation, even from itself";[76] and when Parliament was dissolved the struggle went on in the towns and shires. Yet if left to themselves the opponents of the Protectorate would have fought each other, and if Cromwell's difficulties were increased by the number of groups ranged against him, his task was simplified by reason of their mutual antipathies.

With the installation of the Protector, however, the object of their hatred had become personified, and there was a noticeable movement among the opposition groups to unite for the purpose of destroying the Protectorate. Perhaps the first step towards the "Major-Generals" can be traced in the Instructions that were sent to Monk when he replaced Robert Lilburne in the Scottish

---

issue for myself, the Lord is engaged to disown me; but if the work be the Lord's, and that they are His purposes which He hath purposed in His own wisdom, He will make His own councils stand." To Lt.-Col. Wilkes, *W.S.*, III, 572; *L-C*, III, 460 (Supp. 98).
75. S.R. Gardiner, *Comm. and Prot.*, III, 249.
76. R.H. Abbott, *W.S.*, III, 596.

command,[77] and which take upon themselves a new significance by reason of the man to whom they were sent. George Monk was an ex-royalist who had made a career in the Army, and who had risen with the rising fortune of his Commander-in-Chief. He could be relied upon to obey commands implicitly. Very soon after he arrived in Scotland he discovered disaffection among his officers which gathered around the person of Colonel Robert Overton. Monk dealt with the matter promptly, and Overton was sent under guard to England. The government was alarmed to discover that meetings of a seditious character had been held in London by a number of republican officers.[78] The government was even more concerned to learn that these activities had connections with a royalist conspiracy,[79] and to keep down the opportunities for sedition, sports-meetings were from time to time forbidden;[80] but it is clear that these measures only partially succeeded. The discovery of the "Overton plot" led to widespread arrests and interrogations throughout January, 1655, which revealed activity on a larger scale than had been supposed. General Monk sent word of a plot to gain control of the Scottish Army, in which a former officer, Miles Sindercombe, was implicated,[81] and Major Wildman was arrested in the very act of dictating a pamphlet inciting general rebellion against the Protector.[82] The general unrest may be judged from Whitelocke's comment that

> Many who viewed this Declaration, knew there was too much of Truth in it, and had not the Design been nipt in the Bud, and timely discovered, it might have caused some disturbance to the

---

77. April 1654. Lilburne had to meet the threat from Glencairn and Middleton, and Council had decided some months previously that at the earliest convenient moment he should be replaced by Monk. In April, with the cessation of hostilities against the Dutch, Monk was relieved of his duties at sea, and his Instructions for Scotland were signed on April 6. His commission was signed two days later. *Ibid.*, 246–8.
78. Including men like Admiral Lawson, and Colonels Okey, Alured and Hacker.
79. See the instructions to the governors of Windsor Castle and the Tower, to the officers of the ordinance, and to Monk, *W.S.*, III, 556 f., 559 f., 567–70. Harrison and some other Fifth Monarchists were examined and taken into custody about this time, probably to prevent their becoming involved. *Ibid.*, 618–20,635.
80. Horse racing was forbidden for six months, July 4, 1654, *Cal. S.P. Dom.* (1654), 242, 245; it was forbidden for a further six months, March 3, 1655, *C.P.III*, 24.
81. Whitelocke, 618 ff. Cf. *W.S.*, III, 60of.
82. *The Declaration of the Free and well-affected People of England now in Arms against the Tyrant Oliver Cromwell, Esq.*, Whitelocke, 618 ff.

Protector. ... Divers wondered most that Wildman and others of his Party who had served the Parliament, should now join in this design with those of the King's Party; but they alledged the strengthening of themselves, and their Power afterwards to suppress the Cavaliers, or any other who should oppose their ends: but divers suspected their Designs at the bottom of it, to intend the bringing in of the King; because they conclude in their Declaration for a truly free Parliament, which was the way for the King's Restauration.[83]

The underground movements came to a head in a royalist insurrection that was planned for March, 1655, and intended to involve the whole country. Thurloe's intelligence service together with prompt military action crushed the outbreak, in many places before it had time even to show itself. Royalists were seized at Gloucester, and a general rising at Shrewsbury was forestalled by some prudent arrests. The government seemed to have full information, if not of the details of the plan, then certainly of its general pattern, and was able to make its dispositions accordingly.[84] The meagre forces raised by Sir Joseph Wagstaffe, Colonel John Penruddock and Major Hugh Grove around Salisbury and Dorchester were easily crushed by a small detachment from Col. Berry's regiment under Captain Unton Croke,[85] who captured about fifty of them including all the leaders except Wagstaffe, who managed to escape.[86] This was the extent of the fighting, but it was not to be dismissed as a single local incident.[87] The rising was wholly in the royalist interest, but if common cause could have been made with the Republicans it would have been much more dangerous. The fact that men like Overton, Wildman, and Lord Grey were already in custody meant that the insurgents could expect no help from that quarter.[88] The nature

---

83. *Ibid.*, 620. Wildman was undoubtedly working with Charles; on the other hand, the old republicans like Ludlow and Hutchinson, to whom it was addressed, would never consent to monarchy.
84. March 5, 10, 12, letters to Colonel William Crowne, Colonel Humphrey Mackworth, Colonel Philip Jones, the Mayor of Newcastle and the J.P.s of Oxford. *W.S.*, III, 644, 647 f., 651. Cf. *L-C*, III, 462-3 (Supp. 100).
85. On March 12, 1655.
86. Newsletters, March 17, 20. *C.P.*, III, 28-9.
87. Similar rendezvous and risings had been planned for the surprise of Nottingham (March 13, *ibid.*, 26; cf. letter to Colonel Berry, *W.S.*, III, 650 f.; *L-C*, III, 463 f.), Shrewsbury, Newcastle, Chester and York, and the Home Counties (*C.P.*, III, 24-30). Some of these rendezvous actually took place, but the insurgents dispersed on seeing the smallness of their numbers (*Ibid.*, 27).
88. *Ibid.*, 23.

of the government and the complexity of the situation which it faced made some form of policing almost inevitable,[89] and a further stage in the move towards the system of local Major-Generals was reached when the appointment of Major-General Desborough over the counties of the south-west was placed on a more or less permanent basis.[90] The insurrection of the spring of 1655 can hardly be said to have endangered the regime, but if it had not revealed royalism to have been powerful, it had revealed it to be still active.

V

The Major-Generals

The fact that no High Court of Justice was set up to try the insurrectionists suggests that Cromwell regarded his government as legalized,[91] and Penruddock and his colleagues were therefore tried under the normal processes of English law, although some, who because of insufficient evidence could not be convicted of treason, were charged with felony (horse-stealing).[92] In June it was reported that Cromwell had conferred with his judges and officials regarding the state of the country. It was clear that if similar risings were to be prevented some form of local control would have to be established. The existing local administration had not been able to prevent the enemies of the state from collecting arms, and there had obviously been considerable royalist activity throughout the country.[93] At the same time Cromwell had to face the problems of reducing the standing Army, and of finding employment and pay for those that remained. Comparatively few of Charles's followers had become implicated in Penruddock's

---

89. Cf. the letter to Unton Croke to investigate the activities of Adjutant- General Allen who "doth very ill offices by multiplying dissatisfactions in the minds of men with the present Government". January 20, 1654/5, W.S., III, 578; L-C, II, 400 (CXCVII). See also the activities of Anthony Hillary as a common informer against Thomas Burton. *Burton's Diary*, I, clxxxii–iv.
90. May 28, 1655. W.S., III, 733 f.
91. Cf. R.H. Abbott's comments, *ibid.*, 670 f.
92. Seven were sentenced for treason, and the same number for felony; three were acquitted. Seven had been sentenced to the full rigour of being hanged, drawn and quartered, but Cromwell ruled that none should suffer any further pains than death by hanging or decapitation. Some of the executions were carried out on May 7; Grove was beheaded on May 9, and Penruddock a short while after.
93. Cf. W.S., III, 794 f.

rising, for the members of the "Sealed Knot"[94] had been opposed to it, and had nothing to do with it, but they were only waiting for a more favourable opportunity, and an invasion from the Spanish Netherlands was not beyond the bounds of possibility. Therefore the idea was conceived of appointing officers with the local rank of Major-General and with command over the local militia, to supervise administration in their districts. The cost of this was to be met by a decimation tax on the estates of those who had made the measure necessary – the royalists.

There was a further reason – -less tangible, but perhaps no less real to Cromwell – which may have prompted his closer dependence on the Army at this time, and this arose out of the attitude of Parliament in matters affecting the militia and religious toleration. Parliament had determined to reduce the military equipment of the country, but Cromwell said they ought "to prefer safety before any manner of charge".[95] The Protector therefore stood between the soldiers and Parliament's demand for their disbandment, just as he had done formerly, and it was clear too that he was their only safeguard in matters of religion. In the face of these threats, the Army closed its ranks behind its General: in November 1654, the Council of Officers meeting at St. James's "resolved to live and die with his Highness and the present government, and sent some of their members to acquaint him therewith",[96] and a few weeks later they petitioned the Protector to grant religious toleration to all but Roman Catholics.[97] If, as we have suggested, the relationship between Cromwell and his fellow officers had a religious basis which was deeper than simply that of a commander and his troops,[98] their influence upon him should not be underestimated. There were times when it appears to have been decisive, and possibly this was such an occasion.

The details of the new system of local control were planned by

---

94. The "Sealed Knot" was a secret royalist organization pledged to the destruction of Cromwell. Sir Richard Willis, one of its members, was in correspondence with Thurloe.
95. To the committee that interviewed him on the subject he said that he lacked precise information of the position in Ireland, but Scotland was "wholly very much disaffected to the present government", and "the Presbyterian and Cavalier interests were so complicated, as he did not see how any forces there could be lessened with any safety". Goddard, *Burton's Diary*, I, xci–iii; cf. *ibid.*, lxxvii.
96. November 30, 1654, *C.P.*, III, 10.
97. An intercepted letter written on December 19, 1654. *Ibid.*, 13.
98. Cf. *supra*. p. 65–7.

Princeps: The Constitution and the Major-Generals

Cromwell, Lambert, Pickering and Desborough early in August, 1655. England was divided up into county groupings or provinces;[99] Desborough had already been appointed to the command of the western counties,[100] and Skippon was made Major-General of London and Middlesex.[101] Henry Cromwell had already supplanted Fleetwood in Ireland, and the latter was now given a large command comprising most of East Anglia and some of the Midland counties,[102] while Lambert was appointed to command the counties of the north.[103] Colonel Kelsey was to command in Kent and Surrey; Goffe in Sussex, Southampton and Bedfordshire;[104] Whalley in Lincoln, Nottinghamshire, Stafford, Leicester and Warwick;[105] Boteler in Rutland, Huntingdon, Northants and Berkshire;[106] Berry in North and South Wales, Hereford and Salop;[107] and Worsley in Derby, Chester and Worcester.[108] All these officers were loyal to the Protector and they were given the power of appointing their own deputies.

It was not intended that the Major-Generals should supersede the existing administration, but rather that they should infuse into it something of the discipline and spirit of the Army. Most of the Instructions given to the Major-Generals were policing measures for the suppression of riot and insurrection, the prevention of highway robbery, control of vagrants and paupers, and the disarming of those who were known to be enemies of the State.[109] Some of the Instructions, such as those which commanded the suppression of certain isolated ale-houses and the supervision of innkeepers, at first sight suggest Puritan morality, until it is realized that Puritans did not become total abstainers until the

---

99. See the map illustrating the division. Gardiner, *Comm. and Prot.*, III, facing 340.
100. Gloucester, Somerset, Devon, Cornwall, Dorset and Wilts.
101. Barkstead was later appointed to the command of Westminster and Middlesex.
102. Norfolk, Suffolk, Cambridge and Ely, Essex, Hertford, Oxford and Buckinghamshire.
103. Yorkshire, Lancashire, Durham, Northumberland, Westmorland and Cumberland; cf. below.
104. Goffe was eventually appointed to Sussex, Hants and Berkshire.
105. Derby was added to his command later.
106. Later Bedford was exchanged for Berkshire.
107. Later South Wales seems to have been taken from his command. Cf. *W.S.*, III, 848 n.
108. He later gained Lancashire from Lambert and gave up Derby to Whalley.
109. *W.S.*, III, 844–8. Other directions were mainly administrative, and they went a good deal further than was usual in requiring the registration and control of foreigners and other potential enemies.

nineteenth century, and that isolated inns were likely places for hatching desperate conspiracy.[110] Apart from an instruction to enforce the ordinance for ejecting unsatisfactory ministers and schoolmasters,[111] and another for the suppression of gaminghouses and houses of ill fame within London and Westminster,[112] there was only one that directly affected religion and public morals, and this was a general instruction to co-operate with local authorities in enforcing the existing laws against drunkenness, blasphemy and profaning the Sabbath.[113]

The provisions, however, left the Major-General a good deal of latitude, and if he wished to interpret his instructions strictly there was sufficient excuse for a considerable amount of interference in the private lives of others. Perhaps the most important point which arises from a perusal of the instructions is the extent to which their surveillance and control extended over the nation at every point, and this must have been as great a factor in making them generally hated as their attempts to effect a reformation of manners.

At the same time, the enforcement of public morality was not the main work of the Major-Generals: by far the greater part of their work was concerned with the maintenance of public peace. There was no police force, and although the exact and careful control of potential enemies to the State was unknown at that stage of English history, the measures taken were certainly no more stringent than those which are invoked now in times of

---

110. Cf. also the instruction that they were "to have a strict eye upon the Conversation and Carriage of all Disaffected persons within the several Counties ... as also that no Horse-races, Cock-fightings, Bear-baitings, Stage-plays or any unlawful Assemblies be suffered or permitted within their Counties. Forasmuch as Treason and Rebellion, is usually hatched and contrived against the State upon such occasions, and much Evil and Wickedness committed." 4th article. Commenting upon a suppression of certain sports, Cromwell said on January 17, 1656/7 that there was "a great deal of grudging in the nation that we cannot have our horse-races, cock-fightings, and the like. I do not think these unlawful, but to make them recreations that they will not endure to be abridged of them, is folly." *W.S.*, IV, 278.
111. 7th article.
112. 19th article.
113. "They shall in their constant Carriage and Conversation, encourage and promote Godliness and Virtue, and Discourage and Discountenance all Profaneness and Ungodliness; and shall endeavour with the other Justices of the Peace, and other Ministers and Officers, who are intrusted with the care of those things that the Laws against Drunkenness, Blaspheming, and taking the Name of God in vain, by swearing and cursing, Plays and Interludes, and prophaning the Lord's day, and such like wickedness and abominations, be put in more effectual execution than they have been hitherto." 6th article.

emergency as a matter of course. Cromwell made it clear that he and his colleagues were not blinded by the fact that so few had appeared in support of Penruddock's rising, for they knew that "persons that carried themselves the most demurely and fairly of any men in England were engaged in this business".[114] During the early days of 1656 news began to percolate through to Thurloe from Spain of Colonel Sexby's intrigues to unite Levellers and royalists in support of an invasion from the Spanish Netherlands, and the government saw in this and other plots the justification for their measures.[115] For these reasons Cromwell defended the appointment of the Major-Generals. Nevertheless, they did more than anything else to make Puritan government feared and detested by the country at large, and for that alone they were a major political blunder.

The second Protectorate Parliament was called for financial reasons. The decimation tax upon royalists had not covered the expenses of the policing system, and the virtual failure of the West Indian expedition, together with the cost of war with Spain and the expenses of administration, had produced an acute financial crisis. After special consultations with the Council and the Major-Generals at the end of May 1656, writs were issued for an election on August 20, and Parliament assembled on September 17.[116]

Cromwell's second period of personal rule was over, and in trying to place it in the context of the Lord Protector's life we must try to understand the background. The first point to notice is that much of the evidence of unpopularity – and there is a good deal – is also evidence that the threat which Cromwell professed to fear was real: the Lord Protector believed he stood between the nation and civil war, and he had good grounds for this view.[117] Secondly, there was a significant change in the personnel

---

114. Speech at the opening of the Second Protectorate Parliament, September 17, 1656. *W.S.*, IV, 266.
115. See the synopsis of the letter to the Major-Generals, August 1656. *W.S.*, IV, 226.
116. How far the Major-Generals influenced the elections is difficult to say. Prof. Abbott offers no evidence on the subject, except to observe that influence must have been exerted because it was the common practice in the seventeenth century. The subsequent history of the first few days of that Parliament indicates that if influence was used to secure the government's nominees, it was not very successful. Cf. *W.S.*, IV, 230.
117. See his words to Ludlow, when Ludlow appeared before the Council of State. Ludlow, *Memoirs*, II, 11.

of Cromwell's supporters. He had won the hatred of former colleagues like Harrison, Ludlow and Vane,[118] but, more significantly, during these months he also lost the support – -certainly for a time – of others who had hitherto been compliant. It was noted at the end of January 1655, that Sir Anthony Ashley Cooper had not sat in the Council recently,[119] and others absented themselves for long periods. Whitelocke and Widdrington gave up their position as Commissioners of the Great Seal in opposition to the Chancery Ordinance, although they returned to office very soon after as Commissioners of the Treasury,[120] and in taking control into his own hands the Protector seems to have quarrelled with a good number of his Council, including Lambert and Desborough.[121]

We must take into account the fact that the Lord Protector was an ageing and sick man, who knew that unless his government could be stabilized, the revolution settlement would disappear at his death. The evidence of his signature is sufficient indication that the strain of his life was beginning to have its effect.[122] Throughout the year 1655 he had been intermittently ill, and his ill health had been aggravated by the illness of his favourite daughter, Elizabeth Claypole.[123] In March 1656, he sustained another coaching accident, although he does not appear to have suffered any injury,[124] but the low state of his health was illustrated in a succession of boils and swellings in the chest, from which he was suffering when Archbishop Ussher visited him in January that year.[125] To the total effect of this ill health we must add the unrelieved pressure of detailed administration, and the threat of assassination. These facts only emphasize that the maintenance of the *status quo* was almost wholly dependent upon his person, and that if it was to be safeguarded for future generations steps must be taken to ensure the succession in the office of

---

118. Cf. *Ibid.*, 10–14.
119. Newsletter, January 27, 1654/5, *C.P.*, III, 20; Ludlow, *Memoirs*, I, lxxi (Errata). The reasons given by Ludlow appear to be incorrect, but the fact is not disputed. Ashley Cooper was excluded from the Second Protectorate Parliament. Cf. *C.P.*, III, 73.
120. Whitelocke, 620, 627.
121. Cf. *W.S.*, IV, 56, 113, 116.
122. See the specimen signatures in *Burton's Diary*, III, frontispiece. There is an interesting reference to the Protector's failing memory in the account of Schlezer's audience in May 1656. Cf. *W.S.*, IV, 152.
123. September 1655. Cf. *W.S.*, III, 832.
124. *W.S.*, IV, III.
125. *Ibid.*, 69 f.

Protector. In summary, all these influences present us with the picture of a man firmly persuaded that without him the nation will dissolve into anarchy, able to govern the situation only as long as he could control the administration, and striving to do that in the face of failing health and onset of age; yet he was bewildered and anxious because he could not discover how to make the principles for which he had fought a permanent part of the nation's life, although he was convinced that he had been ordained by God to accomplish this.

Meanwhile, that conviction was enough: "If I have innocency and integrity the Lord hath mercy and truth." Therefore Cromwell ruled, warning men to "take heed lest they be found fighters against Him", and convinced that he spoke "for God and not for men". It was often arbitrary rule – a dictatorship – but it is surely unjust to contrast the Lord Protector with parliamentary monarchy, which was quite unknown in the seventeenth century,[126] and it is even more unjust to compare him with Charles I, whose circumstances were entirely different. Charles had governed arbitrarily, and by his rule had brought about civil war; Cromwell governed arbitrarily because (right or wrong) he believed that only thus could he avert civil war – or anarchy which was worse. As John Milton shows us, the Lord Protector was not alone in that belief.

---

126. As R.H. Abbott does. *W.S.*, III, 836.

Chapter Eighteen
Princeps: Home and Foreign Policy (1653 – 1656)

I

Scotland and Ireland

If the establishment of a constitution and the maintenance of civil peace were the central problems for Cromwell in home affairs, there were others which were threatening enough, and almost as urgent. In Scotland, for example, the situation had deteriorated during the time that Robert Lilburne was in command there, and if it can be said to have improved under George Monk it was only because Monk was a more efficient commander. His appointment to the command had been signalized by an ordinance of union between England and Scotland,[1] but that could not obscure the fact that to all intents and purposes Scotland was a foreign country under an army of occupation. On his arrival Monk found that he was faced not only with the rising in the highlands under the Earl of Glencairn and Lieutenant-General John Middleton, but with general hostility. The English commander immediately took the offensive, so that by the early days of July (1654) he had crushed all resistance, although the result could not be called peace. Meanwhile the Lord Protector tried to persuade some of the Scottish ministers to visit London to confer with him on the situation,[2] and special ordinances were passed for the support of the Scottish universities and public preachers. There was also an ill-fated attempt to extend the English ecclesiastical system across the border.

In Ireland a far more drastic policy had been started,[3] but the situation was complicated by the hostility of some of the officers

---

1. April 12, 1654. Firth and Rait, *Acts and Ordinances,* II, 871–5.
2. See letter to Robert Lilburne requesting him to pay the expenses of Gillespie, Menzies and Livingstone, March 7, 1654, *W.S.,* III, 211; *L-C,* III, 448 (Supp. 86); also a letter summoning Blair, Douglas and Guthrie to London, May 6, 1654. *W.S.,* III, 284.
3. *Supra,* p. 288 f.

who served there and by Fleetwood's inexpert handling of the position. Henry Cromwell was sent over ostensibly to visit his brother-in-law, but in fact to report on the situation generally, and on April 27, 1654, probably with the idea of strengthening Fleetwood's hand, the latter was appointed Lord Deputy.[4] His troubles continued.[5]

The government did make some attempt to deal with Ireland. The land allocated to the Irish Adventurers had been parcelled out in February 1654, but a new survey was ordered,[6] and trade concessions were offered to the Adventurers in an attempt to encourage Protestant settlers and to restore Ireland's economy. It was soon evident, however, that there was not enough land in Ireland to meet all the conflicting claims, and that Fleetwood was not the man to deal with the situation. The transplantation of the native Irish to Connaught, which was an integral part of the "settlement" of that unhappy country, went forward with indifferent success, for Fleetwood interpreted his instructions a good deal more rigorously than had been intended, since it is clear that Cromwell himself only wanted the more dangerous elements to be removed.[7] When Henry Cromwell returned as Major-General there were rumours that he was to supplant Fleetwood, and the latter seems to have felt that his position was becoming impossible.[8] As Carlyle said, if these rumours were not true they proved to be "prophetic of the truth".[9] Fleetwood sailed for England on September 6, 1655, and Henry virtually took control in Ireland from that date. His appointment as Major-General in Ireland meant a modification of the transportation policy and a real attempt to meet Ireland's urgent problems of population and economy,[10] and the correspondence between

---
4. Letter to Attorney-General. *W.S.*, III, 271.
5. Letter to Fleetwood agreeing to the removal of Colonel Alured, May 16, 1654. *W.S.*, III, 296 f.; *L-C*, II, 329 f. (CXCIII).
6. Under Dr. William Petty.
7. Cf. the letter to Fleetwood protesting that Lord Coursey had been treated the same as "the worst of the Irish ... which certainly was not the intention of the law which enjoins the transplantation". April 26, 1655. *W.S.*, III, 699; *L-C*, III, 465 (Supp. 103).
8. See Cromwell's letter to reassure Fleetwood, June 22, 1655. *W.S.*, III, 756; *L-C*, II, 451 f. (CXCIX).
9. *Ibid.,* 449.
10. The instructions issued from the Council included a suggestion for relieving Ireland's population problem by apprenticing Irish children to English masters. *W.S.*, IV, 125–30. It should be noted that Dr. Bates writes approvingly of Henry's administration in Ireland. *Elenchus Motuum*, Pt. II, 62–4.

the Lord Protector and Henry shows that the former approved the moderate policy carried out by his son.[11]

II

Reformation and the Settlement

In religion and in other home affairs the main task of the Protectorate was to carry out a programme of moderate reform that would reassure the country after the excesses of the Nominated Parliament. Although Whitelocke and Widdrington refused to administer the Ordinance for the reform of Chancery, there was no break with the legal profession, and the Protector was careful to appoint the finest lawyers, without inquiring too closely into their political opinions and with respect for their scruples. The royalist Dr. Bates commended very highly the improvement in the administration of Justice, the reform of morals, and not least, the modesty and good taste of the Protector's court.[12] Oliver's disgust with anyone who lived loosely receives corroboration from Whitelocke, who introduced to the Protector Count Hannibal Sehested, formerly the Danish viceroy of Norway. Oliver seemed to take a good deal of pleasure in the Danish nobleman's company until he discovered that the count was "a very debauched Person: which when the Protector knew, he would not admit him any more in to his Conversation."[13]

The religious settlement of the Protectorate has already been described in broad outline,[14] but, like the Constitution, it had never been ratified by a representative body of the nation, and thus when Cromwell became Protector the establishment of religion was still an outstanding problem in home affairs. On February 28, 1654, Cromwell conferred with a number of ministers, including John Owen, Thomas Goodwin, Sydrach Simpson, and Philip Nye, and on the following day a committee of the Council was ordered to confer with the ministers.[15] From these discussions a commission of thirty-eight members was appointed, both ministerial and lay, to approve new candidates for the

---

11. Letter to Henry, April 21, 1656. *W.S.,* IV, 146; *L-C,* II, 485 f. (CCVII). Henry was not appointed Lord Deputy, however, until November 1657. Cf. Newsletter, November 17, 1657; *C.P.,* III, 127.
12. *Elenchus Motuum,* Pt. II, 190 f.
13. Whitelocke, 627.
14. *Supra,* p. 254–7.
15. March I, 1654.*Cal. S.P. Dom.* (1654)1.

ministry.[16] Side by side with this Committee county commissioners were appointed who, in co-operation with the local ministerial committees, were to be responsible for ejecting ministers and schoolmasters who were unfit or incompetent.[17]

The "Commissioners appointed for the approbation of publique Preachers" were divided into three sections taking duty in turn, and we read that in their trial of candidates "there is no respect had to anything so much as grace in men's hearts". It was observed that "some University men for defect thereof, have been laid by, and some who never were University men, yet furnished with Gifts and Graces, have been received and welcomed";[18] but this did not imply a disrespect for learning. An ordinance was passed for the oversight and visitation of the universities and Public Schools,[19] and from Cromwell's speech to the Lord Mayor and Aldermen of London on September 15, 1654, it seems that the system would work both ways: it ensured that in the future no man would be allowed to preach "under pretence of being gifted before he had been tried and was allowed":[20] if it excluded the dull pedant it also excluded the garrulous ignoramus.

Other ordinances were passed dealing with the maintenance of the ministry, the amalgamation of small parishes, and the prevention of royalists being accepted into livings. In this way the ecclesiastical system was put into operation, and it was remarked that although the Commissioners were of "divers Judgments about Church matters", they acted with unanimity.[21]

The problem of religious toleration was complicated not only by the number, variety, and violence of the sects,[22] but also by the political aspirations which had become woven into the tangled

---

16. March 18. Cf. the "Ordinance for appointing Commissioners for approbation of Publique Preachers", March 20, 1653/4. Firth and Rait, *Acts and Ordinances*, II, 855–8; Whitelocke, 584.
17. Fundamentally the scheme was the same as that suggested in Owen's "Fifteen Fundamentals", presented to Parliament in 1652, but the broad functions of the central and local committees appear to have been reversed. Cf. *supra*, p. 256; W.S., II, 520.
18. *Mercurius Politicus*, April 13–20, 1654, p. 3429.
19. Firth and Rait, *Acts and Ordinances*, II, 1026–9.
20. W.S., III, 466.
21. *Mercurius Politicus*, April 13–20, 1654, p. 3429.
22. The Venetian ambassador, Giovanni Sagredo, reported that there were 246 different sects in London: Eucardio Momigliano, *Cromwell* (translated by L.E. Marshall, 1930), Appendix 299 f.

skein of religious heterodoxy. This is illustrated particularly in Cromwell's dealings with the Fifth Monarchists and with the Episcopalians. The thirty-seventh article of the Instrument of Government expressly excluded Anglicans and Roman Catholics from the benefits of toleration, but there was no theological reason why the former should not have enjoyed liberty of conscience. On October 4, 1655 – the year of the insurrection – a particularly oppressive "Declaration against the Royal Family of the Stuarts, and the true Worship of the Church of England"[23] was issued, which showed how suspiciously the government viewed the relationship between the episcopal Church and the royal cause. By this measure royalists were forbidden to employ as chaplain or schoolmaster any sequestered clergyman, while the latter was forbidden to teach, preach, use the Prayer Book, or to administer the Sacraments.

It was not simply a piece of Puritan vindictiveness. What was being proscribed was not simply a form of worship, but a hierarchy and a Prayer Book that was joined to Stuart monarchy both by loyalty, and to some extent by theology. The declaration was potentially harsh, but to be just, it should be pointed out that it ended with the proviso:

> Nevertheless, his Highness doth declare, that, towards such of the said Persons as have, since their Ejection or Sequestration, given, or shall hereafter give, a real Testimony of their Godliness and good Affection to the present Government, so much Tenderness shall be used, as may consist with the Safety and Good of this Nation.

This shows that the Declaration was more an attempt to curb the activities of political opponents than an integral part of Cromwell's ecclesiastical policy. His relationship with Archbishop Ussher[24] supports the view that the Protector would be willing to grant toleration to Anglicans as soon as he could be

---

23. W.S. III. 839-40. S.R. Gardiner maintained that there is no evidence of this Declaration having been invoked by the Major-Generals; on the other hand, the fact that it *could* be invoked was repressive enough. Cf. *Comm. and Prot.*, III, 336.
24. At the instigation of Ussher, Cromwell wrote to Fleetwood on behalf of Ussher's son-in-law, May II, 1655. *W.S.*, III, 713 f. The Archbishop seems to have been on close enough terms with the Protector to intercede in 1656 on behalf of the sequestered clergy, and secured the promise that they would not be further molested if they did not interfere in matters of civil government. Cf. *ibid.*, IV, 69 f.; Nieupoort to States General, February 22/March 3, 1656. *Add. MSS.* 17,677 W, fol. 232.

certain that it was politically safe to do so.[25] John Evelyn has given a very clear account of the last services to be conducted by sequestered clergy before the Declaration was due to come into effect – "the funeral sermon of preaching"[26] – but it is clear from his subsequent account that Anglican services continued to be held during the Protectorate, and were more or less connived at by the authorities.[27]

Similarly, although Roman Catholics were right outside the limits of toleration and priests who were caught were liable to suffer – and some did suffer – the full penalties of the law, it seems that those who did not give cause for suspicion in other ways enjoyed more freedom than their legal position would suggest. In November 1653 the royalist Roman Catholic, Sir Kenelm Digby, was allowed to return to England and was summoned before the Council of State on January 12. There seems little doubt that at this interview the possibilities of Roman Catholic toleration were discussed, and it should be noted that at the Protector's instigation the Council revoked the penalties under the recusancy laws.[28] Many Roman Catholics managed to hear Mass in the chapels of the foreign ambassadors,[29] and after the treaty with France Cromwell explained to Mazarin that, while he had no power to grant official toleration to Catholics, they had less reason for complaint under his government than they had had under the Commonwealth, and that he had already "plucked many out of … the raging fire of persecution". He promised the cardinal that he would do what he could in the future to mitigate their condition.[30] Sir Charles Firth, who amassed a considerable amount of material bearing upon the Protector's attitude to Anglicans and Catholics, has written:

> To sum up. The position of Catholics and Anglicans under the

---

25. In February 1656 he assured a deputation of Anglican clergymen that all he required of them was the promise that if liberty of worship was granted to them, they on their part would engage not to excite fresh disorders. Cf. S.R. Gardiner, *Comm. and Prot.*, III, 336.
26. December 25, 1655. *Diary of John Evelyn* (edited by William Bray and H. B. Wheatley, 4 vols., 1906), II, 81.
27. Cf. Evelyn's visit to the service conducted by Mr. Gunning, December 25, 1657; *ibid.*, 95 f. See also Newsletters December 28, 29, 1657. *C.P.*, III, 130 f.; *Cal. S.P. Dom.* (1657–58), 226.
28. *Ibid.* (1653–54), 360.
29. See the report by the Venetian ambassador, Sagredo, in Momigliano, *Cromwell* (Appendix), 308.
30. December 26, 1656. *W.S.*, IV, 368 f.; *L-C*, III, 5–7 (CCXVI).

Protectorate was in one respect very similar. Each creed and its adherents was exposed to penalties contained in a number of laws made before the Protectorate came into existence. But in each case the Protector and the government were inclined rather to relax than enforce those laws, though whenever the Puritan parliament got together it urged that they should be enforced or made stronger. ... But the position of the two creeds was better than it looked on paper. Each enjoyed more freedom than the laws allowed it, but it was simply because the executive power happened to be more tolerant than the legislative power.[31]

If Cromwell disliked persecuting those from whom he most of all dissented, he was completely embarrassed by the measures he was forced to adopt against Fifth Monarchists and the Quakers, for they were men with whom he had a great deal in common. The passionate desire of the Fifth Monarchist to see the Kingdom of Christ on earth was something which he shared,[32] and the Quaker's emphasis on the "inner light" was very near the centre of his own religion. On the other hand, he could not allow the civil disturbances caused by George Fox's followers, and between Cromwell's methods of orderly government and the Fifth Monarchist's violent and fanatical ideal of a godly oligarchy there could be no compromise. In the interview between the Lord Protector and the members of John Rogers's congregation,[33] who were petitioning for their minister's release, Cromwell said to the petitioners:

> You told me Mr. R. suffered for the Gospel. I told you he suffered as a Railer, as a Seducer, and as a Busybody in other men's matters, and a Stirrer up of Sedition, which rulers, led by just principles, might suppress. I told you Mr. Rogers suffered justly, and not for the Testimony of Jesus Christ; and, indeed, in some degree it is blasphemy to call suffering for evil-doing suffering for the Gospel.

During this interview the Protector protested to Rogers, "who will hinder your preaching the Gospel of Christ – yea, His Personal Reign, who will hinder?" To their request for liberty of conscience, he declared, "I tell you there was never such Liberty of Conscience, no never such liberty since the days of Antichrist

---

31. Sir Charles Firth's notes were very kindly loaned to the present writer by Professor Norman Sykes of Cambridge. The quotation is from one of these unpublished MSS. Cf. also Bates, *Elenchus*, Pt. II, 192–4.
32. Cf. Ludlow, *Memoirs*, I, 246.
33. The debate is given in *W.S.*, III, 607–16. (Early February 1655).

as is now[34] – for may not men preach and pray what they will? And have not men their liberty of all opinions?"[35] The real issue between them was that they demanded Liberty of Conscience for themselves but were not prepared to grant it to others. The Lord Protector in his own groping but practical way was trying to govern for the whole nation, whereas Rogers and Feake and their colleagues wanted the government to be wholly on behalf of those who shared their opinions. "Why, I tell you," said Cromwell, "there be Anabaptists and they would cut the throats of them that are not under their forms; so would the Presbyterians cut the throats of them that are not of their forms, and so would you Fifth-Monarchy-Men. It is fit to keep all these forms out of power."[36]

Similar issues were raised with regard to the Quakers. The Protector heard their criticisms of his government with a good deal of patience,[37] and his later relationship with George Fox shows that he had a good deal of sympathy with their ideas;[38] but not all of them were pacifist,[39] and for the good of the community he could not tolerate their interference with the services of other Christians, their hostility to the clergy, and their general disrespect towards the civil officers of the commonwealth. Accordingly on February 15, 1655, he issued a "Proclamation prohibiting

---

34. i.e. since before the Reformation.
35. Rogers was quick to reply that there was too much liberty, for it included "drunkards, swearers, and men of vile, debauched principles and evil lives, Common-prayer men and such like".
36. Yet although they were a sore trial to him, Cromwell could not deal hardly with these men, and when Henry complained of the opposition he had to meet in Ireland from the Anabaptists, his father replied, "I have to do with these poor men, and am not without my exercise. I know they are weak, because they are so peremptory in judging others. I quarrel not with them but in their seeking to supplant others, which is done by some, first by branding them with antichristianism, and then taking away their maintenance." April 21, 1656, *W.S.*, IV, 146; *L-C*, II, 485 f. (CCVIII).
37. See the accounts of the interviews with John Camm and Francis Howgill, April 8, 1654, and with Anthony Pearson, July 16, 1654. *W.S.*, III, 250 f., 372 f. Prof. Abbott has suggested that Cromwell's willingness to hear such men was due to his desire to pick up information (*ibid.*, 373), but he ignored the essentially "prophetic" character of such interviews.
38. Fox had interviews with Cromwell in 1654, 1656, 1658. In the first visit Oliver said to him, "Come againe to my house: for if thou & I were butt an houre a day togeather wee should bee neerer one another: & y hee wisht mee noe more ill then hee did to his owne soule." *The Journal of George Fox* (edited by Norman Penney, MS. edition, 2 vols., Cambridge, 1911), I, 166–8, 259 f. 327–8.
39. Cf. *W.S.*, III, 555, 571. Cf. Goddard, *Burton's Diary*, I, cxxv-vi.

The Disturbance of Ministers and other Christians in their Assemblies and Meetings".[40]

He was becoming impatient with the licence claimed in the name of religious liberty, just as he had grown tired of the subjective impertinences which purported to be "prophesying" in the name of the Lord.[41] The case of the Unitarian, John Biddle, illustrates the point, for Biddle had fallen foul of Parliament,[42] and had spent most of the year 1655 in and out of prison. While Cromwell's own controversy with Parliament about liberty of conscience was in progress, there were some signs that Biddle's case would be championed by the Lord Protector. In September 1655 a petition was subscribed on Biddle's behalf, and the Unitarian claimed protection under the thirty-sixth article of the Instrument of Government, which provided that none should be coerced into orthodoxy, but when Cromwell discovered that the petition had, been tampered with, he became exasperated and declared "that the Instrument of Government was never intended to maintain and protect blasphemers from the punishment of the lawes in force against them, neither would hee."[43]

---

40. "His Highness therefore, having had many informations from divers men lately risen up under the names of Quakers, Ranters, and others, who do daily both reproach and disturb the Assemblies and Congregations of Christians, in their Publique and Private Meetings, and interrupt the Preachers in the dispencing the Word, and others in their Worship, contrary to just Liberty, and to the disturbance of the Publique Peace, Doth hold himself obliged by His Trust, to Declare His dislike of all such Practices, as being contrary to the just Freedome and Liberties of the People, which by the Laws and Government of this Commonwealth they ought to be Protected in; And doth hereby strictly Require and Command all Persons whatsoever, That they forbear henceforth all such irregular and disorderly Practices." *W.S.*, III, 626 f.
41. It is clear from Cromwell's interviews with the Quaker, Pearson, the Fifth Monarchist, John Rogers, and from Fox's account of his second visit in 1656 that there was a noticeable change in Cromwell's attitude: "And ye power of ye Lord God risse in mee: & I was moved to bidd him lay doune his crowne att ye feet of Jesus severall times I spoake to ye same effect: & I was standinge by ye table: & hee came & sate upon ye tables syde by mee & said hee would bee as high as I was for the Lords power came over him. And soe hee continued speakinge against ye light of Christ Jesus: & went his ways in a light manner." *Fox's Journal*, I, 260.
42. Biddle's books had been ordered to be burnt publicly, and he had been interviewed at the bar of the House and committed to the Gatehouse. Goddard, *Burton's Diary*, I, cxiv-vii. He was later released on bail, but entered into a heated controversy and was rearrested under the Blasphemy Act, for denying the divinity of Christ.
43. Newsletter, September 29, 1655, *C.P.*, III, 53. Biddle was sent to the Scilly Isles. An interesting epilogue to the story is provided in the fact that three years later he wrote to thank the Protector for the allowance which had been granted to him while there. *W.S.*, IV, 857. Cf. *Cal. S.P. Dom.* (1655), 372.

In the face of the religious rivalries it can be imagined with what opposition the Protector's proposal to bring in and tolerate the Jews was received. Just as his attitude to the Roman Catholics cannot be separated from his foreign policy, so this measure cannot be entirely separated from the financial plight in which the country found itself; but it cannot be summarily dismissed as an expedient for gaining credit, for it seemed likely to lose the Protector the support of City merchants who up to that time had been among his most loyal followers. There can be no doubt that in the matter of religious toleration Cromwell was in advance of his colleagues, and if it is argued that there were also certain material advantages in this policy, it must be answered that there were still more material advantages to be gained from conforming to the spirit of the age. There were reports in September 1655 that Jewish services were being held in London,[44] and when Manasseh ben Israel came to England to petition for the re-admission of his race the matter was brought at once before the Council and a selected company of lawyers and theologians.[45] The Council was divided on the subject, but on December 18 a public conference was held,[46] and the Jews were invited to state their case. They were opposed by the merchants and most of the theologians, but supported by the Lord Protector, who seems to have debated the issue with considerable skill. When the report of the Council of State came out, it was found to be generally against the proposal,[47] but its wording tacitly assumed that as the Jews had been ejected by an act of the royal prerogative, they might be re-admitted by the exercise of protectoral prerogative.[48] There the matter was left.

The Protectorate settlement in religion was not merely an ecclesiastical system which appointed Presbyterian, Independent and Baptist ministers to livings, but the extent of its toleration was often stretched, as we have seen, much wider than the law's provisions by the personal favour of the Protector himself, and it is suggested that the spirit in which the settlement was administered

---

44. Nicholas to Jane, September 14/24, 1655. *Ibid.*, 336.
45. November 21, 1655.
46. *W.S.*, IV, 51-3.
47. *Ibid.*, 54.
48. Abbott suggests that the outcome of the conference on December 18 meant that Cromwell "had suffered a severe defeat". In view of the fact that the matter was left virtually in his hands it is difficult to agree.

is as important as the system itself. Critics may suggest that since the majority of Englishmen were not Puritans this toleration affected a comparatively small part of the nation; but even if one assumes that the greater part of the country was episcopalian or Roman Catholic in sympathy (which is doubtful), the questions we would ask are, did the system give the promise in years to come of an even more comprehensive Establishment in which episcopalians might find a place? Was there hope that, when the civil government felt sufficiently secure, religious toleration would be extended to Roman Catholics, Jews and Unitarians? If the ecclesiastical settlement of the Protectorate did hold out these possibilities – and critics often forget that it had only a bare four years in which to reveal its true nature – then we submit that it was more enlightened than the Establishment which it had supplanted, and which in turn succeeded it.

In November 1654 the case of John Carey came to the fore, in which the judge gave his opinion that although Carey's offence was treasonable by an act passed in Elizabeth's reign, there was no way of proceeding against him because the oath of supremacy named in the act had been repealed and nothing had been put in its place.[49] It is a reminder that although Cromwell in his oath of accession had promised to uphold the provisions of the Instrument of Government, the Lord Protector was not "supreme governor ... in all spiritual and ecclesiastical things"[50] as the kings had been before him. It also reminds us that the ecclesiastical system established was not a "Church" but an official organization for the cure of souls and for national evangelism. The essential principle of the system was that Christians who differed in their doctrine of the Church could co-operate to fulfil the duties of a national Church, and there had been brought into being nothing more than a form of ecclesiastical administration for the selection of men judged fit to exercise the public office of the ministry: the organization as such held no distinctive views on ordination or the doctrine of the Church, and hence it is incorrect to call that system a Church, either in fact or in intention.

This brings us back to Cromwell's churchmanship, for such a system could only have been put into operation by those holding the Congregational or Independent conception of the Church. No other doctrine of the Church would permit Christians to

---

49. *Cal. S.P. Dom.* (1654), 400.
50. The Act of Supremacy, 1 Eliz., cap. 1.

accept the possibility of "Churches" existing side by side indefinitely: Anglicans, Roman Catholics, Presbyterians, Fifth Monarchists and even some Anabaptists thought in like terms of One True Visible Church, and for that reason they were prepared on occasions to persecute everybody else. The Independents, however, thought of the Holy Catholic Church in terms of a unity which was spiritual rather than organic: to them local autonomous "churches" were microcosms of the mystical Church Catholic.[51] Their conception of toleration was an extension of this principle, and enabled them, in the words of the Savoy Declaration, to judge "other Churches (though less pure) to be true Churches".[52]

Dr. Bates noticed that Cromwell, as Head of the State, was careful not to "list himself in any sect", although he was "more inclined towards the Independents".[53] The Protector's reason for this aloofness was given by him in his interview with John Rogers for he said that his work "was to keep all the godly of several judgments in peace, because like men falling out in the street would run their heads one against another, he was as a constable to part them, and keep them in peace."[54] On the other hand, although he appeared to stand aloof from any particular congregation, his own need for an intimate Christian fellowship may very well explain why the Army and its Council continued to exert such a powerful influence upon him.

III

Protestant Union

In theology, however, Cromwell could not stand apart from the religious currents of the time. Apocalyptic ideas were not the monopoly of the Fifth Monarchists, and many sober Christians, including Cromwell's favourite chaplain, Peter Sterry, looked for a great cataclysm in 1656 which would usher in the Millenium and the Day of Judgment.[55] Cromwell shared these views to some

---

51. See Thomas Goodwin, *The Government of the Churches of Christ* (*Works*, XI, 261 f.).
52. *The Savoy Declaration, 1658* (reprint, Cambridge, 1939), 408. (Article XXX of the "Institution of Churches".)
53. *Elenchus Motuum*, Pt. II, 191.
54. *W.S.*, III, 607.
55. *England's Deliverance From the Northern Presbytery compared with its Deliverance from the Roman. Papacy* (1652). Preached before Parliament after

extent,[56] and it would be of very great interest if we could assess the influence of these apocalyptic ideas on his policy during 1655, or discover whether his foreign policy was formulated with Armageddon in prospect.

We have previously noticed that the general trend of Cromwell's foreign policy was directed towards Protestant Union and Catholic war,[57] and because of England's geographical position the two sides of that policy, although closely connected, can be quite clearly defined. In his dealings with nations to the north and east the Protector was concerned primarily with promoting the union, or at least the unity of Protestantism, and in his dealings with nations to the south and west he was mainly concerned with developing an attack on Catholicism.

R.H. Abbott has noted Cromwell's preoccupation with "the Protestant Interest", and says that there seems "no doubt but that his interest in it was genuine",[58] but he suggests that when religious considerations and economic advantages conflicted, the latter won.[59] He submits that "It was at this time and in these hands that England began to turn definitely from its position as an island chiefly agricultural to a world power chiefly industrial and commercial",[60] and he hints that "Protestantism" was used as a cloak for other designs.[61] It might be added that a gradual secularization of the policy abroad was to be expected, as being in line with the growing spirit of the age, but it should be pointed out that Cromwell did not recognize any divorce between the welfare of England (commercial or otherwise) on the one hand, and the interest of Protestantism on the other: everything seems to suggest that the two were identified in his mind. The evidence certainly does not permit us to suggest that economic considerations had pride of place in the Protector's foreign policy, despite his interest in mercantile and naval affairs.[62] It is clear that he

---

Worcester on November 5, 1651. Since the Flood happened in 1656 b.c. a further cataclysm was expected in 1656. Cf. V. de Sola Pinto, *Peter Sterry*, 25.
56. Cf. Ludlow, *Memoirs*, I, 246, and Cromwell's letter to John Cotton, October 2, 1651. *W.S.*, II, 482 f.; *L-C*, II, 240 f. (CLXXXIV), also *supra*, p. 25–8.
57. *Supra*, p. 281–7.
58. *W.S.*, III, 159.
59. *Ibid.*, 159, 339 f.
60. *Ibid.*, 188.
61. *Ibid.*, 365.
62. There is a distinct emphasis on the revival of English trade and on naval matters in early writings about Cromwell Dr. Bates commends his rule in these matters.

regarded England as destined to take the lead in the affairs of Protestantism: she was God's "delight among the nations".[63] As Cromwell said in the Council in reply to Lambert's objections against war with Spain, "Wee consider this attempt, because wee thinke God has not brought us hither where wee are but to consider the worke that wee may doe in the world as well as at home".[64] This is typical of Cromwell when he was thinking of his own vocation, and if he transferred his sense of mission to the English nation, the strength and well-being of England was bound to be at the centre of his scheme for the promotion of the Protestant Interest.

Peace with the Estates of the United Provinces was settled at the beginning of April 1654,[65] and this marks the first step towards Cromwell's object of strengthening politically the common interests of Protestantism. A further development of this policy was seen in the mission of John Dury and John Pell to Switzerland and the Protestant states along the Rhine,[66] but the activities of these unofficial envoys also illustrate the other side of Cromwell's foreign policy for they were admirably placed to survey the borders of France and the German Empire, and their investigations were likely to be an embarrassment to both those Catholic powers.[67]

The next important step was the conclusion of a treaty with Sweden,[68] for which success Whitelocke must take a good deal of the credit, and the treaties with Sweden and Holland brought into line a number of the smaller Protestant states which had

---

Elenchus Motuum, Pt. II, 191, 227 f. Cf. Carrington's *Life and Death of Oliver*, 89 f., 129 f., 136 f.

63. This is illustrated in the opening paragraph of a remarkable declaration issued after the drought of 1654, "That this hath been a Nation of blessings in the midst whereof so many wonders have been brought forth by the outstretched arm of the Almighty, even to astonishment, and wonder, Who can deny? Ask we the Nations of this matter and they will testify, and indeed the dispensations of the Lord have been as if he had said, *England* thou art my first-born, my delight among the Nations, under the whole Heavens the Lord hath not dealt so with any of the people round about us." May 9, 1654, *W.S.*, III, 290 f.
64. July 20, 1654. *C.P.*, III, 207.
65. April 5, 1654; Text of the Treaty, *W.S.*, III, 897–911. Peace proclaimed on April 28. Whitelocke, 589.
66. Cf. *W.S.*, III, 229–33.
67. *Ibid.*, 237.
68. April 11, 1654; text of the treaty. *Ibid.*, 911–5. Cf. Whitelocke's accounts of the preliminary negotiations, Whitelocke, 593 f., 601–4.

been hostile to the Commonwealth.[69] It should be noted, however, that in building up friendship with these states the Protector emphasized that Protestantism was the basis of mutual accord,[70] and in a letter to Charles X of Sweden in October 1654[71] he declared that he considered himself set in his present position "to the end that I ought especially to strive and plan to the best of my ability for the common safety and peace of the Protestants". For that reason he deplored the war between Sweden and Bremen and he offered his own services as a mediator in the dispute.

His words would have had little significance if there were no evidence that he was prepared to back them by deeds. When it became known, however, in the summer of 1655 that the Duke of Savoy had launched a persecution against his Protestant subjects of the Vaudois valleys, the Lord Protector acted with a vigour that astonished Europe. The Duke had used troops to push back the Waldenses to the mountain valleys to which by their original grant of toleration they were supposed to confine themselves. There had been some resistance, and a massacre had developed; but Bulstrode Whitelocke describes how the news sounded in English ears:

> Letters of the Duke of Savoy's cruel persecuting the Protestants in Piedmont, by taking away their Goods and Estates, and putting them in Prison, and carrying away of their Children; using all means with Violence to make them forsake their Religion and the Purity of the Gospel; which when they would not do, the Priests persuaded the Duke to send an Army against them to force them to Conformity, who sent eight thousand Men against these poor quiet People and loyal Subjects; the Army fell upon them, slew many of them, with small Loss, and took many Prisoners, whom they used with all Cruelty and then put them to death. Others of them with their wives and Children, fled unto the Mountains, whilst Soldiers plunder'd their Houses, and then fired them and their Churches.[72]

This is a statement by a sober historian, but the effect on Cromwell – who in all things religious thought emotionally – was so

---

69. Denmark wished to be included in the Dutch treaty, and the Count of Oldenburg and the Prince of Anhalt made approaches to England. W.S., III, 252, 364 f. Cf. Whitelocke, 590.
70. To the Prince of Anhalt, July 6, 1654. W.S., III, 364. Cf. Cromwell's letter to the Senate of Bremen, October 27, 1654. *Ibid.*, 492.
71. October 27, 1654. *Ibid.*, 492 f.
72. Whitelocke, 626. Cf. 625.

much the greater. It never occurred to him that in the transportation of Irish Catholics he was responsible for a form of persecution which, if not so bloody, was directed towards a similar end. To him the Irish were transported as a punishment for their rebellion, but the events in the valley of the Vaudois were just another example of Catholic brutality. That was a conclusion in which his preconceptions about the Inquisition, the persecutions of Queen Mary, the Armada and the Irish massacre of 1640–41 all played their part, and the Piedmontese massacre thus revived all the latent hatred he had of Catholicism.[73]

Cromwell's sympathy was cast in an active mould. A solemn Fast was held throughout the nation, a national collection started for the relief of the sufferers, and Samuel Morland was sent as His Highness's special envoy into France and Savoy to protest against the persecution. In a group of letters that are as emphatic as anything in diplomatic correspondence, he urged the Protestant States to make common cause with him in protesting against Savoy's treatment of the Vaudois. Sweden, Holland, Denmark, the Protestant cantons of Switzerland and the Prince of Transylvania all heard from him,[74] and in the letter to the Dutch he commented:

> we are ready to take such other Course and Counsels with your selves, in common with the rest of our Reformed Friends and Confederates, as may be most necessary for the preservation of Just and Good men upon the brink of inevitable Ruin, and to make the Duke himself sensible, that we can no longer neglect the heavy Oppressions and Calamities of our Orthodox Brethren.[75]

Even his letter to the Duke of Savoy himself[76] was no more pointed than the letters he wrote to the King of France[77] and

---

73. It was reported that some Irish troops had been used in the massacre. *W.S.*, III, 521. Cf. John Milton's poem:
    "Avenge O Lord thy slaughter'd Saints, whose bones
       Lie scatter'd on the Alpine mountains cold,
       Ev'n them who kept thy truth so pure of old
    When all our Fathers worship't Stocks and Stones,
    Forget not: in thy book record their groanes
       Who were thy Sheep and in their antient Fold
       Slayn by the bloody Piemontese that roll'd
       Mother with Infant down the Rocks. ..."
                                            On the late Massacher in Piemont (1655).
74. May 25–28, 1655. *W.S.*, III, 726, 728–32; June 7th, *ibid.*, 741.
75. *Ibid.*, 732.
76. *Ibid.*, 724 f.
77. *Ibid.*, 726 f.

Cardinal Mazarin.[78] The projected treaty with France was still in the balance, and Cromwell made good use of the fact. He pointed out to Louis XIV that if the King of France would use the influence he possessed with the Duke of Savoy it would "engage your Confederates and Allies, which profess the same Religion,[79] in a far greater respect and good affection to your Majesty". The Protector assured Mazarin that it was France's toleration of the Huguenots which made the present accord between France and England possible, and declared that by using his good offices in relieving the plight of the Vaudois the cardinal would "lay the foundations of a stricter Alliance between this Republic and the Kingdom of France". The Anglo-French alliance was still very much in the balance, and the issue would largely depend on France's intervention in Savoy. At the moment Cromwell appeared to be the ring-master of Europe. The States General of the Netherlands sent a formal letter of protest to the Duke of Savoy, and with remarkable promptitude Louis and Mazarin brought pressure to bear. The way in which the Lord Protector on this occasion and others forced the King of France and his chief minister to act against their own inclinations received the ungrudging admiration of Edward Hyde.[80]

It has been suggested that Cromwell interceded on behalf of the Vaudois because it "fitted in well" with his foreign policy,[81] but what practical advantage accrued to England, apart from her heightened prestige, by this defence of the Protestants in Piedmont? Cromwell was far less in a position to dictate terms to France than appears at first sight, for he had already committed himself to war with Spain;[82] in fact the English had already been repulsed before San Domingo and had been forced to turn their attention to Jamaica, and this news was likely to be revealed at any time.[83] In exerting such strong pressure on France at this

---

78. *Ibid.*, 727 f.
79. i.e. as the Vaudois.
80. Cromwell was able to intercede and prevent the punishment of the Protestants of Nimes. Cf. Clarendon, *History*, XV, 152–5.
81. Abbott, *W.S.*, III, 717.
82. General instructions to Penn and Venables had been given on August 18, 1654 (*ibid.*, 413–5), and more detailed instructions on December 4 and 9, 1654 (*ibid.*, 528–38). The expedition set sail soon after, and arrived at Barbados on January 21, 1654/5.
83. Penn and Venables departed from Barbados in March 1655 to attack Hispaniola. They landed there without opposition on April 14, but were defeated before the town of San Domingo on April 25 and left the island on May 5 to take possession of Jamaica on the 17th. Although news of the expedition was not received in England until the middle of June, it will be seen that Cromwell

particular time, when the issue of the Hispaniola expedition was still in doubt, Cromwell was engaging in very dangerous diplomacy, and one is forced to conclude that he was either a very audacious statesman or else he was prepared to risk all things in defence of his religion. Perhaps both are true.

It was his passionate devotion to the cause of Protestantism which made foreign ambassadors find him so difficult to fathom. At the height of the Waldensian crisis the Swedish special envoy, Petrus Coyet, approached Cromwell for permission to recruit more men for Swedish service.[84] He found the Protector a very unsatisfactory listener. His Highness "simply said, 'he would give a respectable answer to it all' and began to talk about the evangelical religion". All Coyet could get from the Protector was "his desire for a closer alliance with Sweden for the sake of evangelical interests". Coyet left the audience bewildered by Cromwell's vagueness about the request for troops and his preoccupations with matters of religion.

One of the most striking features of Cromwell's relationship with other Protestant states was the way in which their diplomats constantly underestimated the unity of Protestantism as a major factor in the Protector's foreign policy. On the continent religion could no longer hold the centre of the stage of foreign policy, and its place was taken by commerce or imperial aggrandizement. The chief aid which Cromwell had in his designs abroad was the dynastic rivalry of the Catholic powers, while his chief hindrance was the conflicting interests of the Protestant states: the rivalry between Sweden and Brandenburg, Denmark and Holland, and the suspicion with which the Dutch regarded England's commercial expansion, were all factors which made Protestant Union as Cromwell envisaged it impossible.[85] The rulers of these

---

was definitely committed to war with Spain. Cf. *infra*, p. 345-7; *C-P*, III, 244; *W.S.*, III, 754. The first news of the Piedmont persecutions was received at the beginning of May. Whitelocke, 624.

84. *W.S.*, III, 718, extracted and translated from J.L. Carlbom, *Sverige och England, 1655-57* (Göteborg, 1900), 16-18.

85. Richelieu provides a contrast. He took the realistic view, and looked for the victory of Catholicism not by means of a Catholic crusade, but in the supremacy of his own nation, France. Cf. Aldous Huxley, *Grey Eminence*, 102. The continuation of this policy under Mazarin and Louis XIV very nearly succeeded. To some extent Cromwell's policy was similar, since he expected England to take the lead in Protestant Union, but his designs did not envisage war with his co-religionists, whereas Richelieu's policy was directed primarily against the Catholic Hapsburg powers.

continental countries took the realistic view that the "Christian Nation" was no more than a convenient political fiction, whereas the Lord Protector of the Commonwealth of England acted as if it were a fact. It was a considerable embarrassment to the world of diplomacy – to England's professed friends no less than to her potential enemies – to find the religious issue brought to the fore once more, and it was the greater embarrassment because the one who introduced this complication was himself in a position to dictate: foreign politicians might wish to ignore the religious issue, but they could not ignore it when it was personified in a general who had effected the conquest of three nations, commanded one of the world's best armies and the world's best navy, and who governed a country whose geographical position enabled her to be a potential danger to others without undertaking the same risks herself. The most embarrassing feature, however, for the ambassadors in London was that although it *seemed* as if Cromwell took religion seriously, they could never quite credit that he did.

However, they soon learned to affect the cause of religion in his presence, and even a Catholic like Sagrado, when appealing for ships to help Venice in her struggle with the Turk, "tried to attract him on the score of religion".[86] The Swedish ambassador, Bonde, noted at once Cromwell's determination to keep peace with all Protestant powers including England's commercial rival, the Dutch,[87] and he later gave it as his considered opinion that it was due to inexperience in foreign affairs.[88] Schlezer, the ambassador from the Elector of Brandenburg, seems to have realized that Cromwell's main object was an alliance of all the Protestant powers;[89] but the other envoys, despite their religious platitudes and professions, never seem to have accepted it as genuine. Bonde told the Protector frankly that he [Bonde] would not be worried about the cause of Protestantism if only England and Sweden formed a military alliance.[90]

R.H. Abbott has suggested that the Protector's insistence on religion "served merely to conceal, if it did conceal, the worldly motives behind these diplomatic professions", and he says that

---

86. November 2/12, 1655, Sagrado to the Doge. *Cal. S.P. Ven.* (1655–56), 136.
87. Conversation with Bonde, November 2, 1655. *W.S.*, IV, 8–10.
88. R.H. Abbott quotes a letter from Bonde in P. Kalling, *Christer Bondes Ambassad till England* (Upsala, 1851), 34 f.; *W.S.*, IV, 28.
89. Cf. *ibid.*, 32.
90. *W.S.*, IV, 47, from Carlbom.

there was not one of the envoys "who did not sense this approach to the more practical issues at stake".[91] With all respect to the late Professor Abbott we must join issue with this conclusion. We submit that Cromwell's policy was by no means clear to the foreign envoys at the time: Bonde regarded England's policy as clear evidence that her leaders were inexperienced in diplomacy, and the Dutch ambassador, Nieupoort, who had as much experience of the Protector as any of the envoys, on hearing Cromwell's wish that Protestants would stop fighting to join "in a common league against the inhuman cruelties of popery", was sceptical of the idea, but added that he neglected "no opportunity of ascertaining the final intention of the Protector"[92] – if he was suspicious of Cromwell's reasons, the Protector's policy was by no means clear to him. It is possible to read through the despatches of the foreign ambassadors and reach a very different conclusion from that offered by Professor Abbott, namely, that it was the ambassadors themselves who confused Cromwell's foreign policy by looking for hidden motives where they did not exist: the underlying motives that the ambassadors "sensed" in their audiences were similar to those which they themselves were seeking, and this prevented them from understanding the true significance of Cromwell's policy. The Lord Protector saw himself as the ordained Instrument of Almighty God; they saw him as a successful military adventurer typical of the age of Gustavus Adolphus, Wallenstein, Condé, Turenne and the Elector Palatine,[93] and in this they did him less than justice, for whatever else Cromwell may have dissembled, he did not dissemble in his championship of Protestantism.

This does not mean, however, that England's material advantages were not an important factor in Cromwell's foreign policy. One cannot read through the mass of diplomatic correspondence in which he engaged on behalf of English trading

---

91. "To them Cromwell's policy seemed clear, however concealed by verbiage or by silence. It was to keep peace with and among Sweden, Holland and Brandenburg while pursuing his own quarrel with Spain; to keep peace with France in the same cause; to use the Protestant Interest in all these designs as a cover or adjunct to those designs of trade, colonies and influence in European affairs. There is not a despatch from any envoy which does not recognize this situation and the continual insistence on the Protestant Interest served only to confuse, not to conceal his true purposes." R.H. Abbott, W.S., IV, 48.
92. Nieupoort to De Witt, January 4/14. *Ibid.*, 67.
93. "Those representatives recognized that they were making engagements not so much with a nation and its ruler as with an army and its general." *Ibid.*, 100.

interests without realizing their importance to the Protectorate. As we have said, in so far as Cromwell identified the Protestant cause with the maintenance of his own power and his own country's supremacy, the aggrandizement of England was bound to have an important place in his foreign policy; but it did not have pride of place. He might well be concerned for England's Baltic trade when the conquests of Charles X against Poland and Brandenburg threatened to turn the Baltic into a Swedish lake, but in spite of the Dutch ambassador's warning of the material dangers,[94] he still pressed for a closer alliance with Sweden.[95] Later, he proposed that the United Netherlands should be included in the proposed Anglo-Swedish alliance,[96] possibly as a first step towards a more comprehensive alignment of Protestant states. Neither Sweden nor the Dutch showed any enthusiasm for the proposal, and the Protector protested to Bonde against the secular attitude of the Dutch,[97] "but he nevertheless gave assurances that the Protestant cause and its security were the grounds upon which he acted and to which he would steadfastly adhere as long as he had anything to say".[98] He accordingly addressed urgent letters to the King of Sweden[99] and the Estates General[100] deploring "some too apparent signs of tottering friendship and growing discord", and although it is not possible to say that these efforts had any decisive influence, the Dutch were able to announce in their reply that they had signed a treaty with Sweden.[101] It is suggested, then, that Cromwell's relationships with other Protestant powers show that he consistently worked for the unity, and possible Union of Protestantism, and that this ideal was at the centre of his policy abroad.

---

94. Cf. *W.S.*, IV, 77 f.
95. He tried to persuade Whitelocke and the merchant Sir Christopher Packe to go to Stockholm as England's ambassadors for a treaty (January 25, 1655, Whitelocke, 631, 632 – misnumbered 634), and the further object of the embassy was to be for the good of the Protestant cause, "which was the uniting of that Interest, and preventing the Differences that were likely to fall between the King and the United Provinces, and the Elector of Brandenburgh" (*Ibid.*, 633). If trade had been the primary consideration, such an embassy would hardly have been envisaged at a time when Sweden's conquests might give rise to justifiable English fears.
96. Whitelocke, 636–7.
97. July 25, 1656, *W.S.*, IV, 214.
98. *Ibid.*, from Bonde's Diary.
99. August [21], 1656, *ibid.*, 235 f.
100. August 21, 1656, *ibid.*, 233 ff.
101. 12/22 September 1656, *ibid.*, 251.

IV

Catholic War

In one way the ambassadors of the Catholic powers found it easier to understand the English Protector than did his coreligionists.[102] They were in little doubt about his intention towards Catholicism; the only question which concerned them immediately was which of them he would fight first. This particularly exercised the minds of the rulers of France and Spain, who were already engaged in their own bitter struggle for the leadership of western Europe, and whose rivalries stretched from Italy in the south, along the banks of the Rhine, to the Low Countries in the north. Spain had been quick to recognize the importance of allying herself with England's naval power. In letters to the Spanish Council of State[103] the Spanish ambassador, Don Alonzo de Cardeñas, pointed out that the expense of subsidizing an alliance with England could not be more than the present cost of Spanish defence, but he warned the Council "it will be absolutely indispensable scrupulously to fulfil towards Cromwell all the stipulations agreed upon," since "the English are very exact and very avaricious". It was proposed in the Council to offer Cromwell ten thousand crowns a month if he would declare war on France,[104] and thirty thousand crowns were to be sent to Cardenas immediately for the purpose of bribing anyone who could bring about this decision, but the Duke of Medina de la Torres thought the security of the State and her dominions was so much at stake that up to one hundred thousand crowns a month should be offered. Another member of the Council, the Marquis de Velada, offered his own possessions to achieve the object. The Count d'Orñate spoke to the same effect, and declared that if the state did not keep its promise to the Protector he would do so personally.

This suggests the importance with which the members of the Spanish government regarded an English alliance, and the

---

102. See the advice of Lamilletière to Mazarin on Cromwell's projected Protestant union and its implications for France, July 11/21. F. Guizot, *History of Oliver Cromwell*, II, 427.
103. March 6 and 13, 1654. Cf. the appendix of F. Guizot, *The History of Oliver Cromwell*, II, 435–9, 441 f.
104. April 2/12, *ibid.*, 441–5. Cf. the letter from Navarro to Cardeñas, March 11/21, where the figure 50,000 crowns a month was suggested.

mention of bribery may explain in part why some members of the Protector's council were so favourable to Spain. On the other hand during the months which followed Cromwell repeatedly wrote to Philip IV to secure payment long overdue to English subjects for their services – notably on behalf of Colonel Christopher Mayo and his colleagues[105] – and Spain's failure to meet her obligations in these smaller matters was no recommendation of her good faith should England engage in war with France on the strength of Spanish promises.[106]

Cromwell had hinted to Mazarin that the toleration granted to the Huguenots was a major reason for his readiness for a treaty with France, but if he could have seen any way of bettering the position of the Huguenots by going to war with France he would probably have done so. As it was, the Huguenots enjoyed a limited amount of toleration which depended upon their good behaviour, and Cromwell probably realized that he could exert more influence on their behalf by friendship with France than by listening to the blandishments of Barrière and the Prince of Condé[107] backed by very doubtful Spanish silver. Later On, in a secret instruction, his ambassador to France, William Lockhart, was told to let the government of France know that Cromwell had taken France for a friend, "not out of necessity, but choice", and that the reason for this was "that one [i.e. France] gives liberty of conscience to the professors of the protestant religion, and the other [Spain] persecuting it with loss of life and estate".[108]

---

105. Letters on behalf of Mayo, July 24, August 8, 1654. W.S., III, 380, 393–4 (947–8). Mayo and his colleagues had transported Irish soldiers to Spain, and it appears from a letter to the Council of Ireland that the money was never paid by Spain, it had to be met from the Irish exchequer (August 7, 1657, ibid., IV, 592 f.). See also the letters to Philip IV (on behalf of Benjamin Wright), February 23, 1655, and on behalf of the heirs of Richard Richaut [or Richant], April 30, 1655, ibid., III, 632 f. (959), 701 f. (960–2). A letter of a similar character sent to the Archduke of Austria, August 4, 1654, on behalf of Luce and Owens, ibid, III, 391 (947).
106. It seems that Spain's bad faith in money matters was well known. Mazarin advised de Baas to make much of it in his negotiations with Cromwell. Mazarin to de Baas, March 17/27, 1654, Guizot, *History of Oliver Cromwell*, II (App.), 450–2.
107. At the suggestion of Barrière, Condé's agent, Cromwell employed a Savoyard minister, Jean Baptiste Stoupe, to make a tour of Protestant communities in France and along her borders. He reported them to be generally contented, and suspicious of Condé's ambitions. W.S., III, 259 f. It appears that Condé was becoming an embarrassment to Spain; cf. the letter from Navarro to Cardenas, March 11/21, cited n. 3, p. 343.
108. April 1656, W.S., IV, 139.

Although the merits and demerits of war with either France or Spain appear to have been discussed in the Council of State quite dispassionately,[109] these considerations, together with the obvious temptation to recoup England's fortunes at the expense of Spain's colonial empire, eventually led to the decision to fight Spain, and to attack her first in the West Indies.[110] In the Council meeting that came to these decisions on April 20, 1654, it was urged that to strengthen Spain at the expense of France would be "the greatest prejudice to the Protestant cause all over Europe, the Spaniard beinge the greatest enemy to the Protestants in the world". On the other hand it is clear from the report of this Council meeting[111] that the decision was taken at the instigation of the Protector and in the face of Lambert's opposition.[112]

Related to the policy towards the two major Catholic powers Was the Protector's conclusion of a commercial treaty with Portugal. Spain still treasured the intention of winning back the throne of Portugal, and the relationship between the two Catholic powers of the Iberian peninsula was not the most cordial. The treaty with Portugal was an oblique blow at the Spaniard, and it is probable that Cromwell hoped to offset the English loss of trade with Spanish dominions by means of trade with Portugal and her colonies.[113]

Although the decision to go to war with Spain appears to have been taken in April 1654, the two ambassadors were kept on tenterhooks. A display of naval strength round their coasts and in the neighbourhood of the Mediterranean was not calculated to do much to reassure them, but it had the advantage of demonstrating the naval might of the Protectorate. Blake sailed on

---

109. Montagu's account of the meeting on July 20, 1654. *C.P.,* III. 203–6.
110. Reports were heard first from Captains Hatsell and Limmery who had lived and traded in those parts. A further reason for this policy was that Spanish possessions might be used for transplanting Scots and Irish. *Ibid.,* 205.
111. See also *ibid.,* 207–8; *W.S.,* III, 377 f.
112. The French ambassador was well aware of Lambert's hostility to France, Bordeaux to Brienne, April 10/20, 1654. Guizot, *History of Oliver Cromwell,* II. (App.), 457 f.
113. *C.P.,* III, 206. The treaty was ready for signature a few hours before the execution of Count Peneguiao's young brother (July 10, 1654, *supra,* p. 285 and n. 3). The Portuguese ambassador immediately left the country after signing the treaty, which had been amended in the light of John IV's criticisms. The King still had objections, however, and it was some months before the ambassador who followed was able to notify Cromwell of the King's acceptance. Even then, the clause granting freedom of worship for English traders was not accepted by the King of Portugal until Blake had made his presence felt in the vicinity (July 11, 1656).

October 8, 1654, but despite the reassurances,[114] there was considerable speculation in Paris and Madrid as to the real purpose of his voyage, France on the whole being more apprehensive in view of her design on Naples,[115] although Spain's concern may be gauged from the fact that the Marquis of Leda was sent as a special envoy to London to assure Cromwell of Spain's friendship.[116] Apart from the reasons given, Blake's expedition seems to have been a part of the general plan which was being developed. It directed attention away from the western project, it would make France even more anxious to come to terms, and it would mean that Blake would be admirably placed to intercept the Spanish plate fleet.[117]

Penn and Venables embarked from England in December with instructions "to assault the Spaniard in the West Indies".[118] At the same time the Protector allowed nothing to disturb his outward relationships towards Spain, although it was clear to all the ambassadors that an expedition against someone had been launched. Cromwell seems to have assumed the common European attitude to colonial war, that war in Asia or America did not necessarily mean war in Europe. The excuse for this particular venture against Spain was unimportant:[119] he had decided to fight a Catholic power and Spain, by reason of her vulnerable possessions, her reputed wealth and her Catholic arrogance, had always been the most likely choice: to him it needed no excuse.[120]

The West Indian expedition was, however, the one great military failure of Cromwell's career. The first news was of complete success,[121] but by July 14, the newsletters were beginning to comment that "Wee have heard nothinge from Generall Blake

---

114. Cf. letter to Philip IV, August 5, 1654. *W.S.*, III, 392.
115. The Duke of Guise's expedition against the Kingdom of Naples was postponed when news came through of Blake's voyage; cf. *W.S.*, III, 493 f., 543 f.
116. Clarendon, *History*, XV, 8.
117. To Blake, September 13, 1655. *W.S.*, III, 823 f.; *L-C*, II, 459–61 (CCII).
118. Instructions to Penn, December 4, 1654. *W.S.*, III, 530 ff.
119. Spain's treatment of native populations, atrocities against English traders, and the exclusively Catholic interest in South and Central America were all brought forward as reasons, which deceived no one, even Cromwell himself.
120. Cromwell's attitude was that of the writer of a newsletter in 1656: "To me it is sufficient that the warre is against the Spanyard, because I am satisfyde he watcheth for nothing lesse than an opportunity to treat us to dirt, and say he doth God good service therein, as did the Irish." September 30, 1656, *C.P.*, III, 75.
121. Newsletter, *C.P.*, III, 44.

or Penn",[122] and when news came through that Major-General Haynes had been killed[123] it was clear that the expedition had not been the unqualified success that the first reports had suggested and when on August 4, the News-writer reported the abandonment of Hispaniola and landing on Jamaica, it was clear that the Western Design had entirely failed in its main purpose.[124] Penn and Venables from the commencement had not been on very cordial terms with each other, but it appeared that they had quarrelled badly. If the Western Design had been badly conceived, it was evident that it had been hopelessly mismanaged.

It was a new experience for Cromwell to have to accept responsibility for a military reverse, and he did not get over his chagrin quickly. To Vice-Admiral Goodson who commanded the rest of the western fleet, he wrote, "It is not to be denied but the Lord hath greatly humbled us in that sad loss sustained at Hispaniola",[125] and the echoes of his anger and disappointment were to be heard in his speech at the opening of his second Parliament on September 17, 1656.[126] It would be interesting to know which emotion was uppermost in his mind, for the reverberations reached Edward Hyde in exile, and he adds the comment that, "He had never such distempers ... as upon the miscarriage at Hispaniola".[127] Cromwell had been humiliated before the whole world; but such contrite reflections did not excuse those officers who had been agents in this humiliation, and Penn and Venables left the Protector's favour for good.[128] Nor did this reverse change his determination against Spain, and in October a lengthy declaration was published, which rehearsed all possible grievances against that kingdom, from the Armada onwards.[129]

---

122. *Ibid.*, 45.
123. July 24, 1655, *ib d.*, 46.
124. August 4 and 11, 1655, *ibid.*, 46–8; Whitelocke, 627. Cf. the "Narrative of the Expedition to San Domingo", *C.P.*, III, 54–60, and cf. Clarendon, *History,* XV, 9–12.
125. October 30 [?], 1655, *W.S.*, III, 859 f.; *L-C,* II, 469–72 (CCIV). To Major-General Fortescue, who had been left to command the troops in Jamaica, he wrote, "We desire to humble ourselves before the Lord, who hath very sorely chastened us". October [10–30] 1655, *W.S.*, III, 857 f.; *L-C,* II, 475–8 (CCVI). He wrote in similar terms to Daniel Searle, the governor of Barbados. October [?] 1655, *W.S.*, III, 874 f.; *L-C,* II, 473 f. (CCV).
126. *W.S.*, IV, 274.
127. Clarendon, *History,* XV, 13.
128. *Ibid.* When they arrived back in England at the beginning of September 1655, they were immediately interviewed by the Protector and sent to the Tower. Whitelocke, 627; Clarendon, *History,* XV, 13.
129. *W.S.*, III, 878–891.

This official declaration of war extended the sphere of conflict to Europe, and it was clear that France and England would probably come together against their common enemy. A preliminary trade treaty between the two countries was celebrated on November 28, 1655.[130] In April the following year Colonel William Lockhart, a Scotsman who had married Cromwell's niece, was sent as official ambassador to the court of Louis XIV, and succeeded in winning the confidence of Cardinal Mazarin.[131] In the meantime Blake had reduced the pirates of Algiers and bombarded the port of Tunis, firing the fleet that sheltered in its harbour – an action which Clarendon later described as one of "the highest conduct and courage, and made the name of the English very terrible and formidable in those seas".[132] Blake and Montagu then deployed their fleet to try and intercept the Spanish plate fleet, but it was not until September 9, 1656 that Captain Stayner met and destroyed a part of it, bringing prizes back to England.[133]

Although a trade treaty had been signed with France, Lockhart encountered some initial difficulties in getting an audience with Mazarin, and discovered the alarming development that Mazarin was exploring the possibilities of a Franco-Spanish peace; the arrival of Cromwell's ambassador was an embarrassment to him. The prospect of peace between France and Spain, to be followed possibly by an alliance to support the pretensions of Charles II, gave cause for real concern in London, and in the face of Portugal's refusal to ratify in full her treaty with England, the prospect of a hostile Catholic League was suddenly a reality. If this had happened Cromwell could only have blamed himself, for he had stated only too clearly his attitude towards the Catholic powers. Sagrado on November 26, 1655, wrote in cypher to the Venetian Senate, "If the Catholic princes knew what is being planned, they would cease fighting with and destroying one another, and would think of themselves and their religion",[134] and this was independently corroborated by Francesco Bernardi, the Genoese minister.[135]

---

130. Signed October 24/November 3. *Ibid.,* 930–8.
131. He was also instructed to use what influence he could to bring France and the Protestant cantons of Switzerland together.
132. *History,* XV, 12.
133. The plunder was not as high as the Protector had hoped, and by no means covered the cost of the employment of the fleet in these operations.
134. Momigliano, *Cromwell,* (Appendix), 259.
135. "By now it is time that the Catholic Princes should give heed to their own affairs, nothing else but the general destruction of the true faith and of those

This was the considered opinion of two experienced diplomats, who, because they served small Italian states far from any immediate threat from England, were able to judge Cromwell's policy fairly objectively. The ambassadors of the Great Powers were not. They were too near the scene, and they read into Cromwell's motives their own ambitions: in the midst of the general secularization of politics they thought it inconceivable that any man who had risen to Cromwell's eminence by means of war and revolution could be unrealistic enough to place religion at the centre of his policy. In doing so they underestimated the part played by religion in the Great Rebellion, and its central place in Cromwell's rise to power.

---

who profess it, being contrived; this, alas! I know as certain." January 17, 1656 (in cypher), *ibid.*, 256.

Chapter Nineteen

The Kingship and the End (September 1656 – September 3, 1658)

I

Parliament, Nayler, and the Militia Bill

The Second Protectorate Parliament has the unique distinction of being the only Parliament in British history which has offered the crown of the three nations to a commoner. Yet there was no sign of any such inclination when first it met on September 17, 1656. The Major-Generals and local officials had exerted their influence to secure the election of those known to be sympathetic to the government, but they had not been nearly as successful in this as they would have liked. Major-General Kelsey had suggested that no member ought to be allowed to take his seat without pledging support to the Protector and to the constitution laid down in the Instrument of Government,[1] and although this suggestion was not adopted, tickets were issued on the authority of the Council without which no member was allowed to enter the House. In this way – according to Cromwell – about one hundred and twenty members were excluded.[2] Even so, the House was by no means docile, as the later debate on the excluded members showed, and the Council's action aroused considerable criticism from the government's supporters – notably from Henry Cromwell,[3] and even from the Lord Protector himself.[4]

Cromwell's opening speech[5] reflected his anxiety at the dangers

---

1. Kelsey to Thurloe, *Thurloe S.P.,* V, 384; Kelsey to Cromwell, *Cal. S.P. Dom.* (1656–57), 87.
2. Speech February 27, 1657, *W.S.,* IV, 418. About 100 signed a protest against the Council's action. This remonstrance and the names of those who signed it appear in Whitelocke, 651–3. The excluded members included Hazelrigge, Scott, Ashley Cooper and Maynard. Cf. Newsletter, September 1, *C.P.,* III, 73.
3. Henry Cromwell to Thurloe, October 6, 1656. *Thurloe S.P.,* V, 477–8.
4. *Burton's Diary,* I, 384. Cf. *infra,* p. 351 f.
5. *W.S.,* IV, 260–79; *L-C,* II, 508–53.

that confronted his country at home and abroad. England's chief enemy was the Spaniard, but other enemies were the Cavaliers, whose cause Spain had embraced, the English Catholics (who "have been accounted, ever since I was born, Spaniolised"), and the discontented Leveller and Fifth Monarchy elements who were being misled by the others. He gave details of Charles II's preparations for invasion from the Spanish Netherlands, and he instanced the insurrection of 1655, the plots against his own life and the intrigues of Sexby as evidence of the existing danger, and he justified the system of Major-Generals on grounds of necessity. At the same time, the country was overwhelmed by debt, and he pointedly urged the members not to waste their time at Westminster. He touched upon the ecclesiastical system and the reformation of manners, and he ended a somewhat rambling speech with a characteristic biblical exhortation.

Sir Thomas Widdrington was chosen to be Speaker, and after some heated debate the question of the excluded members was referred back to the Council;[6] as a result about forty more members seceded from the House.[7] The Protector cannot be blamed for the exclusions. In a private speech to the army officers on February 27, 1657 he charged the Major-Generals with calling the Parliament against his own advice,[8] and with the exclusion of those members who did not suit them, adding the comment "next time for ought I know you may exclude 400".[9] In view of his son Henry's criticism, and of the Protector's disclaimer, it appears that the officers of the Council had tried to secure a Parliament which would establish their own position with conspicuous lack of success.[10]

It is clear that whoever is to be blamed, the arbitrariness of the exclusions not only shook what confidence the country had in the government, but it also shook the confidence of Parliament itself. Denis Bond, in the debate on Saturday, December 20,[11] declared that it was called "a rag of a Parliament" and the rest of that

---

6. Newsletters, September 18, 22, 23, 1656, *C.P.*, III, 73–4.
7. *C.J.*, VII, 426.
8. *Burton's Diary*, I, 384. Cf. *W. S.*, IV, 417; *infra*, p. 407 f.
9. *W.S.*, IV, 418; C.H. Firth in *Eng. Historical Review*, xviii, 60 f; from Anthony Morgan to Henry Cromwell, *Lansdowne MSS.* 821, f. 359.
10. They brought forward a Militia Bill for their own maintenance and for the continuance of the decimation tax. Among the opponents of this were Lord Broghill and Claypole who were firm adherents to Cromwell.
11. *Burton's Diary*, I, 182–96.

debate was devoted to discussing how to enforce the services of those who had abandoned the House without leave. Bond declared that "They say that we are now made up of none but soldiers and courtiers, and I know not what friends to my Lord Protector. This is a scandal to us."[12] Desborough was quick to retort, "I hope no man thinks it a scandal to be a soldier, or my Lord Protector's friend." However, when Thomas Bampfield proposed that all the excluded members should also be summoned to the debate, it was higher officers and their supporters in the Council who opposed the suggestion.[13] Later on in a subsequent debate Lambert "gave the case away"[14] when, having complained that "the Council are, upon all occasions, reflected upon", he went on to say that, "If a Parliament should be chosen according to the general spirit and temper of the nation, and if there should not be a check upon such election, those may creep into this House, who may come to sit as our judges for all we have done in this Parliament, or at any other time or place."[15] This indicates what slender claims this Parliament had to represent the nation, the responsibility for which must go principally to Lambert and his colleagues. As Sir Charles Firth has said, the exclusions were "a high-handed measure which nothing but the necessity of public safety would excuse".[16] Whether in the case of Lambert's associates the motive was public safety or personal ambition we are left in some doubt.

The first few months of the Second Protectorate Parliament seemed to achieve nothing. The disillusionment which set in after the exclusion affected the attendances in the House, and in the debate on December 20, 1656, Nathaniel Fiennes, who spoke several times in the name of the Council, said bluntly: "We had better never have met than to adjourn now. We cannot kill the king of Spain, nor take Spain or Flanders, by a vote. There must be monies provided, and other Bills passed ... I would have all the members called, and fall to our business,"[17]

Two things, however, suddenly brought life into the desultory

---

12. *Ibid.*, 192 f.
13. Lambert, Gilbert Pickering, and Walter Strickland. Pickering and Strickland, although not officers, were both in favour of the Militia Bill, and Strickland was against the Kingship proposal. Cf. *W.S.*, IV, 367, 386.
14. Abbott's comment. *W.S.*, IV, 367.
15. December 30, *Burton's Diary*, I, 281.
16. *The Last Years of the Protectorate 1656–1638* (1909, 2 vols.), I, 16.
17. *Burton's Diary*, I, 191.

The Kingship and the End   353

discussions of the House, and demonstrated with disconcerting effectiveness to both Protector and Council that Parliament still had the vigour to act independently. The first was the case of James Nayler, a Quaker, who by not distinguishing adequately between the Immanence of the Holy Spirit and the Person of Christ, seemed to identify the two in himself. He had made an entry into Bristol which reproduced the features of Christ's entry into Jerusalem on Palm Sunday. For this he was arraigned before the House, and during the days that followed his case took up an undue proportion of Parliament's time.[18]

It seems likely that time was given to Nayler's case because of the prominence it had assumed in the mind of the public.[19] One of the members declared, "The eyes of God, of all the nation, and of all the world, are upon you",[20] and although that might be dismissed as rhetorical hyperbole, it was echoed by others, one of whom added, "the world abroad says it is liberty of conscience has brought this fellow before you".[21] The government could not afford to ignore that kind of warning. If Nayler were punished summarily without being heard (as a good proportion of the House seemed to favour), there would be no guarantee that Parliament would not proceed in a similar way in other ecclesiastical causes. Lambert pointed out to the House, "You are jurors, judges, and all, in this case. I would have you careful in your manner of proceeding".[22] On the other hand Skippon – a

---

18. This is clear from the reports of the debates in *Burton's Diary*: December 5, 1656 (I, 24–37), 6 (I, 38–53); 8 (I, 53–80); 9 (I, 89–92); 10 (I, 96–105); 11 (I, 107–15); 12 (I, 118–26); 13 (I, 128–35); 15 (I, 137–47); 16 (I, 150–9); 17 (I, 161–7). Even after judgment was given on December 17, the House had not finished with the case. It went on to consider the petitions against Nayler's supporters on December 18 (I, 168–74), and on December 20 considered a petition in favour of a temporary stay of execution against Nayler, and appointed ministers to visit him (I, 182–4).
19. R.H. Abbott suggested that James Nayler was used as a "red herring" by the Protector's supporters to postpone the question of the Succession; but it is difficult to see why the Protector's friends should wish to avoid such a discussion by a Parliament as well sifted as this one appears to have been. *W.S.*, IV, 358–9. (Cf. a Newsletter on October 28: "There was started in the House this day a question concerning the elecction of successive Protectors ... butt they adjourned without putting any question." *C.P.*, III, 77.) Those who were likely to be opposed to this move were the officers of the Council and if Nayler's case, therefore, was used to postpone this question it was these men who were responsible.
20. Bampfield, December 5, 1656. *Burton's Diary*, I, 32–3.
21. Colonel Coxe, December 6. *Ibid.*, 38.
22. For two years Nayler had been a Quartermaster in Lambert's regiment. *Ibid.*, 33.

moderate Presbyterian – said, "For my part I am fully satisfied with the matter of fact. If you put it off, I fear Nayler's sin will prove a national sin."[23] The government was thus between the horns of a dilemma: should it grant Parliament the right to judge ecclesiastical cases with all that it might imply, or should it intervene and appear to countenance blasphemy? Nayler's examination at the bar of the House on December 6, 1656 seems to have confirmed some in their condemnation of him, but it raised doubts in others.[24] The debate dragged on. It was eventually voted that Nayler was guilty of "horrid blasphemy", but it was decided not to put him to death,[25] judgment being given on the following day;[26] but the political implications of Parliament's action could not be ignored.

On December 25, the Lord Protector wrote a letter to the Speaker in which, although careful to disclaim Nayler's opinions, he asked the House to let him know "the grounds and reasons whereupon they have proceeded".[27] Opponents of the Protector did not lose the opportunity of representing the intervention as sympathy with Nayler's views, and Nayler's friends interpreted it in the same way, but Thurloe assured Henry Cromwell that "The letter his highnes writt was not on the behalfe of Naylor; and those, who soe represent it, doe it not ingenuously."[28] Whatever assurance was given to the Protector appears to have been given privately. A sentence of branding was carried out on James Nayler, and he remained in prison until 1659, but the distinctions which his case had raised between the respective powers of Protector and Parliament continued to disturb the calm of Westminster, and may have paved the way for the Kingship debates a few months later.[29]

---

23. Ibid., 34.
24. Sir William Strickland spoke of "hell groaning under expectation of the issue" (December 6, ibid., 51); but Walter Strickland confessed that in his view Nayler had said nothing blasphemous (December 8, ibid., 56 f.).
25. Voting 96-82. Ibid., 152.
26. December 17, 1656. Ibid., 161-7; Whitelocke, 654.
27. W.S.,IV, 366. It should be noted that Major Audley had suggested that the Protector's advice should be sought in the matter on the second day of the debate about Nayler, but the suggestion was not accepted. Burton's Diary, I, 39. Cf. also Cromwell's remarks on Nayler to the officers on February 27, 1657. C.P., III, 92 f.
28. January 20, 1656/7. Thurloe S.P., VI, 8.
29. Colonel Sydenham put the issue in its most pointed form: "I grant this House has a judicial power, as to judge of your own members, or to judge of appeals from inferior Courts, for you are the supreme jurisdiction. But to send

The Kingship and the End 355

The second matter in which Parliament asserted itself was in the question of the Militia Bill. The system of the militia-control had been created and maintained on the authority of the Lord Protector and the Council, and the Major-Generals were anxious to get their position regularized. The matter was aired on December 23 when Lord Eure presented a petition from the north against the Assessments. Two days later Desborough asked leave to bring in a short Bill "for continuance of a tax upon some people, for the maintenance of the militia".[30] Further discussion was postponed temporarily, but when it did come before the House on January 7, 1657 it was very bitterly contested.[31] It was noticed that although Desborough and the Council were in favour of the Bill, the Protector's most immediate associates, especially Lord Broghill, John Claypole (Cromwell's son-in-law), and Henry Cromwell (his nephew), were just as emphatically against it, and it appears to have been primarily due to Broghill's opposition that the Bill was decisively defeated.[32] This victory was immediately celebrated by the House voting £400,000 for the war with Spain.[33]

The defeat of their own Bill and the immediate vote of supply

---

for men up out of the country, and to judge them without a law, what encroachment is this upon the liberties of the people!

"My Lord Protector is under an oath, to maintain the laws, and all the articles of the Government. Is not he then to look so far to the good and safety of the people as to see that no man be sentenced but by those laws, not without or aginst them?" December 30, *Burton's, Diary*, 274–5. For modern accounts of Nayler, cf. Matthews, *English Messiahs*, 3–42; Schenk, *Concern for Social Justice*, 91 f.

30. *Burton's Diary*, I, 230. Leave was given to bring in a Bill of Assessments for the maintenance of the militia forces by 88-63 votes. *Ibid.*, 230–43.
31. *Ibid.*, 310–20.
32. 124–88 votes; Newsletter, February 4. *C.P.*, III, 88 n. Whitelocke had become Speaker in view of Widdrington's continued ill health. Cf. under January 27, *Burton's Diary*, I, 369 f.; Whitelocke, 654.
33. January 30, 1656/7. *Ibid.*, 654; *Burton's Diary*, I, 371. A letter to Thurloe (?) said: "The bill was cast out; and thereupon many of the majors 9 2 30 2 16 [generalls], &c. complained to 1000 [H.H.], how much the house thereby reflected on him, and discouraged the godly; and that their ayme was to pass noething, that might tend to his accommodation; and that they wowld rayse no money, &c. To which hee answered, that hee hoped better things of them. Next day the house with a great deale of cheerfullness voted 400000 l. to be forthwith levied to carry on the Spanish war, which his highnesse tooke exceeding kindly, and exprest himself very affectionately to the committee of the parliament sent to him about that business. Those that were for the decimation-bill, it was plainly perceived, were exceeding cold in the debate for raysing money, and seemed to repine, that the parliament did soe well." February 3, 1656/7, from Mr. Vincent Gookin, *Thurloe S.P.*, VI, 37. Cf. Thurloe to Monk, February 3, *ibid.*, 38.

for the war were difficult things for the Major-Generals to swallow. The Lord Protector denied any responsibility for the Militia Bill.[34] The question of Cromwell assuming the crown had already been raised in Parliament, and Thomas Burton heard someone remark that "it was the distinguishing character of those that were against this Bill, that they were for hereditary rank".[35] It seemed that the "civilian party" in the Parliament – if we can so call those opposed to the Major-Generals – were ready to use Cromwell as a counter-balance to the power of the Army Officers. It is reported that after the defeat of the Militia Bill, Cromwell asked Lord Broghill why he had opposed it, and the latter maintained that by doing so he had done Oliver a good service. On being questioned further, Broghill said that the defeat of the bill would prevent the government becoming unpopular at a time when it it had begun to win respect, and he added the comment, "they were your enemies, not your friends, who brought it in". Oliver was so far satisfied with this "that he began to distrust those, who had advised him to it".[36] The stage was set for the offer of the crown.

II

The Offer of Kingship

The possibility of Cromwell becoming King was not a new idea, and as we have seen, it may have been in Cromwell's own mind ever since Worcester. As early as December 1654 it had been mooted when Augustin Garland had "mooved to have my Lord Protectour crowned, which mocion was second[ed] by Sir Anthony Ashley Cooper, Mr. Hen. Cromwell,[37] and others, but waved".[38] There had been signs of a new move in the same direction in May 1655,[39] and at the end of July a certain John Norbury and others presented a petition to the same effect which appears to have received some support from the Army.[40] The Protector was assuming many of the ancient royal prerogatives and

---

34. *Burton's Diary*, I, 384.
35. *Burton's Diary*, I, 321.
36. Morrice, *State Letters of Roger Boyle*, 25 f.
37. His son.
38. Newsletter, December 28, 1654. *C.P.*, III, 15 f.
39. *W.S.*, III, 715.
40. August 11, 1655. *C.P.*, III, 48.

The Kingship and the End

perquisites,[41] and it is noticed that from October 1655 the Protector's Council became referred to as the "Privy Council".[42] The publication of a book which sought to demonstrate "the necessity of H.H. acceptation of the Empire" in January 1656,[43] and Waller's adulatory verses on the occasion of Captain Stainer's victory over the Spanish plate ships on September 9, 1656,[44] indicated that the idea of Cromwell becoming King or Emperor was being seriously considered by an ever-widening circle of people. On October 28 Colonel Jephson, who according to Ludlow suggested to Cromwell himself that he should become King,[45] raised "a question concerning the eleccion of successive Protectors as itt was now settled in the Instrument".[46] From these incidents it will be seen that a return to the monarchy under a Cromwellian dynasty, although publicly disavowed, had been openly discussed for some time, and it is not to be wondered that foreign envoys expected Cromwell to be crowned.[47] At the end of 1656 there were other reasons for bringing the question again to the fore. The case of James Nayler had raised queries regarding the respective powers of the Protector and Parliament, and if Cromwell assumed the crown it would mean a return to the known precedents of the traditional constitution, and a decided blow at the arbitrary power of the Army.

The question was raised in its most acute form, however, by the revelation of a serious plot to assassinate the Protector and set fire to Whitehall. Thurloe told the House on January 19 that John Toop, one of the Protector's Life Guard, confessed to the plot on the very night it was due to take effect. Others arrested were Miles Sindercombe and John Cavil, two former soldiers, the latter of whom had confessed.[48] This brought the House face

---

41. *W.S.*, III, 815; IV, 33.
42. *Ibid.*, IV, 201–2 and n.
43. Ludlow, *Memoirs*, II, 20 f.
44. *Ibid.*, 253.
45. Ludlow, *Memoirs*, II, 20 f.
46. October 28, 1656. *C.P.*, III, 77. Cf. *W.S.*, IV, 316.; *L-C*, III, 18 n.
47. Cf. Giavarina to Doge, November 7/17, 1656. *Cal. S.P. Ven.* (1655–6), 282.
48. *Burton's Diary*, I, 354 ff. Sindercombe committed suicide on the evening before execution. Cf. Thurloe to Henry Cromwell, February 10. *Thurloe S.P.*, VI, 53. It appeared from papers taken from Sir John Peyton that both Levellers and Royalists were implicated, and that the plot had been hatched by Cromwell's old opponent Colonel Sexby, in Flanders. The Judge-Advocate Whalley informed the House that Monk and he had searched Overton's apartment and

to face with the problem of the succession. As one speaker declared, "If either a natural or an accidental death should happen to his Highness, as who can tell how soon, who can tell the consequence?"[49] It was a consideration such as this that induced John Ashe to propose, "that his Highness would be pleased to take upon him the government according to the ancient constitution; so that the hopes of our enemies' plots would be at an end. Both our liberties and peace, and the preservation and privilege of his Highness, would be founded upon an old and sure foundation."[50] This produced a somewhat heated argument, but it was clear that the Parliament had not finished with the proposal.

In February 1657 there was a serious invasion scare. Charles was reported to be in the Spanish Netherlands ready to invade with 5,000 men in Dutch ships.[51] The Dutch representative at Brussels assured the States General that since Blake was at Lisbon, "it is impossible for him to hinder what the Spanyards intend",[52] and Thurloe wrote that since the Dutch had no good intentions towards England, "its more than probable they may be engaged by Spayne to become our enemies".[53] These fears again called in question the stability of the settlement under the Instrument of Government, and on February 23, 1657, Alderman Pack presented a Bill for making Cromwell King, with the right of appointing his successor, and with a return to the traditional estates of King, Peers and Commons. It was decided by a large majority to read the Bill,[54] and a newsletter writer commented that "publique notice is taken that all the Majour Generalls voted against it", but this time it was clear that the House was not going to drop the matter. The army officers met at Whitehall and were invited by the Major-Generals to meet them at Desborough's lodgings, when Lambert "opened the substance of the bill for Kingshipp", called for their unity with the members of

---

    had discovered a sealed paper "wherein was expressed that 600 1. was distributed to six several persons, who should have murdered my Lord Protector." *Burton's Diary,* I, 356 f.
49. Mr. Bodurda. *Ibid.,* I, 365.
50. *Ibid.,* 362 f.
51. Monk to Thurloe, February 10, 1637. *Thurloe S.P.,* VI, 52. Cf. Marigny to Stouppe, February 6/16. *Ibid.,* 41.
52. Van Sasburgh to States General, February 5/15, 1657. *Ibid.,* VI, 41.
53. February 3, to Henry Cromwell. *Ibid.,* 38.
54. Newsletter, February 26. *C.P.,* III, 91. It was actually carried by 144 votes to 54. *Burton's Diary,* I, 378. Cf. Thurloe to Henry Cromwell, February 24. *Thurloe S.P.,* VI, 74.

The Kingship and the End

the Council against the proposal, and counselled "moderacion and patience".[55] On the 27th, "Mr. Galeaspey and Mr. Nye preached in the Parliament House before the Members. The first was bitter, the 2d more moderate against King-shippe".[56] The Protector also interviewed a deputation of officers at Whitehall, and in reply to their request that he should not take the title "because it was not pleasing to his army, and was matter of scandal to the people of God",[57] he presented them with some blunt home-truths. He said:

> the time was, when they boggled not at the word, (King), for the Instrument by which the Government now stands, was presented to his Highness with the title (King) in it, as some there present could witness, pointing at a principal officer, then in his eye,[58] and he refused to accept of the title. But, how it comes to pass that they now startle at that title, they best knew. That, for his part, he loved the title, a feather in a hat, as little as they did. That they had made him their drudge, upon all occasions; to dissolve the Long Parliament, who had contracted evil enough by long sitting; to call a Parliament, or Convention of their naming. ...
>
> Some time after that, you thought it was necessary to have Major-Generals; and the first rise to that motion (then was the late general insurrections) was justifiable; and you, Major-Generals, did your parts well. You might have gone on. Who bid you go to the House with a Bill, and there receive a foil?
>
> After you had exercised this power a while, impatient were you till a Parliament was called. I gave my vote against it; but you [were] confident, by your own strength and interest, to get men chosen to your heart's desire. How you have failed therein, and how much the country hath been disobliged, is well known.[59]

He concluded, "It is time to come to a settlement, and lay aside arbitrary proceedings, so unacceptable to the nation", and it appears that his forthright words were not without their effect;[60]

---

55. February 26, 1657. *C.P.*, III, 92.
56. Ibid.
57. Burton's Diary, *I, 382*.
58. Lambert? (Cf. Ludlow, *Memoirs,* II, 29.) When the Instrument of Government had been first produced, "some were said to have moved that it [the title] might be King". Cf. *Ibid.*, I, 370.
59. *Burton's Diary,* I, 382–4; *W.S.*, IV, 417 f.; *L-C,* III, 487 f. (Supp. 127). Cf. the summary in *C.P.*, III, 92 f., and the other report of the speech sent to Henry Cromwell by Major Anthony Morgan. *W.S.*, IV, 418 f.
60. "His Hignes haveing spoken to them at large the other night, this day they [the officers] sent a Comittee to wayte upon his Highnes to assure him of their

but the opposition of Lambert and some of the others was implacable.[61]

Meanwhile Parliament proceeded to debate the "Remonstrance". It was agreed to describe Parliament in future as "consisting of two Houses", and that Cromwell should have the right of nominating the members of the other House and his own successor,[62] and on March 26 the title of the proposals was changed from "Advice and Remonstrance" to "Petition and Advice".[63] It was also agreed that nothing in it should be effective unless it were accepted *in toto,* and in this form the "Humble Petition and Advice" was presented to Cromwell on March 31, 1657. In his speech to the Protector the Speaker, Thomas Widdrington,[64] said, "It is a change of name only, and you are desired to take it by the agreement of the representatives of three nations in Parliament. It is the ancient way by which good Kings were ever made. All Israel gathered themselves together at Hebron to make David King."[65] The Protector asked that he might have "some short time to ask counsel of God and of my own heart".[66]

On April 4, 1657 the Lord Protector met the Committee of the House, headed by Bulstrode Whitelocke, which had been appointed to confer with him, and began the protracted discussions on the Kingship. Most people expected Cromwell to accept the throne – especially the foreign envoys in London, to whom it appeared to be the proof of his ambition and the summit of his

---

satisfaction in his Highnes, and of their resolutions to acquiesce in what hee should thinke to bee for the good of these nations." Thurloe to General Monk, March 5, 1657. *C.P.,* III. 93f.

61. Lambert was recognized as the centre of resistance to the Kingship. In a letter on February 24, Thurloe told Henry Cromwell that he thought Lambert would try to put the army into a ferment. *Thurloe, S.P.,* VI, 74. Henry Cromwell replied to Thurloe: "As for the matter and meritt of the proposealls themselves, I say in generall, that I doe not like them the worse, because some of the great ones could noe better digest them; for since they cannot allowe of what a parliament of their owne modelling hath done, I looke upon them as persons verry unapt to be quiett, nor able to endure (as I may call it) any settlement whatsoever; ... besides, I looke upon some of them as vainly arrogatinge to themselves too great a share in the right of his Highnesse's government, and to have too high an opinion of their owne meritt in subverting the old." March 4, 1657, *Thurloe S.P.,* VI, 93.
62. *Burton's Diary,* I, 385.
63. *Ibid.,* 394.
64. *Ibid.,* 397–413.
65. *Ibid.,* 398.
66. Speech, *W.S.,* IV, 442–4; *L-C,* III, 25–9 (Speech VII).

success.⁶⁷ Some of his opponents took the same view;⁶⁸ but in discussions on the *Humble Petition and Advice* Cromwell was obviously perplexed in his own mind: he had lived during the latter part of his life in "the fire, in the midst of trouble".⁶⁹ Like many of his countrymen, he was disillusioned and wanted to see the country settled in peace.⁷⁰ He thought the things suggested were "Christian and honourable",⁷¹ but a few considerations "do stick" and the first was that "You have named me by another Title than now I bear". He found difficulty in pursuing the matter further because they had stipulated that the *Petition and Advice* must be accepted in full.

Whitelocke reported back to the House, but it re-affirmed (albeit with a much reduced majority)⁷² its intention that the title of King should remain an integral part of the settlement. The Protector had not made an absolute refusal; it was decided to make another approach to him, to remind him that the *Humble Petition and Advice* had been presented by the Parliament of the three nations, that it embodied matters, "which, in their judgements, are most conducive to the good of the people thereof", and to remind the Protector of the responsibility that rested upon him "in respect of this advice".⁷³ Accordingly it was agreed that the Protector and Parliament should meet at 3 p.m. the next day in the Banqueting Hall at Whitehall.⁷⁴

With respect to Cromwell's speech on the occasion it has been observed that if anyone could understand the Protector's intentions, "he must have been gifted with more insight than those who heard it or than those who have commented on it since".⁷⁵ It is true that Cromwell's intention was obscure, as we should expect if he were still undecided,⁷⁶ but the way in which his mind

---

67. See the citations in *W.S.*, IV, 436.
68. There was a desperate insurrection of Fifth Monarchists which was suppressed on April 9. Cf. *Thurloe S.P.*, VI, 184–6, papers relating to it, *ibid.*, 185–8. Cf. Newsletter, April 12, *C.P.*, III, 104–5, also *ibid.*, 106; Whitelocke, 655.
69. March 31. *W.S.*, IV, 443.
70. During the Militia Bill debate Desborough had said, "I was weary of war, and thought this [the Act of Oblivion] might have begot a union amongst us. I wish we might all have lived as Englishmen, but I see no hopes of it." January 7, *Burton's Diary*, I, 315.
71. Speech, April 8, 1657. *W.S.*, IV, 445 f.; *L-C*, III, 29–33 (Speech VIII).
72. Votes 78–65. *Burton's Diary*, I, 421.
73. *Ibid.*, 421–2.
74. *Ibid.*, 422 f.
75. *W.S.*, IV, 453.
76. *Ibid.*, 453–5; *L-C*, III, 34–8 (Speech IX).

was working and his own inclinations seem quite clear. It was a matter of conscience with him, and if the Parliament offered advice they could not expect him to undertake something contrary to his conscience: to do so would be to act without faith:[77] he had been "before and then and since, lifting up my heart to God, to know what might be my duty at such a time as this".[78] Therefore he said, "I had, and I have, my hesitations to that individual thing. If I undertake anything not in faith, I shall serve you in my own unbelief, and I shall then be the unprofitablest servant[79] that ever a people or nation had." On the other hand he was ready to give his own views "which haply may be over-swayed by better apprehensions". He who had contended for liberty for others asked liberty for himself, and "The liberty I ask is to vent my own doubts, and mine own fears, and mine own scruples, though haply, in such cases as these are, the world hath judged that a man's conscience ought to know no scruples. Surely mine doth, and I dare not dissemble." He requested information and he was prepared to discuss the matter more fully; with that for the time being the House had to be content.

In the discussion on April 11[80] he said he had "a general dissatisfaction at the thing" [i.e. Kingship], and desired the members, "whom I presume are all satisfied persons to the thing", to give their reasons. The lawyers Whitelocke, Glynn and Lenthall, the Commissioners, Fiennes and Lisle, and Lord Broghill then advanced the reasons in favour of returning to a monarchical form of government, and it is worth noting that the same arguments were used to support monarchy that Cromwell had suggested to Whitelocke in 1652.[81] The Lord Protector replied that since these arguments came to him in the name and authority of Parliament, they must be given due weight, but he still asked for time.

---

77. "I should transgress against all reason should I make any other construction than that you did intend advice. I would not lay a burden upon any beast but I would consider his strength to bear it: and if you will lay a burden upon a man that is conscious of his own infirmities and disabilities, and doth make some measure of counsel that may seem to come from Heaven, – counsel in the word of God, who leaves a room for charity, and for men to consider their own strength, – I hope it will be no evil to measure your advice and mine own infirmity together. ..."
78. "Who knoweth whether thou art come to the Kingdom for such a time as this?" Esther 4:14.
79. Cf. Luke 17:10.
80. *W.S.*, III, 456–61; *L-C*, III, 42–52 (Speech X).
81. *W.S.*, II, 590; *supra*, p. 260.

The Kingship and the End

The onus was now on Cromwell to answer the lawyers. He did so in a meeting with the Committee on the 13th.[82] He contended that Kingship was in the Law not by reason of its name "but from what is signified", and he maintained that the name was not necessary, however many arguments might be advanced to show that the office was expedient. There was nothing to prevent the Supreme Authority being vested in other names – indeed, it had been so exercised only recently, both under the form of the "Custodes Libertatis Angliae", and under the title of Lord Protector, and he maintained that, as far as the law was concerned, it had been better administered and less corrupt under his own rule than since Elizabeth. As far as accepting the title King was concerned he said, "the Parliament desires me to have this title, it hath stuck with me, and yet doth stick". He told them frankly, "I am a man standing in the place I am in; which place I undertook not so much out of the hope of doing any good, as out of a desire to prevent mischief and evil, which I did see was imminent upon the nation." He had not sought the position, but he confessed his concern for the peril in which the nation still found itself and urged them to strive:

> for somewhat that may beget a consistency, otherwise the nation will fall to pieces. And in that, as far as I can, I am ready to serve not as a King, but as a constable. For truly I have as before God thought it often, that I could not tell what my business was, nor what I was in the place I stood, save [by] comparing it with a good constable to keep the peace of the parish.

The Lord Protector then went off into what many, at that time and since, must have regarded as an unnecessary digression. He informed the members of the Committee how he had remonstrated with John Hampden about the poor quality of the Parliamentary cavalry in the Earl of Essex's army,[83] and he went on to describe how, after a conversation with John Hampden, he set about raising "such men as had the fear of God before them, and made some conscience of what they did". He reminded his hearers how those same troops had been invincible – "wherever they engaged the enemy they beat them continually". The passage might be dismissed as the reminiscences of an elderly general who was becoming garrulous as well as infirm, but at the back of Oliver's

---

82. *W.S.*, IV, 467–74: *L-C*, III, 53–73 (Speech XI).
83. *Supra*, p. 57.

mind there was the memory of what the relationship with his troops had meant to him, and the knowledge that he owed a duty to his former comrades. The Lord Protector spoke as "a person under the disposition of the providence of God", and that was a material factor in the ascent to his present office. We must understand what Cromwell was doing in his speeches to the Committee: he was not defending or even criticizing any theory of government, but trying to relate the call to monarchy to the vocation which he had accepted hitherto. He was struggling through the fog of constitutional arguments advanced by the lawyers, but he was sure of one thing, the experience he had shared under God with those "russet-coated" Ironsides of the Eastern Association: his vocation had begun there. The relevance of this to his immediate problem can be seen when he goes on to say:

> I must tender this unto you as a thing that sways with my conscience, or else I were a knave and a deceiver. I tell you there are such men in this nation that are godly, men of the same spirit, men that will not be beaten down with a carnal or worldly spirit while they keep their integrity. I deal plainly and faithfully with you, I cannot think that God would bless me in the undertaking of anything, that would justly and with cause, grieve them. ... But if that I know, as indeed I do, that very generally good men do not swallow this title, though really it is no part of their goodness to be unwilling to submit to what a Parliament shall settle over them, yet I must say that it is my duty and my conscience to beg of you, that there may be no hard thing put upon me, things I mean hard to them, that they cannot swallow. If the nation may as well be provided for without these things. ... I think truly it will be no sin to you to seek their favour as it was to David in another case,[84] no grief of heart to you, that you have a tenderness, even possible if it be [to] their weakness, to the weakness of those that have integrity and uprightness. ...

Despite the fact that he had castigated the officers on March 27, it was difficult for him to change the fellowship of men whose religion and loyalty he had always trusted for that of the Broghills and the Claypoles and the gentlemen of the long robe. Providence he declared, could often be a good expositor of the Word of God and "Truly the providence of God has laid this title aside providentially". The family of the Stuarts had been driven from the country by God, and God had seemed to strike not only at the

---

84. The case of Nabal and Abigail (1 Samuel 25:31).

family but also at the very title: "I can make no conclusion but this," he said, "I would not seek to set up that that providence hath destroyed ... I would not build Jericho again."[85]

Cromwell's speeches throughout these discussions do not make easy reading. He was a sick man, and he was also a bewildered man, trying to see his way through to something which would give the nation what it needed. Through all his obscurities, one fact stands out clearly; he could not, at that moment, reconcile monarchy with his own career, although he declared he would rather he were in his grave than hinder them in anything that might be for a settlement, "for the nation needs it and never needed it more".

A period of illness intervened[86] and although a meeting took place on the 16th, it was not until the 20th that Cromwell expressed himself at any length.[87] In his speech on that day the Lord Protector's sentences were no less involved than they were before, but it is evident that he had not shifted from the position he had taken previously. All the legal arguments were in favour of monarchy,[88] but he clearly conceived his own office to be founded upon an ultimate law of necessity for national survival, and "It hath pleased God that I have been instrumental to keep the peace of the nation to this day, and to keep it under a title that some [say] signifies but a keeping it to another's use". He had no illusions about how his motives would be misinterpreted, and he was well aware of the criticism with which he had been reproached because he had not offered any alternative to Kingship: "I know the evil spirits of men may easily obtrude upon a man, that he would have a name that the Law knows not, and that is boundless and is that under which a man exercises more arbitrariness." On the other hand if Parliament decided to set bounds to his title it would be limited sufficiently, "but," he went on to say, "I may say this in answer to that, that doth a little pinch upon me, and the more so when I am told it is my duty. I think it can be no man's duty, nor obligation, but it is between God and himself." He concluded by giving the Committee a document which listed various particulars in the *Humble Petition and Advice*, apart from

---

85. Joshua 6:17–26.
86. The postponements "did strongly build up the faith of the Contrariants". *Burton's Diary*, II, 4.
87. *W.S.*, IV, 480–3; *L-C*, III, 75–84 (Speech XII).
88. "It doth agree with the law, the law knows the office, the people know it, and the people are likelier to receive satisfaction that way".

the title of the Chief Magistrate, in which he asked for further information.[89] On the following day,[90] at the end of what has been described as an "apologia pro vita sua",[91] he offered some criticisms of several articles in the *Humble Petition and Advice*, and told the Committee, "When you will be pleased to let me hear further of your thoughts in these things, then I suppose I shall be in a condition to discharge myself as God shall enable me".

Professor Abbott has wondered what effect the lengthy resume of events had upon the Lord Protector's audience, but it is likely that having lived through these same events they would see more point in them than modern readers are able to do. To Cromwell, such a recital of Providence, far from being redundant, was an important factor in the question of his accepting the throne – in fact, if he could discern its lesson in the present case, it would be for him conclusive.

III

The Refusal

"The Protector often advised about this and other great Businesses," said Whitelocke, "with the Lord Broghill, Pierepoint, my self, Sir Charles Wolseley and Thurloe, and would be shut up three or four Hours together in private discourse, and none were admitted to come in to him."[92] A struggle was going on in the Protector's mind. Whitelocke affirms that, "The Protector was satisfied in his private Judgment that it was fit for him to take upon him the *Title of King*, and Matters were prepared in order thereunto; but afterwards by Solicitation of the Commonwealth's Men, and fearing a Mutiny and Defection of a great part of the Army in case he should assume that Title and Office, his Mind changed."[93] This appears to be corroborated by John

---

89. Delivered to Parliament by Whitelocke on April 21. Whitelocke, 656; *Burton's Diary*, II, 7.
90. W.S., IV, 484–97; L-C, III, 86–123 (Speech XIII). For the paper of objections, cf. W.S., IV, 498–500; L-C, III, 492–4 (Supp. 130).
91. R.H. Abbott, W.S., IV, 497.
92. He added: "He would sometimes be very chearful with us, and laying aside his Greatness, he would be exceeding familiar with us, and by way of diversion, would make Verses with us, and everyone must try his Fancy; he commonly called for Tobacco, Pipes, and a Candle, and would now and then take Tobacco himself; then he would fall again to his serious and great Business, and advise with us in those Affairs; and this he did often with us, and our Counsel was accepted and followed by him, in most of his greatest Affairs." Whitelocke, 656.
93. *Ibid.*

The Kingship and the End

Thurloe who, on May 12, wrote an account of what had happened to Henry Cromwell in Ireland:

> His highnesse hath beene pleased to put an issue to it at last, haveinge upon friday last called the parliament into the banquettinge-house, and there declared, that he could not give his consent to their advise, because of the title *hinge*. I perceive this hath strucke a great damp upon the spirits of some, and much raised and elevated others. H.H. was pleased upon the Wednesday and thursday before,[94] to declare to severall of the house, that he was resolved to accept it with that title; but just in the very nicke of tyme he tooke other resolutions, the three great men [Lambert, Fleetwood and Desborough] professinge their great unfreenes to act, and sayd, that ymediately after his acceptance thereof, they must withdraw from all publique ymployment, and soe they beleeved would severall other officers of quality, that had beene engaged all alonge in this warre. Besides, the very morneinge the house expected H.H. would have come to have given his consent to the bill, some 26 or 27 officers came with a petition to the parliament, to desire them not to press H.H. any further about kingship.[95]

Most people believed that despite his speeches to the Committee Cromwell would accept the crown[96] and this opinion was shared both by those who opposed and those in favour of his doing so.

Ludlow provides us with more details about the soldiers' petition which seems to have played such a spectacular part in the final act of this drama. He says that the idea of a petition was first mooted by Colonel Pride, and that Pride and Desborough "both went to Dr. Owen and having acquainted him with what had hapned, they perswaded him to draw a petition according to their desires".[97] As a sequel to this the petition appeared on the morning of May 8 when Cromwell was due to deliver his answer and he immediately sent for Fleetwood and asked him why he had allowed such a petition to proceed "since he knew it to be his resolution not to accept the crown without the consent of the army". Fleetwood was sent straightway to the House with the request that the petition should not be debated or answered at that time, and then Parliament received notice from Cromwell "that instead of meeting him in the Painted Chamber, which

---
94. i.e. May 6 and 7.
95. *Thurloe S.P.*, VI, 281. Cf. Newsletter, May 9. *C.P.*, III, 107 f.
96. Cf. Newsletter, April 30, 1657. *C.P.*, III, 106–7.
97. Ludlow, *Memoirs*, II, 25. One of John Owen's biographers points out that from this time Owen and Cromwell appear to have been estranged. Andrew Thompson, *The Life of Dr. Owen* (*Works*, I, lxvi–lxvii).

was the place where he used to give his consent, they would meet him in the Banqueting House".[98] He declined to take the title of King.[99] "I lying under this consideration," he said, "think it my duty to let you know, – only I could have wished I had done it sooner. ... I say, I am persuaded to return this answer to you, that I cannot undertake this Government with that title of King. And that is my answer to this great weighty business."

Is Abbott right in suggesting that the petition presented by Lieutenant-Colonel Mason made Cromwell's decision "virtually inevitable"?[100] Lambert had been against the Kingship proposals from the first, and his resignation would remove Cromwell's most ambitious rival – a fact that Thurloe realized, even if the Protector himself did not;[101] Fleetwood, later dubbed by Cromwell "a milksop",[102] was bound to the Protector by marriage; and Desborough, who had been married to Cromwell's sister Jane,[103] had given an undertaking that even if Cromwell accepted the crown "he was resolved never to act against him".[104] It would therefore appear that the Protector had little to fear from the disapproval of "the three great men". Similarly, the petition itself was not very impressive. Ludlow says:

> This petition was subscribed by two colonels, seven lieutenant-colonels, eight majors, and sixteen captains, who with such officers in the House as were of the same opinion, made up the majority of those relating to that part of the army which was then quartered about the town.[105]

But this does not add up to a majority of the whole Army. Although there were men like Captain Bradford who had gone with Cromwell from Edgehill to Dunbar, who had written to dissuade him from accepting the crown,[106] others had become

---

98. Ludlow, *Memoirs*, II, 25-8. Cf. *Burton's Diary*, II, 116f.
99. *W.S.*, IV, 512-4; *L-C*, III, 126-9 (Speech XIV).
100. *W.S.*, IV, 512.
101. *Supra*, p. 360 n. 1.
102. Cf. *W.S.*, IV, 728. Henry Cromwell, on hearing the remark, commented, "I believe the milk, wherein 653 [Fleetwood], was sopt, had much water in it." Henry Cromwell to Broghill, February 17, 1657, *Thurloe S.P.*, VI, 811.
103. *W.S.*, I, 32 notes; IV, 314. Jane had died in the previous October.
104. Ludlow, *Memoirs*, II, 24.
105. *Ibid.*, 27.
106. Cf. C.H. Firth, *Last Years*, I, 162-4.

reconciled to the idea[107] and many more were indifferent. Monk wrote from Scotland on March 10 to say he was glad to hear of the unanimity with which the House had proceeded, and that, "for the officers heere, by soe much as I can perceive as yett by their tempers, they will bee very well satisfied with what his highnesse and the parliament shall thinke fitt for the settlement and peace of the three nations",[108] which is as much an indication of the change in the temper of the Protector's army as proof of General Monk's compliance. It does not appear therefore that the Protector had anything to *fear* from the Army.

It was reported that "his Highness knew nothing of the petition, but when he heard of it was extream angry, cald it a high breach of priviledge, and the greatest injury they could have offered him next cutting his throat",[109] but the grounds for his anger are interesting, for Cromwell protested that "coming in as it did it makes people abroad say he is afraid of his army":[110] he was angry because the petition might seem to suggest that he had been *forced* to refuse the crown instead of having reached the decision of his own volition. From this it appears that the Protector had already made up his mind to decline the kingly title. He may have wavered a day or two before his decision was made public, as Whitelocke and Thurloe suggest – they were close enough to him to be relied upon and their impressions were shared by friend and foe alike – but his speeches throughout the Kingship debates show that he was never fully reconciled to the idea of monarchy.

Why did Cromwell refuse the crown? There was at least one practical reason which must be given due weight, for Desborough and Fleetwood had spoken nothing less than the truth when they warned him, "that those who put him upon it were no enemies to Charles Stewart; and that if he accepted of it, he would infallibly draw ruin on himself and his friends".[111] Those

---

107. "The officers have beene with his highnes this weeke, and exprest all manner of confidence and satisfaction in his highnes; and I verily beleeve they speake the truth, even those, who seemed to be most dissatisfied a little before." Thurloe to Henry Cromwell, March to, *Thurloe S.P.,* VI, 107. Cf. Thurloe to Monk, March 5, *C.P.,* III, 93–4. Cf. Newsletters, March 10, 19, *ibid.,* 97, 98.
108. Monk to Thurloe, March 10, *Thurloe, S.P.,* VI, 106.
109. Major Anthony Morgan to Henry Cromwell, May 12, quoted by Firth in Ludlow's *Memoirs,* II, 26 n.
110. *Ibid.,* 26 n.
111. *Ibid.,* 24.

who offered him the crown on this occasion were within three years equally active in the Restoration of Charles. The cavaliers were quite eager that Cromwell should accept the throne, because it would mean a simple struggle between the legal King and a usurper, and because, "it would be made manifest for what cause the War was in a great part begun, to wit; the sole Ambition of Cromwell".[112]

It cannot, however, be imagined that this was the only factor which influenced Cromwell in his decision. From one point of view the offer of Kingship must have appeared as the vindication of his mission – the final call of God which justified all that he had tried to accomplish. Whatever his dreams in the past, Parliament was freely making the offer on the grounds that only by his acceptance could the constitution of the three nations be finally settled – and he was "hugely taken with the word Settlement". If ever Cromwell had experienced a "call" to the magistracy this occasion would seem to have all the signs of being an authentic call of God; he had the Scriptural example of David before him, with David's experience of divine choice and his conception of prophetic-Kingship so nearly paralleled by his own experience and ideas.[113] Yet there was a doubt. Was this the Supreme Call or the Great Temptation? That is the question that must have perplexed him. Cromwell was not wedded to any doctrinaire political theories[114] – he likened himself to a constable keeping the peace of the parish[115] – a practical politician meeting immediate difficulties by any means that offered reasonable chance of success, but he could not help feeling that to accept the name of "King" was to fly in the face of Providence. As he had told Robert Hammond a few years previously, it was fatally easy to meddle with "an accursed thing". Furthermore, how could monarchy be reconciled with that vocational view of public service which had been his from the first? What of his successors? He had declared to the Nominated Parliament that he wished all magistrates were chosen for their godly principles, but primogeniture made no provision for such an ideal arrangement.

It is in the context of these or similar thoughts that the disapproval of his old colleagues is to be seen. We do not think that their opposition was of itself enough to force him to refuse

---

112. Bates, *Elenchus Motuum*, Pt. II, 216.
113. Cf. *supra*, p. 300 f. Widdrington also had cited David. Cf. *supra*, p. 360.
114. Cf. Major Huntington's remarks, *supra*, p. 178 n. 2.
115. *Supra*, p. 363.

Parliament's offer, and with Monk's Army in Scotland ready to support him and a good proportion of the Army in England compliant, it is probable that he could have ascended the throne by force if he had so desired. If the Lord Protector had been merely a military adventurer, he would probably have taken the risk as the foreign ambassadors expected him to do, but in this they misinterpreted his course of action because they misinterpreted the man himself.[116] Cromwell realized that if he accepted the throne he would have to break entirely with the Independents, perhaps not only those within the Army, but also those within the Church. There is a story recounted of Marchamont Needham, the editor of *Mercurius Politicus,* during the Kingship discussions, which is very much to the point. The Protector is reputed to have met Needham one day at Whitehall and asked him what news there was, to which the editor replied drily that *vox populi* said that Mr. Nye should be Archbishop of Canterbury, and Dr. Owen Archbishop of York.[117] Needham's wit placed a finger on a fact which Cromwell could not afford to disregard – monarchy of the kind known in the seventeenth century appeared to be incompatible with the spirit and temper of much that was good in Independency. Owen and Nye seem to have appreciated this, for despite Needham's cynicism they were both uncompromisingly against Cromwell's assumption of the throne. The opposition of leading Independent ministers must therefore be added to that of Cromwell's colleagues in the Army, and in the midst of his own doubts the threatened break must have appeared a formidable argument against accepting the crown: it would mean exchanging the experience of Christian friendship learned in the only real Church fellowship he had experienced,[118] for the dubious loyalty of the lawyers and the sycophants.

---

116. Abbott gives an unconscious comparison between what Giavarina expected Cromwell to do and what a certain Mr. Hooke, a minister from Boston, Massachusetts expected him to do on the question of the crown *(W.S.,* IV, 474–5). Although Mr. Hooke's opinion was "less objective and much less worldly than that of the Venetian envoy", it should be noted that he was right and Giavarina was wrong. Cf. *ibid.,* 333–4.
117. Robinson to Williamson, March 19. *Cal. S.P. Dom.* (1656–57), 318. Cf. Firth, *Last Years,* I, 156–60.
118. Abbott describes Cromwell's oratory as "cultivated and consolidated by long experience in conventicles" *(W.S.,* IV, 463). There is no proof of Cromwell having belonged to any "conventicle" other than his own Troop of Horse and Council of Officers; but we cannot doubt that to him these represented "the Church". Cf. *supra,* pp. 65–7, 149–50, 159.

IV

Princeps

From the time when Oliver Cromwell declined the throne until his death sixteen months later the Protectorate followed the pattern in which it had already been set. New threats to the security of the State were discovered, and new adventures were undertaken both at home and abroad, but it was all in the course of fulfilling the policy which had been followed hitherto and within limitations with which the government had become all too familiar.

Parliament was completely subdued by Cromwell's refusal, but it was agreed to insert the title "Lord Protector" into the *Humble Petition and Advice*,[119] and in this form it was presented to him on May 25 and received his consent "mutato nomine tantum".[120] An "Additional and Explanatory Petition and Advice" was added later,[121] and on June 26, 1657 the Lord Protector with due solemnity was installed a second time,[122] with provision in the constitution for a "House of Lords" and with power to nominate his own successor. The wheel had come almost full circle: the solemnity and symbolism of the Installation and of the formal proclamation on July 1, no less than the form of the constitution itself, indicated that in all but name England had returned to monarchy, and that Oliver Cromwell was King.

There was, however, something in the situation which Cromwell might refuse to call fate ("that were too paganish a word") but which prevented the country from realizing a permanent settlement. The Protectorate was never secure, and if the pattern of the Protectorate did not alter through these last months, neither did the pattern of opposition. Lambert was already suspect. If he had cherished the ambition of succeeding Cromwell as Protector by election of the Council or of Parliament, as he might very well have done under the Instrument of Government,[123] he knew he had no chance now that the Protector had the

---

119. May 19 and 22, 1657, *Burton's Diary*, II, 118-9. The text of the *Humble Petition and Advice* is in Gardiner, *Const. Docs.*, 447-59; Whitelocke, 657-61.
120. *Burton's Diary*, II, 123 f. For Cromwell's speech see *W.S.*, IV, 535-6; *L-C*, III, 304 f. (App. 30). Cf. Newsletter, May 26, 1657, *C.P.*, III, 111-2.
121. Whitelocke, 663-4; *Const. Docs.*, 459-64.
122. For a contemporary account of the ceremony, cf. *Burton's Diary*, II, 511-5.
123. Cf. Bates, *Elenchus*, II, 165.

right of nomination. He absented himself from the Installation celebrations, and he refused to take the oath required of Council members by the *Humble Petition and Advice* to be faithful to the Protector and the new constitution. Upon his refusal the Protector demanded that he should deliver up his commission,[124] and another enemy was added to the list.[125]

The inveterate intriguer, Edward Sexby, had joined with Colonel Titus to produce a pamphlet entitled *Killing no Murder*, which sought to justify assassinating the Protector. The pamphlet was as sinister as it was witty, and it had begun to circulate in England while the question of the Kingship was in progress. Sexby himself was in England at this time but he was arrested on July 24, just as he was embarking for the Continent.[126] He admitted responsibility for the Sindercombe plot and his complicity in the plans of Charles II and the Spaniards, but he became insane while in prison, and he died there on January 13, 1657/8.[127]

Another cavalier insurrection was feared in December 1657,[128] and Ormonde seems to have arrived in the country at the end of the January following, in connection with royalist plans for a general rebellion. The matter did not come to a head, however, until the spring of 1658,[129] when Sir Henry Slingsby, Dr. John Hewitt, John Mordaunt and others were arrested, and a new High Court of Justice was set up to try these men. Their trial was of more than ordinary interest, for Sir Henry Slingsby was uncle to Lord Falconbridge[130] and Dr. Hewitt had officiated at the marriage of Falconbridge and Mary Cromwell at Hampton Court the previous November – reputedly according to the Book of Common Prayer.[131] Both Slingsby and Hewitt were found guilty and sentenced on June 2, 1658 to be hanged, which by the

---

124. Ludlow, *Memoirs*, II, 29; Newsletter, July 18, 1657, *C.P.*, III, 113 f.
125. Lucy Hutchinson records that her husband revealed a plot by followers of Lambert to assassinate Cromwell, because he judged "that Lambert would be the worst tyrant of the two". *Memoirs of Colonel Hutchinson* (Everyman edn.), 295-7.
126. Newsletter, July 25, 1657, *C.P.*, III, 114.
127. He is reputed to have said that the case for killing Cromwell was altered after the *Humble Petition and Advice* because the Parliament had settled the government upon him.
128. Cf. Instructions to Gloucester, December 2, 1657. *W.S.*, IV, 678; *L-C*, III, 307 f. (App. 31).
129. Whitelocke, 653.
130. For reference to the dubious loyalty of Falconbridge, see Clarendon, *History*, XV, 145.
131. *W.S.*, IV, 664.

intervention of Elizabeth Claypole was changed to beheading;[132] others were acquitted – Mordaunt by only a single vote[133] – and a few suffered the full penalty for treason, which was "the first and only instance in which the Protector had assumed the prerogative of executing thus royally the barbarous sentence pronounced by the treason law of England".[134] Some were reprieved, but the evidence had revealed preparations in the City for a rising of considerable magnitude.[135] Cromwell could not escape the pattern in which the Protectorate was cast: the threat of defiant insurrection, violent death and counter-revolution continued to the end.

In foreign affairs too the policy had been defined, but in this there was a discernible shifting of emphasis during the last months of the Protectorate. The Lord Protector seems to have given up the idea of achieving his ends through a Protestant League, and to have relied upon the extension of British influence by the establishment of bridgeheads on the continental mainland. Early in 1657 Cromwell suggested to George Fleetwood that Bremen might be used in such a way, adding the significant comment that by this means the German Protestant States would be "not a little encouraged to co-operate the more zealously for the common good and to withstand the more resolutely the Catholic menace".[136] In accordance with this policy the Protector looked for an alliance with Sweden,[137] but the one obstacle to its full development was his inability to fulfil the financial obligations that he had contracted.[138]

This more realistic approach to foreign affairs was most marked in the alliance with Catholic France for the capture and annexation of Dunkirk. The dream of an all-embracing Protestant alliance passed quietly away with the return of Dury and Morland from the Rhineland states early in 1657, but at the same time

---

132. Her anxiety for Hewitt, who was a friend of hers, is thought to have been partly responsible for her death a few weeks later. Ludlow, *Memoirs*, II, 41.
133. Abbott has said that "The government's mind had been made up … the result of the trial was a foregone conclusion" (*W.S.*, IV, 820). It is difficult to see how this could have been so in the case of Mordaunt.
134. *Burton's Diary*, II, 474. Sindercombe had been sentenced, but see *supra*, p. 357 n. 8. For Cromwell's clemency in comparison with the Tudors, Stuarts and Hanoverians, see *Burton's Diary*, II, 474–6, note by J.T. Rutt.
135. Whitelocke, 673; *W.S.*, IV, 844.
136. *Circa* January 14–15, 1657. *Ibid.*, 383.
137. He seems particularly to have grown suspicious of Dutch designs. Cf. Schlezer's report, May 15/25, 1657, *ibid.*, 519–20, and the letter to Montagu, October 19, 1657. *Ibid.*, 642; *Thurloe S.P.*, VI, 582.
138. Letter to Charles X, 16/26 July, 1658. *W.S.*, IV, 854–6.

The Kingship and the End

Lockhart was pursuing negotiations in Paris for an Anglo-French military alliance which was concluded on March 13 of the same year.[139] Under this treaty six thousand English troops under the command of Sir John Reynolds and Colonel Thomas Morgan were embarked for Flanders to serve in the summer campaign of Turenne. The aim of this campaign as far as the English were concerned was to capture and annex the Flemish port of Dunkirk. Reynolds's troops joined Turenne's army at S. Quentin on June 1 and were received honourably by the French,[140] but a certain amount of friction developed between the two countries regarding the conduct of the campaign. The French generals conducted war rather like an elaborate game of chess, with siege and countersiege occupying the centre of operations, whereas Cromwell had always tried as soon as possible to destroy the opposing field-force. It is interesting to speculate how successful Cromwell's methods would have been if he had had to meet Condé or Turenne in battle, but he did not hesitate to charge the French with wasting the time of the English troops.[141] The news of the capture of Mardike was received at the end of September 1657, and this port was handed over to an English garrison as a pledge of good faith, but the death of Reynolds[142] and the Protector's tardiness in appointing a successor caused some irritation to the French. The year 1657 closed without the attack on Dunkirk having been attempted.[143]

In May of the following year there was an ill-fated attempt against Ostend, but this opened the way for the attack on Dunkirk. Lockhart was placed in command of the English troops, and the battle of the Dunes was fought on June 4.[144] Dunkirk surrendered ten days later.[145] Cromwell had gained his bridgehead in Europe, and Lockhart at once took steps to consolidate the position

---

139. Cromwell appears to have suggested a comprehensive alliance of England, France, Sweden, Denmark and the United Netherlands, but Mazarin successfully limited it to an Anglo-French treaty. Cf. *W.S.*, IV, 410.
140. Letter from an officer in Flanders to General Monk, May 26, 1657. *C.P.*, III, 110 f.
141. Cf. *W.S.*, IV, 602, 629.
142. He was drowned while returning for a brief visit to England, December 5 /15, 1657.
143. See the accounts of Major-General Morgan to General Monk, August 21 /31, 1657. *C.P.*, III, 116 f., and Vice-Admiral Goodson to General Monk,(?) October 8. *Ibid.*, 121.
144. See Colonel Drummond's account to General Monk, June 5/15, 1658. *C.P.*, III, 153–6.
145. June 14, 1658.

of Protestantism in the port.¹⁴⁶ Only a few days before Reynolds joined Turenne in France, the news of Blake's decisive defeat of the Spanish plate fleet at Santa Cruz became known,¹⁴⁷ and although the Admiral returned only to die within sight of the English coast, his victories had caused English naval power to be feared from the Mediterranean to the North Sea.

In summary, therefore, we may say that the foreign policy of the Protectorate, from Cromwell's second installation until his death, was a continuation of the policy we have traced hitherto. If the ideal of an organic union of Protestantism was abandoned, the defence of Protestantism was still his aim,¹⁴⁸ but we can trace a new emphasis on independent action by the British Commonwealth through the French and Swedish alliances and in the clear intention of the Protector to win a foothold on the European mainland. Perhaps the acquisition of Dunkirk foreshadowed the development of English Protestant imperialism on the Continent: if the triumph of Protestantism could not be achieved by a Protestant League, then other instruments must be forged to the same end.

V

The End

The last days of Oliver Cromwell were no less unsettled than the rest of his public life. He had the task of nominating the "Lords" for the "Other House" under the *Humble Petition and Advice,* and he seems to have exercised considerable care in his choice.¹⁴⁹ It is significant too that when Parliament reassembled on January 20, 1657/8 the guard was removed from it and all members who would take the oath were admitted to the House without further hindrance. In this way many of those who had been excluded were now admitted, including such inveterate opponents of the Lord Protector as Sir Arthur Hazelrigge and Thomas Scot; it is perhaps significant that with the virtual eclipse

---

146. *W.S.,* IV, 839 f. Whitelocke was offered the governorship but declined. Whitelocke, 674.
147. May 28, 1657; the action had taken place on April 20. Cf. June 3, Whitelocke, 661.
148. He offered mediation when the inevitable war between the northern powers broke out, and he continued his intervention on behalf of the Piedmontese. Cf. his letters to Louis XIV and the Swiss Protestant cantons, and the instructions sent to Lockhart, May 26, 1658. *W.S.,* IV, 811–15.
149. Cf. Thurloe to Henry Cromwell, November 10, 1657. *Thurloe S.P.,* VI, 609.

The Kingship and the End

of some of the great officers the policy of selection was noticeably relaxed. Cromwell, however, could not expect to receive any credit for that. By their oath the members had promised to be "true and faithful to the Lord Protector of the Commonwealth ... as chief magistrate thereof",[150] but the Republicans were quick to transfer their attack to the "Other House" which they refused to recognize as a House of Lords either in fact or name.

The Protector himself was in very poor health, and his speech at the re-assembly of Parliament was brief,[151] and has been described as "better suited to a conventicle than to a meeting of Parliament".[152] Something of the gratitude which those who attend "conventicles" feel for their religious freedom is echoed in his exclamation, "Who would have forethought, when we were plunged into the midst of our troubles, that ever the people of God should have had liberty to worship God without fear of enemies? Which is the very acknowledgement of the promise of Christ, that He would deliver his people from fear of enemies, that they might worship Him in holiness and in righteousness all the days of their life."[153] Five days later he called the Houses together and delivered himself at more length.[154] He said that he regarded himself "as being set on a watch-tower,[155] to see what may be for the good of these nations and what may be for the preventing of evil". Having discoursed to them on their dangers abroad and at home he dismissed the Houses to their own business.

The House of Commons immediately fell under the influence of the formerly excluded republicans, most of the Protector's more experienced parliamentarians having been promoted to the "Other House". The republicans reminded the House that the grievances of the people were to be preferred before any vote of Supplies[156] and it was resolved by a narrow margin to exclude all private business for a month, for the discussion of public issues.[157]

---

150. The oath. *W.S.*, IV, 703-4.
151. January 20, 1657/8. *W.S.*, IV, 705-8; *L-C*, III, 150-8 (Speech XVI); *Burton's Diary*, II, 322-30.
152. R.H. Abbott, *W.S.*, IV, 708. Cf. *supra*, p. 371, n. 3.
153. Cf. Luke 1:71, 74 f.
154. January 25, 1657/58. *W.S.*, IV, 712-21; *L-C*, III, 162-85 (Speech XVII); *Burton's Diary*, II, 351-71.
155. Isaiah 21:8. Cf. Ezekiel 3:17-21; 33:1-9.
156. Alderman Gibbe and Mr. Darley, January 28, 1657-58. *Burton's Diary*, II, 374.
157. 92 votes to 84. *Ibid.*, 377.

Sir Arthur Hazelrigge said that they "must live long in a little time", for "it may be questioned whether we shall sit a fortnight".[158] This was an ominous beginning, and Hazelrigge and his colleagues at once launched a general attack on the title, authority and jurisdiction of the "Other House" to such effect that less than a week after Hazelrigge had ventured his prophecy Parliament was dissolved.

The Lord Protector summoned the Houses to him on February 4.[159] He said that when he had met with them previously he had "very comfortable expectations that God would make the calling of this Parliament and the meeting of it a blessing to ourselves and to these nations". He had been disappointed. The House of Commons had itself framed the *Humble Petition and Advice* by virtue of which he occupied the office he then held. "There is ne'er a man", he affirmed, "within these walls that can say, Sir, you sought it, nay not a man nor woman treading upon English ground." He had taken the responsibility of government only on the condition that there should be another authority which could mediate between the Protector and the Commons, and he had been given the right of nominating the members. He said, "you not only have disquieted yourselves, but the whole nation is disquieted", and that within fifteen or sixteen days they had brought the country nearer confusion than it had been since the adjournment in June. He charged them with "playing of the King of Scots his game", and he dissolved Parliament with the words, "Let God judge between you and me", to which the defiant Republicans of the Commons cried "Amen".[160]

The Lord Protector was forced back to government on his own authority and he was not fit enough physically to shoulder it successfully. Whatever the apparent strength of the Protector abroad, the rest of the story of Oliver Cromwell has been shown by Sir Charles Firth[161] and Professor Abbott[162] to have been a struggle for the bare survival of his government in the midst of increasing financial and political difficulties, and in the face of the inevitable breakdown in health. Elizabeth Claypole, his favourite daughter, died on August 6. She had been deeply shocked by the execution of Hewitt and had grieved over the death of her year-

---

158. January 28. *Ibid.*, 375.
159. W.S., IV, 728-32; *L-C*, III, 503-8 (Supp. 138). *Burton's Diary*, II, 465-70.
160. *C.P.*, III, 139.
161. *Last Years*, II, 257-307.
162. W.S., IV, 797-876.

old son Oliver in June. She died in great pain,[163] and the knowledge of her sufferings contributed to Cromwell's own,[164] for after her death in August he took a turn for the worse from which he never really recovered.

It was soon after the death of Elizabeth that George Fox had his last encounter with the Protector, and recounted how, "I saw & felt a wafte of death goe foorth against him, yt he lookt like a deade man".[165] The next day he was too ill for Fox to be allowed to see him, yet even in the midst of this last fatal illness he could not escape the constant pressure of affairs;[166] at the beginning of his last illness he was taken from Hampton Court to Whitehall. We ought to be cautious in accepting the reputed speeches of his death-bed,[167] and perhaps the same restraint is needed towards his death-bed prayer; but whether the following were his actual words or not, this prayer summarizes in a remarkable way his thought and his mission throughout life:

> Lord, though I am a miserable and wretched creature, I am in Covenant with Thee through grace. And I may, I will come to Thee, for Thy People. Thou hast made me, though very unworthy, a mean instrument to do them some good, and Thee service; and many of them have set too high a value upon me, though others wish and would be glad of my death; Lord, however Thou do dispose of me, continue and go on to do good for them. Give them consistency of judgment, one heart, and mutual love; and go on to deliver them, and with the work of reformation; and make the Name of Christ glorious in the world. Teach those who look too much on Thy instruments, to depend more upon Thyself. Pardon such as desire to trample upon the dust of a poor worm, for they are Thy People too. And pardon the folly of this short Prayer: – Even for Jesus Christ's sake. And give us a good night, if it be Thy pleasure. Amen.[168]

After one of the worst storms on record[169] he died on September 3, 1658 at Whitehall, which had been for some years his home and was in some ways the symbol of his government. The date was

---

163. The cause was cancer of the womb. Ludlow, *Memoirs*, II, 41.
164. He was deeply grieved by the death of his friend the Earl of Warwick, and also of the heir to the earldom, Robert Rich, who had married his youngest daughter, Frances. Clarendon, *History*, XV, 145.
165. *Journal of George Fox*, I, 327.
166. *W.S.*, IV, 868–70.
167. Cf. *Ibid.*, 871 f. n.
168. *W.S.*, IV, 872; *L-C*, III, 217.
169. Flagellum, 195.

even more symbolic. It was the date of his greatest military triumphs at Dunbar and Worcester, but it was also the date when the ill-fated first Parliament of the Protectorate had met. As Dr. S.R. Gardiner said, the fact that Cromwell's success as a destructive force stood in the way of his success as a constructive statesman "is too obvious to need much labouring",[170] and in the memory of these previous September 3rds we are presented with the two elements which he had striven to reconcile during his life – the overwhelming success of the rebellion under his generalship, and the insistent demand of the nation for a settlement that would be not only stable but also constitutional. He had spent his life in the attempt: he had achieved the seemingly impossible, but to reconcile these incompatibles was beyond even his prodigious powers.

---

170. *Cromwell's Place in History* (1897), 104.

Chapter Twenty
Judgement

I

Like some great symbolic statue the figure of Oliver Cromwell stands at the mouth of a harbour in world history. Beyond him is a new world – a world of new discoveries in science and politics, a world where the old laws and honoured conventions are superseded, and where new freedoms and perhaps new cynicisms have taken their place. But although he stands at the gateway to modern history, and although he and the Revolution he personified are symbolic of our expanding outlook and new-born liberties, his face is towards the civilizations of the past, and he is firmly set within the great expanse of faith that will ever divide the old world from the new.

That is where this book begins and ends – with the contention that to understand a man who lived in an age of faith, we must treat seriously the faith of his age. Modern research has presented us with a wealth of facts about the seventeenth century quite unknown to Mark Noble living a bare hundred years after the Lord Protector's death; modern methods of literary criticism have made it possible to get to the actual words that were written and spoken in a way which was impossible even to the inspiration of Thomas Carlyle; modern conventions of historical objectivity enable us to break through three hundred years of prejudiced writings by Tories who hated Cromwell for killing Charles Stuart, and Whigs who hated him for destroying the monarchy; but with all these advantages we shall be immeasurably the poorer if we underestimate or ignore the religion which gave Cromwell the incentive to do the things he did, and to be the man he was. Perhaps this is the most serious criticism we have to offer against the writings of the late Professor R.H. Abbott, for although the debt we owe to him is evident from the previous chapters of this book, and although future students of the period will turn gratefully to his researches for many years to come, we would maintain that far more must go into the interpretation of historical character than the systematic collation of material facts, however comprehensively presented or accurately assessed; and in this "the spirit of the age" is an all-important piece of historical evidence which must not be ignored.[1]

Before attempting any assessment of our own, let us go on to consider – apart from whether his contemporaries were in favour or not of his personal rule – what were the characteristics of Cromwell's personality and government which impressed them. Richard Baxter wrote "Never man was highlier extolled, and never man was baselier reported and vilified than he." He himself was of the opinion that Cromwell "meant honestly in the main, and was pious and conscionable in the main course of his life, till Prosperity and Success corrupted him".[2] One thing upon which responsible observers in all camps were agreed was that Cromwell stood head and shoulders above his contemporaries, and that he seemed by his capacities created for government. As Edward Hyde, Earl of Clarendon, pointed out, there was no sign of these inherent qualities when he first appeared upon the military and political scene, "yet as he grew into place and authority, his parts seemed to be renewed, as if he had concealed faculties, till he had occasion to use them; and when he was to act the part of a great man, he did it without any indecency through want of custom."[3] He described him as "one of those men, *quos vituperare ne inimici quidem possunt, nisi aut simul laudent...* for he could never have done half that mischief without great parts of courage and industry and judgment."[4] Dr. Bates, a royalist physician who attended Cromwell on several occasions, said that the Protector was animated by a good and evil genius, the first being active in religion, and the second in his "Traitrous Designs", but he concluded, "he was not unworthy of Government".[5]

As we have seen earlier, there was a widely-held historical convention behind the systematic blackening of Cromwell's character,[6] and it is significant that in damning him his enemies

---

1. A fuller criticism of R.H. Abbott's judgment on Cromwell is given in Appendix VIII.
2. *Reliquiae Baxterianae*, I, 98.
3. *History*, XV, 148.
4. *Ibid.*, 147.
5. *Elenchus Motuum*, Pt. II, 240.
6. *Supra*, p. 104.

could not hide their respect for his qualities. Republicans like Edmund Ludlow found least to commend in him, for to them the Lord Protector was the Great Apostate who had sinned against the light, but Lucy Hutchinson, who was not behind Ludlow in detestation of the Protectorate, compared Cromwell's ambition very favourably with that of Lambert – "the one was gallant and great, the other had nothing but an unworthy pride".[7] Oliver's personal courage and magnanimity, she said, "upheld him against all enemies and malcontents".[8]

All these were among his critics and opponents, yet however much they defame his ambition from their several points of view, they do not deny – and the hint is even in Ludlow – his ability to govern well.[9] This is illustrated not only in the sincere admiration which his foreign policy won from royalists like Edward Hyde and Dr. Bates,[10] but also in their grudging recognition of the law and order that he achieved at home. They both remark upon the impartiality with which the Law was dispensed during the Protectorate in all cases where the security of the regime was not threatened,[11] and Bates says that as a result of Oliver's administration "trade began to prosper; and, in a word, gentle Peace to flourish all over England."

A further characteristic of his government, noted by friend and foe alike, was what Lucy Hutchinson calls his "magnanimity". There was a sympathy and concern for human suffering in Oliver Cromwell which appears to have shown itself to everyone but the Catholic Irish, and this trait is the more remarkable when we consider the age in which he lived, and the military and political arts in which he became adept. However, it was evident not only in personal relationship with those who had some claim upon his sympathy,[12] but also towards many of his enemies. Mrs. Hutchinson described a plot against his life by Colonel Rich and the Commissaries Watson and Staines, and says that having proved their testimony before the Council of State to be false, Oliver straightway spoke up in their defence before the Council.[13] We have seen previously that one who knew him very well described

---

7. *Memoirs of Colonel Hutchinson* (Everyman edn.), 295.
8. *Ibid.*, 296.
9. Cf. Ludlow, *Memoirs*, II, 43 f.
10. Clarendon, *History*, XV, 152–5; Bates, *Elenchus*, Pt. II. 173–5, 227–33.
11. Clarendon, *History*, XV, 151; Bates, *Elenchus*, Pt. II, 190 f.
12. Cf. Carrington, *History of the Life and Death of Oliver*, 261.
13. *Memoirs of Colonel Hutchinson*, 272–3.

him as "naturally compassionate towards objects in distresse";[14] but it was Clarendon, the Secretary of State to Charles II's exiled court, who gave the most striking testimony to the Protector's clemency:[15]

> He was not a man of blood, and totally declined Machiavel's method, which prescribes, upon any alteration of a government, as a thing absolutely necessary, to cut off all the heads of those, and extirpate their families, who are friends to the old [one]. And it was confidently reported, that in the council of officers it was more than once proposed that there might be a general massacre of all the royal party, as the only expedient to secure the government; but Cromwell would never consent to it.

The Protector's government took its temper from the Protector's character, and when we are able to get behind the jumble of eulogy and calumny, the character which is presented to us by Oliver's own contemporaries is that of a man of outstanding ability, of justice and impartiality in anything which did not jeopardize his rule, and of remarkable clemency to many of his enemies.

II

Yet to leave the description of his character without mentioning his religion would be to present the body without a soul. Oliver said of himself, "No man, no man, but a man mistaken and greatly mistaken, could think that I, that hath a burden upon my back for the space of fifteen or sixteen years – unless he would beforehand judge me an atheist – would seek such a place as I bear."[16] And that is the issue: Cromwell's religion was either central within his life, or else he was a cynical unbeliever. No judicious historian could deny that within the Lord Protector's career, often hidden to himself, material considerations, dissembled motives and lesser ends played their part; yet all through his life there is the consistent evidence of sincere personal religion and the influence of his theological and ecclesiastical concepts is too evident to be disregarded or explained away as merely the

---

14. *Supra,* p. 48; *Thurloe S.P.,* I, 766. For other descriptions of Oliver, cf. *supra,* pp. 48–50.
15. *History,* XV, 156.
16. Speech dissolving the second Protectorate Parliament, February 4, 1657/8. W.S., IV, 729.

thought-forms of his day. They were the thought-forms of his day, but there was all Heaven and Hell behind them.

In 1656 the Venetian ambassador wrote of the Protector, "It cannot be denied that by his ability and industry he has contributed to his own greatness", but he added, "with all his abounding courage, good sense and natural prudence, all these qualities would have served him for nothing if circumstances had not opened the way to greatness."[17] The Italian envoy perhaps would not have appreciated the religious significance of his own words, but it was in the amazing circumstances of his own career that Cromwell discerned and tested the validity of the divine call that he believed was his. That strict doctrine of Providence which held with John Calvin that "the righteous are the special objects of His favour, the wicked and profane the special objects of His severity"[18] was not only the stimulus of Cromwell's single-minded purpose throughout the civil wars, and the foundation of his claim to a vocation of statesmanship, but during the vicissitudes of the Protectorate it was also the one sure anchor of hope that God would be with him to the end. It is possible to criticize this interpretation of Providence, or the exclusive view of "Election" and "Grace" in Calvinism, or the literal Biblicism and extravagant apocalyptic hopes of Puritanism, but however much these ideas may be criticized, they were factors, and often governing factors, in conditioning the life and thought of seventeenth century England, and we disregard them only at the expense of misinterpreting the period.

In the same way it is possible to ridicule the idea of a troop of cavalry or Council of Army officers organized as a "gathered Church", but it was recognized by Richard Baxter after Naseby, and that keen critic admitted the honesty of Cromwell's intention when he said, "I conjecture, that at his first choosing such men into his Troop, it was the very Esteem and Love of Religious men that principally moved him."[19] Sir Ernest Barker has commented that "The habit of the Independents was always a habit of congregationalism. Even the Independent army debated, because it was a congregation as well as an army."[20] In Baxter's testimony, in the nature of the Army Council and its discussions,

---

17. Sagrado to Doge. *Cal. S.P. Vert.* (1655–56), 311.
18. Institutes of Religion, *I, v, 7.*
19. *Reliquiae Baxterianae*, I, 98.
20. *Oliver Cromwell*, 64.

and in the continuous influence of the Army's opinion on Cromwell's own decisions, we see that these words were true not only in a general sense, but also in the particular and personal sense of a man's relationship with his "Church".

It is within this kind of setting that Oliver Cromwell saw his own divinely appointed task on behalf of the people of England – or perhaps more accurately, on behalf of the "godly" people of England. He was only accidentally – or "providentially" – a soldier and a statesman, and he owned few political theories that could be regarded as inviolable.[21] It was "lawfull to passe through any formes of Government for the accomplishing his ends",[22] and he reminded the Army officers in 1647 that the Hebrews had experimented with several different kinds of government. "If you should change the government to the best of it," he commented, "it is but, as Paul says, 'dross and dung in comparison of Christ'":[23] forms of government, no less than individuals, were to be brought under the judgment of the Biblical revelation, and the proof of divine approval was to be sought in that "chain of Providence" by which nations and individuals are led.

It might be thought at first that because Cromwell's sense of vocation was based upon personal experience it therefore must have been entirely subjective – an arbitrary declaration of his own purpose that brooked no argument or interference: "Come, come, I will put an end to your prating ... call them in, call them in!"[24] A closer study, however, will show that his sense of vocation is not to be dismissed so summarily, for it was endorsed not only by the actual success of his undertakings, but it was also tested by the Word of Scripture. The importance of these factors can be seen when Cromwell's career is compared with more modern dictators, for whereas his conception of duty might lead him to act dictatorially, it could never lead him to act amorally, much less contrary to Biblical morality in so far as he understood it: Cromwell might misinterpret the Biblical standards, he might be guilty of faulty exegesis, but he could never deliberately mishandle Scripture, for he had placed himself under the judgment of its revelation. Similarly with regard to the doctrine of

---

21. He advanced only one purely political axiom – *salus populi suprema lex esto* – perhaps derived less from Cicero's philosophy than from the Christian doctrine of Man.
22. Major Huntington, quoted *supra*, p. 178 n. 2.
23. *Supra*, p. 145.
24. *Supra*, p. 269.

Providence, he could not believe that God was with him, unless he could assure himself of a clean conscience; for, according to his own beliefs, his success was entirely due to the singleness of purpose with which he and his troops had tried to obey God's will. There may be occasions when we are able to discern beneath Oliver's passionate assertions of high calling the shape of less worthy motives, but he never gives any indication in private letter or public utterance that these motives were consciously recognized by him: Cromwell acted like a prophet, and the true prophet "is one who can say with Paul, 'I was not disobedient to the heavenly vision.'"[25]

Throughout his public life we see the future Lord Protector struggling to reconcile these fundamental convictions first with the military and political needs of the nation, secondly with his own responsibility within the nation, and finally with the position of the English Protectorate within the context of world affairs. Perhaps the way in which he met the circumstances of his time on the basis of his professed beliefs tells us more about his character than any summary of his personal attributes.

III

At this stage we must point out that our study has a relevance to certain theological problems which are often regarded as belonging exclusively to the present century. The continued interest in Cromwell is perhaps due in part to the enigma of character and in part to the unique place he occupied on the threshold of this world of utilitarian science and political pragmatism. He brings theology and politics to a single focus: we think we understand the meaning of his actions only too well, but we are slightly shocked to hear him describe his motives in a language which we have long since forgotten. Perhaps, however, it is in the fact that Cromwell continued to use that language in a society which was beginning to demonstrate many features common to our own, that he continues to be a significant figure with something to say to us.

If – as I would agree – "all political problems are at bottom theological",[26] then the rude entry of the totalitarian State into western Christendom demands that Christian theologians must

---

25. John Skinner, *The Book of Ezekiel* (1895), 42.
26. N. Micklem *The Theology of Politics* (1941), Preface.

re-think the relationship between religion and politics generally, and the theological foundations of the State in particular. It is one of the strange tricks of history that at the time when so many modern questions made their first appearance those who were responsible for government in Britain and America were the spiritual sons of English Puritanism. Fresh from the exclusiveness of the "gathered" churches, and from a separation from the muddy world of affairs which was imposed as much by their beliefs as by exile and proscription, they suddenly found themselves responsible for government in important States. They discovered that they could not avoid participation in secular society and the problems it brought with it, but they had to face these problems without preconceived theories and solely upon the principles of their Biblical faith. For this reason the career of Cromwell forces us to consider seriously the place of the State in Christian theology, and challenges us to define the limitations of politics as a "Christian" vocation.

It also makes us question again our understanding of Providence in history, and the significance of the chain of special circumstances that makes us what we are, in shaping our own personal vocation under God. Baxter said that Cromwell and his men

> thought that God had called them by Successes to Govern and take care of the Commonwealth, and of the Interest of his People in the Land; and that if they stood by and suffered the Parliament to do that which they thought was dangerous, it would be required at their hands, whom they thought God had made Guardians of the Land.[27]

Stated in its crudest form this interpretation of the relationship between Providence and Vocation will be rejected, but we cannot escape the issues which the career of Oliver and his men raised. Is there any inner necessity in the events of Providence which determines the ultimate victory of "Good"? and if so, what relationship does this bear to our individual histories? When Dr. Reinhold Niebuhr says that the Christian "takes the historic struggle for justice and freedom seriously and knows that God will not negate what is good in history",[28] that was precisely

---

27. *Reliquiae Baxterianae*, I, 99.
28. "The Providence of God and the Defence of Civilisation". Supplement to the *Christian Newsletter* (May 21, 1941). In one of his books Dr. Niebuhr shows us that the doctrine of Providence as interpreted in the seventeenth century is still tacitly accepted in the modem world. He demonstrates how this doctrine,

Cromwell's contention; but he believed that to be as true for individuals as it was within the pattern of world history- - with this safeguard, that God's Providence would vindicate his personal vocation only in so far as he could meet it with a clear conscience and an absolute integrity.

In the same way Cromwell's life raises the question of Christian standards of conduct within a secular society, about which Protestantism has had singularly little to say. Dr. J.C. Bennett has shown that the answers of Protestant Christianity are extremely complex, and do not avoid the ultimate responsibility of decision by the individual Christian: "the burden upon the mind and the conscience of the individual Christian is very great for he must finally bring together all of these factors that have been outlined and make his own decision. For the Protestant there is no escape from this burden."[29] It would appear to be quite unscriptural to avoid moral decisions of this kind, but it is one thing to leave the individual Christian free to accept his rightful responsibility, and another thing to leave him so bereft of guidance that he is unable to make his decisions in a Christian and responsible manner. For this reason the wrestlings of Cromwell and his colleagues are of direct relevance to our contemporary understanding of "the Christian in Society". Their answer to the problem was what we have called the "dual ethic".

Again, in its crudest form the theology is obviously unacceptable, but the modification of the principle was just as significant as the principle itself, and in at least two ways the solution put forward by Cromwell and his contemporaries deserves careful consideration by those who are concerned with the problems of moral theology to-day. First, in the recognition of Justice as the norm of public action and the aim of civil society, they seem to have recognized a principle which only recently has been taken seriously by theologians. Secondly, from hints in the speeches of Cromwell, Ireton and others we have seen that they conceived this not as a Hebrew standard, but as Christian. The Old

---

and the development from it of the "Messianic dream", have contributed to America's sense of world mission at the present time. It is perhaps a coincidence that the two chapters "Happiness, Prosperity and Virtue" and "The Master of Destiny" come together in the book; on the other hand, it may be profoundly significant. *The Irony of American History* (New York, 1952), 43-64, 65-88.

29. *Christian Social Action* (1954), 91.

Testament ethic[30] was to be applied only "according to the mind of Christ": Justice was to be the goal of the State, but love was to be the motive of the Christian statesman, or, to see the same idea from a slightly different angle, the State was to seek Justice as its highest good, but it was to be Justice upheld by Mercy, and Law interpreted by Love.[31]

To pass from the theoretical to the practical, perhaps of all the Protector's experiments, the one which would most repay careful study is his settlement of religion. Since 1660 it has never received the attention it deserved, no doubt partly because it had had such a short time in which to justify itself – a matter of five or six years – and partly because it had been brought into being by a discredited government.

By the *Instrument of Government* and the *Humble Petition and Advice*, "the Christian religion as contained in the Scriptures" was established as the officially recognized religion of the three nations of Britain. A Profession of Faith was compiled, and all ministers who agreed with this statement, although differing in matters of worship and discipline, were to be "fit and capable ... of any trust, promotion or employment whatsoever in these nations". By this means the Protector established not a particular Church with its individual orders and theory of Church government, but the Christian Protestant religion;[32] for the first time in history the State had established an ecclesiastical system in which more than one form of churchmanship was recognized and was able to take its full part. What this could teach us within the sphere of church relationships in England, or within the Ecumenical Movement at large, only serious study can reveal; but it certainly issues a challenge. The present system of Establishment in England, which recognizes one Church in nominal control of a country that it is increasingly impotent to evangelize, is an anomaly which is tolerated only because we are afraid that its injudicious exit would open the door to a completely secular

---

30. Cf. *supra*, p. 61, n. 2.
31. In a remarkable way they seem to have foreshadowed the thought of Emil Brunner: "While justice always appears as an inferior value in the ethics of the person, in the ethics of institutions it is the supreme and ultimate standard. The highest requirement of systems, institutions, laws, is that they should be just, while it is required of man that he should meet his fellow men not in justice, but in love." *Justice and the Social Order* (1945), 25; cf. *ibid.*, 22–8.
32. The present writer has pointed this out previously in a paper which was incorporated in *The Free Churches and the State* (1953), edited by A. R. Vine, cf. pp. 45 f.

State; but the time has surely come when the needs of society demand that the conventional basis of national religion should be broadened, so that the responsibilities of pastoral care and of evangelism can be shared.

In the same way, the Cromwellian settlement of religion was a practical experiment in a federal conception of the Catholic Church which as Canon J.E. Fison has suggested may very well be the way ahead in ecumenical relationships.[33] At the heart of the system there was a Congregational – or rather, Biblical – conception of Covenant: just as the individual members were within the Covenant of Grace, so they and their churches recognized that they were in covenant relationship with each other. It was a system which depended for its smooth working upon this mutual recognition of membership in the Body of Christ, and the few years it was allowed were at least sufficient to show that where such recognition exists, the unity of the Church can be made evident by other means than immediate organic union.[34] Whether Episcopacy would ever have found its way into the system, we shall never know, but on the face of it there was no practical reason why it should not have done so, once its political associations had been forgotten, and as soon as it was ready to accept a covenant relationship with others.

IV

Cromwell became a "dictator", but it was not from choice. Events had their own way of pushing him to the fore and ultimately to the head of affairs, and the very circumstances of his rise prevented that popular recognition which would have set the seal to his mission. Nevertheless, although only a person "mistaken and greatly mistaken" would imagine that he consciously schemed for the position which he came to occupy, when the chance of taking the government presented itself he took it firmly. It is within that paradox that what he did sometimes seems to belie what he said.

Yet to suggest a fundamental hypocrisy – whether on the grounds advanced by seventeenth century royalists, or on those put forward by twentieth century realists – is to offer a solution

---

33. *The Blessing of the Holy Spirit* (1950), 169.
34. This does not mean that a system of this kind can take the place of organic union, but that it may be an important step in achieving full union.

too simple to be acceptable. It is too simple because it ignores what is perhaps the most singular fact of Cromwell's career – that throughout the vast accumulation of his uttered thought that has come down to us, never once does he admit a lesser motive in private conversation, public speech, or in his most intimate correspondence. No man could have forwarded his own self-interest to achieve a public career of such magnitude without giving some hints of his ambition in word or letter, if personal ambition were the only or even the predominant motive of the career; and yet few men in history appear to have acted more consistently and with a clearer conscience than Oliver Cromwell. The explanation of this can only be that within Cromwell's own mind his ambition was itself the instrument of a greater cause which he served with absolute sincerity.

When we have given due weight to the motives of self-interest and preservation, and when we have faced the fact that the Independents had either to rule or pay the penalty for their rebellion, there remains a paradox within Cromwell's career which has a religious cause; for although religion was not the original occasion for the outbreak of civil war, "God brought it to that issue at last," Oliver said, "and gave it unto us by way of redundancy, and at last it proved to be that which was most dear to us."[35] To Oliver himself the issue of religion had become central, and it was simply the issue of winning liberty for "all species of Protestants, to worship God according to their own light and consciences",[36] but the paradox is in the fact that this liberty could be guaranteed in no other way but by his own personal rule: Episcopalian King, Presbyterian Parliament, Sectarian Convention – they all gave ample evidence of the "strange itch" of persecution that Cromwell feared and detested. He had to rule, or else be prepared to see the religious freedom that he prized above all other earthly benefits disappear either into the prison of uniformity or into a madhouse of anarchy. It was the major tragedy of his rule that in defending one liberty he seemed to threaten all the rest, that in standing as the champion of freedom he often appeared as the epitome of tyranny.

Nevertheless we must ask ourselves whether at that time religious liberty could have been won in any other way. Amid the

---

35. Speech to Parliament, January 22, 1654/5. W.S., III, 586; L-C, II, 417 (Speech IV).
36. *Ibid.*

political dangers of our own day, if this essential freedom should again be put in jeopardy, who could say now how it could best be defended, or what forms of government would be justifiable in its defence? Perhaps a good dictatorship must always be bad government but Oliver Cromwell believed that both spiritual coercion and political anarchy were infinitely worse. It was for this reason that his deepest convictions and his own advancement became identified, and the Lord's "unprofitable servant" accepted the call to become his country's Lord Protector.

Appendices

Appendix One

The Letter to Mr. Storie, January II, 1635/6

THE letter is to be found in *W.S.*, I, 80 f, *L–C*, I, 79 f. (I) Carlyle noticed that it was in 1633 that Laud managed to get the royal assent for the suppression of a lecture at Huntingdon, and because the date of this letter to Mr. Storie is 1635/6 he rather brusquely dismisses the suggestion made by Mark Noble that the two incidents may very well refer to the same lecture. In defence of Noble, however, it should be pointed out that far from supposing that Cromwell's letter had anything to do with Laud's intervention, he merely suggests that Cromwell was probably trying to get the lecture re-started. This is supported by the fact that the two lectures seem to have had very similar characteristics, and also by Cromwell's hint to Mr. Storie that some lectures "in these times" were suppressed "with too much haste and violence by the enemies of God his truth". Cf. *L–C*, I, 81, Noble, *Protectoral-House* I. 258 f., *supra* p. 45.

Mr. Storie,
Among the catalogue of those good works which your fellow-citizens and our countrymen have done, this will not be reckoned for the least, that they have provided for the feeding of souls.[1] Building of hospitals provides for men's bodies; to build material temples is judged a work of piety; but they that procure spiritual food,[2] they that build up spiritual temples,[3] they are men truly charitable, truly pious. Such a work as this was your erecting the lecture in our country; in the which you placed Dr. Welles, a man for goodness and industry, and ability to do good every way, not short of any I know in England; and I am persuaded that, sithence his coming, the Lord hath by him wrought much good among us.

It only remains now that He who first moved you to this, put you forward to the continuance thereof: it was the Lord;[4] and therefore

---

1. Cf. John 21:15 ff.
2. Cf. 1 Corinthians 10:3.
3. Cf. 1 Peter 2:5.
4. Cf. John 21:7.

to Him lift we up our hearts[5] that He would perfect it.[6] And surely, Mr. Storie, it were a piteous thing to see a lecture fall, in the hands of so many able and godly men as I am persuaded the founders of this are, in these times, wherein we see they are suppressed, with too much haste and violence by the enemies of God his truth. Far be it that so much guilt should stick to your hands, who live in a city so renowned for the clear shining light of the gospel.[7] You know, Mr. Storie, to withdraw the pay is to let fall the lecture; for who goeth to warfare at his own cost?[8] I beseech you therefore in the bowels of Christ Jesus[9] put it forward, and let the good man have his pay. The souls of God his children will bless you for it; and so shall I; and ever rest,

Your loving Friend in the Lord,
Oliver Cromwell.

St. Ives,
January 11, 1635.

[P.S.] Commend my hearty love to Mr. Busse, Mr. Bradly, and my other good friends. I would have written to Mr. Busse; but I was loath to trouble him with a long letter, and I feared I should not receive an answer from him. From you I expect one so soon as conveniently you may. Vale.

---

5. Lamentations 3:41, or *Sursum Corda*.
6. Cf. Ephesians 4:12.
7. Cf. 2 Corinthians 4:4.
8. 1 Corinthians 9:7 (G.V.); "charges" in A.V.
9. Philippians 1:8.

Appendix Two

Biblical Analysis of Cromwell's Letter to Mrs. St. John, October 23, 1638

The text of the letter is almost entirely couched in Biblical phrases, which are so interwoven as to make the task of tracing some of them to any particular passage or version virtually impossible. For example, the phrase "I have had plentiful wages" may refer equally to the wages of eternal life (John 4:36), or to the wages of sin (Romans 6:23).

In the following analysis, where Cromwell quotes from either the Genevan or the Authorised Versions the words are italicized. In most cases, it will be seen, it is not possible to attribute his quotations specifically to one version or the other.

Cromwell	Reference	The Versions
"in this I am confident".	Ps. 27:3	"*in this will I be confident*". (A.V.)
		"I will trust in this". (G.V.)
"He giveth springs in a dry and barren wilderness where no water is."	Ps. 63:1	"*in a dry and* thirsty land, *where no water is.*" (A.V.)
		"in a *barren* and dry land without water." (G.V.)
"I live … in Meshek … in Kedar."	Ps. 120:5f	A.V. or G.V.
"Congregation of the firstborn."	Heb. 12:23	"general assembly and church of the firstborn." (A.V.)
		"*Congregation of the first-borne*" (G.V.)
"my body rests in hope."	Ps. 16:9	"my flesh also shall rest in hope." (A.V.)
		"my flesh also doth rest in hope." (G.V.)
"if I may honour my God either by doing or by suffering, I shall be most glad."	Philippians 4:11 (?)	A.V. or G.V.
"give us to walk in the light, as he is in the light."	Cf. 1 John 1:7	A.V. or G.V.
"He it is that enlighteneth our blackness, our darkness."	II Sam. 22:29	"the Lord will lighten my darkness." (A.V. or G.V.)
"I dare not say, He hideth His face from me."	Ps. 10:11	"*he hideth his face.*" (A.V.)
		"*he hideth away his face.*" (G.V.)

"Oh, I lived in and loved darkness, and hated the light."	John 3:19	"And this is the condemnation, that light is come into the world, and men loved darkness rather than light, because their deeds were evil." (A.V. or G.V.)
"I was a chief, the chief of sinners."	1 Tim. 1:15	"Christ Jesus came into the world to save sinners; of whom I am chief." (A.V. or G.V.)
"that He who hath begun a good work would perfect it to the day of Christ."	Philippians 1:6	"that he which hath begun a good work in you will perform it until the day of Jesus Christ." (A.V. or G.V.)

Appendix Three

Extract from "Vindiciae Veritatis"

This pamphlet was written as a reply to *Truth its Manifest,* (by the Scot, David Buchanan,) which was published in 1645. Cf. also Edward Bowles's *Manifest Truths, or an Inversion of Truths Manifest* (1646). The author is thought to have been Nathaniel Fiennes, Lord Say and Sele, who was the only member of the House of Lords known to have been an Independent in religion, and was written for the most part in 1647, although it was not published until 1654. The extract printed is from pp. 78f. of the pamphlet, and also appears in the *English Historical Review* No. 18 (April 1890), Vol. V. 351 f.

> In speaking soon after, of their taking *New-castle,* he confesses *their running away at Marston-moor,* when he hopes to make amends for it, by relating what valour they shewed there: in his storie of this Battle (which for his end, that is, the magnifying of his Countrey-men, it had been better for him to have skipped over) that he might extol *David Lesley* (a man whose worth needs not his lyes, and impudent shameless detractions from the worth of other men, and their known services that day, to help set forth the same, neither can a man, who knows true worth, endure it) he tels such *an infamous lye* of Cromwell (for that is the man his Presbyterian spleen, in every place where he comes near him, riseth up and bursts forth against) as I think *David Lesley* himself hath so much Honor in him, that he will give him the lye in it, and rather spit in his face than thank him for it ... his [Buchanan's] words are, *that those of the partie he spake of a little before, to indear themselves to the people* (poor fellow they needed no lyes like his to do that) *attributed to themselves the Honor of the day, and did not stick to call one of theirs,* THE SAVIOUR OF THE THREE KINGDOMS, *when God knoweth* (for he will take the name of God in vain to countenance a lye) *he, that they did there extol so much, did not at all appear in the heat of the business, but having at first a little skar, kept off till the worst was passed:* then he adds, *this had not been spoken at all, if some idle men, to gull the world, had not given the honor of the day to those, who had but little share in it.* Can there be a more palpable gross lye than this, his own Countrey-men (those who staid in the Field)

being Judges, whether we respect *Cromwell,* the man he means, or the Regiments of Horse commanded by him, which are those, he will have, to have little or no share in the honor of that day? it is well known to all that were present, and by their report to all other, who are not willing to believe lyes, rather than receive what is true, that both the General of the *Scots* Armie, and also Lord *Fairfax,* gave the day for lost, and so lost, that the one stayed not till he came to *Hull,* the other, as it is said, went further from the place where the Battle was fought, before he made a stay, and as it is reported by those that were present, at least 10,000 ran away, most of them the *Scots* Armie, if not all, but those I formerly mentioned, were run out of the Field, and the day theirs in the Enemies opinion that were on that side of the Field, as also in the opinion of ours, both Generals and Soldiers, who thereupon left the Field: when things were brought into this condition, it pleased God to use, as instruments under him, *Cromwell,* who Commanded them and the Regiments of Horse that were in my Lord of *Manchesters* Armie, to give the turn, win the day, and take the Victorie out of the enemies hands. This was the Lords doing, to whom belong the issues of War, and it was indeed a mervailous mercy; and these were the instruments he was pleased chiefly to use therein, which he, that out of envie will not acknowledge, but rather, as this man doth, belye and disgrace, is not onely false and injurious towards men, but opposeth God by disliking that choice which he thinks fit to make of Instruments, by whom he will please to work and give deliverance. Now, as for that which concerneth *Cromwell* himself, *that he did not appear at all in the heat of the business, but for a little skar kept himself off, till the worst was past;* what a man is there, *English* or *Scot,* that hath either worth or honestie in him, who was present, that will not abhor such an envious, malicious falsehood as this, fit to be fathered by none but the father of lyes himself? for it is known, that *Cromwell* charged in the Head of those Regiments of Horse in my Lord *Manchesters* Army, which Horse he Commanded, and with those Regiments brake all the Regiments of the Enemies Army, first the Horse, and after that the Foot, and that he continued with them, untill the victory was fully obtained (yea, and the Psalm of praise for it sung to God, to whom alone the Glory was due) commanding all while they charged, and taking special care to see it observed, that the Regiments of Horse, when they had broken a Regiment of the Enemies, should not divide. ...

Appendix Four

Letter to Robert Hammond, November 6, 1648

This letter is to be found in W.S., I, 676–8, L–C, III, 389–92 (Supp. 35), C.P, II, 49–53. C.H. Firth and S.R. Gardiner were the first to identify it as written by Cromwell. For their reasons and for the identification of the pseudonymous names cf. C.P. II loc. cit., G.C.W., IV, 248 and notes, L–C, III, 388 f., W.S., 1, 676.

Knottingley, November 6, 1648.

Dear Robin,
    I trust the same spirit that guided thee heretofore is still with thee; look to thy heart, thou art where temptations multiply. I fear lest our friends should burn their fingers, as some others did not long since, whose hearts have ached since for it.[1]

How easy is it to find arguments for what we would have; how easy to take offence at things called Levellers, and run into an extremity on the other hand, meddling with an accursed thing. Peace is only good when we receive it out of our Father's hand, it's dangerous to snatch it, most dangerous to go against the will of God to attain it. War is good when led to by our Father, most evil when it comes from the lusts that are in our members. We wait upon the Lord, who will teach us and lead us whether to doing or suffering.

Tell my brother Herne[2] I smiled at his expression concerning my wise friend's opinion,[3] who thinks that enthroning the King with presbytery brings spiritual slavery, but with a moderate episcopacy works a good peace. Both are a hard choice. I trust there's no necessity of either, except our base unbelief and fleshly wisdom make it so; but if I have any logic it will be easier to tyrannise having that he likes and serves his turn, than what you know and all believe he so much dislikes.

But as to my brother himself, tell him indeed I think some of my friends have advanced too far, and need make an honourable retreat, Scots treaties having wrought some perplexities;[4] and hindering matters from going so glib as otherwise was hoped, especially taking

---

1. This may be a reference to either his own or the Scots' dealings with Charles.
2. Sir Henry Vane.
3. Pierrepont? Cf. *G.C.W.*, IV, 248 n.
4. In view of the treaty with Argyle, the Independents ought to reconsider their favourable attitude to moderate episcopacy.

in some doubts that Sir Roger[5] and brother Fountayne are also turned Presbyterians. Dear Robin, tell brother Herne that we have the witnesses of our consciences that we have walked in this thing (whatsoever surmises are to the contrary) in plainness and godly simplicity, according to our weak measure, and we trust our daily business is to approve our consciences to Godward, and not to shift and shark,[6] which were exceeding baseness in us to do, having had such favour from the Lord, and such manifestations of His presence, and I hope the same experience will keep their hearts and hands from him, against whom God hath so witnessed, though reason should suggest things never so plausible.

I pray thee tell my brother Herne this much from me; and if a mistake concerning our compliance with presbytery perplex an evil business (for so I account it), and make the wheels of such a chariot go heavy, I can be passive and let it go, knowing that innocency and integrity loses nothing by a patient waiting upon the Lord. Our papers are public; let us be judged by them. Answers do not involve us. I profess to thee I desire from my heart, I have prayed for it, I have waited for the day to see union and right understanding between the godly people (Scots, English, Jews, Gentiles, Presbyterians, Independents, Anabaptists, and all). Our brothers of Scotland (really Presbyterians) were our greatest enemies. God hath justified us in their sight, caused us to requite good for evil, caused them to acknowledge it publicly by acts of state, and privately, and the thing is true in the sight of the sun. It is an high conviction upon them. Was it not fit to be civil, to profess love, to deal with clearness with them for removing of prejudice, to ask them what they had against us, and to give them an honest answer? This we have done, and not more. And herein is a more glorious work in our eyes than if we had gotten the sacking and plunder of Edinburgh, the strong castles into our hands, and made conquest from Tweed to the Orcades; and we can say, through God we have left by the grace of God such a witness amongst them, as if it work not yet there is that conviction upon them that will undoubtedly bear its fruit in due time.

Tell my brother Herne, I believe my wise friends would have had a conquest, or if not, things put in a balance; the first was not very unfeasible, but I think not Christian, and I was commanded the contrary by the two Houses; as for the latter, by the providence of God it is perfectly come to pass, not by our wisdom, for I durst not design it, I durst not admit of so mixed, so low a consideration; we

---

5. Lambert or Hazelrigge. Abbott suggests the formeR.W.S., I, 676. "Brother Fountayne" was Cromwell himself.
6. Firth and Mrs. Lomas suggest "shirk" as the reading here. Cf. *L-C,* III, 390 n.; *C.P.,* II, 51 n.

were led out (to the praise of our God be it spoken) to more sincere, more spiritual considerations; but I said before the Lord hath brought it to a balance; if there be any dangerous disproportion it is that the honest party (if I may without offence so call them) in my apprehension are the weaker, and have manifold difficulties to conflict withal. I wish our unworthiness here cast not the scale both there and here the wrong way. I have but one word more to say. Thy friends, dear Robin, are in heart and in profession what they were, have not dissembled their principles at all. Are they not a little justified in this, that a lesser party of the Parliament hath made it lawful to declare the greater part a faction, and made the Parliament null, and call a new one, and to do this by force, and this by the same mouths that condemned it in others.

Think of the example and of the consequence, and let others think of it too, if they be not drenched too deep in their one [own] reason and opinions. Robin, be honest still. God keep thee in the midst of snares. Thou hast naturally a valiant spirit. Listen to God, and He shall increase it upon thee, and make thee valiant for the truth. I am a poor creature that write to thee, the poorest in the work, but I have hope in God, and desire from my heart to love His people, and if thou hast opportunity and a free heart, let me hear from thee how it is with thee. This bearer is faithful, you may be very free to communicate with him; my service to all my friends, and to my dear brother Herne whom I love in the Lord, I rest,

Thy true and faithful friend.
Heron[s] Brother.

Appendix Five

Letter to Robert Hammond, November 25, 1648 (W.S., I, 696–9, L–C, I, 393–400, LXXXV)

Dear Robin,

No man rejoiceth more to see a line from thee than myself. I know thou hast long been under trial. Thou shalt be no loser by it. All must work for the best.[1]

Thou desirest to hear of my experiences. I can tell thee: I am such a one as thou didst formerly know, having a body of sin and death,[2] but I thank God, through Jesus Christ our Lord there is no condemnation, though much infirmity, and I wait for the redemption.[3] And in this poor condition I obtain mercy,[4] and sweet consolation through the Spirit, and find abundant cause every day to exalt the Lord, and abase flesh, and herein I have some exercise.

As to outward dispensations, if we may so call them, we have not been without our share of beholding some remarkable providences, and appearances of the Lord. His presence hath been amongst us, and by the light of His countenance we have prevailed.[5] We are sure the good-will of Him who dwelt in the bush has shined upon us,[6] and we can humbly say, We know in whom we have believed,[7] who is able and will perfect what remaineth,[8] and us also in doing what is well-pleasing in His eyesight.[9]

I find some trouble in your spirit; occasioned first, not only by the continuance of your sad and heavy burden, as you call it, upon you, but by the dissatisfaction you take at the ways of some good men whom you love with your heart, who through this principle, That it is lawful for a lesser part, if in the right, to force [a numerical majority] &c.

To the first: call not your burden sad or heavy. If your Father

---

1. Cf. Romans 8:28.
2. Romans 6:6.
3. Romans 8 is obviously in his mind, cf. vv:21–5.
4. 1 Timothy 1:13.
5. Psalm 44:3.
6. Cf. Exodus 3:1–6. Deut. 33:16.
7. 2 Timothy 1:12.
8. He conflates the "He is able" of 2 Timothy 1:12 with the idea of perfection in Hebrews 13:20 f.
9. Hebrews 13:21.

laid it upon you, He intended neither. He is the Father of lights, from whom comes every good and perfect gift, who of His own will begot us,[10] and bade us count it all joy when such things befall *us;* they being for the exercise of faith and patience, whereby in the end we shall be made perfect (James i).[11]

Dear Robin, our fleshly reasonings ensnare us.[12] These make us say, heavy, sad, pleasant, easy. Was there not a little of this when Robert Hammond, through dissatisfaction too, desired retirement from the Army, and thought of quiet in the Isle of Wight? Did not God find him out there?[13] I believe he will never forget this. And now I perceive he is to seek again; partly through his sad and heavy burden, and partly through his dissatisfaction with friends' actings.

Dear Robin, thou and I were never worthy to be door-keepers in this service.[14] If thou wilt seek, seek to know the mind of God in all that chain of Providence, whereby God brought thee thither, and that person to thee;[15] how before and since, God has ordered him, and affairs concerning him: and then tell me, whether there be not some glorious and high meaning in all this, above what thou hast yet attained? And laying aside thy fleshly reason, seek of the Lord to teach thee what that is; and He will do it. I dare be positive to say, it is not that the wicked should be exalted, that God should so appear as indeed He hath done. For there is no peace to them.[16] No, it is set upon the hearts of such as fear the Lord, and we have witness upon witness, That it shall go ill with them and their partakers. I say again, seek that spirit to teach thee;[17] which is the spirit of knowledge and understanding, the spirit of counsel and might, of wisdom and of the fear of the Lord.[18] That spirit will close thine eyes and stop thine ears, so that thou shalt not judge by them, but thou shalt judge for the meek of the earth,[19] and thou shalt be made able to do accordingly. The Lord direct thee to that which is well-pleasing in His eyesight.[20]

As to thy dissatisfaction with friends' actings upon that supposed principle, I wonder not at that. If a man take not his own burden well, he shall hardly others', especially if involved by so near a relation of love and Christian brotherhood as thou art. I shall not

---

10. James 1:17 f.
11. Free paraphrase of James 1:2–6.
12. 2 Corinthians 1:12.
13. Cf. Psalm 139:7–13.
14. Psalm 84:10.
15. The King.
16. Isaiah 57:21; cf. 48:22.
17. Cf. John 14:26.
18. Isaiah 11:2.
19. Isaiah 11:4; cf. Psalm 25:9; 37:11; Matthew 5:5.
20. Cl. Hebrews 13:21.

take upon me to satisfy, but I hold myself bound to lay my thoughts before so dear a friend. The Lord do His own will.

You say: God hath appointed authorities among the nations, to which active or passive obedience is to be yielded. This resides in England in the Parliament. Therefore active or passive, &c.

Authorities and powers are the ordinance of God. This or that species is of human institution, and limited, some with larger, others stricter bands, each one according to its constitution. I do not think the authorities may do anything, and yet such obedience [be] due, but all agree there are cases in which it is lawful to resist. If so. Your ground fails, and so likewise the inference. Indede, dear Robin, not to multiply words, the query is, Whether ours be such a case? This ingenuously is the true question.

To this I shall say nothing, though I could say very much; but only desire thee to see what thou findest in they own heart as to two or three plain considerations. First wither Salus Populi be a sound position? Secondly, whether in the way in hand, really and before the Lord, before whom conscience must stand, this be provided for, or the whole fruit of the war like to be frustrated, and all most like to turn to what it was, and worse?[21] And this, contrary to engagements, declarations, implicit covenants with those who ventured their lives upon those covenants and engagements, without whom perhaps, in equity, relaxation ought not to be? Thirdly, Whether this Army be not a lawful power, called by God to oppose and fight against the King upon some stated grounds; and being in power to such ends, may not oppose one name of authority, for those ends, as well as another, the outward authority that called them,[22] not by their power making the quarrel lawful, but it being so in itself? If so it may be acting will be justified in foro humano – But truly these kinds of reasoning may be but fleshly, either with or against: only it is good to try what truth may be in them. And the Lord teach us.

My dear friend, let us look into providences; surely they mean somewhat. They hang together; have been so constant, so clear and unclouded. Malice, swoln malice against God's people, now called Saints, to root out their name; and yet they, by providence, having arms, and therein blessed with defence and more. I desire, he that is for a principle of suffering would not too much slight this. I slight not him who is so minded: but let us beware lest fleshly reasoning see more safety in making use of this principle than in acting. Who acts, and resolves not through God to be willing to part

---

21. Worse, because the royalists would never forgive what had been done.
22. The inference being that although the Parliament was the outward authority that had called the Army to its task, there was a stronger inward authority which they must obey, because it was given them by God Himself.

with all? Our hearts are very deceitful, on the right and on the left.[23]

What think you of Providence disposing the hearts of so many of God's people this way, especially this poor Army, wherein the great God has vouchsafed to appear. I know not one officer among us but is on the increasing hand. And let me say it is here in the North, after much patience, we trust the same Lord who hath framed our minds in our actings, is with us in this also. And this contrary to a natural tendency, and to those comforts our hearts could wish to enjoy with others. And the difficultuies probably to be encountered with, and the enemies, not a few, even all that is glorious in this world, with appearance of united names, titles and authorities, and yet not terrified, only desiring to fear our great God, that we do nothing against His will. Truly this is our condition.

And to conlcude. We in this northern Army were in a waiting posture, desiring to see what the Lord would lead us to. And a Declaration is put out, at which many are shaken:[24] although we could perhaps have wished the stay of it till after the treaty, yet seeing it is come out, we trust to rejoice in the will of the Lord, waiting His further pleasure. Dear Robin, beware of men, look up to the Lord. Let Him be free to speak and commance in thy heart. Take heed of the things I fear thou hast reasoned thyself into, and thou shalt be able though Him, without consulting flesh and blood, to do valiantly for Him and for His people.

Thou mentionest somewhat as if, by acting against such opposition as is like to be, there will be a tempting of God. Dear Robin, tempting of God ordinarily is either by acting presumptuously in carnel confidence, or in unbelief through diffidence: both these ways Israel tempted God in the wilderness, and He was grieved by them. The encountering difficulties, therefore, makes us not to tempt God; but acting before and without faith. If the Lord have in any measure persuaded His people, as generally He hath, of the lawfulness, nay of the duty, this persuasion prevailing upon the heart is faith, and acting thereupon is acting in faith, and the more the difficulties are, the more faith. And it is most sweet that he that is not persuaded have patience towards them that are, and judge not: and this will free thee from the trouble of others' actings, which, thou sayest, adds to thy grief. Only let me offer two or three thigns and I have done.

Dost thou not think this fear of the Levellers (of whom there is no fear) that they would destroy the nobility, had cased some to rake up corruption; to find it lawful to make this ruining hypocritical agreement, on one part. Hath not this biased even some good men? I will

---

23. Jeremiah 17:9.
24. Remonstrance of the Army presented by Ewer. Not by Carlyle. *L-C*, I, 397.

not say their fear will come upon them; but if it do, they will themselves bring it upon themselves. Have not some of our friends, by their passive principle (which I judge not, only I think it liable to temptation as well as the active, and neither good but as we are led into them by God, – either to be reasoned into because the heart is deceitful), been occasioned to overlook what is just and honest, and [to] think the people of God may have as much or more good the one way than the other? Good by this man, against whom the Lord hath witnessed; and whom thou knowest. Is this so in their hearts or is it reasoned, forced in?[25]

Robin, I have done. Ask we our hearts, whether we think that, after all, these dispensations, the like to which many generations cannot afford, should end in so corrupt reasonings of good men, and should so hit the designings of bad? Thinkest thou, in thy heart, that the glorious dispensations of God point out to this? Or to teach his people to trust in Him, and to wait for better things, when, it may be, better are sealed to many of their spirits? And as a poor looker- on, I had rather live in the hope of that spirit, and take my share with them, expecting a good issue, than be led away with the other.

This trouble I have been at, because my soul loves thee, and I would not have thee swerve, nor lose any glorious opportunity the Lord puts into thy hand. The Lord be thy counsellor. Dear Robin, I rest thine,
November 25, 1648.

Oliver Cromwell.

---

25. Or as Dr. Gardiner punctuated it – "Good, by this man, against whom the Lord hath witnessed, and whom thou knowest! Is this so in their hearts, or is it reasoned, forced in?" *G.C.W.*, IV, 253.

Appendix Six

The "Saddle Letter" Account
from "State Letters of Roger Boyle ... the Life of the Earl of Orrery" (1742) by Thomas Morrice; pages 14–16

After all this was done Cromwell made Youghall the head quarters; from whence they marched out several times to several places; and on one time particularly, when Lord Broghill was riding, with Cromwell one side of him, and Ireton on the other, at the head of their army, they fell into discourse about the late king's death. Cromwell declared, that if the king had followed his own mind, and had had trusty servants about him, he had fooled them all. And further said, that once they had a mind to have closed with him; but upon something that happened, they fell off from that design again. My Lord, finding Cromwell and Ireton in a good humour, and no other person being within hearing, asked them if he might be so bold, as to desire an account, 1st, Why they once would have closed with the king? and 2dly, Why they did not? Cromwell very freely told him, he would satisfy him in both his queries.

The reason, says he, why we would once have closed with the king, was this: We found the Scots and the presbyterians began to be more powerful than we; and if they made up matters with the king, we should have been left in the lurch: therefore we thought it best to prevent them, by offering first to come in, upon any reasonable conditions. But while we were busied in these thoughts, there came a letter from one of our spies, who was of the king's bedchamber, which acquainted us, that on that day our final doom was decreed; that he could not possibly tell what it was, but we might find out, if we could intercept a letter, sent from the king to the queen, wherein he declared what he would do. The letter, he said, was sewed up in the skirt of a saddle, and the bearer of it would come with the saddle upon his head, about ten of the clock that night, to the Blue-Boar inn in Holborn; for there he was to take horse and go to Dover with it. This messenger knew nothing of the letter in the saddle, but some persons in Dover did. We were at Windsor, when we received this letter; and immediately upon receipt of it, Ireton and I resolved to take one trusty fellow with us, and with troopers habits to go to the inn in Holborn; which accordingly we did, and set our man at the gate of the inn, where the wicket only was open, to let people in and out. Our man was to give us notice, when any person came there with a saddle, whilst we, in disguise of common troopers, called for canns of beer, and continued drinking till about ten o'clock: the centinel at the gate then gave notice that the man with the saddle was come in. Upon this, we immediately arose, and, as the man was leading out his horse saddled, came up to him, with drawn swords, and told him, we were to search all that went in and out there; but, as he looked like an honest man, we would only search his saddle, and so dismiss him. Upon that, we ungirt his saddle, and carried it into the stall, where we had been drinking, and left the horseman with our centinel: then ripping up one of the skirts of the saddle, we there found the letter, of which we had been informed; and having got it into our own hands, we delivered the saddle again to the man, telling him, he was an honest man, and bidding him go about his business. The man, not knowing what had been done, went away to Dover. As soon as we had the letter, we opened it, in which we found the king had acquainted the queen that he was now courted by both factions, the Scotch presbyterians, and the army; and which bid fairest for him, should have him; but he thought he should close with the Scots, sooner than the other, &. Upon this (added Cromwell) we took horse, and went to Windsor; and finding we were not likely to have any tolerable terms from the king, we immediately, from that time forward, resolved his ruin.

Appendix Seven

Selected Letters

A. Letter to Mr. Henry Downhall, of St. John's College, Cambridge, October 14, 1626. (W.S., I, 50 f., L-C, III, 221, Appendix 1.)

Loving Sir,
    Make me so much your servant by being Godfather unto my child. I would myself have come over to have made a more formal invitation, but my occasions would not permit me; and therefore hold me in that excused. The day of your trouble is Thursday next. Let me entreat your company on Wednesday.

    By this time it appears, I am more apt to encroach upon you for new favours than to show my thankfulness for the love I have already found. But I know your patience and your goodness cannot be exhausted by,

Your friend and servant,
Oliver Cromwell.

B. Letter to Col. Valentine Walton, July 5, 1644. (W.S., I, 287 f., L-C, I, 176, XXI.)

Dear Sir,
    It's our duty to sympathise in all mercies; that we may praise the Lord together in chastisements or trials, that so we may sorrow together.

    Truly England and the Church of God hath had a great favour from the Lord, in this great victory given unto us, such as the like never was since this war began. It had all the evidences of an absolute victory obtained by the Lord's blessing upon the godly party principally. We never charged but we routed the enemy. The left wing, which I commanded, being our own horse, saving a few Scots in our rear, beat all the Prince's horse. God made them as stubble to our swords,[1] we charged their regiments of foot with our horse, routed all we charged. The particulars I cannot relate now, but I believe, of twenty-thousand the Prince hath not four-thousand left. Give glory, all the glory, to God.

---

1. Cf. Psalm 83:13.

Sir, God hath taken away your eldest son by a cannon-shot. It brake his leg. We were necessitated to have it cut off, whereof he died.

Sir, you know my trials this way; but the Lord supported me with this, that the Lord took him into the happiness we all pant after[2] and live for. There is your precious child full of glory, to know sin nor sorrow any more. He was a gallant young man, exceeding gracious. God give you His comfort. Before his death he was so full of comfort that to Frank Russel and myself he could not express it, it was so great above his pain. This he said to us. Indeed it was admirable. A little after he said one thing lay upon his spirit. I asked him, what that was. He told me that it was, that God had not suffered him to be no more the executioner of His enemies. At his fall, his horse being killed with the bullet, and as I am informed three horses more, I am told he bid them open to the right and left, that he might see the rogues run. Truly he was exceedingly beloved in the Army, of all that knew him. But few knew him, for he was a precious young man, fit for God. You have cause to bless the Lord. He is a glorious saint in Heaven, wherein you ought exceedingly to rejoice. Let this drink up your sorrow; seeing these are not feigned words to comfort you, but the thing is so real and undoubted a truth. You may do all things by the strength of Christ.[3] Seek that, and you shall easily bear your trial. Let this public mercy to the Church of God make you to forget your private sorrow. The Lord be your strength: so prays

Your truly faithful and loving brother,
Oliver Cromwell.

My love to your daughter, and to my Cousin Percevall, Sister Desbrowe and all friends with you.

---

2. Cf. Psalm 42:1.
3. Philippians 4:13.

Appendix Eight
Professor W.C. Abbott and Oliver Cromwell

In *The Writings and Speeches of Oliver Cromwell* the late W.C. Abbott of Harvard has gathered together an invaluable corpus of material relating to the Lord Protector which is as complete and exhaustive as modern scholarship and American thoroughness can make it, and he has thereby put every succeeding biographer of Cromwell immeasurably in his debt.

However, the interpretation of human character involves not only the enumeration of material facts, but also qualities of spirit and emotion – less tangible influences within our environment, but none the less important in our final estimate of character. In this respect, and in one important particular, W.C. Abbott did less than justice to the man about whom he wrote, for he underestimated the fact that religion – sincere religion – was an indispensable feature of the seventeenth-century scene in England, and that in view of the almost universal change in attitude to the conception of Heaven and Hell we cannot interpret the religion of Cromwell and his contemporaries by twentieth century motives. W.C. Abbott did not avoid this fault, and it immediately stamps his own assessment of Oliver as a product of the present century, just as surely as the Protector's letters and speeches show him to have been a child of his own century.

The omission also led Abbott into too close an identification of the Lord Protector with the twentieth century dictators – an identification which becomes increasingly and embarrassingly marked through his work: the publication of his volumes through the years 1937–47 seems to keep pace with America's own increasing preoccupation with the war against dictatorship, until at last the author is led to declare that "the events of the past twenty years were required to find an appropriate descriptive phrase to fit the position which Cromwell held. ... It is no mere accident that comparisons have been made between Cromwell, Hitler and Mussolini."[1]

---

1. *W.S.*, IV, 898.

The comparison is, of course, no accident since there are obvious parallels to be drawn between all revolutionary periods in history and their sequels, but, as Sir Ernest Barker has shown, the differences between the Puritan Rebellion in England and the National Socialist Revolution in Germany are more significant than their similarities, because "the core of Cromwell's doctrine of the nature of the people is a religious core".[2] If, as Dr. W. Schenk has shown, religion was the main source of social and political incentive in the seventeenth century, and if this fact separates the Levellers and the Diggers from the Socialists and Communists who have appeared since 1789,[3] then the same fact separates Cromwell from all forms of twentieth century Fascism. He undoubtedly spoke to the nation in the name of the Lord, and believed that God had called him to do so, but he did not fail to bring himself under the moral judgments of the Word of God which he sought to proclaim. For this reason, if for no other, too close an identification of the Lord Protector with modern forms of dictatorship is likely to be a hindrance rather than a help in our understanding of him.[4]

This unfortunate reading of contemporary history into the seventeenth century has led to a good deal of unconscious distortion. For example, W.C. Abbott says that the narrowness of the voting and the bitterness of the debates on the *Instrument of Government* "revealed how nearly England came to the absolute dictatorship at which, apparently, some if not all the Cromwellians aimed".[5] This sounds convincing until it is realized that the limits of the Protector's power – considerably less than that of the Crown – had already been laid down in the *Instrument of Government*. It is true that the "court party" were trying to get nearer the ancient constitution and to interpret the Protector's powers in terms of the royal prerogative, and that the republicans opposed it, but it must be remembered that there were limits beyond which Cromwell's supporters in Parliament could not go, and those limits had been defined in a written constitution for which they had been responsible.

---

2. *Oliver Cromwell*, 81; cf. 88 f.
3. *The Concern for Social Justice in the Puritan Revolution* (1848), 161–7.
4. This reflects a good deal of the late Dr. Albert Peel's criticism in his review of *The Writings and Speeches;* cf. *The Congregational Quarterly* (July 1948), 234–7. An independent study of R.H. Abbott's book has confirmed these criticisms.
5. *W.S.*, III, 527.

A further example of the same kind of distortion is seen in the passage where Abbott suggests that apart from the dreams of Fifth Monarchy, "the only real alternatives to the old system of parliamentary monarchy were offered by the Levellers and the Republicans."[6] It would be fatally easy to read into this sentence a conception of Tudor and Stuart administration very far from the truth, for what was the "old system of parliamentary monarchy" of which Professor Abbott is speaking? The form of monarchy that England enjoyed prior to the Great Rebellion must never be confused with the form of constitutional monarchy that Britain enjoys to-day: parliamentary monarchy had yet to be born, and began to show itself about one hundred years after the death of Cromwell. The Tudors and Stuarts regarded themselves as no more bound by their Parliaments than Louis XIV considered himself tied to the decisions of the *Parlement* of Paris – if they had, the Civil Wars would never have been fought.

Professor Abbott ought to have seen, however, that the real foundations of a constitutional monarchy in our modern sense were to be found in the *Instrument of Government* and the *Humble Petition and Advice*. Conjectures of what might have happened if Oliver had accepted the crown in 1657 may very well be relegated to Carlyle's "Rushworthian Elysium", but it should at least be noted that if the Lord Protector had accepted the throne he would have done so with powers limited, defined, and granted by Parliament in a sense unknown to any of those monarchs who had ascended the throne by "divine right".

His acceptance of the throne might thus have solved the great dilemma of his rule – to reconcile military power with constitutional authority, but that must remain one of the great guesses of history. The salient fact is that there was in the Protectorate no such clear-cut issue between arbitrary power and constitutional monarchy as W.C. Abbott suggests: whatever else Cromwell was, he was not a dictator in our modern understanding of that word.

---

6. *Ibid.*, IV, 374.

Select Bibliography

Abbott, W.C., A Bibliography of Oliver Cromwell, Harvard U.P., U.S.A., 1929
The Writings and Speeches of Oliver Cromwell (4 vols.), Harvard U.P., U.S.A., 1937-47
Ainsworth, Henry, Annotations on the Booke of the Psalmes, 1627
Apologeticall Narration humbly submitted to the Honourable Houses of Parliament, 1646
Ashe, Simeon, A true Relation of the most Chiefe Occurrences at, and since the late Battell at Newbery, 1644
Ashley, Maurice, Oliver Cromwell: The Conservative Dictator, 1937 Cromwell's Generals, 1954
Aspinwal, William, Description of the Fifth Monarchy, 1653
Aubrey, John, Miscellanies (5th edn. Library of Old Authors), 1890

Baillie, Robert, The Letters and Journals of Robert Baillie, A.M. (ed. David Laing, 3 vols.), Edinburgh, 1841
Bampfield, Joseph, Apologie, 1684
Banks, John, A short critical review of the political life of Oliver Cromwell (by "a Gentleman of the Middle Temple"), 1739
Barker, Sir Ernest, Oliver Cromwell (Cambridge Miscellany XVIII), Cambridge, 1937
Barth, Karl, Church and State (translation by G.R. Howe of "Rechtfertigung und Recht"), 1939
Bates, Dr. George, Elenchus Motuum Nuperorum in Anglia: Or, a short Historical Account of The Rise and Progress of the Late Troubles in England ... Made English, 1685
Baxter, Richard, Reformed Pastor, 1655 Reliquiae Baxterianae (ed. Matthew Sylvester), 1696
Beard, Dr. Thomas, The Theatre of Gods Judgements, 1597
Belloc, Hilaire, Cromwell, 1934
Bennett, J.C., Christian Social Action, 1954
Berkeley, Sir John, Memoirs, 1699
berry, Sir James and Lee, S.G., A Cromwellian Major General, 1938
Blencowe, R.W. (ed), Sydney Papers, 1825
Bowles, Edward, Manifest Truths, or an Inversion of Truths Manifest, 1646

de Bracton, Henrici, De Legibus et Consuetudinibus Angliae (ed. Sir Travers Twiss, 6 vols.), 1878–83

Browne, Robert, Booke which Sheweth the life and manners of all true Christians (Middleburg), 1582

Treatise of Reformation without tarrying for anie (Middleburg), 1582

Bruce, John and Masson, David (ed.), The Quarrel between the Earl of Manchester and Oliver Cromwell (Camden Society), 1875

Brunner, Emil, Justice and the Social Order (translated by Mary Hottinger), 1945

Buchan, John, Oliver Cromwell, 1934

Bulstrode, Sir Richard, Memoirs and reflections upon the reign and government of King Charles I and Charles II, 1721

Burnet, Bishop, History of My Own Time (ed. O. Airy, 2 vols.), 1897–1900

Memoires of ... James & William, dukes of Hamilton, 1677

Burroughes, Jeremiah, Irenicum, to the Lovers of Truth and Peace, 1646

A Vindication of Mr. Burroughes Against Mr. Edwards his foule Aspersions in his spreading Gangraena, and his angry Antiapologia, etc., 1644

Sermon preached before the House of Commons, 1646

Burton, Thomas, Diary of Thomas Burton (ed. J.T. Rutt, 4 vols.) 1828

Calamy (sen.), Edmund, The Souldiers Pocket Bible, 1643

Calamy, Edmund, Historical Account of my own Life (2 vols.), 1829

Calendar of State Papers Domestic

Calendar of State Papers Venetian

Calvin, John, Institutes of the Christian Religion (translated by Henry Beveridge, 2 vols., Edinburgh), 1863

Carlyle, Thomas, Letters and Speeches of Oliver Cromwell (ed. Mrs. S.C. Lomas, 3 vols. New York and London), 1904

Carrington, Samuel, The History of the Life and Death of His most Serene Highness, Oliver, Late Lord Protector, 1659

Carte, Thomas, An History of the life of James, duke of Ormonde (3 vols.), 1735–86

Collection of Original Letters found among the Duke of Ormonde's papers (2 vols.), 1739

Cary, Henry, Memorials of the great Civil War in England, 1646–52 (2 vols.), 1842

Caulfield, James, Cromwelliana (ed.), 1810

Clarendon State Papers, 1767–86

Clarendon, Earl of, History of the Rebellion and Civil Wars in England (ed. Bishop Warburton, 7 vols., Oxford), 1849

The Life of Edward Earl of Clarendon (Oxford), 1857

Dale, R.W., History of English Congregationalism, 1907

d'Ewes, Sir S., The Autobiography and Correspondence of Sir Simonds D'Ewes,

Bart., during the reigns of James I and Charles I (ed. J.O. Halliwell, 2 vols.), 1845

The Journal of Sir Simonds D'Ewes (ed. Wallace Notestein, New Haven, U.S.A.), 1923

Dexter, H.M., The Congregationalism of the last three hundred years as seen in its literature (U.S.A.), 1879

Dugdale, Sir William, A Short View of the Late Troubles in England (Oxford), 1681

Edwards, G.M., Sidney Sussex College, 1899

Ellis, Sir Henry, Original Letters illustrative of English History (2nd series, 4 vols.), 1827 English Historical Review

Evelyn, John, Diary of John Evelyn (ed. William Bracy and H.B. Wheatley, 4 vols.), 1906

Fairfax, Brian (ed.), Short Memorials of Thomas Lord Fairfax, 1699

[Fiennes, N., *see* Vindiciae Veritatis]

[Finch, Heneage-] The Exact and Impartial Account of the Arraignment, Trial and Judgment of the nine and twenty regicides, 1660

Firth, C.H. (ed.), Clarke Papers, 1891–1901

Firth, C.H., Cromwell's Army, 1902
  Oliver Cromwell, 1903
  The Last Years of the Protectorate, 1656–1658 (2 vols.), 1909

Firth, C.H. and Tait, R.S. (ed.), Acts and Ordinances of the Interregnum (3 vols.), 1911

Flecknoe, Richard, The Idea of His Highness Oliver, late Lord Protector ... with certain Reflexions on His Life, 1659

Fleming, (ed.), Diary of Sir Archibald Johnston of Wariston (Edinburgh), 1919

[Fletcher, Henry], The Perfect Politician: Or a Full View of the Life and Actions (Military and Civil) of O. Cromwell, 1660

Fox, George, The Journal of George Fox (ed. by Norman Penny, MS. ed., 2 vols., Cambridge), 1911

Fuller, Thomas, Worthies of England, 1602

Gardiner, S.R. (ed.), Camden Miscellany, 1852.

Gardiner, S.R., History of the Great Civil War 1642–49 (4 volume edition), 1893
  Cromwell's Place in History, 1897
  History of the Commonwealth and Protectorate 1649–60 (4 volume edition), 1903
  Constitutional Documents of the Puritan Revolution 1625–60 (Oxford), 1906
  Oliver Cromwell (New Impression), 1925

Gilbert, J.T., Contemporary History of Ireland (3 vols.), 1879–80

Goodwin, Thomas, The Government of the Churches of Christ (Works, 12 vols.), 1865
Guizot, F., The History of Oliver Cromwell and the English Commonwealth (trans. by A. Scoble, 2nd ed., 2 vols.), 1854
Harleian Miscellany, 1746

Harrison, Frederick, Oliver Cromwell, 1888
Heath, James, Flagellum: Or the Life and Death, Birth and Burial of Oliver Cromwell The Late Usurper, 1663
    A Chronicle of the Late Intestine War, 1663
Herbert, Thomas, Threnodia Carolina, 1839
Holles, Lord Denzil, Memoirs, 1699
Huntington, Robert, Sundry reasons inducing Major Huntington to lay down his Commission, 1648
Hutchinson, Lucy, Memoirs of the Life of Colonel Hutchinson (Everyman edition), 1913
Huxley, Aldous, Grey Eminence, 1941
    Journals of the House of Commons, 1742
    Journals of the House of Lords, 1742

Kiffin, William, Walwyn's Wiles, 1649
Kimber, Isaac, The Life of Oliver Cromwell, Lord Protector of the Commonwealth of England, impartially collected (published anon.), 1724
Kirk, K.E. (ed.), The Study of Theology, 1939
Knappen, M.M. (ed.), Two Elizabethan Puritan Diaries (Chicago), 1933

Lilburne, John, Jonah's Cry out of the Whales belley, 1647
    An Additional Plea, 1647
    Two Letters, 1647
    The legal Fundamental Liberties of the People of England, 1647
    The Picture of the Council of State, 1649
Lomas, Mrs. S.C., see Carlyle
Ludlow, Edmund, Memoirs (ed. C.H. Firth, 2 vols.), 1894

Masson, David, The Life of Milton (7 vols.), 1859–80
Mathew, David, The Social Structure in Caroline England (Oxford), 1948
Matthews, Ronald, English Messiahs, 1936
Micklem, Nathaniel, The Theology of Politics, 1941
Milton, John, Defensio Secunda pro populo Anglicano, 1654 Tenure of Kings and Magistrates, 1649
Momigliano, Eucardio, Cromwell (trans. by L.E. Marshall), 1930
Morley, John, Oliver Cromwell, 1900
Morrice, Rev. Thomas, A Collection of State Letters of Roger Boyle … first Earl of Orrery, 1743

Select Bibliography

Mullinger, J.B., History of Cambridge University (Cambridge, 3 vols.), 1873-1911

Niebuhr, Reinhold, The Irony of American History (New York), 1952
Noble, Rev. Mark, Memoirs of the Protectoral-House of Cromwell (2 vols., 3rd edition), 1787
The lives of the English Regicides and other commissioners of the pretended High Court of Justice, 1798
Nuttall, G.F., The Holy Spirit in Puritan Faith and Experience, 1946

Owen, John, Works (24 vols.), 1850-55

Peel, Albert, Contemporary History (in the Congregational Quarterly, July 1948), 1948
Picton, J. Allanson, Oliver Cromwell: the man and his mission (2nd edition), 1883
Prothero, G.W., Select Statutes and other Constitutional Documents illustrative of the reigns of Elizabeth and James I (Oxford, 4th edition), 1913
Prothero, R.E., The Psalms in Human Life (2nd edition), 1904

de Retz, Memoires du Cardinal de Retz (Amsterdam), 1719
Row, William, Life of Robert Blair (ed. Thomas M'Crie), 1848
Rushworth, John, Historical Collections (7 vols.), 1659-1701

Sanford, J.L., Studies and Illustrations of the Great Rebellion, 1858
The Savoy Declaration 1658 (Reprint, Cambridge), 1939
Schenk W., The Concern for Social Justice in the Puritan Revolution, 1948
Scott, Sir W. (ed.), Original Memoirs written during the Great Civil War (including Hodgson's Memoir), 1806
Skinner, John, The Book of Ezekiel (Expositors' Bible), 1895
de Sola Pinto, Vincent Peter Sterry (Cambridge), 1934
Spence, Joseph, Anecdotes, 1820
Sprigge, Joshua, Anglia Rediviva: England's Recovery, 1647
State Trials, 1810
Sterry, Peter, The Spirits Conviction of Sinne, 1645
Stirling-Taylor, G., Oliver Cromwell, 1928
St. John, Wallace, The Contest for Liberty of Conscience in England (Chicago, U.S.A.), 1900

Tawney, R.H., Religion and the Rise of Capitalism, 1926
Thurloe State Papers (ed. Thomas Birch, 7 vols.), 1742
Trevelyan, G.M., English Social History (London edition), 1944
Troeltsch, Ernst, The Social Teaching of the Christian Churches (trans. by Olive Wyon), 1931

Varley, F.J., Cambridge during the Civil War (Cambridge), 1935
Vicars, john, Englands Parliamentary Chronicle (Parts 1–4), 1644–46
N.F[iennes], Vindiciae Veritatis; the Scots' designe discovered, 1654

Walker, Clement, The Compleat History of Independency, 1648
Walker, Williston, The Creeds and Platforms of Congregationalism (New York), 1893
Waller, Sir William, Vindication of the Character and Conduct of Sir William Waller, Knight, 1793
Ward, Samuel, *see* Knappen
Wariston, *see* Fleming
Warwick, Sir Philip, Memoires of the reigne of King Charles I, 1701
Whitelocke, Bulstrode, Memorials of English Affairs (corrected and enlarged edition), 1732
    Journal of the Swedish Ambassy, 1653–4 (ed. C. Morton, 2 vols.), 1772
Wildman, John, Putney Projects, 1647
Woodhouse, A.S.P., Puritanism and Liberty, 1938

Index

NOTE: Names appearing only in the footnotes have in general not been included in this Index. Authorities quoted are listed in the Select Bibliography.

Abingdon, 95
Adwalton Moor, 59
Agreement of the People, 137, 143, 154, 181, 182, 186, 197, 256–7, 277
Alablaster, Doctor, 24, 40
Algiers, 348
Allen, William, 115, 128, 129, 144–5, 269; Adjutant-General, 315
Alnwick, 170
Alured, Colonel, 239, 313, 323
America, 54, 72, 346
Anabaptists, 64–5, 160, 291, 333
Andover, 200
Anhalt, Prince of, 336
Apocalyptic, 27, 141, 333; *see also* Eschatology
Apologeticall Narration, 54, 62, 223
Apsley, Sir Allen, 124, 126
Argyle, Marquis of, 170–1, 173–4 403
Armada, 17, 19, 43, 337, 347
Ascham, 237, 286
Ashburnham, John, 131, 151–3, 160
Ash(e), Simeon, 74, 79, 80, 176; Ashe, John, 358
Aston, Sit Arthur, 209
Aylesbury, 96
Ayscough, 201, 258

Baillie, Rev. Robert, 66, 73, 74, 79, 82, 84, 85, 88–91, 97–100, 104, 170, 220, 230, 235, 236; Lt.-Gen. William, 78, 168
Balfour, 86–7
Baltic, 286
Bampfield, Thomas, 352
Bampton Bush, 95

Banbury, 200, 244
Baptists, 255, 292, 331
Barbados, 237, 338, 347
Barnstaple, 124
Barrington family, 20; Sir Thomas, 64, 68
Basing House, 87, 102, 103, 207
Bates, Doctor, 238
Bath, 101
Baxter, Richard, 20, 39, 52, 66, 67, 132, 207, 222, 382, 385, 388
Beard, Doctor Thomas, 21, 24–9, 33, 38, 40–1
Bedford, 101; Earl of, 47
Bellièvre, 109, 110, 117, 125
Berkeley, Sir John, 124–6, 129, 131–2, 134, 151–3 158–60
Bernardi, Francesco, 348
Berry, Major-General, 64, 67, 314, 317
Berwick, 164, 170–1, 225, 227
Bible, 39, 45, 148, 149, 168–9, 221–2, 231, 274, 279, 300, 302, 386, 397–9; Authorized Version, 27–8, 169, 399; Genevan Bible, 27, 28, 169, 399; *Souldiers Pocket Bible,* 60–2
Biddle, John, 330
Bishops' Wars, 39, 48–9
Blackfriars, 291, 292
Blackness Castle, 236
Blair, Rev. Robert, 172, 174, 322
Blake, Admiral, 234, 237, 261, 263, 311, 345, 346, 348, 358, 376
Bletchingdon House, 94
Bond, Denis, 351–2
Bonde, 340–2

Bordeaux, 286
Boston (New England), 251, 371
Boteler, 317
Bourchier, Sir James, 34-5; Sir John, 34; John, 35; Elizabeth; see Cromwell
Boyne, 209
Bradford, Captain, 368
Bradshaw, 186-8, 197, 202, 209, 224, 228, 238, 304
Bramhall, Doctor, Bishop of Derry, 30
Brandenburg, 339, 341, 342; Elector of, 340, 342
Bray, Captain, 147
Breitenfeld, 43
Bremen, 336, 374
Brereton, Sir William, 186
Bridgewater, 101
Bristol, 101, 102, 165, 167, 205, 244, 353
Brock Burn, 226
Broghill, Lord, 156, 351, 355, 356, 362, 364, 366, 368, 411; Castle, 239
Brown, Major-General, 95, 96
Browne, Major-General Sir John, 182, 240
Brussels, 358
Buckden, 45
Buckingham, Duke of, 161, 289
Bunyan, John, 270
Burford Bridge, 200
Burleigh House, 59
Burton, Thomas, 315, 356
Bury St. Edmunds, 19, 118
Bushell, Captain Browne, 235
Butler, Sir Edmund, 210
Byron, 78

Calamy, Edmund, 236, 264
Callander, 167
Calvin, 24, 31, 37, 61, 75-6, 385
Cambridge, 49, 56-9, 63, 66, 92, 122; Cambridgeshire, 115, 317
Cambridge University, 20-4, 29-34, 57, 74; Christ's College, 31; Emmanuel, 30-2, 74; St. Catherine's, 33; St. John's, 39, 413; Sidney Sussex, 19, 22, 29-31, 33; Trinity, 21
Campbell, John, Earl of Loudoun, 85, 90, 136, 151, 170-1
Capel, Lord, 58, 165
Carey, John, 332
Carisbrooke, 151-3, 157, 162, 176
Carlisle, 164, 170-1, 242
Carrell; see Caryl
Carter, Captain John, 144
Cartwright, Thomas, 20, 29
Caryl, Joseph, 204, 232, 250, 266
Case, Thomas, 236
Castle, Colonel, 209
Cavendish, 59, 266
Cavil, John, 357
Cecil family, 19
Chalgrove Field, 69
Channel Islands, 108, 201
Charles I of England; Puritan attitude to home and ecclesiastical policy, 43-4; Attempt to impose episcopacy on Scots, 46; Cromwell sees Scots army as ally against Charles, 51; Parliamentary pressure on Grand Remonstrance, 52-3; Separatists' Struggle, 54; Attitude of Presbyterians and Independents in 1644, 71-2, 75; "Parliament" at Oxford, 74; Independent compromise unthinkable, 77; Civil War Campaign, 85-6; Oxford raid, 94-5; Advance against Eastern Counties, 96; Naseby, 98, 230; Scots regard Cromwell as greater menace than king, 100; On Welsh Border, 101; Escape from Oxford, 103; In custody of Scots, 106; Negotiations with Scots and Parliament, 108-110; Third Answer to Newcastle Propositions, 115; Invited to Oatlands, 117; Army seeks to prevent agreement between King and Parliament, 118;

Index

Cornet Joyce's exploit, 119-121; Leaves Newmarket for Royston, 124; Distrust of Cromwell, 125; *Heads of Proposals*, 129-30; London Riots, 130-3; Army Agitators, 134; Army Debates, Chapter Seven; Preparations for Escape, 151-2; At Carisbrooke, 152-3; Seeks to settle differences with Parliament, 154-5; Saddle Letter, 156-7; Cromwell reported to favour restoration, 157; "Engagement" with Scots, 159-60; Cromwell's attack in Parliament, 160-2; Essex agitation for restoration, 164; Defeat of Hamilton, 171; Army's disillusion about King, 172-3; Support for Ormonde's invasion, 173; Cromwell's views on kingship, 174-5; Contrast with Cromwell, 179, 306, 321; Events leading to trial, 179-87; Trial, 187-8; Execution, 189-91; Legality of trial, 192; Estimate of his reign, 193-4

Charles Stuart, Prince of Wales, Presbyterian message on Scots' aid, 121; Cromwell's approach, 124-5; King's letter on escape, 173; King's letter on coming fate, 179-80; Attempts to save King's life, 186, 188; Proclaimed king in Edinburgh, 219-20; Visits Lesley's army, 224; Relations with leaders of the Kirk, 225; Cromwell's Scottish campaign, 230-2, 241-2; Coronation at Scone, 233; Barbados declares for Charles, 237; Proclaimed King of England at Carlisle, 242-3; Worcester, 243-6; Suggested Cromwellian agreement, 261; Sindercombe's plot, 313-14; Fear of Franco-Spanish support, 348; Preparations for invasion from Spanish Netherlands, 351, 358, 373; and offer of crown to Cromwell, 359; Clarendon, his Secretary of State, 384

Charles X of Sweden, 336, 342, 374
Chelmsford, 118
Chester, 201, 287, 314, 317
Chichely, Sir Thomas, 50
Childerley, 121
Cholmley, Sir Henry, 169
Church and State, 50, 56, 280, 390-1
Church Meeting, 146, 149, 280
Church of England, 30, 43, 46, 53, 56, 66, 131, 155, 326
Cinque Ports, 122
Clarke, Captain, 127-8
Clay pole, 351, 355, 364
Clonmacnoise, 212, 214, 244
Clonmel, 213
Cobbett, Lt.-Col., 182
Cockburnspath, 224, 226
Coggleshall, 204
Coke, Thomas, 236
Colchester, 168, 171
Colnbrook, 131-2
Committee of Both Kingdoms, 69, 77, 81-2, 86-7, 89, 95-6
Condé, 257, 341, 344, 375
Congregationalists, 175, 204, 222, 280, 292, 332, 385; *see also* Independents
Connaught, 323
Connecticut, 280
Cook, Captain, 158
Cooper, Anthony Ashley, 294, 297, 350, 356
Cork, 212
Corkbush Field, 153-4
Cornwall, 103, 243, 311, 317
Cotton, Rev. John, 72, 251, 334; Sir Robert, 111
Coursey, Lord, 323
Covell, Captain, 232
Coventry, 66-7
Cowling, Commissary-General, 144
Coxe, Colonel, 353
Coyet, Petrus, 339
Cranford, 99

Crawford, Major-General Laurence, 65, 73–5, 78–80, 84–5, 89; Lt.-Col. William, of Skeldon, 79

Crofts, 243

Croke, Captain Unton, 314–15

Cromwell, family, 20; Bridget (Mrs. Ireton), 107, 108, 252; Elizabeth (Oliver's mother), 18–19, 311; Elizabeth (Oliver's wife), 34–5, 41, 228–30, 236, 311; Elizabeth (Mrs. Claypole), 108, 320, 374, 378–9; Frances (Lady Rich), 379; Henry (Oliver's brother), 20; Henry (Oliver's son), 317, 323–4, 329, 350–1, 354, 356–60, 367–8, 376; Henry (Oliver's nephew), 355; Sir Henry, 17; Jane, 368; Colonel John, 186; Mary, 373; Richard, 28, 162, 203, 239; Robert (Oliver's father), 17–19, 24, 28; Robert (Oliver's brother), 20; Robert (Oliver's son), 46; Sir Oliver, 17; Thomas, Earl of Essex, 17; Walter, 18

Cromwell, Oliver, ancestry, 17–20; Birth and childhood, 20–3; At Cambridge, 22–3, 29–33; Influence of Thomas Beard, 24–9, 38; Influence of Samuel Ward, 31–3, 38; At Lincoln's Inn (?), 34; Marriage, 34–5, 41; Conversion, 35–41; Local Government, 44; Farming at St. Ives, 44–5; Move to Ely, 46; Fen Drainage Scheme, 46–8; Appearance, 48; Elected to Parliament, 49; In Long Parliament, 49–53; At Outbreak of War, 56–7; Defence of Eastern Counties, 58; Battle at Grantham, 58, 60; Battle at Gainsborough, 59–60; Lieutenant-General to Manchester and Committee of Both Kingdoms, 69; Disagreements with Crawford and Manchester 73 ff., 87–91; Marston Moor, 78–81; Newbury, 86; Self-Denying Ordinance, 91–4; Raid on Oxford, 94–5; Second-in-Command to Fairfax, 97–8; Naseby, 98–100; Langport, 100; Successes in the West, 101–3; Position after defeat of King, 104–5; Attitude towards Parliament, 107–8; Illness, 109–10; Attitude towards Army's demands, 111 ff., 122–3; Cornet Joyce's exploit, 119–20; Sides with Army, 122–4; Negotiations with Charles, 124–6; Army Debates of 1647, Chapter Seven; Mistrusts Charles, 131–2; Dislikes use of force against Parliament, 128, 133; Aims at unity and discipline of Army, 133; Ireton's influence, 134; Distrusted by King, Parliament and Levellers, 134–5; Urges treaty between King and Parliament, 136; Charges against Cromwell, 137–8; Disagreement with Levellers' position, 143–4; On forms of government, 145; Expounds unity and differences in Army debate, 146–7; "Carisbrooke Trap", 152–3; Overcomes mutiny at Corkbush Field, 153–4; *Rapprochement* with Levellers, 158–9; Prayer Meeting at Windsor, 160; On Charles's guilt, 160–3; Campaign in Wales, 164–6; March North, 166–7; Battle at Preston, 167–8; Moves towards Scotland, 171–3; Letters to Robert Hammond, 174, 177–9, 403–5; at Pontefract, 176; Pride's Purge, 181; Events leading to King's trial, 182–7; King's trial and execution, 187–191; Cromwell's attitude to King's death, 191–2, 195; Leveller agitation, 197–201; Appointed Commander in Ireland, 202–3; Sets out for Ireland, 205; Massacre at Drogheda, 209–10; and at Wexford, 210–11; Successes and setbacks in Ireland, 211–13; Moral

Index

considerations of Irish campaign, 214–18; Displaces Fairfax as Commander-in-Chief, 219–21; Invasion of Scotland, 222–5; Dunbar, 225–30; Edinburgh, 230–3; Winter in Scotland, 234–6; Illness, 235, 238; Scottish campaign, 242–8; Honoured by Parliament, 249; Suspicion of Parliament, 252; Increasing influence, 254; Opposition to war with Holland, 257–8; On the dangerous situation to the Commonwealth, 259–60; Relations with Parliament, 260–70; Ejection of the Rump, 270; His motives, 270–4; Personal popularity, 272–3; Problems, 275–6; Nominated Parliament, 276 ff.; Foreign policy, 281–7; Domestic policy, 287–95; Settlement of Ireland, 288; Policy in Scotland, 288–9; Dissolution of Nominated Parliament, 293–5; Installed as Lord Protector, 297; Rule by ordinance, 298–9; First Protectorate Parliament called, 301; Opening address, 302; Defines three fundamentals of Government, 305–6; Attacks on Protector's powers, 308–9; Parliament dissolved, 309–12; Insurrection of 1655, 312–15; Appointment of Major-Generals, 315–19; Assembly of Second Protectorate Parliament, 319; Position of Cromwell, 319–21; Policy in Scotland and Ireland, 322–4; Church Settlement, 324–33, 390–1; Foreign Policy, 333–42; Relations with France and Spain: Catholic War, 343–6, 348–9; West Indian Expedition, 346–7; Case of James Nayler, 353–4, 357; Militia Bill, 355–6; Offer of kingship, 356 ff.; Threat of Invasion, 358; Attitude to kingship and reasons for refusal, 363–71; State of Protectorate, 372–4; Foreign Affairs, 374–6; Last days, illness and death, 376–80; Characteristics of personality and government, 382–7; As dictator, 391–3; Estimates of, 11–12, 34, 48–9, 104, 319–21, 381–4; Influence of religion, 12, 53–5, 148–50, 247, 251, 270, 384–9; Independency, 12, 45, 64–7, 73, 107, 113, 222, 274, 332–3, 391–2; Providence, 69, 104, 125, 138–9, 146–7, 149–50, 166, 177–9, 216–17, 271, 278, 300–1, 370, 385; Use of Bible, 27–8, 36–7, 45, 60–2, 221–2, 279, 300–1, 397–400, 406–7, 409; And the Established Church, 46, 53–4, 326–8; Moral Theology, 139, 148, 295, 389; Sense of Vocation, 148, 179, 271–2, 295, 300, 305, 386, 388–9; Toleration, 325–33, 344

Crowland, 58
Crowne, Colonel William, 314

Dalbier, Colonel, 102
Dean, Colonel, 182, 238
De Baas, 344
de Cardeñas, Alonzo, 343, 345
Dell, William, 255
Denbigh, Earl of, 97, 184
Denmark, 283, 286, 302, 336, 339, 375
Denne, Corporal, 200
Denton, Doctor, 120
Derby, Lord, 244, 266
Derby House, 82, 84–6, 90, 94, 96, 118, 166, 169, 171
De Retz, Cardinal, 125, 272
Dering, Sir Edward, 51
Desborough, 263, 297, 315, 317, 320, 352, 355, 367–9
De Velada, Marquis, 343
Devereux family, 20; Robert, *see* Essex
Devizes, 102
de With, 283
De Witt, 234, 281, 341

Dickson, 76
Digby, Lord, 49, 106; Sir John, 176
Dives, Sir Lewis, 134, 182
Doncaster, 101
Donnington, 86-90
Doon Hill, 225, 227
Dorchester, 314
Dorislaus, Doctor, 183, 205, 258, 286
D'Orñate, Count, 343
Dorset, 57, 314
Dort, Synod of, 33
Dover, 411-12
Downes, Colonel John, 188, 193
Downhall, Henry, 39, 413
Drogheda, 52, 204-5, 207, 209-11, 214, 217-18, 246
Drury Lane, 48, 118
Dryden, 190
Dublin, 52, 199, 205, 209, 299; Trinity College, 255
Dugdale, Sir William, 22, 156, 273
Dunbar, 100, 224-30, 234, 240-1, 243, 245. 301, 368, 380
Duncannon, 212
Dundalk, 204, 209
Dundas, Sir Walter, 231-2
Dungan Hill, 135
Dunkirk, 374-6
Durham, 235, 317
Dury, John, 335, 374

Edgehill, 57, 67, 80, 368
Edinburgh, 27, 170-2, 219, 225, 230-2, 235, 237-8
Election, Doctrine of, 32, 37, 38, 42, 68, 271, 385
Elector Palatine, 43, 111, 341
Eliot, 43
Elizabeth, Queen, 18, 26, 52, 71-2, 332, 363
Ely, 18, 46, 50, 57, 69, 92, 96, 317
Eschatology, 27; *see also* Apocalyptic
Essex, 63, 111, 123, 164, 187, 245, 246, 317
Essex, Robert Devereux, Earl of, 57-8, 71, 75-6, 82-5, 90-2, 95-9, 107, 122, 363
Eure, Lord, 355

Evelyn, John, 327
Ewer, Colonel, 176, 179, 409
Exeter, 103, 124

Fairfax, 58-9, 63; Lord, 69, 78; Sir Thomas, Victory at Wakefield, 59; Defeat at Adwalton Moor, 59; Action at York, 78; Prepares New Model Army, 94; Seeks out the King, 97, 103; Naseby, 98; At Bristol, 101-2; Need for Cavalry Commander, 104; Death of Essex, 107; Negotiations with Scots, 108-9; To be only officer above rank of Colonel, 109; Ordered to suppress Army petition, 113; Regiment avoid disbandment, 118; Joyce's exploit, 120-1; Reports to Parliament on Army riots, 122; Army's demands, 123; Appoints Army representatives to meet Parliament, 124; his "incredible Army", 127; Heads of Proposals, 129; Confirmed as Commander of all land forces, 130; London Riots, 131; Agreement with certain Members of Parliament, 132; Governor of the Tower, 133; Putney Debates Chairman, 147; Action in S.E. Counties, Second Civil War, 164, 166, 168; Ireton urges him to purge Commons, 171; Sends Rainsborough to Pontefract, 173; Urges King's trial, 175; Judge at trial, 185; King's execution, 189; Suppresses Diggers, 199; Suppression of mutiny in Whalley's Regiment, 199-200; Cromwell his second-in-command, 202; Opposes invasion of Scotland, 220; Weakened position, 219, 221; Organizes Yorkshire militia, 243; Battle at Worcester, 245; *also* 81, 96, 99, 110, 116, 135, 136, 137, 153, 158, 165, 176, 181, 204, 211, 244, 402

Index

Falconbridge, Lord, 373
Falkirk, 240
Falkland, Lord, 53
Farnham, 181
Farringdon House, 95
Feake, Christopher, 291–2, 299, 329
Felstead, 35, 46
Fen Drainage Scheme, 40, 46–7
Fen Drayton, 58
Fiennes, Nathaniel, Lord Saye and Sele, 80, 136, 352, 362, 401
Fife, 231–2, 235, 238, 239–41, 243
Fifth Monarchy, 141, 152, 199, 221, 252, 254, 262, 265, 276, 284, 291–2, 297–9, 302, 308, 311–13, 326, 328, 333, 351, 361, 417
Flanders, 352, 357, 375
Fleckno, Richard, 22
Fleetwood, Lt.-Gen. Charles, 115–16, 118–19, 154, 223, 238, 243–5, 252, 311, 317, 323, 326, 367–9, 374
Fleming, Adjutant, 104, 163
Folkestone, 281
Forth, the, 230, 238, 242
Fort Royal, 246
Fox, George, 254, 328–30, 379
France, 98, 124, 151–2, 234, 250, 257, 285–6, 295, 302, 327, 335, 337–8, 341, 343–6, 348, 374–6
Frederick, Elector Palatine, 43

Gabbard Sands, 281
Gainsborough, 59–60, 62, 69
Garland, Augustin, 356
Geneva, 75
German Empire, 335; Protestant states, 374
Gillespie, 322, 359
Glasgow, 101, 232, 236–7
Glencairn, Earl of, 313, 322
Gloucester, 57, 165, 243, 287, 314, 317, 373; Duke of, 263
Glynn, 362
Goddard, Guibon, 301, 303–4, 309
Goffe, Lt.-Col., 140–1, 149, 221, 258, 317
Gogar, 225
Goode, 74

Goodson, Vice-Admiral, 347, 375
Goodwin, Thomas, 61, 204, 251, 255, 297, 301, 324; John, 112, 221
Goring, George, Earl of Norwich, 78, 98, 100, 165, 167
Grace, Doctrine of, 32, 37–8, 64, 148, 385
Grand Remonstrance, 52–3
Grantham, 58, 60
Graves, Colonel, 119–20
Gray's Inn, 34
Grey, Lord, of Groby, 169, 181, 314; Lord, of Wark, 68
Grove, Major Hugh, 314–15
Gunpowder Plot, 19, 43
Gustavus Adolphus, 43, 341

Hacker, Colonel, 245, 258, 313
Hamilton, 166–8, 170, 172, 174, 182, 202, 225, 243–3, 246
Hammond, Robert, 113, 116, 130, 151–2, 157–8, 160–2, 174–5, 177–9, 181, 237, 244, 370, 403, 406; Doctor Henry, 124, 152
Hampden family, 20, 35; John, 17, 48–9, 53, 57, 69, 152, 363
Hampton Court, 147, 151–2, 156, 249, 261, 373, 379; Conference, 19, 27, 29, 32, 50
Harris, John, 118–19
Harrison, Major-Gen. Thomas, 152, 183, 189, 200, 220–1, 227, 237, 242–3, 245–6, 252, 262, 264–5, 268, 270, 275–7, 293, 297, 313, 320
Haynes, Major-Gen., 347
Hazelrigge, Sir Arthur, 87–9, 119, 171, 226, 228, 230, 265, 289, 304, 350, 376, 378, 404
Heads of Proposals, 129, 137
Henrietta Maria, Queen, 109, 281
Henry VIII, 17
Hepburne, Sir Adam of Humby, 79
Hereford, 317
Hertfordshire, 57, 317
Hewitt, Doctor John, 373–4, 378
Hinchinbrook, 17, 20
Hiroshima, 218
Hispaniola, 338–9, 347

Hitler, 415
Holland, 19, 98, 134, 188, 234, 249, 253, 257–8, 262–3, 275, 276, 281–7, 298, 302, 313, 335, 337, 339–42; Cornelius, 167, 182, 202
Holies, Denzil, 53, 89–90, 102, 104, 112–14, 119, 121, 123, 181
Holmby House, 109, 115, 119–21, 155, 220
Hopkins, William, 173
Hopton, Sir Ralph, 103
Horton, Colonel, 164–5, 206, 212
Hotham family, 58; Sir John, 65; Captain John, 59, 65
Hounslow Heath, 132
Howlett, Richard, 30
Hull, 57, 63, 68–9, 136, 402
Humble Petition and Advice, 360–1, 365–6, 372–3, 376, 378, 390, 417
Hunks, Colonel, 189
Huntingdon, 20–1, 24–5, 35, 39–40, 44–5, 82–3, 101, 317, 397
Huntington, Major Robert, 116, 119, 131, 133, 155, 166–7, 178, 370, 386
Hurst Castle, 176, 179, 181–2
Hutchinson, Colonel, 193, 221, 247, 298–9, 314
Hyde, Edward, Earl of Clarendon, 48, 131–2, 135–6, 189, 208, 272, 286, 289–90, 338, 347–8, 382–4
Hyde Park, 134

Inchiquin 205
Independents, 45, 54, 64, 66, 71–2, 77–80, 84–5, 89, 92, 95, 97–8, 101–2, 104, 106–7, 112–13, 120, 124, 135, 137, 155–7, 160–1, 165, 167, 172, 174, 181, 197–8, 204, 220, 222–3, 232, 251–6, 274, 278, 292, 331–3, 385, 392, 403; *see also* Congregationalists
Ingoldsby, Colonel Richard, 188, 245
Inquisition, Spanish, 216
Inverkeithing, 239–40
Ipswich, 115
Ireland, 28, 52, 98, 107, 109, 114, 116–17, 162, 199–206, Chapter Twelve, 223, 225, 234, 237, 250, 252, 262, 265, 275, 288, 299, 311–12, 316–17, 322–4, 337, 344, 367, 383
Ireton, Henry, Injured at Naseby, 98; Marriage to Bridget Cromwell, 107; Cromwell's criticism, 107; Presbyterian move against officers, 109; Dealings with Army agitators, 111–17; Cornet Joyce's exploit, 119–20; Supports Army's demands, 123, 128–9; Presents Heads of Proposals, 129; London Riots, 131; Levellers regarded as embarrassment, 133; Influence on Cromwell, 134, 250, 275; 1647 Army Debates, 135–50; Attitude to Charles, 155, 158, 171, 176; Saddle Letter, 156–7, 411; Prayer Meeting at Windsor, 160; Action in Kent, 165; On liberty of conscience, 172; Part in events leading to King's trial, 181, 183–4, 186, 191; His regiment refuses to go to Ireland, 200; Second-in-Command to Cromwell, 205; Irish campaign, 209, 213, 234; Death 250; Ideas on Moral Theology, 389
Isle of Wight, 151–2, 177
Italian States, 349

Jamaica, 338, 347
James I of England, 17, 19, 20, 26, 29, 43, 50, 161
Jenkins, Williams, 236
Jephson, Colonel, 357
Jessey, Henry, 292
Jesuits, 302
Jews, 331–2
John IV of Portugal, 285, 345
Johnston, Archibald, of Wariston, 224, 232, 236–8
Jones, Michael, 135, 199, 201, 204–6, 212
Joyce, Cornet, 119–21, 158
Jubbes, Lt.-Colonel John, 127, 145, 149
Juxon, Doctor, Bishop of London, 186, 189

Index 433

Kelsey, Major-General, 317, 350
Kent, 165, 187, 317
Kentford Heath, 121
Kerr, 231, 236
Kilsyth, 235
Kingston, 133, 155
Kinsale, 201
Knottingley, 178-9

Lambert, John, assists in drafting Heads of Proposals, 129; Action in Second Civil War, 164-6, 168; Deputation to Fairfax, 220; Scottish campaign, 223, 227-8, 240-1, 243; Wounded and taken prisoner, 224; Promoted Lt.-General, 238; Battle of Worcester, 245-6; Abolition of Deputyship of Ireland, 252; Presses for dismissal of Rump, 262; Commission to command in Scotland, 265; Expulsion of Rump, 270; Helps check Cromwell's power, 275; Appointed to decemvirate, 276; Prepares Instrument of Government, 296; One of Cromwell's advisers, 297; Influence over Cromwell, 298; Major-General in North, 317; Quarrel with Cromwell, 320; Objections to war with Spain, 335, 345; In Second Protectorate Parliament, 352-3; Opposes Kingship proposals, 358-60, 367-8; Opposition to Comwell, 372-3; His ambition, 372, 383; *see also* 124, 404
Lanark, Earl of, 136, 151, 171
Lancashire, 57, 81, 167, 168, 317
Langdale, Sir Marmaduke, 98, 164, 167-8
Langport, Battle of, 99-101, 103
La Rochelle, 43
Laud, William, 30, 43, 45, 51, 397
Lauderdale, 99, 117, 131, 136, 151
Laugharne, Colonel, 164
Leda, Marquis of, 346

Legge, 160
Leicester, 67, 97, 104, 166, 244, 317
Leith, 224, 232, 240
Lenthall, William, 59, 99, 102-3, 116, 119, 168, 209, 211-12, 214, 219, 226, 228-9, 232, 235, 240-2, 246, 254, 303, 362
Lesley, David, 78-80, 224-8, 230, 232, 240-2, 401; Lodovic, 170-1
Levellers, 112, 133-4, 137, 139-40, 143-8, 153-4, 157-8, 160, 164, 173-4, 181, 197-201, 205-6, 219, 244, 250, 291, 293, 302, 311, 351, 357, 403, 409, 416
Leven, Earl of, 78, 81, 101, 170, 224
Lilburne, Henry, 104; John, 49, 81, 112-14, 118-19, 123, 134-5, 140, 166, 172, 175-6, 198-9, 208, 235, 289, 293; Colonel Robert, 154, 244, 288, 312-13, 322
Lincoln, 20, 69, 81-2, 317;
Lincolnshire, 58, 311
Lincoln's Inn, 34
Linlithgow, 235
Lisle, Lord, 286, 297, 362
Lloyd, Jenkin, 236
Lockhart, William, 344, 348, 375-6
Lockyer, Robert, 200
Lostwithiel, 82
Loudon; *see* Campbell.
Louis XIV, 188, 338, 348, 376, 417
Love, Christopher, 236
Lowestoft, 58
Lucas, Sir Charles, 78
Ludlow, Edmund, 111, 133, 171, 181, 207, 209, 220-1, 229, 247, 252, 263, 299, 314, 319-20, 357, 367-8, 383
Lützen, 43
Lynn (King's), 58

Machiavelli, 270, 384
Madrid, 286, 346
Manasseh ben Israel, 331
Manchester, Henry, first Earl of, 44, 47, 68; Edward, Lord Mandevilie, second Earl of, 47, 69, 71-5, 78-9, 81-9, 91-2, 97, 107, 130

Manton, 33, 266
Mardike, 375
Margery, Captain, 64
Marshall, Stephen, 204, 292
Marston Moor, 78, 80–1, 179, 401
Marten, Henry, 135, 153, 161, 186, 264
Marvell, Andrew, 152–3, 189
Mary, Queen of England, 19, 43, 285, 337
Mason, Lt.-Colonel, 368
Massachusetts, 251, 280
Massey, Edward, 114, 121–2, 181
Mayerne, Sir Theodore, 38
Maynard, Sir John, 90, 181, 350
Mayo, Colonel Christopher, 344
Mayor, Richard, 28, 162, 203, 206, 212, 228, 239; Dorothy, his daughter, 162, 203
Mazarin, 109, 110, 117, 286, 295, 327, 338, 343–4, 348, 375
Medina de la Torres, Duke of, 343
Melanchthon, 204
Melcombe Regis, 94
Meldrum, Sir John, 59
Meyrick, Sir John, 90
Middlesex, 187, 317
Middleton, John, 167, 313, 322
Mildmay, Sir Henry, 186, 202
Militia Bill, 355–6, 361
Millenary Petition, 29
Milton, John, 197, 266, 298, 321, 337
Molineux, 78
Monk, George, 204–6, 227–8, 234, 236, 238, 263, 283, 297, 312–13, 322, 357–8, 369, 371, 375
Monro, 167, 171
Montagu, family, 17, 19; Edward, Earl of Sandwich, 297, 345, 348, 374; Edward and Henry, see Manchester
Montgomery, 205, 224
Montrose, 101, 103–4
Moral Theology, 55, 61, 142, 198, 389–90; Dual Ethic, 62, 139, 294–5
Mordaunt, John, 373–4
Morgan, Major Anthony, 351, 359, 369; Thomas, 375

Morland, Samuel, 337, 374
Morrice, Thomas, 156
Munster, 212
Musgrave, Sir Philip, 164
Musselburgh, 224–5
Mussolini, 415

Nagasaki, 218
Naples, 346
Naseby, Battle of, 26, 98–101, 104, 132, 230, 385
Nayler, James, 353–4, 357
Needham, Marchamont, 371
Newark, 58–9, 103, 176
Newbury, 86, 88
Newcastle, 64, 171, 223, 265, 314, 401; Marquis of, 58–9, 63, 69, 78–9
New England, 40, 280
Newgate Prison, 289
Newmarket, 121, 124, 199, 262
Newport, 171, 173, 182
Nieuport, 281–3, 341
Norbury, John, 356
Norfolk, 58, 123, 307, 317
Norway, 324
Norwich, 19
Nottingham, 220, 314
Nye, 204, 251, 292, 297, 324, 359, 371

Oatlands, 117
Orrery, Earl of, 156–7, 411–12
Ostend, 375
Overton, Colonel Robert, 136, 199, 221, 227, 240, 313–14, 357
Owen, John, 61, 204, 220, 222, 232, 251, 255–7, 266, 292, 297, 324, 367, 371
Oxford, 59, 74, 86, 94–5, 97, 101, 103, 106, 119, 158, 209, 220, 244, 314, 317; University, 20, 235, 302; Magdalen College, 255, 302; Christ Church, 255; Oxfordshire, 173

Pack, Alderman, 358
Packe, Sir Christopher, 297, 342
Paris, 346, 375

Index

Paulet, John, Marquis of Winchester, 102
Pell, John, 335
Pembroke, 166–7
Penn, 311, 338, 346–7
Penrith, 243
Penruddock, Colonel John, 314–16, 319
Perth, 230, 241–2, 245
Peterborough, 59
Peters, Hugh, 103, 186, 204, 247, 251, 258
Philip IV, King of Spain, 344, 346
Philiphaugh, 103
Pickering, Colonel, 84, 102, 226, 317
Piedmont, 336–9
Pierrepoint, 366, 403
Plymouth, 57
Poland, 255, 342
Pontefract, 165, 167–8, 173, 176
Pope, the, 27, 212
Portugal, 285, 302, 345, 348
Powell, Vavasour, 254, 291, 299
Powick, 245
Poyer, Colonel, 164–7
Poyntz, 127, 181
Presbyterians, 33, 71, 74, 89–90, 102, 106–7, 117–18, 121, 130–1, 133, 135, 151, 155, 160–1, 164–7, 171, 181–2, 198–9, 203–4, 231, 236, 255, 278–9, 292, 316, 329, 331, 333, 354, 411; Presbyterianism, 51, 54, 65, 69, 72–3, 75–9, 100, 157, 172, 174–5, 220, 223, 225
Preston, 167–8, 171
Pride, Colonel Thomas, 113, 181–2, 227, 367
Priesthood of All Believers, 216
Propositions of Newcastle, 106, 109, 115, 134, 136–7, 156
Protestant League, 280, 334, 339, 343
Providence, Doctrine of, 25, 28, 32, 38, 59, 97, 103, 125, 129, 137–8, 142–3, 147–8, 150, 166, 177–9, 216–18, 236, 239, 271, 278, 300–1, 304, 370, 385–9, 409
Prynne, William, 49–50

Putney, 127, 137, 147, 152, 154
Pym, John, 53, 69

Quakers, 254–5, 274, 308, 328–30, 353
Queen, the, 98, 121, 125, 157
Queensferry, 240

Rainsborough, Colonel Thomas, 84, 102, 118, 131–2, 134–5, 138, 143–5, 147, 153, 173
Rathmines, 206
Raughleye, Sir Walter, 28
Reading, 127, 133, 244
Red Hill, 246
Reynolds, Colonel Sir John, 200, 375–6
Rhine, River, 335, 343
Ribble, River, 167
Rich, family, 20; Sir Robert, 118, 130, 379; Colonel Robert, 383
Richelieu, Cardinal, 43, 61, 295, 339
Ripon, 74, 243
Rogers, John, 328–30, 333
Roman Catholicism, 27, 44, 61, 157, 208–9, 211–12, 214–16, 225, 244, 256, 288, 295, 326–7, 343 ff., 383
Root and Branch Petition, 50–1
Ross, 211–12
Roundaway Down, 77
Roxburgh, Earl of, 227
Royston, 122, 124
Rupert, Prince, 78, 81–2, 92, 94, 101, 134, 199, 201, 205, 234–5, 237
Rushworth, John, 104, 120, 127, 132, 223
Russell, Colonel Frank, 84, 414

Saddle Letter, 156–7, 411–12
Saffron Walden, 111, 114–15, 117, 130
Sagredo, Giovanni, 262, 264, 288, 325, 327, 340, 348–?
St. Albans, 57, 123, 175
St. Fagan's, 164–5, 206
St. Ives, 40, 44–5, 125
St. James's Palace, 186
St. John, Oliver, 63–4, 76, 84, 113, 136, 220, 230, 257, 266, 287; Mrs. –, 36–9, 46, 398

St. John's, 245
S. Quentin, 375
Salisbury, 200, 314
Salvetti, 250–2
Santa Cruz, 376
San Domingo, 338
Savoy, 337–8; Duke of, 336–8; Declaration, 336–8
Scarborough, 64, 165
Scheveningen, 283
Schlezer, 320, 374
Scilly Isles, 205, 330
Scone, 233
Scotland, 48–9, 51–2, 65, 73, 76, 101, 120, 131, 152, 170–1, 174, 202, 208, Chapter Thirteen, Chapter Fourteen, 252, 275, 288, 311–13, 316, 322, 369, 371; Scottish National Covenant, 36, 46, 164–5
Scot, Thomas, 304, 350, 376
Scrope, Colonel, 200
Sehested, Count Hannibal, 324
Selden, 161
Self-Denying Ordinance, 66, 73, 91–9, 104
Severn, River, 245
Sexby, Edward, 115, 129, 137, 143, 145, 148, 319, 351, 357, 373
Shepperd, Trooper, 115
Sherborne Castle, 101
Ship Money, 49
Shrewsbury, 314
Simcott, Doctor, 38–9
Simpson, Sydrach, 324
Sindercombe, Miles, 313, 357, 373–4
Skinners' Hall, 130
Skippon, Major-General Philip, 84, 98, 114–16, 118, 122, 200, 317, 353
Slingsby, Sir Henry, 373
Solemn Engagement, 121–2
Solemn League and Covenant, 73, 75–6, 223
Southampton, 317; Lord, 195
Spain, 19, 43, 98, 237, 250, 257, 285–7, 319, 335, 338, 343–8, 351–2, 357, 373, 376
Sprigge, Joshua, 59, 94–5, 102
Stafford, Captain, 211

Staines, William, 92, 134, 383
Stamford, 59
Stapleton, Sir Philip, 57, 90, 112, 181
Stayner, Captain, 348
Sterry, Peter, 208, 255, 292, 333
Steward, Robert, 18–19; Sir Thomas, 40, 44–7; William, 18
Stirling, 225, 230, 240–1
Stockholm, 342
Storie, 40, 45, 397–8
Strachan, 231–2
Strafford; *see* Wentworth
Strangways, Sir John, 50
Streater, Major John, 265
Strickland, Walter, 257, 287, 352, 354
Suffolk, 59–60, 63–4, 111, 115, 123, 245, 317
Surrey, 164, 187, 317
Sussex, 187, 317
Sweden, 286, 302, 335–7, 339–42, 374–6
Switzerland, 335, 337, 348, 376
Sydney, Algernon, 187, 268–9
Synnott, Colonel David, 210

Taafe, Sir Lucas, 211
Tate, Zouch, 89–92
Teme, River, 245
The Hague, 205, 287
Thompson, Corporal William, 200
Thurloe, John, 287, 297, 311, 314, 316, 319, 350, 354, 357–8, 360, 366–9, 376
Tichborne, Colonel Robert, 133, 294, 297
Tickhill Castle, 81
Tilly, 43
Titus, Silius, 220, 373
Toleration, 56, 72, 75–6, 84–5, 156–7, 172, 223, 316, 325, 331, 344
Tomlinson, Colonel, 183
Toop, John, 357
Torqemada, Tomás de, 216
Torwood, 240
Transylvania, Prince of, 337
Trim, 209
Triploe Heath, 122, 199

Index

Tunis, 348
Tweed, River, 171, 224
Twickenham, 131

Ulster, 52, 208
Unitarians, 332
Ussher, Archbishop, 30, 320, 326
Uttoxeter, 168

Van Beverning, 281–3, 292
Van de Perre, 281–2, 284
Vane, Sir Henry, 51, 69, 76, 84, 91–2, 113, 136, 161, 169, 201, 223, 252, 257, 264, 270, 320, 403
Van Tromp, 261, 263, 281, 283
Vaudois Valley, 336–8
Venables, 311, 338, 346–7
Venice, 340, 348
Vermuydin, Sir Cornelius, 47, 284; Colonel, 96
Vocation, 148, 207, 271–2, 295, 300, 305, 386–9

Wagstaffe, Sir Joseph, 314
Wakefield, 59
Waldenses, 336, 339
Wales, 162–6, 176, 243, 317; Welsh Border, 101
Wallenstein, 43, 341
Waller, Edmund, 33, 357; Sir Hardress, 164; Sir William, 77, 82, 86–8, 91, 94, 96–7, 122, 130, 181–2
Walton, Valentine, 80, 83, 302, 413–14
Walwyn, William, 199, 293
Ward, Samuel, 30–3, 38, 239
Ware, 153
Wariston, Archibald Johnston of, 224, 231–2, 236
Warrington, 168
Warwick, 29, 244, 317; Lord, 20, 379; Sir Philip, 38, 41, 48–50, 119, 190; Warwickshire, 293
Waterford, 212–13
Watson, 134, 383
Welles, Doctor, 397

Wentworth, Peter, 26, 269; Thomas, Earl of Strafford, 49, 51, 131, 303
West Friesland, 281
West Indies, 311, 319, 345–6
Westminster Assembly, 33, 54, 69, 72–4, 89, 99, 172
Wexford, 207, 210, 214, 217
Whalley, Major-General, 17, 116, 121, 124, 151–2, 199, 223, 227, 258, 317, 357
Wharton, Lord, 169, 213, 217, 228, 244
Whigs, 381
Whitchcott, Colonel, 183
White, Major Francis, 135
Whitelock, Bulstrode, 90, 182–4, 220, 239, 247, 249, 254, 258–61, 263, 265, 276, 287–8, 297, 320, 324, 335–6, 342, 355, 360–2, 366, 369
Widdrington, Sir Thomas, 182–3, 254, 297, 320, 324, 351, 355, 360, 370
Wigan, 167, 244
Wildman, Major John, 147, 313–14
Williams, John, Bishop of Lincoln, 45
Williams, Richard, 17
Willoughby, Lord, 59, 63, 71
Wilstrop Wood, 78
Wiltshire, 235, 317
Winceby, 68
Winchester, 102; Bishop of, 24; Marquis of; *see* Paulet
Windsor, 94, 131, 154, 158, 160, 163, 172, 176, 181–3, 186, 299, 313, 412
Winwick, 168
Wolseley, 294, 297, 366
Worcester, 26, 100, 244–53, 259, 261, 271, 273, 301, 317, 334, 356, 380
Worsley, Colonel, 258, 269, 317
Wrath, Mr., 36
Wren, Bishop of Ely, 20, 50, 57
Wright, Doctor, 238

York, 59, 78, 87, 169, 314; Yorkshire, 58, 243, 317